DISTINCTION WITHOUT PRETENSION:

The Little School That Did

James L. Brunnemer
Nineveh, Indiana
August, 2003

© 2004 by James L. Brunnemer. All rights reserved.

No part of this book may be reproduced, stored in a retrieval system, or transmitted by any means, electronic, mechanical, photocopying, recording, or otherwise, without written permission from the author.

ISBN: 1-4140-4165-9 (e-book)
ISBN: 1-4140-4164-0 (Paperback)
ISBN: 1-4140-4163-2 (Dust Jacket)

Library of Congress Control Number: 2003099373

This book is printed on acid free paper.

Printed in the United States of America
Bloomington, IN

Cover photos, clockwise, from upper left:

Former president Dr. I. Lynd Esch, placing the green beanie on an eager freshman; Pulitzer Prize-winning columnist and 1958 ICC graduate, William Raspberry; basketball star Tom Moran and his legendary Greyhound coach, Angus Nicoson; beloved 1950 graduate, Dr. Charles Dill; former president Gene E. Sease; and all-time leading Greyhound point-maker, Bailey Robertson, class of 1957.

1stBooks - rev. 02/18/04

To my darling Lu, who understands.

Spoken for me, in song, by Ben E. King:

When the night has come,
And the land is dark,
And the moon is the only light we see.
Oh, I won't be afraid,
No, I won't be afraid,
Just as long as you stand by me.

To Robbie, whose talent is only surpassed by his kind and gentle nature. Admire you, my friend,

Table of Contents

FOREWORD	By Gene W. Lausch	vii
PROLOGUE	By Dr. Carl R. Stockton	ix
INTRODUCTION		xi
CHAPTER I	THE ROAD TO HANNA	1
CHAPTER II	BUTLER DAZE	9
CHAPTER III	TWO ROADS DIVERGED	17
CHAPTER IV	THE GOOD LIFE	25
CHAPTER V	A LENGTHENED SHADOW	35
CHAPTER VI	IN SEARCH OF GOD'S DAUGHTER	45
CHAPTER VII	THE MILLERS: ORDINARY ACTS, DONE EXTRAORDINARILY WELL	53
CHAPTER VIII	SUBLIME IGNORANCE	63
CHAPTER IX	MAN SHALL NOT LIVE BY BREAD ALONE	71
CHAPTER X	VERY BUSY—WITH THE UNIMPORTANT	85
CHAPTER XI	PLAYING FOR BRIGHT	93
CHAPTER XII	WHO'S ON FIRST?	107
CHAPTER XIII	AN ASS LADEN WITH BOOKS	119
CHAPTER XIV	FUTILITY WRAPPED IN INCOMPETENCE INSIDE HOPELESSNESS	133
CHAPTER XV	WHY SHOULD I SAY I SEE WHAT I SEE NOT?	147
CHAPTER XVI	RETURN OF THE NATIVE	159
CHAPTER XVII	A SUSPENSION OF HOSTILITIES	177
CHAPTER XVIII	YEARNING FOR YESTERDAY	193

CHAPTER XIX	ATHLETICS IN THE ACADEMY	211
CHAPTER XX	THE LADY GREYHOUNDS	227
CHAPTER XXI	THE ELYSIAN FIELDS	239
CHAPTER XXII	NICK	259
CHAPTER XXIII	THE ATHLETICISTS	275
CHAPTER XXIV	ZUP	299
CHAPTER XXV	ALL THE PRESIDENTS' (CAUCASIAN, PROTESTANT, ALUMNI) MEN	313
CHAPTER XXVI	PRINCES I HAVE KNOWN	327
CHAPTER XXVII	GENIUS FUELED BY EGO	339
CHAPTER XXVII	BEN 'N JERRY	353
CHAPTER XXIX	GRAY HAIR AND HEMORRHOIDS	369
CHAPTER XXX	ARE THERE NO MORE HEROES?	383
ACKNOWLEDGMENTS		395

Photographs Courtesy of

Louis E. Gerig

Sondra D. Raspberry

Frederick D. Hill Archives,
University of Indianapolis

Personal collection of James L. Brunnemeer

Foreword

By Gene W. Lausch

In October 2002, the University of Indianapolis celebrated the 100th anniversary of its chartering. In *Distinction Without Pretension: The Little School That Did*, James Brunnemer provides his personal perspective on this institution, his alma mater.

Jim brings a rich background to the task of writing about the University. He has seen the school from many vantage points during the forty-year period from 1963 to the present time: as a young person aspiring to attend college, student, athletic participant, alumnus, administrator, husband of a graduate, and parent of a student.

Because Jim's life has been so intertwined with the University, this book is not merely about that school. It is also about Jim. The book describes how both an institution and a person have changed over time and reflects the evolving relationship between the two.

And each has changed substantially over time. When Jim came to the campus in early 1963, the institution was called Indiana Central College and had fewer than a dozen buildings and eight-hundred students. It did not have a graduate program. Later, its name was changed to Indiana Central University and later still to the University of Indianapolis. When Jim left in fall of 2000, the main University buildings and grounds were worth over $60 million and more than 10,000 students from over seventy countries were taking credit and non-credit coursework at the main campus in Indianapolis, and at branch campuses in Cyprus and in Greece. A well-regarded graduate program included doctoral degrees in physical and occupational therapy, and clinical psychology.

Jim's life has also involved change. Adopted at twenty-two months of age by a family whose male head was a foundry worker, Jim was raised in Martinsville, a small Indiana town south of Indianapolis. College attendance was not a family expectation. Jim was a bright, but not academically oriented boy. At least in part, Jim was propelled to college by his interest in and skill at athletics. He discovered leadership skills and academic talents as a student at the University. Ultimately, he earned a doctorate at Indiana University.

Dr. Brunnemer has had a distinguished career in higher education, serving administrative positions at the U. of I., St. Norbert College, Eastern Michigan University, and Albion College. At the U. of I., the positions he held included a stint as director of alumni relations (where as an Alumni Board member I met him in the early 1970s) and dean/vice president for institutional advancement from 1989 to 1999.

Two features of *Distinction Without Pretension* stand out. Despite being about an institution, the book focuses on people and their stories, including University heroes (some flawed) and villains (some well meaning). In writing the book, Jim penetrates beneath surface appearances and writes perceptively and candidly about many aspects of the University, ranging from athletics and student pranks to teaching and University governance. He writes about the mundane reality of day-to-day life as well as follies, successes, mishaps, and triumphs.

The book reflects the temperament of the author. Jim likes people: he is gregarious and has a disarmingly friendly manner. Jim is also forthright and direct. He is a bit less than six feet tall and is well muscled. Jim is a man of action: he was an excellent athlete as a boy and young man and as I was writing this foreword had just completed a 1,200-mile solo motorcycle trip around Lake Erie. He does not believe in pretense and is not impressed by titles or puffed up accomplishments. He has an "aw shucks" manner, but does not miss much. And, Jim resists evasion: he tells things the way he sees them.

It is, I think, important that a complete picture of the University of Indianapolis be presented. As a graduate (1960) and the child of graduates (1935 and 1936), I feel a deep loyalty to the institution but have long deplored the view that only the "best side" of University life should be recorded and disclosed. Any institution that has survived adversity and succeeded over a one-hundred-year period should be honest with itself. And the story that Jim tells—taken in one piece—is a story of triumph over adversity, of service to others, remarkable dedication by able persons, and of achievement without arrogance. In Jim's account of his durable affection for his University there is much to appreciate and celebrate. Such a school should welcome a full depiction.

In the future when those interested in the institution want to gain a sense of "the way things were" at the University in the second half of the twentieth century, I believe that they will consult this book. In the meantime, those of us who lived part of that experience will enjoy reading about the University and the people who comprised it, and perhaps will feel a new appreciation for it and them.

PROLOGUE

This book is a love song. It has rich melodic chords, with some discordant passages, and some jazzy variations that always come back to a familiar theme: Indiana Central College. It evokes the sounds of the sixties and seventies combining in a popular 45 record, played on the juke box, echoing from the student center. Another era. But recognizable to all who were undergraduates in those halcyon days. More innocent days? Perhaps not as innocent as one is often romantically led to believe, as we shall see in this narrative. But always fascinating in retrospect.

The book goes beyond formative student days. It is a collection of memories, recalled honestly and skillfully with a smile, sometimes erupting in irrepressible laughter. It overflows with humor that is affecting. The recollections have an authentic voice, and a perspective that gets our attention.

I know of no other writer who can relate sports statistics with such confidence and interest. You may learn more about collegiate athletics than you ever wanted to know. And you will get the feeling that no one else could tell these stories like this author, a passionate athlete, a fierce competitor and a consummate observer. Brunnemer has written an impressive history of sport at Indiana Central College/University of Indianapolis that will be definitive, consulted by all who are interested in years to come. It will offer motivation for aspiring athletes. This is no mean achievement.

But this collection is much more than a history of athletics. It is a highly personal recollection of so many people who have been associated with this extraordinary place. And through it all, the reader will get a picture of the writer himself as he grows up from relatively carefree student days to secondary teaching and coaching, graduate school, and responsible roles in institutional advancement in Michigan and Wisconsin, but particularly at his *alma mater*. In this he personifies *distinction without pretension*. His is a remarkable story.

It is a great testimony to religiously sponsored liberal arts education at its best. I wish that I had known Jim as an undergraduate in one of my history classes, but I shudder to think of the description of me as a teacher that might have emerged in print! His writing has helped me to have a broader perspective of my own vocation, and of my eighteen years as a dean of Indiana Central University/University of Indianapolis. I was an outsider among a closely-knit group of administrators who were alumni. Brunnemer, another insider, reentered this world with great ease in 1989. It was homecoming. Although our professional contact became severely limited after the dissolution of the Administrative Council (each in his corner), I came to appreciate Jim for his engaging sense of humor, realistic assessments, and admirable focus. But it wasn't until I received a personal note from him—perhaps a Christmas letter?—that I saw a new and unsuspected facet. He could write! And in our subsequent associations, I saw a remarkably articulate and civilized person whom I admired and respected. Reading this manuscript has only strengthened my estimation of him.

I have liked the insights this book offers. I have learned a lot. I do not always agree with his conclusions, nor do I recall some of the events as he does. But when it comes to the

University of Indianapolis, his memory is usually far superior to mine, and much broader. He sees people and events with his own marvelous lenses and what he sees is never dull.

It is a great love song. All of us who have been associated with higher education and especially with the University will be grateful for this troubadour who sings it so well.

                                            Carl R. Stockton,
                                            Sometime Dean and Professor of History,
                                            University of Indianapolis

INTRODUCTION

[S]o there ain't nothing more to write about, and I am rotten glad of it, because if I'd a knowed what a trouble it was to make a book I wouldn't a tackled it, and ain't a-going to no more.

Huck Finn
The Adventures of Huckleberry Finn

Exiting Interstate 94 at Chippewa Falls, Wisconsin, I steered my 1600-cc Goldwing into the Pilot Truck Stop. When traveling by motorcycle on venerable trips across our USA, it is my practice to take a break after every two-hour stretch. I had discovered during my solo sojourns atop a two-wheeled vehicle that life is a routine and placid continuum interrupted periodically by people and events that disturb or augment the sameness of one's days.

It was during this road trip in late June 1999 that I scribbled the first of scores of reminiscences about friends and foes, and of adventures both sublime and ridiculous, in the journal that I filled during my peregrinations. After saturating three such diaries with accounts of episodes humorous and grave, inane and weighty, routine and shocking, it struck me that the great majority of my stories and anecdotes had some confluence with my *alma mater*.

That so many of my recollections emerged from days at Indiana Central College-Indiana Central University-University of Indianapolis* should not have surprised me. After all, I had spent more than a third of my fifty-four years as either a student or an administrator on the lilliputian campus at 1400 East Hanna Avenue in Indianapolis, Indiana.

Two bookend events—the assassination of President John Kennedy on November 23, 1963, and 9/11/01, that awful day when fanatical terrorists attacked the Pentagon and destroyed the twin towers of New York City's World Trade Center with three flying bombs—roughly marked my intimate association with the college in University Heights. ICC-ICU-U of I has been a central theme running through my life. If Sam Clemens were me, Indiana Central would be his Mississippi River.

No single event or memory inspired me to organize the etchings of my mind into this manuscript. While by his own account, Professor Marvin Henricks's *From Parochialism To Community* was "a word painting to catch the essence of the experience" at Indiana Central, the *modus operandi* for me was more like that of when you were a kid in summer, lying on your back on the grass with friends and saying things like, "That cloud reminds me of a ... ," and writing it down.

---

* *The original title of the college chartered in 1902 was Indiana Central University. In 1921, after a ruling by the Indiana State Board of Education, the board of trustees began to use "Indiana Central College" as the name of the school, despite the fact that the college's legal title remained Indiana Central University. In 1976, the title Indiana Central University was restored. Finally, in 1986, President Gene Sease and the board changed the institution's legal name to the "University of Indianapolis."*

I was part of, or an eyewitness to, most of the events described in this book. Historical and anecdotal accounts of events that I did not personally observe were derived from many sources. I especially drew upon a rich body of conversations through the years with an untold number of friends, colleagues, and acquaintances. Many of these tales are owned by others and deserve telling. On these accounts I am at the mercy of the veracity of those who have shared with me. And everyone acquainted with Leo Miller, for example, knows he never let facts get in the way of a good yarn.

I do seem to have an exceptional recall. Why I remember our first telephone number (4-5-2-W) in Martinsville, which my parents taught me in 1950, I cannot say. In writing this account, I didn't have to look up the fielding average (.956) of the 1964 Greyhound baseball team of which I was a member. Thirty-nine years ago we were, statistically at least, the third-best defensive team in the nation. Dad's beer of choice when I was a preteen was Falls City, brewed in Louisville, Kentucky. I haven't seen that label in decades.

Despite my proclivity to call up vivid portraits of past events, as one ages, some facts become fuzzy. In writing my accounts of the life and people at the college, I've taken the advice of no less a poetic icon than Emily Dickinson, who said, "Tell the truth/But tell it slant."

That's what you get in this book: my "slant." The contents of the tract are told from my viewpoint, which automatically limits, and perhaps, distorts, the information. It is through my personal prism that you will view the Indiana Central that I came to know and love.

So if you find in this book something you consider apocryphal (a decorative word I learned in Fred Hill's Old Testament class), consider that it may be. As American humorist Irvin Cobb said, "A good storyteller is a person who has a good memory and hopes other people haven't." And it is well known that two persons witnessing the same incident may render vastly different versions of the occurrence. Winston Churchill described one political foe not as a liar but as one who suffered from a case of "terminological inexactitude."

A school, like any social organization, is ultimately defined by its people. Writing in the *Chicago Tribune*, historian Janet Ginsburg commented that, "History inevitably comes down to the stories of individuals and moments that made a difference." Whether a memorable lab partner, a teammate on the football squad, your college roommate, an especially attractive member of the school's debate team, a sassy and clever waitress in the cafeteria, your strictest, most intimidating instructor, or a particularly helpful person in the alumni network, a school comes to life through the human beings one encounters there. My intent is to describe a college's growth and development through its community (some would say *family*), whom I learned about from others or from my own experiences.

Indiana Central has provided me with much of the good in my life. First, I received an undergraduate education that opened doors of opportunity and a new way of looking at life's possibilities. Not long after graduation, I married a woman I met at Indiana Central, and with her I have reared two sons and enjoyed 36 years of marriage. I earned my livelihood over two separate terms totaling twenty-one years at the university. Lifelong friends are strewn across this nation, and it is amazing how often I meet up with familiar faces of former students and classmates of those college days in interesting and intriguing ways.

But the college has given me much, much more.

The spiritual aspect of the institution was imparted in subtle and not-so-subtle ways by the faculty, staff, alumni, and an abundance of the students with whom I trod the grounds of Indiana Central. In a way that may only be understood at a visceral level, it was the serious and uncompromising message, delivered as if by osmosis through the atmosphere pervading ICC, that one's educational contract included a clause binding one to others' sustenance. The eminent lawyer, legislator, and educator, Horace Mann, recognized the critical import of an educated populace in a democratic republic. But beyond that, he decried the trend of American public education to teach facts by rote, without the accompanying spiritual and ethical context:

> [F]ailure to undergird that knowledge ... with a sense of justice, a love of mankind, and a devotion to duty ... only makes students grander savages ... more dangerous barbarians.

After over a century of honing its educational mission, the leaders of the University of Indianapolis continue to maintain that it is not enough to become a "learned" people, as significant a goal as that is. We must integrate, within our body of knowledge, an awareness of our accountability to a higher calling, a sense of duty to our fellow travelers in the journey of life.

Michael P. Maxwell, Jr., vice president for academic affairs at Marian College in Indianapolis, expertly phrased the test of education:

> For citizens to engage in responsible self-governance, they need an ethically informed and spiritually mature perspective on the world. The opportunity to develop this perspective is more often a part of the educational experience offered by religion-sponsored colleges and universities.

Indiana Central College-Indiana Central University-University of Indianapolis wasn't—indeed, isn't—a university for everyone. I'm only happy that I was privileged to have been associated with the college.

It was a stage upon which I portrayed "myself"—and that was okay with the rest of the cast of characters in which the comedy and drama of our related lives played out. I was but a bit player in the history of the University of Indianapolis. But when I exited that stage, I did so with the fondest of memories.

Read on, should you wish to learn why.

CHAPTER I
THE ROAD TO HANNA

Life is better left to chance.
I could have missed the pain,
But I'd have had to miss the dance.

Garth Brooks
popular country and Western singer

July 1956

Even from our seats in the farthest corner of the upper-deck bleachers in left field, one could clearly see he was a man of remarkable physical proportions. With a deliberate gait he approached home plate carrying an amber-toned Louisville Slugger in his massive hands. He dwarfed the Brooklyn catcher. Even the burly umpire behind the plate seemed diminutive by comparison. Arms bulging out of the short sleeves of his uniform as he stepped gingerly into the left side of the batter's box, the Cincinnati hitter had a menacing quality about him. The stern confidence of the black man was impressive as he prepared to face tenacious Don Drysdale, ace of the Dodger's pitching staff.

I was 11 years old, attending my first Major League Baseball game at historic Crosley Field in Cincinnati. Brought there along with several other teammates by two of my youth league baseball coaches, I was certain that I *had* died. This *was* Heaven.

Two score and seven years later, vivid recollections of that first trip to the cathedral that was Crosley Field, home of the Cincinnati Redlegs, still linger in my mind. The contrasts in sight, sound, and smell were nearly enough to overwhelm a young worshiper of baseball lore. The verdant outfield and infield grass contrasted keenly with the smooth brown basepaths and immaculate white stripes of the baselines and batter's box.

A steady hum of 30,000 fans turned into a deafening roar whenever a Redleg's hero registered a base hit, struck out an opposing batter, or made an admirable defensive play. A timeless ballpark stench that blended stale beer and red-hots and popcorn and sweat-soaked bodies assaulted the nostrils.

Below us was Crosley's famous left field terrace. Parallel to the outfield fence, it was a rising grass-covered slope, unique and beautiful to the fan's eye, but treacherous to a major-league outfielder pursuing at top speed a batted ball. Dominating the outfield wall was a huge scoreboard, still hand-operated in those days by some lucky Cincinnati teenagers hidden behind the slots where they hung the numerals. Hovering just outside the left field fence was an immense building, ugly and soot-begrimed, the sign of a laundry atop it. Scores of baseball-sized craters dotted the flat, tarred surface of the roof of the establishment, attesting to the many "dingers" that had landed there.

Beyond the centerfield fence stood a block of nineteenth century brick industrial buildings, multi-windowed, weatherworn. And in right field was the imposing and storied "Sun Deck," an immense, towering stanchion of bleachers, the cheapest seats in the park at 50 cents each. *This* was where the real Reds fans sat. There was no seat in the Sun Deck without a fanny in it.

James L. Brunnemer

On the field, my baseball cards had come to life. The Brooklyn team of Reese, Snider, Robinson, Hodges, Furillo, and Campanella was splendid in grey visiting uniforms trimmed in "Dodger blue" with scarlet numerals beneath the scripted "Brooklyn" across the chest. The home-team Reds wore sleeveless white jerseys with red shirt-tops underneath, red stirrup hose, and red caps with the distinctive white "C" above the bill.

Through the bottom of the fifth inning neither team had scored. A future Hall of Famer, the six-foot-six-inch Drysdale and his wicked sidearm style seemed invincible on the pitcher's mound. As he wound up and whipped the baseball homeward, I wondered how anyone could yank around a piece of wood 34 inches long and weighing forty ounces in time to hit the ball. On the third pitch of this inning the giant at the plate answered my question with emphasis. Striking with stunningly swift violence, his bat was a blur as he aimed it at a waist-high fastball. Having never seen, in person, a duel between a professional pitcher and hitter, I was awestruck at how majestic is the sight of a baseball leaving the park when powered by a swing so prodigious as that of George Crowe. The towering drive ended when the baseball splashed amid the humanity in the Sun Deck.

As he slowly jogged around the bases, I made a mental note of the man who hit the first home run I ever witnessed live at a ballpark.

That evening when the coaches dropped me off at home I retrieved the box that held my extensive baseball card collection. Finding a Topps pasteboard of the muscular Mr. Crowe, I turned it over to where batting statistics and personal information were found. He had been among the first handful of black players to enter major league baseball after Jackie Robinson shattered the invisible barrier that had prohibited African-Americans from playing in the major leagues for nearly half a century. A 29-year-old rookie when he broke into the majors in 1949 with the Boston Braves, Crowe was to have his best season the summer following that first game I attended. In 1957, Big George led the Reds, which included Hall of Famer Frank Robinson, Ted Kluszewski, Wally Post, Gus Bell, and Ed Bailey, sluggers and All-Stars all, with 31 home runs, 92 runs batted in, and a .271 batting average. Scanning his personal information I learned he was 6'3", 225 pounds, born in 1920 in Whiteland, Indiana. His college? Indiana Central.

September 1956

As was the case of my adolescent peers in 1956, basketball was more than a game to me. I spent countless hours shooting baskets on the asphalt court at the junior high school in my hometown of Martinsville, Indiana, dreaming of one day making the varsity team. It was a warm September Sunday following my first week as a seventh grader at the lone junior high school in town. Typically, I was practicing hoops. I recall the baskets had nearly indestructible chain nets rather than seine twine required in the indoor gymnasiums. The court was nestled in a corner of the L-shaped school building, about twenty feet from the red brick edifice.

Anyone who played on such outdoor facilities in those days will remember that, inevitably, at the endline of the court, craters would develop in the dirt where players would frequently pass beneath the backboard. Often, if a shot missed and dropped straight down it would hit the border of the asphalt where dirt had been kicked and washed away, and bound away from the court. If that happened more than a few times one became annoyed, for the ball had to be retrieved each time before continuing play. I developed a time- and energy-saving method that I executed when my ball hit the curb and started on its wayward journey toward the school building. I would run, and, with a swift kick of the ball, aim at a spot beneath the windows of the brick school building so the ball would carom back to me. Seemed simple enough. And it saved my lazy adolescent self a few steps. I had repeated the maneuver scores of times. However, on this occasion I inexplicably caught the ball a bit lower than I had intended, so that it was propelled upward, striking the window and shattering one of the panes of glass. The ball deflected away, fortunately landing outside the building. I looked around for witnesses. Seeing no one I collected my basketball, jumped on my bike, and raced for home.

Next day I was unexpectedly called into the school's main office. Throat dry, heart pounding, I entered the office of the new principal, Mr. Lloyd Hiatt. Obviously, someone *had* seen my transgression and reported me. As I sat down at Mr. Hiatt's invitation, I saw over his shoulder the very window that had been broken by my wayward ball! The cool breeze emanating from the opening only increased my discomfort and dread. Great way to meet the new boss man.

In the subdued tones and measured pace of his speech that I was later to find so characteristic of Mr. Hiatt, he asked if I was responsible for the accident that had resulted in the window of his office being broken.

It was useless to lie—although I wasn't above that—because it seemed he had the goods on me. I confessed and explained how it happened. (Some years afterward I learned that my explanation coincided with what Mr. Hiatt himself had witnessed. He had been working in his office that Sunday when I kicked the ball into his window!)

"Why didn't you report it?" the principal softly queried, tightening the noose of guilt around my neck.

"I guess I was afraid to," I replied meekly, and truthfully.

After a gentle but firm lecture ("Accidents will happen but we must always own up to them and accept responsibility"), he let me go. No paddling, no payment for the damage, and most importantly, no call to my parents. In those days, punishment at school was doubled or tripled at home—the "embarrassing-the-family" factor, I guess.

Despite my profligate youth, Lloyd Hiatt was to hire me to teach physical education and English to junior high students at Belzer Middle School ten years later, my first job after college. He was a 1942 graduate of ... Indiana Central.

March 1957

Mrs. Phyllis Wershing was my seventh grade English teacher; her husband, Ralph, was the superintendent of the Eminence, Indiana, School Corporation. There was a small group of us adolescent boys who, for some reason, found favor in the eyes of the Wershings. Mr. and Mrs. Wershing were great sports fans, so they would take us to Martinsville High School ballgames away from home. What a treasure for us poor kids who had hardly been out of Morgan County to travel to Terre Haute, Jeffersonville, Shelbyville, and other destinations to follow our high school heroes of the day. The Wershings paid for our dinners at restaurants, a treat that we rarely got to experience. Meals in those days were all taken at home, except, for my family, on wondrous fishing vacation trips to Wisconsin.

So when on a March day Mrs. Wershing asked if I wanted to go to the Eminence High School post-season basketball awards banquet, I was eager. My parents gave approval,

James L. Brunnemer

so I was scrubbed up and excited when the Wershings arrived to take me and two other of my buddies to the event.

What we didn't know until we arrived was the identity of the guest speaker for the banquet, the already legendary coach of the Indianapolis Crispus Attucks "Flying Tigers," Ray Crowe. The vaunted Attucks team, led by the incomparable Oscar Robertson, had won consecutive Indiana State High School basketball championships in 1955 and 1956. After retiring two years later to become athletic director at Attucks, Ray Crowe had, in eight seasons, amassed a nearly inconceivable record of 179 wins against only 20 losses, a ninety percent winning ledger!

Unbelievable! We peons were to be in the presence of greatness that night. It might sound strange that in those "Jim Crow" days in Indiana, four white kids from Martinsville would idolize the black coach of the all-black high school. But sports transcended society's despicable practice of denying the African-American his rights. I would have traded skins to be Oscar Robertson, just as we all wanted to be Ray Crowe. Basketball was the common denominator and those men had achieved what each of us would have given anything to have. We were naïve about the politics of race in those innocent days. It wasn't until later that we would discover the ugliness of racial hatred, not only in alleged "sundown towns" such as Martinsville, but throughout society.

I don't remember what Coach Crowe said to the crowd that evening. I recall only that an adoring audience from the little hamlet of Eminence warmly embraced him. We stood in line to introduce ourselves and receive his handshake. Ray Crowe was someone I would never be as good as, in my mind, which was the reverse of the prevailing racist view of that day.

I had no idea Coach Ray Crowe was the brother of George Crowe, nor that he and the Martinsville High School basketball coach from whom I would later learn much, Henry Potter, were teammates and *roommates*, an unusual arrangement for a white and black student at most colleges and universities in 1939 … except at Indiana Central.

September 1957

Unable to solve the mystery of the built-in combination lock of my locker in the basement of the old MHS building, I looked around for help. Entering the high school for the first time, I was embarrassed to ask assistance of the tall man with the blond crew cut who was rumored to be the new eighth grade basketball coach (if I couldn't figure out how to open a simple combination lock, how could I hope to understand offensive and defensive play?). But I was going to be late for the first bell if I couldn't get this infernal thing opened.

Mr. Rich Reasoner must have sensed my distress as he strode toward me. He asked for my combination numbers, then explained as he spun the lock dial: "Go to the first number, then spin it clockwise. Pass by the second number before returning to it, then turn the knob counterclockwise again and go directly to the third number." *Voila*! With a sweet-sounding "click" the lock unlatched.

That fall I made the team, playing for Mr. Reasoner. Years later we became teaching colleagues at Belzer Middle School, establishing an intimate friendship that has lasted to this day. In June prior to our meeting at my locker Mr. Reasoner had received his bachelor of science degree from Indiana Central.

Distinction Without Pretension

The influence of the small, spartan college located on Indianapolis's Southside abounded in my small world, the limits of which were essentially the four county lines of Morgan. I had no notion that I was being mysteriously, inexorably drawn toward Indiana Central College (ICC) on Hanna Avenue.

Coach Reasoner was my basketball mentor both during the eighth grade and the jayvee season during my sophomore year. In 1957, our junior high basketball schedule included a two-game home-and-away set with Franklin Township. The Flashes' coach, Bob Theil, Indiana Central class of '57, was one of Coach Reasoner's best friends. The first time the two teams met, it was obvious from Coach Reasoner's nervous demeanor that this game was special to him. He didn't want to lose to Coach Theil. Officiating the game were two other close friends and former teammates of the opposing coaches, Don Shambaugh '57 and Larry Hanni '58. Both Theil and Reasoner rode the hapless officials throughout the game, accusing them, facetiously, of favoring the other coach, depending upon which way a call went.

At that time, we had an eighth grader who had "missed being promoted" a couple of times. In contrast to most of the junior high kids on the court that day who were 12 or 13 years of age, "Butch" was, at 15, nearly a head taller than everyone else, muscular, and he had *hair* on his chest! It wasn't a stretch to say he was a man among boys. But unlike in Indiana High School Athletic Association rules, there was no maximum age regulation in junior high. So "Butch" played. Oh, how he played! He scored the same number of points as the opposing team in a 44-26 waltz over the Franklin Township boys and gobbled up most of the rebounds of shots missed that day. Theil was frantic, trying to find some way of stopping our version of Wilt "the Stilt" Chamberlain. After the game, Theil was steamed. Only half-jokingly, he accused Coach Reasoner of "using your bus driver" in the pivot.

Coach Reasoner just grinned.

There were others from our small community who were graduates of Indiana Central, or soon to be. Donel Bisesi '61 had been a varsity basketball player for the Martinsville High School Artesians during my elementary school days. A spunky 5'8" guard, it was his two-handed set shot that I tried to emulate until I grew strong and athletic enough to launch a jump shot. His name frequently found the headlines of the sports pages of the *Martinsville Reporter* every spring as one of the top prep golfers in Indiana and later as a PGA professional. In recognition of his outstanding contributions to college and professional golf, Don was inducted into the university's Athletics Hall of Fame in 2000.

As a young fan I observed numerous times an outstanding Artesian distance runner, Marshall Goss '60. Marshall would invariably speed past his opponents in the mile run on the fourth and final turn, lunge through the tape, then collapse in an exhausted heap on the cinder oval. He was a champion runner both at Martinsville and later at Indiana Central. Ultimately Marshall became head men's track coach at Indiana University.

His brother Gordon '63 captained the varsity cheer squad at Martinsville. Interestingly, when the cheerleaders took the floor for their routines during the game, the crowd's attention did not wane. Gordon's vertical jump was superior to any of the team's varsity players of that time! He was genuinely gifted athletically, even though he didn't compete in varsity sports.

Despite my being intimidated because of his position as high school principal, I

James L. Brunnemer

found Mr. Ray Kennedy '49 to be very friendly to shy and awkward students like me. I learned that Mr. Kennedy had played basketball for Coach Angus Nicoson '42 at Indiana Central. "You mean the Coach Nicoson who coaches the Indiana All-Star Team every summer?" I gushed.

"Yes, the very one," Mr. Kennedy replied. I was impressed, because in those days every kid in Indiana dreamed of playing in the Indiana-Kentucky high school basketball series and certainly knew who Coach Nicoson was.

Hubert Bastin '48 was assistant coach during my baseball playing days at Martinsville. Hugh also had played for Nick and his Greyhounds and became a friend and advisor to me over the years.

But the individual I most admired during my adolescent years was varsity basketball coach Henry "Hank" Potter '39. Coach Potter epitomized all that coaches can be as positive role models for young men. He was a gentleman, but fiercely competitive. He taught us to play within the rules but to play hard always. My first contact with Mr. Potter was as a fifth grader when, as the high school varsity coach, he organized the youth basketball "feeder system" at Martinsville. We practiced at the old Main Street Armory twice weekly and then played games on Saturdays in the Glenn Curtis Gymnasium, upon the same floor that Johnny Wooden once romped on. Coach Potter had an easy, warm manner. Always encouraging, he never missed an opportunity to uplift a youngster with a kind word, and it always provided us insecure, self-conscious youth a boost to be recognized by the head coach.

"Hey, young man," he would call out to me. "I saw you got 16 last Saturday. Way to go. But don't forget your defense. And be a good teammate!"

I learned more about how a man faces unfairness and adversity in life with class and dignity from an incident that occurred at the end of my sophomore basketball season. The school board fired Hank that year. After leading the Artesians to the semi-state the previous year, Coach Potter was left with only two senior players and virtually no junior class. So he filled the roster with promising freshmen and sophomores to build toward the next year. Following our second game in a season in which we would win only three of 21 games, our best player, a senior, broke a cardinal training rule by drinking alcohol. In those days such an infraction meant automatic expulsion from the team—expulsion, that is, if the coach had the integrity to enforce the rule uniformly. The young man's parents wielded much influence in Martinsville. Hank stood by his decision, and despite the protestations of most of the town and emotional appeals from several of his ex-players, the parent prevailed upon the school board not to renew Coach Potter's contract. Not once did Mr. Potter engage in self-pity or name-calling or in any way handle himself but with utmost character and class.

Ironically, Mr. Potter's economic situation changed significantly for he turned a part-time job intended to supplement his income into a full-time career in Franklin Life Insurance sales. After twenty-five years in that second career, during which he was named to the company's Salesman's Hall of Fame, Hank retired to the fairway along the ninth hole at Sugarloaf Country Club in New Smyrna Beach, Florida. In 1991, Coach Potter was honored with induction into the university's Athletics Hall of Fame.

Later, Mr. Potter recruited into the Franklin Life Company another individual who suffered a similar episode in the coaching ranks. Seaborn Hillis '57 went on to become one of America's top salesmen at his agency in Montgomery, Alabama, after being fired as basketball coach at Connersville, Indiana. For his accomplishments in business and philanthropy, Mr. Hillis was accorded the highest honor that the U of I Alumni Association may present to one of its graduates, the Distinguished Alumnus Award, in 1976.

And who replaced our beloved Coach Potter at the helm of Martinsville's varsity team in 1961? Lee Perry '42, a gentle giant of a man who was a stalwart on the storied 1941-42 Greyhound basketball squad.

Those men and those incidents were the first exposure I had to the educational institution with which I was to develop a lifelong love affair. It seemed predestined that I would attend Indiana Central. By the second semester of our senior year of high school, three of my closest pals and teammates—Jack Leonard '66, Dick Elmore '66, and Bob Riffel (who later transferred from ICC, ultimately graduating from the University of Virginia)—had all declared their intention to attend Indiana Central College.

That Great Crimson and Grey Admissions Director in the sky beckoned.

So how—*tell me how*—in the fall of 1962, did I find myself enrolled at ...

CHAPTER II
BUTLER DAZE

*He had the heart of a thoroughbred,
trapped inside the body of a jackass.*
Anonymous

... BUTLER UNIVERSITY?

What seemed a foregone promise of marriage to Indiana Central was delayed by a semester-long flirtation with Butler. Now, anyone with whom I've been even casually associated over the past thirty years might suggest I have an unequivocal, if irrational, loathing of all things Butler. Actually, what appears to be an unbridled contempt for people connected with the school in the Butler-Tarkington neighborhood is actually a tongue-in-cheek joy of tweaking our supercilious northside rivals. Truly, I've always considered Butler University to be among the top four institutions of higher learning ... in Marion County.

A decision late in my final year of high school to attend Butler was primarily the product of a dream that had no chance to succeed. I just didn't know it at the time. With an unrealistic assessment of my very modest athletic assets coupled with foolish optimism, I chose to follow my idol of that day, Tom Bowman, to the north-side campus in the hope of playing basketball for the noted Coach Tony Hinkle. Tom, three years my senior, had taken me under his wing while at Martinsville. He was one of the top high school players in the state and had been recruited by Coach Hinkle to attend Butler.

Why I had the temerity to believe that I might one day play basketball for Tony Hinkle (or any other *college* coach, for that matter) made as much sense as saying Al Gore and I were partners in inventing the Internet. I was very much an average high school player. Nonetheless, I determined to go to Butler as a "walk-on." I would impress Hinkle with my determination and growing, if limited, basketball skills, earn a scholarship, and while not becoming another Bowman, certainly would contribute in the image of Butler playmaker and defender Dick Haslam.

Bowman would ultimately be recognized as one of the Bulldogs' five greatest players when he was named to the school's All-Century Team in 1999. My highlight in a Butler uniform was making a 10-foot jumper against the "Rinky-Dinks"* in a long-forgotten pre-varsity game on a cold October night in 1962.

My one-semester stay at Butler was not without its moments, though. Along with Martinsville teammate Jim Branham, who *had* earned a basketball scholarship from Coach Hinkle out of high school, I pledged Kappa Sigma fraternity at a summer pig roast held to "rush" freshmen identified as potential "brothers." Bowman was a senior active.

* *"Rinky-Dinks" was the deprecating moniker bestowed on the collection of sophomore basketball players who did not play regularly for the varsity. The freshmen team played the "Dinks" prior to most home basketball games at a normally empty Butler Fieldhouse.*

James L. Brunnemer

Fraternity life was a blur of mostly mock-harassment by upper-class actives; required attendance at exchange dinners and other social events with stiffly-coifed sorority girls beaming with insincere smiles; forging long-lasting friendships with fellow pledges like Jim "Blackie" Hohlt and Jeff Cougill; maintaining my "dry" stance regarding alcohol consumption while always buying my share of the rounds for brothers at local bars (illicitly, of course); and, over nightly "study table," realizing how truly inadequate was my preparation for college academics.

My initial college examination was to demonstrate, swiftly and completely, that perhaps I hadn't caught on to how seriously some faculty seemed to take the material they tried to impart daily to their students.

Enrolled in a History of Western Civilization class, Branham and I were three weeks into our college experience when assistant professor Douglas McManus provided the measuring stick of our academic readiness at Butler. I remember McManus well, for up to that time I'd never seen anything quite like him. The memory of Dr. McManus conjures up, most nearly, the image of the pompous "Professor Phil," a character in a Rodney Dangerfield movie of the eighties entitled *Back to School*.

A Kent State graduate, McManus affected a stiff and haughty British persona, with the regal and often bored expression of the superior intellect who must, of necessity, painfully endure the ignorance of his freshman charges. He wore a cap with two brims, front and back, like Sherlock Holmes. While lecturing he would puff periodically from a meerschaum. He sniffed, audibly, that he only read the *New York Times* and *Wall Street Journal*, as every other newspaper in the world was hopelessly inferior in quality, especially Hoosier rags such as the *Star, Times,* and *News* of Indianapolis. Had he just once glanced at the *Martinsville Reporter*, he might have swooned.

The self-styled "Oxfordian" prof—from Ohio—loved to pounce on students brash or naïve enough to challenge any of his novel ideas. More than one insolent freshman was reduced to blubbering non sequiturs when engaged in debate with Dr. McManus. I never ventured the first audible word in class. He scared the hell out of me.

On the day of our first test we brought "blue books," as instructed. This was the accepted practice of the day for examinations. McManus distributed the test paper and as I quickly scanned the twenty essay questions, of which we were to choose fifteen to answer thoroughly, panic seized me. My first thought was that perhaps I had wandered into the wrong classroom, for I had little familiarity with the contents of the paper interrogation now lying on my desk. But as I looked around the room I noted these were the same students who had been showing up at 8 a.m. every Monday, Wednesday, and Friday the past three weeks, along with me. So unless I was dreaming, this was Western Civilization 101, and a test of which I was expected to have some understanding. Uh-oh.

I plodded through, occasionally finding a question to which I could apply some mustard seed of information. But mostly, it was like groping through room after room in an unfamiliar house, in darkness, bumping into walls. Mercifully, time was called at one hour, or approximately fifty-six minutes after I had exhausted my entire knowledge of Western Civilization.

A week later McManus had the test results for us. Now, Jim and I were seated side by side in those turn-of-the-twentieth-century-vintage wooden desks. You know the ones. A hole in the upper right corner for an inkwell that was never used, a pencil slot carved into the wood at the top center, and a black cast iron base supporting the flip-up seat.

As McManus passed down my row his face revealed neither encouraging nor discouraging signs to the students now receiving their tests from his hands. When he dropped my closed booklet onto the desk I took a deep breath, slowly peeled back the cover, and ... my heart sank! At the top of the page were two gracefully penned fives, as in "55." The bottom of the passing scale was 65, so I had flunked my very first college examination.

I looked to my left to see Branham grinning coyly. "Way to go, Einstein," he hissed. "A 'flag' on your first try."

Still with that satisfied smirk on his countenance, certain that his grade couldn't be worse than mine, Jim looked hopeful when McManus came up the row to return his test paper.

Whatever satisfaction he took in my futility was summarily dashed when he found a sad, lonely-looking single digit—a "9"—at the top of his paper. It was followed by a blunt, if neatly scripted, phrase: "You obviously didn't understand the task."

I learned right then that misery doesn't just *love* company; the first in misery becomes *hysterically* elated by the second. Compared to Branham, I was a modern day Copernicus (wasn't he the expert on Western Civ.?).

We had to report our scores that evening to the fraternity house study table monitor, Allen Youmans. Al, a junior Kappa Sig who would later return to his hometown of Sheridan, Indiana, to become principal of its high school, immediately created an apt moniker for Branham and me. He dubbed us the "Ass brothers": "Jack" and "Dumb." (Al was later to prove Butler had not entirely warped his judgment. He married Indiana Central coed Pat Gunter '67.) And Branham? After a nomadic educational trek, Jim ended up a sterling coach and respected high school educator.)

Similarly, my earliest efforts in English composition were, to be kind, below standard. If the grading scale was the world and C-level really was sea level, you would find me in the Mariana Trench, 35,000 feet down, buried beneath the sand and silt, along with some long-forgotten sixteenth-century Spanish galleon.

Dr. Margaret Fisher, rest her soul, was a most prim and proper professor of English. She could have been my grandma. With my Morgan County nasal twang and country slang, the pedantic Dr. Fisher most likely would have recommended me for an English-as-a-Second-Language class, had it been available. Hey, it wasn't my fault that she couldn't speak "Morgan County."

Her appraisal of my first theme left the paper looking like a botched transfusion. There was crimson all over the place. The rumor that local office supply stores were stocking extra red-ink pens turned out to be false, but the point was made that Dr. Fisher was of the opinion that I had only a slim chance of rising to a state of semi-literacy by the end of the semester.

It was with great anticipation that I enrolled in Coach Tony Hinkle's Theory of Coaching class that first semester. Paul D. "Tony" Hinkle was then in the midst of building his reputation as a coaching legend. Like his counterpart at Indiana Central, Angus Nicoson, Hinkle at one time simultaneously coached football, basketball, baseball, track, and golf as well as directed the university's entire athletics program. The local media revered him.

Many of his former players went on to coach in high schools across Indiana. The

James L. Brunnemer

"Hinkle System" was portrayed as the genesis of team basketball in Indiana. My desire was to play at Butler and become, under Mr. Hinkle's tutelage, one of those great Hoosier cage coaches that I so admired and envied.

I was a bit disappointed, subsequently, that there did not appear to be great profundity in Coach Hinkle's lectures. Now I admit I wasn't an intellectual giant, but I was devoted to and studied the game of basketball. When Coach Hinkle didn't drip genius in that first class session, I became a bit disillusioned, especially when he proclaimed early on his credo of athletics: "The team with the most points when the game is over will win." I didn't have the stones to ask him if that pertained to golf and cross country, too.

Puerile youth that I was, I still couldn't help but notice Emperor Hinkle's clothing. It appeared he might be naked. I do recall him declaring that "whoever puts the ball into the end zone determines whether the outcome is a touchdown, a touchback, or a safety in football." And of his proclaiming that basketball is a game of turns: "We get a turn, they get a turn, and the team that makes the most of its turns usually wins."

That's reasonably profound, come to think of it, especially compared with some of Coach Hinkle's classic utterances during telecasts of the Indiana High School State Tournament. You may recall the time he said to esteemed broadcast partner Tom Carnegie: "Tom, that tall kid there has a better chance to score than the little guys because he's closer to the basket." Huh?

Athletes could count on favorable treatment in the various physical education and coaching courses that Hinkle taught. Half the semester was devoted to the game of football, the other to basketball. Basically, if they showed up, basketball players received an A in Hinkle's Coaching of Basketball class. Football players, likewise, did not find it taxing to achieve an A in Coaching of Football. If you played both basketball and football, you had three hours of A in the coaching curricula. I received an A in the basketball-coaching course, but because I didn't play football, settled for a B grade in that course.

Coach Hinkle could never remember anyone's name. Everyone that he didn't call "Keed" (for "kid") he addressed by a nickname for which that individual was most closely associated in his mind. For example, he referred to Bowman as "Defense" because Tom couldn't guard a lamppost if it was stationed at center court.

I witnessed one fascinating exchange between the dour-faced coach and a local character who hung around the Butler program. John Bayliss was a popular eccentric known to all around the Butler Fieldhouse in those days as "Crazy John." It was common knowledge that this cuddly middle-aged child had only 51 cards in his deck. He was sort of an unofficial manager, or something, whom the coaches and crusty old trainer Charlie McElfresh had adopted. I couldn't help but notice that often Crazy John's mumblings were more illuminating than the coaches' revelations.

One afternoon we freshmen were dressing in the locker room deep in the bowels of the fieldhouse when Coach Hinkle walked into the vicinity. Crazy John was there, bouncing a basketball and spinning it on one finger, trying to attract attention from those around him. Hinkle walked over, put his arm around John's shoulders, and said, his droopy-eyed and wizened countenance stolid, "Keed, if you're still thinkin' about takin' up elephant huntin', give it up. The decoys are too damned heavy." John soberly nodded, as if that truly made sense.

Coach Hinkle's lifetime basketball coaching record, for which he was enshrined

Distinction Without Pretension

in multiple halls of honor, speaks more to longevity than genius. Of the 952 games he coached in his 41 basketball seasons, his team lost nearly 400 times. A .588 winning percentage would certainly not place him among the upper echelon of coaches. His repute as a basketball guru seemed to be built upon the strength of his occasional upsets of larger universities with national renown, mostly in games scheduled at the storied Butler arena.

Perhaps it was merely the naïveté of a seventeen-year-old that enjoined me from following the legions of worshipers of the exalted Butler coach. And I've no doubt that Coach Hinkle will rest in peace notwithstanding that I didn't see all that much special about him.

In the swirl of required fraternity social activities, classes, and daily basketball practice, we typical frosh hardly knew, or cared, what was happening outside the campus confines. Hanging out at the campus club, where Butler students gathered in much the same way as generations of ICC students did at Mary Streets's grill, our limited scope of conversation usually included how greasy the French fries were, what an asshole McManus was, and, of course, girls. While upperclass women were off-limits to frosh like me, more than once I would be tardy for class while sneaking longing gazes at drop-dead gorgeous junior Marsha Pinkstaff or cute and perky little Dee Hunt, another campus queen. Hormones of eighteen-year-olds raged in those halcyon days.

We were rudely yanked into reality, however, on the afternoon of October 22, 1962, when frat president Tom Kunkle ordered everyone into the TV lounge. What did he mean, "We might all be wearing khaki in a few weeks"? We gathered there, peering at the fuzzy black-and-white television screen as a sober President John Kennedy announced the United States' embargo on Cuba. Missiles in Communist hands twenty-eight miles from American shores were problematic. Even I understood the seriousness of that. Those were tense days until we were to learn, as Secretary of State Dean Rusk phrased it, "We're eyeball to eyeball, and I think the other fellow [Kruschev] just blinked."

Basketball was the constant for me, however. In 1962, Frank "Pop" Hedden doubled as assistant football and basketball coach at Butler. While Pop completed the football season, a Butler alum and former All-American, Bob Dietz, handled the frosh basketball hopefuls in tryouts. More than forty young men showed up to try to make the squad. Most were like me, without basketball aid, and the security that gave to those actually recruited by Hinkle. Surviving the final cut, which honed the squad down to fifteen of us, encouraged me.

Enter Pop. If you ever watched the "Star Wars" series of movies created by George Lucas, you will likely remember a character named Jabba the Hutt. Picture Jabba and you have a head start on my description of Pop Hedden.

Pop's massive head was shaved completely bald, long before that became a popular style among men (and some *women*) at the turn of the twenty-first century. Pop was an immense, fleshy hulk of a man, unsmiling and sardonic, who preferred communicating through grunts rather than articulate sentences.

Among the nicer and intelligible comments Pop directed my way during my term as a freshman basketball hopeful was this thoughtful encouragement: "Yer pretty damned slow fer a short little shit."

Thanks, Pop. Such a charmer.

At the end of the football season, along with Pop came several basketball hopefuls

James L. Brunnemer

who had also played football during the fall. Fellows like Joe Purichia and Jeff Cougill took off the pads and joined us on the hardwood. Those who had played freshman football for Pop in the fall had immediate and lasting advantage over anyone in the following three categories:

1. One who did not play football, or
2. One who did not have a basketball scholarship, or
3. Anyone under six feet tall who played basketball unspectacularly.

As I looked around at those of us still on the squad, I noted I was among the few meeting all three criteria.

Before Pop had ever seen us practice, I found myself at the bottom of the pecking order. Over subsequent weeks basketball would become less and less fun, and, as a result, less important to me.

But there was one inspiring anomaly to the scene. Like me, fellow Kappa Sig pledge Jim Hohlt harbored a dream of walking on and playing at Butler. A Southport High School grad, Jim was known as "Blackie," nicknamed by our fraternity mates after his very able high school coach, Carl "Blackie" Braden.

I had already come to the realization that I just didn't have the talent to succeed at Butler basketball, but Jim kept his dream alive even in the darkest moments when it made no sense to believe he would ever wear a varsity uniform. He was the most competitive and determined guy in our group. His spirit was indefatigable and his work ethic surreal. He had been born with a clubfoot, but like many obstacles he overcame in his life, Jim compensated for his slight limp. I was so proud of him when he defied all odds to earn a starting position on the Butler varsity as a junior. (Later, at Indiana Central, I was to encounter another with Hohlt DNA, Jim's younger brother, Fredrick '72. "Fritz" would become a champion cross-country runner for Coach Bill Bright.)

An incident during our freshman season demonstrated Jim's almost fanatical drive to play. It was near the end of the first semester during a Rinky Dink game between the freshmen and sophomores who were not playing for the varsity. As had become our custom, Jim and I were seated as far from Coach Hedden as possible. We claimed our seats at the end of a bench containing fifteen players, volunteer assistant coach Dietz, a trainer, a student manager, and Pop Hedden. In only a few short weeks, Pop had eradicated the youthful desire and enthusiasm for basketball most of us had brought to Butler. That is, everyone but the guys who got to play regularly. And "Blackie" Hohlt. I was passing time watching the cheerleaders, especially Ina Sue Cross, who had once deigned to go out with me. Guys nicknamed her "Double." It was apropos.

The ever-present energy field that surrounded Hohlt whenever he was near a basketball court interrupted my reverie. Jim was literally twitching there beside me, yearning to get into this meaningless Rinkie Dink game. He wanted it bad.

So, about five minutes into the contest, I nudged Hohlt and hissed "Blackie! Pop's callin' for ya' to go in for Larry Shade. Git goin'!"

Without even considering who said that—a prevaricator like me—Jim exploded from his seat. Dashing down the length of the bench in front of the other bored freshmen, Hohlt had already stripped off his warm-up jacket, presenting himself eagerly to Jabba the Pop, whose ample butt spilled over the narrow bench almost to the floor behind him. Looking upward with those sad eyes engulfed by immense jowls, Pop, annoyed because this person who wasn't supposed to be standing there was no doubt interrupting a sound sleep, bellowed, "What ta' hell you want?"

"Coach, Brum said … "

Confronted by Pop's dull gaze of disgust, Blackie realized then that he was on a fool's mission. Turning away without another word, the embarrassed Hohlt slunk back toward his seat far in the distance. His teammates and the few fans seated in rows behind us snickered in derision. Jim had a sickly grin on his face and homicide in his heart.

"You're dead meat after this game, Brunnemer. D.O.A."

I left hastily after the contest, eschewing my normal shower. I avoided Jim for a couple of days until he had regained perspective.

Fraternity high jinks were ever present. Pledges would endure agonizing "lineups" after midnight in the basement of the old Kappa Sig house on 46th Street, where the "actives" would test their creativity for devising newer and more brutal humiliations to gauge our mettle.

At one particularly agonizing lineup, my fraternity "father," Bob Angell, sidled over to me and whispered a strategy that would gain me "points" with the older "brothers." Like all my fellow pledges, my eyes were directed toward the ceiling. Some moron was pouring molasses from a can stolen from the kitchen stores over the head of each pledge. With great sincerity in his voice, Angell told me that when it came my time to be baptized with syrup, "keep your eyes open. The senior actives will love it. It'll show you got balls."

Ever had molasses poured in your eyes? Let me assure you it isn't pleasant. As the sticky goo slid onto my hair, seeped down my forehead, and breached my eyebrows, I steadfastly kept my eyelids open. Then something like napalm exploded in the cavities of my eyes. As I unabashedly yelled in pain, and in a rage at being so betrayed by my future "fraternity father," I heard Angell's familiar voice: "That's my dumb-ass son, trying to gain brownie points. I can't believe this pathetic ass-kissing, Brunnemer!" Thanks, dad.

Occasionally we turned the tables on the actives, especially during a "walkout," when our entire pledge class left the house to stay at one of our pledge brothers' homes. We stayed together as actives on the prowl tried to capture one or more of us. The poor unfortunate wretches who were kidnapped by actives would endure punishment intended for all of us.

On the night of our first walkout, during which we would secretly depart, leaving the frat house in a mess by trashing rooms and stealing cookware, Jim Branham and I decided to provide a special surprise for the nastiest pledge-harasser of all. Tom Schendel of Plainfield was a sullen knave with the personal charm of Vlad the Impaler. His pseudo-teasing of pledges often crossed the line of fun to cruelty. The Ass Brothers were two of his favorite targets.

It was just before the midnight hour of the evening the pledges were to skip out. Branham and I were in the study room and Schendel was monitor that evening. As usual he had brought along his favorite pipe for a relaxing smoke as he hovered over us.

As Schendel began to tamp his tobacco, Jim and I exchanged conspiratorial looks. Tom tried to light the pipe, but as he inhaled he became confused as to why he could draw no smoke.

James L. Brunnemer

    Jack and Dumb weren't surprised, though. Only that evening we had sneaked into Vlad's room, unscrewed the pipe stem from the bowl, stuck the stem into Schendel's toothpaste tube and filled the narrow hole with Pepsodent. We cleaned off the excess toothpaste, screwed the two pieces back together and placed it on his desk.

    Angry now that the pipe wasn't functioning, Schendel sucked harder and harder until his nose started to turn in upon itself. Jim and I picked that moment to exit and join our fellow pledges in the great escape. It couldn't have taken Schendel long to discover the problem and subsequently the chief suspects who did the deed. We paid for it later, of course. But our revenge on him was heady for a time.

    By the first day of December, 1962, I had determined to leave Butler. Despite genuinely enjoying the guys in the fraternity, and the silliness of it all, I wasn't sure I wanted to continue in college. Homesick, disillusioned with basketball, and saturated with too many new discoveries too quickly, I found myself on the phone. After a second ring, the voice on the other end of the line said, "Hello, this is Rich Reasoner."

CHAPTER III
TWO ROADS DIVERGED

... in a wood, and I—
I took the one less traveled by,
And that has made all the difference.
Robert Frost

It was my old junior high and jayvee basketball coach to whom I turned for counsel in December of 1962. I wasn't sure that I was college material; I *was* certain that I didn't want to be at Butler. We weren't meant for each other.

When I discussed my misgivings about college with Mr. Reasoner, he listened graciously, solicitously. He suggested I might want to consider Indiana Central College, and if I wished, he would accompany me there and introduce me to people who could assist in my transferring schools.

Coach Reasoner, my dad, and me convened at what was later named Nicoson Hall in honor of the man we met that day. It was the Christmas break between semesters at both Butler and Indiana Central. We first talked with Angus Nicoson, whose winning smile and warm demeanor made us feel instantly welcome. My decision to transplant myself from Butler to Indiana Central would be a life-changing event, although I had no inkling of its significance then.

A visit to the admissions office brought Don Fleenor into my life. Changing from one university to another wasn't an automatic thing. In order to enroll at ICC I needed a transcript of my grades from the first semester at Butler to verify I had earned at least a C accumulative average in my coursework. Since the semesters overlapped, and it was not feasible to get an official transcript of my grades in the brief time between then and the beginning of the second semester, Mr. Fleenor offered an alternative. I was to see each of my Butler professors immediately, have them put my semester grades on 3" by 5" cards and sign their respective names. If the accumulated grades equaled a C average or better I could enroll in time for the second semester at ICC. The official transcript would follow.

I knew I didn't have "or better." The C standard was the best I could hope for, and it wasn't a slam-dunk. It was evident that I was borderline in English and Western Civilization. The transfer hinged on my grades in those two classes. I was okay in the rest of my courses, receiving the expected B from Coach Hinkle, and I did just well enough to garner a C grade in zoology. In McManus's class, I had scratched and clawed upward from that ignominious first exam to get my eyelids at C level. But my lower lip was solidly at a D. The final examination that I had just taken would decide my fate.

I contacted my profs and explained my transfer dilemma. Each graciously agreed to cooperate by providing my grade prior to the official transcript being completed. At the predetermined date I appeared in their respective offices with my cards, and a hopeful, if not confident, expression on my face.

Clutching any ray of sunshine, I had some self-assurance as I entered the office of Dr. Margaret Fisher. I thought I glimpsed at least once during the semester a glimmer of compassion in her staid and stern demeanor. I knocked on the door and in her soft, grandmotherly voice, she invited me in. Smiling sweetly at me, she wished me well in my future endeavors, and then icily marked a D for my efforts in her English class. Nice lady. Unbending and very objective evaluator. A stone for a heart.

Now it came down to the menace, McManus. I almost decided not to go to his office after my hope was squashed that Fisher would cut me some slack. But, with nothing else to do, and it being a short walk to his office, I sullenly plodded toward my doom. I think I know what condemned sailors feel like walking the plank. I wouldn't be transferring this semester.

I stopped sweating and my nervousness subsided, so sure was I now of the inevitable verdict. As I entered his office McManus was heading out the door, on his way to another destination. I could tell from his slightly surprised expression that he had forgotten our appointment. I just happened to be there before he had departed to somewhere and to something far more important than providing the final proof that I was an idiot, especially as regards the nuances of Western Civilization.

Without a word he snatched the card I held forth. With that same patronizing sneer I'd seen so often during the semester, and with a flourish of his pen, he marked my grade on the card. My fate was sealed.

But as he handed me the card, he uttered a curious thing: "See, I'm not such a *bastard* after all, am I?"

McManus turned on his heel and was striding from my presence even before I could peek at the dog-eared card.

A C! A Holy-Blessed-Lord-God-Almighty C! I was eligible to enroll at Indiana Central!

I could have kissed McManus square on the lips.

My first day as a student at Indiana Central College is as clear in my memory as if it were yesterday. Dad drove our 1959 Mercury Monterrey carrying my sparse belongings and me eastward down the two-lane pot-holed street that was Hanna Avenue. We turned left into the campus, looking for the underclass males' dormitory. While the narrow lane we traveled was called the "horseshoe," it was actually the northernmost section of an oval bisected east to west by the thoroughfare. Except for Buxton Hall, reserved for senior men, all living quarters located south of Hanna were for women students.

As we turned there, on the right was the gymnasium, practically brand-new and not as yet named for the legendary Coach Nicoson. It had been completed and dedicated less than twenty-four months earlier. There was no Ruth Lilly Fitness Center, meaning no pool, no auxiliary gym, no weight and exercise rooms, nor any racquetball courts, and far fewer locker rooms, classrooms, and offices. Looking to our left, or west, we saw in the interior of the horseshoe a wide expanse of grass bordered by a few tall, aged trees. Hundreds of impromptu student football and softball games would be played here over the years. Golfers practiced iron shots there. Student activities of all kinds would take place in that vast outdoor arena, night and day. Then one day the administration had a sidewalk constructed right down the middle, west to east, and trees planted flanking the sidewalk. That halted *most* student games there.

As we proceeded north, there was no Key Stadium. Ancient scaffold-like bleachers with splintery wooden seats, leftovers purchased cheaply from Southport High School,

Distinction Without Pretension

flanked the sidelines of the football field at the same location where Key Stadium sits today. As we began to turn slowly north to west around the northeast corner of the giant oval, Wilmore Hall, the sophomore and junior men's dorm, came into sight.

Now turning back south, the car halted in the extreme northwest section of the circuit. There stood the freshman men's dormitory, Dailey Hall, where I would spend the rest of the semester. Only a marker is there now indicating where Dailey Hall once stood. A student facility, Schwitzer Center, would later force the removal of the Dailey dormitory. Yet another addition to Schwitzer, completed in 2001, would obliterate any physical sign that this living unit, so familiar to generations of students, ever occupied that acreage.

Awaiting my arrival was lifelong buddy and new roommate Jack Leonard. I recall being so pleased to be reunited with Jack and my other two Martinsville pals, Dick Elmore and Bob Riffel.

Jack and I had the corner room on the first floor, south wing, last door on the left of Dailey Hall. The 16' by 12' space was austere, containing a bunk bed, one desk with an aged brass lamp in the middle of it, plain wooden chairs on either side of the desk, and one closet that had enough space maybe for the wardrobe of the average itinerant. The Martinsville trio helped me move my stuff in. (A delicious quirk of the English language: rearranging the letters of "dormitory" in a particular way gives you "dirty room," which basically describes our abode for the subsequent four years.)

I appeared on time for an appointment that had been scheduled with Ken Hottell, then a young curriculum counselor and aide to Leo Miller in the business office. In a most impressive and efficient feat of advising, a man who was to become a close friend and colleague in subsequent years settled the next three-and-one-half years of my academic life in our fifteen-minute session together.

"What would you like to major in, Jim?" Hottell inquired.

"I wanna be a coach," I offered.

"Physical education," he said and wrote in the requirements through spring 1966.

"Minor?"

"Don't know yet."

"Okay, we'll just fill out all of your required liberal arts coursework. You can come back later when you've decided." (That took care of the next two years.)

Hottell relentlessly pushed forward: "What electives would you be interested in?"

"Uh. I like to write a little bit."

"Okay. I'll put you in English Composition this term, then Advanced Composition, American Literature second semester of your junior year ... " and, zipidee-doo-dah, my entire college schedule was laid out before my eyes.

At the end of the long registration line was the college registrar. Tuition, room and board, books and fees were slightly less than $2,000. At the turn of the second millennium those costs would exceed ten times that amount.

I was one of approximately 775 students enrolled for the second semester of the 1962-63 school term. One hundred and fifty seniors, the great majority of whom would go on to become educators, nurses, ministers, and other social servants, received associate's or bachelor's degrees at the June commencement. Over ninety percent of that graduating

James L. Brunnemer

class matriculated from high schools within the borders of Indiana.

By the commencement ceremony of 2000, the University of Indianapolis would grant more than 800 degrees, including associate's, bachelor's, master's, and doctorates. Four thousand two hundred students, hailing from 62 countries around the globe, sought degrees in nearly seventy major areas of study.

In 1963 all classes took place on the campus. At the turn of the twenty-first century the U of I was offering education at many sites off campus, including "exported learning" to locations in Cyprus and Greece.

My first class was in the old Administration Building (now Good Hall) across the two (not four) lanes of Hanna Avenue. It wasn't until 1968 that the street that divided our campus into sections north and south would be widened to four lanes.

Students who matriculated at Indiana Central College from 1970 to the present are likely to be unaware that the college was not located at 1400 East Hanna prior to that time. Correspondence was received, deliveries were made, and students lived at 4001 Otterbein up to then. Not until President Gene Sease decided that the college would raise its visibility by affiliating with the more heavily traveled artery, Hanna Avenue, rather than the University Heights neighborhood spur, Otterbein Avenue, was the address change consummated. It really didn't make all that much difference, however. For most northsiders, and to much of the downtown business mentality, the southernmost city limit of Indianapolis was still Washington Street, or U.S. Route 40. The college's Southside location has always hampered its quest to be noticed by the Indianapolis community.

That first afternoon I explored the campus. I circumnavigated the oval that was at the center of life at ICC. South of Dailey, across Hanna Avenue, one found Krannert Hall (now Cravens Hall), which housed sophomore, junior, and senior women. This comparatively new dorm, a gift of Herman and Elnora Krannert, was constructed in 1960.

Next, one found Trimble Hall on the extreme south end of the circle. Our female counterparts in the freshman class lived here in what was Men's Hall prior to 1961. Trimble would burn down in 1988. By good fortune the dorm was virtually empty of people when it succumbed to the flames. A parking lot occupies that space now.

Just east of Trimble stood Noblitt Observatory. The small block building was designed, built, and funded by the brothers Noblitt, Loren and Quentin. (Loren went on to be a respected faculty member at ICC; Quentin would become fabulously wealthy as a cofounder of Arvin Industries in Columbus, Indiana.) With the construction of Lilly Science Hall the little observatory was torn down and the telescope transported to the top floor of the new science facility. Warren Hall was constructed on that section of the campus in 1969. A couple of blocks south on Mathews Avenue stood an additional facility for married students fortunate enough to escape the barracks (more about *those* deluxe accommodations shortly).

Across Windermire Avenue and to the west was Buxton Hall, then a dormitory reserved for senior men. Buxton was mercifully razed in 1999 to make way for the Stierwalt Alumni House, a comfortable facility housing the institutional advancement staff. South of Buxton, still standing today, was Nelson House, the residence for the president of the university since 1954.

The school's original all-purpose facility, the "Old Ad Building," stood directly

Distinction Without Pretension

north across Windermire from Buxton. To the west, across Otterbein, was the University Heights Evangelical United Brethren Church (later a United Methodist Church as a result of the 1968 merger).

North, across Hanna from the church, was a Perry Township elementary school. Hundreds of ICC student teachers received their practice training in that building. The stunning new Christel DeHaan Fine Arts Center would later fill the space where that old brick elementary building stood.

The "New Ad Building," later named for President Esch, was directly east of the elementary school and abutted a huge asphalt parking lot on its north side. Students now comfortably strolling the striking Smith Mall cannot appreciate how students often frantically dodged cars coming in and out of that parking lot in our days there.

Off in the distance to the north were the decrepit army barracks, brought to the campus following World War II to provide housing for married students. I think those crumbling hovels eventually collapsed of old age. But the couples who endured the stifling hot summers and frigid winters within the walls of the tarpaper and thin lath shacks have vivid, if not affectionate, memories of those humble abodes.

Finally, out in the corner bordered by National Avenue and State Street was the baseball diamond where lessons joyous and painful—depending upon how we performed— would be imprinted in my consciousness in coming years.

Dailey, Wilmore, and Buxton are all gone now, replaced by residence halls called North, New, Warren, and the newest dorm, Central Hall, completed in 2001. The old "horseshoe" was ultimately replaced by parking lots. Yet to grace the campus were such structures as Martin Hall for sciences, the Krannert Memorial Library, Schwitzer Student Center and its additions, the Zerfas wing of the Lilly Science Hall, Ruth Lilly Center for Health and Recreation, a modern maintenance building, and the Stierwalt Alumni House.

That was Indiana Central College in January 1963.

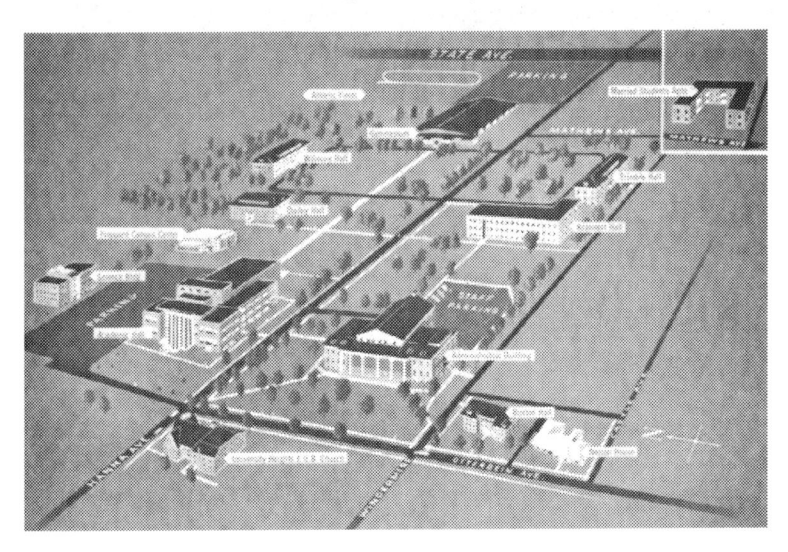

Indiana Central College, 1962-63.

James L. Brunnemer

At noon I joined other students shuffling through the halls of "New Ad" down two flights of stairs toward Mary Streets' Campus Cupboard at the basement level. Student mailboxes were located there. Across the hall was the Rec Room. The noise and number of fellow Centralites passing in and out of that place drew me inside.

Filling the sizeable room were the strains of the Four Seasons' "Walk Like A Man," emanating from a jukebox abutting the east wall, which was stocked with the most current 45-rpm recordings. As I stepped onto the alternating brown-and-beige-tile floor of the Rec Room, students were engaged in various and sundry activities. Numbers of men were gathered around the single pool table at the north end. Several card tables were in the center of the room where students were engaged in the favored card game in the first month of 1963, euchre. It had been only a few years since the university administration had succumbed to allow its youthful charges to play the "devil's game." Other students were milling about, "hanging out," in the parlance of today.

The steady chatter of one particular fellow absorbed in a game of table tennis could plainly be heard, even above the loud music in the hall. He was defending the south end of the Ping-Pong table just inside the doorway. The tall, lithe figure wielded his paddle with extraordinary dexterity as amazed students, heads moving in concert, followed the ball back and forth. Blue-eyed, with a "Hollywood burr" haircut, the confident looking player in a green letter jacket with "I-XL" on the back carried on a steady stream of competitive banter—"talking trash," it would come to be called a couple of decades later—further infuriating his obviously frustrated opponent.

It was then, for the first time, I saw his amazing hands. Yes, hands. It was the magical coordination between his hands and his brain which most contributed to the extraordinary athleticism of Clark Crafton. His paddle seemed to be a living extension of his fingers as he adroitly countered every return of the ball. The flat wooden implement was a blur as Crafton slashed at the ball and consistently drove winners to the corners of the opponent's table. Clark was unbeatable. I was to see the same swiftness and grace of those hands in action on the basketball court over the next three years, swatting the ball from opponents, snatching rebounds away from taller foes, and shooting the basketball with deadly accuracy.

I next moved toward the pool table, where two students were locked in a spirited game of eight ball. Having witnessed my best friend, Jack Leonard, manipulate a cue stick from the time we were in junior high school together, I felt confident I knew at least one of the best billiards players on campus. How many times had I gone into Rube's Pool Parlor in Martinsville with my nondrinking, nonsmoking, nonswearing buddy Jack (he with nary a dime in his pocket) and watch him play for hours? That was impressive, because house rules called for the loser to pay the ten-cent-per-game charge. Jack rarely lost. He had great skill and uncanny foresight that enabled him to visualize where all the pool balls would run on the table *before* he took his shot.

Jack was to win the championship in all three annual campus-wide pool tournaments he entered at Indiana Central.

Having met fellow freshman Steve Lemme, I walked over to where the carrot-topped and gregarious lad was playing a hand of euchre. Around the table were three coeds

Distinction Without Pretension

I was to see in similar poses over the next four years: Phyllis Freed, Judy McClimans, and Jo Ellen Walden welcomed the new kid graciously. Another of my high school chums, Dick Elmore, was at Steve's elbow. Steve and Dick would become inseparable friends through their college years. Likewise, the women assembled there, as did so many persons of varied backgrounds who met at Indiana Central, forged bonds of friendship that would extend across time and space.

Returning to my room, I was to meet a man who would spend the greater part of the next forty years building an unprecedented portfolio of service and achievement at the U of I. Lynn "Gar" Youngblood would become one of my closest friends in the intervening years. At that time he was a senior student and dorm monitor, responsible for keeping feral Dailey Hall freshmen at least reasonably anesthetized. In 2001, he would retire as senior vice president and provost after thirty-five sterling years as a U of I administrator.

Our first encounter, however, would not portend a cozy relationship. Lynn had graduated three years before from Terre Haute Garfield High School, which at that time boasted one of the top basketball teams in the state of Indiana. Terry Dischinger, who went on to All-American status at Purdue and became an All-Pro with the Detroit Pistons in the NBA, was the star player for Garfield and a close acquaintance of Lynn's.

When Jack introduced me as yet another graduate of Martinsville High School, Youngblood retorted, "How many of you outlaws from Martinsville did we let in here?"

He was still rankled over what he perceived as a "home job" his beloved Terre Haute Garfield basketball team had gotten at Martinsville High School in 1959. I was at that game, and Lynn was right. Frank and Jesse James officiated that night. An objective observer would, I believe, admit that Garfield had gotten hosed by the referees in that contest. But we weren't about to admit that to Lynn. Whenever we wanted a "rise" out of Father Superior, we would just bring up that game. In a whit, "Gar" would be foaming at the mouth.

It was time for dinner, so I joined Jack, Dick, Bob, Sam James, and Steve Lemme for the walk to the dining hall, at that time located in the westernmost basement area of the New Ad building. One floor above the dining hall was the library. Librarians Edna Miller and Florabelle Wilson stood sentinel over their beloved books and blissful quietude with relish and thoroughness.

That evening a dance was held at the gymnasium. No, it wasn't a "sock hop" with rock 'n' roll tunes, but a square dance. Modesty and morality prevailed. "Modern" rock and teen dances were still banned on campus. It would be a couple of years in the future before rock 'n' roll would be tolerated by church representatives on the Board of Trustees, so students had to go down the street to the local YMCA for that suspect activity. So I found myself at the gym, and, not caring to square dance, sat in the bleachers with a beautiful young woman with raven hair and eyes to match. Joylyn Hague was one of the college intellectuals, a bit haughty toward a freshman like me, but a lady I would ultimately come to know as a genuinely nice person.

Later on that evening several of us walked across the barren field next to the IGA Foodliner, which antedated Marsh's by several years, and the Lo-Bill by decades. It stood next to a laundromat, where many students chose to wash and dry their clothes instead of using one of the few machines in Dailey Hall. We then crossed Shelby Street to the McDonald's hamburger joint there. The burgers were 15 cents, and if I'm not mistaken,

James L. Brunnemer

the sign beneath the arches proclaimed that half a million had been sold. I have wished so often since that night in 1963 that I had taken my college tuition and invested its entirety in stock in the "golden arches."

Just after midnight that evening, we jumped into Lemme's car and went for the first of many visits to the TeePee Drive-in Restaurant on Madison Avenue. There was a crowd and it was loud. Heavenly!

At 2 a.m. I finally lay down that night to sleep, on a bed in a building at the grounds that would be my second home throughout the next forty-one months, and where a piece of my heart remains to this very day.

CHAPTER IV
THE GOOD LIFE

*Education belongs predominantly to the church
...neutral or lay schools from which religion is
excluded are contrary to the fundamental
principles of education.*
Pope Pius XI

At least three books about the University of Indianapolis have been published.
Commissioned by the Golden Anniversary Committee in 1955, Russell E. Vance, Jr., a graduate of the ICC class of 1947, authored *Fifty Years of Christian Education*. Just eighty pages in length, including numerous period photographs, the book is symbolic of the simple, austere institution it describes. In a straightforward and succinct manner, the author traces the lineage of Indiana Central University from its inception through the celebration of its fifth decade of existence.

The Reverend Professor Vance captures the constant struggles on all fronts that had to be confronted and overcome by the founders and those who followed them as caretakers of the fledgling institution. It was through uncommon determination that a collection of early heroes kept alive the often-flickering flame of an idea to "provide Christian scholarship to its constituents in order that the state and nation might have better educated Christian leaders." Judging by the college records of its graduates, that concept was taken seriously by the visionaries, the faculty and the students. Of a total of 2,422 students who earned diplomas from 1908-55, forty graduates became college professors, two-hundred went on to become ministers, and 1,900 taught kindergarten through 12th grade, meaning fully eighty-eight percent went into education or the ministry. Until well into the 1950s, it was an exception to the rule when a graduate of Indiana Central chose business, commerce, or other professions besides service for his or her life's work.

The second book, *From Parochialism to Community*, was termed by its author, the distinguished graduate and thirty-four-year member of the Indiana Central faculty, Marvin Henricks, as a "socio-historical interpretation of Indiana Central." Professor Henricks fashioned a biography of the university, not seeking to capture the "minutes" of the official history of Indiana Central, but to create "a word painting to catch the essence of the experience" of engaging with the greater university community. Written with candor, poignancy, and humor, the work is consistent with the winsome character of Henricks. Popular with students, he was likened by his charges to the beloved professor who was the central character of James Hilton's novel *Goodbye Mr. Chips*.

A third account of the university, *'Downright Devotion to the Cause': A History of the University of Indianapolis and Its Legacy of Service*, has been painstakingly researched and written by eminent history professor emeritus Dr. Frederick Hill. This exhaustive study of historical documents of the university, presidential papers and official records of the Board of Trustees long laid away in dusty archives, weaves a fascinating account of the men and women who planted the seed, nurtured the sprig, and cultivated the tree that grew

James L. Brunnemer

into the University of Indianapolis.

Additionally, those seeking to know more about the Indiana Central ethos, particularly between the years 1940 through 1970, should read *The McBride Family History*, a book of memoirs written by former dean and professor of philosophy Dr. Robert McBride. A 1947 ICC graduate who later became president at Simpson (Iowa) College, Dr. McBride intended his autobiographical account to be a record for relatives who came after him to know better the family into which they had been born. In recording the McBride family journey, Dr. McBride provides a substantial body of anecdotal information about ICC that is precious. Weaving throughout his life was the modest little college upon which he ultimately left a significant legacy. Dr. McBride's book may be found in Krannert Memorial Library on the campus.

Yet another treatise that finds its author immersed in the life of Indiana Central is *Charting the Elements*. Dr. Robert Munro Brooker, a renowned professor of chemistry remembered as a quirky but fair and generous man, gave the greater years of his life to student advocacy. From 1950 until his death on New Year's Day 2001, Brooker was a constant presence on the campus and in the lives of students, alumni, colleagues, and administrators, always spreading his message that "whatever is good for students, I am for."

What one gleans from each of these perspectives of the modest but perseverant little college reverberates today to the credit of those hardy individuals who sustained it. Through their sacrifice and determination, devoted servants of the school kept alive the concept that a values-centered education was worthy of the selflessness they demonstrated.

As the twentieth century dawned, America was a seething, dynamic mixture of the past and of future promise. Our national banner bore forty-five stars. Oklahoma, New Mexico, Arizona, Alaska, and Hawaii were yet to join their sister states in the Union.

The entry of thirteen million immigrants during the last decade of the nineteenth and the first decade of the twentieth centuries increased the United States' population to more than seventy-six million citizens. Sixty percent of Americans still lived on farms or in small country towns whose inhabitants were steadfastly provincial, most having lived and died within close proximity of the place of their birth. Horse-drawn carriages traveled over predominantly dirt roads (Henry Ford's first "Tin Lizzy" would not be available until 1908). Outhouses, kerosene lamps, and tight corsets were the norm. In one-room schoolhouses, *McGuffey's Readers* were the primary source of education for the five years of schooling that the average American adult completed at the time.

In contrast to the austere life of rural America, in the cities ostentatious lifestyles were in vogue. Top hats and boaters were seen in the smoke-filled men's clubs. Great fortunes were made in railroads, oil, land deals, construction, and Wall Street commercial trading. Although the sinking of the *Titanic* in April of 1912 verified that even man's most stupendous accomplishments could be flawed, it was an optimistic world for the wealthy class of America.

Ironically, those millions from foreign shores seeking freedom and a better life in America would more likely find abject poverty and ethnic and racial prejudice than the carefree life of their dreams. After all, in 1900 America was only seven years removed from a massacre of native Americans at Wounded Knee, South Dakota. It would be another twenty years before women were allowed to vote. The ignominious assassination of

Distinction Without Pretension

William McKinley by the son of a Polish immigrant propelled Theodore Roosevelt to the presidency. At age 42, Roosevelt would be the youngest president to lead our nation. To gauge the racial climate of the time one only need read the 1901 headline of a mainstream American newspaper when Booker T. Washington visited the White House:

"ROOSEVELT DINES WITH A NIGGER"

"Jim Crow" meant separate schools, public transportation, restaurants, hotels, swimming pools, the Ku Klux Klan, and public lynchings.

It was in this era of contradictions, and amidst the backdrop of a national crisis (the Great Coal Strike of 1902, when 145,000 Pennsylvania anthracite coal miners walked off the job), that Indiana Central University was born.

What was to become an important educational enterprise on Indianapolis's south side was a vision in the minds of members of the Whitewater Conference of the Church of the United Brethren in Christ. These church leaders were seeking a site to build a college in central Indiana as a complement to Otterbein College, a related school in Westerville, Ohio. The collision of two powerful forces—an intrepid group of religious leaders and a business-savvy entrepreneur—resulted in an amalgamation that became Indiana Central University.

Recognizing the value of an institution of higher learning as an anchor in a community, and, pragmatically, as a catalyst in selling residential lots that he owned, Indianapolis businessman William Elder proposed an arrangement to the Whitewater Conference members. Mr. Elder offered to provide eight acres of land and to construct a "modern college building" if the members would agree to sell 446 residential lots in the area surrounding the proposed university campus. In 1901, the deal was sealed.

Despite the fact that not all of the lots had been sold, Mr. Elder and the United Brethren churchmen were optimistic enough about the prospects of completion of the terms of the agreement that on October 6, 1902, they signed the articles of incorporation of Indiana Central University. So it was that Indiana Central University became a reality fully fourteen months before two sons of a United Brethren bishop, bicycle-building brothers Orville and Wilbur Wright, would successfully experiment with the first power-driven, heavier-than-air flying machine at a place called Kitty Hawk, North Carolina.

A modern, three-story (four stories in the center section), neoclassical building of approximately 60,000 square feet was constructed, costing Elder the princely sum of $40,000. Some corners were shaved, as anyone who has ever rapped his knuckles on the stately looking but *faux* Ionic columns would know. The resplendent pillars actually consisted of painted metal, not marble as would be found in the "real thing." After all, Elder promised the trustees a useful building, not a palace.

The value of the building and grounds at the completion of construction was $55,000. On Wednesday, June 13, 1905, Elder presented to ICU's first president, J. T. Roberts, and its trustees the deed to the structure and accompanying acreage. (An interesting clause in the original contract prohibited the sale of "intoxicating liquors" in all future buildings to be erected on the original lots!) Just over one hundred days later students entered Indiana Central for the first time.

Through the accounts of Vance, Henricks, and Hill we gain insight into the

James L. Brunnemer

somewhat revolutionary vision of a church denomination to found an educational institution serving not just its own particular doctrine, but "the promotion of a liberal education ... not to any constrained interpretation of religious belief." The founders did desire an "emphasis on Christ" in religious teaching at the school, but they obviously were ahead of their time in encouraging academic freedom to explore thought unfettered by a particular church dogma.

Such a liberal position in that day did not mean, however, that students would be freed of the responsibility the institution felt for the moral and spiritual fueling of its charges. A paternalistic attitude toward its students, characteristic of every administration through at least the end of the twentieth century, was present in the earliest days at Indiana Central. Any student who requested, for example, extra classes, permission to go out of town, employment on or off campus, or other similar mundane exigencies had to go before the entire faculty of ten, which would discuss and decide the merits of those requests.

An account in the first school yearbook, the *Oracle*, described the inaugural student body in this way:

> When on the 27th of September, 1905, the doors of Indiana Central were for the first time opened to students, there was not a large crowd awaiting entrance; it was not composed of the sons of the rich, who come to squander money and time in luxury and idleness. But there was a small group of students, who knew the value of time, the necessity of toil, and the disadvantages of want. However, that which was lacking in numbers and wealth was easily supplied in the indomitable will and courage of those present.

Tuition costs in the first year one hundred autumns ago? Fall and winter semesters required a $12 payment, plus an additional sum of $10 for the spring term. Attending summer school cost the student six dollars more. Including the matriculation fee of three dollars, the student could earn credits in each term offered during the 1905-06 school year for a total of $31.

Room and board for the student staying in what meager and modest housing was available in the University Heights neighborhood totaled two dollars weekly.

The first commencement was held on June 18, 1908, at about the same time five-year-old English immigrant Leslie Townes Hope (later known as Bob) passed through Ellis Island, New York, in the company of his parents. ICU's inaugural graduating class of two—Charles P. Martin and a 1905 transfer from Otterbein College and native of Marion, Indiana, Irby J. Good—each received Bachelor of Arts degrees. At that time, Good surely could not have foreseen how he was destined to leave his own distinctive mark on the soul of the university.

Those early years were characterized by the suffocating debt that burdened the institution and the heroic struggle of the university's constituents to cope with it. In a remarkably prescient statement, ICU's second president, L. D. Bonebrake, observed in 1913, " ... only lack of money (stands) in the way of greatness for Indiana Central University."

Throughout its first four decades, trustees, presidents, administrators, faculty and staff, and supporters among its alumni and friends sparred continuously with a shortfall of funds and resources. Today, as we look across a campus with more than two dozen separate buildings, a college with full enrollment, and 56 consecutive years of balanced budgets, we can only stand in admiration of those early church and educational leaders. What fortitude and determination it must have required to keep alive their vision for Indiana Central University with the nearly insurmountable obstacles they encountered daily.

Naturally, the onus for dealing with the pressing debt of the first four decades of the university's existence fell upon its chief executives, Roberts, Bonebrake and I. J. Good, respectively. Those stalwart men spent the greater portion of their terms in office wrestling with a deficiency of capital and operating revenue brought on by meager enrollments, ambivalence of the United Brethren Church for the need of higher education for its followers, and frustrating failure in nearly every fund-raising campaign or venture. Dodging lawsuits from unpaid creditors, unsuccessfully pleading with church conferences to assume their financial responsibilities on behalf of the college, launching one futile fund-raising campaign after another, and, in too many instances to believe, avoiding receivership, the leaders of Indiana Central pressed on.

Individual and collective heroics sustained the school and its mission. Early faculty and administrators turned profound acts of sacrifice into commonplace occurrences. They accepted stunningly small salaries, or mere promises when the payroll could not be met. As described in an early admissions publication, the "faculty of the school is a well-selected body of *painstaking* [emphasis mine] men and women."

Epitomizing such noble sacrifice were two early graduates who joined the faculty after graduation, Dr. Sibyl Weaver '16 and Dr. William P. Morgan '19. Each taught at Indiana Central for more than forty years, through some of the most barren eras in the university's history.

Not every member of the faculty was willing to make radical sacrifices, however. After receiving no satisfaction in seeking reimbursement for late wages, Louise Alger '11 hired an attorney to collect the salary due her. Writing in frustration to President Good, Ms. Alger declared, "a church college should be built upon more honorable foundations." She seemed not to be impressed that ICU's "sea (of red ink) was so vast, and (Dr. Good's) rowboat was so small."

Early philanthropists and friends of the university were a small but genuinely dedicated cadre of supporters. Certainly Mr. Elder's initial investment in providing land and the first building, today an historic landmark of the state of Indiana honoring the name of President Good, was the catalyst for the realization of the dream.

The gift of Mr. and Mrs. Porter A. Dailey in the amount of $20,000 led to the construction of ICU's first residence hall. Tacie Ann Buxton gave $12,982 in honor of her husband, Dr. Albert J. Buxton, a timely and most significant gift. Brothers Loren and Quintin Noblitt together were responsible for the Noblitt Observatory, which stood for decades in the vicinity of where the current Warren Hall dormitory is now. Loren, an ICU faculty member, designed the observatory and even ground the lens of the telescope, while his brother funded its construction. Quintin frequently paid off notes for the university, contributed and loaned money, then refused any repayment or acknowledgment in return.

A $40,000 bequest from the estate of Roy Nelson was clearly a major windfall for the school. The president's residence, Nelson House, was named for him.

James L. Brunnemer

The president of Railroadmen's Savings and Loan Association, F. S. Cannon, could have virtually put the college out of business in the 1920s, but with great magnanimity, he and President Good always found a way to get an extension on the enormous debt. Cannon's confidence in Dr. Good would be rewarded some twenty years in the future.

But there was never enough cash. Constant reminders of the school's financial vulnerability came in the form of missed paydays by faculty and staff. True stories abound of faculty paid in garden produce or in spartan housing instead of cash. They accepted piteously meager salaries, sometimes supplementing their pay in creative ways. Professor Brandenburg, for example, supplemented his less than $1,000 annual compensation with a grocery store in his house on Bowman Avenue.

The constant lack of financial resources led to the first ICC fund-raising campaign, announced on November 10, 1915, with a goal of $250,000. It failed.

While the first and second chief executives, John T. Roberts and Lewis D. Bonebrake, respectively, unquestionably made their individual contributions to launching and tending to the college in its infancy, their combined terms as president were a relatively brief ten years. In 1915, Bonebrake faced one of the most serious challenges yet from an impatient creditor. Attorney Charles Dryer, on behalf of Foley Brothers, Incorporated, which remodeled the college heating plant for about $500, informed Bonebrake of his intention to "order foreclosure if payment is not received immediately." Although that threat was deterred, trustees determined Bonebrake was not the man to lead ICU out of the financial woods. By not renewing his contract in 1915, the board turned to business manager and instructor I. J. Good, who didn't want the job. But loyalty to his struggling alma mater compelled Good to reluctantly accept the trustees' overture.

Many may share credit for keeping open the doors of the infant enterprise in the early days, but it was one man's iron will and Christian commitment that held together all the parts of a shaky coalition for three decades.

Irby J. Good returned to his alma mater to teach following graduation and was considered "quite excellent in the classroom." Later, he was asked to become business manager in hopes his intellect and sound judgment could solve the troubled financial ledger of the university. In a sober report to the Board of Trustees on March 12, 1915, I. J. Good informed the body that Indiana Central was $85,000 in debt, a staggering amount at that time. This report was a foreboding of a trend that was to be Dr. Good's singular challenge throughout the subsequent twenty-nine years he would serve as president.

It's not hard to speculate, in retrospect, that had not that man and that mission conjoined during a critical time in its history, there might be no University of Indianapolis today on Hanna Avenue. Following Good's first year as president a lay trustee, G. N. Moyer, wrote to him: "Good you have been to this institution as the hero in rescuing a drowning man going down for the third time." Had Dr. Good only known then that for the next twenty-nine years he would, symbolically, have to stay immersed in the water to keep his university's financial head above the red tide.

Abetting President Good in his valorous struggle to keep the college solvent was his quiet lieutenant, treasurer Evan Kek. Few were aware of the lengths to which Mr. Kek would go to meet ICC's financial obligations at times of severe fiscal crisis. Kek's successor as business manager, Leo Miller, is one of those few who are aware of the debt of gratitude the college owes to the valiant financial manager. To understand the commitment

Distinction Without Pretension

of Mr. Kek to keep ICC afloat, consider this: While he was an assistant to Kek, Mr. Miller witnessed several instances of a month-end when there simply was not enough cash on hand to pay the bills. Without even knowing it, faculty and staff often were in jeopardy because the payroll wasn't available on the days preceding payday.

Dr. Kek would quietly borrow $30,000 to $40,000 from a local lending source. He did this on his own signature, not as business manager of the college, which meant that should the money not be paid on time it would be Kek's life ruined, not the college in default. Naturally, few knew of this practice. In each instance, Kek managed to repay the loan on the date it was due, usually because overdue tuition payments or contributions would appear, as if timely answers to prayer. More than once, however, Mr. Kek made up a deficit from his own meager salary. Leo marveled at the personal devotion of this humble man.

President Good no doubt would have enthusiastically endorsed the sentiments of Pius XI regarding education, as summarized in the quotation at the head of this chapter. Good zealously believed that the "most important work [of the college] was the development and maintenance of religious attitudes and high moral standards of faculty and students." He further maintained that it was the affiliated church's responsibility to provide the bulwark of financing the college if the institution were to remain distinctively Christian, as he fervently believed it should. Sherman Cravens, who came to ICU in 1938 as an older student and stayed after graduation to direct admissions and church relations, recalled fundraising forays to the United Brethren churches, some of which attempted lovingly, if meagerly, to support the struggling school.

Because the university had only one vehicle, Dr. Good, Dr. Cravens, and Treasurer Kek would travel together long distances to serve as guest preachers and plead for money for the college. The first of the three would get out at a church, the other two would travel onward, and then the last, after preaching, would return to pick up the other two for the trip back to campus.

At one United Brethren Church in an Illinois village, Dr. Cravens and Mr. Kek left President Good to do his work. It was a bitterly cold December day. The small church had a pot-bellied stove in the center of its sanctuary. Prior to the service a group of men, farmers all, warmed themselves, all the while chewing tobacco and spitting into the fire. When he arrived, Dr. Good became outraged at such behavior, and on the spot delivered an extemporaneous, scathing homily on the evils of demon tobacco. Needless to say, the churchmen took offense and Dr. Good came up empty-handed at plate-passing time.

After that, Cravens and Kek prudently conspired to prohibit Dr. Good from appearing again at that church. The noble purpose of saving souls had to be tempered with the practical cause of raising money for the survival of the college. And the pious Dr. Good could not be trusted to stay on task where sin was afoot.

One enormously crucial accomplishment growing out of Dr. Good's vision for the future was the purchase of real estate surrounding the campus. Through dogged determination at the height of the Great Depression, President Good managed, despite the sparse assets of the college, to turn the original eight acres granted by Mr. Elder into a campus of nearly 100 acres before his administration ended. His foresight enabled the college to have space to add buildings, and the teaching and technology within them, to provide the broad-based education students of the modern University of Indianapolis now receive.

The Good presidency, beginning with his inaugural in 1915, spanned three of the most noteworthy eras of American history. From 1914-18, as the college struggled mightily to gain a foothold as a viable educational institution, the "War to End All Wars" took a horrific toll of lives and property as it played out on the European continent.

In 1920, Indiana Central obtained fifty additional acres for campus expansion and the first "clean-up day" found the entire student body painting, landscaping, and scrubbing all over the grounds. In August of that year, the Nineteenth Amendment to the United States Constitution gave women the vote, and the very first radio broadcast, of the Harding-Cox election returns, was heard on November 2 on station KDKA, Pittsburgh.

A relatively unknown, disenchanted survivor of World War I was writing *Mein Kampf* from his German prison cell as the first campus dormitory, Dailey Hall for women (later renamed Buxton Hall) was erected. In 1921, Indiana Central University became Indiana Central College in response to the State Board of Education accrediting the institution as a "standard college" rather than a university. As supervisor of teacher training for the state of Indiana, Oscar Williams glumly reported that the "university" in ICU was an "unfortunate misnomer." He found Indiana Central to be "a substandard school offering an ordinary liberal arts curriculum ... and does not measure up to the standards of a university." Although the trustees retained Indiana Central University as its legal name, they changed its public moniker to Indiana Central College that year.

Eager students published the first issue of the student newspaper, *Reflector*, in 1922. A few months later Men's Hall (later Trimble Hall) was built. Athletics were becoming popular, so the first athletics director, John George, was hired to provide guidance to the men's and women's sports programs. Yet another student living unit, New Hall (later to become Wilmore Hall) was completed in 1926.

On May 20, 1927, just days before the twentieth graduating class of the neophyte college held its commencement ceremony, a daring young aviator lifted off from Roosevelt Field in Long Island, New York, attempting to become the first man to fly across the Atlantic Ocean. After thirty-three and one-half hours in the air, Charles Lindbergh landed in Paris, becoming an American icon overnight. And even if the stern faculty allowed it, there were few ICC students that year who could afford to see the first full-length "talkie," featuring popular vaudeville star Al Jolson in *The Jazz Singer*.

What passed through the mind of Dr. Good on October 24, 1929—"Black Thursday"—when the New York Stock Exchange crashed? That event was the precursor of a worldwide depression that would find 25 million Americans, or fully thirty percent of the workforce, without jobs. School went on, even though many students could pay their tuition only if the college accepted farm produce in trade. Faculty occasionally went without even their puny compensation. Ironically, only four days shy of exactly fifty-eight years later, another "black" day, Monday, October 19, 1987, would see the Dow Jones lose 22.6% of its value, or $500 billion in stock overnight. Fortunately, federal regulations protected our country against the economic free-fall felt by our ancestors in the thirties.

Interestingly, it was just prior to "the Crash" that President Good considered departing from his preferred policy of isolating the school from Indianapolis. Cautious that the moral character of the college risked unseemly influence from the secular capital city

Distinction Without Pretension

community if he accepted financial help from its leaders, Good had nonetheless determined to begin a crusade to seek just such support from Indianapolis businessmen. Unfortunately, the cataclysm of the stock market and the onset of the Great Depression ended a Good initiative before it began.

The president's nephew, Harry Good '25, was in his third year as coach, preparing his young baseball team for its intercollegiate schedule, when a dramatic news flash hit the campus. The world was stunned on April 4, 1931, when Knute Rockne, Notre Dame football coach and symbol of the "Golden Age" of sports heroes, died at age 33 in a plane crash in Bazaar, Kansas. The entire nation mourned his death.

Dark clouds gathered in Germany on the night of October 30, 1938, foretelling another worldwide conflagration. ICC students returning to their dormitory rooms that evening likely did not suspect that the *Kristallnacht* pogrom 8,000 miles to the east would lead ultimately to war, a conflict that would alter their lives irrevocably.

In 1940, Tupperware was invented, penicillin developed, and a mechanism was discovered that helped turn the tide for the Allies against the Axis powers in World War II: radar. A quiet, unassuming graduate of Indiana Central College, Navy lieutenant Ralph Hiatt '30, played an intentionally invisible but significant role in the development and use of radar during the war.

With the onset of World War II, enrollments in colleges and universities nationwide, including ICC, plummeted as millions of American boys and men went off to fight for freedom. As noncombatant members of the services, women filled jobs on the home front heretofore held by men. This would further the cause of emancipation of women following the war. The consequence for Indiana Central was a campus virtually devoid of male students. Total enrollment was fewer than one-hundred-and-fifty in 1943, many of them males excused from military service for reasons of religious conviction.

Retired Bishop H. H. Fout, who appears to have been the chief thorn in President Good's side for the greater part of his presidency, triggered Good's demise as president in the spring of 1942. With the approval of other trustees, Fout established the Greater Indiana Central College Committee for the stated purpose of studying "the entire situation of the college with problems that now confront the Board as to its future." This was an affront to Dr. Good. He perceived Fout's committee as a threat to undermine his authority and felt as if he "was being put on trial." So he simply refused to cooperate with the committee. When trustee leaders moved forward with the initiative anyway, tensions between them and Dr. Good heightened. Many faculty members applauded the committee, as they had long resented Good's authoritarian management style.

Highly respected alumnus and Indiana University professor Dr. William Breneman '30 found Dr. Good to be "extremely bigoted … dictatorial and not foresighted." He added, however, this accolade: "It is difficult for me to conceive of anyone who could have done a much better job of holding a tottering institution together than he did."

By 1944, with Dr. Good's vitality drained, and impatient, fretting trustees eager for a new direction for the school, the president was asked to step down. The tenacity fueled by this great man's moral strength had been tapped out. Bishop C. S. Denny probably captured the feelings of the majority of the trustees when he observed, "the college probably would not have lasted as long as it had without Good; but probably would not last much longer with him [in command]." Good's twenty-nine-year tenure as president ended on July 1,

James L. Brunnemer

1944.

But his thirty-three year crusade on behalf of Indiana Central was not in vain. Through utter self-will, Dr. Good handed the college back to the trustees, struggling but alive. Though the original flame may now have been but an ember, growing dimmer by the day, ICC had survived. And, on January 9, 1945, just over six months after he was released from the job he had come to love with all his heart, a final payment of $10,000 was made to Railroadmen's Savings and Loan Association. In a large part because of the devotion of Dr. Good, the college was debt-free for the first time in its history.

The esteemed Indiana historian Dr. Donald Carmony, a 1929 Indiana Central graduate and member of its Board of Trustees for nearly forty years, said of President Good: "He sacrificed beyond any reasonable call of duty for the welfare of the school he loved. And his vision proved to be better than that of the trustees."

Now came the arrival of one who was a rising star in American industry but had spurned that promising career to serve God. His ministry led him to a career in Christian higher education and to the portals of Indiana Central College. With his coming, Indiana Central was finally to emerge from the formidable debt that nipped always at its heels, and onward to prosperity and growth unprecedented in the school's forty years of existence.

CHAPTER V
A LENGTHENED SHADOW

*Back of every noble life are principles that
have fashioned it.*
George Horace Lorimer

In November of 1944, events of World War II were changing our society for all time. That same month and year in Indianapolis, Dr. I. Lynd Esch was elected president of Indiana Central College. When Dr. Esch accepted the challenge that the Trustees laid before him, no one could foresee the singular impact this great man would have on the little school in University Heights.

Following his graduation from high school at age 15, Lynd Esch enrolled at Goodyear Industrial University. He was to earn a higher scholastic index than any student who had theretofore enrolled at that noted engineering school. After an impressive contribution in advanced research in rubber production, he was asked to teach at GIU. Following seven years as a faculty member, Esch determined to broaden his educational credentials. He entered junior college in Oakland, California, and there, in a required economics course, found his textbook to be the same one he had taught at GIU ("I did make an A in the course," he noted later). Following the two-year course of study, he earned his A.B. at Chapman (California) College, achieving academic majors in philosophy, psychology, and English, plus a minor in German!

It was while he was a student at Chapman that he felt called to the ministry. After earning his doctorate at the University of Southern California and being elected there to four scholastic honorary societies, including Phi Beta Kappa, he was then ordained a United Brethren minister. Dr. Esch distinguished himself as a pastor, serving pulpits for twelve years in two different UB churches in California before he received a telephone call from a tiny United Brethren church college in mid-America. Indiana Central was searching for a president to succeed Dr. I. J. Good.

Though heartbroken to accept the Trustees' decision to take the college from him, the bane of Dr. Good's presidency, suffocating debt, had finally been settled during his lifetime. Fifty-two days afterward, on February 25, 1945—four days before Dr. Esch began his term as president on March 1—Dr. Irby J. Good's staunch heart beat its last.

The monumental task confronting Dr. Esch in 1945 might have dispirited a lesser man. The few buildings on campus were in grievous shape. The previous graduating class totaled twenty-six members, and prospects for student admissions were grim. The projected budget for the 1945-46 school term was $100,000, yet no one seemed to know how it would be met.

During interviews leading to his appointment, Dr. Esch addressed the challenges by asking the trustees this question: "Are you now willing to engage with the city of Indianapolis?"

Prior to then, previous chief executives had felt it their duty to protect the little

James L. Brunnemer

Christian enclave and its students from the "den of iniquity" known as Indianapolis. In Dr. Esch's vision, its proximity to the state capital's downtown was one of ICC's few substantive *advantages*! Through intervening years the wisdom of that view was proven again and again. The evening division established during the mid-fifties for adult learners drew an entire new niche of students to the campus. Pre-professional curricula in law, nursing, medicine, and engineering blossomed, and undergraduate and graduate business and management courses became flagship programs.

President Esch joined dozens of civic organizations in Marion County, accepted appointments to numerous boards of corporations, and spoke at literally hundreds of luncheons and other events in a frenetic pace to connect ICC to the Indianapolis business and social community. He carried the college with him as the respect and admiration for his character and ability grew among city leaders.

Because the original mission of Indiana Central College avowed to deliver an education for "professional training and development of students as first quality Christian citizens," Dr. Esch coined the phrase in 1947 that became the school's motto: "Education for Service."

Immediate and urgent problems facing the new president on the campus were manifold. But if the college were to gain credibility and attract students, the first order of business had to be accreditation. Without the stamp of legitimacy that the North Central Association placed upon colleges and universities in the United States, a degree from ICC would not have value in the business and professional world.

The college applied for that accreditation in March 1946. Accompanied by business manager Evan Kek, Dr. Esch drove to the North Central Association offices in Chicago. Under mercilessly pointed interrogation by NCA staff, Dr. Esch boldly and candidly articulated the case for accrediting Indiana Central College. Given the appalling state of the campus facilities, sparse and stagnant enrollment, a faculty—while enormously dedicated—that lacked requisite academic credentials, a miniscule endowment, and other related difficulties, there was no plausible reason to expect the esteemed examiners of the NCA to grant Indiana Central academic endorsement.

Following the group grilling, Dr. Esch took the floor. He didn't beg. He didn't grovel. But the sanguine young leader expressed passionately his belief in the institution and what it could become. He gave the investigative team his personal assurance that not only would ICC survive—given a seal of approval by the NCA—the college would become a center of learning that would fill a key niche in central Indiana and would ultimately affect its state and the Midwest with a commitment to melding education with service. Dr. Kek immediately felt that Dr. Esch made an uncommon impression on the accreditation officials with his calm but steely resolve. He was committed to triumph. And the accrediting officials took notice.

The accreditors *were* impressed, not by the college, but by its president. Certainly the investigating team noted Dr. Esch's sterling academic vitae. Most likely they looked positively at his impressive accomplishments in industry at Goodyear. His conversion to the ministry, abandoning what promised to be an extraordinary, and lucrative, career in industry, could not be overlooked.

ICC received that life-sustaining accreditation, but hardly in the usual manner. You see, the team essentially accredited Dr. Esch, rather than the institution. Later, Mr.

Distinction Without Pretension

Harry Gage, a member of NCA's executive board, admitted to Dr. Esch that ICC, on its merits, did not meet the standards for the North Central Association's endorsement. They accorded Indiana Central probationary accreditation on the performance and promise of one man: its extraordinary chief executive officer.

Another example of the presence and weight of moral authority that Dr. Esch wore like raiment occurred during the construction of the "new administration" building in 1957, later to be named I. Lynd Esch Hall. A campaign to raise funds for the building and its maintenance was initiated in 1956.

Despite the best efforts of President Esch and those benefactors who stretched themselves beyond their own capacity to give, it was evident the school would need to borrow a substantial amount of money to complete its construction. Approximately $500,000 of the final cost of the building had yet to be raised. With all philanthropic sources exhausted, it became necessary to approach local lending agencies for help. Cash flow, always shaky at best, left the college in a perilous position relative to securing this much-needed advance. Living at the edge of viability, from semester to semester, the university had no significant collateral to offer.

Otto Frenzel, a steadfast friend of both President Esch and the college, brought together decision-makers of six insurance companies and four banks to listen to Dr. Esch's plea for assistance. Leo Miller and President Esch appeared at the appointed hour in the offices at the bank where the meeting was scheduled. Sober-faced, shark-eyed bank and insurance company executives were there to hear the appeal for funds. Attending as well was Frenzel, president of Merchants National Bank and Trust Company.

Dr. Esch outlined straightforwardly the precarious financial position in which the university found itself, but vowed to be personally responsible for meeting the terms of the loan, if it were approved. All the while the representatives probed President Esch and Mr. Miller liberally with very tough, and several humiliating, questions. Mr. Frenzel offered not the slightest comment during the entire grueling session, preferring to remain an observer. The insurance and bank officials were unmoved. It wasn't a sensible deal. The exposure would be too risky because the university had only promises, not hard evidence, that it could pay the money back.

When the time came to render a decision, Dr. Esch and Mr. Miller were prepared to hear the inevitable. The handwriting was on the wall. There would be no loan.

As the nasal-voiced spokesman for the financial entities began to deliver the bad news, Otto Frenzel chose that moment to speak for the first time. Succinctly, he pronounced, as he rose to leave, "I think we can lend the good doctor the money he needs."

The other reps' mouths were agape.

The university received the loan and ultimately paid off the mortgage. But the financial executives did exact their pound of flesh. Insisting on an unusual condition to the loan, the university had to execute an insurance policy, in the amount of $500,000, on the life of its key player, President I. Lynd Esch.

Once again, as with the accreditation team a decade earlier in Chicago, the loan was made on faith in Dr. Esch. The president of Merchants believed in him, if not in the college.

To those of us who were students, Dr. Esch was the epitome of the classic college president. Sagacious, decisive, visionary, inventive, keenly discerning, highly moral, intellectual, optimistic, and of cheerful temperament, he possessed an aura of strength and dignity befitting our image of what a college president should be. While one never expected to see President Esch in a T-shirt and jeans (I doubt that he even owned such casual attire), he did have a healthy sense of humor and was tolerant of youthful shenanigans, up to a point.

An esteemed Indiana secondary school educator who had attended but did not graduate from Indiana Central, Dr. Robert Hanni, attested to the wisdom and quiet but firm manner with which President Esch handled discipline.

Following World War II and the Korean conflict, every American college and university had a "vets" group consisting of veterans of military service now enrolling in schools on the GI Bill. Foreseeing an opportunity to recruit to the college married veterans, Dr. Esch acquired six portable, weather-beaten army barracks to be used for family housing. Bob Hanni was one of a number of ex-soldiers at Indiana Central who were beneficiaries of this act of Congress.

These men and women who had served their country on foreign soil were not your standard freshman enrollees. Unlike their comparatively sheltered 17- and 18-year-old freshman counterparts, these people were older by four or five years, and worldlier by decades. They smoked and drank alcohol, cursed, danced, and played cards, all practices that ran counter to the rules of church-affiliated schools like Indiana Central. While Dr. Esch was partial to and fond of those young people who had served their country, he insisted they adhere to rules of conduct of the college, which prohibited *all* of the above.

Dr. Hanni related to the author the story of his final days as a student on the ICC campus:

"We had a poker party in the basement of Men's Hall, and I had brought in some beer and cigars to add to the atmosphere. Word got back to Dr. Esch about this event, so he called me in.

"He asked me if it was true that I had supplied alcohol and tobacco for an episode of gambling on the campus premises? Of course, I admitted I had, indeed, done all of that.

"Dr. Esch didn't offend, didn't toss moral judgments at me. He said, simply, that the school couldn't tolerate one standard for the vets and another for the rest of the students, and then very respectfully suggested that I go elsewhere for my education.

"There was genuine mutual respect in that conversation. Dr. Esch profoundly appreciated men and women of the military and the sacrifices they made on behalf of the nation. We shook hands and I transferred to Ball State, where I later earned my bachelor's, master's, and doctoral degrees."

The power of the story lies in the fact that although Bob Hanni left ICC, children Cary '69, Karen '71, and Kevin '74, as well as his younger brother Larry Hanni '58, would earn degrees there with his encouragement. The Hanni family legacy now extends beyond the children of both Bob and Joyce, and Larry and Marilyn Hanni's children to Bob's great-granddaughter Kena, class of '07.

Dr. Esch was a father figure to the campus much as FDR had been to the country through the Depression and World War II. He was esteemed, trusted, feared, and in some cases resented just because he was a strong moral leader and a character model. Of course, Dr. Esch would likely spin in his grave to hear himself being linked with this famous

Distinction Without Pretension

Democrat. President Esch was a staunch Republican, and, as affable former academic dean Dr. Carl Stockton noted, "probably considered FDR an incipient Communist!"

While on campus, students hardly noticed, I believe, that one never saw Mrs. Esch accompanying the president. At some point during my term at the university I heard obscure references to a grievous event that took Mrs. Esch. I gave it little thought, thinking, I suppose, that she had died of a disease, or worse, an automobile accident. It wasn't until years later I learned that the truth was much more tragic than I could have imagined.

According to Dr. Robert McBride, Elverda Esch was "gracious in manner and impeccable in appearance," but tended to be reclusive and never seemed to embrace her role as the first lady of the college. In part, she was plagued by a medical condition characterized by debilitating headaches. It is also true that like many women of her generation she had not completed high school and was keenly sensitive about it. Legend has it that some in the university community, including a number of faculty and their wives, "snubbed" Mrs. Esch because of her "lack of refinement."

Returning from a speaking engagement on Good Friday in April of 1954, Dr. Esch discovered his wife's body in their kitchen, her head in the oven with the gas still turned on, an apparent suicide. Dr. Esch never remarried.

President Esch overlooked a lot of harmless pranks and student high jinks, but when what Dr. Esch deemed a moral law or a sacred protocol had been breached, he could come down with devastating commitment and authority. Consider the case of a creative student musician who chose the wrong song to make sport with. During a long-forgotten basketball game, sometime during my junior year I believe it was, a clever member of the student pep band saluted a sure win by the Greyhounds with a rendition of "Taps."

Ken Burns produced and directed the award-winning documentary, *The Civil War*, initially broadcast on PBS in 1998. Burns reported on the Seven Days' battle at Richmond, Virginia, from June 26 through July 1, 1862. So moved by the valor of troops of both the Northern and Southern armies during that horrific struggle, Union General Daniel Butterfield requested that a special tribute be composed to honor the dead of both sides. A Union soldier, Private Oliver Norton, wrote the 24 notes to "Taps," which was played over the field where the honored dead were interred. "Taps" became a military signal in army camps that the end of the day had come, and it continues to be played for ceremonial tributes to fallen soldiers at funerals today.

With under a minute to go and Nick's boys winning by a comfortable margin, the cornet player stood above his fellow band members—who always sat in the northwest section of the gymnasium—and tolled out the mournful tones of the very recognizable military dirge. It was a way of pronouncing "checkmate" to the opponent that Nick's basketball team had in a hopeless stranglehold—sort of an early version of the "Nah-Nah-Nah-Nah, Nah-Nah-Nah-Nah, Hey-Hey-Hey, Gooooooood-bye!" chant of the nineties.

The students in the crowd arose and cheered at the sound of the familiar notes signaling a triumph by the Hounds. Lights out, Manchester, Hanover, Franklin—whichever we were playing. This promised to become a tradition, like Red Auerbach's victory cigar when the champion Boston Celtics had an opponent in an inescapable grip.

But "Taps" was to be played, actually, *twice* at once that evening—for the *first* time, and the *last* time. You see, Dr. Esch happened to be at the game that night. As the unsuspecting student began his rendition of "Taps" to put an exclamation point on the

James L. Brunnemer

Hounds victory, Dr. Esch became incensed.

The next day the student was called into the president's office for a history lesson. He learned about the solemnity of that particular piece and its significance to veterans of American wars and families who had lost loved ones in combat.

Our generation didn't appreciate sufficiently the important symbolism attached to this sacred tribute. Dr. Esch was to educate all of us, via comments in Chapel, about the lack of respect demonstrated through using that time-honored salute in an athletic milieu.

Dr. Esch was a patriot. And many of us attached the requisite approbation to "Taps" after that incident.

President Esch took great personal joy in ferreting out perpetrators of student chicanery, even if he chose not to penalize the act in the aftermath. Once, a group of students managed to place a rusty, dirty old car in the Ad Building, now Good Hall. Students anticipated an indignant explosion from the president. As students gathered in anticipation of a typhoon-class storm, Dr. Esch casually took a look and observed, "You know, you could get a lot more money for this car if you'd just washed it before putting it in the showroom!"

With the tension relieved, Dr. Esch left the vehicle there until the end of the day, allowing the student body to admire the mischief. Later that afternoon, he gathered a half-dozen or so male students to assist in removing the car. As they pondered how to maneuver the auto down the front steps of the building, Dr. Esch remarked, "If we just had a couple of planks, we could easily guide the car down these steps."

One disingenuous male student stepped forward to eagerly suggest, "I know right where a couple of boards are that will work."

President Esch grinned slightly, chuckling in the knowledge that at least one of the rascals had unwittingly implicated himself.

Dr. Esch, likewise, was genial and unprovoked when a later generation of students absconded silverware from the dining hall and neatly set all the tables for dinner—in the library.

Some incidents backfired on students. Once, when Dr. Esch was away on a fundraising trip, a group of enterprising students "borrowed" a goat from a farm on the outskirts of Marion County, sneaked it into President Esch's office and roped it to his desk.

Unbeknownst to the students, the president had returned from his trip a day earlier than intended, on a Sunday afternoon, and went directly to his workplace to check the mail. He found there, of course, the foul-smelling beast grazing on his office carpet.

Dr. Esch called a local farmer, Howard Turley, who, at the president's request, arrived after dark and surreptitiously extricated the animal. On Monday morning, as curious students gleefully awaited the expected uproar and subsequent investigation by the campus Gestapo, there was, surprisingly, no reaction forthcoming. Dr. Esch didn't mention to anyone that anything out of the ordinary was afoot in his office. Student assistants delivering documents to Dr. Esch's secretary emerged to report nothing unusual in the president's demeanor—and the goat was nowhere to be seen.

The students were mystified and the pranksters had a dilemma: They needed to return the missing goat to its owner.

Distinction Without Pretension

After allowing the students to sweat it out for a couple of days, Dr. Esch put out the word through his lieutenants that a stray goat had somehow shown up at the Turley farm and its owner, if he could be located, could pick it up there.

Acts of generosity by Dr. Esch in assisting students were commonplace but committed secretly. How many times Dr. Esch went to his own hip pocket to help a student in need only he, God, and the student beneficiaries know. But one example might serve as a clue to many other similar acts of kindness and compassion Dr. Esch performed for his students.

During his senior year in 1962, Bill Bless and wife Beverly were living in the dilapidated old army barracks. They had an infant daughter, Jenny, and Bev was pregnant with their second child, Mark '83 (who would, twenty-one years hence, earn NCAA Division II All-American honors as a defensive tackle for the Hounds).

With graduation just weeks away, Bill was taking a full load of classes in order to graduate and be eligible to apply for a teaching and coaching job. To support his family he was working the "graveyard shift," midnight to 8 a.m., in the foundry at International Harvester (for, ironically, a foreman named Ernie Brunnemer, my dad). With this arrangement, something had to suffer. In Bill's case it was sleep—he didn't get much—and his classwork. A professor who noticed Bill wasn't performing up to his usual standards called him in to discuss it. When Bill confided to his teacher that he was working a full shift at Harvester, the prof advised him to quit his job to focus on classwork, believing if he did so he could recover and receive the grade of which he was capable. Otherwise, Bill likely would receive a less-than-satisfactory mark. The dutiful senior replied that he simply couldn't give up his employment: "I need this job to feed my family."

Unobtrusively, the genuinely concerned instructor approached President Esch and explained Bless's dilemma.

Later that week Dr. Esch asked Bill to visit him at his office. Bless entered and took a seat across the desk from the president.

"Bill," Dr. Esch began, "Some of your professors are concerned that you aren't doing as well as you should in your classes."

Bill repeated to Dr. Esch what he had explained to his professor.

Countered Dr. Esch: "Why don't you take time off and concentrate on your studies until graduation? You can go back to your job after you complete the requirements for your degree."

Bill could only repeat the facts of necessity that kept him from doing that. He had bills to pay, his family had to eat, and there was no other support forthcoming.

At that point, Dr. Esch reached into a rear pocket of his trousers, took his wallet out, opened it and counted out $100—not an insignificant sum in the spring of 1962—then handed it to Bill. The amount was equivalent to the "take home" pay Bill would earn during the balance of the semester.

Dr. Esch was stern but in some cases could be persuaded to stretch his patience with student behavioral problems. A young student from "the Region" in northwest Indiana, Ted Hermann, was a benefactor of Dr. Esch's openness to reason. For whatever missteps he had committed to warrant it, Ted was ordered to appear at the president's office to be told personally and officially that he was dismissed from the college. At the appointed time, Ted trod morosely into the office. Surprisingly, the colorful chemistry professor Dr. Robert Brooker accompanied the student. Neither said a word as they took their seats opposite Dr. Esch. The president was unsparing in his criticism of Ted's behavior. He addressed aloud the list of transgressions committed, ending with the pronouncement that Mr. Hermann was to leave school immediately.

It was at that moment Professor Brooker asked if he might speak. Dr. Esch nodded. Dr. Brooker first agreed with everything that the president had said to justify the student's release. There was no question that Mr. Hermann had earned his dismissal from school. But Dr. Brooker interjected that the student was a very bright and able individual who, given proper guidance, might yet turn out to have a promising future. Brooker then asked if President Esch might allow him to be a quasi-parole officer for Hermann. He would, daily, have Ted report to him with evidence that he was timely in his studies and was free from trouble in and out of class.

Pausing for what Ted Hermann must have felt was far too long an interval, President Esch agreed to allow Dr. Brooker to serve in that capacity if he was willing to give the effort on behalf of the wayward student. A relieved Hermann did, indeed, remain in school and ultimately graduated, with honors.

Some years afterward, Dr. Esch was in the audience as Dr. Theodore Hermann was inaugurated as president of the prestigious Carnegie Mellon Institute in Pittsburgh, Pennsylvania.

A minor mystery surrounding Dr. Esch's name intrigued some folks associated with the college. No one seemed to know what the "I" in I. Lynd Esch stood for. The president guarded this secret closely, for his own personal reasons, even from trustees and close friends.

Dr. Esch's days as a mortal ended on February 10, 1994. At the funeral services as he delivered a eulogy, then-President Emeritus Gene Sease announced that Dr. Esch had given his blessing before dying to reveal what the "I" in his name represented. When Dr. Sease revealed to the assembled mourners that it was *Isaiah* Lynd Esch, Gene thought that only he had had the information. However, there *was* another, unbeknownst to Gene, who also knew: Leo Miller. In 1958 the trustees had presented to Dr. Esch, with their gratitude, the opportunity to travel around the world after the completion of construction on the new administration building. The signature of the business manager needed to be on the passport of Dr. Esch, so the president unwittingly presented his document to Leo Miller for authorization. International documents such as passports require full names. Initials were unacceptable, unless, of course, you were Harry S. Truman, whose middle initial stood for nothing. As President Esch signed his name, Leo couldn't help but notice the passport registered to Isaiah Lynd Esch. Leo never told anyone, not even his wife, Alberta.

President Esch would artfully preside over all aspects of ICC for a score and five years.

In the 1953 *Oracle* the student editorial staff paid what could be called a prescient tribute to Dr. I. Lynd Esch. Acknowledging the strength, dignity, and perseverance of this extraordinary man in his daily rigor, the students turned to the poet Emerson for words of tribute to him. Affixed beneath a picture of then-president Esch was this: "An institution is a lengthened shadow of one man."

That simple phrase is quite appropriate in saluting the contributions of Dr. Esch to the university. Indeed, that shadow measures every president who subsequently wears the chief executive officer's medallion at the university on Hanna Avenue.

CHAPTER VI
IN SEARCH OF GOD'S DAUGHTER

The larger my island of knowledge,
the longer my shoreline of wonder.
Ralph W. Sockman

Among the distinguished alumni of the University of Indianapolis is Pulitzer Prize-winning journalist William Raspberry '58. A syndicated columnist for the *Washington Post,* Bill is that rare exception among celebrated American writers whose public speaking skills are equal to that of his pen (or, in this age, word-processor).

In his penetrating address before the 1992 senior class—the only time I've witnessed a commencement speaker receive a standing ovation from the graduates—Mr. Raspberry asserted, only slightly facetiously, that college is a "place where you stand for four years while you decide what you're going to do with your life."

Not a bad description of a period of time when a teenager becomes an adult; when new experiences deepen the student's understanding of life; when information is imparted in a systematic way and the student learns how to absorb it; when the possibilities of life as an independent adult are first really glimpsed; when self awareness is increased (and limits are discerned and potential is discovered); and when bonds of lasting friendships are established. While important learning occurs in the formal classroom setting and in attendant academic activities, much learning occurs through informal interchanges with faculty and fellow students, and in uncustomary circumstances.

Considering the subtle subtext of Mr. Raspberry's cogent comment in the light of my own education at Indiana Central, I would ask you: "What constitutes an education?" Like fingerprints, the components of an "education" are as varied as the number of people who exist. Each of us lives in a window of time separate and distinct from any other. World, national, regional, and local events that alter the social, cultural, and political balance in an era in which one happens to live modify each of us, separately.

Higher education is a living, growing, and developing montage of discovery. Learning takes place on many levels, acquired through all the senses one possesses. College life is virtually a rehearsal, in a reasonably protected environment, for the "real" life to come.

There is, during the time one is enrolled in a college, an increased awareness and a heightened sense of expectation, resulting in greater attention to formal classroom instruction and receptivity to all forms of learning. Pathways are opened. Whether through planned instruction or serendipitous occurrences, private introspection or openly shared thoughts, triumph or humiliation, love gained or lost, learning is earned through a collection of experiences, individualized to each student.

Always complementing the prescribed classroom experience is one's personal panorama of life experiences that helps shape who we are at any given point in our life, until death.

James L. Brunnemer

English historian Dame C. V. Wedgwood (1910-97) described the educated man as one who "should know everything about something ... and something about everything." The attainment of such a lofty goal is improbable, but the opportunity to maximize one's breadth of understanding of the world is best advanced in a conventional way at the college or university.

As Sockman noted in his exquisite observation that launched this chapter, the more one learns, the greater the realization of how vast the ocean of knowledge truly is.

Every institution of higher education is unique. Those responsible for providing the educational experience at the University of Indianapolis hold that two objectives stand out as most critical: to learn to *think* and to use one's education to make the world a better place. Or as the second president of the United States, John Adams, succinctly said more than 225 years ago on the purpose of an education: "To *be* good, and to *do* good."

Faculty and staff who would help to shape the lives and minds of the approximately 800 full-time students during my undergraduate days were a stalwart and dedicated group. Terminal degrees were the exception to the norm on that faculty. However, there were a number of instructors who might have taught in the finest institutions in America, choosing instead to stay at Indiana Central because their first love was teaching rather than research. Student enlightenment, including advising their pupils beyond the classroom, has always been the cardinal commodity of faculty at ICC. Faculty members have accepted suffocatingly low recompense to focus on teaching rather than follow the "publish or perish" mindset of larger institutions. Professors genuinely cared about students' personal and moral growth as much as their academic progress.

This is not to suggest that staying abreast of evolving trends, knowledge, and technology in one's discipline was dismissed as unimportant by faculty and administrators. But members of the faculty were encouraged to first succeed at their most significant role: helping students to learn in an environment that included accepting one's responsibility to use education to improve society.

Those roots in the service ethos of an education at ICC still run deep at the U of I.

(Many students resented the paternalistic attitude of administration and faculty. Having the adults on campus attending to students' personal and moral conduct was offensive to some. But the moralistic climate at ICC was not objectionable to me. Actually, I was grateful that college personnel would care enough to look after students' personal lives beyond the classroom. All college student bodies are by nature an irresistible force crashing against the immovable object of the administration. Testing, always looking for a tiny hole in the dike of authority, students will seize every opportunity to exploit any mote of inconsistency or hypocrisy in the moral leadership of the elders. And the elders at Indiana Central were constantly on the lookout to rectify shaky behavior by the students.)

All curricular offerings in 1960s Indiana Central were encompassed, basically, in eight separate departments: art, music, and drama; language and literature; science, math, and home economics; social sciences; nursing; physical education and coaching; education; and business and economics. Each department had instructors with extraordinary gifts for teaching, along with a few members who truly should have chosen a different profession.

Overseeing the five dozen full-time faculty was straitlaced Dean Cramer. Dr.

Distinction Without Pretension

Robert Cramer—"aloof, dogmatic, arbitrary, self-conscious, esoteric, intellectual," as described by one colleague—had, with the encouragement of President Esch, taken a sabbatical to earn his Ph.D. at Yale University in 1950. He returned to Indiana Central as its chief academic officer. Dr. Cramer was unquestionably brilliant of intellect and loved beauty and refinement. Socially, he was stiff of bearing, especially among students. Many were ill at ease in his presence. A man of paradoxes, he was at the same time a graceful writer and a terrible lecturer. Years later, as I traveled on behalf of the university as an administrator, Dr. Cramer was one of a handful of faculty and staff who engendered feelings of polarity among alumni.

Among the intellectual giants on the faculty was Dr. Robert McBride. A 1947 graduate of Indiana Central who earned his degree following a tour of duty in the European theatre in World War II, McBride went on to achieve the Doctor of Philosophy degree at the University of Chicago in 1959. Students of Professor McBride speak in awe of him even today. His intellect was nonpareil, his curiosity legendary, and his expectations of students daunting, yet inspiring. His reputation for intellectual integrity was forged by an unrelenting search for "God's daughter," Truth. He was fiercely dedicated to his students' intellectual growth.

Dr. McBride established an extracurricular "philosophy club" that met at his home, attracting some of the brightest and most creative minds within the student body. This initially informal gathering developed into the "senior colloquium," spawning scholars who would compete with America's best and brightest. Professor McBride fought tirelessly for recognition for his promising students. In the late fifties he unabashedly challenged the Danforth Scholarship Foundation for what he perceived as bias against students from small institutions such as Indiana Central. No doubt because of Dr. McBride's reputation as a scholar and a Danforth Associate on the campus, committee members reviewed their decisions. In 1956, Dan Rhoades emerged as ICC's first winner of that prestigious scholarship. Later, Dr. Rhoades would join the faculty at Yale University, where he became a respected instructor in social ethics.

Following in Rhoades' footsteps was David Young '57, the second ICC Danforth Scholar. Other protégés of McBride who would achieve Danforth grants, Fulbright Fellowships, or Woodrow Wilson Scholarships were Virgil Keefer '59, Larry Miller '62—"the most brilliant student I ever had," McBride would later say—and Ty Inbody '62.

"A shy, black student" named Rita Hobbs '56 had "one of the sharpest minds of all my students," he would add. The aforementioned William Raspberry, who studied under McBride, was yet another superb scholar.

University of Michigan Law School graduate Gene Lausch '60—"another extraordinarily bright thinker," according to McBride—says of McBride's influence on him and his fellow students:

> *Dr. McBride was, like Socrates in ancient Athens, a 'corrupter of the minds of the young.' The kinds of 'infections' that were passed on? The importance of the life of the mind; the elusiveness of truth; the need to think carefully and rigorously; and the pleasure of 'thinking well.' Dr. McBride took his subject seriously and expected others to do so as well. He worked hard. Most of us who*

James L. Brunnemer

> *studied under Dr. McBride have been subjected to his withering gaze when we failed to perform to capacity. But his intensity was balanced with qualities of gentleness, humor and compassion. Dr. McBride treated us with respect, callow youth that we were, because he saw a potential in us that we did not ourselves understand. It inspired us to reach beyond ourselves.*

McBride's closest friend on the faculty was Marvin Henricks. Professor Henricks was enormously popular among students because of his genuinely unpretentious nature. He was always thoughtful and respectful of students and had an engaging sense of humor punctuated by an infectious laugh.

He could be deliciously irreverent, a trait that especially endeared him to students. While occasionally using his rapier wit to disarm haughty, naïve scholars, he generally sympathized with his young people's intellectual, emotional, and social struggles. Students' creative independence of reason and logic always found safe harbor in Henricks's classroom.

Prof Henricks would occasionally wander off in thought during discussions in class, pondering painfully, it appeared, issues that were highly personal to him. I shall never forget during one engrossing class discussion in Sociology regarding the application of one's faith to real-life decision-making and reason. Mr. Henricks looked over our heads, as if concentrating on a higher plane of thought, beyond the classroom and his students. Revealing his internal struggle—indeed, verbalizing what seemed to be a still-unfinished resolution of his theological bent—Henricks admitted that "emotionally, I'm a Christian … but intellectually, I think I'm agnostic."

It wasn't the shock of his proclaiming a theological position that would be controversial for a faculty member of ICC at that time, but the undisguised conflict within that he candidly revealed to his students that was fascinating and inspiring.

Along with McBride and Henricks, the Department of Social Sciences had the very able history instructors Dr. Roland Nelson and Dr. Frederick Hill. The feared "conscience of student moral behavior," Dr. James Weber, began classes in Old and New Testament each day by calling on a student to lead fellow classmates in prayer. Weber was noted for a seventeen-page final examination of the most wretched sort, designed to humble even the most pious and clean-living souls among the multitude.

Later, Ruth House, a tall and flamboyant redhead who once gave me a most unlikely perfect score of one hundred percent on an essay final exam in psychology, joined her very able colleagues in this department.

Dorothy Munger, a wonderfully talented and genuinely nice woman, and voice teacher Farrell Scott led a small but most respected music faculty. Gerald Boyce, a brilliant thinker and an eclectic artist, would anchor the art department for more than thirty years. Morbid curiosities manifested in his art were gravestone etchings and the recurrent theme of hypocritical, evil medieval priests. Gerry could be wickedly funny and acidly cynical in his observations of the human condition.

Business and economics majors would be instructed by a true gentleman and scholar, Dr. George Humbarger, and by a woman who was as much a mother superior as a teacher. Alberta Miller was to make contributions to her students that never saw the light of day because of the personal nature of students' problems in which she became involved. Alberta had a sixth sense for discovering turmoil lurking beneath a young person's outward demeanor; and she was a master at the loving and gentle craft of providing appropriate measures of tough-minded advice and compassionate understanding.

Marvin Baker, Russel Merkel, Russell Rayburn, Kermit Todd, and Roy Davis bolstered the Education Department. These were kind gentlemen who sent their students into the teaching profession having imparted a clear understanding that above all, teaching was about *loving students*.

Possessing perhaps the soundest reputation as an educator on the faculty, at least from those outside the college, was Dr. William Pitt Morgan. Himself a graduate of ICC, Professor Morgan was a demanding, eccentric instructor of biology who could reduce a student to tears in class with his brutal sarcasm or inspire a student beyond his known capacity for learning with a rare smile or compliment. It was known that a recommendation from Dr. Morgan for a student applying to medical school was as close to a guarantee for admission as one could have. He was highly esteemed among his peers at other institutions. Scores of Dr. Morgan's protégés went on to become fine physicians and to other medical careers.

A well-known fact was the acrimony existing between the traditional, rules-fixated Dean Cramer and the oft-times unorthodox teaching methods of Dr. Morgan. In truth, they loathed one another. A tribute to both men is that they endured for decades as colleagues, enabling each to make extraordinary contributions to the lives of Indiana Central students.

Another member of the science department who would evoke intense emotions from students during his more than fifty-year association with the college was chemistry professor Dr. Robert Brooker. His bombastic, brusque exterior and caustic humor masked a kind heart and profound love of his students, particularly those underprivileged or out-of-the-mainstream types. Because Brooker wanted no recognition for them, his kindnesses can be enumerated only by those who were beneficiaries. He had a large sense of self and certainly *did* demand credit for being an outstanding professor and chemist. But in matters such as his generosity, he preferred to remain anonymous. Over the years, he and wife Ruth Brooker assisted hundreds of young people by providing thousands of tuition dollars directly to them, as well as providing shelter and comfort in some extreme cases where students had no place to go.

Dr. Brooker was influenced significantly by his impoverished background in rural Missouri and by his military experience. He credited his time in the armed forces with bringing out dormant qualities of leadership that had previously gone untapped. What many did not know was the torment and suffering that same military experience exacted in his private hours. His memories included being under terrifying enemy fire during World War II at the Remagen Bridge, seeing men blown apart only inches from where he was. Frightening flashbacks afflicted him all his adult life.

"Do it right, or do it wrong. But, dammit, do *something*!" was his motto. Sometimes that *modus operandi* resulted in humorous outcomes. Ed Lindley, in chemistry class under Brooker in 1962, described an incident that demonstrated Brooker's bent for creative "field expediency." As he entered the classroom, with the students dutifully seated and quiet, Dr. Brooker was grappling with his necktie, a required faculty habiliment that he despised in the extreme. Again and again he attempted, without success, to bring the two ends of the neckwear to reasonably acceptable lengths. Each time he tried, one end or the other would drape far below its counterpart. Finally, the professor gave up. Opening a drawer of his desk, Brooker reached in, pulled out a pair of scissors and with a look of utter satisfaction, proceeded to clip the unruly cravat at navel length. With no reference to his stunt, he then began to lecture to the giggling class.

Tough as the battle-tested warrior that he was, Dr. Brooker would accept no lame excuses from the student who was late with assignments and was especially hard on those he thought were not fulfilling their potential. Often brutally candid, Brooker offered this opinion to one student about his chances of qualifying for medical school:

"Brunnemer, the only way you'll ever get into medical school is as a cadaver!"

His quiet, almost reclusive wife, Ruth, played an equally heroic role in the lives of Dr. Brooker's students. Often it was she who would persuade her husband to offer a "second chance" (and occasionally, a third and a fourth) to wayward students over Bob's objections. The Brookers were among the couples that served the university in ways that simply cannot be replicated.

If you enrolled at Indiana Central College to become a nurse in the decade of the sixties, you would have experienced the unforgettable tutelage of Virginia Sims. Dictatorial and uncommonly assertive for a female faculty member of that day, Miss Sims's characteristics were more associated with her male counterparts. She could scare a snarling dog with a self-righteous diatribe.

Stanley Linkel, then the chief custodian for the campus, related a dressing-down Miss Sims laid on one of the architects of the new Lilly Science Hall as it neared completion in 1963. It seems the designer of nursing labs was giving a tour to the nursing staff of the spanking new facility, obviously with a sense of pride and an air of self-satisfaction. At the first classroom designed especially for the nursing curriculum, paper towel dispensers had been hung in all the appropriate spots. With one visual sweep of the room, Miss Sims unleashed a withering assessment upon seeing the hand-turned cranks on the dispensers: "Do you mean that after my nurses have sterilized their hands by washing, they must re-infect themselves by turning *germ-infested* cranks before drying them? Get these useless pieces of tin off my walls! Replace these immediately with towel dispensers that have buttons which my nurses can push with their elbows, so their hands will remain aseptic. NOW!"

Needless to say, the fully chastised architect skulked away to remonstrate with his distributor of towel dispensers.

A colleague shared a story involving Miss Sims and one of her archenemies on the campus. Arnold Hodgson was a genial assistant to President Esch. His primary responsibility was the raising of private donations for the school. A native of New York, Mr. Hodgson had a devilish sense of humor, characterized by the wry cynicism of an Easterner. Virginia didn't like Arnold for a number of reasons, but mostly because he had the audacity to consider all other departments on campus of equal weight and importance to hers. Since his fund-raising took that attitude into account and he didn't spend every waking hour in the pursuit of money to make Virginia's nursing department better, she had little use for him.

It was during an administrative meeting with department heads and administrators that a long-festering dispute between the two played out. Miss Sims was being her usual passionate, indignant, and defiant self as she offered her opinion on some matter. Arnold, deftly joining the fray, offered clever and cutting remarks to offset Miss Sims's argument.

Sensing a condescending attitude on her colleague's part, Virginia cut loose.

"Now look here, Arnold Hodgson," scolded the nervy nurse. "You'll not patronize *me*! I've been here a lot longer than you have, so don't you try to lecture me! If you think I'm going to let you run over me, you're mistaken, sir! I'll give you 'tit-for-tat!'"

With the merest hint of the Cheshire cat in his eyes and sly grin, Arnold replied, adroitly,

"Tat."

For extraordinary intellectual quality, no department on campus could top that of the English faculty. Allen Kellogg, who earned his Ph.D. at the University of Chicago in 1943, possessed a brilliant mind, reciting classical poetry and prose or offerings of the most arcane authors in the English language, on cue. I recall Dr. Kellogg once saying, in defense of the classics, "If you don't read good books, you're no better off than one who can't read." At the time, I was thumbing through an issue of *Mad* magazine, so I didn't fully appreciate the wisdom of his words.

Dr. Kellogg, Mrs. Martha Waller, and other members of the ICC English department would entertain themselves at parties by reciting parts of Shakespearean couplets or quatrains from memory, challenging others to then complete the phrase. Waller, herself a member of MENSA, lectured entire class periods, often citing lines and lines of poetry, *sans* notes. Typically, she would sit on the edge of her desk, cross the longest legs from knee to ankle I had seen in my young life, and proceed to amaze us with her recall of facts of English literature.

Lois Fouts, a kind lady and grammarian, Frieda Bedwell, and Sibyl Weaver were other stalwarts of that department, along with a professor who would alter my path to learning, Dr. Ray Warden.

The beloved Marga Meier was the one-person language department, teaching German, French and Spanish. She could probably have faked it if a student wanted to learn a mountain dialect of Upper Silesia.

Kenneth Sidebottom was a living embodiment of the familiar cliché of the absent-minded professor. His capacity for stumbling over the most elementary physical movements belied his brilliance as a mathematician.

An intimidating presence on the faculty was Konstantin Kolitschew, a 1928 graduate of Tomsk Chemical Technological Institute, Siberia. Most students could hardly understand Dr. Kolitschew's mangled English, let alone the labyrinthine theories of physics upon which he expounded in class.

To many outside the college, Angus Nicoson *was* Indiana Central. The popular Hall of Fame coach earned acclaim from the wider public through his association with the Indiana High School All-Star basketball team in its annual classic against its counterparts in Kentucky. We'll visit Nick and his longtime loyal assistant, Bill Bright, in subsequent chapters.

The library—"The treasury of wisdom, the heart of the university"—was not a place with which I was to become overly familiar. I went there only to meet girls or to get in out of the rain. Edna Miller was the chief librarian, supported ably by her assistants Florabelle Wilson and Rella Walden.

The administrative staff ranks in 1963 were thin, but able. Leo Miller, with whom we'll get more familiar later, was the business manager, and his assistant was Bob Barrick. Ken Hottell was the amazing "three-years-in-two-minutes" curriculum counselor. Wilmer Lawrence served as registrar. Heading up the admissions department was Don Fleenor, assisted by Dale Robinson. Mary Huey was Dr. McBride's counterpart as dean of women. Leonard Pearson handled public relations for the school.

The fledgling evening division, which would ultimately outnumber full-time day students at the college, was established at Dr. Esch's behest by Harry McGuff. Dean Ransburg, later to become director of alumni relations, assisted Dr. McGuff, while Jim Birdcell headed the industrial relations department.

Assorted secretaries supported the administration, and Vesta Hill dispensed love and medication as the school nurse. Madge Bright met students' needs as bookstore manager, and cafeteria manager Don Ewing patiently and with good humor handled massive student complaints about the institutional cuisine.

A staff of nine maintenance workers kept the campus physical plant running.

Each residence had a house mom. In 1963, those dear and patient ladies were Melissa Rider (Krannert), Grace Miller (Trimble Hall), Alice Reid (Wilmore), Henrietta Hapeman (Dailey Hall), and Dortha Hamsher (Buxton).

There was one unofficial administrator who may have been the most significant influence many students encountered while at Indiana Central. Mary Streets managed the campus cupboard, intended as a haven for commuters, but which in fact became a regular hangout for all students. Mary sympathetically dispensed common sense and wisdom with equal doses of truthful and constructive criticism to confused, homesick, and lovesick students. She had an especial fondness for married students, mostly athletes, who lived with their young families in the old army barracks. Often, when students like Jerry England or Bill Bless or Jim Ware, all married with children, would come into the cupboard and ask for a Coke and a free packet of crackers, she knew they had not more than the dime for the Coke in their pockets. She would quietly tell them to come back after closing time, when she would unlock her door and prepare each of them a hamburger, French fries, and a drink, *gratis*.

Back then, Indiana Central may have lacked the user-friendly facilities, state-of-the-art technology, and the sophisticated and highly qualified faculty of which its progeny, the University of Indianapolis, rightfully boasts in 2003. But the people—faculty, staff, and others one encountered while living at Indiana Central College, circa 1963—were, if nothing else, *student-friendly*. And that made a meaningful difference in the lives of those of us on the scene then.

CHAPTER VII
THE MILLERS: ORDINARY ACTS, DONE EXTRAORDINARILY WELL

> *That best portion of a good man's life,*
> *his little nameless, unremembered acts*
> *of kindness and love.*
> — William Wordsworth

Among many unheralded heroes of the U of I legacy was a husband-and-wife team, Leo and Alberta Miller. For nearly 30 years, the Millers served the university in steady, if unspectacular ways.

Leo came to Indiana Central College in 1946 as an understudy to Evan Kek, half of yet another married couple who played significant roles in the life of the college. Evan's wife, Anna Dale Kek, was an instructor of foreign languages and one of but a handful of faculty in the mid-forties with an earned doctorate.

During the turbulent years of assisting President Good in keeping Indiana Central financially solvent, Mr. Kek's constitution had been severely tested. He had determined he would leave the college at the end of the 1947 school term. Confiding candidly with Leo about a weakness that had burdened him during much of his career at Indiana Central, Mr. Kek said, simply, "It's 'demon rum.' I just can't lick it."

Of Dr. Kek it might have been said, as Winston Churchill remarked of military genius and close friend Sir John Dill, at his wake: "He did all he could to make things go well, and they went well."

Leo replaced this courageous and faithful man in June of 1947.

Despite his deeply lined face and a sad, almost pained countenance, as if he had a lifetime sentence of hemorrhoids, Leo Miller was a deceptively humorous man. He could spin a story that would leave the Mona Lisa cackling. A stern pillar of fiscal responsibility and integrity as the college business manager, Leo was a chief advisor to presidents Lynd Esch and Gene Sease during his career. For the better part of three decades Leo achieved balanced, if austere, annual budgets. Financial responsibility was a simple process to Leo: "Don't spend more than you have." He threw quarters around like they were manhole covers.

Although her position as an instructor of business was not as visible as her husband's, Alberta Miller's influence on the university's students was profound. With an angelic smile and irresistible warmth, Mrs. Miller was quiet and unassuming, but certainly not passive. Alberta stepped into students' lives with wise counsel and a mother's love when necessary, along with solid educational directions and stern discipline when called for.

Nepotism in the workplace was never a problem with the Millers. In fact, Alberta complained that she was always last among faculty and staff to get upgrades in her office. Leo was responsible for that irritation, as he wanted no one to have reason to believe his

James L. Brunnemer

spouse received favorable treatment from the business office when it came to amenities at her workstation. So when others would get new carpet, office furniture, or other comforts long before she did, Alberta groused about her husband's discriminatory behavior, despite knowing the reason why.

Don Ray '50 credits Mr. Miller for his early education in the fundamentals of business and for preparing him for the success he later enjoyed as president of L. S. Ayres. He recalls, with great fondness, Leo's guidance as an instructor as well as his razor-like sense of humor:

> *It was my privilege to be in the first graduating class of the Department of Business Administration. When I look back, I realize now Leo Miller **was** the Department of Business. I could never believe a statistics class could be made interesting or fun until I had that course with Leo Miller. He had a way of making a game of it as he did all subjects he taught. In Business Law we argued cases; in Finance, we were investors. We once toured the Chicago Commodities Market, and thanks to Mr. Miller, we were treated like royalty. I'm not sure what he told them, but I have a feeling he expanded the truth, as was his wont. He was young, a great storyteller, and enjoyed his work.*
>
> *During my senior year, Alberta joined Leo in Indianapolis to teach at Franklin Central. She was a year late in coming because she had replaced him at Spencer High School. The only way he was able to get out of his Spencer contract* [to come to Indiana Central] *was if he would agree to let Alberta replace him. That might tell you something about Leo. Nevertheless, her arrival provided me with much-appreciated income. My job was to get the keys each day from Mr. Miller, go to Franklin Central and pick up Alberta. After my own riding experiences with Leo, I'm sure Alberta appreciated the quiet ride home with me. After fifty years, the Millers remain our dear friends. If it had not been for the Millers' constant encouragement, it is likely I would not have stuck it out at Indiana Central.*

Don went on to tell about his class's Golden Anniversary reunion in May of 2000. Leo and Alberta were invited as honored guests, along with several other faculty and administrators. Time constraints prohibited any remarks from the guests, so emcee and class president Ray thought he might catch Leo unprepared. After prefacing Mr. Miller's introduction with a few uncomplimentary comments, to roil the waters a bit, Mr. Ray turned the mike over to Leo. Not surprisingly, Leo reached into his coat pocket for notes he had, indeed, prepared for the occasion. For the next thirty minutes Mr. Miller proceeded to, according to Mr. Ray, "dominate, entertain, and tell truths, half-truths, and bald-faced lies!" Leo concluded by saying, "I had a feeling you might do something like this so I wanted to be prepared."

"Mr. Miller," says Don Ray, "was *always* prepared."

Distinction Without Pretension

Among the many hats Leo wore during his thirty-three years at ICC was a brief term as dean of men. It wasn't long before Leo recognized that his most consistent cluster of problems as dean was in dealing with Angus Nicoson's athletes. In 1955, President Esch had decided that the best means of handling the off-court problems of the athletes was to assign Nick as assistant dean of men, reporting to Leo.

While this arrangement was short-lived, it wasn't without its entertaining moments. One spring, mild weather had arrived and with it the usual stirrings among the young men of the campus.

Leo sniffed out a rumor that a panty raid, the organizers and leaders of which was a cadre of athletes, was to be executed after the women retired to the dormitory at the required nine o'clock hour that evening. Shortly before the curfew, Leo and Nick arrived, having concealed their car a couple of blocks away. The two crept furtively around to the side of Men's (later Trimble) Hall, expecting a herd of prospective panty pilferers to emerge. As Leo and Nick concealed their presence in the bushes, about sixty male collegians, in heat, and with a mob mentality, poured out of the dorms.

The destination was Wilmore Hall, at that time the women's residence.

The campus then, in contrast to today, was essentially a black hole after the sun went down. Virtually without security lighting and far from the dim glow of downtown Indianapolis, the campus provided Leo and Nick the perfect cover of darkness from which to observe the band of horny he-men who were now moving as quietly as a herd of stallions toward the tantalizing objective beyond the tree-lined and grassy field they were traversing.

Like two specters in the night Leo and Nick kept up with the men, stealthily slipping from shrub to tree to flower bed, as all advanced steadily across the campus. Never more than fifteen yards from the unsuspecting horde, the administrators remained undetected behind the dense foliage, accelerating their pace to keep up with the increasingly rowdy collegians.

Finally, with the guts of cat burglars, Leo and Nick merged into the aft end of the conglomerate of male students just as the whole crowd arrived at the front steps of the entrance to the women's dormitory. As the group prepared its assault on fortress Wilmore, Leo stepped boldly to the front and knocked on the door. The astonished men (according to one possibly unreliable witness), noting the presence of Coach Nicoson as well as Dean Miller in the dim light at the door, executed a collective gasp, sucking the very leaves off the trees under which they stood.

Miss Huey, the dean of women and housemother in charge of protecting young coed virtue, appeared at the door, and to the surprise of all gathered there, invited the men inside! With a bit of advance warning, Miss Huey and her girls had prepared a nice array of refreshments in the basement rec room, where all now amassed. Cider and cookies were neatly laid out in expectation of these gentlemen callers.

Their mischief diffused, the men settled in with the women for an enjoyable interlude, their own little surprise party, compliments of Leo, Nick, and Miss Huey.

And as far as Leo could report, no one lost his or her undergarments, at least that evening. The bold surveillance and timely action in thwarting the wayward men took the starch right out of their shorts.

Leo once told of a most bizarre episode of student recruiting he experienced when

James L. Brunnemer

he was asked by Dr. Esch to serve, part-time, as an admissions counselor. He was in the Ft. Wayne area for an 8 a.m. appointment to recruit a Southside High School senior named Dean Ransburg and to meet his parents.

Upon arriving, and after knocking on the Ransburg front door several times with no response from inside save the barking of the family dog, Leo turned to go back to his car. About that time a sleepy-eyed parent, Dean Ransburg's father, opened the door and, somewhat disheveled, yelled for Leo to come in. The household, now up and alive, was a scene of some chaos. The Ransburgs had overslept and were late for work and school.

Leo offered to return at a more convenient time, but Mr. and Mrs. Ransburg insisted that he stay.

"No, please. Talk to us as we get ready."

So as one Ransburg listened while showering and dressing, a second gathered up necessaries for work, and still another threw down a quick bite of breakfast, Leo steadfastly extolled the virtues of the education the younger Ransburg would receive as a student at ICC. He had not quite finished his canned presentation when the patriarch of the family apologized, but everyone had to depart *immediately* lest they be late! Leo quickly gathered his promotional materials, bid the family a hasty adieu, and closed the door, hearing it lock behind him.

While backing his car out of the driveway, Leo looked up to see Mrs. Ransburg running toward his car, frantically waving for him to halt. Something was terribly wrong. With a breathless explanation, she quickly apprised Leo that the family sedan would not start. The baffled recruiter wound up driving the entire family to their separate destinations across the city of Ft. Wayne.

Of course, Dean enrolled at Indiana Central. He went on to compile an admirable record as a student-athlete, graduating in 1954. After a stellar career as an administrator at the college, Dean was accorded ICC's highest honor, the Distinguished Alumnus Award in 1971.

In the early 1960s, an Indianapolis citizen named Minnie Richey approached Mr. Miller with an offer to contribute to Indiana Central twenty-one separate pieces of real estate in Marion County. All were located in depressed areas of the inner city, mostly between Indiana Avenue and California Street, and marked by west 9th and 10th streets. Never one to look a gift horse in the chops, Leo accepted with a goal of rapidly turning the land into cash.

Mr. Miller drove President Esch on a tour of the donated assets through the seedy neighborhoods where each was located. As they advanced from property to property, Leo noticed in his rearview mirror they had picked up an escort. An Indianapolis sheriff's deputy, undoubtedly curious as to why two middle-aged white guys in ties would be prowling around this particular inner-city area, had decided to put them under surveillance. Leo had a list of each separate lot and its address. As he cruised from one to the other, stopping to view each with Dr. Esch from the car, the police officer would furtively move with them, staying about a half block behind. Leo supposed the cop assumed they didn't see his very obvious tracking of their every move.

All the while, Mr. Miller was preparing his defense in the event that he and President Esch were busted on suspicion of drug dealing by this overly zealous lawman.

Finally, the canny cop must have gotten bored, because he simply drove away.

While the combined value of the twenty-one properties was not a bonanza, it was, nonetheless, a generous and welcomed gift, except for one problem.

The donated real estate on 10th Street and Virginia Avenue included an old hotel, the first floor of which was dominated by a bar. You need only reflect back to the early sixties to surmise what the attitude of the Evangelical United Brethren Church fathers would have been about Indiana Central owning an establishment that dispensed "Satan's brew."

"And I didn't even want to *think* about what might be going on in the $2-per night rooms upstairs!" Leo said.

Not long after the college had accepted the gift, the university's insurance representative called to alert Leo about an occurrence at the hotel.

"Well, Mr. Miller," the rep intoned fatalistically, "We had a fire at the building at 1010 East 9th Street last night, and …"

Leo interrupted, and with his usual deadpan intonation, queried, "Successfully, I hope?"

Unfortunately, the fire had burned only an old couch and singed a wall.

On the evening of the very day the gift was transferred, making Indiana Central College the legal proprietor of this asset, there was a major brawl and stabbing at the bar, which made news in the local papers next morning. Of course, it was not publicly known that ICC was the legal owner of this enterprise, so that fact, fortunately, didn't make the story.

Leo was quaking in his cheap loafers during the entire interim of a few weeks until a buyer was found and the property disposed of.

Alberta Miller helped untold numbers of students behind the scenes. Stanley Warren, a standout scholar and African-American, was one. Near the end of his senior year he was to take an important examination in Mrs. Miller's class. Wearing a grim countenance upon entering the classroom, Stanley appeared to Mrs. Miller to be uncharacteristically forlorn. He left long before the other students in the class had finished with their tests. Afterward, Alberta discovered he had completed only half of his examination. He was one of her brightest students and had obviously mastered the material in her class, but he mysteriously turned in an incomplete exam.

Alberta waited outside the door of his next class and when he emerged at its conclusion, she confronted him. "Stanley, why did you finish only half your test when you obviously know the material? Is there something wrong?"

"Just give me an F," Warren replied. "I don't want to talk about it."

But Alberta persisted. Finally, Stanley Warren revealed the cause for his depressed attitude. In 1959, there were very few teaching jobs available for African-Americans in Indiana, even those with master's and doctoral degrees. Because blacks had little chance to teach in all-white or even mixed-race schools, Crispus Attucks (segregated) High School, Stan's *alma mater*, had one of the finest faculties in the state.

Stan fervently desired to return to his former high school, but had recently learned he would be unable to get the job there that he wanted. His alternative was to "go south" where teaching positions, in inferior schools for poverty-level wages, were available. That alternative was unacceptable to Warren, because motivating his anger and frustration was a hidden dilemma.

When Stan had determined to go to college to become a teacher his father told him he was wasting his time and money.

"And now it's turned out he was right," the younger Warren confessed.

Alberta listened, then reasoned with this bright and proud young man. She convinced him not to give up on his dream. She arranged for him to re-take the examination and continued to monitor his progress.

Stanley Warren would complete his bachelor of science degree at Indiana Central in 1959 and his Ph.D. in education at Indiana University in 1973. He later forged an impressive career in education as a professor and associate academic dean at DePauw University. In 1998, Dr. Warren was honored as a Distinguished Alumnus of the University of Indianapolis. Today, Stan remains grateful for the quiet but resolute business instructor who refused to allow a talented student to become a victim of his own discouragement.

Not all of Mrs. Miller's students heeded her advice, however. During a 1968 business economics class, Alberta asked of her students, "Where do you expect to be five years from now?" Junior accounting student Steve Carson '68, a graduate of Southport High School, replied, "I expect to be making $10,000 as an accountant for one of the major CPA firms."

That was rather bold talk on the part of a twenty-two-year-old business major at Indiana Central in the mid-sixties. To imagine himself with one of the Big Seven making *ten thousand dollars* within five years of graduation was rather presumptuous, at least to the modest Mrs. Miller.

Not wishing her students to set themselves up for failure, Alberta cautioned the enthusiastic young student: "Now, Mr. Carson, I'm afraid you may have your sights set a little high."

In 1993, just before becoming a member of the U of I board of trustees, Steve, as vice president for ATT Worldwide Network Systems, managed over *$20 billion* of American Telephone and Telegraph assets and was earning *75 times* his ambitious senior prediction, annually. While he esteemed Mrs. Miller as an important influence in his education, Steve Carson didn't rate her high in prognostication.

An unmatched teller of funny tales, Leo often regaled colleagues with self-deprecating humor, especially in regard to his natural tendency to be a klutz. Once, when Leo was moving his and Alberta's automobiles in their driveway in order to wash one of them, an unusual episode occurred. Leo moved one vehicle out of the garage and then entered the second car to move it behind the first. He apparently hadn't gotten the emergency brake set properly while parking the first car, because as he turned the ignition off in the second, he looked up horrified to see the driverless car in front moving backwards on the steeply inclined driveway, heading directly toward him. With a sickening bang, Car #1 collided with Car #2, leaving significant dents in both vehicles. Leo went indoors to call his insurance agent to report the mishap.

As he probed for information about the accident, the agent asked for the name of the driver of the first car?

"I was," Leo replied.

The agent dutifully inquired after the driver of the second vehicle.

Distinction Without Pretension

"I guess that was me, too," Leo answered, honestly.

Thoroughly confused, the agent and Mr. Miller went back and forth like an Abbott and Costello routine before Leo was finally able to convince the insurance man that he was both drivers in a two-car collision. Only Leo can tell that story and do it justice. Believe me, the juice is in the details and in the way Leo squeezes the fruit.

Many students didn't know Leo and Alberta were husband and wife, and while the pair avoided discussions about their mutual knowledge of students, Alberta would occasionally share something particularly clever, humorous, or vile a student said of Leo, without revealing the student's name. As the enforcer and collector of monies from students who often were scarcely able to afford college costs, he was an easy and frequent target of their frustrations.

On one occasion, however, knowing of Leo's futile and tiresome efforts to collect tuition from a particularly lax and evasive student, Alberta knowingly abetted Leo in a way the unwitting student probably doesn't know even as he reads this.

For six semesters this student was continually delinquent with his tuition or room and board payments. Leo would send letters and reminders, would call the student in, phone his parents, and threaten to kick him out in an endless and exasperating pattern. Typically, the scrounge would grudgingly respond to these periodic duns with a dribble of money, enough to justify Leo extending his time a few more days or weeks.

It so happened one day before a typing class in which the student was enrolled that Alberta overheard the cleverly evasive scofflaw boasting to some classmates how he had won $800 in a poker game the night before. Hager St. Clair '56 once related to me how he and this student would play poker with a group of "not-so-brilliant gamblers" at a local club, often bringing home a fistful of cash, sometimes as much as $1,000. On one of the rare occasions in which she shared personal student information with her husband, Alberta reported this young man's good fortune to Leo.

That afternoon Mr. Miller called the student into his office and with feigned resignation, and a sorrowful sigh, said, as much as he hated to do it, he simply couldn't carry the student's debt any further. The young man would have to discontinue classes and vacate the dorm immediately. Considering his plight only a moment, the student, sullenly and without comment, reached into his billfold and counted out $500 in cash to pay the accumulated debt on the spot.

For obvious reasons the lucky gambler will go unnamed. But he will now know that his good-fortune-turned-sour has been a source of great glee through the years for Leo and Alberta!

Both Millers would frequently, and quietly, pay tuition or other fees from their own pockets to enable kids to stay in school (unbeknownst to the particular students in need). Now, having been married well past their golden wedding anniversary, the Millers have never been financially wealthy. However, the memories each must have of the literally hundreds of students who were on the receiving end of some act of personal kindness and generosity makes each rich, indeed.

One grateful graduate related a story of his good fortune as the result of the Millers.

Gene Perkins attended Southport High School where he was a self-described "hellion." A laid-back sort with an impish grin, Gene loves a practical joke and pulled many of them in his younger days. He was a preacher's kid, like so many of the students who attended Indiana Central.

When I first met Gene in 1991 at his office in Johnson County, I knew little about him. Constructing custom homes was his trade and he had gained a reputation as a builder of integrity and skill.

At the time of my first appointment with Gene, I arrived at a modest ranch house in Greenwood, which served as his company offices. He met me at the door dressed in faded jeans, a flannel shirt and stocking feet.

After a few introductory comments Gene and I sat down and we began to reminisce about our common school, Indiana Central. As he talked he seemed to drift away to another time. I became a spectator to a man's personal reverie of days past.

Self-effacing while quietly self-confident, Gene told me of his love for his father, a Methodist minister, and his mother, and of his passion to assist his younger brothers, Thornton and Wayne. He had helped both young men financially to enable them to earn their college degrees, Thornton at Indiana Central, Wayne at Boston University. At the time of our conversation, Thornton was a physician in Chattanooga, Tennessee, Wayne a professor in philosophy and religion at the University of Evansville.

Gene was interrupted at one point in his ruminations by a phone call. I asked Gene if I should step outside. He shook his head, indicating I should stay.

I noticed at one time during his telephone conversation, Gene scribbled a figure on a piece of scrap paper. When he hung up he chuckled to himself, then revealed to me that the caller was the editor of the *Los Angeles Times* newspaper, a classic car enthusiast, who "has been trying to buy one of my Duesenbergs."

Gene was at that time serving the second year of a term as president of National Classic Cars of America. In a barn next door was his collection of two Duesenbergs—1933 and 1934 models—seventeen Packards, and several other classic vehicles that Gene had purchased and restored. Among those was a 1937 vintage touring car once owned by movie idol Errol Flynn and Elvis Presley's Packard Caribbean.

When asked what defines a "classic car," Gene launched into a history of America's car industry, including his love of classic automobiles. The brief definition: "They don't make 'em anymore!"

Gene detailed the purchase, restoration, and history of his Duesenbergs, the rarest and most valuable of his collection. When I asked the value of such a car, Gene slid that scrap of paper upon which he had jotted a figure across his desk, saying, "That's what the guy in Los Angeles offered me over the phone."

The penciled figure on Gene's note a dozen years ago was $750,000.

Gene then turned his thoughts back to ICC. He seemed to want to tell me something he had been pondering in his mind, something significant he had experienced there.

Gene was married during his undergraduate years at ICC, which was fairly uncommon in the fifties. It was not easy to go to college and support a partner, too, plus Gene and his wife had an infant son. Gene was not a stranger to hard work, so he held things together.

But then tragedy struck. The couple's baby died.

As if the attendant devastation and grief of such an event on young newlyweds wasn't enough, Gene had an additional problem: finding a way to replace tuition he would

Distinction Without Pretension

need for the second semester at ICC. You see, he had spent the money intended for his school on funeral expenses for the baby.

Alberta learned of this woeful situation and that Gene was not likely to return to school for the spring semester. She lamented to Leo, "It would be a shame to lose Gene. He's such a fine boy."

Gene hadn't planned to enroll for the second term, but Alberta suggested to him that he go ahead through the registration process. While he knew it was futile because he didn't have money to pay the tuition, Gene acceded to Alberta's pleading and was there on registration day.

He thought perhaps he could somehow borrow the money or find some accommodation for his dilemma. He really wasn't sure what he would do. He just showed up.

The last stop in the registration line, of course, was where employees of the Treasurer's Office sat to receive payment for the classes for which one had registered. When Gene came to this final point he said, "I'm Gene Perkins, and ..."

Before he could finish the sentence the young lady charged with accepting student payments interrupted saying, "Oh, Mr. Perkins, you're to see Mr. Miller. Your tuition has been paid."

Stunned, Gene slipped into the office of university treasurer Leo Miller. Upon entering Leo's office, Gene, embarrassed, softly said, "Mr. Miller, there must be some mistake. The girl out there said my tuition had been paid, and ..."

For the second time in a matter of minutes, Perkins was interrupted in mid-sentence. Leo Miller told Gene of a benefactor to the university who, from time to time, provided financial assistance for students in difficult circumstances. A local businessman, Frank Meek, had established a fund in memory of his son who died in combat during the Korean War. Mr. Meek asked that Mr. Miller use the fund to help worthy students who had special needs for assistance. Quietly, without fanfare, Leo told Gene that Mr. Meek would be his benefactor.

"Mr. Miller, how does he know me?" Gene asked.

"He doesn't. But *we* know you, Gene," was all Leo Miller said.

At that moment, Gene Perkins vowed that his first earnings after graduation would be used to repay the school, and, in effect, that benefactor, the money that enabled him to complete his education and graduate with a bachelor's degree in 1959.

Gene never met Mr. Meek, but years later during a meeting at the Indianapolis Realtors' Association saw a portrait in memory of him hanging on the wall. He recognized the name as the same man responsible for his staying in school.

On the word of the Millers, the Frank Meek Memorial Trust Fund helped many students at Indiana Central that way, without ever knowing their identities.

Gene became a member of the U of I board of trustees in 1992 and has been a wise counselor and benefactor himself since.

Leo and Alberta reside in a modest retirement community near Indianapolis, returning regularly to the campus, the scene of so many quietly heroic deeds of which only they and those who received their help may recall.

CHAPTER VIII
SUBLIME IGNORANCE

There are three kinds of people in the world: those who can't stand Picasso, those who can't stand Raphael, and those who've never heard of either of them.

John White

Stsssssss-*CLANK-stsssss-ZONK-stsssss-CRONK-CLANK-stsssss-ZINK-stsssss-CLUNK-CLANK-CLONK-stsssss.*

Awaking with a start at the rude noise, in an unfamiliar bed, I thought, "Where am I?" As the 1920s-vintage radiator near my head groaned and growled, the cold metal wrenching as the steam entered its valves, it all came back. It was dawn of my second day as a student at Indiana Central, a bleak, raw Monday in the first month of 1963. My Bendix alarm clock was an unnecessary accoutrement. The harsh sound of the primitive heating system would rouse me from slumber every cold day over the next three winters.

Rolling out of the lower bunk, I stretched, and noticed roomie Jack Leonard wasn't even slightly disturbed by the noise. He could sleep through an earthquake, 5.4 on the Richter.

Addressing him by his high school nickname while shaking him vigorously, I said, "Moose! Get up! Let's go."

Classes started promptly at 7:45 a.m. So I stumbled down the corridor to the communal showers and restroom where other sleepy-eyed residents of Dailey Hall were in various stages of their morning rituals.

Striding into the frigid January air, I was covered by the only wrap I owned. My high school letter jacket provided a modicum of warmth. Of course, I had remembered to remove the block letter "M." That was to avoid being tagged a "High School Harry" by upperclassmen, a moniker reserved for those clueless freshmen who hadn't let go of their high school athletic accomplishments.

Our first stop was the dining hall, located in the basement of the New Ad Building (later Esch Hall). It was this day I was to observe for the first time a dining hall phenomenon, a human computer named Larry McCarty. All students in the residence halls, or approximately three-fourths of the student body in 1963, were required to purchase a meal ticket. Few exceptions were made. A number was assigned that you duly reported to McCarty before picking up your plastic tray and proceeding through the cafeteria line.

By the third week of any semester Larry knew every student in the school, not by name, but by meal ticket number. "Let's see ... you're 961 ... 322 ... next! ... 63 ... 375 ... " and so on. Larry passed away not long ago, rest his soul. If he were alive today and we met on the street, I would bet a bundle he wouldn't remember my name but could recite my dining ticket number!

I headed up the stairway to my first college class following "Breakfast by ARA

James L. Brunnemer

Slaters." (To my knowledge, cafeteria manager Don Ewing escaped his term at Indiana Central without one lawsuit being filed for endangering the lives of students; but the food *was* awful! Especially reviled by students was Sunday's special, "Roast Roadkill," as young diners labeled it.)

At ten o'clock my schedule called for me to report to the second floor for a course in English Composition. I was a bit late finding the room, so upon entering I scanned the rows toward the back for an empty desk. Finding all but a seat in the front row filled, I approached to ask a curly-haired, square-jawed student, "Is this seat saved?"

"No," he replied. Then, with a smile you could have poured on a waffle, he added, "But if you want, I'll pray real hard for it."

It was then I discovered that Chuck Shultz, not unlike many of his pre-theological pals, could be a regular wiseass.

And that morning I encountered an individual who would play a pivotal role in changing my attitude about learning. Ray Warden was only a name on a class entrance card when I passed into his classroom. I had no idea he would be a major catalyst in my educational journey.

In the United States the residential college environment is as much a part of one's cultural identity as neighborhoods once were. Of the 2,300 four-year colleges and universities in America, more than 1,500 are independent, private institutions, with the remainder being publicly supported schools. The result is an educational system unmatched by any other country in the world.

"Young people, barely beyond adolescence, really, are seduced into a community bond that will affect them for a lifetime. Every college advertises a 'distinctive environment' that will produce a graduate stamped with the college persona as firmly as a seal in hot wax," commented J. Linn Allen in the *Chicago Tribune*.

The residential campus serves to bring together into a community impressionable and vulnerable young people whose self-concept becomes linked with the mores of the college they attend. Like so many of its kindred schools, the U of I was established by a religious sect, the mission of which included the promulgation of its values through the education of its youthful students.

Richard Freeland, president of Boston's Northeastern University, says of education in America: "Where do you get social standing, which is what most people crave as their primary dignity? The answer in this country is where you got your college degree!"

Attachment to a university does not accrue only through knowledge acquired using state-of-the-art technology imparted by learned professors in gleaming, modern facilities. Would I donate to the Alumni Fund today if reminded that <u>L</u>ight <u>A</u>mplification by <u>S</u>timulated <u>E</u>mission of <u>R</u>adiation, first proposed in 1958, was being discussed in my science classes?

Most assuredly, graduates of the so-called "elite institutions"—Ivy League schools, the universities of Michigan, California at Berkeley, Stanford, and Notre Dame, for example—may gain added prestige for the degree earned there, and entrée to doors opened by their glitter. But the people who comprise a university community make the most lasting impressions. As with so many small schools like the U of I, one may become misty-eyed about warm relationships with persons who shared the joys and the miseries characteristic of the roller coaster of emotions during that very impressionable period of one's life. My memories are saturated with stories of athletes and athletics, because that was the milieu where I learned most thoroughly life's lessons at ICC. The same men against whom one competed later commiserated with you. The guy you challenged on the baseball field shared your most private thoughts and vulnerabilities in the dormitory.

Typical of young people my age, my college experience would be a time of metamorphosis. Over the ensuing 1,200 days of my life, I would change in various and sundry ways. Physically, I would grow two inches in height and add twenty pounds to my frame. Intellectually, faculty and advisors would make their collective contributions to diversifying my somewhat retarded collection of learning. Emotionally, I would experience hundreds of situations—some more significant than others—that would reveal to me my own unspectacular character and impel me to know more about myself and my place in the world. Socially, I was dislodged from the narrow, conservative, and protected cocoon of Morgan County to a place where a broader sector of humanity lived and interacted.

Despite the fact that ICC was over ninety-five percent Caucasian, many of us were exposed for the first time in a meaningful way to fellow students of differing races and cultures. Klaus Deiter-Tietz, from Germany, played "football" in the corridors of Dailey Hall, controlling with his feet a soccer ball, surpassing in skill my practiced dribbling of a basketball. I was to learn more about the "Dark Continent" of Africa from one of its residents, fellow freshman Max Gorvie, than from any geography book I would read. And there was baseball teammate Tim Giles, a bright and proud African-American, whose defiant attitude I initially detested, but who was the first of my friends to arrive at my wedding in Cincinnati five years later.

Politically, my innate and practiced conservatism collided with the values of committed liberals. After several instances of being annihilated with words during discussions of political issues, I learned if I were to disagree legitimately with others, I first had to understand my side of the argument. Initially, I didn't *have* a side, except that I didn't like their position, meaning they were wrong. It's a humbling, even humiliating experience to be so thoroughly trounced verbally, intellectually, and politically by others who think differently than you because you haven't formulated your own positions.

There was an abundance of serious students at ICC in 1963, but I wasn't one of them. Like many of my fellow white, Anglo-Saxon, heterosexual, Protestant brethren on the campus then, my focus was on much more provincial and mundane matters. Naïve, lacking the sophistication of adults, my generation had enrolled in college for the purpose of advancing our status in life and to embrace all the silliness and seriousness in that environment.

Now let me ask you: can you pinpoint a specific incident, or a precise moment in time in your life when you were inspired to learn, when you consciously determined to make a commitment to serious study?

I can.

It started on this first day of classes at Indiana Central. After breakfast, I was to brush lives with the man who would be an inspiration, a special person who didn't assume I had nothing to offer a thoughtful discussion. Although at the time my intellectual horizons were essentially limited to the sports world and little else, Ray Warden allowed himself no preconceived notions of students' capabilities, whether one had a sterling academic

James L. Brunnemer

record or moved his lips while reading. He became the greatest influence in advancing my heretofore undistinguished academic interests.

Schoolwork had always taken a distant second to athletics in my life. It's not that I had a terminal case of nescience. But as a youngster, with a common trait of the adoptee—lack of self-esteem—my persona was salved by my athletic prowess. During the formative years of my youth, ages six to twelve, my ego received its "strokes" through competition in sports. My interests ranged roughly the width of a baseball field or the length of a basketball court, depending on the season of the year. My cultural appreciation extended to watching Senor Wences on the "Ed Sullivan Show." (I thought French fries and French toast *really were* ethnic foods.) Upon entering Indiana Central, I was a typical, intellectually stunted, teenaged jock.

Among the many intellectuals of whom I stood in awe as an undergraduate was Ron Scott. The anti-athlete, Scott was pale and frail, a six-footer who weighed—counting spare change in his pocket—140 pounds, with no discernible muscular definition. But he had an aura of the sage about him, punctuated by a superior and quixotic look of genius. Often, I observed him looking at me bemusedly, studying my witlessness carefully, up close, as if I were a laboratory animal. Looking back on it, I believe others considered him of higher intelligence because he rarely said anything. He just appeared to be smart.

Wise old King David said as much over 2,500 years ago:
> *He who restrains his words has knowledge, and he*
> *who has a cool spirit is a man of understanding.*
> *Even a fool who keeps silent is considered wise;*
> *when he closes his lips, he is deemed intelligent.*
> [The Proverbs 17: 27-28]

I *still* don't know if Ron Scott was a genius or not. But he was a genuinely nice person with whom I would never have gotten acquainted if it weren't for the cozy environment of Indiana Central.

So the trend toward giving my best effort and energies to my dream of being an outstanding athlete took precedence over school texts. A requirement of athletic participation was academic eligibility, of course, so I always made certain my grades were at an acceptable level. In high school, I had no difficulty maintaining a B average, with As in subjects I enjoyed and Cs in those I tolerated. The occasional D was met with stern measures at home. My mom once created her own one-game suspension for me as a result of the only dreaded F-level grade I ever received, in a long-forgotten course when I was in junior high school. I never again let that happen. The penalty of watching my team play a game without me was too painful.

So as I went to my first class at ICC on that January day, I took the seat next to the witty Shultz. I could see immediately English Comp wasn't a freshman survey course. Seated shoulder to shoulder across the front of the class was an ICC academic all-star team, with folks like Ed Riley, Shultz, Mary Dee Meyer, Elena Sue Hiatt, Barbara Sullivan, *et al*, majestic with confident expressions, their kinetic brainpower short-circuiting the electric lights in the room.

I suddenly felt an acute sense of dread at being placed in a class among the intellectual elite of the college. My low spirits sagged even more when the intimidating

Distinction Without Pretension

Dr. Warden gave us our first assignment. We were to write a five-page paper on an incident during our lives that stirred us emotionally.

Pondering the task, the one incident that had moved me deeply in my recent history was the feeling that lingered too long after we were defeated in the previous high school sectional basketball tournament. That loss was a devastating blow at the time to an immature adolescent who had seen so little of the world. It was then that I realized my days as a carefree high schooler, a teenager, were unalterably fleeting.

I was aware enough to recognize that something as insignificant, as mundane, as being on the losing side in a silly game would not pass muster with the assemblage of scholars in this class, let alone its learned professor. Despite knowing I would be scorned for writing about such an inane event, I was desperate, down to the final hours. So, at 1 a.m. on the morning the assignment was due, I wrote about that sectional loss. At the end of class that day, I submitted my handwritten paper.

At our next class meeting two days later, Professor Warden had our compositions graded and ready to hand back to us. One by one he returned the papers to my classmates until there were none left in his hands. I could feel my face flush with embarrassment. My effort must have been so bad he didn't even grade it! My thoughts turned to the "drop and add" process, wherein a student could withdraw from a class and pick up another without penalty if done within the first week of the semester.

It was at that moment when Prof Warden began: "For a first effort there were several good papers, and a couple of outstanding ones."

"But," he continued, "there was one piece of writing that was truly exceptional in certain important aspects. It is rough, to be sure, and in need of much polish. But the passion in the author's words compels the reader to feel the intense and painful emotions as he did. Let me read from it."

I swear to God, he began to read phrases I recognized as those I had written! He was using *my* writing as an example of something worthy!

Perhaps you might imagine the pride I felt at that moment. No one had really told me before that I might possess some talent for expression, that writing with feeling was as important as the topic at hand. It was then that I determined to explore my possibilities. And it was with great pride and satisfaction that upon completing my doctoral thesis on the sociology and psychology of sport in 1980, I contacted Dr. Warden. He was at that time employed as an editor for Bobbs Merrill publishing company. It was gratifying to share my accomplishment with him.

I later learned that Ray Warden had not received his education from a life of privilege. He could relate to the kid from the less affluent side of town, because he'd been one, too. He told the story of how he was inspired to learning:

> My aunt, Miss Nora Meers, who had been a country
> schoolteacher in Kentucky, gave me her library, and
> my mother taught me how to read from McGuffey and
> how to spell from the Blueback Speller. I remember
> that my one-room school (High View) did not own a
> single book, not even a dictionary. All the school owned
> was a pot-bellied stove, a water container, a map and

James L. Brunnemer

> *an ample supply of hickory switches which lay about in abundance. But Miss Sally, who had taught the entire family, didn't need a library; she was a walking encyclopedia of information and moral platitudes. So this is how it all began!*

It was an educator named William A. Ward who noted, "The mediocre teacher tells. The good teacher explains. The superior teacher demonstrates. The great teacher inspires." By Ward's definition Dr. Warden was, in my view anyway, a *great* teacher. And while the results of his influence on my urge to learn would ultimately require an extended gestation period, it was Dr. Warden's encouragement that day at which I mark the beginning of my formal education.

Any Indiana Central student who has passed beneath the portals of Good Hall—and that would be every one of us—can likely point to a professor or staff member at the college who provided important inspiration as Ray Warden did for me. That was the beauty of that time and that place.

Enhancing formal classroom learning in the early to mid-1960s were manifold extracurricular activities for those who wished to participate. These were so bland that they would likely bore to distraction today's more urbane students.

Many chose not to become involved in campus life, contending, "There is nothing to do at Indiana Central." A great number of students went home during weekends, giving evidence to the claim that ICC was a "suitcase college." More likely it was an affirmation that the student body would rather retreat to comfortable surroundings and high school friends than become immersed in the social life offered at the college.

Do these lines from a student's letter to the editor of the *Reflector* of February 10, 1965, sound familiar?

> *We need Fraternities and Sorority houses on our campus, to give ICC students an increased self-discipline, an increased academic competitiveness, and an increased social competitiveness.*

That same plea for social organizations, with living quarters, would be heard by the administration annually from legions of students over the next forty years. I would wager that a number of current students have asked the same consideration of the administration of 2003!

During the first months at ICC, required "green beanies" identified freshman students on the campus. There was purpose behind this silliness that escaped our immature selves. We had left behind parents, the familiarity of our hometown high school friendships, young love relationships, and elevated positions in our teenage social strata. The common experience of being hazed by upperclassmen helped to bond us puerile "rhinies" together during what for most was our first extended period of time away from the comforts of home. The shared misery of being harassed by older students helped us not to notice, quite as much, the strange new surroundings and the loneliness and melancholia of it all.

Distinction Without Pretension

A tug-of-war between seniors and the beanie-clad frosh, once held at a community park in Beech Grove and later at Brown County Park, determined if freshmen would have to wear the silly round piece of cloth another month.

Sports, especially basketball and football, were social occasions as we rallied behind the Greyhounds. Both varsity and intramural sports were available in abundance, although in this pre-Title IX era athletic opportunities for women were far fewer in number than those for the male students.

Initiated in 1952, Brown County Day was a unique custom composed of a daylong adventure in the beautiful hills of that idyllic countryside. All classes were canceled, and the combination of fun, food, and games brought together the entire student body, current and emeriti faculty, staff, and even a few alumni. It broke my heart to learn that the student body in 2002 voted to eliminate this tradition of a half-century.

Homecoming activities generated class competitions with floats, dorm decorations, and a dance reigned over by the queen selected by the student body. (I married one, 1965 Homecoming Queen Luella Sauer.)

We enjoyed nighttime forays to McDonald's on Shelby Street (by the time I graduated in 1966, the electric sign on the Golden Arches had changed dramatically, proclaiming one *billion* burgers had been sold) and to the Teepee on Madison Avenue. An occasional lunch at Mona's Restaurant at the corner of Shelby and Hanna broke up the monotony of the cafeteria menu.

A scant year before my arrival on campus Dr. Esch and the trustees had loosened the institution's social and moral bindings slightly. On December 16, 1961, the administration sanctioned the *very first* on-campus dance, the Christmas Ball. This was a huge breakthrough for those liberal enough to think that college-aged men and women dancing together would not compromise the moral standing of the college.

So by this time, Leap Week concluded with *coeds asking the boys* (takes your breath away, doesn't it?) to the Sadie Hawkins Dance, and later in the semester we would attend the Sweetheart Dance.

As the leaves turned color and fell away, basketball season arrived. So it was over to the gym (later named in honor of Coach Nicoson) to cheer on Nick's boys.

There were Thanksgiving Dinner and vacation, and Christmas dinners, and the welcomed three weeks of Christmas and New Year's break.

Then May Festival and another queen named.

Geneva Stunts, Class Skits, and the annual Junior Carnival were other diversions provided for students. Everyone participated in Religious Emphasis Week. And there were drama productions and the Artist Series to attend, with noted celebrities like actor Basil Rathbone, vocalist Odetta, plus popular musical groups such as the Brothers Four and the New Christy Minstrels performing.

Commencement was held on the lawn in front of the old ad building, weather almost always permitting, beneath the spreading branches of huge oak trees.

Student organizations were aplenty. There were no separate feminist clubs, Black Student Association, or P.R.I.D.E. for gay and lesbian students, however. With the obvious exceptions of Young Democrats and Young Republicans, organizations in those days favored bringing people together rather than dividing them by political suasions.

One could join clubs for Art, Drama, International Relations, Spanish, French,

James L. Brunnemer

German, Business, Philosophy, and Science. For one day I joined one of the clubs named after a game for the campus intelligentsia. I learned that day that life is too short for chess.

Band and orchestra troupes and student choirs were full. Deputation teams served as singing ambassadors in churches and other venues off campus, and the Centralaires held concerts to perform pop tunes of the day along with old standards. There was the Christian Vocation Association; the debating society, Philalethea; Sigma Zeta, the science honorary society; Alpha Phi Gamma for budding journalists; Young Democrats and Young Republicans; Phi Alpha Epsilon for freshman honor students (I never was invited to even one of *their* meetings); the auspiciously titled Society for the Advancement of Management; and M.E.N.C. (Music Educators National Conference). The college radio station, WICR-FM, broadcast on 10 watts in those days, which meant that with a strong wind programming could be picked up as far away as U.S. 31 to the west and Keystone Avenue to the east.

For women there was Theacallosia, the women's literary society, and IAY (only girls who belonged knew what those letters stood for. What is IAY, girls?). The Crimson Steppers, who some curs disparaged as the "Crimson Stumblers," performed crisp dance routines at home athletic contests. Student nurses could join Kaduceans (occasionally a male nurse would be enrolled, but seldom in those days); PEMM Club for women with majors or minors in physical education; and Gamma Gamma Omicron, established to bring together women living on and off campus.

For men there was Lambda Chi Phalanx, a service fraternity without a separate living unit; Alpha Phi Omega, for Boy Scouts; and the lettermen's club, "C" Association. A full slate of athletics for men filled the bill, while women's athletics were less pronounced.

For all there was the Student Recreation Room, or simply the "rec room," where students found fellowship in games of cards, billiards, table tennis, and the jukebox. It was our version of the campus "mall," where students "hung out."

And then there was Chapel ...

CHAPTER IX
MAN SHALL NOT LIVE BY BREAD ALONE

The joy of the young is to disobey—but the
trouble is, there are no longer any orders.
                                            Jean Cocteau

Okay, listen carefully, Dr. Cramer, wherever your immortal soul resides. I'll say this only once:
I MISS CHAPEL!
There. It's out. As a former student, alumnus, and a twenty-year employee of the U of I, I confess that the once-nettlesome ritual of reporting to Ransburg Hall at 9 a.m. every Monday, Wednesday, and Friday for a required hour of spiritual and cultural nourishment, interspersed by occasional student mischief, was, in retrospect, a valuable and unique component of the Indiana Central experience.

What remains of chapel, or "convocation" as it was later termed, is hardly recognizable today. The last time I looked, sophomores attending a variety of campus cultural events a few times during the year satisfy the requirement for what is now termed the "Lecture and Performance Series."

Chapel originated at the earliest beginnings of the college when all students, as well as *faculty and staff,* gathered for one hour *every day*, Monday through Friday for a required sermon or religiously related address.

By the time I entered ICC, chapel had been reduced to three days weekly, and usually only one of those resembled a Christian religious service. A couple of times a week one was exposed to cultural presentations, and about every fourth chapel hour was dedicated to a student presentation or event.

During four years of chapel, I was exposed to varied and diverse experiences I would not have voluntarily sought out. Musicians, theologians, social reformers, politicians, philosophers, and community leaders of note each added to my widening view of the world through presentations in chapel. I was to learn in a powerful way, for example, how volatile and profoundly implacable are emotions between Jew and Arab in the Middle East long before suicide bombers terrorized the citizens of Israel, and Palestinians of all ages became victims of retaliatory strikes by the modern Israeli army. It was during a chapel hour that a Palestinian Moslem and an Israeli Jew debated passionately the perplexing questions of that conflict, exposing roots of hatred bred in Biblical times.

I didn't know Aaron Copland from Jimmy Hoffa, nor did I appreciate American composing until Mr. Copland's appearance in chapel. Drew Pearson, the renowned author and lecturer, shared his controversial views with wide-eyed students in Ransburg Auditorium while members of the John Birch Society placed anti-Pearson pamphlets on cars parked outside.

"That's the villain in 'Zorro,'" was the first comment out of my mouth when Basil Rathbone was introduced to sleepy-eyed students. The esteemed, Shakespearean actor would likely have taken issue with the fact that he was recognized only because of

James L. Brunnemer

his appearance as a supporting actor to Tyrone Power in that 1940s-era movie of the folk hero.

And I once asked a fellow naïve freshman sitting in the seat next to mine, "What makes a 'strata various' violin so special?" as celebrated violinist Joseph Fuchs evoked mysterious and wonderful sounds from one of the original masterpieces on the Ransburg Hall stage.

The administration probably equated the forced ritual of chapel/convocation with spooning castor oil into a sick child: "It tastes bad, but trust me, it's good for you." While many lecturers were merely talking in someone else's sleep, the thrice-weekly programming was, looking back on it, enlightening to us uninformed young people. Nevertheless, we students fought it all the way.

We did tolerate, even enjoyed, actually, "chapel lite": class election campaigns and other student competitions; faculty and student talent shows; and performances by the Centralaires and the College Choir. And always there lurked the potential for student chicanery orchestrated by daring and inventive types among us intended to mock the sanctity with which Dr. Cramer held chapel hour.

The World University Service (WUS) auctions were always lively. Students dug deep into shallow pockets, following auctioneer Jack Caster's steady banter, for all manner of objects, tickets, and privileges, the proceeds from which went to the less fortunate in foreign countries. Along with other students I made my bids, hoping to have Dr. Esch shine my shoes or to buy a seat at Marvin and Sylvia Henricks's table when they prepared a five-course dinner at their home.

Class academic competitions, among which was the "Brain Game," were intense. It was especially intriguing to watch the faculty defeated in the mid-1970s by a virtual one-man junior class team, Steve Nontell. His knowledge of esoteric and arcane information was truly astounding as he answered nearly every question before either his teammates or the opposing faculty fivesome could even respond. Only music professor John Gates, a true scholar, saved the faculty from total embarrassment that day.

It was during Class Skits that I first saw the beautiful freshman with long blonde hair and shapely legs who would change my life. Her two-word part as a Swedish maid ("Ja! Ja!") was not impressive, but the walk across the stage captivated me. Her name was Luella Sauer, and we've become close friends since that October day in 1965. Two sons and five grandchildren share our mutual blood and genes, and we marked the thirty-sixth anniversary of our wedding in July 2003.

Daring chapel pranks by Central students of yore were fabled. Alumni would speak of the time dozens of clocks were hidden in various locations around the stage, the alarms set to blare at staggered times throughout a long-forgotten speaker's address, as forlorn faculty looked on helplessly. And there was a terrified chicken that flapped wildly onto the stage from the nether regions, squawking to the hilarity of the assembly as a disconcerted speaker and mortified administrators and faculty attempted to subdue the poor fryer.

Catholics did not attend, of course, because of the religious nature of the hour, but that did not excuse them from the discipline. They were locked in the library as we were *locked* in the auditorium, and attendance was taken. Surely any self-respecting fire marshal today would close the school down at the thought of nearly a thousand students secured behind bolted doors in an auditorium and library within the same building.

Many students chose chapel hour to catch up on sleep. As soon as the stage lights went up and the house lights dimmed, one could almost hear dozens of eyelids snapping shut in tandem. I was cursed in that I could never sleep, but large football players, next to whom I would invariably be seated, would lean heavily on my shoulders in slumber. Never did a beautiful coed press her soft tresses onto what would have been a most accommodating shoulder. It was always guys like Mo Barnes or Steve Carson—huge, ugly men—who used me for a pillow.

Chapel was, in retrospect, a unique activity, the only hour the entire school body gathered in one place. Amity prevailed among those gathered there in a common disdain for the regimen. We shared gloom or laughter or appreciation, by turns, at whatever was taking place on the stage.

One noteworthy interlude occurred in the fall semester of 1964. The chapel committee had booked the renowned anthropologist Ashley Montagu for a presentation. Dr. Montagu was one of the more prestigious intellectuals of international repute who accepted an invitation to address our student body.

As usual, I had no inkling who this person was, but he was obviously a notable guest, familiar to many faculty and to some of the brighter students in the audience. His visit had provoked a mild sense of anticipation, in light of his reputation for trenchant delivery and his forthright, and what some would consider his controversial, views on the origin of Man. For the many in the Indiana Central student audience who were reared to the Christian belief that "all men are created equal," Montagu's observation that
> [I]t is the mark of the cultured man that he is aware
> of the fact that equality is an ethical, and not a
> biological principle ...

was certain to generate some consternation.

The speech was brisk, intriguing, and wildly controversial for a conservative, traditional student body such as that in residence at Indiana Central in the early sixties. He was especially frightening to the pre-theologians in the audience. You could feel the atmosphere thicken with tension as Dr. Montagu, *sans* emotion, unswerving, and coldly efficient, led us unceremoniously down the road of mankind's emergence through natural selection. That man ascended from a lower form of life was not a theory with Dr. Montagu, but a mere factual detail, almost offhandedly interjected into the bigger story of evolution that he weaved for us. With no deference to the slightest possibility of Divine Intervention in the process, Dr. Montagu cogently wrapped up his address and opened it up for questions.

I had caught telling glimpses of senior "pre-The" student Chuck Shultz for perhaps the last fifteen minutes of Dr. Montagu's remarks. Shultz was a genuinely bright student, if somewhat smug in his intellectuality. As president of the student academic honorary society, Phi Alpha Epsilon, he had earned the right to be haughty, in my view. During the presentation Chuck's facial expressions and body language betrayed his increasing outrage that Darwin's theory of evolution would be seriously presented as an alternative to his traditional Christian beliefs. Chuck didn't charge the stage, but waited civilly, if impatiently, until Dr. Montagu concluded his remarks.

When the invitation for questions was presented the self-appointed defender of

James L. Brunnemer

this student body's theological dignity fairly leapt to his feet, cast a cold and patronizing eye at the speaker, rocked slightly on his heels and inquired, "This is all well and good, Dr. Montagu, but where does *GOD* fit into this picture?"

Hardly a millisecond elapsed before Montagu spat back, "Of which 'god' are you speaking, young man? There are hundreds, you know."

A flummoxed Chuck's face turned livid. He sputtered something unintelligible and, frustrated, it seems, at the provocative theory the speaker was purveying, plopped down in his seat. The other future ministers in the house were equally apoplectic at such heresy. I don't remember what happened after that, but there were very few follow-up questions of Dr. Montagu. No one wanted to be verbally strafed so publicly as Chuck had been.

We once were entertained by a hypnotist (Bernard Nall, I believe) who performed his craft while explaining that particular phenomenon to an appreciative audience. After expounding on the science of hypnosis, he requested volunteers from the audience who would submit to being hypnotized. "How painful could this be?" I thought to myself, so it took little prodding from a couple of my buddies to get me onto the stage for the experiment.

There were about fifteen of us who stood in a row across the front of the stage when Nall asked us to concentrate fully on a stationary object in the hall. I selected the chandeliers, which hung unimposing above the audience. He continued to speak softly as he moved slowly before us, looking intently at each.

The dim bulbs of the chandelier became fuzzy. Then I felt a tap on my shoulder.

"If you are not asleep, you may leave the stage now," he whispered.

Confusion gripped me: Am I hypnotized? Am I asleep? Is this a command, which I cannot avoid, that I'll carry out involuntarily? I began to move, zombie-like, toward the stage steps. My feet and legs were working, so I walked down the steps leading away from the stage. As I returned to my seat, grinning faces in the section affirmed that I was fully conscious. There were ten students remaining on the stage, in various poses, eyes closed, obviously under some degree of hypnosis.

It was then that the mesmerizer declaimed, "I could have, given time, hypnotized each one of the original students. However, those with lesser powers of concentration are more difficult to put to sleep."

Thanks a ton, Bernie, for sharing with the entire student body who the dumb guys are!

The highlight of the demonstration for me was seeing Steve Lemme, sound asleep, it appeared, grimacing, with tears flowing down his cheeks while "eating" a pretend onion.

Spontaneous standing ovations by the student body were a rarity in chapel. In my more than thirty-year connection with the university I witnessed three such unplanned standing tributes saluting the stage performer or performers.

The budget to attract high-quality speakers was paltry, of course. The fact that chapel was a requirement and come hell or high-water Dean Cramer was going to see to it that you were in your assigned seat was an automatic trigger for resentment. And the

Distinction Without Pretension

audience of eighteen- to twenty-two-year olds generally wouldn't be impressed if a meteor came through the roof of Ransburg Hall, anyway.

So when an announcement that the day's "cultural" event was to be a performance by a junior high band, I can tell you I wasn't prepared for the ultimate tribute that would be made that day.

Here's how it happened.

It was a Friday, the absolute worst of the three days for student attention. The usual list of announcements preceding the program concluded, then the casual and very brief introduction was made of a band from McLean Junior High School, located somewhere in southern Indiana.

Ho-hum.

The only students on the edge of their seats were a number sitting toward the rear of the hall who had figured out how to slip out the exit doors *after* the student reps had taken attendance but *before* Dean Cramer could batten the hatches.

For those who were too polite, or unable, to sleep or study, the lights were dimmed and a spotlight was trained on the middle of the stage drapes. The curtains slowly parted to reveal seventy-five young musicians on the stage. A loud and proud rendition of "The Star Spangled Banner" got us off our feet and elicited a long and loud ovation from the viewers. But standing for the anthem was tradition and duty.

It was what made the entire audience leap to its feet simultaneously the second time that was special.

At the conclusion of the national anthem, the band gained our increasing attention with a well-played medley of George Gershwin tunes. "The Bells of St. Mary's" was performed poignantly and expertly. "Pivot Man March" was rousing, and as the curtains closed on the talented adolescents the re-energized audience showed its approval with hearty applause. We noticed the concert had ended ten minutes early—that was a plus—so we continued to applaud, expecting the curtain to open one last time in order that the youngsters could take their collective bow.

The drapes parted again, but only wide enough for a small person to pass through.

Then, the tapping sounds—lonely, slow, and rhythmic—of a snare drum. And now a youngster in a blue band uniform with yellow trim appeared at the opening of the drapes, striding slowly and deliberately, directly toward the audience, as he tapped out a rhythm to ... something.

He marched perhaps ten feet onto the stage apron, sharply executed a perfectly square "right face," and proceeded with military precision, stage right. Then a second youngster playing her flute emerged, marching with the same measured pace as the drummer, who had, upon reaching the furthest point stage right, turned to face the audience. The flautist followed the path of the drummer to the front of the footlights, pivoted crisply, ninety degrees left, in the *opposite* direction of the first youngster.

The individual musicians began to play only when passing through the curtain. One by one, spaced with exacting care, youngsters stepped out while playing trumpets, French horn, oboe, violins, cymbals, clarinet, trombones, saxophone, piccolo, and tuba. Each instrument added to the growing texture of sound. The young people alternately proceeded stage left, then stage right, in precise cadence, balancing perfectly the musical

James L. Brunnemer

assemblage.

The tempo was captivating and the music built steadily with each additional performer who joined his fellow musicians. It wasn't long before the unmistakable classical piece with the throbbing beat was identifiable to the audience: Ravel's sensual, enthralling *Bolero*!

Finally, when the last of the seventy-five junior high musicians fairly filled the boards, a crescendo was reached that the by-now rapt collegians could feel in their very bone marrow. The throbbing, intoxicating, raw sensuality and power of that classic had this college audience swaying involuntarily in its seats. This was before the world had ever heard of Bo (Ten) Derek.

We were ready to reward the surprisingly fetching entertainers with an appropriate and enthusiastic salute.

But this sassy bunch of munchkins wasn't finished.

They had only set us up for the climax of their artistry. The full complement of musicians played the score once through, then reversed their entrance. One by one, with movements masterfully coordinated, the adolescents marched back through the curtains, each one muting his instrument as he passed through the gap in the drapes. As each exited, the music became less vigorous, reducing artfully the fullness of sound, until only the drummer, tapping out the rhythm in lonely beats, identical to his beginning, was left to follow his mates. When he turned his back on the audience and marched through the curtains, all music stopped. There was not a sound in the house.

Stunned, the audience received its cue at the closure of the drapes. Bedlam prevailed, as Indiana Central students cheered, whistled, clapped, and stomped their feet in tribute to the performance these young people had offered. At last the curtain parted completely to reveal the youngsters at attention, in neat rows, accepting graciously the standing accolades of their new college-age admirers.

I don't know where Stanford Gilley, the director of that band, is; but his kids broke down all resistance that college students had toward being in chapel that day. We all knew we had experienced something special.

In 1975 I was a member of the convocation committee that was responsible for recommending speakers. I had read an item about Don Newcombe, the great former pitcher for the Brooklyn Dodgers, who was a volunteer speaker for the National Center for Alcoholism in Washington, D.C. The article indicated that speakers for the Center would make presentations at no fee, expenses only. Even Leo the Frugal would have difficulty resisting that price.

The Bums of Brooklyn were my favorite baseball team when I was a lad, and Newcombe had been one of my boyhood heroes. I might have been the only person at the university who knew "Newk" had posted a 27-8 record for the Dodgers in his sensational National League MVP season in 1957, eighteen years previously. It's possible that I was the only one on campus who gave a rip, too. (I did learn later that Alice Friman, award-winning poet and faculty member, grew up in Brooklyn and actually attended games at Ebbets Field in the mid-fifties when Newk, and Pee Wee, and Campy and Gil and the Duke were gods in Dodger Blue. Alice lovingly referred to Anderson, Indiana, native and Brooklyn pitcher of that era, Carl Erskine, as "Oisk," in the New York idiom.)

In an assembly of college students, who would really care about a washed up, fifty-some-year-old former big league pitcher whose weakness for alcohol drove him out of the game?

Nevertheless, I wrote the Center for Alcoholism, secured a date on Mr. Newcombe's schedule, and met his flight from Los Angeles on the day of his arrival. On the route from the airport to the Holiday Inn on Thompson Road where we had reserved a room for him, I pried fascinating (to me) tales about his days as a big leaguer from an initially shy, reluctant, and somewhat sardonic Newcombe. Too soon, it was time to leave.

Next morning I returned to bring Mr. Newcombe back to the campus.

During my introduction of Don Newcombe to the assembly next morning, the usual rustling of students seeking a relaxed position was heard. As I recited his baseball resume I beheld ennui in their eyes. As fabulous as his record as an All-Star pitcher for the Dodgers had been, I could sense the usual air of inattention, attended by yawning, whispered conversations, and noses in books. Some were already sagging in their chairs preparing for slumber. There was a slight stir when I closed my remarks by telling them this former great was now a recovering alcoholic here to share his thoughts about drinking.

Tall and imposing at 6'5" and 250 pounds, the African-American rose to stand behind the podium, addressing the students with a commanding basso profundo. For nearly forty minutes Don Newcombe masterfully wove his words into a beautiful tapestry, using humor, pathos, irony, and drama to draw these young people forward in their seats. He told of what it was like to be the third black in the history of baseball to have a place on a major league roster and the racist indignities that he and teammates Jackie Robinson and Roy Campanella endured. He spoke of pitching in what many have called the "Game of the Century," the 1951 National League playoff game between the archrival Giants and his Dodgers. It was Newcombe who was relieved by Ralph Branca, who then delivered the pitch that Bobby Thomson crushed for the "Shot Heard 'Round the World." He related tales of the rough-and-tumble nature of the game in those days, when his only weapon of retaliation to unspeakable racist acts by opponents was an occasional ninety-mile-an-hour fastball under a white batter's chin.

The students became enthralled. It was when he began to speak of his growing dependence on alcohol and its wickedly calming effects that he closed his fist around his young listeners. He spoke of the false sense of strength and serenity drinking gave him, the deception of friends and loved ones he increasingly relied upon, and the debilitating toll drinking extracted on his once proud and superior physicality. With the audience barely breathing, he told of the incredible strength and moral will of his petite wife, Donna, in the final episode of a very long chapter of Don's drinking bouts.

Newcombe had straggled home filthy, unkempt, and blind drunk after a forty-eight-hour binge of drinking. His wife put him to bed. In measured, painfully blunt words, Don Newcombe told of being roused from sleep the next morning, hung over, with Donna demanding that he come to the front room hallway. In his drunken stupor, he had difficulty rising from the bed; but she insisted. Newcombe told of literally crawling on all fours to the door of the bedroom, confused at seeing his wife and two daughters dressed with coats on and baggage at their sides.

Eyes flashing indignantly, Donna wasted no words: "I want you to see what you've done to yourself and to me and to these girls before we leave. I won't let you sleep through

James L. Brunnemer

this. I want you to remember how this feels when you watch us walk out this door. I want you to know what you've lost because you can't handle your drinking."

With that she took both girls by the hand and began a defiant march toward the door.

Sobered by the shock of what his wife was saying, Don rose up and began to plead with his wife not to go, that he'd change, he would give it up. He repeated all the same excuses he'd used many times before. But this time Donna was unbending. The door was opened and she and the girls halfway out when Newcombe staggered across the living room carpet and returned to his knees. Placing his massive right hand—the one with his World Series Championship ring on the third finger—atop his youngest daughter's head, Newcombe swore through stinging tears on the life of this precious child that he would never drink again.

And to that day more than fifteen years later when he spoke to the students of Indiana Central University, he had remained dry. After closing this wrenching account about his very personal encounter with the effects of alcohol, he pivoted quickly and sat down. At first, too stunned to react, the audience was mute, the hall soundless. Then suddenly, as one, the students rose in a thundering salute to this brave man's steely courage.

A college president (Gene Sease), an award-winning poet (Alice Friman) and a former National League Most Valuable Player (Don Newcombe) following Mr. Newcombe's penetrating convocation address about his fall into alcoholism. Ms. Friman was a Brooklyn native and avid follower of Newk's Dodgers back in the '50s.

Over the years faculty would occasionally sing, play instruments, and perform skits in chapel. Students always looked forward to those rare instances when faculty would step outside the safety of their traditional, staid roles in the classroom to demonstrate

Distinction Without Pretension

talents or frivolity unexpected by the students. A barrier would temporarily dissolve and the students could stand in judgment of the faculty member. The courage to make oneself vulnerable in this way was invariably rewarded with warm student applause or, at the least, polite acceptance.

One individual who never showed such openness was ramrod straight and always proper Dr. Robert Cramer. Dean Cramer was the epitome of decorum, consistently aloof, serious, always by-the-book rules-conscious.

So a titter of surprise wafted through the student audience at a convo presentation featuring faculty and staff talent when Dean Cramer appeared on stage. Without advance notice, the lanky Dr. Cramer walked into the stage lights in those understated, clipped strides so familiar to students. He approached the podium at the side of the stage, settled behind it, cleared his throat and launched into a dramatic reading of some nondescript poet. This is what students would expect of Cramer. It was as close to loosening up as he would ever allow: a public rendering of a work by a long-dead and dull bard.

Curiously though, Dr. Cramer began to wince as he read. Finally, an exasperated countenance preceded a pause, and then he stopped reading. His eyes glanced nervously across the stage at the Steinway piano. Then, his face brightening, he glided across the boards, took a seat on the piano stool, stretched his arms skyward, placed his fingers gently onto the piano keys, and began to play a classical score.

"Rachmananov," whispered a music major sitting behind me. So it was a classical score, not a dramatic reading we were to hear from our esteemed dean. And he played well, as far as I could tell.

But wait. Perhaps four measures into the highbrow piece, Dean Cramer again looked troubled. With a flash of chagrin and one last heavy thrust on the keys, his music prematurely ended. Seemingly abashed and uncomfortable, he just couldn't seem to be satisfied with his performance. Once again the willowy dean shook his head in dismay.

Standing behind the piano, peering into the space of the auditorium ceiling, it seemed a light bulb switched on in his brain. A broad smile now filled his face, a sight students rarely saw on his puss. It was at this moment he removed something from his shoes that had gone unnoticed by unsuspecting students. Hidden by the piano, Dr. Cramer deftly removed the rubber overshoes covering his patent leather loafers.

From the amplifiers surrounding the auditorium now emitted a snappy jazz tune, and Cramer began to … to … *NO!*

Damned if Cramer didn't burst into a spirited dance routine! These were not ordinary loafers. He was wearing **tap shoes!**

Now let me not deceive you. This wasn't Fred Astaire that sixteen hundred eyes were following. Cramer cut more of an Ichabod Crane figure as he stiffly, but gamely, pranced about the stage, *almost* to the beat of the music. To his credit, Cramer was obviously not performing this routine without practice. He had necessarily gone through great effort to put himself before the mercy of students. And it didn't go unrewarded.

As the final notes of the song wound down, Cramer performed his denouement, ending his frolic with an awkward but lively flourish. The house unraveled! Thunderous applause and a spontaneous leap of the assembly to its feet greeted a somewhat startled but obviously pleased Dean Cramer.

Leo Miller added this epilogue to the tale: Mr. Miller had returned to the school

James L. Brunnemer

at 11 p.m. one evening the prior week, and hearing music in the auditorium, unlocked the door to investigate. There he found a fully surprised Dean Cramer practicing his dance while a student controlled the electronic equipment out of which the taped music emitted. Cramer immediately demanded that Leo promise, on the spot, that he would not reveal his discovery to anyone.

Because the dean needed assistance to play the recorded music for weeks as he rehearsed his routine, the student was under a similar sentence. The young sound technician knew if he breathed even a word of what he'd seen, not only would he never graduate from ICC, Cramer would see to it that no university in the solar system would allow him admission. Both Leo and the student kept their promises, resulting in one of the most shocking and remarkable chapel events ever.

My most memorable chapel program was one in which an incident altered the planned program, resulting in a frenetic scene that every member of that audience will forever recall.

It was formal opening chapel, circa 1963. I was seated in the fourth row, our seats being assigned alphabetically in those days.

Formal opening chapel was a sacrament filled with grand ceremony and dignity. It was an opportunity to indoctrinate freshmen with their first exposure to this thrice-weekly ritual and to remind upperclassmen that the college still held chapel as an important contribution to their educational and moral well-being.

The program was always identical and predictably decorous. First, the college choir, scrubbed and robed and sounding angelic, sang the opening hymn. Next came the faculty processional, accompanied with a spirited movement on the organ. Appropriately dignified, the faculty, in full academic regalia, marched down the aisles to take their places in folding chairs on the stage. Finally, the address by President Esch had the purpose of pointing students in the appropriate direction on their educational and moral compasses.

However, on this day, a problem occurred early in the agenda. The choir was on stage, maroon choir robes vivid against the blue backdrop, bursting forth in religious song. Suddenly, out of the heavens came an obtrusive *"whooooooosh."* What seemed like a veritable avalanche of confetti descended on the unsuspecting singers. The main barrage fell swiftly, without warning.

I remember that I was focused on Linda Jackson, a striking blonde with large beautiful blue eyes. When the falling paper shreds engulfed her she momentarily became indistinct in the whiteness all around. Like all the other choir members, she did her best to persevere despite the rude distraction. None of the singers reacted overtly to the paper blizzard falling on their heads, but Linda's quizzical expression at least acknowledged that something extraordinary, and unrehearsed, was occurring on stage.

The sound of the choir I cannot duplicate in words, but if you've ever had a record (not a CD or a cassette tape) on a stereo and the power goes off, you can understand how the sound of that group was interrupted. One second they were synchronic, harmonious, their rich intonation emanating throughout the hall. When the confetti cloud descended upon them they slowed, in vocal lockstep, with an elongated "Ho---o----o-------o----ly," like a 78-rpm record played at thirty-three-and-a-third speed (only people born before 1950 will understand what I'm attempting to convey here). Admirably, they regrouped, with their voices returning to the appropriate tempo.

Bravely, the choir completed its number, as snippets of confetti continued to trickle down, wafting as feathers, from wherever it originated.

The parade of faculty was short-circuited. They remained out in the theater lobby. No signal was given, no orders to change the itinerary. The faculty just seemed to know they should not move. Not now.

With no sense of urgency, no hurried movement to betray his inner thoughts and emotions, Dr. Esch appeared from a place at the side of the hall and walked slowly, deliberately, almost funereally toward the lectern at the side of the stage.

The student body, which only moments before had been stifling giggles, amazed at this stunning prank, became still as death as Dr. Esch somberly mounted the steps leading to the stage. Tom Anthony, always one of the usual suspects in such antics, recalled leaning over to the student next to him and saying, "God Himself knows I had nothing to do with this, but right now I'm in big trouble!"

Arriving, finally, at the dais, President Esch looked out over the assembly of students before him. With taut jaw and a withering glare, Dr. Esch said nothing for what seemed an eternity. Slowly, he swept his eyes across the entire assembly. It seemed that he made direct eye contact with every student there. After this agonizing millenium, he still uttered nary a word.

His countenance bespoke that he had been deeply offended, personally wounded, by the event that had upset the grandeur and solemnity of this rite. His fixed scowl seared into each of our youthful souls.

Then, in a low, firm voice—"What God would sound like if we could hear him," Jerry England once described it—Dr. Esch began to express his profound disappointment that a student in his fine, Christian institution would dare be part of a calculated and dastardly act such as this.

Honestly, I don't remember a word of what he said to us frightened, contrite students at that moment, but I can tell you this: His indignation was so profound, and so genuine was his pain and regret, that although I had played no role whatsoever in the outrageous blot on the ceremony so dear to Dr. Esch, I was ready to confess to the crime for the student body. I felt guilty, just as if I were an accomplice. Dr. Esch's smoldering anger and Churchillian presence could move one in that way.

Ordinarily, the perpetrators of such an ingenious ruse as the chapel confetti caper would be revealed soon after the event. When cast across the campus, Dr. Esch's dragnet always snared first those known to be especially predisposed to such mischief.

The president, Dean Cramer, and other administrators each had their own underground network of operatives upon whom they relied for information if the culprit wasn't found among the immediately obvious suspects. Or often, the guilty party, fearing he would inevitably be found out and knowing the measure of the penalty would escalate according to the amount of elapsed time between the act and the confession, would come forward voluntarily. The downside to that was obvious. Generally the guilty party would be threatened within a dollop of his life, an appropriate slap on the wrist would follow, and the incident would be forgotten by the administration. The upside, of course, was instant fame and even legendary status for the daring miscreant.

But in this instance, though the event was the subject of dining hall conversations for months and the potential suspects were many, no one was convicted of the crime.

Rumors of the execution of the perfectly timed stunt abounded. It was said that the amount of paper shredded would have consumed weeks of toil if four to six students laboring eight hours daily were engaged. Conveying that amount of paper into the auditorium, carrying it into the "crow's nest" above the stage, and concealing it in a huge bag overhead without discovery by someone in the theatre department seemed an impossible feat. It had to be a conspiracy of many students, it seemed. And the more persons involved, the greater the likelihood someone would talk.

The most intricate part of the entire drama was the firing mechanism. Those who viewed the crime scene afterward spoke of a candle that was lit, burned down to a particular level, which resulted in the flame igniting a thin rope-fuse. The rope burned slowly until it could no longer bear the weight of the huge paper flap that, once pressured into flying open, emptied the contents of the bag onto the unsuspecting students below. The timing from ignition of the fuse to the release of the paper had to be calculated precisely.

The favored theory was that several students, perhaps up to ten or a dozen, had been involved, and the inventors of the complex fuse system were smart.

As days turned into weeks, then to months afterward, the prevailing campus mystery faded as a topic of conversation. Campus life ground on, and other fresher, if less intriguing, events replaced the great confetti caper in the frontal lobes of the students.

Years passed. Occasionally when at Homecoming or a similar event where alumni of that era would gather someone might remark, "Remember the time when … " followed by a description of the chaotic scene, and, invariably, "Did they ever find out who did it?"

And no one ever knew.

We thought.

It was years later, summer 1971, that this incident was to be recalled in a most surprising way.

I returned to ICC in June of that year to become director of alumni relations. One of my first responsibilities was to organize a "farewell tour" for the recently retired President Esch in order that alumni from around the state might pay him tribute. Many evenings found Dr. Esch and me driving through the Midwestern countryside to various cities where alumni gathered to bid him Godspeed in retirement.

Typically we would gather for a sumptuous meal prepared by the church ladies' societies in the social room of one of the small Evangelical United Brethren churches that supported ICC. Afterward, Dr. Esch would regale the gathering with stories from his quarter-century memory book as president. Often the proposed two-hour event would stretch at least an hour beyond that as alumni, enthralled with the Esch tales, would beg for more. Great memories were recalled, and made, on those junkets.

One of our stops was a church in Kokomo. On this particular evening, Dr. Esch was doing his usual enchanting soliloquy when, with a chuckle, he began to tell in great detail his version of the confetti caper of 1963. Dr. Esch embellished the yarn, his eyes lively, enjoying his hold on the rapt audience.

As he came to the climax of the story, he paused. With a wicked grin, Dr. Esch bore his gaze in upon one rather shy, unimposing member of his audience and thundered, "Jim Peck, you and Gary Palmer really did a remarkable job on that trick!"

Distinction Without Pretension

Words are too feeble to describe the stunned look that covered Jim Peck's face.

Perhaps my look of complete disbelief might have competed with Peck's visage, though. Jim Peck and Gary Palmer? The two campus science nerds pulled off the most notable chapel mischief of all time? It couldn't be!

Had an objective and infallible scoring system of character traits been available to detect who of all the students at ICC were most likely to pull off such a stunt, only on superior intelligence would either of those two have qualified even remotely for the suspects list.

Quiet, unassuming and upright, their moral miens had eliminated the devious duo from any possible suspicion.

My amazement that those two Elmers had actually engineered one of the most celebrated and inventive pranks in the annals of such outlandish acts at Indiana Central was eclipsed only by the stunning realization that Dr. Esch knew all along the two perpetrators, but had kept it secret for more than ten years.

Later, as we drove back to Indianapolis, with Dr. Esch grinning in self-satisfied bliss all the way home, I asked how he knew it was those two who did the deed. Even then, safely in retirement, Dr. Esch refused to reveal his sources or means of detecting the guilty jesters. But he did tell me the rationale he adopted for not revealing to the world of ICC who had sabotaged his precious formal convocation.

"If I had told anyone that I knew who did it," Dr. Esch explained, "I would have had to appropriately punish them." With the fulsome laugh that shook his ample tummy like Santa Claus, Dr. Esch said simply, "I couldn't very well kick out of school our two brightest science students, now could I?"

Classic Dr. Esch.

It's a shame, really, that current and future U of I students will never experience the drab and boring programs, the hilarity, and the maturing and educational moments one experienced in thirty-six chapel programs per annum at ICC.

Yes, I *do* miss chapel.

CHAPTER X
VERY BUSY—WITH THE UNIMPORTANT

> *From Antigone through Martin Luther to*
> *Martin Luther King the issue of liberty has*
> *turned on the existence of a higher law than*
> *that of The State.*
> — Milton Mayer

The balance of my seven semesters at Indiana Central College would play out against a backdrop of the most significant social movement in American history, an undeclared "war" in Southeast Asia, and the assassination of one of the nation's most popular presidents. Each would wrench the soul of America.

As late winter turned to spring in 1963, Martin Luther King and his followers were gaining ever-increasing momentum in the struggle for civil rights. Although the acceleration of the Vietnam conflict lay a few years into the future for all but a relatively small number of citizen soldiers, it was now on the radar screen of the American consciousness. John Kennedy had less than seven months to live.

Comfortable within the peaceful sanctuary that was the ICC campus, I wasn't paying much attention to events 500 miles to the south, where infamous police chief "Bull" Conner was using high-pressure water hoses to contain and abase civil rights protesters in Birmingham, Alabama. Nor was I consumed by the deadly jungle conflict half a world away. The struggle among social and political factions that would alter the American culture as surely as did the Great Depression, or any of the wars in which our nation had been involved up to that time, was not yet of meaningful consequence to most students on the ICC campus.

Looking in the rearview mirror of history, it may seem astounding to thinking people today that we were relatively oblivious to the turmoil of the times. For the most part, college-age students in the early sixties simply weren't aware, let alone immersed in, the world-altering events into which our country was becoming embroiled. I think this was especially true at small, conservative, church-affiliated, independent colleges and universities. Maintaining at least an acceptable academic average under the strain of an overload of new information and experiences, understanding confusing emotions of all kinds novel to adults-in-the-making who hadn't seen much of the world, and having as much fun interacting with males and females in campus life as possible—these occupied the time and energies of the great majority of college students while apocalyptic events played out on the world stage.

Amidst the turmoil of the 1960s, when fundamental American principles, traditions, and institutions were challenged in unprecedented ways, the Indiana Central campus was, in contrast, a virtual haven of peace and tranquility. While schools such as Berkeley, Kent State, Wisconsin, and Columbia became bitter battlegrounds between students and "the system," one witnessed very little activity or unrest within the Indiana Central student body.

James L. Brunnemer

Certainly a number of faculty were chagrined to find such inertia for protest among their charges, wondering how the students at Indiana Central could allow major social issues to be played out on the national and international stage without being part of it.

Why weren't the collegians at Indiana Central more involved in such salient events of that historic time?

One can fairly surmise that the basic conservative nature of the campus population itself was the chief factor. Few volatile activists sought admission at ICC. For the most part students came from backgrounds that didn't lend themselves to the luxury of placing political activity ahead of study. These young people, under the watchful eyes of the families that spawned them, were intent on earning degrees and having opportunities for better lives than had their forebears.

Perhaps the most important reason for campus calm at ICC, however, was a directive from President I. Lynd Esch. The "Esch Rule," very simply stated, went like this: "Any student found attempting to disrupt the business of the university by occupying by protest classrooms, administrative offices, or other university facilities will first be expelled from school on the spot. Then, that *former* student will be arrested and prosecuted for trespassing." A tribute to the stature of the patriotic and paternal president was that the "Esch Rule" never had to be invoked.

There were a few students who carried out tentative, mostly inane protests of the "unjust American system," but most of us were simply focused on events within the narrow vista of the 67-acre ICC campus.

Most weeks during the spring semester at Indiana Central in 1963 included, for me, a routine of fifteen hours of classes (did anyone really study "two hours for every credit hour of class" as we were told we should?); harassing the congenial Dailey dorm monitor, Youngblood; engaging in baseball practice and games; learning about life with fellow students over meals in the dining hall and late-night discourse in the dorms; and engaging in lots of vacuous merriment.

As an example, only days into the semester, a group of us committed one of the hundreds of harmless pranks that we worked so hard to commit upon one another. Between one and two a.m. on a frosty morning, two residents of Dailey Hall stealthily and brazenly tiptoed by Mom Hapeman's door, the old floors creaking beneath the paper-thin carpet. Every piece of furniture in the lounge, including the one television set in the dormitory, we transferred and stacked before the doorway of Steve Lemme and Dick Elmore's room. The next morning when they arose for their usual routine, Steve and Dick opened the door to view furniture weighing the equivalent of a Volkswagen blocking every square inch of the doorframe. They had to climb out a window to extricate themselves from their cell. Clad only in pajamas, the pair dropped the ten feet or so into four inches of snow on the ground. Then they returned the furnishings to the lounge, piece by piece, under the stern gaze of house matron Fraulein Hapeman.

Retribution was swift, however. Two nights later, a waste can full of water was placed, leaning against the inwardly opening door of the room Jack Leonard and I shared. The next morning we spent hours mopping up the two inches of liquid spilling into our small abode, a flood triggered when I opened the door.

Distinction Without Pretension

Recalling that episode prompts me to share an earlier incident that surely would rate an A+ on the grading scale of clever antics. A beloved icon through whose veins flowed the crimson and grey of ICC was Charles Dill. A 1950 graduate and a student of Dr. William Pitt Morgan, "Doc" Dill earned his medical degree from Indiana University and then returned to settle with wife Maryrose and raise his family in University Heights. Large of frame and possessing a boundless sense of humor, Doc Dill served for many years as a volunteer physician for Greyhound athletic teams. When he died, suddenly, of a coronary in 1981, the Indianapolis community and the Indiana Central family universally mourned Charlie.

Among many acts of deviltry he captained during his undergraduate days was a lulu Doc related to a group of us once. Accompanied by the usual Dill flair for telling stories with a rapid-fire delivery and a mischievous twinkle perpetually dancing in his eyes, Doc told of a discovery made by him and a few fellow residents of the third floor of Men's Hall when he was a senior.

Doc and his cronies somehow discovered that if all the toilets on third floor were flushed simultaneously, water pressure of the outdated system would turn the first floor johns into geysers, shooting water upward three to four feet. (How in the world they found this out only God and superintendent of buildings and grounds Birtle Allen would know!)

There happened to be, at that time, a cadre of men who regularly, and annoyingly to fellow first floor residents, occupied the stalls, casually reading the Sunday newspaper while seated for nature's call. The "Sunday Morning Sitters," as they were dubbed, would linger for forty-five minutes to an hour, occupying each of the six johns.

So, the obvious plan was concocted. Doc and five other miscreants met in the third floor men's room at nine a.m. on a Sunday. A "scout" passed the message upstairs when all the "Sitters" had settled comfortably into their customary poses.

At the agreed upon signal, Doc and his mates, as one, jammed the flush handles forcefully downward. Immediately, angry howls could be heard clearly, even up on third floor. Wisely assuming that the victims would eventually figure out who had so rudely interrupted their routine, Charlie and the boys wasted no time. It was out the door and down the fire escape and into the pews of the nearby University Heights Church to ask for forgiveness.

Ummm. I doubt that last part.

With the warm spring weather came baseball season. Having apparently impressed Coach Bill Bright with my high school-honed skills, I found myself a starter at first base. I batted clean-up for the Greyhounds in my first college game as a freshman, in Lafayette, against Purdue. Like Nick in basketball, Bill believed in a tough pre-Hoosier College Conference schedule, so we played the likes of Purdue, Indiana, Louisville, Cincinnati, Xavier, Indiana State, Eastern Illinois, Miami (Ohio), and other larger programs to prepare us for Franklin, Manchester, and other schools more our size.

What I faced in the batter's box that day was truly unfair. A veteran Purdue left-handed pitcher by the name of Joe Cagiano threw a pitiless curve ball along with his overpowering fastball, rendering this eighteen-year-old offenseless, despite the bat that I'd carried into the box. I'd not seen anything so scary in all my playing days up to then. Needless to say, I didn't help the squad much against him. I managed a weak bloop hit in four times at bat that day and learned in the process that college baseball was going to be

James L. Brunnemer

a real challenge for me.

Later that week we played Eastern Illinois University at Charleston. A nightmare became reality for me in that third game of my college career. Our team had played well, and I managed to produce a run-scoring single in the top of the ninth inning to bring us into a 6-6 tie. In the bottom of the inning, Jerry Mullinix walked a batter and then struck a man out. Consecutive singles loaded the bases. Bright signaled us infielders to play "in"—which meant a position to the inside of the bases—in order to attempt to cut the winning run off at home if the batter hit a ground ball.

Well, that opportunity presented itself.

The hardest smash I'd ever seen came my way on the very first pitch. Actually, I don't recall *seeing* the ball. I just heard the *POK* of bat striking ball and perceived a blur streaking toward me. Instinctively I reached down and the baseball smacked into my glove after one skip off the ground. That ball was struck so hard I still can't believe I caught it. But there was the baseball, in my glove!

The runner on third had broken for home at the crack of the bat but was only about halfway there. A quick toss to catcher Armen Cobb, coupled with a return throw to me at first base for the double play, and we would play extra innings with a chance to win.

So surprised was I to actually feel the ball in my glove, I came up quickly—too quickly—hurrying my throw to Armen. Actually, the adrenalin rush that occurred must have had something to do with the fact that my fling to the plate, hurled with all my might, sailed three-fourths of the way up the backstop screen! So errant was the throw, Cobb couldn't even attempt a jump for it. He simply turned his head as the ball sailed far above him. The runner relaxed and trotted across the plate. The game was over. EIU 7, ICC 6. The truly remarkable stop of the horsehide missile was wasted with the wildest heave anyone living west of the Appalachians could recall seeing.

We won more than we lost that season, without much help from my bat. I hit .200-and-change, not an auspicious beginning to my collegiate baseball career.

There was one final memorable event in which I played a role before moving back home and starting my summer job as one of the lowest members in the food chain of laborers in the foundry at International Harvester Company.

That was initiation into the C-Association at the conclusion of finals week.

During the last day of the spring semester those of us who were first-time letter winners during the 1962-63 school year were "invited" to be inducted into the brotherhood of fellow athletes by the veteran lettermen. (A sign of the times: the C-Association was an all-male society.)

Following the spring athletic banquet, we who would be the "guests" for the ceremony met in front of Wilmore Hall at 10 p.m. Through the darkness, we could hear from the eighty-or-so upperclassmen amassed on the steps of the gymnasium an eerie and ominous "clack-clack-clack" echoing across the campus. We had been required to fashion for any veteran letter winner who requested it paddles of approximately eighteen inches in length. Some of these wooden weapons were creatively ornate, carefully crafted by us in the hope the recipient would consider the time and energy put into the "gift" and might persuade the donee to go lightly on us. Yeah, right. Like the chances of a man with one leg in an ass-kicking contest.

Distinction Without Pretension

As the testosterone flowing through their veins began to increase, the wild men awaiting us at the gym brought their paddles together, rhythmically, creating an unsettling noise. One of our now-cowering companions likened the intimidating sound to that of fierce Zulus thumping battle shields with their weapons prior to attacking a foe. Quaking like leaves of an Aspen tree in the wind, we thirty new inductees nervously considered our fate.

At the appointed time we trudged sullenly to the gym and waded into the by-now crazed and hostile horde there. We weren't sure, at this point, that this custom that was intended to be fun hadn't degenerated into a dangerous mob mentality with uncertain outcomes. I quickly scanned my memory to recall if there were stories of past events that resulted in fatalities.

The first order of business was to don the blindfold we'd been instructed to bring; the second, to strip completely, save for the jockstrap each of us wore beneath our clothing. We'd subsequently lose even this slight article of apparel as the evening-from-hell unfolded. Seated, cramped and unseeing, on the dank cement floor of a classroom, insults and threats were hurled at us from all directions. Vituperations were delivered at the tops of voices we recognized as belonging to individuals whom we had heretofore mistaken as civil human beings. Real doubt chilled our blood as each of us silently considered the question: We will be okay, won't we?

An individual among us especially singled out was one of the kindest, most gentlemanly, and brightest of the inductees. My good friend and high school teammate Dick Elmore had received the Robert Brooker Award as the top scholar among *all* athletes at ICC for the year.

Dick's antagonist was one who would be found at the opposite end of the academic scale. President of the C-Association, John Koontz, at 6'5" and 240 pounds, was literally the "BMOC"—the biggest man on campus. An all-conference football player known for his surly attitude toward newcomers, few underclassmen earned John's respect. At this moment, as he growled menacingly at us, we weren't positive that rumors he'd killed a freshman drama major by dropping him out a third-floor window of Buxton Hall was a joke after all. (John was later to have a notable teaching and coaching career, culminating in his selection to both the Indiana Wrestling and Indiana Track halls of fame.)

Above the din, as we trembled unseeing on the cold concrete floor considering our fate, Koontz's voice was clearly definable: **"Let me tell you scumbags what I hate most in the world! It's a goddamn smartass who makes all As"!** (Whew! I'd dodged *that* bullet, anyway.)

Then: **"Where the hell is *Gilmore*?"**

Dick *Elmore* had no doubt as to whom Koontz was referring. He was to endure an especially humiliating screed from his football teammate before we were herded to the lower regions of the gymnasium for a gantlet of diabolical tortures.

The least abasing of these was sitting on a block of ice—"buck nekkid"—and attempting to pick up a grape using only one's sphincter muscles. If you haven't tried this, I'd recommend passing on it. It's not pleasant.

We survived all the various and sundry tortures a group of college athletes can conjure up—including the ritual painting of private parts in a rich crimson enamel that would remain with us for many days afterward despite delicate but painful scrubbing and showering—to face, in a manner of speaking, the "Senior Swing." Graduating seniors were honored with this one final rite. The command: "Alright, dung-heap, let me see elbows and butt-holes!" The two dozen of us lined up side-by-side, still blindfolded, and grabbing our ankles with our hands, presented our shiny posteriors as targets for the seniors' tribute.

Every senior, as he came down the line, leaned over and whispered encouragement in your ear. He challenged you to always be loyal and proud to be a Greyhound. Following the debasement we'd endured, those words made one feel ecstatic, and accepted into this select fraternity. After that meaningful chat, he would gently tap your rear with his paddle.

Except for one. There was a jaunty Greyhound senior whom each 1963 C-Association inductee will always remember.

Strolling last down the line, pausing behind each of us, was Walt Lyon. Walt didn't bother to whisper his valedictory.

A loud smack and either a muffled grunt of stifled pain or a surprised screech of overt outrage by the recipient followed, "**Remember 'Big Walt.'**"

I shall *never* forget "Big Walt."

Despite my struggles adapting to college-level athletics and academics, memories of those days are sublime. I was among millions of American boys whose lives were *not* at risk daily of being killed by an Asian enemy on foreign soil. Though naïve and removed from the sociopolitical turmoil embracing the nation and world, I was gaining new understandings of people and learning how constrained my small-town existence had been. A part-time job and my middle class family enabled me to exist without great financial stress, and I was healthy and vital as I would ever be. In short, my situation as a teenage freshman at ICC was not unlike so many of my generation. We had it made, really.

The school term moved inevitably toward its conclusion. I witnessed in May of 1963 what, if my memory serves, was the last outdoor commencement ceremony held at Indiana Central. The site was directly west of the portico of what is now Good Hall, with the enrobed faculty and graduates, families, and friends seated on folding chairs. President Esch presided over the ceremony. On this warm and breezy day, the shade of the huge trees and fresh aroma of budding shrubs and flowers added a unique character to the scene. It was a proud moment for parents of the graduates because the vast majority of seniors receiving degrees that day, as with virtually all ICC alumni at that time, were the very first to earn a college degree in their families.

Following the end of the school term I joined a team of college baseball players from schools across the state to play in the summer amateur league in Indianapolis. We were called the College All-Stars, as flattering a description as it was inaccurate. In fact, dominant pitchers much older and more seasoned than us fresh-faced collegians led the two best teams in the league. One was named Del Harris (yes, *that* Del Harris) and the other was Bill Bright.

The first summer game as a college player helped to further my understanding of the chasm between my high opinion of my baseball skills and that of reality. At that time Del Harris was head baseball and basketball coach at Earlham College in Richmond. That was a "fer piece" from coaching the Houston Rockets to an NBA championship, and later as the headman for the Los Angeles Lakers. He pitched in that summer league for a team from his hometown of Plainfield, Indiana.

Distinction Without Pretension

Batting against the rangy Mr. Harris at Garfield Park provided me with an education. On my first time at bat, as Harris began his wind-up, I was focused on the spot over his right shoulder where I would pick up the baseball on its flight to home plate. I immediately surmised he'd thrown a fastball, and that it was comfortably outside the strike zone. I relaxed and waited for the umpire to signal, "Ball one."

"Steeeeeee-rike!" bellowed the man in blue, Bob Wolfe, a man I heretofore didn't know, but would come to appreciate later as an outstanding official.

That pitch was a foot outside!

I turned briefly to shoot an impugnable glance at the ump, then resumed my batting position to await the second Harris offering. This pitch was a carbon copy of the first. A fastball again (I'd seen more "giddy-up" from high school pitchers) and this toss was well outside, too.

"Steeeee-rike two!" roared Wolfe.

"What the hell, man, are you blind? That pit- ... "

"*Shut your trap, Rook*, and get back in the box!" the umpire rudely interrupted. "And this time watch the pitch all the way."

Hmmm. An odd thing for an umpire to say. Must be a frustrated coach.

But I heeded his words. Bearing down now with two strikes on me, I did, indeed, earnestly scrutinize the next pitch from Del Harris all the way into the catcher's glove. Again, the ball appeared to be a fastball of average velocity. But as it neared the plate, seemingly six to eight inches wide of the strike zone, it suddenly defied physics, darting sidewise to cross the outside corner of the plate.

Wolfe's "Steeee-rike three, yer out!" call was anticlimactic. No argument from me this time. I wasn't certain what I had seen as I walked away. But after a couple of the older players noted the puzzlement in my eyes, they informed me I'd seen my first real slider.

Harris treated me like a stepchild that day. I went 0-for-4 against his assortment of pitches—including a fastball that really *was*—and discovered why he had been an outstanding pitcher in the minor leagues.

It was the very next game at Riverside Park that I stepped into the rectangular batter's area to face for the first time in competition my coach, Bill Bright.

As I took my stance, I glanced at Coach Bright and grinned. After all, only days ago at the college he had encouraged and taught me. Bill's expression remained, as it was before I acknowledged him, stoic, if not contemptuous.

Oh, okay, let's get serious here. Be that way, coach. It will be fun to feast on the "old man's" (he was 32) *pitches.*

Grimly now I settled into the box, coiled to drive the first pitch that crossed the plate to the outfield. Bill's left arm whipped around, and the pitch—letter high, an aspirin tablet—hurtled homeward. And it was coming straight at my ribs! As the projectile bore down on me I bailed out, sprawling in the dust as it whizzed by. I rose up, a bit confused, and irked that my own coach would "dust me off." I looked out toward the mound to see Bright, displaying no emotion, rolling the ball in his fist, waiting for me to resume my place in the batter's box. He proceeded to strike me out with the ease he would have a ten-year-old.

"Awe," proclaimed Northwestern University's noted sociologist Bernard Beck, "is respect, tinged with fear." At that moment, I was in awe of Bill Bright.

CHAPTER XI
PLAYING FOR BRIGHT

*Dignity does not consist in possessing honors,
but in deserving them.*
                    Aristotle

There is no one to whom I am personally more indebted for my growth during the college years than Bill Bright. Coach Bright is one of the most remarkable individuals I've had the privilege of knowing in my lifetime. Highly respected by most, and despised by a few who encountered him as a competitor in athletics, an instructor, a coach, or an athletics administrator, he is an able and incisive individual. I first met Bill Bright shortly after my transfer from Butler. Bill coached the junior varsity basketball team that I immediately joined upon my enrollment at ICC. But it was through baseball that I became intimately acquainted with Bill and benefited most from his expertise and kindness.

An intensely shy man, Bill chose a profession that constantly challenged him to try to understand and deal with the idiosyncrasies of people. His strict adherence to rules and his reliance on detail and organization often brought him into conflict with those with lesser standards of behavior. Bill's exterior of self-control and his acute sense of fairness often resulted in harsh and blunt observations and actions that concealed a genuinely caring heart capable of great compassion. His was a sensitivity that most never saw because of how closely he guarded it. I was privileged to get behind Bill's mask.

As a teacher he should be remembered with professors Nelson, Henricks, and McBride, among other high-quality educators at the college. There were few courses in the college curriculum at Indiana Central more demanding than Bill's "Tests and Measurements" class. Despite the reputation of health and physical education as the "toy store" of college academics, each class taught by Bill was an exercise in respectable intellectual pursuit. He took his job seriously.

As a coach, Bill preached and practiced preparation and mastery of the fundamentals. No athletic leader I've observed demanded more of himself than Bill Bright at knowing the rules of the game, teaching the basics and intricacies of sport, and living up to his own exacting standards in preparing his players for competition. Not even Nick. Of all those I've known, maybe Royce Waltman equaled Bill's intensity and attention to detail. Bright was a superb coach.

Those who played baseball with Bill during his undergraduate days in the early fifties will recall how predominant he was as a pitcher for the Greyhounds. Angus Nicoson was coach for the 1952 squad, which, behind Bright's superb pitching, won all thirteen of its games.

Bill signed to play professionally with the Philadelphia Phillies following his junior season in 1953. At the end of that year Bill was drafted into the army for a two-year hitch. When he came out of the service he suffered from a mysterious malady resulting in a loss of strength in his pitching arm. Newly married to Pat (Hunt) '57 and with a child

James L. Brunnemer

on the way, Bill foreswore his promising baseball career to return to ICC and a steady job coaching and teaching. Not long afterwards it was discovered that an abscessed tooth was the source of the poison that had settled in Bill's elbow, rendering the natural whip useless.

Once the tooth was extracted, Bill's left arm became as lethal as ever. Now securely ensconced at ICC, however, Bill didn't return to professional baseball to fulfill his dream. Few who saw Bill pitch in those days doubted that he would have made the major leagues.

I never saw Bill in his prime as an athlete, although we were teammates in summer competition during my college years. At that time he was in his early thirties. Bill was a lithe six-footer, blessed with great quickness and athleticism. His dark, penetrating eyes hidden beneath heavy brows missed nothing on the field of play. He has remained trim and physically fit into his seventh decade.

I have impressions of his competitive fire that I'll forever recall. Though his best years as a pitcher were behind him, standing in a batter's box as he threw a baseball from 60'6" away was utterly petrifying. I know what it was like as a left-handed hitter to face, first, his devastating fastball, second, his menacing curveball, and most imposing, his acute competitiveness when he strode onto that pitcher's mound.

Bill's comprehension of how to play the game of baseball was profound. Until learning it from Coach Bright, I didn't know that *every* player had a responsibility on *every* play of *every* inning of *every* game. He not only knew intimately the rules of baseball but commanded immediate recall on the field of play. No umpire who ever worked a Greyhound baseball game had better knowledge of the rules than Bill.

We found ourselves in a tight game once with Anderson College, coached then by former Brooklyn Dodger great Carl Erskine. In the final inning, Steve McGee led off with a hit and Tom McNamara doubled, bringing to bat our hottest hitter, Larry Spurgeon. Coach Erskine called time in order to settle his rattled pitcher down. With the potential winning run on third, the decision was made to intentionally walk Spurgeon to set up a possibility of a double play.

Erskine then employed a defensive tactic none of us had seen before. He ordered his right fielder to come all the way in to take a position about fifteen feet *behind* his catcher! The ploy sacrificed an outfielder to prevent the winning run from scoring on a wild pitch or passed ball.

As this was occurring, Coach Bright had been engaged in checking his roster for possible pinch-hitters or substitute fielders. Looking up just as the umpire cried, "*Play ball,*" Bright fairly blew out of our dugout as if molten residue from a volcanic explosion.

"**Time-out!**" he shrieked.

As a sly smile curled from a corner of Carl Erskine's mouth, Bright proceeded to cite line and verse from the rules of baseball that prohibited any defensive player with the exception of the catcher from standing anywhere but in fair territory when a pitch is delivered. The crafty Erskine no doubt knew he couldn't get away with this trick, but tested Bill nonetheless.

Don Ireland ended all suspense with a clean hit to win the game.

One of the subtleties of playing for Coach Bright was observing how much he gave of himself to his coaching responsibilities. His work ethic was nonpareil. As a player, you felt ashamed if you didn't attempt to meet, in some measure, that same fervor he brought to the game. That is one reason, I believe, that Bill's teams overachieved on the baseball field.

Bright insisted that his players appeared orderly and professional on the field. When uniforms were issued, Bill spent time teaching proper dress, down to appropriate folding of the knickers over the knee, proper positioning of the cap, and so forth.

Time-efficiency may have been perfected by Henry Ford, but no one I've known paid more attention to economy of time and effort than Coach Bright. This included packing one's duffel bag for road trips to achieve maximum efficacy in getting into uniform and onto the field. We were always amazed at how much more quickly Bill was dressed and ready for pre-game warm-ups and practice than the rest of us. Invariably, Bill would be nervously pacing, impatiently waiting for the rest of us to get into our baseball gear and out of the locker room. He'd bark at anyone he thought dawdling. I felt more pressure to get properly and quickly attired for a game than I did playing.

It was a real breakthrough when one of my teammates, stealing furtive looks as Bright buzzed through his dressing ritual, discovered the coach's secret. Bright organized his duffel bag, layering his baseball uniform *in the order* in which he would don the various articles of clothing. Baseball spikes, of course, went in the bag first, being the last piece of Bright's apparel that he would put on. Lying atop the spikes were his uniform pants, accompanied by the wide red baseball belt. In succession were his precisely folded baseball jersey, the red outer baseball stirrups placed neatly on the shirt, with the white sanitary hose above that to slip on before his exterior socks. Next came a pair of athletic shorts (for the players it would be shorts with "sliding pads" to protect one's flanks), and then the baseball undershirt with long sleeves. If it were cold, as was common during spring days in Indiana, a cutoff "dickey" that covered the neck would be slipped over the sweatshirt. Atop the undershirt in his bag was a jock strap ("comfort shorts" had not been thought of yet).

His only nod to anything out of order was the baseball cap. It was the last item placed in the bag so that it wouldn't be crushed out of the neatly curved shape into which Bill had molded the bill of the cap. He was an artful ecdysiast, in reverse.

His routine was interrupted but once, to my knowledge, in the four years I played for Coach Bright.

Our squad had made the 125-mile journey by bus from Indianapolis to Charleston, Illinois, for our annual rivalry with Eastern Illinois University. Eastern's coach, Joe McCabe, was an excellent baseball man. Bill was always "up" for those teams whose coaches were exceptional, like Carl Erskine at Anderson University and Earlham's Del Harris. Bill's insecurities, manifested by his fierce pride, would make him especially testy with the players on these outings. He wanted his team to look like pros, behave like pros, and play like pros. And he intended to demonstrate he was a pro, as well, in everything he did. His reaction to mental lapses and physical misplays was intensified. My oh my, you didn't want to overthrow the cut-off man, miss a signal, or fail to back up a play properly when Bill faced a counterpart who he suspected might know and appreciate the game as much as he.

So it is that you may appreciate Bill's reactions when he began his time-honored dressing ritual in the locker room at EIU that Saturday in 1965, and found that he had failed to pack an important item of his baseball uniform. By coincidence, I had ended up with the locker next to Bill's. Things started out normally. Bill had peeled his "civvies" in his usual time of less than half a minute, saying nothing. Bill never talked as he undressed or dressed for the game. Idle chatter was distracting, wasteful of valuable milliseconds.

I was proceeding at a pace a little faster than normal, being in proximity to the dressing cyclone, when from the corner of my eye I noted an uncharacteristic pause in the usual flurry of Bright's metamorphosis from civilian to baseball coach. Looking to my left I saw that Coach Bright's countenance revealed an expression both quizzical and horrified. Stealing a quick glance downward into his duffel bag, it suddenly dawned on me: Bill didn't have his stirrups, the red outer hose that covered the sanitary socks. Without those one would look like George Washington in a baseball outfit. Bill simply would not have gone onto the field in knickers and white hose.

In typical Bright fashion, he made an instantaneous analysis of his dilemma and arrived at a decision.

Silently, those piercing dark eyes moved around the room from player to player. In a burst of clarity I realized he was doing a rapid-fire skill-rating of the athletes in the room, assessing their rank order value to the team! I could almost see the computer working in his mind: dit-dit-dit ... Bill Tutterow, starting second baseman. Bright's head moved slightly, his gaze falling on the player next to Tut. Dit-dit-dit ... Mike Terrell, backup catcher. Dit-dit-dit ... Jerry Seay, right field, bats third. Dit-dit-dit ... and so on through the entire twenty-five-man roster. Within the space of half-a-minute, Coach Bright's gaze returned to that player who in Bill's hierarchy was least important to our effort on the field:

"CUSTER!" Bright barked.

Jon, a freshman, looked up, startled, wondering what offense he may have committed. Or maybe it was his turn to carry the bat bag to the field.

"Yes, sir, Coach?" Jon replied meekly.

"Hand me your socks!" Bill tersely intoned, emotionless.

Custer, wide-eyed now, wasn't sure that he heard correctly.

"What socks, Coach?"

"Your stirrups. Hurry up!"

Unaware of Coach Bright's quandary and his solution for it, Jon walked over and in confusion handed his red stirrups to the coach.

Without explanation, and not the slightest sign of remorse, Bill grabbed the red hosiery. Quickly sliding them over his sanitary socks, he completed dressing in a matter of seconds and departed wordlessly for the field.

As the locker room door closed behind Bright, Custer still stood near the spot Bill had just vacated, his hand out and mouth agape. Perhaps Jon's genuine distant relative—the *other* Custer—had a similar expression when he saw Crazy Horse and the boys thundering toward him from the Little Big Horn River eighty-eight years previously.

At that moment it hit Jon that he had now inherited Bright's conundrum. The rest of us began to giggle. We could envision what the freshman would face that day. It was Jon Custer who would look like one of the signers of the Declaration of Independence during the game.

We gathered at the diamond, and with a slight acknowledgment of Jon's embarrassing condition, Bright allowed him to stay in the dugout while the rest of us went through our pre-game warm-ups.

Distinction Without Pretension

The dugout was a "below ground" type, enabling Custer to stand without revealing the sight which would mark him for abuse should the opponents see that he wasn't dressed properly for the game. This may seem a minor thing to the civilian, but looking "bush league" always brought contemptuous and ceaseless "razzing" from opponents.

The game began, Bright looking his usual splendid athlete's self in the third base coaching box, while Custer was safely hidden in the shadows of the dugout.

Now Jon *did* add value to the team. His ability to taunt opponents was a noticeable commodity in our team's success. He had a real talent for it. Custer could get under the skin of even the most stoic of players. That afternoon Jon's annoying voice and clever repertoire of insults had a clear effect on certain of our opponents.

Through the early innings of this game he was doing an even better job than usual. His booming voice carried to all parts of the park. On one play the opposing first baseman, a familiar competitor from Franklin, Indiana, Tad Hemminger, neared our dugout in pursuit of a foul pop-up. Jon's insults as Tad settled under the ball so unnerved him that he dropped the easy catch. Custer then heaped more abuse on the player when a weak ground ball slid through his legs for another error. Even Tad's teammates could see he was rattled at our motor-mouth's verbal onslaught. Ironically, up to that time Jon might have been considered our most valuable player.

Then he made a grievous mistake.

An EIU batter whom Custer was abusing mercilessly swung late on a pitch, lining the ball off the screen that covered our dugout, precisely where Jon was standing. Reflexively, Jon jumped out of the dugout to retrieve the ball and return it to the umpire, maintaining a steady chatter of insults directed at the batter as he did so.

When the sudden, simultaneous howls of laughter went up from the EIU players and fans, Jon knew he'd made a devastating error. It wouldn't show up in the box score, but it was a grave blunder, nonetheless.

"HEY, BEN! BEN FRANKLIN! LOOKIN' GOOD, BABY!" was the first and kindest insult that began a torrent of profane abuse for the ridiculous-looking Custer. As the cacophony of contempt increased Jon dutifully tossed the ball to the umpire, who himself couldn't contain a chuckle. The abashed Custer trotted back to the dugout, trying with no success to appear dignified.

He refrained the rest of the game from any taunting of opponents.

And Bill continued to look good from the coaches' box.

During summers our ICC team played together in a league of other teams dominated by college-age players from Anderson, Kokomo, Lafayette, Marion, Lebanon, and the Camp Atterbury Job Corps. Bill pitched and played outfield for us. Nick, who had gotten Schuster Block Company to sponsor the team, was coach. One of the rewards of playing summer ball with your college team, having Bill Bright as a teammate and Nick as coach, was seeing them in a different light. Even though Nick tried to make it seem as if these summer contests were the equivalent of war, he was generally more laid-back. Laughing, telling stories, he allowed us to peer into Nick, the normal guy. Angus was witty and fun.

Likewise, Bill enjoyed the relaxed atmosphere that our summer circumstance allowed. He didn't feel the need to maintain the façade of teacher/coach who constantly monitored his miscreant children for bad behavior. Bright was more like a friend, a big brother, than a mentor. Normally serious in demeanor, it was a joy to hear Bill's child-like giggle that he emitted when allowing himself to be "one of the guys." His high-pitched laughter and teasing were a refreshing change. He could, to the extent that his disciplined self would allow, relate stories, laugh at ours, and occasionally even needle Nick. That summer we all got to know another side of Bill, and it was special since he rarely let his guard down during the regular school year.

Bill occasionally provided some guarded mirth for us teammates as well. He was not a wellspring of patience, to which anyone who knows Bill can attest. Although he had developed pinpoint control of his pitches through years of practice, once in a while his rein over his amazing arm would abandon him. Bill might miss the strike zone with dozens of pitches, consecutively. One such incident occurred with Bob Wolfe, the superlative official referenced previously, behind the plate at Riverside Park in the summer league.

The game began in a very light rain, not enough to disturb play on the field. Bill opened the game by walking the first three batters on the minimum twelve pitches, all outside the strike zone. Bill grumbled mildly on a couple of Wolfe's calls of pitches that were marginally close. But we all knew we were witnessing one of those spells when Bill was struggling with his control. As the rain picked up a bit over the next couple of innings and Bill continued to have problems throwing strikes, he began to complain to Wolfe about the condition of the baseballs. The balls had become soiled and a little sodden because of the rainy conditions. Miffed, Bright began returning balls to Wolfe, insisting on a cleaner baseball. Having witnessed such snits by Bill before, Wolfe knew Bright wanted to blame his lack of pitching location on the semi-damp baseballs rather than his unwieldy pitching arm.

Now Bill knew as well as Wolfe that the Indianapolis Parks Department, which sponsored the amateur league, provided only three new baseballs for each game. So when Bill would angrily return a ball that he felt was not suitable for play, Wolfe would patiently towel much of the mud and wetness from the ball and toss it back to Bright. Finally, after Bill had walked in a couple of runs, he and the umpire began an uproarious routine (to those of us observing the farce) of "pitch and catch." Bright would indignantly toss a ball he felt was unqualified to throw. Wolfe would dutifully wipe it off, toss it back, only to have Bright flip it right back to him. Finally, Wolfe sarcastically asked Bill, "What do you want me to do? I only got these three baseballs. And there's no Jamaican sweat shop near here to make any new ones."

Bill remained adamant that in order to pitch he had to have dry baseballs. Espying our team's canvas bag of well-worn balls—the ones we used for pre-game batting and fielding practice—the recalcitrant Bright marched over to our bench, picked up the bag, and returned to the mound.

"We'll use these," he announced. The opposing coach offered no opposition. He was enjoying this comedy far too much.

Play continued. And Bright still couldn't get the ball over. He'd throw a ball through the light mist.

"Ball one!" Wolfe would bark.

Bill would disgustedly throw *that* offending ball over to our dugout, reach into the bag and grab a dry one. Wind up, rock, and fire:

"Ball two!"

And so on, until the natural outcome occurred: Bill reached into the bag, and it was empty. He'd used up the approximately three-dozen practice balls in our bag.

Wolfe wisely scanned the skies at this point, declared the field unplayable, and the game ended.

Preseason baseball practice indoors, 1965. From left, first baseman Brunnemer, Coach Bill Bright, pitcher Jerry Mullinix, shortstop Phil Paswater, and Jack Leonard, my lifelong best friend until his tragic death at age thirty-four.

Bill's mercurial temper was legendary. Those who have observed Bill in high dudgeon will attest to the intensity of those blazing dark brown eyes, of the veins bulging out of his neck, and the taut lines and florid hue of his face. At times such as these, Bill's tongue sliced with precision, his high-pitched, staccato voice rising several octaves above his normal tone.

Coaches use anger, feigned or bona fide, to motivate athletes. While their wrath is

James L. Brunnemer

sometimes genuine, coaches many times "perform fury" for effect. Fueled by his enormous competitive passion, Bill Bright became more authentically vexed than any coach I've ever observed. You didn't embarrass him, as an opponent or as a player on his team.

One of the most dramatic examples of Bill Bright's competitive fire I was to observe occurred during the summer of 1964. Despite Nick's constant belief that any athletic contest should be approached as if lives of our family were in peril if we lost, we were a bit more relaxed in our approach to the games in the summer. Most of us had jobs—Tut, Roger, and I worked at the International Harvester plant, in the foundry—so our baseball skills and conditioning were not as crisp as during the regular collegiate season. It was great fun, this team and this league, despite Nick's constant carping and "I told you so!" if we lost because he was convinced we weren't dedicated enough to our tasks.

In addition to having most of the starting players from our college squad, and Bright, we also had a former Greyhound pitcher/outfielder and coach at Jeffersonville High School. Don Poole, who was later selected to the Indiana High School Baseball and University of Indianapolis halls of fame, was second only to Bright as an athlete. So we had a pretty good team.

It was a Saturday when we made our first road trip to Columbian Park in Lafayette for a game. A goodly crowd came out to watch because first, it was a fairly entertaining level of amateur play, and more importantly, the Lafayette team featured one of that city's all-time great athletes and the current Indiana "Mr. Basketball," Denny Brady.

Brady, who led Lafayette to the 1964 Indiana State High School Basketball championship in March, was a fine left-handed pitcher with great belief in himself (read "cocky"). He was to go on to stardom as a guard for the Purdue Boilermakers, but what he brought to this summer game was a sharp-breaking left-handed curveball and some serious zip on his fastball.

Bill Bright always rose to a challenge, so he was pumped up as we prepared to take on the Lafayette team and their hometown hero

What a game it turned out to be!

Both Bright and Brady were exceedingly sharp through seven innings. Denny had one of those nasty curves we used to call a "drop ball." As it approached the plate the ball just seemed to break downward, or "fall off the table." We found ourselves flailing awkwardly at more than one pitch that seemed to start at the waist but would bounce into the dirt as you tried to uppercut with your swing. His hot fastball made the curve even more effective.

Bill, as usual, was "rockin' 'n' firin'." No wasted motion from him. He would no sooner catch the return throw from catcher Dan Nicoson than he'd begin his rhythmic wind-up. Kicking his right leg nearly above his head, his body would rotate and as he thrust off the pitching rubber with his left leg, he'd drive toward the plate, whipping that left arm around. At the end of his fingertips was a missile that, when released, became a heinous challenge to a batter. Bill had absolutely the most picture-perfect pitching form of anyone I ever played behind.

Neither team had scored as we entered the top of the eighth inning. Both Bright and Brady were in double digits in opponents fanned. Brady revealed a crack in his composure when Steve McGee led off the inning with an infield single. The next hitter laid down a sacrifice bunt, moving McGee to second. Donnie Poole answered our need, driving

Distinction Without Pretension

a double into the gap in right to push McGee home, giving Schuster the lead, 1-0. Brady settled down and allowed no more runs.

Bottom of the eighth. Bill fanned the first hitter, but walked the second man in the lineup. With a two-strike count on the next hitter, Bill threw a wicked curve and in trying to check his futile swing the batter accidentally made contact. The ball squiggled toward third base. Charging the slowly rolling sphere, Jack Leonard came up with the ball but made a hurried throw from an awkward position. Jack's powerful arm made even more emphatic the off-target throw. The ball sailed over my head into the first base bleachers.

Then came the controversy. An overthrow out of play meant the runner on first base would advance, by rules of baseball, to the base to which he was running (second), plus another (to third). The batter, meanwhile, was awarded first, plus one (to second base). At least that was the rule for any baseball game except the one played that evening in Columbian Park.

The home plate umpire stopped play as the ball rattled around the concrete stands behind first. He was okay so far. But then he proceeded to order the runner from first all the way home, and the batter to third base!

Bill's protest started off simple enough. Knowing it was just an oversight on the part of the ump, Bill quoted the proper interpretation of the play from his nearly photographic memory of the rulebook, fully expecting the ump to put the runners back one base each, to third and second.

Didn't happen.

The ump, perhaps feeling patronized by the authoritative recitation of the rules by the pitcher, offered his own interpretation of the play. One runner scored and the second would stay where he was.

Bazookas went off. Artillery fire from the mound. Stukas dived, shrieking. Bill, then Nick, both got in the face of the errant umpire, screaming their protests, but to no avail. Despite being obviously incorrect, the ump got stubborn about it and refused to change the call. His partner remained mute.

"His call," was all the base ump would offer.

The disagreement went on a full ten minutes before we accepted reluctantly the inevitable and returned to our respective positions.

It was 1-1.

Bill stalked to the mound and the expression on his face was fierce. The flame on his subsequent pitches matched the heat in his veins. I almost felt sorry for the poor young man in the batter's box as Bright threw three hellacious heaters right by him. Two outs. Lead run on third. Bright's the Man.

But the Lafayette coach was clever. With two outs, the "suicide squeeze" is just that. The runner breaks from third for home at the first movement of the pitcher in his delivery. The batter *must* get the bat on the ball and the ball bunted into fair territory. Otherwise, the runner is a dead duck. If, with two down, the bunt is not placed well, any player among the pitcher, catcher or third or first baseman can easily field the ball and toss it to first to end the inning on a force out.

But this surprise bunt was placed perfectly. The batter dropped it dead, with a little backspin in front and slightly left of the plate. Dan Nicoson stayed at the plate to give himself some chance of tagging the runner if someone could reach the ball. At third, Jack

James L. Brunnemer

was playing deep, so he couldn't get there in time. I went to the first base bag to await a possible inning-ending throw there.

It was inconceivable for Bill to stop the impetus of his body after delivering a pitch. The follow-through of the lefthander compelled Bill to rotate his weight toward third base. It simply wasn't humanly possible to halt that involuntary shift, at least for *most* athletes, anyway. Bill Bright somehow put the brakes on his pitching momentum and with the quickness of a panther pounced toward the baseball trickling along the ground fifty feet from him.

With the runner bearing down on the plate there was no time for Bill to field the ball and toss it to Danny. With a sweeping movement of his right hand Bill *scooped* the ball in the webbing of his glove and flipped it to a startled Nicoson as the runner began his slide.

No one this side of the major leagues could have even gotten to the ball in time in that circumstance, let alone make a close play of it. Instinctively Danny caught the thigh-high toss and dropped his glove straight downward, blocking the plate. Dust obscured the play as the runner toppled our catcher with a hard slide across the plate. It's close, but I think we got him.

"SAAAAAAAFE!" hollered the ump emphatically.

This just threw gasoline on the smoldering fire that was Bright. Again he went chin to chin with the optically challenged grunt behind the plate. But Bill was not going to win any battle with this guy. The score remained 2-1, Columbians.

The top of the ninth was tense. Brady retired the first two of our hitters quickly on a ground out and a pop up. Up came Bright, especially dangerous in this situation. After a called strike, two balls, and a foul ball, Bill took a monstrous cut at a Brady chest-high fastball. I swear the pennants around the park rippled at the gust created by Bill's swing. Strike three.

The home team and its fans jumped for joy, cheering loudly. One player celebrated, in fact, just a bit *too* exuberantly. Brady pumped his arm two or three times while looking defiantly at Bright. Bill's stoic expression didn't change. He walked away like the pro he was.

But a mental note had been taken. In the game of baseball, if one displays more than an acceptable amount of jubilation at defeating a foe "between the lines," it hints of "showing one up." Ballplayers tend to file those incidents away for future reference (read "what goes around, comes around").

End of story? Nope. Just a prelude to the *real* one.

Exactly one week later, by a quirk in the schedule, we found ourselves in Indianapolis, meeting at the gymnasium in preparation for the drive back to Lafayette to play the Columbians again.

Here we were, not having seen one another since the previous Saturday. Coupled with our jobs and the number of games scheduled, we didn't have practices. Just played the games.

So when we gathered for the one-hour journey, the usual banter began. We were in a light mood as we prepared to embark on the trip. The events of last week were forgotten—except by one of our entourage.

We loaded our equipment into three cars and squeezed ourselves in. Bill entered

Distinction Without Pretension

our car, sitting in the right front seat as usual. Someone told a harmless joke, at which we chuckled—except for one of us. Bill Bright was staring ahead, oblivious to the commotion around him. Someone asked him a question about some inanity or another. He grunted a quick retort, making it obvious he was in no mood for levity.

The atmosphere in our car chilled. All chatter ended. Something ominous was exuding from that right front seat.

Bill's demeanor portended a gathering thunderstorm. We were all affected by his bearing. For the next hour there was total silence in our vehicle. We weren't sure what caused his pother, but no one dared invade the eerie mood that possessed him.

It was customary on trips like these for us to stop along the highway to get a sandwich and a Coke. Bill preferred the Burger Chef Restaurant, the second word of which Bill always called Chef, with a hard CH (like "CHop), rather than "sheff." It always sounded funny to hear it pronounced that way. But since Bill failed to suggest that we stop, we didn't. We were all afraid to recommend it. So on we went.

Arriving at the park, we emulated our very businesslike teammate. We stepped lively to get the equipment out of the car trunk and began to loosen up with purpose. Bright's moods affected others around him in that way.

After pre-game batting and infield practice, Bill went to the bullpen mound to get himself readied to face the Lafayette team that had beaten us seven days earlier in that controversial game.

Bright was even more focused than usual. His deportment was that of a man on a mission. Nick went over and said a few quiet words to him. Bill never looked away from his catcher, just nodded almost imperceptibly.

Coach Nicoson walked away, and as he passed by me I swear I saw the slightest hint of a knowing smile on his face. The twinkle in Nick's eye meant that he knew something the rest of us didn't. Nick had seen Bill Bright like this before. He knew what was coming.

I've observed over the years that superior athletes seem to have an ability to raise their play to another level in given situations. While the great ones are generally just better than those around them, special challenges periodically call on stars to raise the stakes. For example, I was in the stands in June of 1969 at Louisville's Freedom Hall the night George McGinnis, angered at what he perceived as disrespect from the Kentucky High School All-Star team, dismantled them with 53 points and 31 rebounds. This warm night in Lafayette I was to witness another example of what can happen when the competitive juices of a surpassing athlete are aroused. It was amazing to behold.

Pitching for the Columbians, as expected, was Mr. Brady. He appeared a bit smug as he took the mound to open the game. After retiring the first batter, Brady walked McGee. Up came Bright, hitting as usual in the third slot.

On Brady's first delivery, Bright hopped on the fastball with those cobra-quick wrists of his, sending a laser-beam into the alley in right field. Bill ended up on second base with the runner scoring. Brady blinked at the ferocity behind that swing. We were retired with only that run, and the Columbians came to bat.

The first hitter watched two Bright fastballs split the plate for strikes. On the third, the leadoff hitter waved futilely at the ball, and as he left the batter's box dragging his bat behind him, he peered for just a moment toward the man on the mound. He seemed to sense

James L. Brunnemer

that something out of the ordinary was going on out there.

The second batter had a similar fate. These were the days before radar-guns tracked the speed of the baseball crossing the plate. Bill had to be throwing more than 90 miles per hour. His hurling would be nearly impregnable in this game. Coach Bright once told me his approach to pitching was to simply throw fastballs for the first six or seven innings of a game, until fatigue reduced the speed of his heater. Only then would he bring out that devastating curveball. But tonight he violated that strategy, at least for the third batter in the Lafayette lineup.

With two outs, up strode Mr. Brady, looking arrogantly at the man on the mound as he dug in at the left side of the plate. This kid hadn't earned his extraordinary success in athletics by being easily intimidated. His competitive drive appeared to be as keen as the man he was facing. It was *mano a mano*. Well, not really.

Bright wound up and threw a fastball ... directly beneath Denny Brady's chin. Instinctively falling away from the terrifying missile, Brady's helmet flew off, his bat went thataway, and the young competitor sprawled ignominiously in the dust and chalk of the batters box.

That was the first message Bill delivered to the young man who had been so self-satisfied in victory the week before.

The second pitch, same as the first. Brady glared out toward Bright as he picked himself up and dusted his uniform off for a second time. Beneath the agitation of his demeanor, however, a seed had been planted in the batter's sub-conscious. There is a certain amount of real danger in the game of baseball, and Brady wasn't certain this man with a lethal weapon in his hand was playing a game any longer. There was something sinister in the look and manner of the lefthander, now standing erect, anxiously awaiting Brady's return to the batter's box.

Brady dug in again, but human nature now involuntarily controlled his inner being. Self-preservation can overcome the spirit of even the most valorous of warriors. So when Bright violated his customary pitching plan and threw a pernicious curve ball, Brady did the natural thing. As the ball appeared to be coming at his head once again, Brady bailed out for a third time. The difference this time was that the Bright pitch arced about three feet—right to left in Brady's field of vision—across the plate. Brady's knees buckled.

"Strike one!"

Bill threw a second unholy hook on the next pitch. Although Brady summoned up the moxie to stay in the batters box, he couldn't move the wood from his shoulder. Strike two.

Brady, now expecting the curve, flailed futilely at a Bright fastball that darted knee high. By the time the young man began his embarrassing swing, the ball was already safely in the catcher's mitt. This was *mano a nino*.

Bright had struck out the side.

This is how the game went from that point. Brady, obviously shaken, began to have control problems. When he did get the ball over we feasted on his fat pitches.

When Bill Bright came up for his second time at bat, two runners were on and the score was 3-0. Brady bore down, and tried to return the favor by throwing a pitch in tight on Bright. Bill just leaned away, and reestablished his stance for the next pitch. It was the Brady special, one of his best curves of the night, seemingly dropping like a meteor as it approached the plate. Bright put all his agitated energy into an explosive uppercut and SOK! The ball headed high and far toward right field. It hit the earth well beyond the 368-foot sign in right field. This was the exclamation point to his other telegrams to Mr. Brady.

The rest was anti-climactic. Donny Poole hit a two-run homer in the eighth inning to make the final score 10-0. For the night Mr. Bright had three hits in four at bats, including a double and a home run, five runs-batted-in, three runs scored.

His pitching line: 0 runs, 2 hits, 0 walks, 15 strikeouts. A man among boys.

Immediately after the game ended, the metamorphosis in Bill's disposition was remarkable. The high-pitched giggle returned, he teased Donnie Poole for being thrown out trying to steal a base, then said "Anybody for a Burger CHef?"

Nick just grinned, and shook his head.

CHAPTER XII
WHO'S ON FIRST?

> *Take a look around, 'Ski.' Where the (bleep) you gonna' put 'im?*
> Herman Franks, Cubs manager, to pitcher Moe Drabowsky, who walked the first three batters of the game on 12 consecutive pitches outside the strike zone and had a 3-0 count on the fourth hitter.

Part of the fun of playing baseball at Indiana Central was getting to know the umpires who officiated our games. Fellows like Eddie Hoyt, Buck "Peaches" Emory, Dave Shiflet, and Bob Wolfe worked for a local umpire's association that assigned them regularly to our games. For the most part these men succeeded at being impartial. We became acquainted with and liked them all and really didn't expect to receive any favorable calls. But the familiarity bred by the regularity with which they worked our games sometimes had embarrassing side effects.

Like the time we were playing Miami (Ohio) University on the old ICC diamond, which was enclosed by State Street and National Avenue. Roger Walter had singled and while on first base received a rare steal sign from Coach Bright. Eager to succeed on this opportunity, Rog was off as the hurler fired his pitch to the plate. What Roger and Coach Bright had not anticipated was the bazooka the Miami catcher had for an arm. When he caught the pitch he rose up from a squat to throw a streak to the shortstop covering the bag.

Roger had no chance. *Nada*.

As he dashed toward second and prepared to go into his headfirst slide, the ball had already arrived. The shortstop had time to call home for money by the time Roger got there. But, doing his duty, Roger dove into second anyway, raising a lot of dust. The Miami player swiped his glove cleanly across Walter's hand about a foot on the first-base side of second. It was not close. Roger's momentum carried him across the bag and he reflexively bounced up with one foot on second, expecting to hear the obvious call.

Instead, Peaches yelled "**SAAAAAA-FE!**"

Before the shortstop could even begin to protest this miscarriage of baseball justice, and to Roger's bemusement, "Peaches" began dusting Roger's shirt off with both hands, saying, "Y'all right, Rog?"

The bewildered opponent could only stammer, "Who ... who the hell is this? Your uncle?"

One afternoon Peaches and Eddie were apparently not available, and we noted the familiar stride of the gentle Dave Shiflet entering the ballpark. With him was another ump whom none of us had ever seen before. It was the home opener for the Hounds. The opponent was the Indiana State branch campus at Evansville, which was later to become

James L. Brunnemer

the University of Southern Indiana.

About the fifth inning, ICC had base runners on first and second with two outs, no score. A sharp single to right field sent both runners flying and as the Greyhound player rounded third base Bright was giving the all-out green sign, pointing toward home with his straight right arm while wheeling his left arm swiftly in a counter-clockwise circle. It looked to be Greyhounds 1, ISUE 0.

The right fielder made a strong, accurate throw, if a bit late, and a mist of dust raised as the runner slid over the plate. Nabbing the one-hop toss, the catcher made a futile swipe at the sliding runner with his glove, clearly missing him.

"**Yer out!**" bellowed the official, reaching skyward with his right arm, thumb extended, fingers clasped in a fist.

Bill looked as if he'd been shot from a cannon as he covered the distance between the third base coach's box and home plate in about four strides. Immediately he was in the face of the umpire who had not yet removed his protective mask. Through his metal bars the quiescent ump saw a Bill Bright fusillade of grand proportions. It wasn't the best I'd ever seen. But it was better than par, if not an eagle.

Bill pointed precisely at the track in the dirt left by the player who had slid there just seconds before. He vividly reenacted the missed tag of the catcher. He enumerated the qualifications of umpires in this league, chief among those that they be able to see. He demonstrated for the edification of the umpire the correct position from which to make that particular call, adding that the umpire hadn't been in it. He questioned if the ump recognized he was not at home in front of the TV set, but on a real live baseball diamond with the responsibility for making accurate and serious calls. After Bill summarized his case, knowing the call would not be changed, but alerting the ump that he'd tolerate no more slacking behind the plate, he began to walk away. But typical of Bright when so irked, he lobbed one final verbal grenade over his shoulder in the ump's direction: "Now get back in there and *call the game right, Busher!*"

All this was delivered with nary a "cuss word," not one. In all the years I was around Bill as a student, player, assistant coach, and as an administrative colleague, I never once heard him say even a "damn" or "hell." But he could trim your sails with all the other words available in the English language.

The storm passed. The wind died down. In that ramrod straight posture he always maintained, Bill arrived at the coach's box, when with an almost offhanded gesture, a rather weak afterthought, the umpire lamely waggled his left hand and delivered in a half-whisper, this: "You're out of the game."

Only the catcher and the next batter entering the box even heard this declamation that meant Bill had been tossed.

Back at his command post, Bill looked toward home plate for action to resume. The ump, however, was not in his position to call pitches, but was, rather, standing to the side with his mask off, peering down at Bright.

Confused, Bill glanced back impatiently, wondering what the problem was. When Bright saw the ump's lips move again with a voice hardly discernible at a distance of ninety feet, he called out to his hitter. "What's the hold-up?"

The ICC player with the wood in his hand meekly replied, "The ump kicked you out, coach."

Distinction Without Pretension

"**WHAT!**" Bright roared, and like a streak was on his way toward home plate and the idiot in blue once again. He reached the umpire in about half the time as the first trip.

When Bill got really exercised, his words—venom, actually—spewed forth unintelligibly. Too fast. Sounds in word form couldn't keep up with the indignation bursting from his brain.

Ranting, raging, Bright could not believe this nimrod would have the audacity to expel him from the game for the ump's own incompetence. Bill might have, some times in the past, deserved to be booted from a game, but this wasn't one of them.

After charring the man's ears with unbroken invective for a minute or so, Bright decided this official wasn't worthy of further dialogue. He did a perfect military left face, striding rapidly toward first base umpire Dave Shiflet, a veteran official who had umpired many contests in which Bill Bright coached or played. He'd seen all this before. With arms folded, Dave calmly listened to two more minutes of Bright's diatribe about the ineptitude of Dave's fellow official.

As Bill moved toward the culmination of his protest, he ordered Dave to "**Straighten that 'busher' out.** Tell him he isn't kicking **me** out of this baseball game. **This** isn't Little League. **This** is **college** baseball. You **tell him** to just go back there and call the game."

Bill then started that same familiar stride across the diamond from first to third on his way back to the coach's box. As he trod over the pitcher's mound on his defiant journey, he turned his head just slightly and in a clear voice that removed all doubt regarding his commitment to coach this game, delivered the key words of the entire dispute. With laser-like efficacy directly into the eyes of the now-befuddled home plate ump, Bill shot this rejoinder: "*You won't be paid.* **YOU WON'T BE PAID!**"

Dave Shiflet walked slowly from his position behind the first base bag and motioned subtly for the young umpire to meet him at a spot between home and first. A lengthy conference ensued in which Shiflet seemed to be doing most of the talking. A calm voice in this tempest of emotions, Dave imparted reassuring words and gestures to his umpiring partner.

All this time the Evansville bench was observing this surreal scene with unrestrained mirth. Watching Bill Bright fume was either unnerving or a cause for humor, depending upon where you were and what connection you had to the issue. The visiting team was obviously relishing every minute of this.

With a final pat on the shoulder of the rattled umpire from Shiflet, each official returned to his proper position on the field.

As he stepped behind the catcher, the disconsolate home plate umpire placed his protective mask over his face and in a meek and trembling voice, proclaimed, "Play ball."

Erupting out of the visitor's dugout, in total shock at what he suddenly realized he was witnessing, was the ISUE coach.

"**What the hell is going on here?** You can't '**unkick**' a man *back* into the game! There's no '**Get-out-of-jail-free' cards** in baseball!" he ranted.

So now ensued another, equally acerbic interchange between a near-rabid coach of the Greyhounds' opposition and the totally discombobulated ump. The man in blue simply hung his head as the ISUE coach verbally eviscerated him.

The veteran Shiflet rushed to rescue the poor wretch again. He pulled the frothing

James L. Brunnemer

ISUE coach to the side, diplomatically persuaded him that the ICC runner *was* ruled out, the coach probably *didn't* deserve to be tossed out on such a trivial protest, and wouldn't we all be better off if we just returned to playing baseball?

Though he wouldn't fail to remind the home plate official time and again during the balance of the afternoon that he had made a travesty of the game by his failure to maintain his authority, the ISUE coach finally relented and the game continued.

The Greyhounds pushed across five runs in the next inning and won the game handily.

The rookie ump managed to make it through the rest of the day without further controversy.

He and Dave Shiflet *both* received their checks after the game ended.

And I never saw that guy umpire another baseball contest at ICC.

The Greyhounds had a junior varsity basketball squad in those days. Bill's responsibility as Nick's assistant included coaching that team of freshmen. Most students and other fans wouldn't get to the gym until shortly before the varsity was to play, so as a general rule, not many people saw the first-year lads in action. But I recall a memorable "curtain raiser" at Anderson College. As student sports information director I often kept the scorebook for the jayvee games on the road. The scorer's bench was on the sideline just to the right of the Greyhound bench. As usual when the Hounds were being beaten I felt it had to be that we were getting screwed by the refs.

With about two and a half minutes remaining in the game, the Hounds' jayvees had shot fewer than ten free throws, Anderson more than thirty. I couldn't help but notice this imbalance and as I continued to mark successive free tosses time after time on the Ravens' side of the scorebook ledger, I became increasingly agitated.

While the scoring table protocol called for official members to remain quiet and unbiased, this practice was rarely followed in the arenas and gymnasiums around the Hoosier College Conference in those days. Typically, locals keeping the official scorebooks, statistics, and game reports would make partisan comments and openly cheer for the home team. Even the public address announcer made no secret about who was his favorite.

About this time an errant shot bounced high and long toward the foul line and Bob Curless, a lanky 6'4" freshman for the Hounds, went straight up to retrieve the rebound. As Bob clutched the ball high above his head, two Anderson rhinies sandwiched him and knocked him to the floor, causing Bob to lose control of the ball. As the basketball bounded away, the shrill whistle of an official halted play. The referee, appearing far too serious for jayvee officiating, raced over and pointed demonstratively at the prone figure on the floor. He signaled a foul on *Curless* rather than either of the two AC bullies who had leveled him.

I know I don't have a soft voice, and when used in an emotional manner, it probably carries more loudly than I imagine. But I rather felt my analysis was not improper when I directed to the official this statement: **"That's the *worst* call I've ever seen!"**

Actually, I *had* seen worse calls. And I didn't even cuss him.

Nonetheless, he took offense at my critique. Suddenly, the offended official strode truculently toward me, brought his hands together perpendicularly in the classic signal, and shouted, "Technical foul on you!"

Distinction Without Pretension

My mouth dropped open.

Bright was already on his feet to protest the call on Curless when this second item was added to his agenda.

"You can't call a technical foul on *him*!" Bill exclaimed. "*He's* just a *scorekeeper*!"

I'm not sure I appreciated *that* demeaning description. After all, I was the only other person in the hall besides a few parents and the rest of the team rooting for his squad. But Bill wasn't paying much attention to whether my feelings would be bruised right then.

After the usual abrasive give-and-take between an irate coach and an offended official, the referee stepped back and sneered, "Okay, now it's one on him and one on you."

Demonstrating his authority, the stripe-shirted popinjay made a dramatic gesture signaling a technical on Bright. Now Bright was livid. He screeched at the arbiter, told him how ridiculous this entire fiasco was, and wondered aloud how he could have received his official's license.

Up came the by-now very practiced technical signal again.

"That's two technicals, coach. You're outta here!"

Bright stared in mute disbelief for several seconds. Then he simply announced to the referee that "If I go, so does my team."

Without comment, the official walked to the timekeeper and asked to borrow a stopwatch, which is kept for potential emergencies with the scoreboard clock. To Bright, he said mordantly, "You have one minute to vacate, coach."

Bright fired back, "You won't need that stopwatch."

He turned to the team, which was both bemused and bewildered at the scene, and said, tersely, "Let's go."

Off marched the Greyhound jayvees behind their fuming coach, leaving the game eleven points behind with about 150 seconds still to be played. That game hasn't ended yet.

I could have crawled under a turtle. It was my big mouth that started the whole escapade.

Strangely enough, this wasn't the end of the episode.

Pete Bullard '65 was a track and football athlete who went on to a stellar thirty-year teaching and coaching career in the Lawrence Township system. He and I earned a few bucks officiating junior varsity games on the ICC court. Thus, we were officiating games that involved a coach who also was our professor and fellow athletes with whom we interacted or were, in some cases, teammates in other sports. Despite the obvious loyalties Pete and I had for ICC, we generally held to the official's nonpartisan code, trying to "call 'em as we saw 'em." We walked that fine line of official objectivity for the eight dollars per game we were paid. That was good money for two hours' work in those days.

But when Anderson's jayvee team took the floor for a return match only three weeks after the game in which Bright removed his team from the floor, it was a bit bizarre.

For that particular game, Pete was not available. So John Patterson, a local high school official who occasionally filled in for Pete or me, was my partner for the rematch. We took the court in our black-and-white striped officials' shirts, ebony pants and referee's shoes, and whistles around our necks.

When the two teams came out for their pre-game warm-ups, John and I were standing at mid-court near the scorer's bench. As is traditional, the visiting coach came over to us to offer his handshake and greetings. He introduced himself to John, wished him a good game, and then turned to clasp my hand. As the coach looked at my face for the first time, he did a double take. I smiled slightly, saying with my expression that, "Yes, I am who you think I am."

The young Raven's assistant coach offered no comment, no protest that the opponent's student sports information guy, the one whose comment caused the game of twenty-one days ago to be prematurely terminated, was to officiate tonight's rematch. He just looked stunned, like he'd encountered a strong gust of flatulence and didn't feel it polite to comment.

He walked away.

The game was interesting and intense. Both teams were shooting exceptionally well, so there were not a lot of violations or fouls to call. The game moved quickly, the teams rushing up and down the court in a fast tempo. The Greyhounds moved out to a big lead—for which I was most grateful—so there was little significance to our calls.

Then the inevitable happened. Anderson's frosh mounted a comeback. The Greyhounds' lead dwindled from a high of twenty-two early in the second half to a mere point with less than a minute to play.

By now the crowd, coming early for the varsity game, was sizable and the Greyhound fans were especially vocal in rooting for their rhinies to stave off the gallant Raven comeback.

Anderson called timeout after rebounding a missed Greyhound shot. They would have a chance to go ahead. With but nine seconds left in the game, the Ravens were plotting their final play. John and I checked signals during the time-out to be certain we had our assignments covered. Suddenly, the eight bucks I was getting for this contest didn't seem near enough.

The ICC team defended the Raven players like white on rice as Anderson tossed the ball in to begin the finale of the drama. A pass, a dribble, another pass as the clock moved inexorably toward double zeros. Now a lob pass into the pivot where the Anderson player snared the ball, turned, and let fly a jump shot. Almost simultaneous to his release of the ball I heard the horn sounding the end of the game. The ball, airborne, floated up, arced downward, and SWISH! Nothing but net.

Pandemonium broke loose, the home crowd screaming "**NO BASKET!**" while the Anderson players jumped for joy in expectation that this split second was favoring them.

From my position directly beneath the basket, I peered confidently out to John Patterson, relieved that the call on a game-ender such as that was the responsibility of the *outside* official. Did the player release the ball *before* the horn sounded, John?

Patterson's eyes met mine, but not with the firm confidence I had expected. His eyes were wide, and almost imperceptibly he shrugged his shoulders while shaking quickly his head from side-to-side. He was looking to *me* for the call on the last-second shot.

It's a good thing I acted reflexively, because had I taken time to ponder what had occurred to this ICC jayvee squad at Anderson, my wayward ethics might have caused me

Distinction Without Pretension

to commit basketball perjury. But the call was a no-brainer. I knew that the Anderson player had clearly released the ball before the sound of the horn.

My left arm went up and came down definitively. Basket good! Anderson wins by one point. Fans booed, but I knew the call was the correct one. A few of the Greyhound frosh protested, but only mildly. They knew the truth as well.

The Anderson team and coach rushed jubilantly off the court. For a fleeting second the Raven jayvee coach caught my eye.

"Good call," he offered.

"Screw you," I muttered under my breath.

Bill's coaching decisions weren't always popular with his players. One of those decisions was the source of much humor and an ultimate comeuppance for me.

Each year we played Marian College, a team we were expected to handle easily. The previously all-women's Catholic college had begun admitting men only a few years earlier, so their athletic program was in its infancy. But in 1965 their baseball team was a scrappy bunch. We undoubtedly regarded them too lightly and found ourselves locked in a struggle to win and salvage our pride at our home diamond.

The Knights rallied in the ninth inning to force extra innings and then scored two runs to put us in a real hole as we came to bat in the bottom of the 10th inning. Bill was incensed with us for our overconfident attitude and lackadaisical play.

Fortunately, we countered Marian's rally with one of our own, tying the game at 12-12. With one out we had the bases loaded. I happened to be on third base representing the winning run when Roger Walter came to the plate. Belying his slight build at 5'10" and 160 pounds, Roger had quick hands that enabled him to drive the ball great distances. It was precisely this kind of situation Roger lived for: the winning run on base, himself at bat.

Now Roger had been struggling at the plate for a few games. He had made outs in his last 10 times at bat. Nonetheless, his confidence was buoyant and this scenario demanded his focus. He was eager, with that shark-eyed look he got when he was most intense.

Stepping into the batter's box, Roger dug his spikes into the dirt and took a couple of warm-up swings. Peering coldly at the pitcher, who was toeing the rubber nervously, Walter became a taut, coiled spring ready to lash at the first pitch over the plate. As the pitcher began his wind-up to deliver his first offering, suddenly:

"TIME!"

It was Bright. He was moving rapidly from the coaches' box along the third baseline toward home plate. Everything stopped. The pitcher interrupted his delivery. The ump raised his hand to halt further action.

With a swift gesture, Bill signaled to the dugout for ... a *pinch hitter?*

"Fox. Batting for Walter," Bill informed the umpire.

Roger was stunned. Never, ever, had someone batted for him in a crucial situation. During the extra inning game our roster had been depleted of substitutes who had come into the game as pinch-hitters, pinch runners, and replacements in the field for defensive purposes. Only two players were eligible to enter the game at this juncture. Especially insulting was the fact that the batter Bright selected to replace Roger was not even a position player. Denny Fox was a pitcher—and an *awful* batter!

James L. Brunnemer

It was amazing that Bill chose to supplant Roger, who was one of our best hitters, with Fox. Nevertheless, Bill's tactic was obvious if one knew him. He had a left-handed hitter who was struggling at the plate batting against a left-handed pitcher. Baseball percentages call for a right-handed batter to face a lefty pitcher, despite the fact that the Marian portsider couldn't break a breakfast plate from fifteen feet away.

Walter was to reveal the real indignity later: "He waited until I got into the damned batter's box," Roger snarled. It was a rule of the grand old game that you never intentionally embarrassed a player between the lines. Baseball protocol called for Bill to have made his decision while Roger was in the on-deck circle, not after he'd assumed his stance at the plate.

After Walter disappeared into the dugout, Fox, unaccustomed to being in a game for offensive purposes, swung a couple of bats to warm up, then stepped in to face the pitcher.

The Knights' lefty fired his best seventy-five-mile-an-hour fastball and Denny took a mighty, robust cut. The result was a "swinging bunt," which occurs when a batter gets just enough of the ball to squirt it along the ground. The squiggler got beyond the pitcher but the first baseman couldn't get to the ball in time to throw me out before I slid across the plate.

We had avoided the ignominy of defeat with a 13-12 victory over an obviously inferior opponent. Bill was so disgusted with our listless effort, however, that he kept us after the game to run bases repeatedly as punishment before letting us retire to the shower room.

But a win is a win. That night in the dorm several of us congregated to celebrate on the second floor of Wilmore Hall, where most of our rooms were located. Roger was sitting on the lower bunk in his chamber, refusing to join in the levity with his teammates outside in the hallway. Finally, one of the guys asked Roger what was wrong. Almost inaudibly he growled something about "never once having been pinch-hit for in his whole baseball life."

"Damn Bright let me get clear into the box before putting Fox in," Roger blathered, "against that porker who couldn't throw hard enough to bruise a baby's ass."

Now understand this: No one respected Coach Bright more than Roger Walter. But in this instance, no matter what we said or did, Roger wouldn't come out of his snit. I mean, ever!

Year after year, whenever members of that 1965 team would get together, talk would eventually get around to the Marian game when we played so badly that Bright made us run bases for hours. (After about twenty years, the story had stretched until the post-game punishment had Bright making us run to Bloomington and back.)

After a few years, Roger's continued ranting about that incident really became a highlight of our gatherings. Inevitably, someone (usually me, of course) would casually say, "Roger, remember the Marian game in '65 ... " and Roger would raise hell. He never saw humor in it. Three decades after the incident he was still pissed at Bright for waiting until he got into the batter's box before "bringing in a (bleeping) non-hitter, Denny Fox, against a (bleepity-bleep) porky pig of a left-handed weenie arm for (bleeping) Marian College with the (bleepity-bleeping) winning run on (bleepity-bleep-bleeping) third base!"

But the day would come when Roger's grievance would be redressed.

After college, the dream of my very early life to be a professional baseball player had gone south. Nonetheless, I continued to play in the local industrial league in the city. I had stayed in reasonably good condition. The confederation was a competitive one, comparable to the old independent town teams of earlier days, which consisted of a couple of ex-major leaguers, some minor leaguers who never quite got to the "bigs," and a number of ex-college players like myself.

After five or six years, one's foot speed deteriorates and reflexes become less sharp. So I bowed out of baseball and accepted an invitation to play on a competitive fast-pitch softball team. The team won a few local championships, earning its way to regional and national tournaments.

After another three or four years of playing fast-pitch, the skills eroded enough that I quit *that* level of play and joined a serious slow-pitch league. Again, this slip down the ladder was gradual but certain.

Finally, in 1983 I found myself playing my first base position on a coed church-league slow-pitch softball team in Saline, Michigan.

I had bottomed out in my playing career. This was as low as it gets. One of my sons, Beau, 15, played outfield while Kyle (age 13 at the time) played second base for this recreational-league team. Guys still competed, even at that level. Because I had been a former college player, my teammates had some expectations of my abilities. We had a so-so season, losing as many as we won, and I didn't do anything spectacular, despite the reputation.

Our player-coach, Bob, a young guy half my age, was gung ho about the team (he'd never played anything higher than this church league). His temperament was always at a Knute Rockne-fevered pitch despite the meaningless outcome of these games.

Mercifully, we were playing the final contest of the season. To my coach's dismay, I had dribbled weak ground balls to second base each of my most recent fourteen times at bat. I was *awful*. But my purported stature as an ex-collegiate player was always a consideration, so Bob had, in his mind, an obligation to play me.

It was the final inning and we were losing something like 24-11 when I came up with two outs, no one on base.

I took my place in the batter's box, when suddenly Bob called time-out from the third base coaching box, and started walking toward me. He seemed a bit uneasy, saying, haltingly, "Uh, Jim ... let's ... would you mind ... uh, Sally (a twelve-year-old lass with one arm in a cast) hasn't gotten to bat. Do you mind ... if she, uh ... *pinch hits* for you?"

The coach was doing everything he could not to offend me. He must have wondered what he'd said when, convulsing in laughter at an irony only I could appreciate, I gasped, "Sure, Bob, get Sally in here."

I carried my aluminum bludgeon back to the bench, realizing that my previous appearance at the plate would be the final time I would ever bat in competition.

Driving straight home following the game, I dialed the phone to contact Roger at his Indianapolis home. When I heard the familiar voice on the other end I enunciated slowly and distinctly, "Roger ... Brum. Listen carefully. Today, I was pinch hit for ... in a coed ... church league ... slo-pitch ... softball game ... by a 12-year old girl ... with a broken arm!"

The laughter, accompanied by his body and the phone hitting the floor simultaneously, let me know that Roger had finally been vindicated, after all these years.

Most people of my generation remember the spring day in 1968 when Martin Luther King, Jr., was assassinated. I shall never forget the day *after*.

I was teaching junior high school when Bright invited me to be a part-time volunteer assistant coach. A southern trip had been scheduled and, despite the turmoil in the country, the Greyhound baseball team loaded into four vehicles, seeking warmer temperatures and the chance to play during the week of spring vacation. How eerie it was traveling through Nashville, Tennessee, on an interstate bereft of traffic. Martial law had been declared in most major southern cities after Dr. King's murder, but we were on the road, nonetheless. From our cars we could look up into the tenements that lined the highway to see sober black faces peering back at us.

We arrived that day at Berry College, near Rome, Georgia. After a practice, the team went into the small village for a meal. Our four vehicles brandishing Indiana license plates loaded with twenty-five white guys and one black man pulled into parking spots outside the restaurant. Instantly, three Rome police squad cars descended upon us, emergency lights blazing. Dean of students Nathan Wooden was traveling with us. After a short conversation during which Dean Wooden explained to the police that we were a baseball team and not freedom marchers, they let us proceed.

Georgia Tech, a Southeastern Conference baseball power, was a daunting opponent. Our team had a raw-boned, 6'3" left-handed freshman, Bill Smock, who had not seen action thus far and was eager to pitch. When Coach Bright made the unusual decision to start Smock, the rookie, with his pronounced speech impediment, uttered "Now you're g-g-g-gonna s-s-s-s-see some p-p-p-p-p-pitchin'!" And we d-d-d-d-d-d-d-did!

In the first inning John Wirtz, Roger Walter, and Bill Tutterow rattled consecutive hits off the Engineers pitcher, giving the Greyhounds a surprising early lead. Smock, meanwhile, kept the powerful Tech lineup off-balance, varying off-speed junk and a sneaky fastball.

Into the bottom of the ninth we held a 4-1 lead. Tech, embarrassed at trailing the hayseeds from a tiny school in Indianapolis that none of them had ever heard of, struck back in their final at-bats. The first two batters lashed vicious base hits that would have gone far out of the park, had they been elevated rather than line drives. Two runners on. The next hitter launched another bullet, this time in the gap to left—both runners scored—leaving a man on second and no one out.

With the Hounds in increasing jeopardy, Bright visited the mound to reassure Smock. After the brief confab, the coach decided to "dance with what brung him," leaving the freshman in to finish what he'd started, win or lose.

Smock struck out the next hitter and then walked the following batter. Tech's clean-up man then hit a scorcher that reached our left fielder so quickly the runner on second could only advance to third. With the bases loaded and only one out, there was no doubt the determined Tech team would score. But could we hold them to one run and get into extra innings?

The gangly freshman threw two pitches wide of the plate to Tech's shortstop, an NCAA All-American the previous season. The Georgia Tech hitter had to be salivating at what he knew the next pitch would be—a fastball in the strike zone. And Smock's fastball

Distinction Without Pretension

wasn't getting anyone out.

Surprise, batter! Smock threw that slow curve of his and the overly eager Tech batsman shifted his weight forward too early. Swinging lamely at the pitch, he lifted an innocuous foul ball down the right field line. The lazy floater was beyond the reach of the infielders and certainly out of the range of this day's right fielder, Dan Nicoson. Danny was, first, a catcher, whom Coach Bright occasionally played in right field. Swift of feet he wasn't.

As those of us in the dugout watched the ball in its descent toward a spot where it would fall harmlessly, we mentally moved to the next situation: count two balls, one strike on the batter. Can we possibly get a ground ball to turn a miracle double play? But suddenly our thinking was invaded by the realization that Nicoson was breaking on the ball. He was *actually* making an effort to catch it!

At first, all players in the dugout, watching as one, thought the same thing: "Danny can't possibly reach it."

The second thought collectively entering our minds was one of horror: "My God, Dan, *don't catch it!*"

If Nicoson somehow does snare that ball, the runner on third base, already tagged up and ready to fly toward home as soon as the catch is made, will coast in from third with the tying run! Otherwise, it's just a foul ball, a strike on the batter, and a chance to get the final two outs without them scoring.

Now the entire team verbalized—at the tops of our voices—that very thought: **"Let it drop, Dan, let it go!"**

But with his characteristic plodding gait, Nicoson and the ball, now almost colliding with the earth, intersected. Reaching downward without slowing, Danny somehow snagged the ball right off the tops of his spikes! Out *two*!

The Tech runner got just what he had wanted. The coach shrieked **"*Go!*"** and the speedy Techster sprinted toward home plate and a tie game.

As his momentum carried him crosswise to the infield, Danny looked to have zero chance of even making a throw to our catcher, Mike Terrell. Accepting that the tying run was inevitable, Terrell stood semi-relaxed at the plate. Those of us in the dugout could only groan.

But get this! Dan managed to contort his body and cock his arm despite his drifting away from the target, which was nearly two hundred feet away. Out of an impossibly awkward position he launched a rocket toward home plate.

A dumbfounded Terrell recovered to position himself to the third-base side of home plate. Danny's sizzling toss hurtled toward Terrell as the runner, now realizing his anticipated cakewalk home had turned into a legitimate contest, leaped into his slide about six feet from home. The burly ICC catcher braced himself for the inevitable collision with the base runner.

The runner slid and dust exploded as the ball smacked into Terrell's waiting mitt. Snagging the dead-perfect throw six inches above the ground and a foot to the third base side of the plate, Terrell applied a tag as the runner's lead leg slashed across the hard-rubber base.

Partly concealed in the dust cloud enveloping the three most important characters in the drama, the umpire hesitated slightly. Then, with full-bodied histrionics, threw his

James L. Brunnemer

right arm skyward and bellowed "You're **OUUUUUUUUUUTTTTT!**"

Out *three*! And that's all you get in baseball!

Hoarse yells lifted skyward as two dozen players and coaches spilled out of the Greyhound dugout and sprinted toward the mound to celebrate a huge win. One guy, the most competitive of all those wearing a Greyhound uniform, tried subtly to quell his teammates' joyous celebration: "Act like we do this all the time," hissed Bill Tutterow, not wanting to give Georgia Tech the slightest indication but that we expected to win all along. (You'll learn more about the consummate competitor we called "Tut" later.)

Bill Bright was among the most honest, loyal, and capable professionals the institution ever employed. After a more than forty-year association with Indiana Central as an honor student, an electee to both the University of Indianapolis and Indiana Baseball halls of fame, and a gifted instructor and coach, he retired at the end of the school term in 1996. In truth, he was "nudged" by the administration.

Institutional politics is a fact of life in any organization. Perhaps out of naiveté or simply an unbending adherence to his own sense of fairness, Bill always did what he thought was right rather than bow to political diplomacy. I remember, for example, his posting a warning sign in one of the men's locker rooms used by those who were members of the fitness center: "Personal locks are not permitted on the lockers in this room. Any locks remaining on lockers will be removed by Friday at 5 p.m."

At the hour indicated, athletic director Bright took a bolt cutter to several locks and removed all the articles of equipment from those lockers. It mattered not to Bill that a trustee of the university was riled about being one of those whose locker had been emptied.

Bill's uncompromising attitudes often put him in breach with some of his coaches. One had to admire his commitment to equal treatment of all, but it wasn't always the most prudent course to take.

With some justification, Bill could hold me at least partially responsible for his early departure. Although it was the university president's action to recommend that Bill accept an early retirement, I admit that, when asked my opinion as a vice president of the university, I didn't voice support of his continuing in his role.

This from one who counted Bill among the most positive influences on his life.

I've had a lot of time to think about my decision to render the judgment that I did. And I truly regret it. But there *is* an irony to the scenario. From Bill Bright, more than any other teacher I'd ever had, I learned to strive to be objective, regardless of emotional attachment. "Do what you think is right, despite your personal feelings," Bill had counseled us many times. In the end, that is the course I took. I put the importance of the job over the man.

I had forgotten a more important factor: loyalty. I was wrong to do that.

CHAPTER XIII
AN ASS LADEN WITH BOOKS

*The first step to knowledge is to
know we are ignorant.*
                  Lord David Cecil

"Hey, Brum!"
A familiar voice emanated from inside a mid-fifties vintage car as it slowed, pulling alongside me. The driver was ICC classmate Bob Williams, a congenial lad from Decatur Central High School.

"C'mon. Take a ride downtown with me."

Since I didn't have anything more urgent to do than to attend a class in three minutes, I thought, what the hey? I don't recall why Bob needed to go to the City, or where we were going. I just know we got downtown, but not where Bob intended.

Traveling north on Madison Avenue in Bob's old '56 Pontiac, we were exceeding abundantly the 45-mph speed limit posted on a stretch near Manual High School. Then, almost perfunctorily, Bob observed, "Got a red-light in my rearview mirror."

I looked back to see an Indianapolis sheriff's deputy astride a motorcycle closing on us, his red flashing light rotating garishly.

Bob slowed and then pulled over to the side of the road. As we sat there the cop stepped off his cycle, and, pulling a citation booklet out of his rear pocket, approached the driver's side where Bob had already rolled his window down.

The officer stopped next to the driver's door. With pencil and ticket book in hand he leaned down, peering inside at Bob and me.

Before the man in blue could say a word, Bob announced, nonchalantly, "I'll take a hamburger, French fries, and a Coke."

The burly cop, whose face already had the pained expression of a man wearing too-tight shoes, winced ever so slightly before retrieving his bored countenance. He obviously wasn't amused at this brash college-boy humor. Without a hint of emotion, he sniffed, and simply said, "Follow me, boys."

As the cop returned to his Harley Davidson, I gasped, "Ohmygod, Williams! We're going to jail!"

"Screw him if he can't take a joke," the unruffled Williams said with a grin.

I hammered Bob all the way to Alabama Street, site of the Indianapolis lock-up, where the uniformed motorcyclist led us. Once inside the police station the officer delivered a stern lecture, none of which I heard. I was consumed by thoughts of spending this night in the tank with derelicts, drunks, and horse thieves. However, after reaming us out, but good, the cop gave Bob a ticket and let us go.

Such was the seriousness with which I held my academic responsibilities at the beginning of my sophomore year at Indiana Central College. I hadn't caught on yet to Lord Cecil's wisdom. I wasn't aware that I was ignorant, a naïf sharing tuition payments with my parents. Looking back now, it is painful to know how cavalierly I regarded the opportunities for cultivating knowledge in those days. It wasn't that my gun was without bullets. But I

James L. Brunnemer

couldn't be bothered with learning the firing mechanism and pulling the academic trigger. That would come later. Further, it wasn't that my uncultivated intellectual habits drifted two standard deviations from the norm; I was probably very near the statistical mean of ICC students when it came to devoting energy and time to the elevation of the mind.

But there were serious scholars who seized the precious academic jewels offered them, who applied themselves in meaningful ways to learning. While I was contemplating how to solve my weakness for hitting a curve ball, or what prank might next be executed to harass Dick Elmore and Steve Lemme, folks like Dick Rodebaugh, Steve Maple, Marydee Meyer, Andy Moore, and Alice Sue Findley were on their way to becoming adept thinkers and genuine scholars.

At the beginning of the first semester of 1963, the ground of American society was shifting beneath our feet. Only a week before the adventure with that pleasant representative of the Indianapolis Sheriff's Department, August 28, Martin Luther King delivered a speech that has become immortalized as his "I Have A Dream" address. His hortative brilliance in that moment remains a perpetual inspiration to those who have benefited from his courage. The words he spoke that day hadn't yet become the hallowed symbol of the African-American struggle for equality that they would. Unfortunately, that would happen, subsequently, with his martyrdom.

Just as an earlier era of Indiana Central students can recall precisely where they were and what they were doing when news of the Japanese attack on Pearl Harbor was announced—or a later generation, 9/11/01—so, too, can many of us remember vividly the events of the assassination of President Kennedy.

It was Thursday, November 22, 1963, the first of four consecutive surreal days when our senses would be overwhelmed. I had just stepped into the hallway on the third floor of the Ad Building following Martha Waller's class in Shakespeare that ended at 1:45 p.m. (12:45 Dallas time). A passing student said, more casually than the occasion seemed to have called for, "President Kennedy has just been shot." It was from junior Darrell Hoyer (later principal at Decatur Central High School) that I was to learn of the event that would alter history.

Stunned—remember, this was the *first* of three American political murders my generation would witness in the sixties—I hurried immediately to Wilmore Hall to join about fifty other residents glued to the black-and-white television screen there. Not long afterward, to our collective disbelief, a choked-up Walter Cronkite would pronounce: "At 1 p.m. Central Standard Time, President John Fitzgerald Kennedy died at Dallas' Parkland Hospital."

Every radio and television network followed the events of the day. Cameras captured painful images of American citizens' very public mourning. Men and women wept openly on city streets, clutching one another in utter grief. Arriving at Andrews Air Force Base, Mrs. Kennedy, still clad in the outfit stained with her husband's blood, stood by bravely as his coffin was removed from the plane to a waiting ambulance to be returned to the White House. Programming was interrupted to announce that Dallas police had cornered an unknown named Lee Harvey Oswald in a Dallas movie theater and taken him into custody as the chief suspect.

On Sunday morning, November 24, I was at home, sitting with my parents in front of our TV, preparing to watch the transfer of the Kennedy coffin in Washington, D.C.

Television cameras were focused on the caisson upon which rested the flag-draped coffin of the president. A saddled, but riderless, black horse, with empty boots reversed in the stirrups, stood restively behind, occasionally rearing slightly. In ten minutes, the funeral cortege would begin its solemn journey along Pennsylvania Avenue to the Capitol, where President Kennedy's remains were to lie in state.

Suddenly the broadcast switched to the Dallas city hall. We watched as several brawny officers escorted a pale, thin Oswald, his face swollen and distorted by bruises from the beating he'd taken while being subdued. Inexplicably, from the right side of the screen, a rotund figure, later identified as Dallas nightclub owner Jack Ruby, appeared. Clearly visible, the barrel of a handgun pointed directly at Oswald's side. Ruby pulled the trigger. Oswald's visage contorted in surprise and pain, and then chaos commenced. America had watched its first murder on live TV. It was dumbfounding.

The final act of this great American tragedy would unfold on Monday, November 25. In a scene that would sear the souls of all of us who witnessed it, three-year-old "John-John" saluted as his father's coffin passed by on its way to Arlington Cemetery following the requiem mass at the Cathedral of St. Mathew the Apostle. In light of the plane crash that snuffed out John Jr.'s life at age 38, reviewing that image of a little boy paying final respects to his fallen father evokes the same haunting visceral reaction that it did in 1963.

Youthful rebellion, with the new, edgier rock 'n' roll as a driving force, was at the forefront of sixties society. The outrage of parents and conservative guardians of the morals of youth at the swiveling pelvis of Elvis a decade earlier was now focused on four mop-haired lads from England, who would ultimately become cultural icons for their generation. Consider that in March 2002, 46 million people in the United States would see one of television's most acclaimed productions, the Academy of Motion Pictures Oscars presentation from Hollywood. Thirty-eight years earlier on February 2, 1964, Ed Sullivan introduced the Beatles as "four boys from Liverpool" on his nationally televised show, "Toast of the Town." When the rag-topped foursome made that first appearance in America, more than *73 million viewers* would tune in, making it to this day one of the highest-rated programs in television annals.

For some of us who had grown up in the fifties the Beatles represented something too radical for comfort. It wasn't just their music, but the rebelliousness they stood for. According to historian Eric Forbes, the "redefinition of freedom in the sixties was a rejection of all authority." Most of us born prior to baby-boomers *did* believe father knew best.

The chief spokesman for the group, John Lennon, shocked those in the pulpits of American churches by saying, "The Beatles are bigger than Jesus." The Beatles may have been, but they weren't bigger than Elvis. We defenders of our own icon can point out that in terms of the number of tunes that reached #1 on record charts, Elvis had 33, the Beatles 27! No other individual or group is even close.

It was an age of hallucinogenic drugs, fascination with Eastern religions, and the expanding Vietnam War. Parents skirmished with their children over music, hair length— indeed, nearly everything adults in that culture held dear.

No less an authoritarian figure and hero to many embattled parents and public defenders of the status quo, Green Bay Packer coach Vince Lombardi, observed:

> *... ancient traditions, congealed creeds and despotic states*

James L. Brunnemer

> ... necessarily idealized (freedom) against order, the new against the old, and genius against discipline. Everything was done to strengthen the rights of the individual and weaken the state, and weaken the church, and weaken all authority. I think we all shared in this rebellion, but maybe we have too much freedom. Maybe we have so long ridiculed authority in the family, discipline in education, and decency in conduct and law that our freedom has brought us close to chaos.

At campuses across the nation, subtle shifts in student attitudes were occurring toward perceived injustices in the world. Momentum for social change was manifested in increasing incidents of student dissent at colleges and universities. Creative protests were played out on the national scene over great social issues, with the war in Southeast Asia as an accompanying catalyst.

Out of this restless, often lawless, backlash of its younger generation, two of the most significant and far-reaching acts of legislation defining the rights of United States' citizens—the Civil Rights Act (1964) and the Voting Rights Act (1965)—would be enacted.

And what occupied the mind and time of the ICC student during that historic era? I can't say that I was the prototypical pupil, but then in my third semester of higher education, I still wasn't immersed in either intellectual pursuit or political activism. While I had become learned enough to trust no longer even my own dog to guard my food, Sisyphus had nothing on my futile attempts to scale the academic mountain. The panorama of my perspective on national and international events could be measured in feet, and my depth of understanding, in inches.

While students at Berkeley spent afternoons among masses of fellow demonstrators, absorbing fiery rhetoric from righteously indignant insurrectionists, I was likely to be engaged in a spirited game of euchre, or futilely grappling with Dick Elmore in a game of Ping-Pong.

Dick was a far better table tennis player than me, but his gentlemanly comportment combined with my uncompromising (and boorish) competitiveness led to a heated rivalry. In truth, Dick beat me 19 out of every twenty matches. I'm not certain he didn't purposefully allow me to win from time to time, just so he could get away from my insistence that we play "one more game."

A day came, though, when the Ping-Pong gods smiled on me. It seemed that I returned every smash Elmore propelled my way. I lost count of the number of my shots that nipped the edge of my opponent's end of the table, rendering them unreturnable.

Naturally, as was my wont, I was impossibly smug and ill-mannered when winning. Not for me to be gracious. I talked "trash" to Dick before that term was even invented.

Distinction Without Pretension

And for once I could see it drove a knife through "Elmo's" ordinarily tranquil and complaisant core. He was pissed. And demanded of me another game.

I responded by placing my paddle on the table and walking away.

Over the next several days, Dick tried to engage me in a rematch, but I chose to let him suffer the degradation of losing. Hankering for vengeance was not characteristic of Dick Elmore. I took a kind of pride in being so obnoxious as to push him out of his normal gentility.

Finally, days later, I gave in to his pleadings and there we stood, the length of the Wilmore Hall Ping-Pong table between us. I won the toss for serve.

Perhaps four minutes later, tops, it was over.

Elmore, 21-zip.

Yapping at the self-satisfied conqueror, like some tiny hyperactive Chihuahua biting at Dick's ankles, it was my turn to plead for another game. Rather than concede to my raucous taunts, Dick, instead, uttered these uncharacteristically bold and brazen words:

"You'll *never* beat me again!"

What? Did I hear you correctly? You have thrown down a gauntlet, wrapped in an infinite adverb, to this warrior? To this person who lives for any sort of competition, you've made a declaration of permanent subjugation to your preeminence?

"Write it down."

"What?" responded my friend and foe.

"Put that in writing. I'll make you eat those words one day," I snarled.

So he did. I can show it to you. Because for the nearly thirty-seven years since Dick made that ill-fated promise, I've carried the now-tattered scrap of lined paper in my wallet, with "Mo's" vow written in pencil:

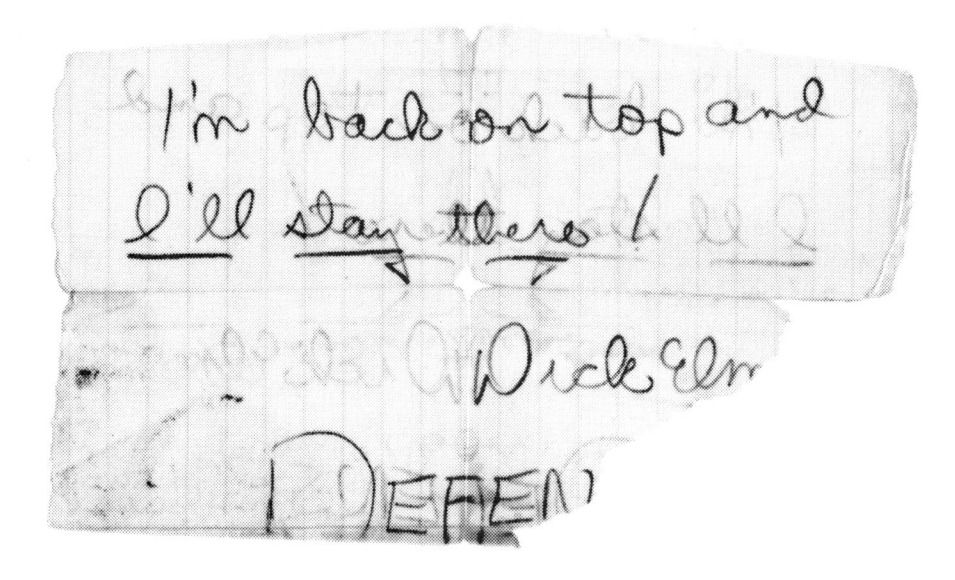

James L. Brunnemer

Okay, so I've *not* beaten him since that glorious and awful day in Wilmore Hall. In truth, we haven't played table tennis in more than three decades.

But I haven't forgotten.

He doesn't know it, but I'm tracking my friend Dick Elmore as we both age. You see, I'll find out the name of the retirement community he and his wife, Angie (Rogers) '69, eventually choose. And one day, I'll show up there. I will have surreptitiously scouted his game. I'll know his physical infirmities, any vulnerability. An arthritic elbow? Diminished eyesight? A prosthesis of some sort?

I'll know.

And at the right moment, I'll appear, Ping Pong paddle in one hand, his insulting note in the other!

I'll beat him. And never play him again!

And if I don't win? I'll chase him to the grave.

Other cosmically important events filled our idle hours at ICC, besides table tennis. But lest you think that we paid no heed to scholarship, let me offer this:

On a night before a major history final, authored by the supremely respected Dr. Roland Nelson, a group of us gathered to pool our inconsiderable collection of wisdom in anticipation of a sturdy challenge.

Steve Wischmeier, a baseball teammate and a prototype of the catcher, which meant a squat physique and gnarly hands like a troll, was among our study group. Intelligence was not a problem for "Wisch," but apathy was. His college experience was like a heart transplant. Professors tried to educate him, but his head rejected it.

Having been up until half past three that morning, we all looked like we'd been "rode hard and put up wet" when we gathered for the 8:45 a.m. test.

With little introduction, Nelson distributed the test and took his seat at the front of the classroom. Wisch and I retreated to the last row and slid into desks side by side. Only minutes after the exam started I caught a glimpse of my burly buddy lowering his head onto crossed arms over his test paper. Thinking this was a temporary respite from the mental rigors of our long night of study, I continued writing in my blue test booklet.

Then I heard Wisch's breathing. At first it was but a light sounding exhalation. However, no more than half-a-minute later, his quiet expiration became a wheeze, then built upward into a full-blown, audible snore.

At my own peril, I reached across the aisle, and shaking him gently, whispered, "Wisch. Wisch. Wake up."

No response.

A bit harder this time I nudged his arm. "Wisch. Wake up! Wisch!"

Without opening his eyes, Wischmeier barked, "Leemedahellalone!" Then nodded back into slumber.

He was still in Never-Never Land when I handed my test paper to Dr. Nelson and departed.

During that fall term I would be exposed to the Virginia Cravens School of Etiquette. Miss Cravens looked to be about the age of Methuselah's grandmother. Some claimed with seriousness that she was *born* seventy-seven years old.

Distinction Without Pretension

Evening and Sunday meals at Indiana Central in the fall of 1963 called for coats and ties for male students, prim dresses for women. Miss Cravens occupied a seat at a different table every evening to impart proper table manners to us savages.

First, however, I had to master the terminology. It took several weeks for me to unlearn nineteen years of Morgan County lexicon. I discovered that what I'd been calling "dinner" was actually "lunch." And even more confusing, "supper" was "dinner" in the elite world of Indiana Central. I caught on to that rather quickly, but then they threw "brunch" at me, a cross, I was told, between "breakfast" and "dinner" (I mean, "lunch").

I recall clearly the first time Miss Cravens' presence graced the table at which I sat. I thought I was on top of things when I held my right pinky outward, *sipping*—not *slurping* obstreperously, in the usual fashion—iced tea. But as I ladled a second redskin potato out of the community bowl, I felt inexplicable heat from some unknown source searing my brow. I looked up to see the fierce countenance of Miss Cravens scowling directly at me.

Flustered, my mind raced to determine what *faux pas* I might have committed. Mentally tallying the number of my tablemates, it dawned on me that there were only potatoes enough for one apiece! With the subtlety of a dervish, I scooped the extra spud off my plate with a spoon and proceeded to drop it onto the tablecloth. (Under the pressure of Miss Craven's incredulous expression, returning that potato to the bowl was like nailing Jell-O to a tree.) Forlornly watching as it rolled over the precipice that was the edge of the table, I stretched to make a barehanded save before the wayward tater bounced on the floor. My hope to return the vegetable without stirring much ado went for naught. Seven pairs of eyes now observed my increasingly clumsy attempts at *savoir faire*. My dilemma had expanded, too, for the small round tuber felt like a smoldering ember in my palm. With a paucity of dignity, I exclaimed, "Ooo! Ooo! Hot! Hot!"

My second attempt was a hurried lob of the potato that rimmed out of the bowl. Stretching once again to retrieve the unobliging redskin, I made certain it would stay in place by slam-dunking it on the third try. It was only then that I assessed what I thought to be third-degree burns on my fingers.

From her sullen expression, I concluded that Miss Cravens was not impressed either with my dexterity or my comportment at table.

I suppose I was far too naïve to appreciate the significance of an event I observed after sundown one evening. A van had pulled up to the rear of Lilly Science Hall, while I lurked near there, probably walking with a coed in the woods behind the building. The deliverymen, I guess one would term them, were carrying lengthy bags of some mysterious contents into the building. Only later would I learn that cadavers were delivered after dark to the anatomy laboratories. Some United Brethren leaders might have been horrified to know that real human bodies were being dissected in the name of education on the hallowed grounds of Indiana Central College.

Not all of my class time was wasted in idleness. As Professor Ruth House animatedly lectured on educational psychology, a classmate handed me a note, with a quote, following which was the question: "What is unusual about this sentence?"

The sentence was: "The quick brown fox jumps over the lazy dog."

I spent the better part of the lecture pondering the mystery, without arriving at the foggiest notion why this sentence was special. Slyly, as Dr. House turned to write an

James L. Brunnemer

abstruse psychological theorem on the slate blackboard, my classmate informed me that every letter in the alphabet appeared in the sentence. It had been developed by Western Union to test its Telex Communication system. Don't tell *me* you can't pick up key information in a classroom.

When a smartass psychology major noted that I had a "grossly inferior hippocampus," I was indignant, but I wasn't sure what to be offended at. My brain matter may have suffered from a lack of curiosity, but within other organs and chemicals there was constant agitation.

So, let's be unabashedly forthright. We were preoccupied with sex.

It would be one of Indiana Central's genuine scholars who most accurately defined for me the essence of the male college experience.

Once, this *summa cum laude* graduate and I were sharing our college experiences, his of the late fifties, and mine of the early to mid-sixties, when my friend attempted to put his perspective into words. Wrestling with just how to phrase his description of campus life and his intellectual take on it, he said, after a deep breath and a sigh, in even tones: "College life was four years of desperate and protracted horniness."

Lots of guys certainly felt the same. But I didn't quite expect a student of Bob McBride's to phrase it quite that unambiguously.

Interspersed amongst the grandiloquent intellectual information put forth in the classrooms were practical lessons gleaned from informal chats with fellow students. For example, adolescent males would learn this tidbit, shockingly communicated to me by a coed with whom I was sharing a Coke one evening: "When it comes to romance, whatever you guys want, we girls want, too."

Just as none of our generation ever experienced "the Mound"—the acclaimed "passion pit" of earlier generations of ICC students—current and future students will never know the bliss of the "horseshoe" on a Sunday night. Men returning from home met their girlfriends and those lucky enough to get a parking spot on the horseshoe would be wrapped in passion inside the locked automobiles.

Not every tryst at the campus love nest ended satisfactorily. Like the time I returned to campus on a Sunday night, late, to catch a half hour with my favorite girl of the moment. I picked "Roz" up at eight in the evening, two hours before she had to be in the dorm. It was time enough to make out on the horseshoe and still get her back by the ten o'clock curfew.

My problem this night was that I was ravenously hungry—for full-body contact with Roz, sure, but legitimately, desperately hungry in my stomach. And I had only ninety-five cents to my name, enough for a Coke and fries for two, or a Coke, fries, and a *Steakburger* for one!

The noble side of me leaned toward taking Roz out and sharing the soft drinks and fries, but the lesser angels of my nature pleaded for the burger. Knowing that the Steak n Shake restaurant on Madison Avenue closed at 10 p.m.—exactly the hour the girls were required to be in the dormitory—I returned her, uncharacteristically early, at nine-fifteen. This allowed me enough time to get my jollies, and still make it to the restaurant to claim a charcoal-broiled prize. I made a lame excuse about a pop quiz or something that I needed to study for, dropped her off with a kiss, and drove madly to the Steak n Shake. Arriving at about nine-thirty or so, I ordered, via the electronic box there, the deluxe cheeseburger, fries, and Coke that I so desperately craved.

As I took the *first* bite from the delectable sandwich, imagine my mortification when I looked to my left to see Roz with three other friends pulling into the parking spot adjacent to mine. And she was riding "shotgun" in the front seat of the red Chevy, which, when they backed into the stall next to mine, placed us exactly adjacent to one another.

Apparently the girls had decided to make a quick run to the Steak n Shake, too. I choked on the bite as I feebly nodded to acknowledge their presence. I didn't have the *cojones* to roll my window down and converse. I knew my gauche act ended any further relationship I might have had with Roz.

A worm. A slimy worm.

These days preceded, of course, the serious movement by women for equality. There was an abundance of ordained ministers on the faculty. So eyebrows raised, and some members of the faculty/clergy were especially outraged, when a letter from a rather progressive female student to the editor of the *Reflector* in 1965 posed this rhetorical question: "And just how long *will* it be for women to be seen as something besides a receptacle for a man's penis?"

Talk of sex was the constant among students, at least the male population. Trust me. It was, with some exceptions, mostly just male bravado and braggadocio when Indiana Central men talked of sexual adventures in 1963. The vast majority of such palaver was the product of mere fantasy. The Federal Drug Administration had approved use of "the pill" for birth control in 1960, amid great moral misgivings of much of the American populace. At small Christian colleges (some would add "for small Christians"), the specter of guilt-free sex hovered darkly over that scientific breakthrough, which would ultimately have an irrevocable effect on American socio-sexual mores.

And every spring, when the first warm evening appeared after a long bleak winter, inevitably the sap stirring in the campus trees in anticipation of the oncoming summer was matched by the gurgling hormones of horny residents in the men's dorms.

Before women attained some semblance of equity with their male counterparts on campus, they were required to be in the dorm behind locked doors at ten p.m. weeknights, midnight on Friday and Saturdays, and 11 p.m. Sundays, unless they had prior permission to do otherwise.

So an annual ritual played out, almost serendipitously: the "panty raid."

Obviously, this ceremonial custom was really more huff and puff and bluff than any serious notion of actually encountering females and physically removing their undies. You knew *that* from the number of ministerial students taking part. In fact, it was usually a pre-theology major who initiated the whole silly affair.

Anyway, at about eleven o'clock one unseasonably warm April evening, with the women safely behind locked doors, about sixty of us trekked across the horseshoe loudly announcing our intentions.

Most of the men gathered below the three floors of windows at the northwest corner of Trimble Hall, where several freshmen girls hung out of open and unscreened windows. Innocent, naughty threats were lofted from the men below, demanding the girls toss souvenirs to the predators. Tantalizingly, the girls challenged the men to "come up and get 'em yourselves!"

James L. Brunnemer

At that time, a freshman coed had already become, if not a legend on campus, certainly a major curiosity. I will nobly refrain from revealing her name, but those on campus at that time will know to whom I refer as possessing a stunning pair of boobs, the most spectacular knockers to grace the campus in memory. Hers were Dolly Parton-class, and dorm-mates of hers let it be known there was nothing false about them. They were the real deal.

As the fervor of the banter between the guys below and the girls above intensified, Geneva (I'll call her) got into the emotion of the moment, appearing at the window to offer, not her panties, but an article of apparel much more impressive: one of her bras.

What happened next has become hazy through the years. It was at this point Jack Leonard and I drifted away from the mass of males, so we missed the main event. The story, told and retold at subsequent alumni gatherings, had Geneva, with the help of two members of the ladies field hockey team, launching the cones into the night air. Billowing downward, the customized double D-sized cups filled with air like two parachutes attached to one another.

It is said that when the bra finally alit, the cheers of the adolescents below turned to panic. Two terrified freshmen were trapped in the tepees. An emergency call to maintenance was sounded, and with a forklift they freed the trapped students after about 45 minutes.

I can't swear by this. But that's what I was told.

While this was happening, Jack and I had begun to walk eastward when, glancing toward the dimly lit entrance to Trimble, I made a breathtaking discovery. I suppose it was because of the welcomed warmness of the evening, but the window to the room just at the top of the stairs that served as a waiting area for gentleman callers at Trimble was open. Wide open, *sans* screen!

This was a bonanza unexpected. Entry into the inner sanctum would be ecstasy, surely; but better than that, we'd punch a ticket to campus stardom. If we could breach the barriers of the women's dorm while all the attention was focused elsewhere, we'd be folk heroes! Jack and I would join all those before us who became renowned for daring feats. They'd talk about us for years as the two freshman guys who got into the girl's dorm during the panty raid of '63. Hell, they'd write songs about us!

The window ledge was about seven feet from the ground. I suggested that because of his impressive arm strength, Jack should jump up and grab the windowsill, and then I would support him as he crawled through. Then he could help me in after. Agreed.

He leaped upward. I supported Jack's weight on my shoulders as he grabbed onto the windowsill. As I stood there, my heart pounding at the prospect of the adventure that lay ahead, there came from my buddy an audible gasp. Bewildered at his confusing reaction, I whispered, "Moose, what's goin' on?"

I knew we had trouble when Jack's reply was a polite, "Hi, Mom Miller." As my surprised roommate gripped the bottom sill of the window, the figure of the Trimble Hall house matron suddenly loomed above him.

Grace Miller was a gentle and kindly woman who loved the students of Indiana Central. She had a natural angelic visage, which emanated from her sweet disposition. However, she took seriously her duty to protect the virtue of her freshman girls of Trimble from the unruly hormones of barbarian males on the campus. When confronted with

Distinction Without Pretension

the slightest threat to the chastity of her feminine charges, Mom Miller could become a formidable foe.

With no trace of a change in her sweet face, Mom Miller reached upward and, showing surprising strength for a frail sixty-some-year-old lady, cold-bloodedly brought down the window frame with the swiftness of a guillotine onto Jack's eight fingers and both thumbs.

Jack tried gallantly to suppress his natural inclination to respond to the piercing pain he felt in his digits. It wouldn't be honorable to scream like a banshee in the presence of a house mom.

But his anguish showed in the kick he delivered to the human stepladder beneath him.

I stepped back. But curiously, Jack didn't immediately drop to the ground, as I expected. He couldn't.

I've wondered more than once what Mom Miller's view was as she surveyed the scene from inside. Below her in the dim light that shone outward into the night, there was a male student, ten terminal parts of his hands clamped in the vice made by the window frame and the windowsill. As he looked up at her through the dark his face was contorted in agony, yet appeared apologetic for the inconvenience. Helpless, forlorn, Jack pleaded with his eyes: "Please open the damned window, Mom!"

After what must have seemed an eternity—or like sitting through one of Bill Gommel's lectures, anyway—Mom Miller lifted the window slightly and my unfortunate friend slithered down the outer brick wall.

Cuddling his mangled fingers next to his body, he muttered, "Brunnemer, you are a dead man when my fingers heal enough to get 'em around yer throat! DEAD. MAN!"

It wasn't the first time, or the last, that I had heard, or would hear, such threats.

Memories of the sophomore and junior years meld together in my mind. But I can offer a brief story that might provide for the reader an assessment of my maturity level. In the wide world of sport today, my competitive behaviors might seem tame, blending in with today's mayhem in athletics. But in 1964, intentionally throwing a baseball at a base runner was considered at least moderately deviant, certainly not the act of a sportsman.

I haven't been in a baseball dugout for over a quarter of a century, so I'm not familiar with the terminology used by collegiate players of today. But I had in the mid-sixties what was called "rabbit ears" on the baseball field. For those of you who know little about baseball, having "rabbit ears" is not a good thing, for that term refers to one who hears, and is affected by, jocular razzing from opponents. Me? I had the ears of an elephant. I could hear whispers in an opponent's dugout and swear they were ripping on me. Hearing derogatory remarks always fueled my competitive zeal, sometimes inspiring me to better performance, but more often leading to disaster.

At West Lafayette that season of my junior year, during pre-game infield practice before the Purdue game, I overheard an opposing coach telling his players, "That ICC first baseman is the best glove man we've ever played against." Hearing that, I began to preen like a peacock, attempting a baseball ballet around first befitting his opinion. I made three errors in the first two innings of the game.

Despite my fumbling in the field, we were leading the Boilermakers, 2-0, after six

James L. Brunnemer

innings, thanks to masterful pitching by Jerry Mullinix.

In the Purdue half of the seventh inning, Jerry had wavered, giving up a two-out single and then walking the next two batters. With the bases now loaded, up to the plate strode PU's best hitter, a shortstop named Del (whose last name I can't recall). His father was a scout for the Minnesota Twins at the time.

On the first pitch, the overly eager Boiler batter bounced an easy ground ball right back to Mullinix. Fielding it ably, Jerry lobbed the ball softly to me at first base. The throw was slightly awry, necessitating my moving to the home plate side and into the baseline to retrieve the throw. Dashing vainly up the base path was the frustrated Del. He and the ball arrived at about the same time, but I was able to snag the toss, brush my toe across the base, and quickly step out of the path of the runner. Out three.

However, as Del raced by me he intentionally flailed his right elbow sharply into my chest.

Instinctively, I spun toward right field as he ran across the base and began to slow. Without thought I cocked my left arm with the intention of putting the baseball directly between the numeral "1" and "0" on the back of his jersey.

Something, however, clicked in my brain, suggesting that hitting a defenseless opponent in the back with the ball might not be an appropriate retaliation despite his show of ill will. With my arm already moving forward, I attempted to stop the throw. The result was a desultory lob that arced just over his left shoulder. I turned to cross the diamond to our dugout along the third base line when howls of indignation blew out of the Purdue dugout. I recall Randy Minnear, a former Broad Ripple High School star, being especially outraged at my boorish action. Players started to pour out, and the possibility that my senseless act would trigger a brawl was bona fide.

As I crossed over the pitcher's mound, I saw out of the corner of my eye a Purdue player who'd been on second base, running directly at me, a menacing expression on his face. It was Gordon Teter, who was an All-Big Ten running back for PU's football team. Remembering the lesson most boys of my era learned in childhood—"If a fight's going to happen, get in the first blow"—I turned to do just that. Teter and I collided like two mini-sumo wrestlers, trying to jounce one another to the ground. By now, players from both teams had sprinted to the mound area, engaging in verbal sparring and some scuffling. Cooler heads separated me and a man who likely would have eaten my lunch. Teter was a tough boy.

Purdue's coach, Joe Sexson, got right in my face to verbalize his incredulity that a player would throw a ball at one of his own. It was then that Bill Bright demonstrated, as he so often would, support for one of his men.

"I saw what your player did, Joe, so get away from my kid! You take care of yours and I'll take care of mine!" Bill said threateningly. Sexson backed off like a spurned suitor.

Bill can't know how I appreciated that. It wasn't the first time I'd embarrassed myself in that way and though Bill didn't condone my rash act, he stood up for me in the heat of the moment. He was that kind of man.

The story doesn't end here. It so happened that I was scheduled to bat first in the next inning. A hint of tension beneath the surface of the Purdue lads was still detectable when I took my stance in the batter's box. Hitting a very playable ground ball to the

Boilermaker first baseman, I sprinted toward first. Purdue's pitcher dutifully came over to cover the bag. Normally, a first baseman will toss the ball to the pitcher, who would touch the bag with his foot as he ran along the base line. But since I had attracted some measure of bile among some of the Purdue players, the first sacker determined to make the play himself and teach me a lesson. Also a Boilermaker football standout, but unlike Teter a lineman of large proportions, the player timed his arrival at the base with my own.

When we met at the bag, I remember flying head-over-hindquarters, and little else. After a ride in an ambulance, I was to spend the night in the Purdue infirmary with a slight concussion. Vengeance was thine, Black and Gold.

A number of the Purdue players demonstrated an abundance of class that evening, as a parade of my opponents came to the bedside to wish me well. Included in that group was Del, a true sportsman, who apologized for igniting the whole affair.

And who would chauffeur me back to Indianapolis the following day? Coach Sexson. We mutually discovered during that sixty-mile trip that the other guy wasn't so bad after all.

CHAPTER XIV
FUTILITY WRAPPED IN INCOMPETENCE INSIDE HOPELESSNESS

Cain't anybody here play this game?
Casey Stengel, manager of the
pathetic New York Mets, which would
lose a record 120 games in 1962.

In contrast to the seriousness of the times, one could always find hilarity or agony, depending upon one's emotional investment, in watching Indiana Central's intercollegiate football team.

Following ICC football during my undergraduate days, and as a young alumnus, was a source of continual frustration. Fall in Indiana was inevitably tainted for Greyhound grid fans. From 1962 through 1969, under the coaching of, first, Paul Velez (1962-66, 14-29-2) and then Ed Dwyer (1967-69, 4-21-1), the Greyhounds overwhelmed eighteen opponents, underwhelmed fifty, and "whelmed" three. Our team won roughly one of every four games during those years, with one aberrant season (1965) when the Hounds went 6-3. During that year when the Hounds won more than they lost, their play often made us forget for brief moments how low our football program had sunk.

The reasons for such consistent futility on the gridiron? Velez and Dwyer were enormously decent men who apparently didn't recruit enough good players, or if they did, couldn't find the ingredients to win. Some blamed the administration for not having a commitment to excellence. Others suggested that Nick, as director of athletics, slighted football in favor of his basketball program.

Regardless, the bottom line is that our football teams had their helmets handed to them in most games, and it was agonizing to witness.

In eighteen contests during the 1966 and 1967 seasons, ICC scored a total of 132 points. That paltry offensive production, barely a touchdown per game, was odious enough. But in that same set of encounters, the opponents scored *three times* as many points, resulting in two Greyhound wins, 15 losses and a tie.

Our team was so inept that team doctor Charlie Dill, as loyal a supporter as the Greyhound football program ever had, once described the predictability of our offense in this way: "When we came out of the huddle, three backs would be laughing out loud, while one was pale as a ghost."

Velez was as consistently successful as a wrestling coach as he was dismal as a football mentor. Why he couldn't seem to transfer the good fortune he had coaching guys in tights to those in pads no one was quite sure. (Paul is a member of the Indiana Wrestling Hall of Fame.) He certainly had numbers of fine athletes in both sports. Paul's wrestling teams of that era had champions like Cleo Moore, Maurice Barnes, Larry McCloud, Mike Watkins, Dave Paino, Tim Giles, Dale Sidebottom, and others. On the gridiron were

James L. Brunnemer

talented and hard-nosed players such as Dave Scheib, Vasco Walton, Herb Lepper, John Deal, Bill Tutterow, Jim Ware, Bill Bless, Jack Schuck, Dave Smith, Pat Koers, and John Egenolf, to mention a handful.

As student sports information director, it was my duty to report results of the games to the Indianapolis newspapers. For this I earned thirty dollars a month from ICC public relations director Leonard Pearson, and five bucks per report from the *Star* and the *News*.

I recall one particular game during the 3-6 season of 1964, when a slow-footed left-handed not-very-accurate-throwing quarterback named Charlie Miller received a major headline in the *Indianapolis Star* sports section.

"*ICC's MILLER TOSSES FOUR TD PASSES*," screamed the banner. The staffer who wrote that headline obviously did not see the game or he might have qualified what this true, but deceptive, headline implied.

I was there, manning the statistics book as usual. The game, versus Chicago Illini (now the University of Illinois-Chicago), was played at historic Soldier Field. The combined total of about ninety-eight fans rattled around in the 60,000-seat venue like BBs in a boxcar.

ICC won the contest, 34-24, over CIU. Miller might have been the statistical star, but he had more than ample help on the scoring passes.

Vasco Walton, a multi-sport athlete who later would be twice named the Most Valuable Player for the minor league Indianapolis Capitals pro football team, played wide receiver on the Hounds' offensive unit. Miller's first touchdown was a slant pass that Charlie threw like a bullet a full two yards *behind* Walton, who was running in the *opposite* direction in which Miller threw the ball. Defying whatever law of physics that says an object going one direction at top speed cannot reverse and go the other way without first stopping, Vasco half-spun while putting on his brakes, reached out with his right hand and somehow got his fingertips on the point of the football. Continuing to turn back toward the direction from which he had just come, Vasco drew the ball into his body without touching it with his left hand, and cradled it under his arm. Regaining his equilibrium, he now began to sprint in a direction ninety degrees from his original path. Naturally the defender was still trying to change his own momentum. No contest. After doing the impossible, Vasco merely sprinted the remaining forty yards into the end zone.

The next TD pass Miller "created" was a desperation toss as Charlie evaded a fierce rush by the opponents. Walton, with his body fully extended inches off the grass, dove to snag the wobbly lob with the tips of his fingers. Securing the pigskin, Vasco skidded along the ground in a fetal position tucked around the football. Six points. That catch would have made ESPN SportsCenter highlight clips today.

Touchdown toss number three was what would be called a "Hail Mary" today, except that the wild fling was generally standard operating procedure for the Greyhounds offense under Paul Velez. This wounded duck of a throw turned into a spectacular score, thanks this time to the extraordinary athleticism of David Scheib.

Miller's pass resembled a forty-yard pop fly, with Scheib and not one, not two, but three CIU defenders waiting hungrily for the pigskin. It was INT all the way, except that Scheib timed his thirty-six-inch vertical leap precisely, literally stole the ball from six CIU hands, and strolled into pay dirt as the three opponents crumpled in a heap. Way to

Distinction Without Pretension

go, Charlie!

The fourth and last TD pass found Miller running for his life fifteen yards behind the line of scrimmage. "Running" is a relative term for what passed for movement from Charlie Miller. Top speed for Miller was somewhere between a slow lope and a mild walk.

Anyway, a dying quail of a throw he had hurled in desperation looked to fall harmlessly to the ground, when out of nowhere came the indomitable Walton. If you've seen tennis players, having lobbed a ball backward while running full tilt away from the court, suddenly brake and return to the net, you have an idea of the play Vasco made. As Charlie's hapless toss wafted earthward, Vasco reversed himself, and, running full tilt, bent at the waist to snag the ball off his shoe tops. Skidding to a halt while pirouetting, Walton weaved, darted, and dodged fifty-five yards down the field for the score. Another great play by Miller.

Dave Scheib was one of the high-quality athletes at ICC during my years there. Dave played a key role for the state-finalist Manual High School basketball team featuring the VanArsdale twins, Dick and Tom. Both would go on to sterling careers at Indiana University and in the NBA. Scheib was a pretty fair player on the hardcourt but football was his real game. Coach Jay Windell, who moved on following Dave's freshman year, had recruited him. In his final three years, Dave was to labor ably as a quarterback, running back, and wide receiver for Coach Velez. Following his senior season he was drafted by the Philadelphia Eagles of the NFL, only to be among the last of the rookies cut by the team.

Representative of Scheib's career at ICC was another 1964 game, this one versus Olivet College near Marshall, Michigan. It was a miserable November day. Snow mixed with freezing rain made what passed for a football field there a quagmire. Scheib was aware that a number of NFL scouts were in the stands that day to watch two players: himself and George Pyne, a 6'6", 290-pound defensive lineman for Olivet.

Allow me to digress a moment to add this information, which would become relevant to events of the Olivet game. The week before the Olivet trip, following the inevitable defeat at Anderson College, I was in the Ravens' athletic complex searching for a telephone to call the *Indianapolis Star* with the report of the game. Anderson's athletic director kindly led me to the office of one of the football coaches, unlocked the door, and left me to complete my task. Discovering I had left my pen in the press box, I opened the desk drawer in search of a writing implement. There lay a copy of Anderson's scouting report on the Greyhounds that had played a role in our 27-7 loss that day.

Here was a genuine ethical dilemma: Do I read the report here, or steal it and read it on the bus back to campus? With an utter lack of scruples, I sneakily thumbed through the pages, reading coaches' remarks on team tendencies, plus strengths and weaknesses of individual Greyhound players.

My eyes fell on an interesting question posed in the report: "Do they have any 'weak sisters?'"

In bold strokes, the scout rendered this frank opinion of a particular Greyhound gridder: "#69 – Looks like Tarzan, plays like Jane!"

I would suspect I was the only person affiliated with Indiana Central who had that information, so I had a greater appreciation of an incident that would take place on the Olivet field the following Saturday. We lost, of course, 34-0. Despite the conditions of

James L. Brunnemer

the field—or maybe *because* of them—an Olivet wide receiver named Dominic Livedotti would run pass patterns unfettered through the Greyhound secondary to snare a record number of pass receptions, including four touchdowns.

Scheib, meanwhile, was experiencing the worst day of his sparkling career. The Comets' defense, led by future New York Giant pro Pyne and aided by inept blocking by the ICC offensive line, had smothered Scheib the entire game. Pyne, now a NASCAR executive whose son Jim later followed his father into the NFL, tossed ICC blockers around like rag dolls. What he did to Scheib that day would be grounds for assault in civilian life.

With only minutes remaining in the game, Scheib leaned over in the Hounds' huddle, hands on knees, gasping for breath, with ribs so sore he could barely inhale. Black and blue circles covered his body; blood seeped out of his nose and mouth, and his knuckles and shins were skinned raw from the beating he had taken.

He was near tears in frustration and pain, praying for the game to just end, when he heard a challenge to the team coming from a most unlikely source. It was #69, an offensive lineman chattering at his teammates, with "C'mon, guys, don't be a bunch of quitters! Now's the time to suck it up! Let's go!"

Scheib lifted a weary head in the direction of this bothersome prattle. The speaker, who had played nearly the entire game in the miasma, was cloaked in a football uniform that had barely a trace of mud on it! The white of his jersey and pants were a drastic contrast to Scheib and the rest of the team, whose uniforms were soaked throughout with the muck and ooze of combat. Ten players were identically soiled, their numbers indistinguishable. However, #69 was clearly identifiable.

With a fury born of the realization that this white knight was challenging *his* manhood, Scheib stepped out of the huddle. In full view of the fans in the stands, he swiftly swung his cleated shoe upwards, kicking his chatty teammate squarely in the ass. Surveying the fully surprised lineman through eyes that were slits, Scheib, a minister's son, snarled, "Trade places, sumbitch. Now I'll block and you carry the goddam ball!"

Bill Tutterow, who played both football and baseball outstandingly in his four years at ICC, related an incident during his sophomore year that was emblematic of the Velez era. In one of the few games that the Greyhounds still had a chance to win by halftime, the squad left the field trailing only 7-6 after the first thirty minutes.

In the days before Key Stadium, players would file into one of the two classrooms in what is now Nicoson Hall to receive instructions during the halftime break. This particular day Paul squeezed the seventy-five-man squad into the 12' by 16' classroom. The first twenty-five players to enter the room each commandeered one of the armchair desks and sat down. The other fifty men dispersed around the walls, shoulder to shoulder.

It was an early fall game, and the temperature outside was in the high eighties. Seventy-five sweating, heated athletes in the cramped room made for a sweltering environment. Paul was at his most energetic, which meant his usual monotone occasionally changed pitch slightly. He spent the better part of the twenty-minute halftime break droning on about X's and O's before he moved toward what was intended to be a stirring crescendo to pump the lads up and on to victory in the second half.

As the by-now drowsy-eyed players attempted to retain some focus on what Paul was saying, the largest player on the team was in an irrevocable pattern of diminishing

Distinction Without Pretension

consciousness. Wally Bishop, 6'6" and 245 pounds of practice fodder standing near the closed classroom door, was slumping slowly—but irresistibly—into the arms of Morpheus. He was giving in grudgingly, but giving in he was.

Precisely as Paul ended his halftime pep talk with a less-than-energizing "Now fellas, let's go out there and knock the **_daylights_** out of 'em," the slumbering Wally slid downward, eyes closed in blissful peace. His shoulder pads brushed the room's light switch on his trip toward the floor, extinguishing the lights and leaving the team and Paul's message in pitch-black ignominy.

Naturally, a group of seventy-five eighteen- to twenty-two-year-old men could do no other than literally convulse in cacophonic laughter at the surprising ironic twist.

Poor Wally. His slumber ended as he crumpled to the floor. He'd knocked the "daylights" out of his own team.

Poor Paul. His version of a Knute Rockne speech was not only uninspiring, but was drowned in the laughter of his own squad.

Poor Hounds. They were to absorb once more a losing effort in that second half.

My stomach still gets queasy when I recall what happened to lifelong friend Bill Tutterow against Chicago-Illini in the fall of 1965. Known familiarly as "Tut," he was a freshman, not big at 5'8" and 160 pounds, but skillful, tough as nails and unyieldingly competitive.

Bill was versatile, which meant he could do most things on a football field as well as or better than nearly all his teammates. Early in the season the Indiana Central team had had an epidemic of fumbled or misplayed punt returns. So Velez turned to Tut, and, as in all things athletic or competitive, he excelled.

Tut was at about the Greyhound thirty-yard line, awaiting an Illini punt. I was standing on the home sidelines, parallel to where he was when he settled under the opponent's kick. It was an abnormally high floater, and with several of the opponents thundering toward him, I expected Tut to raise his hand to signal a fair catch. But, you know, Tut wasn't a fair-catch kind of guy. No, he had already determined he could catch the punt, elude the initial tacklers, and advance the ball.

But at the instant the ball settled into his hands, two huge Illini linemen, at top speed, steamrolled the vulnerable Tutterow. The impact, which could be heard above the sounds of traffic over on Hanna Avenue, was sickening. Bill disappeared beneath the first two black jerseys, then three more who roared in closely on the heels of the initial duo.

My first thought after the Illini players, one by one, untangled themselves and rose celebrating over the prone Greyhound was, "How did he hold onto the football after being hit like that?"

But then I noticed Tut—flat on his back—wasn't moving. A couple of Greyhounds, arriving on the scene like sheriff's deputies at a car crash, began to signal frantically for Doc Dill and the medical crew to come quick.

Later, Tut told me the rest of the story. When he snared the ball he had tried to turn away from the Illini players and one of his cleated shoes had been planted at the time of impact. As they collided with him he felt a searing pain in his left leg and hip.

Bill sensed immediately this was no ordinary football injury. The excruciating paroxysm of pain emanating from his hip joint was like nothing he'd experienced before.

James L. Brunnemer

As the opponents, frothing at the mouth, celebrated over him, Tut lifted his head slightly to peek at the source of the astounding fire now spreading through his left lower extremity. He didn't really want to look, but as a moth is drawn to flame, he had to see.

What he took in with just a glance made him retch. His right leg was in its normal position, his grass-stained pants and muddy shoe positioned as they were supposed to be.

But his left extremity was in a place it shouldn't have been. Lying grotesquely at nearly a 90-degree angle to his right leg, the limb seemed almost as if it weren't his own. Later he was to learn it was a complete dislocation of the hip. Wave upon wave of tortuous pain from the agitated neurons serving that part of his body rolled through him.

He passed out.

When Bill regained consciousness, he observed Coach Velez, who had reached him first, moving his left foot from side to side, saying to no one in particular, "I think it's his ankle."

The primal scream of an animal escaped Bill's lips, startling the obviously not-a-med-school-grad Paul in its vociferousness. Doc Dill arrived next and waved Coach Velez to the sideline. Tut was in able hands now. Doc did whatever a physician does in those circumstances, and then supervised Tut's teammates as they gingerly lifted him onto a stretcher. The ambulance was on the stadium track awaiting the stricken player.

Applause, which always served to salute an injured player when he is removed from the field of play, emerged behind me as I moved toward the procession transporting Tut to the ambulance.

I touched Bill's arm and quietly said something of an encouraging nature. His face was contorted in agony, and while he moved his head slightly toward me, when our eyes met it was clear he didn't recognize me.

I then moved toward the bleachers where Bill's mother, Dellie, would be anxiously awaiting news of her son's condition.

As they prepared to place him in the ambulance, the stretcher and its occupant were jostled a bit, adding to the convulsions of pain. It was at that time a man not known to the disabled player poked his face to within inches of Bill's and blurted out these comforting words:

"Does it hurt, my son?"

Only one emotion could distract Bill from his physical discomfort: consummate rage. This lout, whom Tut didn't know, didn't care about, and surely didn't want in his face at this crucial time, had tripped Tut's trigger:

"(Bleep) no, Sherlock!" Bill sneered, forgetting for an instant his condition. "I'm going (bleeping) dancing tonight, right after I get out of the (bleepity-bleeping) emergency room!"

The man was thunderstruck by the venom spewing from the injured young man. His startled, almost hurt expression, revealed his dismay. He'd only been trying to help, offering comfort. It was then Tut became aware the man in black was wearing a white collar.

As the bumbling priest slithered away to nurse his *own* wounds, Tut felt guilt and shame. He'd just cussed out and abased a man of God!

But as another spectacular spasm of pain shot through his hip, Tut forgot about the man. "I'll pay penance for that sin later," he thought. And passed out again.

Distinction Without Pretension

A wiry defensive back from Arsenal Technical High School in Indianapolis, Tom Heitzman, was knocked silly executing a helmet-first tackle of a Hanover player on that Ohio River campus during the Velez era. When he arose, his wild, wide-eyed look convinced his teammates that Tom was not in the conscious world. When one of his mates attempted to help him to the sidelines for a break, Heitzman became indignant, insisting that "I play defense!"

Despite the pleas of his teammates, he wouldn't leave the field, repeating over and again, "I play defense! I play defense!" One burly defensive lineman grabbed Heitzman to try to remove him from the field as confused fans wondered why the ICC players would be fighting amongst themselves.

Suddenly, Heitzman broke free and began to run from his other ten teammates, who, as a group, gave chase, trying futilely to subdue him. The chaotic scene resembled a spontaneous snake dance as Heitzman dodged and weaved to avoid capture by his own mates. Adding further hilarity to the already bizarre scene, a Labrador retriever that had wandered onto the gridiron joined in the chase, nipping at Heitzman's shifty heels. The amazing thing was that Heitzman was much more athletic and elusive under the influence of that blow to the head than when he was in possession of his faculties. After nearly a minute of these antics, someone finally managed to tackle the loony Heitzman, and five of his teammates toted him, kicking and screaming, to Doc Dill on the bench.

In 1948 President Esch authored a policy to address equity issues of faculty with additional duties separate from their teaching loads. Coaches were considered members of the faculty so President Esch's policy allowed them teaching credit for coaching. Theoretically, their jobs did not depend on winning. Nonetheless, even Dr. Esch couldn't overlook the fact that the ICC football program had become the laughingstock of the Hoosier College Conference. So, Velez acquiesced and stepped down as a head coach with a 14-29-2 record to become an *assistant* to the newly hired *head* coach, Ed Dwyer!

Tutterow, a junior at the time, recalls the first pre-season practices under Coach Dwyer. Nicknamed "Biggie" by his players, Coach Dwyer was a huge man, 6' 6" and more than 300 pounds. He had been a very fine player at Purdue, earning All-Big Ten honors as an offensive lineman. But he tended, regularly, to confuse his eager lads with commands at practice such as:

"Okay, gentlemen! Half of ya' over here, half of ya' over there, and the rest of you come with me!"

Or, "Okay, gentlemen! Pair off by threes!"

During a class following a rare Saturday triumph under the Dwyer regime, one student reported that an obviously elated Biggie opined that the close victory for the Hounds had been a "real cliff-dweller."

In his first year, in an attempt to inspire those returning from the 1-8 team of 1966, Coach Dwyer decided to start the season with a theme, a slogan, for the defensive unit. He would call the ICC defense the "bloodhounds." Scary.

Early in a pre-season workout, with the team gathered around his massive frame, Coach Dwyer explained: "Now, men, the first part of that word is 'blood.' We're gonna be so damn mean and physical we'll swim in our opponents blood."

James L. Brunnemer

"The second part is 'Hounds.'" The coach then drew himself up into his best professorial pose and continued, "Now you freshmen won't understand this, but the upperclassmen and us literary men have all read *The Hounds of the Bastille*, and ..."

Tut stopped listening at that point as he searched his mind. "Doc Warden made us read *The Hounds of the Baskerville*, but I don't remem- ..."

At that moment he became aware of his teammates' failing attempts to stifle their community giggles, and realized that the Master of Malaprops had struck again.

The "Bloodhound" defense that season proved to be as porous as Biggie's recall of the classics. Opponents averaged 30 points a game to ICC's 16.

Coach Dwyer took his pedagogy in the classroom to heart. One morning Roger Walter and Bill Tutterow arrived at their 7:45 a.m. class for a unit in the Coaching of Track and Field. Neatly drawn with chalk on the 10' by 6' green slate board was an oval that covered the entire space. Ed had laboriously created an eight-lane replication of a running track. It had obviously taken a great amount of time to draw fastidiously each of the straightaways. The precise curvature of the turns explained the string tied to a piece of chalk on Biggie's desk. He had used it to depict the arc of the turns with authenticity.

This was an instructional work of art with which the Coach was visibly delighted. He announced to the class that the topic of his coaching lesson today would be the half-mile run event and the necessity of "staggering" the runners' starting spots. He had dutifully marked with lines crossing the lane at each spot where the runners would begin. The idea, of course, was to negate the advantage of runners placed in the lanes closer to the inside of the track as they ran around the first two turns.

Ed plunged into the lecture, making certain the budding coaches in the class noted the reasoning behind the staggered start, going through each lane to demonstrate how the distance between each starting spot neutralized any advantage by the time the runners were through the second turn.

There was just one problem.

While listening carefully to the professor, Roger and Tut began to examine the starting positions on the drawing. Each quickly came to the same conclusion: Biggie had *reversed* the starting spots. The staggered start on Dwyer's track had the inside runner several yards *ahead* of the competitor in the second lane, the second-lane competitor the same distance in front of the third-lane starter, and so on through each of the eight lanes. This meant that when the runners entered the second turn, instead of eliminating the advantage to the inside runners, the competitors starting on the inside lanes would have an outlandishly superior lead over those in the outer ones.

Tut raised his hand. "Coach Dwyer, I have a question."

"Yeah," Biggie grunted.

"Don't you have the staggered start backwards?"

Biggie scowled. He peered for a full half-minute at this work he had so painstakingly and lovingly created.

"Dammit," he groused, picking up an eraser. With a flourish, he swiped it violently across the track, smearing his work beyond repair. Without turning around, he said to his bemused pupils, "Class dismissed!"

Distinction Without Pretension

Biggie was always on the lookout for pranksters. He didn't suffer mildly wise guys in his midst, though he gave anyone with a modicum of sensitivity to humor tons of reasons to be tickled.

One fall semester during the first day of classes Prof Dwyer circulated a clipboard with blank lines for listing names. He instructed the eighteen students in the room to put the surname, followed by only the initial of one's first name.

Ed launched into his expectations for the class, when the clipboard, all names completed, was handed forward to him.

He read aloud the list, each person raising his hand to be identified when Biggie called his name. All went well until Ed got to the last name on the list: Virgin, J.

"Awright, who's the smartass? You guys think you're so damn cute. I'm sick and tired of baby-sitting and I won't have anybody in here who can't check his silliness at the door. Don't you people know you're not in high school anymore? Now because of one immature moron in this class all of you get to read the first five chapters in the book and I want a five-page report on those chapters, due Wednesday! If I have to ... "

The hand of a shy student in the rear of the room was waving, trying to get Mr. Dwyer's attention.

"**What?**" Biggie snapped.

"I'm Virgin, sir. Joe Virgin."

At first, thinking this kid was still trying to put one over on him, Biggie tied into The Virgin with a vengeance.

"But Coach Dwyer," the young man pleaded, "My name really *is* Joe Virgin. Here it is on my driver's license."

"Uh ... Oh," Biggie conceded, without apology. He changed the topic back to his expectations of the class and didn't say another word about "smartass freshmen."

Joseph E. Virgin earned his bachelor's degree in 1967.

Desperately looking for solutions to end one of the typically spiraling losing streaks, Coach Dwyer determined that a change of coaching venue might be the answer.

Those who remember the pre-Key Stadium days at Indiana Central will recall the tower behind the home bleachers. Resembling a scaffold, the four-posted structure consisted of four levels rising approximately forty feet above the ground at its highest point. It passed for what today would be called the press box.

On the first level, at a height just above the top of the home bleachers, was a table and folding chairs for the scoreboard operator, scorers, and statisticians. On level two, about eight feet above them, was another table and chairs where the radio station announcers and their crew observed the game. Levels three and four were reserved for the cameramen who filmed the game and for the assistant coaches of both teams, who communicated with the head coach on the sideline via headphones.

This day, in hopes of turning around the fortunes of the lowly Hounds, Coach Dwyer had decided *he* would view the action on the gridiron from that lofty perch, transmitting his orders to his top assistant at field level.

The structure was open on all four sides, allowing wind, rain, snow, and other elements to challenge further each of the occupants in their various responsibilities. Access to the tower was a simple unenclosed ladder. One climbed at his own risk, so "acrophobes beware." And handicapped access wasn't even a passing thought.

It was Homecoming Day at Indiana Central, so when "Biggie" mounted the ladder for the trek upward he was to look out over the largest crowd of the season seated in the bleachers just below him. The opponent was archrival Franklin College, with its vaunted passing attack under their wily coach Red Faught. There were always offensive fireworks when the Hounds and the Faught-coached Grizzlies got together, with most of the explosives provided by Faught's wide-open, high-scoring aerial show.

Faught was considered a genius by his coaching peers for his innovations in the passing game. He designed the "run-and-shoot" offense, a commitment to a wide-open passing game that was emulated by major college and professional coaches alike. He took teams with inferior athletes, placed them in his system, and literally outscored his frustrated opponents. His commitment to offense was total, so the opposition always had to be prepared for anything that might come out of his arsenal. During a particularly brutal three-year stretch, Faught-coached teams outscored the Greyhounds by a total of 113 points to 22: 1967, 32-0; 1968, 41-14; and 1969, 40-8.

Keyed up for the challenge Faught and his lads presented, Coach Dwyer couldn't stand still. As the kickoff neared, everyone on that tower was aware of his presence, because when the massive 300-pound coach paced about like a caged lion, the tower trembled.

During the initial quarter of the game, Biggie's new coaching tactic from on high seemed to be paying off. Communicating through headphones to his assistants below, coach Dwyer was calling plays masterfully, anticipating the Baptists' defenses so well that the Hounds marched flawlessly down the field on their first possession to score a touchdown for an early lead.

Defensively, Biggie's calls stymied Faught's clever passing attack, resulting in Franklin being forced to punt the first three times they possessed the ball.

When the Hounds drove down and scored again to take a 14-0 lead, it seemed Coach Dwyer had struck the equivalent of football nuclear fission.

But Faught had a deep bag of tricks, along with a speedy wide receiver whose athleticism was superior to any one of the Hounds' defenders. The Franklin coach began to call plays to utilize the small but crafty pass catcher, exploiting ICC's weakness.

Twice on identical plays, which had the wideout opposing man-to-man coverage by the Greyhound defense, the Grizzly quarterback laid the ball in the receiver's hands behind the defense for long touchdowns.

The Hounds adjusted, though, at Biggie's command to "double team" the fleet Franklin receiver. So the leak in the dike was at least temporarily stanched.

Late in the third quarter, however, with the Hounds clinging to a precarious 14-14 tie, Franklin broke the huddle. The slender gazelle in football pads came loping toward the Greyhound side of the field with the Hounds in single, man-to-man coverage! That the time bomb in blue was lined up with only one Greyhound defender between him and the goal line didn't escape the shrewd eye of Coach Dwyer. He hissed into the mouthpiece of his headset, "Get Ruster over to help on number 26."

Seeing no response to his directive as the Franklin players got into their stances at the line of scrimmage, Dwyer shouted more fervently into the microphone "Get help on 26! Double up! Double up!"

At that moment the Greyhound assistant on the field with whom Biggie had been communicating removed his headset, turned, and looked up alarmingly at the coach in the tower. The distraught aide pointed to the headset with a bewildered look on his face, then shrugged to signal that he couldn't hear Coach Dwyer. The electronic communication system had malfunctioned.

The Franklin QB began to bark signals. Noticing that the Greyhounds had only one defender within twenty yards of this favorite target, he stood up, cupped his hands around his mouth and shouted a predetermined command to change the play he had called in the huddle. He was obviously going to throw to #26.

Biggie, frantic now, put his hands around his mouth as well and hollered to the coach on the sideline, "Double 26! 26! Get help on him!"

The confused assistant, unable to make out what Coach Dwyer was trying to say over the noise of the crowd, simply shrugged again, putting a hand to his ear to indicate he didn't understand.

The Franklin signal caller began: "Blue—49! Hut! ... Hut!"

Now Biggie, panicked: "Number 26! **Double!** *Double!*"

The confused sideline coach: "Huh?"

Biggie: **"26! 26! GET THAT *SONUVABITCHIN'* 26!"**

An expensive public address system—which Indiana Central didn't have—could not have carried Coach Dwyer's comments more clearly to the crowd below him. As his booming voice swept over the multitude, about 2,000 heads turned quickly upward to see from where came the anguished, and profane, plea.

I'll leave it to those of you familiar with the demographics of Indiana Central alumni in 1969 to calculate how many of that Homecoming crowd were members of ... uh ... the "cloth." Disapproving scowls bore into that huge figure of a man as he forlornly watched fleet #26 speed right by the desperate ICC defender. The blue-clad lad was a full fifteen yards behind everyone when the ball launched by his teammate nestled softly into his waiting arms. He crossed the goal line with the score that doomed the home team to another disappointing loss, a play that the indignant alumni ministers completely missed in their duty to express their silent stares of disapproval at the impiety of the coach.

To my knowledge, Biggie never again ventured up the tower during a game he coached.

Every small college coach dreams of recruiting that one great athlete who will make a dramatic impact on his program. For instance, in 1994, new Greyhound mentor Joe Polizzi recruited Kevin Kreinhagen, who had originally signed to attend the University of Louisville. When Louisville's Howard Snellenberger departed to become head coach at Oklahoma, Kreinhagen accepted Polizzi's offer to come to Indianapolis. Kevin would be the catalyst for one of the finest four-year stints in U of I football history. Kreinhagen still holds most of the U of I career passing records and led the Greyhounds to records of 8-3 (1997) and 8-2 (1998). But athletes such as this were rare at our school in the Dwyer days.

So covetous was the coach of landing a prize recruit, he pored over the various Associated Press and United Press International High School All-State teams in 1968 with the intent of perhaps persuading one of Indiana's elite high school players to energize the struggling NAIA program on Indy's Southside.

James L. Brunnemer

As he read the names of the all-state first team in the *Indianapolis Star*, his eyes fell on the quarterback at South Bend Adams High School. This teenager was the standout player on one of the best high school teams in Indiana.

As the first team selection at quarterback by sportswriters across the state, he was a highly sought-after prize. IU, Purdue, perhaps even Notre Dame in his hometown would pursue this top athlete.

Getting this boy's name on a grant-in-aid at Indiana Central would be akin to my dialing up Bill Gates, "cold," asking for a million dollars for our school, and his agreeing to write the check! Long shot. Lotto-like odds. Lonnnnnng shot.

But what did he have to lose? figured Biggie. So he looked up the telephone number of the high school one afternoon and dialed the coach's office. When the high school football head coach answered the phone, Biggie got right to the point. (I wasn't there, but this is the gist of the conversation.)

"This is Ed Dwyer, and I'm the football coach down here at Indiana Central. I wanna know if your quarterback has signed with anybody yet?"

There was a pregnant pause at the other end of the line when the coach answered, "Well, no, he hasn't."

"Good," Ed responded, "If the kid will come down here I'll offer him a full ride right here on the phone."

The high school coach, a bit puzzled at this unusual offer for a player of his, "sight-unseen," replied, "Coach, I'm sure he'd be happy to consider your offer. Are you pretty confident he can play in your league?"

Sensing a possibility to land what could be perhaps the best high school prospect in the history of the school, Biggie began to wax eloquently about the youngster and his potential not only to play, but also to dominate our league.

Dwyer no doubt could visualize conference champions, national playoffs, and unbeaten seasons with such a stalwart field general at the head of his offense.

The high school coach was a bit overwhelmed at the loquaciousness of the ICC coach, but he promised to talk with his quarterback about the offer.

That same day, the coach of the quarterback called back to Dwyer, with the young recruit in his office. Then he put the teenager on the phone.

"Hello, Coach," a somewhat shy and trembling voice said from the other end.

"Hi, kid," a confident Dwyer replied, then launched into perhaps his finest recruiting pitch ever. Biggie was not deterred, even when the youngster questioned his own ability to play at the ICC level. In fact, Biggie was pleased at the lad's modesty.

"He's a great prospect and humble as well," thought Ed.

So the offer for a full grant-in-aid was made by the elder, and accepted by the younger. A date for a visit to the campus by the prospect was agreed upon. That night Biggie Dwyer no doubt went to bed a happy man, visions of championships dancing in his head.

The day came when Ed Dwyer's savior at quarterback arrived on the Indiana Central campus. Accompanied by his high school coach, the happily smiling quarterback walked into the football office.

Thrusting a huge right hand toward the youngster, a gregarious Biggie said, "Coach Ed Dwyer. Nice to meet you!"

Distinction Without Pretension

Accepting the handshake, the young man responded, "Russ Flueckiger. Great to meet you, too, coach!"

No one knows if this was the moment that Biggie realized the quarterback prospect standing in front of him—the one to whom he had, by phone, committed a fully paid athletic scholarship—was not the first team all-state quarterback for South Bend Adams High School, but Russ Flueckiger of *South Adams High School.*

Biggie had recruited a quarterback from Geneva, Indiana, whose high school was about one-tenth the size of the South Bend school.

Russ was not a bad quarterback. And he was truly an outstanding individual, bright, hard-working, with great integrity. He was pleased as any young competitor his age would be with an athletic scholarship from a college. Fleuckiger became a minor celebrity in his small town, "the kid with the full ride from Indiana Central."

When Russ arrived in the fall at the campus, his initial shock came in the locker room.

"I'd never seen players this big before," he was to say years later. "And when we went onto the field, I could see I was out of my league. These were *men,* and they could *play*!"

To his enormous credit, and characteristic of the true gentleman that he is, Coach Dwyer never once implied that Flueckiger didn't belong. Nor did he ever consider negating Russ's scholarship, even though it was within NAIA rules to do that. Russ was faithful in his commitment to the team, never complaining, never missing practice, and doing his job to the best of his ability. And he never took one snap from center in a real game in four years.

Russ has made a very comfortable living as an insurance representative in his hometown of Geneva.

Without doubt, the lowlight of those years occurred in the 1969 game against Anderson College when the Hounds offense scored 43 points—and still lost by five touchdowns! The 78-43 pasting by the Ravens was emblematic of U of I's porous defense, which allowed an all-time record 41 points per game to the opposition for the season. One wag reading the score asked if the basketball season had started early!

Finally, in 1970, in desperation, President Sease called upon Dick Nyers to resuscitate the by-now nearly comatose Greyhound football program.

CHAPTER XV
WHY SHOULD I SAY I SEE WHAT I SEE NOT?

You can observe a lot just by watching.
Yogi Berra, Hall of Fame baseball
player and noted philosopher

As a result of riots provoked by perceived LAPD brutality of a young black drunken driver, ashes in the Watts section of Los Angeles were still smoldering when I returned for my senior year at Indiana Central. Reverberating on college campuses across the land were echoes of protesters shouting in cadence, "Hey, hey, LBJ! How many kids did you kill today?" Such was the American socio-political climate in September of 1965.

Except for the fact that I would join my good friend and mentor, Rich Reasoner, as his student teacher at Belzer Junior High School, the fall term seemed little different from the previous six. The real students continued in their studious ways while we children of a lesser ilk parlayed our college refinement into more novel and ingenious larks.

Prior to returning for the fall semester, Roger Walter had purchased a rusty, smoke-belching '55 Pontiac Bonneville for the princely sum of fifty bucks. He got what he paid for. Hissing and coughing the better part of the 150 miles from his home in Butler, Indiana, to Indianapolis, the bucket of bolts and bailing wire made it to the corner of Otterbein and Windermire, wheezed its death rattle, and stopped cold. Roger persuaded a couple of fellow Buxton Hall residents to push the clunker to the front of the dorm, where he proceeded to unload his things and carry them into the dormitory.

Now, Roger had neither the money nor the intent to have the car repaired. He'd only spent what he did for one-way transportation to college. So the lifeless pale blue Pontiac sat where it died, in September, through the end of Christmas vacation.

Because the junker was located directly in front of the walkway leading from the front door steps of Buxton to the street, seniors residing there had to detour around the car on the way to class. Although it took but a few extra steps to bypass the pile of rubble, college students, being the energy-economists that they are, grew steadily agitated at Roger's old wreck. So after a few weeks, enormous dents appeared in the side of the vehicle. What had been the headlights were kicked out and some irate student had broken the radio antenna off, for a fishing pole or something.

Guys even defied the antagonizing pile of iron by simply leaping onto the hood and stomping over the top of it!

It was alleged that Roger's cousin, Morris Walter '67, made lemonade out of the blue lemon. Rumor was that he'd started renting the backseat of the Bonneville to eager lovers who had no private accommodations elsewhere on campus to share *amour*. Such numbers of hot-blooded students were desperate for cheap space for their trysts that Morrie

James L. Brunnemer

had to start taking reservations.

At the beginning of the spring semester, Roger was in his usual impecunious state. He called several used car dealers, hoping to sell the car for cash to purchase his books for second semester. To his surprise, no one wanted to buy the bargain-basement Bonneville. Finally, Roger hooked up with a junk dealer in Beech Grove who offered to come take it away for ten dollars. Roger's zoology textbook alone cost twenty-five. Never before or since have I heard of a guy selling a car worth less than a schoolbook.

Meanwhile, the student I expected to be my roommate had decided not to return to school. On registration day, I was in search of another to share my modest abode in Wilmore Hall. After having my favored option overruled (Dean Wooden would not allow me to set precedent by inviting any of a number of coeds I would have been happy to room with), a male sophomore student in a similar bind and I were brought together.

For reasons of delicacy I'll call my delightful new residence-sharer "Bobby Ray." A preacher's kid, B. R. was an affable sort whose face was perpetually adorned with a mischievous grin. His wasn't a handsome face, but in a rough-hewn, country sort of way he was irresistible to women. It was Bobby Ray whom Mark Twain was describing when he invented Huckleberry Finn.

B. R. didn't differ from most other guys at the college, except in one way: every evening he disappeared from the campus. He was a real ladies' man. Some guys took to calling Bobby Ray's 1958 Chevy the "Mayflower," because so many Puritans came across in it. He purportedly juggled his schedule to meet his women ("nude, lewd, and tattooed," he described them) in various locations around Indianapolis.

I would see him twice a day. The first time was usually about eleven o'clock in the evening when I returned to the room just as Bobby Ray was heading out for the evening. I'd be in the bathroom next morning, before class, when the boy would drag in, a broad grin covering his face and a gratified gleam in his eyes.

One wintry morning as a group of us stood outside the door of Wilmore complaining about traversing a snow-covered campus in a ten-degree chill for our 7:45 a.m. class, B. R. came to the rescue. He offered to drive us there, as his car was still warm from the previous evening. He had just gotten in.

God, how we envied him!

During the last week of the semester the dreaded final exams were looming. Those of you who were like me, and unlike the dedicated students such as Dick Cravens or Joe Hughes who actually stayed even with the material *during* the semester, know the drill. "Goof off," pay only enough attention in class to get by, then cram like Hades in the two nights before finals to try to save your academic be-hind.

So it was that I found myself toiling miserably at three a.m. on a Tuesday night studying for the terror-test of all: Professor James Weber's seventeen-page final in Old Testament. I've wondered since about God's role in inspiring the premierly pious Dr. Weber's efforts that produced such an examination from Hell. If anything was the work of the Devil it was this torturous exercise. It was the intellectual equivalent of the Bataan death march. I mean no disrespect, but there were casualties, many casualties, as a result of Weber's fiendish exam.

My resistant brain was saturated with as much biblical information as it could absorb, including all the kings of Israel (chronologically); that the Pentateuch was the five books of Moses; who "Bar-jesus" was; that Noah was 600 years old when the floods came; and that why you never see a unicorn today isn't really because "them silly unicorns was playin'" and got left behind, like the Irish Rovers tried to convince us in song. At just after the third hour that morning, I slogged to my bed to get what rest a shameful procrastinator could in the few hours left before the 7:45 a.m. reporting time.

I had just turned down the covers of my top bunk and was walking toward the light switch when the door to my room swept open and there stood Bobby Ray, a picture of utter bliss spread across his face. It was apparent B. R. was *walkin' down Main and feelin' no pain.* The satisfaction expressed on his countenance implied that his night out had been hedonistically fulfilling. His brain was as besotted as mine, but not with Biblical facts.

Before he could launch into details of his escapades of the past several hours, I reminded him of something he'd no doubt forgotten in his revelry: "B. R., are you ready for Doc Weber's Old Testament final tomorrow?"

Stunned silence answered my query. The look of satisfaction in his eyes turned to anguish. His shoulders sagged. One might say his look even revealed a bit of fear. He still didn't reply.

Bobby Ray sidled slowly over to his bunk, dropped to his knees, folded his hands, and lowered his head as he placed his elbows on the mattress top.

This was a total surprise. Had B. R. become repentant of his behaviors? Had his conscience finally overcome his tendency to pleasure? Did the corner in which he had painted himself bring him to his knees in confession, seeking forgiveness? I was witnessing a real-live epiphany here.

B. R. began to pray softly, respectfully. But the substance was probably not that which he had learned from his preacher-father:

"Lord, you and me both know I gotta have at least a B on Weber's final tomorrow," B. R. whispered, mournfully. Then, "Lord, please don't let Doc ketch me cribbin' on that test."

With an "Amen" to punctuate his plea, Bobby Ray crawled into his bunk and was fast asleep before I could turn out the light. He slept as peacefully as an innocent babe over whom God provides his loving grace.

B. R. passed the test. With a B. I got a C+.

Last time I looked, he was providing moral teachings and admonitions as a teacher of high school youth in a south-central Indiana village.

In four years at Indiana Central I had only one evening division class. Most of the instructors in the night school were "adjunct," not regular faculty members. The attraction of "tuition lite" and the close proximity of the college to downtown Indy resulted in a steady stream of eager working adults invading the campus after regular hours as part-time students to boost their academic and employment status.

One cold and wet November evening I was listening to the lecture of a president of an Indianapolis bank. It was an awful night. The temperature had plummeted, in the space of an hour, from a tolerable thirty degrees to a frigid five below zero. Howling wind and rain turned to sleet, rendering the icy streets of Indianapolis nearly impassable. Most of the students, being adult, nonresidential learners, had not made the effort to show up.

James L. Brunnemer

About fifteen minutes into the lecture, however, the door to the class suddenly flew open, banging against the wall, revealing a pregnant commuter in the doorway. She was soaked to the bone, her hair was drenched, and water dripped off her jacket to form puddles beneath the hemline of her shift. Stumbling upon entering, she dropped her armload of books with a loud, embarrassing clatter. At that moment all pretensions of instructor-student protocol dissolved. This conscientious coed had been pushed beyond the limits of endurance and decorum by this final humiliation. With a withering glare leveled at the bemused prof, she fairly snarled, "This better be *good*!"

In order to attend to all the various jobs necessary to run the athletic program at Indiana Central, an obvious pool of cheap labor was the athletes themselves. Thus, players having athletic grants-in-aid were assigned to clean latrines, mop and vacuum floors, and, supervised by the head of the Maintenance Department, to paint the sports facilities. Sometimes you got lucky and drew an easy assignment, such as popping corn for home athletic contests.

In December of 1965, Bill Tutterow and I found ourselves in charge of the popcorn machine at a basketball game. We were novices at the intricacies of producing popped corn from the kernels put in our command. Our inexperience resulted in a disaster and a windfall on the same night. After successfully popping two batches of corn, with just the right amount of oil and butter added, we thought this wasn't a bad deal. Having eaten about half of our product, we were stuffed as we neared completion of the third go-round. However, this time, while adding salt to the mix, the perforated lid on the eight-ounce saltshaker fell off, spilling the entire contents of the container into the corn we had popped. Panicked, we were considering our options when we saw Nick scaling the steps from the floor of the gym to the concourse surrounding the arena. He was headed right toward us.

We had mere seconds to refill the container before the athletic director/coach joined us behind the popping machine. Without a word, Nick lifted the pewter salt container and began to add, liberally, to the already salt-saturated corn.

"Sells more Cokes if the popcorn is on the salty side," he said.

Nick had no idea how salty *all* sides of *that* corn were now.

We filled the cardboard boxes as folks lined up to pay twenty-five cents for a twelve-ounce serving. Within minutes, our customers began to return, gasping for liquid relief. Throughout the game, queues snaked outward from the concession stand as every ounce of Coke products in the fountains was bought and consumed by the parched-mouth popcorn purchasers. Lines at the water fountains held more fans than the bleachers.

Nick mentioned to me on Monday how pleased he was that we had completely sold out every ounce of soda. Across the campus, Leo Miller was surely perplexed as to why the university water bill for that month was astronomically high!

Just before Christmas vacation I received a telephone call that every senior on the cusp of graduation desires. Mr. Lloyd Hiatt, my junior high school principal of whom you read earlier, called to invite me to interview for a teaching and coaching position at Belzer Junior High School for the following fall. All went well, and before the Christmas holidays I had a signed contract in my possession.

Knowing where I would be working after graduation did not increase my attention

Distinction Without Pretension

or motivation toward outstanding scholarship in the spring. I sloughed off even more. In my newfound status as an assured wage earner, I had become a bit haughty toward my professors' attempts to further enlighten me. But in a way I couldn't have foreseen, a simple interrogatory sentence, from an obscure poet, would have a lasting effect on how I would henceforth view the world.

To complete a minor in English, I had enrolled in an elective class entitled Victorian Poetry. Victorian poetry was like a foreign language to me. I just never could get it. Furthermore, I was of the opinion that this arcane poesy had little application to how I would be earning my living come fall.

Dr. Kellogg took great pleasure in reciting verses from the dais while the rest of us followed along in our textbooks. The erudite Dr. K. was willowy, even delicate of frame, with a long face devoid of emotion most of the time. He would somberly recite a stanza of Victorian darkness. Learned aesthete that I was, thinking those particular lyrics to be humorous, I would break out into loud and most embarrassing laughter. Conversely, Kellogg might be reading lines that evoked tears in my eyes, only to see him pause, place delicate but long and bony fingers to his mouth, and, to my amazement, begin to titter, indicating, of course, that I'd swung and missed again.

Now at least once, every student has regurgitated material without really understanding it. Me, I made a science out of the practice. But while committing to memory verselets from an esoteric poet, I came across a line that described precisely how I felt about Victorian poetry.

From a quite unrenowned bard of the Victorian era, Arthur Hugh Clough (1819-61), I read this: "Why should I say I see what I see not?" This lament pertained to his skepticism of the prevailing intellectual thought of the age and his refusal to accept that which clashed with his logic. A more celebrated poet of that day, Matthew Arnold (1822-88), eulogized his friend, Clough, in verse. It was Clough's single-minded search for truth that Arnold extolled in *Thyrsis*, calling his contemporary the "Gypsy Scholar."

For me, it was an illuminating concept leading me to an honest assessment of my shallow understanding of Victorian poetry. Further, for me that simple logic and its reverse—"Why should I not say what I see?"—provided a basis for inquiry with which I would, in the future, test those great imposters: pretense, hypocrisy and falsehood.

Even Al Capone, crass criminal and murderer that he was, could be excused for revealing a truth about the duplicity of law and justice in the 1920s when he observed:

> When I sell liquor, it's called 'bootlegging.' When my
> patrons serve it on silver trays on Lake Shore Drive,
> it's called hospitality.

Dr. Kellogg assigned a final paper that would count twenty-five percent of our semester grade. It was then I determined to declare my academic independence by challenging the renowned scholar. With the courage of "a Christian holding four aces," in Twain's words, I wrote an earnest assessment of my lack of understanding of the subject. With energy and conviction, I discussed why college students like me would pretend that we both knew and *liked* the subject. Despite the fact that I could manipulate my way to a passing grade without cheating, it seemed wrong to have to resort to simple rote memory to be appraised by the professor to have a certain level of expertise, when in fact I did not.

I thought that out of my honest attempt to engage Dr. Kellogg in some form of debate regarding academic integrity, he might view me as a student with a legitimate and respectable point of view. To my chagrin, he merely graded the paper of which I was so proud for grammatical structure. He made no comments nor offered congratulations for my attempt to provide worthy feedback. He gave me a C grade. That was worse than getting an F for a rebellious act. I felt as I if I had authored a candid observation, dripping with principle, but received no reward.

I must admit I think Dr. Kellogg considered me too much of an intellectual lightweight to invest his time.

That exercise was not wasted, however. An important lesson was learned. Even I, undistinguished thinker that I was, could choose to question authority. I decided to no longer surrender my curiosity or skepticism for the sake of convenience or avoiding confrontation. Basically, I determined not to accept at face value another's views without knowing the facts. Simply because a person was, or was perceived to be, of higher intellect or station in life than I, did not relieve me of the responsibility of *thinking*. I learned to distinguish between shit and Shinola.

My eighth grade-educated Dad, who was and is yet my greatest hero, would be proud that somewhere in the college experience I had begun to use "common sense." According to Marilyn Vos Savant, common sense is:

> [g]ood judgment that arises from no particular source of learning and is present in varying degrees from person to person, regardless of his or her intelligence. People are capable of all kinds of good thinking, but some just don't see what's right in front of their noses.

Famed author Gertrude Stein said it a different way decades ago: "Today information is plentiful, but wisdom is scarce."

That was Dad's specialty, his unfathomable homespun wisdom.

The obscure poet, Clough, served to encourage me to inquire about, rather than accept, that which figures of authority claimed to be true. It was a critical lesson for me and has been useful in cutting to the truth throughout my life.

As winter days rotated into spring, my focus turned to my final season of intercollegiate baseball. Steve Lemme was among those I met at ICC whose friendship I came to cherish during our four years together. He played an extraneous role in one of my memorable incidents on the baseball field.

When we traveled to Terre Haute in March that season to play the Indiana State Sycamores, snow flurries were swirling in the old Three-I League Stadium that ISU used as its home field. The dugouts were below ground and the roof was a flat concrete shelf projecting outward to shield players further from the elements.

In the fourth inning, Steve Hollenbeck of ISU lifted a towering pop fly into foul territory along the first base side of the infield. At the crack of the bat I picked up the flight of the ball. It was headed toward the grandstands behind our dugout, about thirty feet from where I had positioned myself on the diamond. Thinking I had a chance to catch the ball, I pursued it, gathering speed as I closed on it. But just as the ball fell into my glove, the lights went out.

I had plowed amain into the protruding dugout roof, chest high. Needless to say the dugout didn't budge. When I woke up seconds after the collision, I was certain I'd never breathe again. My lungs weren't working. What little oxygen I could inhale came in wee gasps.

An ambulance was called to take me to the ISU infirmary, where X-rays revealed a badly bruised sternum but no broken ribs.

What remains of this mundane event is the response of Steve Lemme. The big redhead was a backup to me at first base all four years. He rarely had the opportunity to play. As I lay on the ground, Bright signaled Lemme to warm up. He would be my replacement.

As they gingerly lifted the stretcher to put me in the ambulance, my teammates filed by. Steve, now ready to enter the game for one of his infrequent appearances, stopped long enough to lean over and confess, "I'm sorry, pal. That was me, hollering 'Plenty o' room, Brum. *Plenty* o' room!'"

Any former Greyhound who played basketball in the old Taylor University gymnasium will remember that the floor was about twenty feet short of the standard length (ninety-four feet) of a college court. Also, an ancient circular game clock there, which resembled an ordinary wall clock, had an unusual characteristic. When that particular time clock with the second-hand moving around toward 00:00 reached the three-second marker, it would suddenly lurch to zero, eliminating the final three seconds of the contest. It was important only when a team was trying to score a tying or winning basket at the end of a game.

Once, in an intense affray in the unfriendly confines there, the Greyhounds had control of the basketball, behind one point, with ten seconds showing on the Taylor scoreboard clock. Nick must have forgotten to remind his boys of the clock's flaw, or else he designed an eight-second play. With Clark Crafton dribbling the ball, preparing to pass or shoot the last-second shot, the clock reached the three-second mark and characteristically leapt to 00:00 before a shot was taken! Stunned, the team, Nick, and the Greyhound fans screamed for justice. But the officials left the floor, and Nick's coaching arch rival, Don Odle, walked across to offer a handshake to his counterpart.

Stalking into the visitors' dressing room where the players were fuming, an irate Nick offered this: "What you get when you come to Taylor is a good Christian screwin'!"

It was that remark I recalled during our baseball game with Taylor in my final season. Mike Mancini was an outstanding football and baseball player for the Trojans. He stood about 6'4" and weighed on the north side of 240 pounds. Prior to our taking the field, Mancini approached me, stuck out a friendly hand and said, in a genuine tone, "Good luck to you today, brother, and may God bless you and keep you."

"Uh, may ... uh ... God ... yeah. You, too, Mike," I managed to stammer, in reply. I'd never had an opponent invoke God's blessings on me prior to a game. That was cool, I thought.

In the first inning, Mancini came to bat with two outs, no runners on. He hit a ball to third base, where Roger Walter handled the pick-up and fired it to me at first. His throw, however, was wide to the home plate side of first base, necessitating my stepping into the baseline to retrieve the throw and try to get back to tag the bag to retire Mancini. Never having been inside a bullring with an angry *toro* trying to impale me on his horns, I

James L. Brunnemer

cannot say for sure what happened next is in any way similar. But the snorting and heaving emanating from Mancini as he crunched up the base path, I can still recall. And when his head, then shoulders collided with my rib cage, I swear those bones on the left side of my chest melded with the ribs on the right. The last thing I remember was his size twelve baseball cleats branding my head as he tromped over me. (Today Mike serves ably as a representative of Holy Cross College near South Bend, Indiana.)

I recollected then what Nick had said about good Taylor Christians.

A memory was made when I was on the other side of the blindfold for the rite of passage of athletes receiving their first C-letter award. One part of the hazing during the letterman's club initiation entailed mass mayhem. The new letter-winners always wondered why one item they were required to bring to the ritual was a newspaper. They were about to find out.

Some forty fear-filled and fresh letter-winners trekked to the gym to join the C-Association the evening following the spring sports banquet. Inside, blindfolds securely in place, the by-now jockstrap-only-clad inductees were herded by us veteran lettermen into one corner of the basketball court. The nervous horde was instructed to kneel down and cluster together in a tight circle.

At a given signal, each of the athletes would use his newspaper as a weapon, swinging randomly in the attempt to thrash all those in his vicinity. As far as I know, no one was ever seriously hurt by this newspaper gang-fight. It made for a lively interchange among the new men and a wildly funny sight for the upperclassmen. Rookies were warned to swing like they meant it, else the paddles they had fashioned for the veterans would be used on them instead.

So they always went at it with a will.

As they knelt there, shoulder-to-shoulder, the eager young naked men were coiled in anticipation of the mayhem. Suddenly, baseball teammate Jerry Mullinix noticed something amiss.

"Hold it!" he cried out. All those poised for the start of the spectacle froze.

Steve David, who had won his initial moniker as a cager for Nick, was wielding a newspaper that resembled a medieval mace. He had purchased a Sunday *Indianapolis Star*, rolled it tightly into a club of about three feet in length, and wrapped electrical tape around and around the thick paper. This wasn't a newspaper. It was a lethal war club Geronimo would have been proud to use on white settlers in the Arizona Territory.

Someone had obviously tipped off Steve as to why he was to bring a newspaper with him.

Directly in front of Mr. David knelt Jerry Seay, a freshman baseball letterman and teammate of Mullinix and me. His position suggested he was prepared for beheading by an executioner. Confused as the rest of the horde gathered there on the gym floor because of Mullinix's interruption of the proceedings, Jerry prepared to do his duty armed with a *Perry Township Weekly*. Not to denigrate that Southside publication, but as a weapon it had about the strength and thickness of two-ply toilet tissue. Rolled up in Jerry Seay's hand, the flaccid newsprint folded in the middle and drooped downward.

Mullinix stepped down from our observation post in the first row of the gym bleachers and made his way through the packed humanity to where David and Seay were.

Distinction Without Pretension

"David!" Mullinix commanded when he reached the armed ocean of nudity. "Trade papers with Seay!"

I think I heard an audible "Gulp!" from Steve David.

Neither David nor Seay could see the other, of course, because of the blindfolds. But even though one could only observe the lower half of his face, David's look of chagrin at this turn of events was easily apparent. When, with Mullinix's help, the two unseeing men swapped papers, David realized the advance warning he'd received had backfired ominously.

When he traded his toilet tissue for David's war club, Seay's startled expression quickly turned sinister. He surmised in a heartbeat that before that exchange the playing field for at least one of his fellow inductees had been tilted grossly in that rogue's favor. You had to believe Jerry Seay was motivated to exact a hefty payment for the scofflaw's scheme.

Mullinix turned Seay around to face David, lining him up perfectly square with a target he couldn't see but wouldn't miss when the action started. A contrite David was no doubt trying to think of some plan to avoid the inevitable.

Leaning over to whisper a last bit of information to Seay, Mullinix then told the group leader, "Okay, we're ready now!"

In a whit, Goliath had become David.

At the signal, Seay, who batted cleanup for our baseball team, used his experience with a Louisville Slugger with maximum efficiency and devastating results on the body of his fellow inductee.

Steve didn't even attempt to swing the pathetic Perry newspaper. He assumed a fetal position to fend off the blows raining down on his head, neck, shoulders, ribs, arms, and legs by the powerful and accurate swings of Seay.

When the group leader finally halted the sea of naked humanity from pummeling one another further, Steve David had sustained bruises he wouldn't forget for a while.

Jerry Seay had beaten the dog-poop out of David with Steve's own weapon.

In May of my senior year, days before Commencement, I was surprised by a call from President Esch asking me to meet with him in his office. (What had I done? Could he rescind my diploma at this late hour?) Dr. Esch flattered me with an offer to become an admissions counselor for the institution and to begin immediately. Dr. Esch was not aware that I'd been offered a teaching position by ICC graduate Lloyd Hiatt at Belzer Junior High School, where I had done my student teaching under two other ICC alumni, Bob Theil and Rich Reasoner. When he learned that I had already signed that contract, all discussion of the possibility of my joining the university ended. President Esch was far too principled to suggest I negate that contract, even if I had been tempted to do so, which I wasn't.

Of course, five years later, in May 1971, my old coach Bill Bright would call on behalf of President Sease to ask if I would be interested in returning to the college as its alumni director.

It was a warm and humid day when I found my place in line along with more than two hundred of my fellow black-robed graduates-to-be of the Class of '66. Following the student marshals directing us to rows of folding chairs on the gymnasium floor, we marched to the processional "God of the Ages." The organist played briskly and trumpeters blared majestically "da ... dadadada-da-da-da" as proud parents and family looked on.

Under the east basketball stanchion in the school's gymnasium a stage had been constructed where sat President Esch, a couple of dignitaries who would receive honorary degrees from the college, and the Commencement speaker.

Roe Bartle was a huge man, well in excess of three-hundred pounds on a frame over six feet-four inches in height. His reputation as an orator was just as large. Known as "the Chief" in Kansas City, where he had served ably as the most popular conservative politician in that city for many years, he had traveled to ICC in May 1966 to address our graduating class. As mayor of Kansas City, Bartle's influence and persistence had secured the old American Football League franchise for his city and state. In gratitude, the team took their official name, "Chiefs," from Mr. Bartle's moniker.

Highly sought-after as a speaker, Roe Bartle had an impressive stentorian voice, which he manipulated artfully from barely a whisper to a booming baritone.

With students in rebellion and campus disruptions common all over the nation, Bartle could hardly believe his eyes as he observed the clean-cut ICC crowd. On most college campuses, the Beatles' influence upon hairstyles among the young men of the day was instantly apparent, as was the scruffy facial hair of the hippie that many male students emulated. But not at Indiana Central.

After being introduced by Dr. Esch, the Chief stepped behind the dais and cast his eyes slowly across the two hundred pairs of eyes beneath the mortarboards before him. As a preamble to his prepared remarks, he spoke resonantly, carefully enunciating each word:

"IT'S A PLEASANT CHANGE FOR ME-A ... TO BE IN THE PRESENCE-A ... OF A COLLECTION-A ... OF YOUNG PEOPLE-A ... WITH WHOM I CAN DISTINGUISH-A ... THE GIRLZ-A .... FROM THE BOYZ-A!"

Grateful parents, gathered to see the fruits of their labors, not to speak of a considerable cash investment, exploded in applause. They were proud of the Chief's acknowledgment that at least in this audience the decadence of student defiance across the rest of the country had not despoiled the morals of *their* offspring.

As I joined with lifelong friends and fellow graduates Jack Leonard and Dick Elmore for post-Commencement pictures on the ICC lawn, we began to peak over the horizon. The future looked rosy. All three of us, and another baseball teammate, Steve McGee, had purchased our first new cars the previous month. Four brand-new 1966 Pontiac LeManses, each of a different color, were parked side-by-side in the lot, attesting to our new freedom and promise of good things to come. Symbolic of our common naïveté, the LeMans model would prove to burn nearly as much oil per mile as gasoline, just as our futures would engage us in realities unforeseen.

It was a volatile world awaiting us ingenuous youths. At about the same time I was walking across the platform to receive my diploma from President Esch, a man named Larry Gwin, 25, was performing on another stage half a world away. On May 6, 1966, Gwin, who would survive to earn his law degree at Boston University, was a combatant in the "battle" of Thanh Son 2, Vietnam. The carnage included a number of children and old couples, unintentionally killed and maimed in a U.S. artillery barrage.

Gwin's valedictory on the war in Vietnam: "Everything we did over there was a waste."

Only weeks after we left the safe confines of Indiana Central, a black sharecropper, Ben Chester White, was lured into the Homochitto National Forest near Jackson, Mississippi, ostensibly for a day's work. His last words before being slaughtered by a shotgun blast were "Lord, what have I done to deserve this?" His crime was the same as Medgar Evers', and that of four pre-pubescent black girls in Birmingham, Alabama, all of whom died because of the color of their skin. Justice would prevail in each of these murderous acts. For Mr. White's family, it would come on February 28, 2003, when white supremacist Ernest Avants, 72, was convicted, thirty-seven years after the crime he committed the same month of my graduation from college.

Still in our future were events of universal significance: An American named Armstrong would bounce along the surface of the moon three years and two months after we had graduated. A decision by the United States Supreme Court, in the case of Roe vs. Wade, would create a schism in our culture in 1973. One year after that, Richard Nixon's resignation would follow what would become known as the Watergate scandal. We would witness an American humiliation with the fall of South Vietnam in 1975, and America's first brush with the terror of a near nuclear meltdown occurred, in 1979, at a place called Three Mile Island in Pennsylvania.

Nineteen-eighty would be the year America would elect as its president a former actor who would come to be called "the Great Communicator." The year Ronald Reagan became chief executive, scientists first detected a virus called "AIDS." On a chilly January day in 1986, a nationwide television audience saluted elementary teacher Christa McAuliffe and her NASA mates with a *bon voyage*, only to watch in horror minutes later as the space ship *Challenger* exploded and fell into the sea.

"Black Monday," when the Dow Jones Industrial Average fell by 22.6 percent, preceded by a month the breakup of the Soviet Union in 1987. And millions around the globe became ecstatic just two years later, celebrating and cheering Germans on as the Berlin Wall fell. The first high-tech war, "Desert Storm," would be beamed into American homes in brilliant color by CNN in 1991. Multi-billionaire Bill Gates in 1993 would proclaim the Internet to be comparable to the printing of the Gutenberg Bible in terms of communications advancements.

Not long after the twentieth century turned into the 21st, international terrorism would come to the shores of America. The hijacking of four commercial aircraft, two of which slammed into both towers of the World Trade Center in New York in 2001, triggered a reaction in America not seen since Pearl Harbor.

In 2003, the anniversary of my birth, February 1, was altered for all time. Never again will I celebrate a birthday without sharing that day with memories of the catastrophic fate of the crew of the space shuttle *Columbia*. And war with Iraq became a reality after the United States broke ranks with the United Nations to, in essence, eliminate the evil dictator, Saddam Hussein.

These were events yet to be lived by a naïf who went to sleep that warm May evening in 1966 dreaming of changing the young lives of junior high kids who were clamoring, "Teach me concepts! Teach me concepts!"

Gee. Ya' think?

CHAPTER XVI
RETURN OF THE NATIVE

*The past is the present, isn't it? It's
the future, too. We all tried to lie out
of that—but life won't let us.*
                    Eugene O'Neill

In June 1971 Richard Nixon was in the White House. Fewer than ninety days previously, the Supreme Court had unanimously upheld busing as a means of achieving racial balance in U.S. schools. Living, and still collecting government pensions, was a handful of widows of veterans of the *Civil War*.

After four years of teaching and coaching at Belzer Junior High School in Lawrence, Indiana, I took a leave of absence to complete a master's degree in education. It was after completing studies at Indiana University that my plan to resume a teaching career took an unexpected turn. A telephone call from my former coach at Indiana Central, Bill Bright, ignited the chain of events that led me back to my alma mater.

Dean Ransburg, who had earned the Distinguished Alumnus Award for his work as alumni director at ICC, had accepted a job at another institution. Coach Bright called on behalf of new president Gene Sease to ask if I might have interest in succeeding my friend Dean.

Shortly afterwards, I found myself in President Sease's office, trying to fathom why I might be considered college administrative material. Recognizing that I would have no great difficulty returning to the teaching profession if things didn't work out, I agreed to give it a try. The salary offer of $10,500 was about the same as my combined salaries as a teacher and summertime director of Lawrence Parks.

Following the initial interview with any applicant for an administrative position, it was the practice of Dr. Sease to invite a serious candidate to a second session accompanied by his or her spouse, if the candidate was married. I remember only one comment President Sease made to Lu and me as we arose to depart at the conclusion of the joint interview:

"Very nice to have met you, Luella," he pleasantly offered. Turning to address me, Dr. Sease continued, "After having visited with the two of you, it's apparent, Jim, that you over-married."

I could have told him that. But he hired me anyway.

The Indiana Central College to which I returned in late spring of '71 had not changed drastically since my graduation five years earlier. Answering machines were live people. You didn't leave voice-mail messages. You just called back or left a note with a human person intended for the staff member with whom you desired to speak. E-mail, with all its wonders and pitfalls, was decades away. Our computers were barely more than glorified card files, as I recall. Personal communication, agreeable or otherwise, brought people together to solve or clarify issues without impersonal, antiseptic, sometimes-hostile electronic transmissions confusing the issue.

James L. Brunnemer

The author as a thirty-something director of alumni relations at Indiana Central, circa 1977.

      PCs? CDs? DVDs? Are you kidding? We used typewriters or stenography to produce written correspondence. We were still listening to 45s, 78s, and 33 and a 1/3rd synthetic discs on "record players." Stereophonic sound was a recent development, and LPs (long playing records) were in vogue.

      Each dormitory was equipped with a single black-and-white television in the lounge. Students could watch any channel they wished, as long as it was WTTV-4, WFBM-6, WISH-8, or WLWI-13. Cable TV and its hundreds of choices was well beyond the horizon.

      A study by Royal Phillips Electronics in 2000 revealed that forty-four percent of America's homes had at least six TV/stereo remote controls. In 1971, I was only a few years removed from having *been* a "human remote." (If a channel were to be changed, my Dad would turn to me from his favorite "Archie Bunker" chair and say, "Change that over to channel six." I'd rise up from my comfy spot on the couch, spin the dial, and adjust the "rabbit ears" antenna.)

      Johnny Carson, not David Letterman or Jay Leno, was King of the Night after the late news. Mary Stuart was reigning soap opera queen and "Search For Tomorrow" her popular medium. Unlike the occupants in dormitories (are they still called "dormitories?") on campuses today, with personal televisions in every room, students in the early seventies didn't spend much time following those daytime dramas.

      Students still wore hard contact lenses then. I heard the term "microwave" only in terms of some mysterious radio or television transmission. A "church key" opened bottles,

Distinction Without Pretension

the caps of which could not be screwed off by hand. Families with children usually drove the un-chic "station wagon," forerunner of today's multipurpose vans.

In 1971, 435 high school teams were eliminated from the Indiana State High School Basketball Tournament before *one* state champion was crowned (East Chicago Washington). This was down from six-hundred-eighty-eight hopefuls only a decade before, but far more than the three hundred high school teams competing for *four* championship trophies in 2003.

Dr. Sease introduced, as hosts and guides for various campus events, a group of personable and bright students he called "presidential aides." That would be changed to "president's assistants" in the 1980s with the discovery and subsequent epidemic of Acquired Immune Deficiency Syndrome.

Michael Jackson was just a sprite of a lad, still one of the Jackson Five.

America and President Nixon were desperately seeking an honorable means of pulling out of Vietnam. While I have few regrets in life, never serving in the military is one. The military draft was reinstated in 1968. Thousands of young Americans crossed the border into Canada in order to avoid military service. As an educator with a wife and two young dependents, I was classified 4-A by the draft board in my native Morgan County. I didn't enlist but expected to be drafted.

Many men of that era who were not called to military service felt grateful. I rue never having served my country in uniform, although my feeling doesn't stem from a sense of guilt. I just have an enormous respect and sense of appreciation for those who interrupted or gave their lives to serve on behalf of our country.

This was a day when the number of faculty and staff of ICC was still small enough to gather on a daily basis for a ritual long gone now. Beginning at nine a.m. in the faculty dining room we bonded as a community, if not a family, over coffee and rolls. Discussing topics both inane and material, from the superiority of Brand X over Tide to how one coped with a dying relative, there was a true sense of *esprit de corps* among the maintenance personnel, support staff, administration, and faculty that engaged in mutual labors for our modest school.

That is the ICC and the America I remember at the time I accepted the position of director of alumni relations in the spring of 1971. Over the following nine years it would be my privilege to become acquainted with literally thousands of alumni and friends of ICC/ICU/U of I.

Now that I was an administrator and faculty member, I wondered how I would address Dr. Robert Cramer, the austere, intimidating, Yale-educated academic dean. On the second day of my new employ I rounded the corner on the first floor of Esch Hall, nearly running over the eminent Dr. Cramer. Immaculately dressed, the unruffled dean smiled wryly and with the nonchalance of one who might have been my colleague for years, said, "Hi, Jim."

"Uh … hi … uh … Dean Cramer. How are you?" I managed to stutter. This was the guy who once threatened to kick me out of school for excessive Chapel cuts.

"Fine, fine. Say, that's a nice suit you're wearing," he kindly commented. But before I could thank him for a genuinely nice remark that made me feel comfortable in his presence, he added coyly, "Too bad it doesn't fit."

With a chuckle of one who knew he had disarmed me and altered the image I had of him as a stiff, humorless, and unreachable superior, he turned and continued down the hall.

All those years that dignified exterior had hidden a regular wiseass. From then on Dr. Cramer and I would get along just fine.

Initially, I really wasn't certain what my job was at the college. I guess I was sort of an ambassador to the alumni constituency, charged with making friends and identifying potential prospects for financial support of the college. I enjoyed the friend-raising part, but I wasn't sure about fund-raising. Seemed kind of oily to me. Little did I know then how I would come to embrace the importance of private support for independent colleges and spend more than thirty years in college advancement.

Among the first junkets to the land of the alumni on which I embarked was a gathering at a now-forgotten EUB church in a northern Indiana town. I had persuaded Ken Partridge to accompany me as the program speaker for the evening.

It was the practice then to hold our alumni chapter meetings at churches affiliated with the institution, generally in the basement social room. In coordination with the host, usually an alumnus who was a member of the church, the college would provide the main entrée. Generally this included a baked ham or fried chicken, along with the beverage, iced tea. Folks attending would bring a covered dish of some kind to share. And believe me, ICC had many wonderful cooks among its alumni.

On this particular trip I didn't expect a deviation from the norm. Although the gathering took place more than thirty years ago, this event is one that Partridge has never let me forget.

When Ken and I entered the church social room we couldn't help but notice all the elderly ladies escorted by equally grizzled men, most of whom were attached to aluminum walkers. I mean, the youngsters in the crowd were octogenarians.

The real significance of this didn't strike Ken and me until after the customary ten-minute pre-meal prayer, when we were sent to the front of the food line. Guests first, you know.

Arrayed beautifully before us were (I swear) twenty-seven different kinds of Jell-O salads. All the colors of the rainbow were represented in the chilled fare on the table. Nary a potato was in sight, not even mashed. No green beans, no corn, no broccoli, no trace of baked beans or anything else that might fill a hungry man's stomach. Nothing but yards and yards of soft and easily digestible Jell-O.

I sampled, perhaps, a baker's dozen of the gelatinous cubes while piling a liberal helping of the sliced ham onto my dish. Ken, likewise, forked onto his plate about a seven-inch high stack of pork. We were the only alums present who would savor the pithy part of the meal. Denture danger, no doubt, for the rest of the multitude. I had never appreciated more that gang in the Bible who had only fish and bread to eat while listening to Jesus' Sermon on the Mount.

When the time came for the program, it was traditional to invite each of those present to introduce themselves and say "a word or two" about their experience at ICC.

Typically, older alumni rhapsodized about the hallowed days at their dear old school. Often, en masse, the group would break out, a cappella, in the *Alma Mater*. It was a real and heartwarming extemporaneous salute to memories of days gone by.

What I hadn't anticipated was the rather remarkable performance of an alumnus,

Distinction Without Pretension

whose fifty-fifth class reunion would be celebrated at Homecoming a couple of weeks afterward. He began by telling about his freshman semester in 1913, then continued to regale the elderly audience with recollections from every subsequent year up to this September day in 1971. The man had Alzheimer's in *reverse*: he remembered *everything* that had ever happened to him. Forty-five minutes later, with half the crowd now in slumber, alumna number two introduced herself.

By the time it was Ken's turn to make his presentation, fully three-fourths of the audience had nodded off.

I can't swear by it, but I think Ken's carefully crafted address was condensed to, "Hi. I'm Ken Partridge, director of management programs at the college. Good night, and drive safely."

"Indy's Top Dog"—now there's a subject to ponder. Over the decades students, faculty, and alumni at the U of I have quietly and patiently endured the misperception that Butler University is somehow superior in quality to their institution. The local media, among whom have been and are found numerous grads of Butler, have perpetuated the puffed-up image that the Butler community has of itself. U of I has ceded the propaganda war to our "elite" northside neighbors, while taking satisfaction in its own reputation, as one visiting accreditation team described it, as having "distinction without pretension." U of I people simply do not take themselves nearly so seriously as our picayunish neighbors to the north.

In 1969, under the leadership of President Gene Sease and athletics director Angus Nicoson, Indiana Central joined the National Collegiate Athletic Association (NCAA) and, subsequently, the Indiana Collegiate Conference. Prior to that, Indiana Central was affiliated, athletically, with the National Association of Intercollegiate Athletics (NAIA), which existed primarily for small independent colleges and universities. A charter member of the Hoosier College Conference, Indiana Central had competed with Earlham, Hanover, Taylor, Franklin, Anderson, and Manchester since 1947.

Entering the new conference, the Greyhounds would vie with Butler, Evansville, DePauw, St. Joseph, Wabash, and Valparaiso in intercollegiate athletics. The move from the NAIA to NCAA membership was considered to be a step forward for our sports program.

From 1971 through 1993—1992 according to Butler, but I'll explain that discrepancy later—the Greyhounds of ICC played the Bulldogs of Butler in football for the Indy "Top Dog" trophy. For a couple of decades this game came to symbolize the genuine respect (and of some, the enmity) existing between members of the two rival institutions that are located on opposite ends of the city of Indianapolis.

In November 1971 the Indy Top Dog football series between the Bulldogs and the Greyhounds was inaugurated. The Top Dog activities proved to be instantly popular as alumni from both schools, numerous in and around the state of Indiana, took up the cry for annual bragging rights. Each fall the game drew the attention of local media and alumni of the schools. The respective alumni letterwinners' associations of the two schools combined to sponsor the Top Dog trophy, which featured a chain of links made of emblems of Bulldogs and Greyhounds.

The match between the two Indianapolis universities was a natural, now that the U of I was a peer conference member with Butler. The intensity of the action and perennial

James L. Brunnemer

closeness of the games provided attractive entertainment. Many Indianapolis-area players who had opposed one another in high school rivalries would renew their competition in this small-college football series. This was before the NCAA messed up a great thing by surrendering to the King Football lobby to establish divisions based on the amount of money colleges were willing to invest in their intercollegiate athletic programs.

The initial game in the series was preceded by a luncheon at the Murat Shrine to promote the contest. Coaches Dick Nyers of ICC and Bill Sylvester of Butler and their teams were hot topics of local media in a buildup to the game. The Greyhounds, of course, were huge underdogs. In the two previous years the Bulldogs had trounced ICC by 57-0 and 35-0 whitewashes.

Emotions were high by the 1 p.m. starting time at Butler Bowl on Saturday. The game would prove to exceed the hype.

The day was cold and dank, with leaden skies hanging low over Butler Bowl. A determined Nyers had his team prepared for what would be his finale as Greyhound coach.

The game was conspicuous for the punishing defense by both teams. Greyhounds Doug Seminick, D. J. Hines, Steve Wheatley, and Oscar Gardner stymied the Bulldog offense, allowing no points through the first three quarters of the game.

Behind fullback Rick Sidebottom, who carried the football a school-record forty-one times that day, a determined offensive line and the passing duo of brothers Phil (quarterback) and Mike (flanker) Eads, Coach Nyers's lads held a 17-0 lead as the fourth quarter began.

Butler, stung by the fact it was being beaten up on its home turf, came alive. When the Bulldogs pulled to within five points at 17-12, momentum was clearly with the Northsiders. Late in the final period Butler was driving relentlessly toward what could be the winning score when the Greyhounds' superb linebacker Oscar Gardner slipped inside Bulldog receiver Tom Redmond to make a diving, skidding interception at the ICC eleven yard line.

With time running out, the Hounds failed to move the football against the now very stubborn Bulldog defense. With only twenty seconds remaining in the game, punter John Mitney retreated on fourth down inside his own nine yard line. BU put all eleven men on the line of scrimmage in a last-ditch effort to block the kick. As the ball was snapped to Mitney, the entire Bulldog eleven charged ferociously through the Greyhound line. Mitney strode forward, sweeping his leg into the football as the swarm of navy blue jerseys converged on him. Obliterated by the flying mass of Bulldogs, Mitney somehow exploded the ball out of the human wreckage.

The ball soared, the longest and highest punt of Mitney's career. Finally, it hit the turf, bounced, rolled and rolled, inching now, finally stopping dead on BU's twelve yard line. The seventy-nine-yard punt would set a new school record!

However, nine seconds remained, still enough time for a desperation pass. And as long as Butler had life, this game was not over!

But wait. Crumpled on the ground next to Mitney, who lay entangled among the seven Bulldogs who smothered him, was an official's yellow flag! What glimmer of hope BU had nurtured was now snuffed! Given a first down by the roughing-the-kicker penalty, the Greyhounds had only to hike the ball, quarterback Eads drop to his knees, and the game

Distinction Without Pretension

would result in a monumental upset! And that is just how the first Indy Top Dog game ended.

More than thirty years later, Coach Nyers, his voice choking up even then, related to the writer the emotions he had felt before, during, and after that game:

"I had already decided to leave Indiana Central," Nyers recounted. "And I told that to the team in the locker room just before we went out for the opening kickoff. I never had a team that so committed itself to winning a game for me as that bunch of guys did that day.

"There was no reason to believe we could beat Butler. Their program was far in advance of ours at that time. But Oscar, D. J., the Eads brothers, Rick, Steve, Doug, all of them, put their hearts and minds together for the victory. I've never been prouder of a team as I was of them."

The 17-12 triumph assured the first link of the Top Dog trophy chain would be a Greyhound. That game was to be a measuring stick for succeeding Top Dog contests. It was always bloody and spirited when the Dogs and the Hounds clashed on the gridiron.

Nyers resigned following that historic win. He and Nick, then athletics director and basketball coach, could not coexist. The competitive fires that fueled each man were no doubt a major factor in their inability to get along. It was a classic clash of men with remarkably similar personalities having different agendas.

Riding back to the campus with Nick following the momentous upset, I expressed concern about the outcome of the football game. The Bulldogs would have extra incentive to avenge this defeat in our basketball game later in the year. Ever the competitor, Nick confided, "They won't have an excuse when we beat 'em then, will they?"

That November at Hinkle Fieldhouse, Indiana Central played its first game as an Indiana Collegiate Conference basketball opponent against Butler, which was led by Billy Shepherd and Oscar Evans, two standout performers. Nick's Greyhounds took a surprising early lead over the Bulldogs, but behind the slick 6'4" Evans, who would score 44 points that night, Butler rallied, slicing a twenty-point lead to five with under three minutes to go. The wily Nick called time, switched to a zone defense that completely befuddled Coach George Theofanis's team, and the Greyhounds pulled away for a 105-95 triumph. J. D. Layman '73 and Todd Whitten '72 were catalysts for the Hounds in the upset win.

And Butler really didn't have any excuses.

The rivalry was made even keener from the Bulldog standpoint because of another pre-game event established the second year of the Top Dog series. It was proposed that representatives of the two varsity club associations be brought together for a golf match on the Friday prior to the game. Each team was to bring eight players to the event that was held at a local country club.

This proved to be a huge mistake by the Bulldog alums! I don't remember whom they brought to compete with our team. As alumni director, I had the responsibility for recruiting Greyhound graduates for the match. At tee time of the appointed day, a squad of ICC alumni had assembled who I felt confident would be the equal of any similar collection of golfers that Butler could put on the links.

Mickey Powell '61 and Don Bisesi '61, each of whom had won the Indiana PGA individual tournament multiple times, were our top players. Dave Baril '76, Denny Dennett '72, and Mike Dickey '72 each was a club pro who, like Powell and Bisesi, were among the

James L. Brunnemer

finer players in Indiana professional ranks. Adding top-flight amateurs such as Jack Noone '67, Woody McBride '52, and Fred Belser '63, we fielded an excellent team. I made certain I was the "coach" of these alumni, because victory was as certain as the sunrise.

We stomped them, with Mickey Powell carding a 33 on the back nine for a medallist score of sixty-eight. The best score from a Bulldog alum was sixth-best in the field.

Members of the ICU alumni golf team that humbled a similar group of graduates from Butler prior to the 1973 Indy Top Dog football game. Led by Mickey Powell (center, holding the winners' plaque), who would later serve two terms as president of the Professional Golfers Association (PGA), the team members were (from left) Jack Noone, Mike Dickey, Fred Belser, Woody McBride, Powell, Denny Dennett, Don Bisesi, Dave Baril, and "coach" Brunnemer.

Of course, that would be the first and the last Butler-Indiana Central Alumni Varsity Club Top Dog Golf Classic. After absorbing that humiliating defeat and no doubt recognizing that our players would still be in top form for years to come—we weren't graduating any seniors, after all—Butler simply refused to play us anymore. Pounds of class, Butler. Pounds.

After The U of I won the initial Top Dog football game, Butler would win fourteen of the next twenty renewals of the rivalry, with two contests ending in ties. A gauge of the closeness of the two schools' teams is that thirteen of the games were decided by a touchdown or less.

The 1972 Top Dog game was a classic. It also was the debut of a young Butler quarterback who would be the primary reason his team would not lose to the Greyhounds in the four years he played. Billy Lynch's mastery in the Indy Top Dog series was one in

Distinction Without Pretension

which even the most ardent Greyhound fan had to admire.

Another brutal defensive struggle in the second Top Dog Game played at the new Key Stadium found ICC clinging to a 7-0 lead in the final minutes of the game. Dodging here and there to escape flying Greyhound tacklers again and again on a final march down the field, Lynch found back Bob Grenda streaking down the sidelines with a perfect pass with less than a minute to play for twenty yards and a touchdown. Eschewing the kicked extra point and a tie, Coach Bill Sylvester called the play to try for two points and a win.

Rolling to his right, Lynch was almost run out of bounds by the Greyhounds when he spotted Grenda, in the endzone only inches from the sideline. Lynch's precise bullet pass was snared by Grenda as he sprawled earthward, toes of both feet clinging to the turf scarcely inches inside the white lines of the end zone. Two points. Butler wins, 8-7!

The following year, at the 1973 Top Dog pre-game banquet, I was sitting with Doc Dill, as then-Bulldog captain Bob Grenda spoke for the Butler team.

Doc muttered, "That sonuvabitch cost me $150 in last year's game!"

"Doc," I said, "I didn't know you bet on the games."

"Hell, I didn't lose a bet," he countered. "I gnashed my damn teeth so hard on that winning conversion last year that I broke a cap!"

The Top Dog rivalry ended ignominiously twenty years later. Butler had a dilemma. In the early nineties, Butler's administration had determined no longer to offer grants-in-aid in football because the program had become too expensive. This was an unpopular decision among many of their alumni like Lee Grimm, Ronnie Adams, and other former Bulldog gridiron greats.

However, in order to maintain its Division I-A status in basketball, Butler either had to drop football altogether or disguise itself as a Division I-AA football program by agreeing with other schools with a similar predicament to play one another while not offering football scholarships. The Indianapolis media has conveniently looked the other way at this hypocrisy.

The transparent Division III Bulldog football program has not escaped the unrelenting eye of Jeff Sagarin, however. A 1970 M.I.T. mathematics graduate, the Sagarin Rating System is a complex formula that is one measurement used by the NCAA to determine teams for the Bowl Championship Series to determine the national champion. In the Sagarin ranking of all two-hundred-forty Division I-A and I-AA in 2003, the Bulldogs were recognized as the 239th best, with lowly Siena College the only Division I-A and I-AA football program worse than the Bulldogs.

One difficulty with the ruse in 1993 was that Butler could find too few schools in similar straits to fill its schedule. They found it necessary to travel from coast to coast to schedule enough opponents. So after unceremoniously dropping the Greyhounds after the 1992 season, BU's football coach called the U of I in late summer of 1993 seeking a game. Greyhound coach Bill Bless readily agreed to the contest.

As a member of NCAA Division I-AA, Butler could have offered as many as sixty-three grants-in-aid, but, of course, was offering none. The Butler athletic honchos apparently reasoned that the competition in the Top Dog game was somehow not fair because the U of I offered the allowed complement of thirty-six scholarships under Division II rules. So they audaciously let it be known through the local media that the game wasn't "official." Anticipating inevitable defeat, the Butler sports media unilaterally announced,

James L. Brunnemer

casually, a week before the 1993 Butler-U of I football game that the contest was just an "exhibition." To their way of thinking, the Top Dog Trophy—emblematic of superiority on the gridiron between the schools—would not be a prize to the winner of the game. Of course, U of I kicked Bulldog butts, 34-21, but the memorial to victory stayed in the BU trophy case. And no one out there even had a red face.

As director of alumni relations, promoting the institution to its graduates was my primary function. Aiding me in this task was a staff of four, including Wilma Kyriasis '63. A charming graduate of Indiana Central, Wilma replaced my classmate and friend Beverly Gorbett '66 as editor of the alumni periodical in 1972. One summer day as I was passing Wilma's office I heard her laughing uncontrollably. This seemed a bit odd, for she was alone at her desk. After composing herself, she told me of a strange phone call she had just received. Wilma explained that when she picked up the telephone to make a call outside the campus, someone was on the line. In those days that kind of thing occasionally happened. Why, no one ever knew. After realizing she didn't have a dial tone but a breathing human being on the line, Wilma asked, "Who is this?"

"Who's this?" replied a male voice at the other end.

"I asked you first," countered Wilma.

"I'm Tom," the stranger partly identified himself. "And you?"

"I'm Wilma," my colleague replied.

There was a brief pause, when Tom asked, "Well ... now that we know each other Wilma, let's have an affair."

A somewhat discombobulated Wilma, convulsing with laughter, managed to reply, "Are you married, Tom?"

A short pause. "Yes. But I'm not *fanatic* about it."

Peals of laughter from Wilma. "As much as I'd love to, Tom, I just don't have time," she said, with finality.

"Well, then, bye, Wilma. Have a great life!"

"You, too, Tom! Bye!"

Annually facing the challenge of filling the freshman class, admissions director Dave Huffman was under constant pressure, competing with counterparts at other schools for the pool of high school graduates available. Remember, with Indiana Central's miniscule endowment, student tuition was critical to paying the bills.

As with most professions, admissions people seek out peers at other colleges to share successes, techniques, new concepts, and, in some cases, mutual woes. Dave once related, with a chuckle, the results of an informal survey he and his fellow admissions officers from other Indiana independent schools conducted at one of their annual conferences.

It had been a rough year for all, and as each admissions head reported the percentage of students enrolled that fall at his or her college, the statistics became successively grimmer.

Earlham College: "We're down four percent from last year."

Butler, down five percent.

Indiana Central, off five and a half percent.

Taylor: "We're in a panic. Our numbers are down twelve percent compared to last year!"

Franklin College: "We're up fifteen percent."

Hold it!

Heads around the table, until then bowed in communal distress, jerked upward. The speaker was Edward "Eddie" Teets, the slight Franklin admissions director whose horn-rimmed glasses over shifty eyes gave him the appearance of an owl.

As others expressed astonishment at this implausible report of success, Teets, who would later be elected mayor of Franklin, Indiana, elaborated: "Well, we expected to be down by twenty percent in student enrollment, but we're only down five percent. So we're up by fifteen percent, aren't we?"

Statistics are all about how one reports them, Huffman learned that day.

An uplifting reunion of two friends one spring afternoon led me to discover that I am bilingual in the English language. Really.

Jim Shaw earned his bachelor's degree at Indiana Central in 1964. At the time of this incident he was visiting my office as a newly confirmed member of the Alumni Association Board of Directors. In his real job Jim was vice president of Midwest Financial, the first banking institution in Indianapolis with majority African-American ownership. A terribly bright and engaging man, Jim was preparing to leave following our meeting when the name of Mary Busch was mentioned in relation to a program sponsored by the university.

"Does Mary *work* here?" Jim asked.

"Sure, Jim," I replied, "Mary coordinates our Community Relations program."

"No kidding? I haven't seen Mary in years," he commented.

"Would you like to say 'hi'? Her office is on the next floor."

"I'd love to see Mary," Shaw said enthusiastically.

So off we went.

Before I share what happened next, let me say to you that Jim Shaw and Mary Busch are immaculate practitioners of the English language. Each articulates flawlessly, with grace and dignity, and is unfailingly correct in linguistic communication.

We arrived at Mary's office and the secretary waved us through the doorway. When the two old friends first saw one another, their faces expanded into broad, warm, enthusiastic smiles. Jim moved to embrace Mary in a massive hug, face beaming, and said something that sounded like, "OohbabyIcain'tbleeveyoumommayoulookinsoooogooodmaryhowyoudoinchile?"

Mary's voice went up two octaves as she nearly shouted back, "Omanwareyoubeehidinyougoodlookingdogyoulaintneverlordysakes!"

I was stunned at how these two pillars of proper parse had so easily fallen into a singsong, giddy, black street jive. It seemed obvious that, upon seeing one another after so long, their speech patterns had reverted to an earlier day, to a time when there was no pretense, no need to be "proper," when each lived by another linguistic standard. It was enchanting to see how very fond of one another they were, how genuine the feeling of friendship between them, and to see the sheer, unbridled joy they shared in meeting again.

Somehow, for me, this scenario rang a tiny bell in my subconscious. There was something familiar in this exchange between two old friends.

James L. Brunnemer

Later it struck me. Being the only graduate of my family to have attended college, I often felt self-conscious when I returned to my Morgan County home. Something within me was uncomfortable in wearing my "college-educated" veneer when in the presence of my parents, sisters, brothers-in-law, aunts, uncles, cousins, and other family members. That attained "educated" language of mine served, in my unconscious mind, to divide, to separate me from my family. So I would mask that by regressing into the patois of my pre-college days. My word endings were dropped ("nothing" became "nuthin'") and "ain'ts" returned to my speech. I said "them there," instead of "those." Even my tone became more nasal, which traditionally accompanies the familiar central Indiana idiom. It was an entirely different dialect within the English language.

I hadn't really thought about it, nor examined the phenomenon of "slang-uage," until observing that remarkable interchange between my friends Jim and Mary.

Wilma Grosskopf is destined to be Saint Wilma in Heaven. She is the wife of George Grosskopf '50, a longtime and enormously popular athletics administrator at Pike High School in Indianapolis. George was among the alumni I met early on in my role as director of alumni relations.

Anyone who has spent even a little time with "Gross George" has a favorite story to tell of his outrageous antics. At more than 350 pounds in his adult years, it might be surprising to know that George Grosskopf was a svelte champion sprinter and pole-vaulter at Indiana Central.

Larry Hanni '58 told of a time that three athletic directors—he (Franklin Central), Marion Fine (Ben Davis), and Grosskopf (Pike)—traveled to Iowa to attend a national conference for high school ADs. George provided the transportation, an aging, rusty, garish pink station wagon, the rear compartment of which was liberally stocked with iced beer and snacks of all sorts.

Being a teetotaler, Hanni was the designated driver (before that term became vogue). Pulling up to the Hanni residence, Big George slid over to the front passenger seat and Hanni took the wheel. As the three traveled along Interstate 70 through the Indiana countryside, George would constantly prod Hanni to speed up to pull alongside other cars, buses, and semi-trailers, where Grosskopf would lift his beer in salute.

Until stopping for fuel at a roadside station in Illinois, Hanni was puzzled by George's tomfoolery, and by the often astonished and sometimes disgusted visages of the other travelers. As he went around the car to pump gas into the tank, Larry read, haphazardly painted in giant orange letters along the entirety of the passenger side of the vehicle, hastily slapped on by the car's owner, this:

INDIANAPOLIS BAPTIST CHURCH GOSPEL SINGERS

Market Square Arena, built in 1974, has come and gone. Along with the Indianapolis Fairgrounds Coliseum, the Hilton U. Brown Theatre, Clowes Hall at Butler University, and the Murat Temple, MSA was among the very few buildings satisfactory for attracting concerts or performances of major entertainers in 1970s Indianapolis. Any follower of Elvis knows he "left the building" into eternity at age 42 following his last concert on earth in MSA in Indianapolis in 1977.

Setting up the stage for the January 29, 1972 performance of Sonny and Cher, whose variety television show had rocketed to #1 nationally only months before they came to Indiana Central. Humor most foul was delivered to the conservative ICC audience by a then-unknown comic who would later become a stage and screen star of legendary proportions.

    With the construction of what was to become Nicoson Hall in 1960 the college was able to take advantage of the seating capacity as a potential venue for entertainment. The student government, Central Council, with support of faculty advisors, annually booked performances through Mr. Bob Young of Sunshine Entertainment. Such events benefited the student body, and, depending upon the appeal of the act, the greater Indianapolis community. It was never the intent to make an enormous profit off the shows. Leo Miller just insisted that the affairs not *lose* money.

    Although the school wouldn't risk the guaranteed front money that major "hot" attractions demanded, entertainers of some note such as Mac Davis, the Lettermen, James Taylor (with a spontaneous appearance of his then-wife, Carly Simon), and others less familiar came to the campus to perform for appreciative audiences.

    In fall of 1971 Central Council signed a contract with an up-and-coming but certainly not nationally acclaimed duo, Sonny and Cher. Salvatore Bono and Cherilyn Sarkisian would make their distinctive marks first in popular music and television as a couple, then later as a congressman (Sonny) and an award-winning actress (Cher).

    At the time they agreed to an appearance in the Indiana Central gym, they were only on the verge of making it big. This was one stop on a "red-eye" tour that they had agreed to for the income. But it was notable that in January of 1972 Sonny and Cher

James L. Brunnemer

debuted with a one-hour variety show on CBS, shortly after recording their first hit, "I Got You, Babe."

Little could the staid Indiana Central community and their student council have imagined that between the signing of the contract and their scheduled appearance at the college, Sonny and Cher would become a national phenomenon. Their weekly gig became one of the highest-rated programs in television history.

Sonny (later Congressman Bono) and Cher, who would become an internationally celebrated entertainer and actress, as they appeared before their appearance at the Indiana Central gymnasium in January, 1972.

On the twenty-ninth of January, Indiana Central would host the hottest act in show business in its gymnasium! (The stock contract for that evening likely guaranteed less than they now paid their chauffeur!)

Rumor had it that the agent for Sonny and Cher tried to get out of the contract, but

Distinction Without Pretension

in those days signing your name to a legal document meant you agreed to the terms of the deal. They showed up at ICC the night following another ratings bonanza for CBS.

A raised platform was constructed for the show and placed in the middle of the basketball court to form a stage in-the-round. The house was packed. With seating on the floor of the arena and standing room, there may have been 8,000 in attendance.

When the house lights went down and a young comedian with an oversized head atop a thin six-foot tall body appeared in the spotlight, there was a sense of pride and anticipation by those of us affiliated with the school. Luck and opportunity had collided to enable us to pull off this coup. Indiana Central had hit the big time!

Imagine the collective elation of ICC students, administration, and alumni turning first to shocked surprise, then to chagrin, on to mortification, and finally, to *despair* as this shy-looking man with a fake arrow through his head opened the show for the main act and proceeded to spend one-half of an hour polluting the somewhat sterile air of the conservative Indiana Central environment with a rapid-fire series of the most vile and lewd jokes!

This was not what one heard when watching the "Sonny and Cher Show" on Thursday nights. One realized that the television industry's censors really did have a reason for existing.

But an interesting dilemma was created by the comedian's presentation. This man was **foul**. And *hilarious!* How was one to respond? Did you strike a mildly disgusted, dignified pose, signaling your disapproval of this type of muck being spread on your home court? Or did one give in to natural instincts for detecting humor and convulse with laughter as the situation demanded?

After a particularly gross string of one-liners, the comedian—who by now you have guessed was a young, not-yet-internationally-famous Steve Martin—broke off his muddy monologue with this:

"Okay, let me see. Are there any kids here under six years old?"

Shielding his eyes with his hand against the glare of the spotlights, Martin peered into the crowd. A few scattered little hands were cautiously lifted upward.

"Okay, I got a joke for you. There were these two lesbians walking down the street, and ... " Nervous laughter spilled out of the crowd in response to Martin's spoof.

I caught a glimpse of President Sease and wife Joanne seated about ten rows up near where the west basket was located. Indiana Central's chief executive officer was mortified. His stone-faced expression communicated raw disgust and full-gauged fury. The comedic superstar-to-be was not tickling Dr. Sease's funny bone.

Joanne sat next to him with, I swear, a bemused, if somewhat bewildered, look on her usually beatific face. Always the epitome of grace, she was rolling with the punches. I imagine Gene was trying not to meet eye-to-eye with any of the trustees who might have come for this cultural event, especially those representing the Evangelical United Brethren Church.

The warm-up act left the stage to a smattering of polite applause, or maybe it was a signal of relief from those assembled. Indiana Central audiences were not accustomed to this brand of humor. I've wondered since then if now, after more than thirty years as an entertainer, and considered by many an icon of American comedy, Steve Martin might recall that performance in Indianapolis early in his career. How would he remember Indiana

James L. Brunnemer

Central?

After a bit of fanfare by the band on one side of the stage, on came the main event.

A twenty-something Cher was dazzling in a long sheer white gown slit to her hip, revealing shapely lean, long legs. I haven't mentioned yet that Lu and I were seated in the sixth row, our wooden folding chairs, at most, thirty feet from the stage that rose about six feet above floor level. Lu hadn't questioned when we left home why I would pack my binoculars. And with the lights lowered she wasn't immediately aware that I had brought them up to my eyes. From less than ten yards away, 20' by 40'-powered field glasses revealed every pore of the goddess Cher's body. I had panned slowly upward from her ankles to about mid-thigh when my blatant lust was rudely interrupted by a tomahawk chop across the binocs. The deliverer snarled, "**JIM!**"

What was the problem here? I thought we'd been married long enough by then for her to know I was a crass degenerate.

I have to admit that Sonny and Cher didn't cheat the audience just because they were in "India-no-place" and tiny, and some would say ultraconservative, Indiana Central. They were charming, clever, and witty, delivering a marvelous performance. Neither approached the base humor of the warm-up comedian. They were "naughty, but nice." They left their encore number to a standing ovation.

I didn't see Dr. Sease following the show.

In terms of his commitment to making a difference, no president of the Alumni Association surpassed Gene Lausch '60. Gene was the first president in memory actually to "run" for the office. Most of those who became the head officer of the organization needed to be cajoled or drafted into service. A truly bright and genuinely kind man whose friendship I have enjoyed since we worked together then, Gene was passionate about Indiana Central, but he also had issues with the school and had determined to address those through the alumni organization. He was impelled by a genuine sentiment that the school wasn't living up to its potential. In becoming directly involved, he demonstrated the integrity and use of his intellect and energy toward causes for which he truly cared. He may have been the finest president the association ever had.

A 1960 graduate, Gene went on to earn his law degree at the University of Michigan, and he can be fairly credited with being one of the moving forces behind the scenes in the remarkable growth and development of the city of Indianapolis from 1970 through the turn of the twenty-first century.

I've always admired Gene's command of the English language. A master of the ironic turn of a phrase, he speaks and writes extraordinarily well. To observe Gene responding to a question or comment is, for me, a real treat. Without fail, Gene will pause thoughtfully before reacting to a comment or a query. His visage communicates deep cogitation if confronted with a poser, a quizzical look of bemusement if the question is preposterous or inane, or he'll grin broadly and chortle if he's truly amused. What typically follows is an impressive, pithy, esoteric utterance, perfectly parsed. He's a joy, truly, to josh. Light banter is the only level at which I can ever really engage Gene. He's way too smart for me to spar with on serious issues.

Another most enjoyable Alumni Association leader with whom I was privileged

Distinction Without Pretension

to work was Mary Kay (Coon) Anthony '65. In contrast to Gene's more serious and formal style, Mary Kay used her charm and unabashed down-home common sense to get at the heart of matters. After her election as president, we met to discuss her agenda for the year. When I asked what she would like to accomplish first, Mary Kay avowed without hesitation, "We've *got* to stop the reading of those dreadful 'dead rolls!'"

She was speaking of a tradition embraced by and sacred to a segment of older alumni. Each year, in celebrating the Fifty Year, or "Golden" graduation anniversary, it was customary to read the necrology report. Solemnly, with an alumna playing an excruciating death knell on the organ in Ransburg Hall, the name of each graduate who had "passed on" in the interim between the last meeting and this one would be mournfully read aloud. I think even the dead being honored resented this horrid practice, and Mary Kay decided it would end. And it did.

A similarly tactless tradition that well-meaning members of the board had instituted was the seniors' "welcome" into the alumni association at Commencement. When I was instructed by the chairman of whatever committee was in charge of the first contact from the alumni body to the new graduates, I did as I was told. A card table covered by a cloth was stationed just beyond the stage in the gymnasium where each graduate would pass by after receiving his or her diploma. As the beaming, freshly commenced degree holder approached the table, the Alumni Association president proffered a handshake of congratulations, then pressed an envelope into his hand. For the majority of the graduates, the letter was innocent enough, simply a greeting welcoming the neophyte into the alumni brethren.

But it became a cause for consternation among some of the graduates. Though few students were aware of it, a $2.50 fee was charged each semester to every student for operating expenses of the Alumni Association. If a student attended all eight semesters, he had unknowingly contributed twenty dollars toward the organization into which he was now being invited into membership. However, if a student transferred, say, the first semester of his sophomore year, that graduate was now delinquent in his dues. He owed five bucks to become a member in good standing of the Alumni Association the moment he walked from the stage.

As I stood next to the alumni president, I couldn't help but notice that after returning to their seats, opening and reading the contents of the alumni letter, many students were crumpling the correspondence and angrily dashing it to the floor. I further observed that the word was traveling backward through row upon row of those not yet having crossed the stage. Now new graduates toting their diplomas refused the handshake of the president of the Alumni Association, rushing quickly by, to the rank embarrassment of all of us. I don't recall any of the graduates being so impolite as to literally thumb their noses at us, but the message was clear.

We got rid of that gauche practice, too.

Perhaps in my entire working career, no job I had was more enjoyable or fulfilling than that of director of alumni relations at Indiana Central College, 1971-80. Being relatively close in age to the students walking the halls on the Hanna Avenue campus, relationships were built that I cherish to this day. Memories and lasting friendships were made during Homecomings, Alumni Weekends, alumni chapter meetings, golf outings, and a myriad of other events and activities in which I was privileged to play a role.

James L. Brunnemer

More than that, however, was associating on a daily basis with colleagues I admired. Educator Dr. F. J. Foakes Jackson, in speaking of kinships he had experienced, could have been describing an important lesson that I learned as alumni director at Indiana Central: "It's no use trying to be clever. We are all clever here. Just try to be kind, a little kind."

People were more than a little kind at my alma mater.

CHAPTER XVII
A SUSPENSION OF HOSTILITIES

*How a man wins shows some of his
character. How he loses reveals all of it.*
Anonymous

It has been said that you can learn all you need to know of a man during a round of golf. The American capitalist society, with its dependence upon stoking and rewarding the innate competitive nature of man, might help to explain the nexus between our captains of industry and American country clubs.

What fuels the inner passions, drives, and instincts that manifest themselves in our external actions and behaviors? Competition is the means through which we attempt to satisfy drives impelled by deprivation or abuse in early life, of unmet needs for power and influence, sex, money, or recognition. And it is through competitive activities that others are most likely to see beyond the socially acceptable masks we wear into the essence of who each of us is as a person.

As a member of the administration of Indiana Central from 1971 through 1980, I was privileged to be one among a core of men ranging in age from roughly twenty-five to forty years, with comparable backgrounds, interests, and motivations. This collection of men developed a camaraderie and group loyalty that hasn't been replicated in any workplace I've experienced in the three decades since.

A seemingly innocuous activity that took place nearly every day during the school term on the west end of the basketball court in Nicoson Hall was the primary adhesive that created a bond among these men. Each day, when both hands of the clock pointed north, about a dozen-and-a-half ICC employees gathered there for what we termed, simply, "noon-hour basketball." The endeavor encompassed far more than amusement or recreation, however. What really took place in the gymnasium could have provided enough material for a fascinating doctoral study about the behavior of adult men in competition.

Although a number of people would pass in and out of the games at different times during this nine-year period, it was Lynn Youngblood, Lou Gerig, Dave Huffman, Leonard Grant, Ken Partridge, Mike Watkins, Cary Hanni, Ken Hottell, Larry Collins, Terry Wetherald, Jerry England, Kip Kistler, Ken Borden, George Lake, and Don Cushman who would meld into a group that will forever be known in my memory as the "Faculty Flops."

Our excuse for the games was exercise, and our cardiovascular, muscular, and respiratory systems no doubt benefited to some degree. In general, we were, athletically, the antithesis of the Olympic motto—"swifter, higher, stronger." Collectively, we were slow, fat, and weaker than dining hall tea. But we had enormous fun, and a number of wildly humorous events occurred in the course of it all.

It was the combative and competitive nature of this activity that actually produced a closeness in our group that was remarkable. Without meaning to do so, we laid bare the very core of our individual personalities during the course of these inane contests. On some of our brethren this reflected great credit; on others, including this writer, it could be pretty ugly. But in revealing our basic, most susceptible selves, the group compassion and sensitivity toward the individual human flaws of each of us were extraordinary.

Eighteenth-century observer Comte de Rivarol noted, "Friendship among women is only a suspension of hostilities." For men, shared physical activities that shed light on our natural competitiveness and how we respond to the challenge of our manhood often result in long-lasting friendships.

Comparing this phenomenon to the covenant of soldiers described by author Steven Ambrose in his book *Band of Brothers* might be an exaggeration, but it wasn't coincidence that we enjoyed one another off the court, in social and cultural arenas in the company of our spouses, as well. Over the years the Flops, as a coterie or in lesser fractions of our number, would attend scores of sports outings, parties, concerts, plays, and official school events. We traveled, golfed, fished, and even gigged frogs together.

We could be a cheeky bunch. Bawdy humor and outlandish pranks we played on one another served as a common denominator. Lingering above all, though, was a respect, tolerance, and acceptance among these men of one another's divergent personalities, philosophies, and individual idiosyncrasies that was uncommonly sturdy.

All the while, we worked cooperatively on behalf of the university. Trust, loyalty and mutual respect was reciprocal. Professionally, we were proud of one another as each accomplished the various and sundry tasks for which we had responsibility. Indeed, dare I say it, there was genuine love for one another in this group.

The phenomenon of an aggregation of men battling fiercely, at times uncompromisingly, in an activity so insignificant as lunch-hour basketball was fascinating to behold. It is said that a well-adjusted person is one who can play a game as if it really is. The issue for some of us was bigger than winning or losing a game to twenty hoops or testing our basketball skills. Daily we measured our mettle against one another. Human wars in miniature were fought on the court. Seemingly mature, achieving males became as desperate as adolescents struggling to earn a place in a sort of athletic hierarchy. Calmer, more mature faculty and staff would listen incredulously as we recounted incidents of previous combat on the court. Viewing the many injuries we displayed (not to mention the steady increases in health care premiums removed from their paychecks!) they would shake their heads in disbelief and amusement at the foolishness of it all.

Of the semi-major injuries I can recall, Cary Hanni broke his foot and arm; Ken Hottell incurred one of the most severe ankle sprains our veteran university trainer had ever seen; Mike Watkins broke fingers and suffered a severe gash on his head; and Terry Wetherald had a significant knee injury. In addition to a self-sustained broken wrist (that story later), a fracture of the ankle, and a Hottell elbow that knocked a cap off my tooth, I suffer today from arthritis of the neck incurred when one of the Flops nearly ripped my head off its neck, mistaking it for the basketball. And perhaps most significant of all, Ken Partridge was "de-haired."

Distinction Without Pretension

The original Faculty Flops: (front, from left) Ken Borden, Terry Wetherald, Dave Huffman, and George "Slider" Lake. In back, Terry Taylor, Ken Partridge, the author, Lou Gerig, Jack Noone, Dave Wood Ken Hottell, Don Hecklinski, Wayne Howard, Dave Ivory, Lynn Youngblood, Bill Bright, Kip Kistler, and current athletics director Suzanne Willey. Not especially an intimidating presence, the Flops.

      No written definition of "panache" more clearly defined the essence of the academic dean of that time, Leonard Grant, than watching him in action on a basketball court. Born and bred on the East Coast, Leonard was brash at best, obnoxious and arrogant normally. A brilliant intellect, he was domineering on the court. While he was of average athletic ability, Grant felt his will should prevail in all weathers because of his superior intelligence. Thus, no one, in Leonard's mind, ever stole the ball or blocked one of his shots without fouling him. Playing basketball with Dr. Grant, it's improbable that you'd guess he was an ordained Presbyterian minister.

      Personally, I will be forever indebted to Leonard for his wise counsel, challenging me to reach beyond my limited academic expectations to intellectual levels I hadn't considered before. Without his encouragement it's more than likely I would never have attempted, let alone completed, a doctoral degree. All of us celebrated with Leonard when he accepted the position of president at Elmira College in New York, but each of us, likewise, was sad to see him leave the university.

      No one of us enjoyed our competition more than the dean. Early in the gestation of what became our noontime routine, we emerged as a group from the locker room on a Monday, dressed and ready to begin play. To our collective dismay, Jerry England was instructing a group of physical education students who were spread throughout the entirety of the basketball floor. Dean Grant marched directly toward England, a member of his faculty, and ordered him to clear the west end of the court of students. We had more important business to conduct than England's class, despite the fact that somewhere there were parents convinced the tuition they were paying was relatively important to those

James L. Brunnemer

responsible for the education of their sons and daughters. An accommodating and bemused Prof England moved his class to the east half of the court.

Further, Dr. Grant made it clear to Coach England that he was never again to schedule a P.E. class during the noon hour. As a final act, noting we had an uneven number of players for our game, he pointed to a young man whom he knew played basketball and *removed him from the class* so we would have even sides!

Leonard loved to flaunt his authority in our presence, more for humorous effect than to reflect credit on himself. When some members of the student body approached the Faculty Flops to play a game against the women's basketball team for charity, we agreed to do so. The students insisted that President Sease suit up for the game, so Gene showed up at the court at noon a few times to get at least some semblance of what actually took place on the court rather than in the stands, where he'd always been. As Yoda might have phrased it, "Athletic, Dr. Sease not was."

Grant encouraged and applauded Sease's embarrassing attempts at playing the game of basketball.

"Way to go, Dr. Sease. Nice feed," Dean Grant would fawn, all the while whispering mocking asides to others of us about the faltering play of "Gene the Dream," as Grant dubbed the president. It was a game effort Dr. Sease made to appear in that contest for charity. For Leonard it provided humorous fodder at the president's expense for years afterward.

The Dean saw himself as a reincarnation of his childhood hero, Boston Celtic great Bob Cousy, directing traffic on the court, setting up plays, dictating tempo, controlling the action. He wasn't bad for the average forty-year-old. He had a little runner he liked to throw up to the hoop that went in more often than not.

One winter day the Flops were engaged in the usual tense action. The game was tied, next basket wins. The closer to the decisive score the more physical play became. No one would get an easy lane to the basket without being punished.

However, Leonard broke free for what looked like a "gimme" lay-up. Out of nowhere came the most unlikely of our crew to do a Bill Russell impression. At 5'10" and a delicate 160 pounds, Ken Partridge usually stayed outside on the fringe, away from the heated action underneath the boards. By his own admission, when it came to physical confrontations Ken was afflicted with a back problem ("I've got a yellow streak six inches wide running down my spine," he once announced.) He was more interested in getting a bit of exercise trotting up and down the floor than competing to win. Feigning defense just convincingly enough to make his opponent think he was being guarded, Ken was satisfied to take an occasional push-shot, which was rather accurate and of which he was most proud.

As Leonard went up confidently to lay the ball off the glass for the winner, Partridge sneaked in behind Grant and got enough of his hand on the ball to deflect it cleanly. Leonard prided himself in the fact that nobody could block his shot, so he especially became incensed if someone actually did. He usually called a foul in such a situation, even if there wasn't one. But the Partridge deflection was so unexpected, quick, and precise, even Leonard didn't have the *chutzpah* to call a phantom foul.

On subsequent plays, Leonard tried gamely to redeem himself and avenge the Partridge move that humbled him. Despite Grant's relentless defense, though, Partridge managed to fire off a one-hand shot between Leonard's outstretched arms, and it hit nothing but net. Game, set, and match.

Leonard's fuse blew. "Jesus H. Christ, Partridge, you (bleeping) lucky (bleep), you never hit a (bleeping) shot like that in your whole miserable (bleeping) life!" (He continued from there, but you get the picture.) Leonard was still bitching at Partridge as we all showered and left the locker room, dispersing across the campus to ply whatever trade the college paid us for.

The evening of this episode, the entire faculty and staff gathered in the dining hall for the annual Christmas Dinner, which culminated the end of the first semester. Dr. Sease indicated that we would all now stand for the invocation, to be delivered by the Dean, and very Reverend, Dr. Leonard Grant. Ken Partridge, Mike Watkins, and I, seated at the same table with our wives, bowed reverently as Leonard began his oration, in sweeping religious tones, sounding like I imagined Moses did when he came down off Mt. Sinai with the two broken pieces of that stone tablet.

Filling the hall with his impressive oratory, Dr. Grant fairly bellowed, "**Great God, JEHOVAH!**"

Without looking up, Partridge leaned over, nudged me slightly with his elbow and whispered, "Is that the same guy in the gym at noon today who called me a low-life, fornicating, two-toned (bleepity-bleep-bleeper)?"

The next sound God heard, emanating Heavenward, was the irreverent giggles of Watkins and me in response to Partridge's faux-astonishment at the Reverend Dr. Grant's piety. On the verge of collapse, Watkins and I did our best to stifle the guffaws trying to find a way out. Partridge remained, head bowed, a devilish grin betraying his feigned surprise.

If I had my life to live over again, I would be Ken Partridge. Of all the members of our group, he was the most adept at maintaining his image as a polished gentleman while leading us in madcap and feckless adventures. Director of the Evening Division and men's golf coach, K. P. was older than most of us, albeit only chronologically. While he was, when necessary, a model of decorum, dignity, and class, in the presence of friends Ken could descend into a deliciously sarcastic and hilariously profane adolescent. No one had more fun than Momma Partridge's number one son.

Prematurely bald early in his college years, Ken openly derided his own toupee, which he had worn since his early thirties. He loved to regale his golfers, who adored their coach, with stories of "rug-wrecks."

Active physically and willing to try any sports activity, Ken told how he always wore a headband while waterskiing. He wore the band not in the normal fashion, encircling his head above the ears. Rather, it extended around the top of his head and under his chin, the better to keep his hair in place if he took a tumble whilst blading over the waves.

Partridge related to us an incident that occurred when he and his family were in Wisconsin for a summer vacation, along with fellow alumni Dick and Gloria Hilfiker (class of '56).

The scenic resort area of Wisconsin Dells lies in the central part of that state. The Dells have all manner of tourist attractions, including go-cart tracks that were a rather new phenomenon in the 1950s. To this day, two things Ken Partridge cannot resist: a grand golf course he hasn't yet played, and driving go-carts. He reverts to his childhood when

James L. Brunnemer

he climbs into one of the miniature racers. He probably harbored secret dreams of racing at Indy, but gasoline-powered go-carts had to appease his appetite for speed and noise all his adult life.

When Ken encountered one of the go-cart tracks at the Dells, he used six-year-old daughter Laura as an excuse to enter the cockpit. He strapped the petite redhead in on his lap and they began to circle the eighth-mile oval. Ken felt the joy, as always, coursing through his veins. He was exhilarated as he and Laura dodged in and out of traffic. Challenging juvenile drivers on the straightaway, diving into the turns, Ken coaxed the maximum speed he could out of his racer, which had a top speed of about thirty miles an hour. He enjoyed most forcing prepubescent drivers into the safety tires that ringed the track.

Ken chortled to himself as he deftly pressed the accelerator to the floor, cutting in front of and blowing by one driver after another, outwitting and out-driving the ten- to twelve-year-olds with whom he found himself competing.

Lap after lap Ken charged on, his face fixed in a broad grin, when he noticed wife Roselle waving excitedly to him at the outside rail. As he sped by, she pointed at his head. The incessant bawl of the lawn mower-sized engine drowned out her attempts at communicating, and since he couldn't read lips, Ken simply acknowledged his mate's gesticulations with a return wave and a "Whoooooo-ey!"

"Yes, Roselle," he thought, "I am having a great time. And so is Laura!"

As he next rounded the third turn, he noticed Roselle again gesturing, even more fervently. Pointing now at her own head, she was trying frantically to convey a message. Ken took it to be his wife's approval, so he threw back his head and laughed uproariously whilst roaring by.

What Roselle had seen and was trying to tell Ken was that his hairpiece, with the wind from the speed flowing over him, had begun to roll up in front.

The next time Ken came by, fully one third of the artificial tuft of hair had risen up from his pate. It was held in place only by tape that was fighting a losing battle with the constancy of the airflow caused by the speed of the racer. The small car had no windshield, so the brunt of the air was directly in his face.

On the next trip around Roselle was frantically beckoning him to hold onto his moss. By now the entire front half was arched upward. Ken was unaware that his peruke was flapping in the breeze like Old Glory. He was too engrossed in the rapture he was having as a Walter Mitty version of A. J. Foyt.

It was on the backstretch that the wind triumphed over the adhesive holding Ken's pad in place. As the toupee flew off his head Ken reflexively reached up to snatch the flying hair as it soared backwards. Missed it, though.

The first sign of trouble was a crackling, sizzling sound as the red-hot manifold upon which it had landed fried the hair on the pad. Then a pungent odor of burning synthetic fibers reached his nostrils as he slowed to a stop.

Unbuckling the belts holding him and Laura in, Ken retrieved the smoking pad. A charred stripe clearly delineating where it had been seared on the exhaust pipes of the engine now decorated Ken's hairpiece.

Thenceforward, Ken used the wig with the black racing stripe across it as his "practice" topper in the noon-hour games.

Distinction Without Pretension

A Partridge "mane mishap" in which the Flops shared took place at Butler Fieldhouse, later renamed for Butler's popular coach, Tony Hinkle.

The Faculty Flops were scheduled to oppose a collection of Butler University faculty and staff in the historic Fieldhouse, scene of so many epic high school and college basketball games. On this particular Sunday afternoon, however, never were so few gathered to witness such an insignificant basketball game played by a motley collection of cagers endowed with so little skill.

As always, this avid assemblage of thirty- and forty-ish males went at it with vigor. The "crowd" included four or five wives and maybe half-a-dozen children, most of whom ran and played on and under their choice of the 15,000 empty seats. I well remember seeing a robust rat poke his nose out from under the bleachers, proving once and for all—to my satisfaction, at least—that every Hoosier creature *was* a basketball junkie. But even the rotund rodent quickly lost interest when he saw it was only a ragtag bunch of adults trying to prolong a love for a game that had obviously passed them by.

The contest was spirited. We whipped the Bulldog faculty by some fifteen points. Late in the game, Partridge replaced someone in our lineup. K. P. was, as usual, floating out on the perimeter of the mayhem.

However, on one trip down the floor, when Dave Huffman fired a jumper toward the bucket, Ken uncharacteristically found himself under the basket. He had no choice but to attempt to retrieve the rebound when the missed shot bounced practically into his hands. On his best vertical jump one would have a difficult time slipping an ace of spades between his sneakers and the hardwood; but gamely, Ken did go for the ball.

Three Butler players, all physically bigger than Partridge, were in the vicinity as the basketball skipped off the rim and floated toward Ken's outstretched paws. All leapt simultaneously, entangling K. P. in a mass of hands, arms, elbows, torsos, and legs.

As Partridge stretched upward, one of the six Butler arms swiped wildly at the descending sphere. Unfortunately, the eager Bulldog prof missed the ball, and, instead, raked Ken's toupee from its moorings on his skull. The rug flew off, skidding along the hallowed floor where Oscar Robertson once scored thirty-nine points to lead Crispus Attucks to an Indiana State High School title. There lay Ken's unkempt pad, where Rick Mount and Jimmy Rayl and Larry Bird and Dick and Tom VanArsdale had all demonstrated their basketball artistry to the world.

Immediately, action stopped. The startled Butler guys weren't sure what had happened. They were looking for the blood. Had they injured this gentlemanly ICC administrator? Each stood frozen in disbelief. Unabashed, looking as if he'd been bloodlessly scalped, Ken ambled over, snatched up the brown hairpiece and slapped it on his head. Trouble was, in his haste to return the artificial turf to its appropriate spot, one of the sideburns of the pad covered his left eye. Using both hands, Ken made an expedient adjustment, swiveling the "toup" around into its proper location.

By now the Butler guys were turning away, attempting to suppress their amusement at this unexpected stupefaction. K. P. grinned sheepishly and proceeded to lope back up the court. But from then on, he made certain he navigated clear of the shoals and reefs under the hoop. No more shipwrecks for him.

In the locker room afterward, paraphrasing the legendary sportswriter Grantland Rice, Lou Gerig recited this refrain as he toweled off: "For when that one Great Scorer comes to mark against your name, He writes not whether you won or lost, but did Partridge keep his mane?"

Ken Partridge's closest friend on the ICC staff was John Swank, an ordained minister who served various posts at the college during his two decades there, including director of public relations and as an instructor of speech.

While Swank was not a participant in the lunch-hour madness, he was considered an "honorary Flop" by virtue of his regular attendance at our social functions. He was Partridge's senior in age by about fifteen years, but if anyone was more of a kid at heart than K. P., it was Swank.

We could test the effectiveness of a new joke or humorous story with the John Swank "wheeze-o-meter." John had a distinctive laugh, which, when pushed beyond normal limits, became a breathless gasp as uncontrollable tremors of mirth would convulse his body. Accompanied by tears flowing from his eyes, the full-body spasms and waves of wheezes elicited by the story were far more humorous than any tale I ever heard in Swank's presence. Once you've witnessed John's attempt to tell the "alligator story" to a group of listeners, you would understand.

K. P. and Swank were regular golf buddies. Despite his oath as a cleric to abide by the rules of life with some semblance of honor, it was known to anyone who ever gamboled at golf with Swank that he plays like a union executive. He negotiates his final score.

Some alleged that he had a specially made golf shoe with a metal wedge on the insole, which enabled the good reverend to "find" many of his wayward golf shots thought to have gone in the rough, out on the *fairway*. This generally occurred after a brief search in the high weeds and a poorly concealed swing of his leg. Partridge usually allowed Swank about four "found" balls per round.

Once, leaving a green after the foursome that included Partridge, Swank, and Cary Hanni had putted out, the fourth member of the group and that day's keeper of the scorecard, Dave Huffman, queried, "Swank, what'd you get?"

"Oh, give me a five," replied the diminutive reverend.

"I didn't ask what to *give you*, John," the wary and Swank-experienced Huffman retorted. "What did you *get*?"

"Well, then ... I *got* a seven," Swank announced, truthfully this time.

Each of the Flops had his own singular idiosyncrasies. The director of the computer center, Larry Collins, was remarkably light on his feet for a man 5'9" and 250 pounds. One couldn't budge him with a forklift, but he often "flopped," a tactic intended to draw a charging foul on an opponent. He also was prone to call what we termed "touch fouls," because Larry believed if he missed a shot it had to be because someone had contacted his wrist or arm.

The only thing Collins loved more than noon-hour hoops was noon-hour eats. This, even though he claimed perpetually to be on a diet. Over the eight years of closely observing L. C., I think he lost more than 3,000 pounds. But he gained 3,030. It was in the early seventies that the local Pizza Hut instituted the "all-you-can-eat" noon buffet. Later, in his honor, I believe they termed it the "Larry Collins A-Y-C-E-B." Occasionally, following our game, we'd troop over to the restaurant for lunch. Once, while he began to eliminate the nine slices of pizza stacked on his plate after his first run through the line, Larry looked incredulously at our waitress and chastised her for not bringing him the *diet* Coke he'd clearly ordered.

After a stay of about a decade, Larry got a real job at Eli Lilly Company and has had a sterling career there. No more loyal friend could one have than Larry Collins.

Indiana Central has had an uncommonly high number of long-term, faithful employees, but none more so than Ken Hottell. When Ken retired in the spring of 2002, after forty years on the staff, the university hired about three employees to be responsible for the jobs he performed for decades by himself.

Lanky and lithe at 6'3" and 160 pounds, Ken was quick, but gangly, and not always in control of his body. He hurt people. As the administrator in charge of negotiating our health coverage, Ken had to explain the multitude of insurance claims occurring every day in the gymnasium between the hours of noon and one p.m. There was a delicious irony in the fact that Hottell would be the most likely inflictor of injuries suffered by the other Flops.

One winter, a thirty-ish looking man who was president of a local insurance firm began showing up during our lunch-hour festivities. Because we usually had a full complement of players from our faculty and staff, he was relegated to shooting baskets on the side while our scrimmages took place. Always ready to substitute if needed, he continued to come despite not getting to play in our games.

Then one day Ken Partridge had to leave before the usual one o'clock ending to our daily set-to, providing an opportunity for the eager stand-by to join in. Brief introductions were made, then we quickly returned to the heated action characteristic of our group.

After fewer than five possessions, the action saw our new friend driving the lane to put up his first attempt at a basket. Hottell moved over to block the newcomer's shot. Ken's errant elbow came down across the bridge of the executive's nose with a distinctly audible "*thwack!*"

The man went down, rolled over and looked up, startled by the blood gushing from his proboscis. From the odd angle of his nose one could clearly see it was broken. Refusing any aid, he hurried off to the locker room to shower and then drove off to the hospital.

We never saw our new friend again after that day.

Seizing on an opportunity to make a few bucks from the Indiana Pacers' franchise while meeting a need the pros had for a cheap place to practice, Leo Miller had contracted with general manager Mike Storen to lease our gymnasium for Pacers practice between the hours of 1 and 4 p.m. After finishing our daily basketball routine, we Faculty Flops shared the locker room with Pacer stars like Bob Netolicky, Mel Daniels, and Billy Keller (who later became head coach of the Greyhounds).

The Pacers team had its complement of characters in those days, and we had become somewhat acquainted with them. For example, Darnell Hillman's spectacular Afro coiffure created a perimeter of shade beneath his 6'9" frame that rivaled that of a vintage oak tree. The late Pacer All-Star, Roger Brown, used to drive his car to practice with an Indianapolis Sheriff's Department-issued siren blaring and red lights flashing. Everyone

James L. Brunnemer

pulled over to allow this "emergency" vehicle to pass, meaning no traffic jams for Roger on his way to practice.

After a standout career in the NBA, Gus Johnson spent a season with the Pacers. He had the yarn-spinning presence and stentorian voice of Uncle Remus, and was the most amazingly profane man I have encountered in my entire life. His use of "m----------r" as a catchall, versatile term for every circumstance, was absorbing. As the situation demanded, Johnson used his favorite four-syllable word as a noun, a pronoun, a verb (including the infinitive, the gerund, and the participial forms), an adjective, adverb, preposition, and in all four types of sentences.

Once, in the time it took me to remove my basketball gear, I counted forty-two "m----------rs" emerging from Johnson's mouth. Most of what else Johnson said was unintelligible; but the "M" word was crystalline throughout his discourse.

Not athletic enough to be drawn into fractious indignity on the athletic field, Lynn Youngblood could nonetheless be a feisty competitor. His low-key manner served him well in his routine as vice president, but masked a fire that could reach surprisingly high temperatures under duress.

Anyone who knew Lynn well is aware of his tendency toward being close with his money. Lynn was parsimonious. Or penurious. Look those up if you need to. I just called him "cheap." While we were always challenged to "have your reach exceed your grasp," faced with picking up a tab, Lynn's reach generally fell far *short* of his grasp.

For certain, he never let his success go to his clothing. It will come as no surprise to those closest to him to learn that, having decided to make one of his rare golfing appearances in the 1990 alumni letter-winners outing, Lynn would send wife Janis on a sojourn to local garage sales to find him a pair of golf shoes.

No high-priced pro shop merchandise for *our* boy. After a daylong tour among the jostling yard sale aficionados of Marion County, Janis beamed as she presented her husband with a matched pair of decades-old golf shoes. Fully half the spikes were missing from the scuffed and faded size twelve faux-leather loafers. The fact that Lynn wore a size nine was of no consequence. Janis had invested $2.50 in those bargain-basement beauties, so they fit.

Lynn and I were paired in the same foursome the day of the outing. Someone knew something, because we tied for worst golfers of the field, with identical eighteen-hole scores of 124 strokes. Lynn had to four-putt on the last hole to tie me, however. I putted six times on hole number eighteen.

The real theatre had begun on the eleventh green. During the preceding few holes I'd noticed the sole of Lynn's left shoe separating from the rest of it. By the eleventh hole, the sole had almost completely detached, hanging together only at the heel. A distinct and annoying *slappetta-slappetta-slappetta* forecast Lynn's presence as he walked around the course. But nothing could embarrass him. These shoes, after all, were discount darlings.

He fended off his golf partners' continued insults in his usual good-humored manner. Then, however, the sole of the *other* shoe began to unravel, as well. Now we had an echo effect as Lynn walked: *slap-slappetta-slap-slappetta-slap-slappetta*.

Our barrage of ridicule intensified until even Lynn could stand it no longer. Always resourceful, Youngblood signaled to Kathy Kanable, an ICC senior recruited to drive the beverage cart, to come to the fifteenth tee where we now stood. Handing Kathy a dollar, Lynn whispered something to her, and she tore off in the golf cart for a destination known only to her and Dr. Youngblood.

Less than ten minutes later up drove the dutiful student, her cheeks bulging like Dizzy Gillespie blasting a high note on his trumpet. As we watched in amazement, Kathy disgorged the contents of her mouth—a full pack of chewed gum—into a paper napkin. Lynn proceeded to divide and place the "adhesive" strategically in the space between the flapping of his soles and top portions of those pathetic shoes.

For the balance of the day, we now had to endure the *squish-squish-squish* of Lynn's golf footwear. The primary overseer of academics at the U of I had solved the flapping problem with his usual ingenious practicality!

Among the most successful coaches of athletics in the history of Greyhound sports, Jerry England was the most congenial of our bunch. More so than anyone, Jerry kept in perspective the basketball we played at noon. Coach of numerous NCAA Division II track champions, including an Olympian, Jerry is also an accomplished mason and an award-winning potter.

He stood six feet tall and maintained a sculpted physique and vigorous health. At age fifty-five, Jerry placed fifth in the hammer throw at the 1987 International World Age Group track meet. Slow to anger, Jerry is, however, prone to great agitation when his code as a man is threatened beyond his ability to tolerate it.

I'll reveal here an incident that his wife of over fifty years, Fran, isn't supposed to know. Had she been aware that her husband was in a fistfight not long after his sixty-fourth birthday, she would have scolded him profusely. Sparing the details, I'll confide that Jerry was provoked into a confrontation by a much younger male over a parking spot in downtown Indianapolis. Jerry had unintentionally boxed the man in with his car for a period of fifteen minutes or so. Returning, Jerry was embarrassed at his *faux pas* and tried sincerely to apologize. The thirty-something yuppie refused Jerry's *mea culpa* and began goading him. Becoming increasingly aggressive with the soft-spoken England, the unsuspecting ass shoved Jerry forcibly against his automobile. Bad move. You don't tug on Superman's cape.

When his head struck the car door, a cut was opened on Coach England's temple. Furious at seeing blood flow onto the new shirt that Fran had gotten him for Father's Day, Jerry commenced with three quick and solid punches to the young man's eye, cheek, and mouth. Looking up from his now prone position, the frightened young man must have been relieved to see a friend of Jerry's holding him back before he did further damage. Arriving at home, Jerry tried, without success, to wash away the bloodstains from the garment. Worried that Fran would learn the truth, Jerry burned the offending shirt in the trash container at the side of his garage. As far as I know, reading this will be the first details she has of the incident.

An enormously able coach revered by his athletes, a surprisingly calm, understated approach characterized his teaching of track and field. His success in that sport, noted in another chapter, was extraordinary. A fine football player as an undergraduate at Indiana Central, it was on the gridiron that the competitive embers within England would burst into a blaze. Jerry carried that fiery demeanor into his role as assistant coach in charge of

James L. Brunnemer

linemen for the Greyhounds.

Whenever the Hounds played Valparaiso at Brown Field on that campus, the game was certain to be fiercely competitive. In the 1977 game there, the contest turned ugly early in the first quarter, with players from both teams cursing and scuffling after nearly every play. As the first half ended, a near riot occurred at midfield as a free-for-all broke out among the entire assemblage of players from both squads.

After restoring order, head coach Bill Bless and his assistants herded their angry team into the locker room. Coach England, trailing behind the squad, was distracted by a loud and vicious stream of profanity directed at him from a young man in the Crusader student section behind the players' bench. Jerry couldn't stand a potty-mouth, so he went after the offending Valpo student to teach the lad a lesson he wouldn't learn in Etymology 101. ICU student assistant coach Steve Harding intercepted the outraged coach, coaxing him into the locker room.

Inside, Coach Bless was livid. He knew his players had to return their focus to winning the game rather than the fisticuffs. He expressed his disgust with the lack of mental and emotional discipline of the players, told them to calm down and to get their minds on the real job. He closed with a warning that "the next guy I hear who says a swear word on the field is through for the day! Concentrate on football and shut your mouths!"

The players were dutifully chastised and subdued. Bill looked over the fifty men whose heads were lowered in shame, when the heavy locker room door blasted opened and slammed against the wall, buckling the plaster. Stomping into the room like a mad Pampas bull was Coach England. His blood obviously up, he had the look of a wounded animal in his reddening eyes. He didn't wait to be asked if he had anything to say.

"I want to see some (bleeping) people who are ready to give it back to those Valpo sonsabitches!!! Those (bleepers) think they can intimidate us with that (bleep) every time we come up here!! You wanna be a bunch of pussies and take that (bleepity-bleep-bleep) then stay in the (bleeping) locker room. Anybody who wants to kick some Valpo ass and take names, follow me!"

Bless's right hand went to his forehead and his head drooped downward. He knew well enough that when Jerry got this agitated it would be easier to baptize a cat than to calm him down. Doc Dill turned away to suffocate his need to release a full-out belly laugh.

The room was saturated with an ear-splitting silence. Not a player moved a muscle nor changed the sober expression each had committed to Coach Bless's instruction.

Jerry was bewildered. It was as if the dying Violetta had finished the stirring final notes of *La Traviata* with spectacular flourish, yet the crowd failed to respond. It was awkwardly incongruous for Coach England to have delivered such a passionate call to action and the team to respond only with mute docility.

Enraged at the players' seeming indifference to his personal call to arms, Jerry stormed back to the training room to vent his pent-up vitriol on various and sundry trash cans, rolls of tape, and spare water cups.

It would be a year before the other coaches told Jerry what had preceded his tirade.

A political version of a Las Vegas card-counter, Lou Gerig could read people, categorize them by their idiosyncrasies, likes, and dislikes, and commit to memory their family names down to the third generation. While he was not as intellectual as some others of our group, no one understood power and politics better than Lou. I received an early indication of Lou's political acumen when we teamed up to handle the sports part of public relations, over which he ruled as director until 1980 (when he became press secretary for Senator Richard G. Lugar in Washington, D.C.).

Hired by the university just two weeks after I arrived in the summer of 1971, Lou immediately began to organize his realm. Because of my interest in sports, the two of us approached President Sease about the prospect of my assisting Lou as sports information director, as an adjunct to my responsibilities as director of alumni relations.

Prior to the season opener for football that fall, Lou had determined that no unnecessary personnel would be allowed in the press box. One section of the cramped box above Key Stadium, before its renovation to include ample space for the chief executive and his guests, was reserved for President and Mrs. Sease and the three or four people they had room to host.

In order to enforce the new restraints, Lou himself zealously guarded the locked door at the north end of the chamber reserved for the press. He turned away, to their consternation, several of the usual alumni and interested parties who in past years would drift into the press area, particularly in inclement weather. Lou was getting quite adept at politely persuading such visitors to sit in the regular stands, when there came a light tap on the door. Opening it sternly, Lou looked downward to face a small, beautiful towhead of a girl, who could not have been more than six years old. This was a bit odd, but Lou was determined, announcing to the waif that the press box was off-limits to children like her.

"No, it's not," the sassy little munchkin spoke up.

Befuddled, Lou replied, "Uh, why?"

"'Cause I'm the boss's daughter," Cheri Sease confidently professed.

Lou hardly hesitated, saying, "Come right on in, Honey."

Gerig had *élan*, possessed a clever sense of humor and acute repartee, and was very resourceful. He had to be, because he screwed up liberally.

Like the time he found himself in a pickle with Nick. You must understand that Angus Nicoson really didn't like Lou Gerig. Lou wasn't Nick's first choice for the job of director of public relations at ICC. Angus's son, Danny, was. Nick's attitude about this situation reminded me of the story of Al McGuire, who once coached Marquette University to a national basketball championship. A player of McGuire's cornered the streetwise coach after practice one day, inquiring of McGuire why he didn't start over the coach's son, Allie.

"I'm every bit as good as Allie, coach," the young man pleaded soberly. "Why can't I be on the starting five?"

McGuire retorted, "B. J., you *are* just *as good* a player as Allie. But my son wins all 'pushes,'" (which in the patois of gamblers means a tie). This ended once and for all any dispute about whom McGuire favored.

Anyway, prior to the beginning of basketball season, Lou had requested time of Coach Nicoson to take team and individual photographs for the media. Nick begrudged *any* interruption with practice and was especially chafed to cede such a respite to his P.R. nemesis. But the pragmatist in Nick acknowledged that this was a necessary duty if his team was to get any notice in the local press. The appointment was set and Lou, who was his own photographer, showed up, cameras and leather pouches slung hither and yon on straps around his upper torso.

The players were in their game uniforms as Gerig pulled them to the side, one-by-one, for individual pictures. Those not being photographed would practice foul shots. Finally, Lou assembled them altogether for the team photo. At its completion, the entire session had taken about half an hour. As Lou left the floor, Nick called the team to center court for a brief chat before sending them back to the locker room to don their practice gear and a return to serious business.

As Lou checked his camera and prepared to leave, he noted a rather serious oversight. He had forgotten to put *film* in the chamber. The photo-shoot that Nick had so grudgingly allowed had resulted in absolutely *no* pictures.

But there was no overt panic in the Gerig lad. Turning innocently to Coach Nicoson, Lou said, "Coach, I've still got a few shots left on this roll of film. Do you mind if I get a few more pictures of the boys?"

Flattered that the new guy appreciated the importance of getting plenty of photos of his team, Nick happily agreed. "Sure, take all you want."

At that signal, Gerig quickly repeated the entire procedure, getting all the necessary photos over the next half hour.

It must have been that kind of clever expediency that moved Lou's alma mater, Anderson University, to appoint him chairman of its board of trustees in the late 1990s and proffer him an honorary degree in 2003.

Gerig was the chief organizer of the Flops' social calendar. Often this meant a trip down to the old Indianapolis Fairgrounds Coliseum, long before it became the Pepsi Coliseum, and prior to the Indiana Pacers joining the NBA. We watched many games played with the patriotic-colored basketball, featuring the revolutionary new wrinkle that the American Basketball League gave to the world of hoops: the three-point shot.

One evening Lou had gotten us free tickets for a Pacers game. We should have guessed our seats would be in the very top row of the south bleachers of the Coliseum. Down below, moving about like an active colony of ants, were the players. But even if our view of the court was not ideal, we Flops always found ways in which to entertain ourselves. On this particular night, whatever constitutes the Seven Deadly Sins (I believe that drinking, smoking, gambling, profanity, blasphemy, gluttony, greed, and lying are in there somewhere), we committed all of them, publicly, in four quarters of a pro basketball game.

There was one Pacer fan who was not enamored of our collective buffoonery. A rather corpulent lady in the row directly in front of us was demonstrating, with clear body language, her disgust with our behaviors, especially as the atmosphere up there became fouled with rancid smoke emanating from our cheap cigars—also supplied by LaLou. Affronted that this woman didn't appreciate boys having fun, Gerig responded by directing a steady stream of smoke rings, aimed from close range, at the back of her head. Midway through the first quarter of the game, with a flip of her hair and a withering look, she fled our area and took refuge in an empty seat nearer courtside.

As each of us smoked, drank, gambled, cussed, and generally misbehaved, I noted that to my left, in the same row but about ten seats away, a smiling, congenial-appearing man had leaned forward, observing us. Meeting his smile with one of my own, I nodded a greeting, and sat back, puzzled. He somehow looked familiar. Stealing another glance, I noted the man was still peering our way, a wry smile dominating his countenance.

I leaned back, nudged Partridge and asked if the guy to our left, who appeared to be strangely interested in our gang, was anyone he might know. After a brief glimpse, and acknowledging the man's smile, Partridge leaned back and whispered, "Oh, s--t! That's Ted Murphy, one of the college trustees!"

The information was duly passed and our group transformed itself into one that might pass for a troupe of choirboys. The cigars were snuffed, the plastic containers of beer were subtly slid under bleacher seats, all gambling ceased, and our language improved considerably. None of us could face this man, so before the game ended, we skulked away as one, down the aisle opposite that of brother Murphy.

Not a fortnight later one of the three annual meetings of the college board of trustees was held on the campus. All of the administrators were required to be present for the luncheon prior to the regular meeting, so, with utter dread, we gathered in the side dining hall at the appointed hour. There, with a waggish grin on his chops, was Mr. Murphy, assistant to the bishop of the United Brethren Church.

As each of us entered, Ted would say coyly, smarmily, "Hi, boys! Know anywhere I can get a bet down on the Pacers?"

We tried to ply the wily old churchman with a bribe to keep quiet, but he just held his cards, awaiting a time when he might need to play them.

CHAPTER XVIII
YEARNING FOR YESTERDAY

*The Past ... happy highways where
I went, and cannot come again.*
　　　　　　A.E. Housman

Probably few folks associated with the University of Indianapolis took note of the death in April 2002 of Linda Boreman, age 53, the result of an automobile accident in Denver. An anti-pornography activist for the last two decades of her life, Ms. Boreman was formerly known as Linda Lovelace, star of the 1972 "classic" film, *Deep Throat*. This movie had absolutely nothing to do with the Watergate scandal that toppled Richard Nixon from the presidency, except that the film provided the nickname for the mysterious information source for *Washington Post* writers Bob Woodward and Carl Bernstein.

Deep Throat, the movie, was causing quite a stir across the nation at that time. It didn't take a lot of persuasion when one of the Flops suggested we go to view *Deep Throat*, so that we might find out what all the fuss was about. We were a civic-minded group, the Flops, and where there might be an important sociological event or celebrity impacting national news, we felt it our duty to research it to be informed. (Yeah, right.)

Let me pause to place this bold adventure in perspective. Putting it mildly, pornographic films most assuredly were high on the list of enterprises that the twentieth-century United Brethren Church looked upon unfavorably. For even one, let alone nearly *all*, of the chief administrators at the college in the early seventies to be found inside the walls of a sleazy porno theater no doubt would be grounds for dismissal of the renegades. In this case it might have resulted in mass executions. Remember, at that time in its history, Indiana Central had only recently begun to allow dancing in forms other than square or folk!

Had the Indianapolis Police Department raided the Westside theatre for some reason—lax fire codes, violation of state pornography laws, drug enforcement—the ICC administrative staff would have been noticeably decimated.

The memorable part of the evening occurred prior to the film. We parked our three cars in the muddy lot beside the theater and began to slink into the seedy, tired old building, hoping we wouldn't be seen by anyone who might know us.

Picture this: Sixteen white males trying to appear nonchalant, pacing nervously on the sidewalk in front of a porno theater blanketed in garish neon lights promoting its allure. Moving in unison as a school of guppies, we ambled toward the theater entrance. Upon reaching the door, we ducked suddenly into the lobby. To avoid notice from passersby, the Flops requested admission by standing at the slightly ajar side door of the ticket booth rather than lining up outside the booth in the normal fashion.

Once safely inside, we were as relieved as a bunch of adolescents who had gotten away with some childish prank. Suddenly, a pay phone on the wall began to ring. The ticket seller—who was also the ticket-taker, the usher, the custodian, the concessionaire, and the projectionist—left his booth to answer the phone, leaving a few of us still to purchase our tickets.

He lifted the phone to his ear and after briefly listening to the caller, bellowed in a voice much too loud for the small space of the lobby where we stood, "Is there a **Reverend John Swank** here?"

At that shocking pronouncement, Pastor John bolted from the scene, exploded through the lobby doors and into the darkened theater, finding a private refuge in a seat near a side wall.

Of course, it was Partridge who had set up the call.

This was the man to whom I entrusted the guidance of my younger son, Kyle, after Ken recruited him to play golf at U of I. After their first road trip, Kyle reported of Coach Partridge: "He's so cool, Dad. And just the *crudest!* We love him!"

Kyle would play a pivotal role in an incident that I held closely for more than seventeen years before revealing it to a special group of U of I alumni.

It was a Saturday in November 1972 when the usual gang, including Partridge, Youngblood, Gerig, Watkins, Collins, Huffman, *et al.* entered Brown Field at Valparaiso University to find a huge Homecoming crowd there expecting to cheer the Crusaders on to victory. Kyle, at that time just three years old, came along with us for his first road trip.

We found room in the last row of the rickety, glorified scaffolding that passed for bleachers, open for icy breezes to lap at one's legs. Three flimsy metal bars at your back were all that prevented a fifteen-foot fall to the ground below.

The raw, bleak November day, with slate gray clouds boiling above, threatened rain or snow. The wind was constant, blowing north to south, parallel to the sidelines. The flags across the way were rigid, as if made of plastic.

The game was ferociously contested, but by the end of the third quarter our boys were on the lean end of a 9-22 score. At this point, from about four seats to my left, Ken Partridge, casting a wary eye to the darkening heavens, grumbled, "If this game doesn't get over soon we're going to get wet."

The Greyhounds rallied furiously, however. With a little over three minutes to play a touchdown and a conversion narrowed the Hounds' deficit to six points, 16-22. The Valpo crowd, spilling out of the regular seats now into the aisles, began to get nervous. Still concerned about the impending rain storm, Partridge checked the sky and urged, "Hurry up, or we're gonna get drenched!"

Indiana Central's stubborn defense held deep in its own territory, turning the ball back to the offense on their own fifteen-yard line. The Greyhounds began a relentless, hair-raising drive back toward the Valpo goal. With less than two minutes remaining in the game, Coach Bless made a simple tactical move that the Crusaders couldn't seem to counter. He inserted lightweight flanker Mickey Sisk at the tailback position, from where Mickey would loop into the flat. Quarterback Rod Pawlik would flick a little eight- to ten-yard pass to him. Sisk would then advance another five or ten yards down the field. It was simple yet devastating to the Crusader defenders. Pawlik to Sisk, eight yards. Fullback Steve Montgomery, run off tackle, one-yard loss. Pawlik to Sisk, 13 yards, first down. Tailback Dick Nalley, around end, two-yard gain. Pawlik sacked for a loss of seven. Pawlik to Sisk, 14 yards, another first down. Sisk again, this time for twenty-one yards and a first

Distinction Without Pretension

down on the Valpo thirty-five! Under a minute to play now. The crowd is going wild!

The Hounds are stuffed on the next play at the thirty-two yard line. Thirty-four seconds remain in the game.

"**Time out!**" Coach Bless screams from the sidelines.

Then, a tug at my pant leg. Another. Another, and finally, "WHAT?"

I turned to my son, who has behaved so well as to be invisible.

"I gotta use it," Kyle whispers, shyly.

"What?"

"I GOTTA USE IT!" he replies, not whispering and not shyly.

I look at the aisle below me, which is now overflowing with Valpo fans. I know the restrooms are in the gymnasium, at least two hundred yards to the north of the field.

"I tell ya it's gonna pour!" laments Partridge.

The referee signals it is time to play. The Hounds are in their huddle. I make a feeble try at convincing a three-year-old that he is in control of his bladder.

"You can wait just a little while, can't you, son?" I plead. "The game's almost over."

But this little boy needs instant relief: "No, Dad, I GOTTA GO NOW!"

Okay, I'm not a low-paid middle manager at the college for nothing. Decisions are my business. So I glance furtively around me. The frenzied crowd is engrossed in the action at the south end of the field, where Mickey Sisk has snagged yet another pass and is run out of bounds at the Valparaiso ten yard line. Less than fifteen seconds left!

Another glance over my shoulder at the area behind the bleachers. No one there. I quietly spin Kyle around. In a flash, I unzip his fly.

"Go!" I whisper hoarsely.

He does, but Newton's Law of Gravity must compete with the ferocity of the wind. So the palliative stream shoots instead directly to our right, carried upward and grandly into a misty spray.

He's finished and I have restored his zipper to the upright position, turned him back toward the field and am smugly satisfied that I've pulled off the trick. Then I hear Ken's voice:

"I told ya. It's starting to rain! I knew it!"

The "rain" had found Ken and no one else.

Mickey Sisk capped the excitement by snaring Pawlik's final pass in the end zone with no time remaining on the clock, tying the game 22-22. John Mitney's conversion kick won the game for the Hounds and the Flops were delirious with excitement. In between his felicitous expressions about Indiana Central's extraordinary victory, Ken was still wondering why the rain hadn't continued. Most of us made it, dry, to the car.

He wasn't to learn the truth until, while addressing the Varsity Club golf outing crowd in 1989, I told, for the first time, the story of how Partridge's current NCAA Division II All-American golfer, Kyle Brunnemer had, as a child, peed on K. P.'s rug.

It's not easy being the father of a golf pro when one is as inept at the game as I am. Since becoming a member of the PGA, Kyle has provided for his dad the best in golf equipment, clothing, and accoutrements. When I approach the first tee I can be a rather intimidating figure to those with whom I have never played golf. With my name hand-sewn on a Titleist bag; wearing the latest in sports attire, including shirts, trousers, shoes, and caps; donning my stylish golf glove; with expensive ball marker and repair kit, I cut a suave figure on the links. Then I tee it up and flail away. All pretension disappears. They know they have a real Elmer in the foursome.

Friend and former teammate Dan Nicoson '68 reminded me not long ago of a memorable shot I executed during the first round of golf I ever played. It was summer prior to my senior, and Dan's sophomore year at Indiana Central. We drove to Friendswood Golf Course north of Mooresville, Indiana. If I'm not mistaken, the Friendswood links had been farmland only a year before. As a milieu for golf, FGC resembled a goat ranch more than the very popular golf course it is today.

As I recall, I had shot par (72), which would have been commendable, except we had finished but seven holes. Standing on the tee at number eight, a par three, Dan and I noted a unique feature of this particular challenge. The green lay about 160 yards away, the fairway as straight as Dr. Cramer's spine. However, about twenty yards in front of the tee area and parallel to one another were two saplings, each perhaps four inches in diameter, one on either side of the driving area. It was evident that if one simply drove his ball between the natural gunsight formed by those trees, the ball would track right toward the green. Dan proved this theory to be valid as his drive split the space between the two young alder trees and landed, pin high, on the green.

While I teed up my ball, it had not yet been observed—as it would be later by my good but brutally candid friend, golf pro Don Bisesi—that, for me, even the tee is "a bad lie." Nevertheless, I was somewhat sanguine that I could smack the ball down the avenue fashioned by the trees and perhaps garner my first par ever!

Alas, what happened next defied belief. Ask Dan sometime if my swing did not produce three distinctly contrasting sounds in less than one second of elapsed time.

POK-THWACK-THUNK!

The first of those was the report created when the 3-wood in my hands struck the teed golf ball.

Number two percussion was the result of a small sphere traveling at high velocity, impacting the solid trunk of the tree on the right side of the tee area.

The third of the reverberations was that same golf ball, having caromed off the tree and rifling directly back whence it originated, striking the initiator squarely on the knee. I dropped like I'd been sacked by Dick Butkus.

Actually, I failed to mention the fourth and fifth noises, which resounded in succeeding seconds.

"*DA-YAMM!*" I shrieked in pain.

"*OMYGAWD!*"

That was my impudent and uncaring golf partner, Nicoson, as he collapsed in swells of laughter.

Despite my ineptitude at,

> *... an outdoor game in which a player attempts to propel a small resilient ball with clubs around a turfed course with widely spaced holes in regular pro-*

gression with the smallest number of strokes ("golf" as defined by Websters)

… golf coach Partridge will admit that he and I have had some of the greatest fun and most intensely competitive rounds together on the links of anyone he's played against. The reason: the hare (Partridge) allows the tortoise (me) a huge head start in the form of strokes.

In golf that means that over eighteen holes he will spot me a shot on the top dozen handicap holes, a stroke advantage on each of what are supposed to be the most difficult challenges on the course. Ken's thrill comes in making up the gift with his superior skills.

One September, K. P., Dave Huffman, and I left Indianapolis at four a.m. to play a round of golf near Renssalaer, Indiana, before going to St. Joseph's College to witness the Puma-Greyhound football game there.

Partridge had staked me to the usual twelve strokes, of which I had taken good advantage. As we teed the ball up on number seventeen, we were even up in match play, eight holes apiece. Ken had to win the final two holes to maintain his dominance over me in our rivalry.

Hitting first on a flat, obstacle-free par three of 150 yards, Huffman lofted a beautifully struck wedge shot that flew the flag, sticking like a dart about seven feet beyond the hole. Dandy shot.

Similarly, Ken's shot soared high and straight at the pin. A bounce and a bit of backspin left his ball less than three feet from the cup, a certain birdie for an able putter like Partridge.

My turn. Enduring Ken's usual scoffing at my 15-wood (honest to God, I had what K. P. called my "sand wood" specially made!) I waggled, gripped and re-gripped, then swung with the usual Force-10 velocity, striking maybe the top third of the ball. The pitiful nubber started its "who knows?" journey by skipping along the ground, a classic "worm burner."

With polite restraint, my playing partners suppressed any derogatory comments that awful shot deserved. But as we waited for it to cough, gasp, and die, the ball surprisingly continued to roll on. The ground was sun-baked hardpan, which aided in the continued momentum of the bouncing ball. As we remained focused on the juggernaut shot, it disappeared in a tractor rut, no doubt left days earlier by a careless groundskeeper who had mowed in a spot too wet to bear the machine's weight. Instead of losing tempo, however, the ball rounded the slightly curving track and shot out as hot as it entered, redirected toward the green. Onward the white orb ran, until it struck a large, protruding shard of rock. Caroming off the stone that had been there long before man thought to build a golf course around it, my ball was now nearly at the fringe of the green, with some life still in it.

Onto the greensward it rolled. We all held our breath. Crawling now, the ball turned slowly, agonizingly as it drew even with the Partridge Titleist. With about five additional rotations, the sphere stopped dead—twelve inches from the hole.

No one said a word as we started toward the green. Suddenly, I noticed Ken was no longer marching along with Dave and me. Instead, he was still on the tee, bent over about five feet *in front* of the tee markers.

"What's wrong?" I called out to K. P.

James L. Brunnemer

"Go ahead. I'll catch up. As soon as I repair your ball mark!"

I got the last laugh this time. So rattled by the fluke shot of mine, Ken missed his birdie try. I tapped in to win the hole. Partridge conceded the match on the spot.

I admired Dave Huffman's on-court demeanor more than that of any of the Flops. Steady of mien and unendingly dependable, the director of the university's student enrollment organization maintained some sense of dignity with all the craziness around him. Analytical by nature, Dave showed a low level of outward passion but fiercely competed to win. Although naturally skilled athletically, Dave went about everything he did in a cerebral, calculating way, virtually analyzing his way to success. His primary sports were baseball and basketball, but he developed into a very fine golfer and tennis player by rehearsing the repetitive skills with great exertion.

Emotionally, Dave maintained a placid outward expression. It was a rare occasion when one witnessed the always proper and unflappable Huffman lose his calm, staid demeanor.

But I saw him lose his cool once, *big time*.

Dave, Mike Watkins, and I were playing golf at the Links, southwest of Indianapolis. I use the term "golfing" with some liberality, for while Dave was a decent golfer, Mike and I, charitably, were pathetic. People actually looked forward to playing with Mike and me because we were entertaining. Either of us was apt, on any given swing, to commit some outrageous act, perhaps something so singularly bizarre as never to have been seen on a golf course before.

This day the three lefties had completed sixteen holes. Despite how excruciating it must have been for a purist such as Dave to observe what Mike and I did to the Royal and Ancient game, not once did he patronize either of us. Even when Watkins sliced one divot that might have served as a nice welcome mat for his doorstep, no disparaging comment escaped Dave's lips. To watch his expression, Dave might have been shooting a round with Nicklaus and Palmer.

Teeing it up on number seventeen, a relatively simple and straight par four, 390-yard challenge, Dave, as always, with honors, delivered his drive right down the middle of the short grass. He stepped to the side of the tee, fixing his gaze down the fairway, awaiting my tee shot and prepared to provide his usual polite encouragement, regardless if I topped it or popped it up as I usually did.

After a couple of warm-up swings, I took my customary turbulent cut at the ball. Without turning his head Dave peered over the fairway expanse to try to pick up the flight of my Titleist. Just at that moment, however, he heard behind him our partner, Mike, say disparagingly, "Aw, Jim, I think that one's in the water."

This confused Huffman, for on this particular hole, there *was* no water hazard. Just grass, tee to green. So he looked over his shoulder to see Watkins and Brunnemer, standing in tandem, cupped hands to foreheads, shading eyes from the sun. Like two Comanche scouts scrutinizing a far-off smoke signal, we were following the flight of my drive, 90 degrees to the right of the hole I was aiming at.

Two fairways over my errant shot did indeed plunk into a pond that was minding its own business, not expecting to receive a ball from *that* direction.

This was the straw that fractured the proverbial back. Huffman dropped his bag

Distinction Without Pretension

where he stood, toppled over as a redwood might under the woodsman's axe, burst out in maniacal laughter as he hit the ground. This one was just too incredible for even Dave to take.

It made me proud, really, that shot. Not many people could say they caused Huff to become totally unglued as I had.

I first met Mike Watkins in 1965 when I witnessed his internal combustion during an ICC wrestling match. Petite, at barely 5'6", Mike was relentless in his pursuit to become a champion wrestler in the 119-pound weight class. And he did, indeed, become a conference champion.

Hilariously self-deprecating and a master of the instantaneous retort, Mike's drive was apparent in the Flops' activities. He was a gamer. Likewise, his fellow admissions counselor Cary Hanni went into overdrive as a competitor. Also an adept golfer, Cary treasured the lunch-hour games.

Watkins and Hanni were ravenous recruiters, ushering in a new era of capable students with their passionate faith and belief that ICC was the finest school any graduating high school senior could select. The energy and charisma emitting from these two would singe the carpet if they stood too long in one place. Their competitive natures and creative student financial aid packaging kept their boss, Dave Huffman, constantly vigilant to be certain they stayed within the limits of the school scholarship budget.

Jovial personalities both, Cary and Mike each possessed a lively sense of humor and a youthful outlook that helped them relate to high school students and parents. Some of U of I's finest and most successful alumni now making the world a better place chose to attend our rather unheralded school precisely because of the personal attention received from Watkins and Hanni.

Mike turned his love of "the deal" to real estate after a stint as dean of men at the university. Establishing his own realty company, Mike is today recognized as one of Indiana's most successful practitioners and is a highly sought-after motivational speaker by his colleagues in the profession. I was proud to nominate Mike as a trustee in 1990. He continues to be a stalwart member of that board today.

Likewise, Dr. Cary Hanni '69 embarked on a similar journey, leaving his position as an admissions counselor at the college to pursue a degree in medicine. He had harbored a dream of attending medical school through his association with the man who would be his model and mentor, Dr. Charles Dill.

Living a sparse existence while making his way through medical school, Cary and wife Vicki raised a family of achievers, including daughter Kristine, a fourth-generation student who graduated from the U of I with honors in 1999. Cary currently practices surgery with the Evansville Surgical Associates medical group. Immensely bright and a sensitive human being, I can think of no one I'd rather have attending to my health than Dr. Cary Hanni.

Among the most nostalgic memories I have of my time at the university were of Cary and me together on combined alumni/admissions sojourns together. Passing time on endless, perfectly straight Illinois highways, uncluttered by traffic, traveling through canyons of cornstalks on combined alumni/admissions trips, we played "Name that Tune," singing oldies into the wee hours of the Illinois morning as we traveled back to Indy.

James L. Brunnemer

It was also my privilege to request that President Lantz and the board of trustees consider Dr. Hanni for membership on that body in 1993, which he continues to serve.

Among the myriad activities in which the Flops engaged, even weight loss became a ferociously competitive activity. Invariably, as we aged and excess pounds would find its way onto midriffs, someone would conclude it was time to drop some of the tonnage.

If one or more of the gang committed to shed a few pounds it became fodder for a contest.

Strong-willed, with the work ethic of a Sherpa, Cary Hanni believed he could accomplish anything if he tried hard enough. Understanding his "motor" is not difficult if you've met his parents and his siblings. Members of the Hanni family are consummately driven to succeed. Cary refused to lose to anyone in any competition. His self-discipline became obsessive once his focus was established.

He had an impressive unbeaten string in weight-loss contests when one day the two of us agreed on a pact to see who could drop twenty pounds the fastest. We were to weigh in at noon on a Friday and the first guy to lose the weight would be the winner.

While Cary will never believe it, I really didn't intend to "liquid up" on a Thursday prior to our Friday weigh-in. It didn't occur to me to drink intentionally eight Pepsi Colas from noon to 9 p.m. on the eve of the onset of the contest. It just happened. I don't remember why.

But the result was that when we stepped on the scales Friday at noon I checked in at 201 pounds, Cary 209. That meant if Cary got to 189 before I got to 181, he would continue his string of weight loss victories.

That weekend Cary was paranoid about his diet and exercise. He told me later he skipped all but a few meals over the weekend and ran two miles each day. By the time of the first weigh-in on Monday he was fully confident that his shed poundage would weaken my resolve.

We approached the scales before going out to play our usual noon-hour basketball game. As Hanni stepped up to check his weight, an astonished Lou Gerig made this observation:

"Cary, you got no *ass*!"

Truly, it appeared that Hanni had basically lost all the excess weight he carried on his posterior. A sly grin spread across Cary's face as he read the scale: a solid six-pound loss in only three days.

It was my turn. When the scale revealed my weight to be exactly one hundred and eighty-six pounds, Hanni turned a pale green. He examined the scale, mounting it again to check his weight. He then had me ascend it for a second audit. Fiddling with the gauges, Cary tried desperately to discern how I could possibly weigh *fifteen pounds less* on Monday than I did at noon Friday!

Cary would usually not become discouraged about anything. He always found a ray of light in any adversity. But this was too much even for the eternal optimist. All the starch seemed to just go out of him. I learned later after basketball that day he went to the Pizza Hut for the "all-you-can-eat" special and tanked back up to his original weight. He tossed in the towel, too disheartened to go on.

I later revealed to Cary that I had played in an amateur basketball tournament over the weekend, playing a total of six games on Saturday and Sunday. The combination of liquid weight I carried to the scale on Friday and the exertion my body went through in the games had resulted in an extraordinary and pseudo loss of poundage. It was kind of a kick to be the one to destroy that seemingly indefatigable will of iron of my good friend Cary Hanni.

Unfortunately, this wasn't the last laugh in these types of competitions. Several of us, including Cary, Lou Gerig, and I were locked in a close weight-losing battle several months later, when Lou wiped us out in the final three days of the contest. We were down to the wire and within a pound or less of one another when Lou contracted a flu bug. During the final three days he dropped eleven pounds to that dastardly illness, winning our contest hands down. Cary and I accused Lou of paying his doctor to inject some kind of virus in him just to win. Lou admitted if he'd thought of that he would have considered it. But this sickness had been real.

Sifting through a raft of old files not long ago, I came across an elementary school "Pupil Progress Report." A harbinger of things to come was evident as I perused the report card for Jimmy Brunnemer, Martinsville Central Elementary School, Grade One, 1950-51.

I suppose report cards were standard in most Indiana elementary schools at that time. The student's progress in reading, language skills, writing, spelling, mathematics, music, and art was indicated by letter grades A, representing "excellent performance," through F, the dreaded failing grade. I don't consider it immodest of me to share that I scored a preponderance of A grades in those subjects, with a few scattered Bs here and there. After all, it *was* first grade.

However, the challenge I would have over succeeding decades of my life was starkly revealed beneath the section entitled "Personal Conduct." Here, grading symbols were numerical, a "1" representing "very good" behavior, while a "3" indicated a definite need for improvement. My scores in personal conduct during the first grading period of my scholastic life:

"Respects the rights of others"	-	2
"Refrains from disturbing others"	-	3
"Works and plays well with others"	-	3
"Is courteous"	-	2
"Exercises self control"	-	3
"Obeys school rules"	-	3

Is this kid headed for the penitentiary, or what?

Throughout my life I've avoided using the excuse that my competitive "overdrive" is a manifestation of having been abandoned as a twenty-two-month-old by my biological parents (along with eight other siblings). I was adopted shortly thereafter by the people who nurtured me and gave me, truly, unconditional love from that early time until their passing when I was an adult. So any excuse rings hollow when I consider how blessed I was to have had Ernie and Gladys Brunnemer as my parents. But one cannot dismiss out of hand the notion that being rejected by one's primary caregivers at an early age makes one hunger for approval.

I was a handful from the start. An unruly temper fed by self-doubt seemed to be at the core of my behavioral challenges. Of course, as I got older, the descriptor changed. It became "temperament." "Temperament," of course, is "temper" too old to spank.

For me, the Faculty Flops games proved to be a time of self-discovery. By far the most emotionally volatile of the Flops, I didn't play for fun and exercise. In truth, I battled to justify my self-worth. I felt inferior in so many ways to Lynn, Ken, Dave and the others, so my quest was to defeat them on the court. This was one arena where I could be superior, most times, to them.

Mark Twain once observed, "In his private heart, no man much respects himself." While I wanted desperately to be a dignified, honorable, and fair competitor, my lesser nature simply wouldn't allow me to achieve that. I was a cross between a junkyard dog and a pit bull in these games. I didn't have to win the collective (team) battle but I simply could not lose personally. To do so was too painful for my lack of self-esteem. Let me cite one example of how mixing two explosive dispositions can lead to an absurd circumstance.

Similar to me in volatility was Coach Terry Wetherald. Beloved by just about every athlete who ever played or wrestled for him and much-liked by his colleagues as well, Terry was as fiercely competitive as any of our guys. His jolly nature and self-derogatory humor hid a strong need to belong, to be approved. Like me, he cared most about something when acting as if he didn't. Though he was short of stature at 5'5", one would best not be deceived by Wetherald's diminutive physical size. He was, as a fellow ex-Marine would aptly describe him, "one tough sumbitch."

Terry and I embodied the adage that "growing old is mandatory; growing up is optional." Our incomprehensible competitiveness simply cannot be understood by the rational mind. The chemicals that raced through our neural synapses are inexplicable, as was our behavior in the lunch-hour basketball games.

The incident I'll now report was the result of repetitive conflicts accumulated over time that erupted into a showdown. I saw Terry Wetherald as a pest on the basketball floor. Because of his size, he couldn't get off many shots at the hoop. He was fast, so could be annoying to a taller, slower person, and he prided himself in blocking out on rebounds to make up for his small stature.

I didn't give Terry much respect on the court, and he noticed. Off the court I loved him like a brother. During competition, if he was on the opposing side, I sneered at his attempts to defend me. (This will give you a hint of the retarded maturity level we're dealing with here.)

On this day Terry and I had encountered one another under the hoop over the course of a couple of games. At those times I had jumped over Terry, no doubt fouling him as I did, to get the rebound and put the ball back in. Terry was too proud to call the contact fouls, and I would have disputed it anyway, most likely calling him a "pussy" or some such. So it became increasingly physical when we met near the basket.

Finally, Lou Gerig let fly with a shot, and, watching the flight of the ball, I moved reflexively toward the hoop. I became aware of someone holding me as I tried to move, blocking my path to the basket. I took my eyes off the ball to see who was interfering with my movement. It was Wetherald, *facing me,* his *back to the basket,* rather than the other way around. He had no intention of rebounding the basketball himself. He just wanted to prevent me from getting to it.

He was clutching the front of my jersey. I tried to edge around him and he simply slid sideways in that direction, maintaining his hold on my shirt. This was perfectly plausible to Terry, in the context of the competition, for undoubtedly he felt I had fouled him earlier. This stretch of the rules was justified in his estimation. Frustrated with his annoying tactic, I reached straight out in a fit of rage with both hands to grab hold of Terry. What I ended up with was his *hair!* Because of the dearth of follicles on top, I seized fists full of hair on both sides of his head.

In an immediate response to my aggressive move, Terry reached out, too, grasping the contents of my jockstrap in a death grip.

"Uhhhggg," I gasped.

Now, I *literally* had the "upper hand" in the fray, but Terry had the decided *advantage*.

The ball bounded away for someone else to retrieve, as we stood there, interlocked, neither willing to release the valuables we held.

Finally, though my negotiating stance was the inferior one, I looked into his unblinking eyes and snarled, "Let go!"

"*You* let go!" replied the other adolescent-brain.

A few seconds elapsed as we stubbornly refused to concede in this *mano a mano* display of testosterone silliness.

Then, slowly, my fingers relaxed, and slowly, ever so slowly, I released his hair from my fingers. Simultaneously, matching my deliberate ungrasping Terry released his prize—actually my "prizes"—slowly, each eyeing the other for treachery as Khrushchev and Kennedy stared one another down during the Cuban missile crisis.

We laughed about it later. It wasn't funny at the time.

On another occasion, the Flops were in the midst of the familiar mayhem that passed for competition at noon.

Now we all have our own special pet peeves that, accrued over an interval of time, can lead us to spasms of temper. For some a dripping faucet might compel one to leap out of bed in the middle of the night in frustration. The person in the line at the grocery who questions the cost of each of his seventy-seven items as you wait impatiently behind him can move one to a fit of pique. Whatever it is that leads you to become surly, you might understand that on the athletic field it was, for me, a specific act: to be hit in the nose. This might have stemmed from childhood, when a baseball finding my schnozz instead of my fielder's glove, or a forearm across my face in a football scrimmage, always resulted in an involuntary flowing of tears from my eyes. I perceived the tears to be seen as a sign of weakness. So when such an event occurred, my reaction, invariably, was defiance and a need to retaliate or vent in some way as a result of the fury aroused in me.

James L. Brunnemer

Brunnemer, left, and Terry Wetherald were pals, almost civilized—away from competition on the basketball court.

    This day I found myself with the basketball and a clear path to the basket. John Beebe was at that time director of placement at the university and a former Greyhound starter for Nick. Like the rest of us adult-impersonators on the court, John was keenly competitive and had learned long ago that there was no such thing as an uncontested charge to the basket. Even though it was apparent he couldn't stop my driving lay-up, John decided he would exact some kind of cost for my wide-open advance to the hoop.

    Flailing at me after I had become airborne to release the ball softly against the glass, he whacked me sharply across the bridge of my nose. It smarted.

    As I landed on the court on the follow-through of my drive, I could already feel the tears welling up in my eyes from the blow. My momentum carried me the remaining eight feet or so to the recessed stanchion to which the backboard and hoop was attached. It was essentially a round metal pole firmly planted to the underflooring, covered during the basketball season with a soft rubber sleeve that protected players who came into contact with it.

    In my rage at being so unnecessarily abused by Beebe, I chose to take my anger out on the pole. Instinctively, I drew back and landed a roundhouse left-handed punch squarely in the middle of the unsympathetic stanchion.

Distinction Without Pretension

There was a problem, though.

At the conclusion of each basketball season, the protective rubber sleeves were removed from the posts at both ends of the arena and stored until the next season. The new basketball season was still a couple of months away.

My fist contacted not soft rubber but cold, hard steel. When the concussion of flesh and bone on metal raced up my arm, I didn't have to be a pre-med major to know something cracked, and it wasn't the pole.

When one makes a mistake, especially an act as stupid as this, one attempts to save face in any way possible. For me, in this instance, it meant covering immediately the fiery pain I felt in my left wrist with feigned nonchalance.

"Sorry," Beebe muttered insincerely.

"That's okay," I replied, equally dissembling.

The game continued, my wrist pulsating with pain. We were nearing the conclusion of this day's third and final game of the lunch-hour league. I can't complete this tale without saluting my own determination (okay, stubborn pride) by revealing that the final, and winning, basket, came on a driving shot that I made with my inflamed left hand.

We returned to the locker room, showered, and proceeded to our civilized jobs at the university. By the time I arrived back at the office my throbbing wrist made further work inadvisable. I couldn't grasp and lift a pencil.

My office door was closed as I sat at the desk reviewing my options. I knew I couldn't drive my car. I picked up the phone receiver with my right hand and laid it aside. Then I dialed Lou Gerig's extension, picked up the phone and placed it to my right ear.

"Lou, have you got a minute? Okay, come on over."

Seconds later Gerig was in my office peering down at the useless left hand resting on my desk.

"Lou, I think I broke it," I said sheepishly.

My friend responded with an unsympathetic shake of his head at the result of the witless display he had observed less than an hour earlier. We got into his car and drove to St. Francis Hospital. X-rays confirmed a fracture of my wrist. A cast covering all but the fingers on my left hand up to just below my elbow was fashioned.

The punch line to this story occurred a few weeks later as Ken Partridge and I watched the Greyhounds' football game at Key Stadium.

The late John Mitney, an exceptional but temperamental kicker for the '75 Hounds, was standing in punt formation on fourth down. As Partridge and I watched, side by side, Mitney miss-hit a punt, resulting in a mediocre kick traveling about ten yards upfield. Visibly upset with himself, Mitney reached up to rip his chin strap from its mooring, kicked angrily at the turf and stomped his way to the sideline, where he jerked his football helmet off and threw it toward the bench.

"C'mon, Mitney," I lectured, "*Act your age!*"

No words were necessary for me to be reminded of the vacuousness of what I had just said when Partridge merely looked downward at the cast on my arm, slowly fixed on my eyes with an omniscient grin, then peered toward the nineteen-year-old Mitney.

I was thirty-four at the time.

James L. Brunnemer

The author shooting a game of eight-ball with students in the Rec Room in Schwitzer Center. Evidence of a burst of temper, which precipitated an ill-advised punch to an iron basketball stanchion, is the cast on the shooter's broken left wrist.

    It was a nasty incident not long afterward that finally convinced me to take a serious inventory of my behaviors and seek constructive change. Bill Coffee '73 is today a very successful businessman living with his wife, Cindee '74, in Louisville, Kentucky. Cindee was a partner in one of Louisville's largest and most prestigious law firms before giving up that lucrative career for church service. The Coffees' daughters, Carree and Courtney, round out a simply admirable family.

    In 1975, Bill was employed at A. B. Dick Company in Indianapolis, frequently joining the regular Flops during our lunchtime games. Bill had a clever, engaging manner that I appreciated when he was on my team. On the opposing side, however, he became in my jaundiced eyes a whiner who fouled incessantly and unnecessarily. Not being a lovable puppy myself and winning no sportsmanship awards, either, Bill and I often clashed.

    I don't remember the specifics of the dispute that impelled Bill and me to exchange blows. All I know is, based on the awkward fisticuffs that ensued, nobody suggested we hurry off to the Golden Gloves. What I do remember is the awful embarrassment of that hideous event. When Bill and I traded punches, play on the court stopped immediately.

Revolted by this display of childishness, with most of their rancor aimed especially at me, the rest of the Flops lost interest in further competition and drifted off to the locker room. Their unease and disgust with me was palpable. They couldn't possibly know how deeply humiliated I felt at my inability to control emotions that would lead me to clout an alumnus on the cheek over a silly basketball scrimmage.

I had finally gone too far.

After that disturbing sequence of events, I sought to understand the process that anger and desperation in those games provoked in me. First, I visited my good and trusted friends, psychiatrist Dr. Jeff Kellams '67. I read the latest brain research being done with Positron Emission Tomography (PET) and Functional Magnetic Resonance Imaging (FMRI). I learned that scientists suggested that the frontal cortex fulfills emotions and higher thoughts, playing a delicate balancing act with our good and bad feelings. The left side of the brain transmits positive emotions, like love, happiness, achievement, friendship, and gratification, while scientists contend that negative emotions (fear, disgust, sadness, apprehension, for example) that are intended to help us avoid danger are located in the right side of the brain.

Subsequently, I began to observe—almost as one in a lab—the chemical rush of emotions as they played out through my veins. I recognized that once chemicals were triggered and released, my anger had no recourse but to be played out. Incredibly, I could almost *feel* the rush of chemicals through my body. I became aware that I was poised to defend myself against whatever threat my brain had established in my consciousness. It seemed that unless I responded in some outward, physically demonstrative way, an unsatisfied, dark mood would linger for varying periods of time. It appeared that unless I allowed the feelings of anger to escape, the chemicals released would not dissipate. I always felt contrition, but couldn't admit it at the time of the episode, lashing out if someone tried to counsel or chastise me.

What caused this anger? Were there frightening, insidious memories from my past lurking in my mind that provoked the outbursts of temper within me? Why did I inevitably despise myself when I behaved badly, boorishly, meanly, nastily, and cruelly? Why did others who acted in similar ways offend me?

I wondered about the other guys. Why were some of them more in control of their passions? Why are some individuals more comfortable with themselves than I seemed able to be?

Over the ensuing months I made a remarkable discovery about my anger. It seemed that when I felt passions begin to rise, if I just backed up, focused on "not caring" about whatever challenge was provoking my personhood, I could stop the anger before it got a foothold on my emotions. It actually seemed as if I could corral the chemicals of passion before they were released and became irretrievable.

I actually learned to *lose on purpose*. When I sensed confrontation with another was leading me beyond my personal danger point, I learned to artfully "back off," without it being obvious to my opponent. It may sound silly, but the ability to disguise my forced disinterest in competing at that point was crucial because, from a competitor's standpoint, having an opponent fighting *too hard* to win is preferable to having your opponent quit in the face of intense competition. This discovery, and the subsequent use of its power, gave me enormous self-satisfaction. I could break the chains of temperament with which my

James L. Brunnemer

inner demons had enslaved me.

Not long afterwards, I happened across these words of Colton, which I now understood:

> *The intoxication of anger, like that of the grape, shows us to others, but hides us from ourselves, and we injure our own cause, in the opinion of the world, when we too passionately and eagerly defend it.*

In April 1979 the second-most influential male in my life died violently on a California roadway when his motorcycle collided with a truck. I was devastated at receiving word of the death of my lifelong friend, Jack Leonard, a classmate both at Martinsville High School (1962) and at Indiana Central College (1966). At the time of his accident I was on sabbatical leave from my position as alumni director to complete my doctoral studies at Indiana University.

The kinship between Jack and me began in first grade. From that time until he died Jack was always the type of person I wanted to be. He was strong and athletic, yet kind and gentle with a smile that lit up the room, and had the heart of a saint. I knew of no one who came into his presence who did not genuinely admire Jack. Bright and a hard worker, he was named the Outstanding Graduate Student at two separate universities. While studying oceanography at Purdue University (which took him to Newport, Rhode Island for diving coursework), he and his new wife, Rebecca, rented a modest trailer home on a horse farm near Lafayette. Although his classmates voted him its outstanding student, Jack had become enchanted with the animals he cared for as part of his rental agreement. So he determined to enter a veterinary science program at the University of California at Davis.

Only two weeks prior to his graduation and becoming a doctor of veterinary science, Jack's fatal accident occurred. As his Purdue classmates had two years earlier, the veterinary class at UC-Davis voted Jack Leonard, posthumously, its outstanding student.

The old saying is so true: "Whom the gods love, die young."

Only days following Jack's memorial service in our hometown of Martinsville, Indiana, I sat down and wrote *"Thoughts at Odd Moments"*:

He's dead now. But memories of him remain. Thoughts of him come to me at odd moments. Like now, as I sit at my office desk poring over a publicity mailer for a university event. Suddenly it is 1957.

> *(Summer in a small, rural Indiana village. Two twelve-year-old youngsters stand some fifteen yards apart, oblivious to the din created by the onlookers filling the wooden bleachers, even to their teammates shouting encouragement from all parts of the little league baseball diamond. The batter peers out to the pitcher's mound, trying to appear relaxed and confident, but his darting eyes and frequent licking of his lips betray his inner turmoil. Standing on the pitcher's mound, his white 'Dodger' uniform contrasting sharply with the vivid green of the outfield grass and the cloudless blue sky, the second youngster*

Distinction Without Pretension

nervously turns the baseball over and over in his right hand. I am that batter. The pitcher is Jack Leonard, my best friend.)

It was only a single pitch, in one insignificant inning, of one inconsequential little league game. But recalling it warms me, gives me comfort, reminds me of a time when life seemed less complicated, less demanding, less confusing. It was before Jack died and I had not yet been forced to confront the awful finality and utter mystery of Death.

My mind moves ahead to April 1979. As I stand over the grave site, unaware of the throng around me that has come to grieve, I am curiously detached from the awful emotions within. While experiencing the deep, crushing emotional hurt of the sudden senseless death of the thirty-three-year-old man I loved as a brother, I am at the same time feeling a sense of childlike joy as I recall a moment that occurred two decades before ...

(The pitcher is in his windup now. The pre-pitch fear that had dominated my conscious mind is gone. No time for fear. I'm looking wide-eyed for the tiny white blur, which will, I know, appear at a point over the pitcher's right shoulder—on a watch dial it would be ten o'clock. I am coiled to swing, knowing I have only the merest fraction of a second to put into motion my twenty-eight-inch long Mickey Mantle-model bat as the pitch explodes toward me. Jack Leonard throws a baseball uncommonly fast from a distance of forty-five feet.

The baseball darts by me. Because I have hesitated ever so slightly, the small percentage of chance in my favor to hit the ball is now gone. I realize in the final few feet of the speeding baseball's journey to home plate that I have no chance to touch that pitch.

It's close. The umpire bellows: "Ball four!"

It could easily have been called strike three.

After a quickly stifled expression of disappointment, Jack's grin flashes simultaneously with mine. Two friends. Two competitors acknowledging a draw in this confrontation. I can't help but wonder as I trot, acting nonchalantly, toward first base if Jack can sense the relief I feel that this brief test of our skill and character has passed?

The gnawing fear of failure that always preceded my facing Jack now has subsided, but I feel he knows the truth that I firmly believed: There was no way I could consistently hit his pitching.

And Jack's perspective? He was to admit to me after that game that he expected every pitch he threw to me to be lined to some distant part of the field. He knew I could hit anything he threw over the plate.)

James L. Brunnemer

The discovery of the essence of competition—mutual respect—was, for both of us, a significant moment. Jack didn't know what he did for my self-esteem, so important to an insecure adolescent, by revealing that to me. And I'm sure that when I confessed my fear of facing him, it boosted his confidence, too.

We were like that, Jack and I. That rare friendship without conditions or restrictions where two young boys could share their innermost thoughts and fears. I've never since had a friend with whom I could be so completely myself.

He's dead now. But the memories of him remain. They come to me at odd moments.

God, how I miss him.

Shortly thereafter, I decided to leave Indiana Central for the second time.

CHAPTER XIX
ATHLETICS IN THE ACADEMY

*Football bears the same relation
to education that bullfighting does
to agriculture.*
             Elbert Hubbard

Can you name a four-year, degree-granting institution of higher learning in the United States that does not subsidize an intercollegiate athletics program?
No? Neither can I.

Given that colleges and universities were established in America to provide formal education beyond the secondary level—to produce an "enlightened clergy," originally—and that such institutions are purported to be innately academic in purpose, why is it that nearly all such institutions are seemingly bound to provide a competitive sports program for its men and women students?

The ostensibly incongruous marriage of athletics and educational institutions has been the focus of countless studies by educators and sociologists as well as the source of endless commentary by popular media over the past hundred years.

An ocean of scholarly and anecdotal literature exists examining America's preoccupation with sport. To understand the roots of this national sports mania, one might look to America's War Between the States of 1861-65. American antebellum culture was altered irrevocably by the great conflict. Among the socially significant changes was the transformation of sport and games as an increasingly acceptable outlet for (mostly) males of that day.

The conflict between northern and southern states brought together into army encampments the largest concentration of American men between the ages of sixteen to forty in the "four score and seven years" of its history. For the first time, on a large scale, the male populace left the farms and small villages of an agrarian society to travel long distances for training, then battle, in faraway places that they heretofore knew only from schoolbooks or hearsay. Aside from frenzied emotional and physical exertions elicited from men on battlefields, life in the squalid camps of the huge armies was one of agonizing repetition and boredom. For every soldier killed in battle, seven died of disease and exposure to the elements.

Emerging games and competitions helped to pass time and provide exercise for the men. Traditional amusements of that day, such as horse racing, wrestling, bare-knuckle boxing, and other feats of strength, speed, and coordination provided activity and entertainment for the troops.

A relatively new game, called "base" or "base-ball," had been adapted from the English sport of "rounders" prior to the War. "Base-ball" became so popular that teams were regularly formed from units within both armies to compete for camp supremacy.

The first intercollegiate game of "base-ball" was held, eighteen players to a side, between Amherst and Williams colleges on July 1, 1859. When Amherst won, 73-32, "there was a universal ringing of bells and firing of cannons," reported the *Amherst Express* student newspaper, "and throats already hoarse shouted again amid the general rejoicing ... The students of Amherst rejoice not merely in the fact that in this contest their Alma Mater has borne away the laurels; but also in the belief that by such encounters as these, a deeper interest will be excited by those amusements, which, while they serve as a relaxation from study, strengthen and develop body and mind."

Following the Civil War, having traveled outside their previously limited geographical constraints, young men were now more mobile and worldly wise. With a growing emphasis on and increased opportunities to pursue higher education, college enrollments expanded significantly. (Similar great migrations to colleges and universities occurred following world wars I and II, especially aided by the GI Bill after WWII.) Hardy, spirited, and virile young men were now cloistered in sedate, ivy-covered sanctuaries in numbers greater than at any previous time in America's history. Baseball had become a mainstream activity among the young blades of the day; however, other games were emerging to serve as outlets for the excess energy of youth as well.

Football, an American amalgamation of the English games of soccer and rugby, was gaining in popularity among students at eastern seaboard colleges. American football was played officially for the first time on November 6, 1869, between Princeton and Rutgers at New Brunswick, New Jersey. About 100 fans attended, including one umbrella-waving prof who warned the participants, "You men will come to no Christian end."

In Springfield, Massachusetts, in 1891, a soft-spoken young teacher of physical culture and the Christian gospel, James Naismith, devised an activity he named "basketball," as a winter diversion for athletes of the day. Just five years after Naismith introduced his new game, the modern Olympic Games, patterned after those of ancient Rome and Greece, was instituted.

The male students themselves, *sans* coaches and sanctions of university administrators, organized the earliest contests. Challenges to counterparts at neighboring educational institutions resulted in spirited competitions, creating ardent rivalries and heightened school spirit among the greater body of students. Cautious administrators cast wary eyes toward these rowdy games, supplying insinuated approval in the absence of their disapprobation.

In other nations sport grew as well. However, rather than invading the academy, the need for athletic competition by the young men in Great Britain, Germany, Italy, and France, among others, gave rise to sports "clubs," which were independent of the universities in those countries.

The movement of sport in American colleges and universities was aided by pivotal social change. Some academicians praised the return of the philosophy of "the development of mind, body, and spirit" of the ancient Greeks. Members of the popular media saw glory in the "pioneer élan" of the young men of the day, mythologizing the ideal of rugged individualism that was the legacy of the American frontier. Others, noting the native competitiveness of man, saw sport as a substitute for war. Elsewhere there was a growing sense of the importance of physical training for young men. More pragmatic was many administrators' belief that physical activity such as that exerted in athletics by young male college students would make them less likely to pursue less acceptable activities in increasingly coeducational institutions. The puritanical constraints of the Victorian Age were being trod upon in the growing liberal society of late nineteenth-century America.

All of this foreshadowed an explosion of sport, which found its natural growth where young, competitive males in the nation collected: in America's colleges and universities.

Contributing to the popularity of intercollegiate sports contests was the prospect of securing "bragging rights" for school supporters through athletic victory. New venues for gamblers were created, of course, and ever since, sport at all levels has continually fought to maintain purity in the spirit of the games against the darker elements of our society.

Teams in early intercollegiate competition were formed by groups of men, which selected a "captain." The duly elected leader had the major responsibilities for organizing the team, selecting its members, and determining strategies and tactics on the field of play. (Today, some major universities employ as many as two dozen coaches to staff intercollegiate football programs alone!)

When a spate of crippling injuries and even fatalities of young men competing in intercollegiate football mounted at the turn of the twentieth century, alarmed university presidents began to seek ways to exercise control and provide standards for the safety and sanctity of the sport. President Theodore Roosevelt, an ardent advocate of the glory of manhood, called a national conference of university officials in 1903. Out of those early ruminations was born the forerunner of the National Collegiate Athletic Association (NCAA).

Close on the heels of university administrators' actions to establish a consistent framework for their schools' competitive sports programs came professionally trained and sanctioned coaches. Next, growing legions of followers approved the concept of erecting huge stadiums and arenas for collegiate teams. The need for universities to attract the best athletes gave rise to the "athletic scholarship," or grant-in-aid, plus widespread under-the-table enticements for the promising sports hero.

As at most schools, students organized the original sports teams at Indiana Central University. It was not long after the doors to the college opened in September 1905 that its young men and some of its female students sought to create an organization to promote and subsidize sports activities. The Athletic Association, with a commitment of dues (twenty-five cents per term in 1909), was formed under the aegis of a faculty advisor.

Students scheduled practices and games, coached themselves (in the beginning), and arranged transportation when playing at other schools. The faculty advisor monitored athletic activities to ensure they were appropriate to the greater mission of the institution.

Students laid out the first baseball diamond in the fall of 1905, and a few hardy souls began to practice shortly thereafter. In the spring of 1906, the first recorded athletic contest between Indiana Central and an organized team, other than those in intramural skirmishes, was held. The diamond was located just west of the Administration Building (now Good Hall), where University Heights United Methodist Church now stands. ICU was victorious in the historic baseball game, defeating the Madison Giants in a slugfest (or perhaps a defensive abomination) 32-31 in nine innings.

In 1907 and 1908, men's and *women's* basketball, and tennis, were introduced, with teams playing and practicing as time, money, and circumstance allowed. One of the early standouts of ICU basketball who later became an acclaimed member of the school faculty was William Pitt Morgan. "Will," as he was known to his teammates, was captain of the 1915-16 ICU cagers, then the "Cardinal and Grey Warriors." It wasn't until 1926 that a group of students chose the name "Greyhounds"—"long, lean animals renowned for speed, jumping prowess, and fighting heart"—as the official sobriquet for ICU athletic teams.

The history of Indiana Central/University of Indianapolis sports is a rich one. Greyhound squads have competed well in every conference or league in which they have played. By 1923, Indiana Central had been accepted as a member of the Indiana Intercollegiate Conference, which served to oversee and regulate play among colleges and universities of Indiana. It was that year a young coach named Johnny George wrote the athletic policy under which Greyhound teams participated. In part, George wrote that athletics at Indiana Central were to:

> ... *provide amply for physical training and to enter into intercollegiate contests, but not to lay such emphasis on this interest as will over-shadow the other features of college life; nor is it the purpose to build up strong athletic teams at great expense and have them give a large portion of their time to winning contests, merely for the sake of winning.*

The university's national affiliations have been, first, with the National Association of Intercollegiate Athletics (NAIA), later the National Collegiate Athletic Association (NCAA), and, after it subdivided into four levels, the NCAA Division II.

Basketball, football, and baseball were to emerge over time as the favored sports in terms of student interest and popularity among alumni. Tennis, track, cross-country, wrestling, golf, and other later additions to the sports program were perceived as "minor" sports, with a lion's share of the athletic attention being reserved for the "big three."

The absence of a gymnasium retarded the growth of basketball as a sport in the early years of the institution. In 1921, the "temporary gymnasium," which would stand for forty-four years, was constructed on the ground where Warren Hall is located today. The first sanctioned season of basketball competition is considered to be the 1922-23 year with John George as coach. In December of 1922, Central won its first official intercollegiate basketball game, defeating Fairbanks-Morse 30-18. The Cardinal and Grey Warriors split its dozen games that initial season for a 6-6 won-lost record.

Southport High School officials allowed Central students to use its football facilities when momentum picked up to organize a football team. With a squad that included almost no one who had even played organized football, ICU students opened its inaugural gridiron season on September 28, 1924, losing to an experienced Franklin College team, 0-28.

It was in that game the first Indiana Central sports legend was born. Apparently the Baptist gridders decided to test the mettle of Central's biggest player, 225-pound pre-ministerial student Alfred "Doc" Emmert. Doc overheard one Grizzly player mutter to a teammate as they lined up to start the contest, "Let's get that big sonuvabitch."

In the summer of 1919, Doc Emmert was thirty-two years old, working in the coalmines of eastern Ohio. It was there that he heard his call to the ministry of God. He journeyed to the ICC campus that fall seeking enrollment at the college. It didn't occur to

Distinction Without Pretension

Doc that the fact he'd only completed the sixth grade might be a slight stumbling block in his quest to become a preacher. Impressed with the gritty, if naive, Emmert, President I. J. Good arranged for this husband and father to attend the Academy. Twice, even thrice, the age of some of his fellow students there, Emmert first completed grades seven through twelve in five years.

He had never seen a football game when he rallied to coach George's call for "able bodied and courageous men" for ICC's first football team in 1924. He had, by then, celebrated his thirty-seventh birthday anniversary.

Despite the costly introduction to the rough-and-tumble gridiron sport, Doc would go on to earn accolades during his four years. He was named to a few all-conference teams as an offensive and defensive lineman at ICC.

Losing a couple of teeth as well as the game, Doc nonetheless played inspired ball against the Grizzly eleven in that first-ever ICC football game, earning the respect of all who witnessed the contest. When Coach George asked the normally gentle giant what had gotten into him, the non-swearing Emmert related to the coach what the Franklin boys had said about him at the outset. Then Doc added, "Prof, goddammit that made me mad!"

Undaunted, that first Cardinal and Grey Warrior squad went on to a 4-2 record for the season, including a victory over Ball State Teachers College. The joyous sensation of that win was tempered by a loss to Southport *High School* the following week!

Such evidence supports the notion that sports were part of the culture of ICU early on. Through the years, sport has grown in proportion to the schools with which the college has historically affiliated. Other institutions with similar missions, grounded in the various church affiliations, have promoted athletic competition as a healthy outlet and as a measurement with other schools in their respective spheres.

After twenty-three years as a member of the Indiana Intercollegiate Conference, Indiana Central joined the Hoosier College Conference when it was inaugurated in 1947. This union brought together into athletic competition private schools of comparable size and kindred origin, each college having been established by a different religious sect. Franklin, Taylor, Manchester, Hanover, Anderson, Earlham, and Indiana Central were charter members of this league.

In 1973, Indiana Central would be accepted into the Indiana Collegiate Conference, considered a step up for the college and its sports program. The league included cross-town rival Butler University and other private schools with storied athletic heritages: DePauw, Wabash, Valparaiso, Evansville, and Saint Joseph's.

Shortly after the Hounds joined the ICC, executives of the NCAA moved to divide intercollegiate athletics into different levels, distinguished not according to the enrollment of the college or university, but the *financial commitment* to which a school was willing to obligate itself. The NCAA offered institutions four categories: Division I-A for major programs like Indiana, Notre Dame, and UCLA; Division I-AA for schools like Western Kentucky and Marshall; Division II, which allowed a smaller reservoir of athletic aid; and Division III, purportedly schools that would offer no financial assistance based on athletic prowess.

This new structure came about because of pressure from a few dozen major football-playing institutions that threatened to pull out of the NCAA unless allowed to pursue the enormous lucre available to them through televised contests. Television revenues, a seemingly bottomless well of cash, were becoming so vast that executives from that industry began to wield great influence on college sports, even affecting the dates and times games would be scheduled. It was not unusual for a conference to agree to have its basketball teams tip off after ten p.m. in order to grab a share of the TV money and exposure. Of course, many small schools, whose programs do not attract super-athletes and are purposely kept modest in proportion to big-time athletics, generally do not share in this largesse.

When it came time for the U of I administration to select among the four levels of competition, the Greyhounds opted for Division II.

Given the new strictures, historic and storied rivalries were now impossible to maintain. While the other Greyhound sports teams competed in the Great Lakes Valley Conference, U of I joined a separate conference for football in order to have enough Division II schools to schedule in its traveling area. The Great Lakes Intercollegiate Athletic Conference, which was made up predominantly of Michigan colleges and universities, accepted our application to enter their league for football only.

One must ask why athletics has enjoyed such a disproportionate amount of attention and funding at U of I, or at any of the schools like ours, for that matter. What benefits have accrued to our university through funding and promoting sports during the past century?

The easier answer to that question might be to focus first on what benefits *have not* come through sports activities at Indiana Central. Sports at the U of I have not resulted in national exposure, as at Notre Dame, Indiana University, Purdue, and lesser NCAA-sanctioned athletic programs in Indiana colleges and universities.

College sports in America have become an enormous industry, spurred by television revenue and the attention of all forms of popular media. Attracting hosts of fans to the university is not achieved through sports contests at U of I. The number of persons who viewed all sports events is not available, because the greatest percentage of the contests scheduled are free to the students and public. Only rough estimates of attendance at university athletic events are available, but no more than 50,000 people witnessed athletics at home contests (or listened to radio or television broadcasts) in *all* sports during the 2001-02 year. That number is the equivalent of about three-fourths the patrons at *one* Indianapolis Colts game.

Healthy revenue as a benefit enjoyed by universities with major athletic programs is not found in the U of I program. In fact, you may be surprised to learn that, exclusive of tuition paid by student athletes, varsity sport is distinctly a deficit on the general operations budget at the University of Indianapolis. In the first year of the millennium, the university spent $3.5 million on athletics for financial aid, expenses for travel, equipment, and coaching personnel for twenty-one men's and women's sports. This is in stark contrast to the Ohio State University, the sports budget ($80 million-plus) of which exceeds the amount the University of Indianapolis spends on its annual operations for the entire school ($44.5 million!)

Against a total of no more than $20,000 in gate receipts for all those sports combined, one can easily see that there must be other reasons for maintaining the sports program at the university, because it certainly does not make money. To my knowledge, members of the administration and board of trustees have never seriously entertained thoughts of subsidizing athletic teams to pursue national repute.

Nor can it be claimed that alumni donations have increased in any significant way because of sports programs at the University of Indianapolis.

Intercollegiate athletics have benefited the American professional sports business, serving as unofficial "minor league" training grounds. A small fraction of college participants actually reach the major league level. According to the National Federation of Interscholastic Sports, of the 6,440,000 high school athletes participating in 2000, five percent, or about 32,000 teenaged males and females, moved on to compete in NCAA Division I-A, I-AA, II, III, and NAIA athletics. Two of every 10,000 of those college athletes were later drafted by the major pro sports teams (the National Football, Basketball, Baseball, and Hockey leagues).

At the U of I, the number of athletes who have gone on to play professionally is even more miniscule. Some who have drawn notice from professional squads over the years and had minor league professional experience include former teammates Henry Potter '39 and William "Tony" Sharpe '39, each of whom played minor league baseball; Bill Bright '54, whose promising career as a Philadelphia Phillies pitching prospect ended when he incurred a sore arm; and Ray Trisler '65, a minor league pitcher in the Milwaukee Braves farm system. Mike Wishnevski '82 spent nine seasons in the Seattle Mariners minor league system. Jim Crowell '97 pitched in relief for the Indianapolis Indians and for a couple years with the Cincinnati Reds. After recording a 12-1 record for the Hounds in the 2001 season, Rick Hummel '01 signed with the Chicago White Sox and is now pitching in their minor league system.

Angus Nicoson '42 played for a time with the Indianapolis Kautskys, a member of the league that was the forerunner of the National Basketball Association. Bailey Robertson '57 tried out for NBA teams after leaving the college and ultimately performed for the famed Harlem Globetrotters. (Along with all former Trotter players, Bailey was inducted with the team into the National Basketball Hall of Fame in 2002.) In recent years, a handful of U of I basketball players have performed in minor American and foreign professional leagues: Ron Rutland '91, Perrell Lucas '96, Tyrone Barksdale '97, Mike Deemer '98, and Cedric Moodie '02 each have earned salaries with teams in leagues in Europe, the Orient, and the United States.

Lee Perry '42 spent a brief time with the Chicago football Cardinals; Dave Scheib '65 was one of the final players cut by the NFL Philadelphia Eagles in 1964; Vasco Walton '67 was twice named the Most Valuable Player for the old Indianapolis Capitals minor league football club; Stan Markle '74 played linebacker for the Philadelphia Bell in the American Football Conference; Stephane Fortin '98 has played in the Canadian Football League for five years as a defensive back for the Saskatchewan Roughriders; and Gary Isza '98 was a wide receiver in the Arena Football League. Following an All-American senior season at U of I, Josh Gentry '99 signed a free agent contract with the Indianapolis Colts.

However, of the thousands of young people who have participated in athletics at the institution, only two spent any appreciable time in the major leagues of sports. George Crowe '42 began his career with the New York Rens professional basketball team and later had an eight-year career as a first baseman with the Milwaukee Braves, Cincinnati Redlegs, and St. Louis Cardinals. Dick Nyers, after graduation in 1956, signed as a free agent with the Baltimore Colts, playing two-and-a-half seasons with that NFL club.

James L. Brunnemer

As far as can be determined, the only Greyhound female athlete to earn money as a professional athlete was Mary "Wimp" Baumgartner '57, a catcher in the women's professional baseball league.

Perhaps the most notable former Greyhound athlete to be associated in the professional leagues was an assistant coach. Tom Zupancic '78 served for fifteen years as coach of strength and conditioning with the Indianapolis Colts and in 1996 was named by his peers as the NFL's Strength and Conditioning Coach of the Year. Tom has since served owner Jim Irsay as vice president for business development for the Colts.

In the arena of international athletic competition, a handful of Greyhound athletes have represented the United States and at least two foreign countries. The aforementioned Zupancic was an alternate on both the 1980 and 1984 United States Olympic Greco-Roman wrestling squads. Randy Heisler '86 was a participant in track and field for the United States Olympic team at Seoul, Korea, in 1988. The amazing story of former Greyhound gridder Dick Nalley, who had never seen a bobsled before making the U.S. Olympic squad in 1988 at Lake Placid, will be recalled in another chapter.

Representing her native country of Sri Lanka, two-time University of Indianapolis NCAA Division II champion Vijitha Amarasekara '89 also competed in the 1988 Olympics in the javelin. At the 2000 Olympiad, Orel Oral '03, U of I All-American swimmer, competed for Turkey, whence he matriculated to the college.

And if one were to count Fred Wilt, yet another Greyhound distinguished himself on the U.S. Olympic team, as a marathon runner in both the 1948 and 1952 Olympiads. Wilt, from Pendleton, Indiana, was recruited to play basketball for the Greyhounds by Harry Good. Following his sophomore year at ICC in 1940, Indiana University's celebrated Coach Earle "Billy" Hayes convinced Wilt his future was in distance running. Wilt won the NCAA national individual title in cross-country and in the two-mile run for Indiana University in 1941. After serving in the Navy during World War II, Wilt returned to footraces, and in 1950 was honored as America's top amateur athlete, winning the coveted Sullivan Award.

The University of Indianapolis has had a mostly positive alliance with its notable adjunct called intercollegiate athletics. Generally, academics and athletics have co-existed well as "sports, in balance" similar to those of our peer colleges and universities. Among the benefits provided by an athletics program for the campus community have been:

Positive public exposure and useful visibility. Although faculty would rather gargle hemlock than admit that an institution of higher learning receives greater public exposure from, say, a championship basketball season than a superior chemistry faculty, the fact remains that sports publicity does help define a college in our culture. Students of William Pitt Morgan were among the top graduates of the Indiana University Medical School for decades. Yet how much did the public know about the demanding and brilliant biology professor compared to basketball star Bailey Robertson? Scoring forty points or more in a game in the 1950s, which Bailey did five times in his hoop career at Indiana Central, was cause for notice in the local newspapers. Although there does seem to be something inherently amiss about sports providing free publicity for a university, as NCAA Hall of Fame football coach Paul "Bear" Bryant of Alabama once observed, "It's hard to get 80,000 people to rally around a math class."

In fact, according to historian Fred Hill, in 1929 Indiana Central tried a novel (for

Distinction Without Pretension

its day) approach in "hopes of luring neighbors and media to the campus" by purchasing lights and holding its football games at night.

Occasionally, University of Indianapolis sports teams or individual athletes manage to earn prominence beyond the normal hometown publicity. In the early 1990s, the Burger King corporation established an award to recognize superior scholarly and athletic performance in intercollegiate football. A $10,000 donation in honor of a college football player is presented to the scholarship program at his college or university. Individual awards are given each week in the four NCAA divisions to encourage high scholarship and outstanding performance on the gridiron. Since its inception, three Indianapolis gridders, Dave Burton '96, Matt Gardner '97, and Jeff Sorg '96 have merited the Burger King award, bringing $30,000 into the general scholarship fund at the university.

In the year 2000-01, the U of I achieved a most remarkable "double" in its athletics program, the kind of recognition presidents and trustees love to boast about. Like Burger King, the Verizon Company sponsors a program in conjunction with the NCAA to recognize athletes in all divisions who perform extraordinarily well in both the classroom and on the athletic field. Annually, nominations for its Academic All-American teams are submitted by nearly all of the 2,000 colleges and universities with intercollegiate athletic programs. Emory University in Atlanta, Georgia, led all colleges and universities in the four NCAA divisions that year with twelve Academic All-Americans, followed by Notre Dame (eleven), Penn State (nine), and Purdue and Nebraska with eight each. Tied for sixth place among all colleges and universities nationally for producing outstanding student-athletes with seven Academic All-Americans were Arizona State, the Massachusetts Institute of Technology, Augustana (Illinois), Calvin (Michigan), Pittsburg State (Kansas) ... and the **University of Indianapolis**! (The highest placing Ivy League schools were Harvard, tied for twenty-sixth, and Yale, fortieth.)

The Sears Directors Cup, also sanctioned by the NCAA, recognizes intercollegiate sports programs for *breadth* and *success*, acknowledging schools for their overall excellence in the total sports program. In 1996-97, the U of I finished fifth nationally among 271 NCAA Division II schools for men's and women's sports in the Sears Cup competition.

In 2000-01, while U of I won no national team championships (the highest finish in a national tournament was the Greyhound baseball team, which placed third in the NCAA Division II National Championships) the success of the total program was attested to by the eighth place finish in all sports compared with other programs in Division II.

With twenty-one sports (11 for women and 10 for men), the University of Indianapolis offers one of the broadest arrays of athletics for its students in the state of Indiana. U of I is well above the national average of thirteen sponsored sports teams for NCAA Division II member schools. This provides solid evidence that U of I is achieving a critical balance of sports success with a breadth of opportunity for all students.

The occasional positive national recognition that schools like the U of I seek and cherish was evidenced in the April 7, 2003, edition of *Sports Illustrated*. The Greyhound program was saluted by that reputable periodical for being only the second NCAA II school in history to have all seven of its winter sports teams competing in NCAA national championship tournaments on the same day. On March 6, 2003, both men's and women's basketball, swimming, and indoor track teams were in the Division II nationals, along with the Hounds' wrestling squad. Ten U of I athletes would earn All-American honors in their

James L. Brunnemer

respective sports at those events.

In consecutive weeks (September 22 and 29) of 2003, *Sports Illustrated* recognized two University of Indianapolis athletes for outstanding accomplishment. Columnist Steve Rushin cited 2003 graduate Kim Moore for winning the women's National Amputee Golf Championships when she shot scores of 76-89-77 in the three-day tournament. Also, U of I quarterback Matt Kohn (an Academic All-American who posted a 3.03 GPA in 2002) was featured in *SI* for setting a host of NCAA Division II records in the Greyhounds' 59-52 overtime win against Michigan Tech. Among the standards set by Kohn, who completed 39 of sixty-one passes and six touchdowns in the game, were passing yards (645) and total offense (652), the latter of which trails only that of David Klinger of Houston, who racked up 732 yards against Arizona State in 1990.

It seems fitting to note here the accomplishments of David Huffman, who, after a sterling twenty-six-year career in admissions at the university, succeeded Bill Bright as director of athletics in 1994-95. Dr. Huffman oversaw what is arguably the greatest decade of Greyhound sports to date. In his initial year as athletics director, the U of I won its first Great Lakes Valley Conference all-sports title. Through the balance of the twentieth century and through the 2002-03 year, his final season before retiring in June, the success of the university's sports programs both on the playing fields and the athletes' performance in the classroom would bring unprecedented credit to the University of Indianapolis.

The finest sports season in school history and one of the best for an NCAA Division II school would be his coaches' and athletes' retirement gift to Huffman. The 2002-03 Greyhounds qualified either teams or individuals in fourteen separate sports and would bring the school its second GLVC all-sports trophy. Men's teams that competed in NCAA postseason play included baseball, basketball, golf, swimming and diving, tennis, and wrestling, plus indoor and outdoor track and field. Six women's teams, including basketball, golf, swimming and diving, tennis, and indoor and outdoor track and field also competed in tournaments for national honors.

During Huffman's tenure, scores of Greyhound athletes have earned All-American honors for their individual skills. More impressive, however, is the forty-two *Academic* All-Americans who have brought acclaim to the U of I sports program. In a typically modest statement of his contributions to the athletics success, Huffman, who hired all of the current Greyhound coaches, said, "It should be noted that I haven't coached any athletes, hit any home runs, made any baskets, or aced any serves. My responsibility as AD ... is to set a table where people can come and be successful, and that's what we've done."

Actually, the ability to "set that table" is the most difficult aspect of leading an athletics program, something that Dave Huffman has done with the aplomb found only in the most gifted of athletics administrators.

It is a substantial pair of shoes into which 1975 graduate Dr. Suzanne Willey will step as successor to Huffman as the new director of athletics at the U of I.

Enhanced admissions. The success or reputation of its athletic teams attracts many students, including non-athletes, to a college or university. Providing a broad selection of varsity sports competition is especially important to schools like the U of I in which more than twenty percent of its undergraduates play at least one varsity sport. The average amount of athletically based financial aid for students attending the U of I in 2000 was $5,000, meaning that the balance of the total room, board, and tuition costs of $15,000 came either through additional financial aid from other sources or from the students themselves.

Among the most significant of federal legislation for enhancing increased availability to women athletes, of course, was the institution of Title IX in 1972. Opportunities for girls and women at all levels of athletic play has had an enormous effect on the number who continue to play sports at the collegiate level. This has resulted in a most positive effect on admissions at colleges and universities that offer the broadest offerings of varsity sports for women. Fully fifteen percent of undergraduate women attending the University of Indianapolis competed in at least one varsity sport last year. With a student gender ratio of nearly two women for every male student at the University of Indianapolis, a wide array of athletic opportunities for women may be a key factor in a female student's choice to come to the U of I.

Constituent attachment. Sports teams come closest to melding all university constituencies, including alumni, friends, faculty, staff, and students, into a community "oneness" than any other recognized entity at the university. Typically, the largest single gathering on campus during the year is Commencement—the next five greatest crowds are the home football games. Part of the social fabric of a college experience for all constituencies of a college or university appears to be attending games and supporting the athletic teams. Competition among and between colleges and universities on athletic fields provides an atmosphere for non-participating students to gather in mutual support for fellow students against a similar collection of collegians from rival colleges. The presence of faculty and staff at sports contests enables students to view them in a different context and often is the basis for the development of more important relationships and understandings outside the classroom. Athletics may be a component in maintaining close ties with alumni and friends that help in a continuing relationship to the benefit of the institution.

The shared emotional aspect of a triumph—spectators cheering their approval, athletic administrators and coaches demonstrating their competence, and the athletes displaying skill and grit—may lead to surpassing unity on behalf of the institution more than any other single activity or event. In 1924, the father of Ed Garbisch wanted his son to be a concert pianist. Observing as his son was carried off the football field by ecstatic fans after leading Army to an upset victory, the elder Garbisch exulted, "No matter how magnificent the performance of Paderewski, the audience does not sweep up onto the stage and bear the artist off in triumph!"

Scenes such as that described by Mr. Garbisch occur regularly on college campuses the nation over.

Lasting lessons. Sport has been called a "microcosm of society." Those who participate as undergraduates point to lessons learned through athletic competition as extremely valuable in later life situations. Bonds are forged with teammates that last lifetimes. Studies have confirmed that the sports experience, for the "scrubs" as well as the "stars," can result in enduring positive contributions to success in life.

More than a century ago, quite unintentionally I would suppose, Rudyard Kipling captured the essence of the athletic challenge in these stanzas from *If*:

If you can force your heart and nerve and sinew
To serve your turn long after they are gone,

James L. Brunnemer

> *And so hold on when there is nothing in you*
> *Except the will which says to them: 'Hold on!'*
>
> *If you can fill the unforgiving minute*
> *With sixty seconds' worth of distance run,*
> *Yours is the Earth and all that's in it,*
> *And, which is more, you'll be a man, my son!*

With all due respect to Mr. Kipling, sport is no longer only for the male species. Pressure on colleges and universities to provide girls and women equal access to all aspects of university life intensified throughout the 1960s. Enacted on June 23, 1972, Title IX essentially prohibits gender-based discrimination of any activity in schools receiving government financial support. President Sease appointed Sue Anne Gilroy, his assistant at that time (who later served as Indiana's Secretary of State), to ensure ICC's sports programs would be in compliance when Title IX became law.

A 2002 study commissioned by Oppenheimer Funds polled 401 adult females, all earning at least $75,000 annually. Researchers found that eighty-one percent of those surveyed had competed in organized athletics after elementary school. Included in that number were such notable leaders as national security advisor Condoleeza Rice and Sue Wellington, president of Gatorade Corporation.

According to the study, sport is a tool for young women that helps them compete in any male-dominated business. Offered Mrs. Wellington, "The main benefit is that you really 'get' what competition is all about: the multiple arts of taking risks in the face of uncertainty; getting and giving team help; pushing hard even when you're behind and things seem hopeless. All those things serve both men and women in their careers."

One last chance to play. The public's fascination with athletics has generated unprecedented attention to (some would say has elevated game-playing grotesquely out of) its appropriate place in our society. Accelerated intensity of sport at all levels has resulted in more competitive athletes across the board.

What happens to all of the youngsters who yearn to continue competing in varsity sports after high school, but who are not talented enough to play at the top level collegiately? These individuals seek, or are impelled by reality, to find their suitable level of competition in a process mirroring "natural selection."

Rosters at schools like the University of Indianapolis are filled by generally able but less talented or physically smaller athletes who compete just as fiercely, enjoy the spirit of competition as avidly, and seek public approval as heartily as their counterparts in programs with greater visibility. With a few notable exceptions, athletes will not go on to professional playing careers after leaving the university. Nonetheless, programs such as those at the U of I provide an opportunity for students to continue to enjoy varsity competition beyond their high school experience.

As former DePauw University coach and athletics director Tommy Mont once boasted about small-college football, "What's different about our football program at DePauw and that of the 'major' schools? We've got all the color and drama—marching bands, cute and lively cheerleaders, great rivalries pitting vigorous and competitive young men against one another, great tailgating, rabid alumni second-guessing the coaches. The

Distinction Without Pretension

only thing big schools have that we don't? Parking problems!"

Influential alumni. A residual but certainly far-reaching benefit of an intercollegiate program is that many athletes enter the teaching and coaching profession after graduation. Studies have indicated that coaches have a disproportionate influence upon young people, and, further, many successful adult men and women rate their athletic mentors among the most positive influences on their lives. The U of I has produced an abundance of exemplary coaches at all levels of sport. Among those who returned to their alma mater to become singularly influential in the lives of thousands of student-athletes were Harry Good '25, Edgar Bright '26, Angus Nicoson '42, Dave Shaw '52, Bill Bright '54, Paul Velez '56, Ken Partridge '58, Willie Martin '59, Doreen St. Clair '61, Bill Bless '63, Gerry England '63, Terry Wetherald '63, Suzanne Willey '75, and Dave Wood '76.

William "Tony" Sharpe '39 was head baseball coach for thirty-one years at the University of Nebraska; Bob Otolski '60 was a successful high school and college coach, including serving as head coach at Northern Illinois University; Mark Reiff '78 coached the women's track team at Stanford University; Dave Wollman '76 is currently head track coach at Southern Methodist University; and both the men's and women's track squads at Indiana University have U of I graduates as their head coaches, Marshall Goss '60 and Randy Heisler '86, respectively.

In the high school ranks, Sharon Most '63 led Martinsville girls' golfers to an amazing nine state titles in eleven years. Also unprecedented is the six state basketball championships coached by 1956 graduate Bill Green '56, including three in a row in 1985-86-87. Ray Crowe's '39 Crispus Attucks Tigers dominated Hoosier basketball in the '50s, with two championships in 1955 and 1956. Jack Colescott '52 and George Marshall '59 are also Indiana Hall of Fame high school basketball mentors. Phil Acton '62 compiled one of the most impressive high school football coaching records in Illinois history, with nineteen of his ex-players making NFL squads. A member of the Indiana Football Hall of Fame, Don Bunge '48 coached superbly for 33 years at Bremen High School, where the football field is now named in his honor. Ray Howard '61, Don Poole '61, Bill Tutterow '69 and John Wirtz '61 have all coached more than 500 wins in high school baseball. Mary "Wimp" Baumgartner '57 and Marilyn Ramsey '63, each a member of the U of I Hall of Fame, produced outstanding teams in long coaching careers.

These are only a handful of the thousands of less heralded graduates of the college who have made a difference in the lives of untold numbers of young athletes who came under their tutelage.

Does athletic competition belong in the academy? The question will continue to be debated in colleges and universities indefinitely.

Dr. Scott S. Cowen, president of Tulane University, is among a growing number of current chief executives at NCAA Division I-A institutions who are dubious about the role of intercollegiate athletics in the university's daily life.

Lamenting that the elite intercollegiate athletic programs are "increasingly out of sync with the goals and values of American higher education," Cowen and his board of trustees recently initiated a re-evaluation of Tulane's athletic division. Despite having a "clean program with one of the highest graduation rates for student-athletes in the nation," Cowen and his colleagues nevertheless have come face-to-face with the daunting reality that sports may no longer have a place in their university:

James L. Brunnemer

> *We had to weigh the cost of running* [athletics] *in light of the disparity in intercollegiate athletics being exacerbated by the presence of the Bowl Championship* [football] *series. It is a student-centered athletics program being run in a national athletics climate that revolves around entertainment and big money. It is time for all of us to think about the real purpose of higher education and where athletics fits into that purpose.*

Hodding Carter III, president of the Knight Foundation, echoed Dr. Cowen's concerns regarding the growing influence of money on intercollegiate athletics when he chided college trustees and administrators: "What's not in doubt is that there are really vast sums being spent ... that further distort the position of sports in higher education."

Generally, the ICC/U of I athletics program has met standards of acceptability as a small-college program offering broad-based opportunities for both men and women. A balance between striving for excellence without over-emphasizing winning at the expense of integrity (U of I has never been cited for a major NCAA violation) seems to characterize the university's commitment to athletics. Its athletes *are* students (athletes generally earn higher grade point averages than that of the rest of the student body) and athletics provides another venue for teaching lessons for life.

The last time I looked, all head, and some assistant, coaches at the U of I were members of the faculty. Dr. Carl Stockton, retired dean at the University of Indianapolis, was not one to allow extracurricular activities to stray too distant from the mission of the school during his eighteen years as chief academic officer. He recently made these observations of coaches regarding the responsibility they assumed for their players' academic performance:

> *My impression was that it was done remarkably well, thanks to the coaches and their staffs, who understood the primacy of academics, and were helpful in extraordinary ways with individual students. Some faculty, of course, always groused about the athletic tail wagging the institutional dog. I did not see this. Indeed, I always had an ally in problem academic deficiencies, and I often wished that all students with academic problems had the strong and unwavering support of the coaching faculty. Their success rate was astounding. I've always believed in the ideal of* mens sana in corpore sano*, *and considered athletics an integral part of the college curricula. Finally, my experience was that coaches were among the most responsible faculty in committee work, those ubiquitous tasks faculty have beyond the classroom in academic governance. This speaks to the integration of athletic faculty into the whole educational fabric.*

> * *"Sound mind, in sound body."*

Distinction Without Pretension

    The U of I sports program has not been the source of widespread prominence, nor has the university reaped great sums of money like many of the Division I-A sports programs. Athletics have generally been kept in balance, providing students and the university community with appropriate benefits without succumbing to the lure of lucre and notoriety, and its oft-times accompanying scandals.

    Nonetheless, between the lines, student-athletes wearing the crimson and grey compete no less fervently than their counterparts at institutions with major sports programs, for,

> *[I]n a race, everyone runs but only one person gets first prize.*
> *So run your race to win ... run straight to the goal with purpose in every step.*
>
>   I Corinthians 9: 24-26

CHAPTER XX
THE LADY GREYHOUNDS

> *[G]ender equity in education[will ensure] that no person will be excluded on the basis of sex from participating in, be denied benefits of, or be subjected to discrimination under any program or activity receiving federal financial assistance.*
>
> Title IX
> June 23, 1972

Should you ever have occasion to visit the Major League Baseball Hall of Fame in Cooperstown, New York, you will find one graduate of Indiana Central College enshrined in the hallowed archives of professional baseball history.

Would you care to guess who that former Greyhound athlete is?

How about Mary Louise "Wimp" Baumgartner of Fremont, Indiana, Class of 1957?

Although sports offerings for women were sparse at ICC in those days, Wimp was ahead of her time as a female student-athlete from 1954-57.

Mary Louise (she'll scold me for using her given name rather than her favored nickname!) participated in all the sports available to women and even played a role in the baseball career of classmate Bill Bright. During the off-season, as Bill perfected his pitching style, he often lacked a catcher. One of the few athletes on campus who would venture behind the plate to accept throws from a guy who threw a more than 90-mile-an-hour fastball, had a devastating curve, and was more than a bit wild, was Wimp. She was tough and athletic enough to handle Bill's offerings.

Baumgartner played five years in the All-American Girls Professional Baseball League, twice making the league's All-Star team at the catcher's position. If you watch closely toward the end of the highly successful motion picture "A League of Their Own," starring Tom Hanks and Geena Davis, you'll see Wimp. In the scene where the women are invited to Cooperstown for a special induction of the league's players into baseball's illustrious hall is Indiana Central's Mary Baumgartner, along with other aging members of that league.

Following her playing days, Mary embarked on a twenty-five-year coaching and teaching career from which she retired in 1990. She was inducted into the University of Indianapolis Athletics Hall of Fame in 2000.

Along with her sisters, Wimp contributed the funds to renovate, modernize, and provide lights for the current U of I women's softball stadium. Baumgartner Field is now one of the finest playing facilities in the Great Lakes Valley Conference.

As Title IX passes the thirty-second anniversary of its enactment, opportunities for women seeking participation in sport have never been greater. I am especially delighted that my six-year-old granddaughter, Julia, and her infant sister, Kaitlyn, will have a near-equal opportunity of playing sports as grandsons Noah, Nate, and Sam as they grow up.

At the University of Indianapolis, women may choose from among eleven different sports teams, one more than the men. Excluding the football squad, the roster of which numbers approximately eighty male students, a greater number of women annually compete in the Greyhound uniform than men.

Despite the gains in opportunity that Title IX has afforded women in interscholastic and intercollegiate athletics, problems do persist. Sports litigation has become commonplace in many American colleges and universities. Ironically, some men who believe the effects of Title IX has deprived them of opportunity to participate in the sport of their choice have been the initiators of legal action. The dilemma, in shorthand, is that because of rising costs at all levels of sport—and the legislation that demands that women have equal access to sport with their male counterparts—many schools are being forced to eliminate some male sports teams to meet Title IX regulations. Usually men's so-called "minor" sports, such as volleyball, wrestling, and golf, for example, are curtailed or abolished altogether.

Can women athletes compete with men in comparable arenas, on the playing fields?

I would maintain that two truths are apparent in regard to women's athletics. First, it is sexist and wrong to deny women equal opportunity to participate in sport. Secondly, it is neither sexist nor wrong to notice that most male athletes are stronger, faster, and more powerful, than their female counterparts and thus superior in athletic performance.

Actually, we need not guess about this. Men and women compete in some sports in which they carry out exactly the same activity and objective measurements are made. For example, in track and field, men and women perform in the long jump and high jump, and run the 100-, 400-, and the 5,000-meter runs. The results are obvious.

Enough examples exist at the interscholastic, intercollegiate, and professional levels to indicate that men are generally stronger, faster, and leap higher and farther than women.

In May 2003 thirty-two-year-old Annika Sorenstam, who has dominated the Ladies Professional Golf Association for several years, was invited to play in the PGA's Colonial tournament. In accepting the sponsor's exemption, Sorenstam became the first woman in fifty-eight years to play in a men's professional tour event. While she shot respectable scores of 71 and 74 (five over par for the two days) she missed the cut, with only eleven out of 111 golfers carding higher scores. The winner of the Colonial event, Kenny Perry, said of Sorenstam, "She showed she's the best woman golfer in the world. She handled the whole experience with dignity."

Assuring all that she enjoyed herself measuring her game against that of her male counterparts, Annika said, "I'm glad I did it."

She was quick to admit, nonetheless, "But this was way over my head. I wasn't as tough as I thought I was."

Accuracy and distance in driving a golf ball from a small tee is considered one of sport's most difficult skills. While topflight female professional golfers may surpass the lowest-rated members of the Professional Golfers Association, the top men consistently out-drive the best women golfers by yards off the tee. Women may possess the perfect swing, and impeccable timing, but they simply do not have the muscle mass and explosive power of the men. Annika's 268-yard average drive was 100th among the 111 players at the Colonial.

Consider the average driving distance, in measured yards, of the best of the men's Professional Golf Association tour, the Senior PGA, and the Ladies' Professional Golf Association over the past five years:

Year	PGA Tour	Senior PGA	LPGA
1998	John Daly (299.4)	John Jacobs (284.9)	Caroline Blaylock (267.0)
1999	John Daly (305.6)	John Jacobs (285.7)	Jean Bartholomew (260.7)
2000	John Daly (301.4)	Terry Dill (286.2)	Caroline Blaylock (270.1)
2001	John Daly (306.7)	Lon Hinkle (289.3)	Wendy Doolan (265.8)
2002	John Daly (305.3)	John Jacobs (285.4)	Akiko Fukushima (270.4)

I would bet the house that similar data will accrue among world-class athletes in any sports that divide men and women in terms of strength and speed.

However, there is no reason why in skills requiring superior hand-eye coordination, like putting in golf, for example, women cannot be equal to, or surpass, males. I regret I don't have putting averages for PGA, Senior PGA, and LPGA players, but I would venture to guess in that aspect of the game of golf, the best women golf pros would compare favorably with the top male players.

Having made the point that in "power-oriented" sports men are dominant, why shouldn't we expect women to be able to compete with men in professional billiards? Shouldn't Jeannette Lee, the "Black Widow," play comparably to her male counterparts in a game that doesn't require great strength, but superior coordination of hand-eye movements and great concentrative powers? Shouldn't professional basketball statistics for, say, free throw shooting accuracy be as high for women as men? Where the primary criterion in an athletic event involves hand-eye coordination and a high degree of focus rather than physical strength and speed, why shouldn't women be able to compete equally with or better than men?

National polls surveying intercollegiate athletics have revealed the obvious: the most popular sports in terms of spectator interest are basketball and football. Men's basketball and football. There are exceptions, but it's fair to say that a large majority of Americans prefer men's sports to that of women's.

At the intercollegiate level, in contrast to the growing popularity of men's basketball, the top-level programs that continue to reap astronomical amounts of cash, only six women's NCAA Division I-A programs out of 114 made money in 2001-02. In fact, in its latest survey of Division I-A, I-AA, and II colleges and universities, among all men's and women's sports, eight of the top ten sports programs ranked by average financial loss were those of women:

Women's basketball	-$711,000
Women's track and field/cross-country	-$398,000
Women's volleyball	-$391,000
Women's rowing	-$385,000
Women's gymnastics	-$378,000
Women's softball	-$377,000
Men's baseball	-$367,000
Men's track and field/cross-country	-$356,000
Women's swimming	-$346,000
Women's field hockey	-$342,000

Sadly, reality caused the collapse of the Womens' United Soccer Association (WUSA) in September 2003. Despite the popularity of such stars as Mia Hamm and Julie Foudy, languishing attendance and television ratings forced the closing of the league before the season was even half-completed.

And finally, consider that through the date of the historic Colonial tourney in which Annika Sorenstam competed, the top ten female professional golfers, led by Se Ri Pak, Sorenstam and Grace Park, had earned a *total* of $3,630,122 in prize money. Davis Love III alone had garnered $3,787,712, more than the top ten women. And the three men behind Love—Mike Weir ($3,365,025), Tiger Woods ($3,067,250), and Vijay Singh ($3,001,255)—had won nearly as much as he. The obvious fact is that in all professional sports, men outrank women in popularity as assessed by the number of viewers and the number of dollars spent.

Why? It is probably an oversimplification to suggest the obvious: that males are, in physical strength and speed, superior to their female counterparts. But therein lies at least part of the answer. Those who participate in or follow athletics with great interest are generally attracted to those athletes who perform at the highest levels of sport. The popularity of sports where speed, strength, and explosive power of musculature are necessary will continue to favor men over women. Why else the appeal of superstars like Michael Jordan, Barry Bonds, and, closer to home, Peyton Manning and Reggie Miller, for endorsing commercial products? Each is considered to be among the best at what he does in professional sports. Many women professionals represent various products to the public as well, but male athletes make many times more, on the average, than females in placing their images in advertising campaigns.

Although I have already made clear my conclusions about the superiority of male athletes over their female counterparts, there have been many outstanding women athletes who have performed for the Crimson and Grey.

Current athletic director Dr. Suzanne Willey came to Indiana Central from her home in Iowa to follow her high school idol, Judy Powell (Birgerson) '67 to Indianapolis. Sue would set school records for participation in sports that might never be surpassed. From 1972-75, Willey earned more letters (nineteen) than any athlete, male or female, in the school's history. Sue garnered four letters each in field hockey, volleyball, basketball, and softball, and three more in tennis. No fewer than eleven times she was named Most Valuable Player in her sport. Graduating cum laude, Sue was honored with induction into the U of I Hall of Fame in 1993, ten years before she would be named director of athletics for her alma mater.

Of the female athletes I've had the opportunity to watch most consistently, one especially stands out for her astounding achievements. From 1991-95, Melissa Graham's performance as a point guard for the Lady Greyhounds was unsurpassed. She may well be the finest all-around basketball player in the history of U of I athletics. Consider the number of categories in which Melissa appears in the U of I record book. Eight years after her final game as a Greyhound, Melissa remains:

- 1st in career **assists** with 593.
- 1st in **steals** for a game (8, twice), season (98, 1992-93), and career (335).
- 1st in career and season **3-point shooting accuracy**, with 224 of 552 attempts (a .406 percentage, which still ranks her seventeenth all-time in NCAA Division II statistics), and 60-136 during the 1994-95 season (.441).
- 1st in number of **3-point shots** made in both a season (64, 1994-95) and career (224).
- 5th in career **scoring**, with 1,464, an average of 15 points per game.
- 8th in all-time U of I **rebounding** with 566 (let me remind you this girl was a point guard!)

Add to this that her record of forty-five consecutive free throws made is still the U of I standard and you begin to grasp that her skills and instincts for the game of basketball were nonpareil. Not one to hand out false praise, men's coach Royce Waltman once paid Melissa a striking compliment. After an outstanding exhibition by his talented point guard, Ty Barksdale, GLVC Player of the Year and a second-team NCAA All-American in 1997, an admiring and enthusiastic news reporter asked Waltman:

"Coach, have you ever seen a better job of handling the basketball by a point guard in your coaching career?"

Deadpanned the coach: "As a matter of fact, I have. Melissa Graham in the game right before ours!"

Despite my presupposition of the superiority of the male athlete, it is my judgment that the single most dominant individual athlete in the history of Greyhound sports was a female. It would be hard to argue that the record of performance compiled in four years (1987-90) on the ICC tennis courts by June Wernke (Rigney) '90 is unequaled by any other single Greyhound athlete, ever. *Sports Illustrated* featured this young woman who won the Great Lakes Valley women's singles championship all four years that she competed; matched that record in women's doubles with different partners; was selected GLVC Tennis Player of the Year each of her four years; and three times qualified for the NCAA Women's National Tennis Tournament.

Along the way, June received the Greyhound Outstanding Female Student-Athlete Award and the Student-Athlete Sportsmanship Award. She was inducted into the U of I Hall of Fame in 2000. The punch line to June's extraordinary career? She was *never beaten* during the regular season in her four seasons at U of I—65 wins, *nada* losses.

James L. Brunnemer

Any doubters?

If there were an Anna Kournikova Most Beautiful Lady Greyhound Athlete Award, Courtney Sands-Gault '93 would be my choice, hands down. The 6'2" lass, who set a record for rebounds in a career with 929 and is still fourth on the all-time women's scoring list in basketball (1,527) was, simply, drop-dead gorgeous. The Kodak All-American, GLVC Player of the Year in 1992-93, and 2002 Greyhound Hall of Fame inductee would step on her mother to get a rebound, then break into a smile so radiant I'm certain Mom would forgive her. If Melissa Graham was the offensive artiste of the 1992-93 Lady Greyhound squad (24-4), Courtney was the stevedore who shored up the defense and was the unspectacular but consistent warrior for Chuck Mallender's greatest team.

LuAnn Humphrey '84, inducted into the University of Indianapolis Athletic Hall of Fame in 2001, was a three-time MVP for the Lady Greyhound basketball team. She remains third on the all-time rebounding list (819) and tenth in scoring (1,092). LuAnn was honored with the 2002 Dr. Charles Bertram Alumni Award of Distinction. The Bertram Award recognizes personal and professional achievements of former Great Lakes Valley Conference student-athletes. An attorney, Humphrey has served as an enforcement representative for the NCAA since 1999.

Just a little squirt, Michelle Faulkner '93 was blessed with a huge heart and an unimposing but valiant competitive drive. Quiet, unassuming, and no bigger than a minute at 5'2" and ninety-five pounds, she looked as frail as Bambi. But this little waif had the steely resolve of a Marine drill instructor. She would earn three All-Little State honors, was twice an All-GLVC selection, and would perform on U of I cross-country teams that compiled a record of 245 wins, fifteen losses in her four years as a letter winner. She missed becoming U of I's first female national champion in the 800-meter run in track and field in 1993, finishing second by a stride, earning All-American honors in that event.

I had the privilege of viewing Pam Rodriguez '96 swat winner after winner, totally frustrating her opponents on the tennis court. And she seemed hardly to be working at it. Her 21-0 record in '96 is the Greyhound women's record for one season.

Although Vijitha Amarasekara '94 competed for the Greyhound women's track team, Jerry England coached her to the individual women's title in the javelin in both 1993 and '94. Another of England's projects from the Lady Greyhound team was Amy Jackson Perryman '88. In her senior year, Jackson was a double All-American under England's tutelage in both the discus and shot put. She was inducted into both the University of Indianapolis Hall of Fame (2001) and the Wall of Fame at her high school, Southport in 2003.

In the relatively brief history of women's athletics at ICC/U of I, Greyhound rooters have had the privilege of observing a number of outstanding women's squads.

Basketball has been a varsity sport played by ICC women since the mid-1950s. Among the gifted athletes of note to perform for the Lady Greyhounds prior to the time the university joined the NCAA in 1972 was Judy Powell Birgeson. A stately six-footer when she stood erect (in the sixties, statuesque women like Judy were self-conscious, and so they often subtly slumped to understate their height), Ms. Powell '67 could outshoot ninety percent of the guys on campus in a game of "H.O.R.S.E." She was an all-around performer on the hardwood as a rebounder and passer, as well as an accurate shooter. Judy Powell Birgerson was inducted into U of I's Hall of Fame in 1999.

Among the successful head coaches for the Lady Greyhounds was a former player for Angus Nicoson, Jack Noone '69. With Debbie Law '85 and LuAnn Humphrey leading the way, the Hounds posted 18-7 and 17-8 campaigns in 1980-81 and 1981-82, respectively.

Replacing Noone after the 1981-82 season, Chuck Mallender would amass a record of 179-101 in eleven seasons as Lady Greyhounds coach. Until 1992-93, Mallender's 20-3 squad of 1983-84 would be the finest single year in women's history. It would be in 1993 that, regrettably, Coach Chuck Mallender died of cancer. In 2000, Coach Mallender was named posthumously to the Greyhound Hall of Fame.

Two years later, with stalwarts Graham and Hensley still in the lineup, new coach Lisa Hicks would lead the women to the NCAA II play-offs on the strength of a 21-7 record.

From 1997-2001, Greyhound fans would thrill at the exploits of Greenfield's Elizabeth Ramsey '01. She would break school marks for points in a season (534) and career (1,887). Ramsey tossed in 39 against IPFW on February 7, 1999, which still stands as the school's one-game record for women cagers. During her stellar career she set records for points per game in a season (21.4) and career (17.6). You'll find Ramsey's name just above Courtney Sands-Gault as the career leader in rebounds with 973 as well.

In her second season since she assumed head coaching duties for the U of I in 2000-01, Coach Teri Moren had her Lady Greyhounds ranked in the nation's NCAA Division II top ten. The former Indiana All-State and Purdue performer recruited a tall and talented group of women, which featured balanced scoring and a suffocating defense. With a record of 29-3, Moren's 2002-03 squad set a record for most wins in a season, placing it at the top of those outstanding teams of the past:

2002-03	29-3	.906	Terri Moren
1983-84	20-3	.870	Chuck Mallender
1992-93	24-4	.857	Chuck Mallender
1987-88	22-5	.815	Chuck Mallender
1994-95	21-7	.750	Lisa Hicks

By all measures the two best women's basketball teams in Greyhound history were the 1992-93 and 2002-03 aggregations. The similarities in talent and style of play were striking, and the team play exhibited by both was extraordinary.

Let's begin with the coaches, Chuck Mallender and Teri Moren, respectively. Both were (are) exceptional judges of talent. Each recruited players of high caliber, both in terms of ability and competitive drive. Both had at least one superior post player surrounded by an array of more petite but highly active teammates. In terms of preparation and game plans, Mallender and Moren should take a place among the upper tier of coaches, male or female, in any sport for the U of I.

After racing to nineteen victories in their first twenty-one games, the Lady Greyhounds of 1992-93 were faced with an agonizing reality. Their beloved coach, Chuck Mallender, was forced to leave the team near the end of the season because of a rapidly advancing cancer. As Chuck's health steadily faltered, his team, under interim coach Mary

James L. Brunnemer

Maravilla '91, dedicated itself to making their coach proud. Their collective grief was excruciatingly evident as they attended Coach Mallender's funeral with but three games remaining on their schedule. Dedicating the season to Coach Mallender, the Lady Hounds won the Great Lakes Valley championship, but the dream of advancing to the Elite Eight ended in the first round of the NCAA Division II regional when they fell to Saginaw Valley State, 81-76.

The team set all-time records for points per game (82.0) and rebounds, averaging 44.9 per contest. Four of the players on that team would ultimately finish their careers among the five all-time top scorers. All-American Courtney Sands completed her four-year stint at center ranked third highest among scorers with 1,527 points and as the women's leader in rebounds with 919. She was, in 2002, inducted into the U of I Athletic Hall of Fame. Crafty playmaker and one of the nation's top three-point shooters, Melissa Graham, finished fourth in career points (1,464) while Lori Morgan '93 was just behind in fifth place with 1,341. Morgan grabbed 775 rebounds in her career to finish in third place all-time. Freshman forward Ann Hensley would end her career three years later as the career leader in points scored with 1,650.

Winning twenty-nine of thirty-two games in 2002-03, Teri Moren's team won more games in one season than any Greyhound basketball squad, male or female.

For Coach Moren, the "go-to" cager under the hoop was the graceful, 6'2" Kristen Lowry '03, who led the team in both scoring (15) and rebounding (7) per game. Lowry, a senior, finished among the top twenty individuals nationally in shooting percentage, bagging sixty percent of her field goal attempts on the year. Balanced scoring was a key for the Lady Greyhounds, who won a record seventeen consecutive games before falling to Northern Kentucky in the NCAA Division II championship tournament. Former Roncalli All-State selection Erin Moran '03 (14 ppg) and sharpshooter Amy Wisser '05(10) both averaged in double figures, with 6'0" Emily Hammes '04 providing assistance on the boards. Also, Moren's women focused on superb team defense, allowing but fifty-eight points a game to their opponents.

If there was one element that separated these two outstanding teams it would be at point guard, where the incomparable Melissa Graham sparkled game after game for Coach Mallender. For all-around play, no one before or since has surpassed the skills of the 5'8" Graham. Although a decade separated the squads, either could wear the title of "greatest Lady Greyhound basketball team ever."

Track and field enjoyed its best decade from 1984-94, during the time that the Greyhound ladies' coach was Dawn Patel. During those ten years, Dawn guided the program to heights not approached previously. In only her second year the Greyhound track squad was 37-3, led by U of I Hall of Famer Amy Jackson Perryman '87. Sandy Hedges, Amy's mother, credited yet another Indiana Central graduate, Tom Hathaway '54, with helping Amy through trying times as a teenager. Hathaway, who later became cross country coach at his alma mater, mentored Amy Jackson as head track coach at Southport High School during a bleak period in her life when she watched her father battle the cancer that ultimately took his life.

"Coach Hathaway and his wife, Carolyn, took Amy under their wings when her father, Russ Jackson, died of cancer while she was in high school," Mrs. Hedges noted. "To cope, she put all her energies into track."

In addition to her induction into the U of I athletic honor group, Amy Jackson Perryman was similarly honored by the Indiana Track and the Southport High School halls of fame.

For three consecutive seasons, Patel's ladies dominated opponents, compiling a combined record of eighty-five wins against only ten losses in 1990 (35-2), 1991 (19-1), and 1992 (31-7). In her final two years as coach, Dawn would have an NCAA II national champion in the javelin event. In '93 and '94, Vijitha Amarasekara was the titleist, and subsequently represented her native land, Thailand, in the 1994 Olympic games.

During the 1995 and '96 seasons, men's coach Jerry England did double duty, coaching the women in addition to his men's squads. There was no drop-off in success, as the women defeated thirty-six foes, losing eleven contests.

When Scott Fangman replaced England in '96 as head of the men's program, he accepted the women's post as well. His 2002 women's team went 38-1 and finished in a dead heat with Lewis University for the first GLVC title for the women. Maria Harriman '03, a distance runner, earned first-team college division Academic All-America honors in track and field that season and is a two-time All-American in the 1500-meter run. Harriman is just the sixth person to earn repeat Academic All-American status and just the second to be chosen to the first team more than once.

Despite the loss of key veterans such as Harriman, Fangman's 2003 squad proved to be dominant again. Winning its tenth consecutive Little State Meet, the women matched the men's 39-1 record for the season. All-American Cari Roush '04 won three field events in the Little State, including the shot put, discus, and the hammer throw. Tiffany Turner '04 was extraordinary in the 100- and 200-meter sprints. Roush, Turner, and 3,000-meter steeplechase competitor Nicole Williams '03 represented U of I in the Division II national meet in Edwardsville, Illinois.

Softball at ICC fielded its first women's team in 1969, under coach Joanne Alexander. Current athletic director Sue Willey would guide the program for eighteen seasons (1978-96), compiling a 256-187-3 record. Led by Julie Joseforsky '91, Kathy Miller '92, Tricia Neely '91, and Cindy Simko '91, the 1990 (24-7) and 1991 (27-9) teams were the most successful in Lady Greyhound annals.

A steadily improving 2003 squad was led by a freshman pitching sensation, Beth Wendlinger '06, who earned All-GLVC First Team honors after compiling a 7-3 record, a 1.24 earned run average and more than ten strikeouts per nine innings pitched in conference play. With Wendlinger available for three more seasons, things bode well for the Greyhounds' softball future.

Swimming and diving for women and men experienced nearly identical success during the coaching stint of Seeman Baugh. Coach Baugh built an enviable record coaching women during his decade at the helm. With dominant All-American performers such as Nicole Rives '94 (1993 and '94 in free style) and Joy Anderson '95, who won one- and three-meter diving in '94 and '95, including the national individual title in the three-meter board in 1995, Coach Baugh and his women defeated nearly eighty percent of their opponents (227-63, .783) during his coaching career.

James L. Brunnemer

Stepping into a well-established program, Coach Gary Kinkead has continued the success of the swimming teams at U of I. His women swimmers finished twelfth in the NCAA Division II national swim meet in both 2001 and 2002. Leading the squad in '02 to a record of 54-15, two-time Great Lakes Intercollegiate Athletic Conference Athlete of the Year Megan Grunert '03 competed in the 200-meter individual medley, the 200-breaststroke, and the 100-butterfly, setting U of I records and earning All-America honors in all three!

In 2003, Grunert again earned GLIAC Athlete of the Year honors, but at this event the six-time All-American led her team to U of I's first conference swimming title in school history. On the heels of the conference championship and on the strong performance of Megan and her mates, the U of I recorded its highest finish ever at the 2003 NCAA Division II championships, held at Grand Forks, North Dakota, at eleventh. With a time of 2:18.25 in the 200 breaststroke, Grunert finished third, yet another All-American performance. Teammate Stephanie McKaig '04, a mere six seconds behind Grunert, claimed ninth place in the same race.

Tennis coach Dawn Patel (1979-2002) stepped down in the spring of '02 after seventeen seasons of unparalleled success. Compiling a 219-138-3 overall record, Dawn's ladies won Heartland Conference titles in 1978 and '81 and GLVC championships seven times. Two of her superlative players were June Wernke (Rigney) and Pam Rodriguez. A four-year GLVC singles champ and four-time GLVC Player of the Year, Wernke-Rigney would end her regular season career with a 65-0 record. Pam Rodriguez, who was the first U of I player ever to win the Rolex Mid-American regional tournament, was undefeated (21-0) in 1996.

Replacing Patel in the spring of 2002, current coach John Venter led his 16-1 women's tennis team to his first GLVC women's tournament championship. The women were undefeated in conference play. Grace Wilhoite '04 ended the season without a single loss in conference singles and doubles play, earning GLVC Player of the Year honors.

With the veteran Wilhoite (19-6 in singles and 21-6 in doubles) and Jessica Broadus '05 (18-6 singles, 15-5 doubles) leading the way, Venter's 2003 team set a new record for team victories with eighteen to earn a bid to the NCAA II national tournament.

Cross-country Coach Tom Hathaway led his women's squad to 398 victories against just sixty losses, an unprecedented .869 winning percentage, from 1988-94. Among the finest lady distance runners in the history of the college was tiny Michelle Faulkner, who earned All-American honors in both cross-country and track. Along with a strong supporting cast of Amy Potts '92, Brenda Liechty '92, Beth Walters '92, and Tracy Smith '90, Faulkner and her mates swept the Little State title three straight times (1990-'91-'92). The 1992 team set a record with a 71-3 mark, and, at fourth place, finished the highest ever in the NCAA II Great Lakes Region.

Coaching both men's and women's cross-country teams is 1990 graduate Kathy Casey '90. Casey, the GLVC individual champion as a competitor in 1988, has mentored Maria Harriman '03, one of twenty-nine recipients in all NCAA divisions to receive an NCAA post-graduate scholarship.

In 1986, Larry Bledsoe '59 fielded the first women's golf team to represent the

Distinction Without Pretension

University of Indianapolis in NCAA Division II play. Christy Federle '90 and aptly named Michelle Swing '93 became the first Lady Greyhounds to earn All-American honors. Bledsoe's ladies won the GLVC in 1999, 2000, and 2001. Courtney Tate '02, twice a GLVC Scholar-athlete of the Year and the first three-time All-GLVC player in school history, set the U of I standard for number of victories in 2002, closing with a 110-35-5.

Former star athlete Kelly Tungate '92 replaced Bledsoe as U of I golf mentor in 2003. Standouts for Tungate were Tate, Kim Moore '03, and Amy Wenning '05.

Under the coaching of Jody Butera, the Lady Hounds won its first GLVC championship ever in volleyball. With an all-time best season record of 29-10, the team made its first trip to the NCAA tournament in 2003. Three-time All GLVC outside hitter Shaun Mcallister '05 was the team leader.

Tallying eighteen goals and forty-one assists-both school records-Jenna Silverman was selected Player of the Year in the Great Lakes Valley Conference in 2003, as well as earning Academic All-District V honors.

In 1972 Title IX legislation opened a door for women who seek competition through athletics. At the University of Indianapolis as at other universities, women have been liberated to express themselves, unchecked by past prejudices, through competitive physical activity. The presence of women athletes at the university has brought to it a completeness not present prior to 1972.

CHAPTER XXI

THE ELYSIAN FIELDS

*The race is not always to the swift, nor the
battle to the strong. But that's the way to bet.*
            Damon Runyon

For athletes, as well as followers of sport, the courts and fields and tracks where games take place are Elysian fields, exceedingly delightful places indeed. In every gymnasium, upon every football field and baseball diamond and golf course, around every track oval and within every tennis court, special recollections are made for and through those who compete and for those who support them.

Indiana Central's "temporary gym"—built in 1921 as a short-term structure that ended up being used through the 1960 season—was one of those memorable venues where generations of Indiana Central students united in common advocacy of their school's teams. It was long gone before I arrived on campus but the really old-timers, the alumni even more grizzled than I, recall extraordinary moments there. The noise of the raucous capacity crowd of probably no more than 1,000 fans in that gym, supporting the Greyhound hoopsters, seemed as deafening as that generated by the 17,000 that regularly gather in IU's Assembly Hall. According to one alumnus who saw his first basketball game there as a boy, "It even *smelled* like a place where basketball should be played."

In my long association with the University of Indianapolis as a player, the father of a U of I athlete, and an avid follower of Greyhound sports, I've compiled a truckload of memories of exceptional teams, stunning athletic plays, and effulgent individual performers.

Appraising nearly a century of Greyhound teams, how does one define its greatest? If you were to choose from all the sports teams at the university, what criteria would you use to judge the best of the best?

I suppose one must start with national champions, the teams that climbed the mountain to win an encompassing elimination tournament, or were a consensus choice as champion of all by a sanctioned voting body. If either of those are the standard, then the only team in the history of U of I to win a national title would be the 1990 Division III University of Indianapolis Forensic Team. The squad, coached by Professor Audrey Cunningham, defeated Colorado State by one-half point at Mankato State University in Minnesota to win the only known and bona fide national team championship of any kind in this university's history.

Forensics, to the unwashed, is not really a sport. Nor is it the examination of a dead body. That is *forensic medicine*. This title was for virtuosity in argumentative discourse—basically a speech contest. And U of I was the best of all in Division III that year! The star of the team was, as one might suspect, a communications major, Steve Dabrowski '92. The team leader placed high in "Impromptu Speaking," "After Dinner Speaking," and a combination of five oratory events called the "Pentathlon."

Other stalwarts on the U of I's only national titleist were Kerri Brinson '90, Amy

James L. Brunnemer

Pacheco '91, and, interestingly, a *nursing major*, Kristina Ganschow '90.

Alas, regarding intercollegiate athletics, the U of I has yet to win a national title in either a women's or a men's sport. That detail aside, Greyhound athletics have had a rich and distinguished history, with many extraordinary teams in its competitive class.

The first truly notable Greyhound teams were the basketball squads recruited and coached by Harry Good. Captain of ICC's 1924 cagers, "Handsome Harry" was the lanky nephew of President I. J. Good. Returning to Indiana Central in 1928 to serve as athletics director, Good would coach, at one time or another, football, track, baseball, and tennis. But it would be in coaching the sport of basketball that he would set a standard of excellence that has been unmatched in the more than sixty years since he left ICC.

Unfettered by cryptic racist rules enforced at other schools and conferences such as the Big Ten, Harry Good was one of the first collegiate coaches to recruit black players. From 1932-35 the Good-led Greyhounds dominated Indiana small colleges with successive season records of 16-3, 16-1, and 15-4, a three-year run of 47-8, an .855 winning percentage.

In basketball, ICC first played Butler, its Indianapolis rival, in the 1928-29 season. Proclaimed by sportswriters of the day as National Collegiate Champions, the 17-2 Bulldogs of a youthful Tony Hinkle drubbed Harry Good and Greyhounds 67-19 that year. The next time the Bulldogs and the Greyhounds met, in 1933-34, Harry and his boys had apparently learned something. Behind big Dave DeJernett, the first of many great African-American athletes to wear the Cardinal and Grey, ICC won sixteen of seventeen games, including a victory over Butler in the storied Fieldhouse, 32-31. The two Indy-based schools would play each of the next five seasons with these results:

1934-35	BU 37, ICC 24
1935-36	ICC 39, BU 34
1936-37	ICC 41, BU 27
1937-38	ICC 43, BU 40
1938-39	BU 37, ICC 33

In their personal duel, Harry Good bested Hall-of-Famer Hinkle, four games to three. Perhaps Coach Hinkle's true wisdom came in his knowledge of when to cut and run. The series ended after the 1939 season, which corresponded with the greatest cycle of winning seasons in Greyhound hardwood history.

On the eve of World War II, Harry Good's teams were nearly unbeatable. Coach Good's combined record of 48 wins and 3 losses from 1939-42 (15-2, 17-1, 16-0) has remained the epitome of Greyhound success on the hardwood in the sixty-one seasons of play since that time.

At the end of February 1942, when Indiana Central capped its only perfect basketball season with a 59-36 win over Manchester, the nation's mood was likely comparable to that of November 2001. Only three months had elapsed since the Japanese attack on Pearl Harbor. America was slowly gathering its momentum to face the challenge of the Japanese Empire and Hitler's Nazis, similar to the United States' response in 2001 to the devastating terrorist attacks on the World Trade Center and the Pentagon.

It was within that historical framework the Greyhounds of Coach Harry Good reached the pinnacle of success in basketball.

In those days, with no nationwide television or sports newsmagazines, nor sports

Distinction Without Pretension

information directors shilling for their school's teams, only one universally accepted ranking system for intercollegiate basketball existed. The era's foremost prognosticator, Dick Dunkel, a nationally syndicated sports columnist, was the recognized expert in evaluating the nation's best squads. There were no NCAA "divisions" in 1941-42, so Dunkel included all colleges and universities in his ratings, with no allowance for size of school. Dunkel's final ranking for America's intercollegiate basketball teams that year was:

1. Wisconsin*	6. Stanford
2. Arkansas	7. Illinois
3. Washington State	8. Southern California
4. Minnesota	**9. Indiana Central**
5. Indiana	10. Santa Clara

(* national champion)

    No, you aren't seeing things. Tiny Indiana Central, coached by Harry Good, was ranked ninth among *all* college and university basketball teams in 1941-42. This was the team of Crowe, Nicoson, Perry, Howe, and Bloomingdale. (Top-rated Wisconsin won the NCAA tournament, lending credence to Dunkel's ratings!)

    The Greyhound team included some strikingly talented players. George Crowe had been selected as Indiana's first "Mr. Basketball" at Franklin High School in 1939. A multitalented athlete, Crowe was the leading scorer for the Hounds. Angus Nicoson of Coal City, Indiana, and later Hall of Fame coach at Indiana Central, was the consummate competitor at guard who led Coach Good's vaunted fast-breaking attack. Big Lee Perry, later to play professional football with the Chicago Cardinals, was the man in the middle at 6'5" and 230 pounds, a huge man in that day. Bill Howe was a hard-nosed forward and fierce rebounder, while top defender Ray Bloomingdale rounded out the starting five.

    In an era when fifty points was a high offensive output for a game, the Greyhounds averaged fifty-seven points to their opponents, thirty-two. The only truly close game of the season was a 25-24 squeaker at Illinois State. Oakland City fell twice to ICC by nearly identical scores of 73-37 and 74-34. Good's squad beat Ball State twice, one a 68-32 rout.

    At the conclusion of its season the Greyhounds were invited to play in the National Invitational Tournament held in Madison Square Garden in New York City. The NIT was a much more prestigious gathering of college basketball teams than the fledgling NCAA national tourney then. However, because of the war (and the less-publicized fact that the school couldn't afford to send the team) the faculty voted the opportunity down.

    Mirroring the decision of many small colleges, ICC discontinued athletics during the Second World War. At about the same time the popular future Hall of Fame coach at Indiana University, Branch McCracken, enlisted in the armed services. IU recruited Good to replace McCracken until his return. After coaching there from 1944-46, Good went on to the University of Nebraska, coaching basketball and golf until his retirement.

    During his fifteen seasons as head basketball coach at Indiana Central, Harry Good compiled a record of 195-52 for a winning percentage of .789, a mark that has never been approached by his seven successors.

    As in the case of Coach John George begetting Coach Harry Good, one of "Handsome Harry's" former players would eventually replace him and establish his own legacy as a coach of basketball. It was 1942 graduate Angus Nicoson to whom his alma mater turned in 1947 to revitalize an athletics program that had been disbanded and lay dormant for the greater part of World War II.

Three decades later, with an unparalleled record of achievement as athletic director, Hall of Fame basketball coach, and esteemed mentor to literally thousands of ICC student-athletes, a tragedy of the most grievous nature would close his legendary career.

We'll talk about Nick in the next chapter.

Greyhound basketball fell on hard times following the illness, retirement, and subsequent death of the beloved Angus Nicoson. From the time of his last season in 1976-77 until the arrival of a fiery, charismatic coach with roots in Maryland, Greyhound teams enjoyed only two winning seasons. In the fifteen-year interim between Nick and Royce Waltman, coaches Bill Bright '54, Bill Green '56, and Bill Keller won but 174 of 406 games, a very un-Greyhound-like .429 pace.

From 1992-97 Royce Waltman led a resurgence of Greyhound basketball. After serving as chief assistant for Coach Bob Knight's 1987 national champions at Indiana University, Waltman became head coach at DePauw University. There, from 1988-92, his Tiger teams compiled a record of 100-43, advancing in 1992 to the title game of the National NCAA Division III Tournament. University of Indianapolis announced the hiring of Coach Waltman in the spring of that year to replace Bill Green (who would return to the high school coaching ranks at Marion and win his unprecedented sixth Indiana state championship).

Following his first season at U of I, at 13-14 the only losing season he had in twenty years of high school and five years of college coaching, Waltman returned the Hounds to winning heights. His 1995-96 team went 20-9, the first twenty-win season for the Greyhounds in thirty-two years.

The next year Waltman's squad would finish 23-5, recording the only back-to-back twenty-win seasons in Greyhound history. With a veteran squad returning and a lightning-quick transfer from Middle Tennessee State, point guard Tyrone Barksdale '97, the Hounds ran through their first eighteen opponents of the 1996-97 season and into the only #1 national ranking for the Greyhounds, ever. On the way, in its ninth game of the year at Wisconsin-Parkside on December 23, 1996, the Greyhounds won the school's 1,000th basketball victory.

At 6'7", forward Terry McBryde '97 glided through the air for slam-dunks that brought ear-splitting roars from Greyhound fans. Freshman Bart Holubar '00, a 6'5" forward, was a defensive stalwart, as was 6'6" Dave Wiese '98. Noi Chay '97 complimented Barksdale at guard with his deadly three-point shooting. Michael Brooks '97, arguably the most accurate three-point shooter in Greyhound annals, was "money" in the clutch.

On January 23, 1997, the Greyhound team of Coach Waltman won its sixteenth game in a row with an 85-67 rout of Southern Illinois-Edwardsville, tying the sixteen-game winning streak for one season of Harry Good's 1941-42 squad. Ironically, the next morning athletic director Dave Huffman learned that on the evening of the Greyhounds' victory over SIUE, Good had died peacefully at his home in Minneapolis at age ninety-five.

Despite losing four games during the second half of the season the Hounds ranked third in the Division II final poll, the highest finish for a Greyhound basketball squad, all time. A disheartening 75-72 loss in the NCAA regional tournament to Oakland (Michigan)

Distinction Without Pretension

University ended one of the greatest seasons ever at U of I.

Having observed Coach Waltman during his five years at the U of I, I would consider him to be the most complete coach with whom I've been closely associated. Possessing a keen sense of discernment and the ability to synthesize information instantly, Royce saw through pretension and was totally without prejudice. Only skill and character mattered in his world. Intense, and passionate about the game of basketball and his players, Waltman did his job as well as any coach I've had the privilege of knowing.

When he was recruited to rescue the basketball fortunes at Indiana State University in 1997 after five seasons at the U of I, Royce Waltman's 89-49 record and sixty-five percent winning ledger surpassed that of Coach Nicoson.

From 1924 through 1931, football at ICC was a diversion from King Basketball. During eight seasons, with a record of 22 wins, 32 losses, and 6 ties, the Greyhounds did not distinguish themselves on the gridiron. At the height of the Great Depression, football was dropped as a sport by the administration.

There were some notable occurrences, nonetheless. During the best year prior to the sport being suspended, Harry Good coached the 1928 team to a 5-1-2 record. One of the victories was over an obviously outmanned Oakland City eleven by a 97-0 score. And on November 9, 1929, Oscar Smith would tally a school-record seven touchdowns in a 53-3 Greyhound romp over Valparaiso.

Following World War II, Indiana Central reinstituted football and it didn't take long for the Greyhounds to make their mark. In 1947, ICC won its first football title in the Hoosier College Conference's inaugural season with a record of 7-1, under (who else?) Angus Nicoson. Among the Greyhound stars on that championship squad were Don Bunge '48, Charles Dill '50, Marion Burleson '53, Bill McGrath '50, Ivan Moreman '50, Verne Chandler '51, and Harold Schutz '50.

The Hounds won three consecutive Hoosier College Conference championships (1953-54-55) under three different coaches. In his second season after having played and graduated from Indiana Central, Indianapolis native Dave Shaw '50 coached the only undefeated ICC football team (8-0 in '53).

Shaw, a Manual High School grad who went to Purdue on a football scholarship, transferred back to the neighborhood to finish his football career after injuries plagued his play at West Lafayette. Dave stayed on as an assistant to Walt Bartkiewicz, who would leave following the 1951 season. After a 5-3 campaign in his first year, Coach Shaw knew he had the makings of a strong team in the fall of 1953. Little did he know that he was about to coach the only football squad at ICC that would finish its season without a loss.

With an offensive tandem in Little All-American Dick Nyers '56 at halfback and field general Dick "Tiger" Schrier '56, the Hounds ran the table on their eight foes, winning the Hoosier College Conference in the process. Led by Little All-American center and linebacker Abie Carter '54, and hardnosed strongman John Hurrle '55, the Indiana Central defense shut out three of its eight opponents, allowing an average of less than a touchdown a game (5.8 points). After opening the season with an 18-6 triumph over Taylor, the Greyhounds recorded consecutive shutouts of Franklin (18-0), Earlham (7-0), and Anderson (18-0). Nyers returned an interception 100 yards—which remains a Greyhound record today—in a 19-7 win over powerful Ferris State. When Manchester fell, 31-14,

James L. Brunnemer

in the final game of the year, ICC had its only undefeated Hoosier College Conference champion (6-0) and season in football history.

Angus Nicoson returned to the sidelines in 1954 to lead the Hounds to a 6-3 record. Jim Wallace (5-3-1) completed the hat trick in 1955. That three-year run remains the second best (19-6-1) in Greyhound football history.

The last Hoosier College Conference title the greyhounds won came under Coach Jay Windell in the 1960 season. It would be a long, dry spell before the Hounds reached eminence in football again, for over the next decade Indiana Central would win less than thirty percent of its games.

It was the former great Nyers who rescued Greyhound football from the doldrums. Following a sterling career as head football coach at Carmel High School near Indianapolis, Dick Nyers transformed ICC's program into one worthy of respect.

His 6-5 team of 1971 was only the second winning season for the Greyhounds in eleven years. Although he coached but two years, Dick Nyers' contribution to the renaissance of football at Indiana Central was profound.

Nyers' chief assistant, Bill Bless '63, replaced him as head coach and for the next twenty-one years stamped the football program with his integrity, grit, and quiet competence. There were great moments under Bless, including the Greyhounds' only trip to the NCAA football play-offs, in 1975. Later there would be two Heartland Conference Champs: 1978 (7-3) and 1981 (7-4), when ICC beat Butler in a 16-14 thriller for the crown.

Among the many great moments this writer witnessed during the Bless years, none was sweeter than the bizarre ending to the 1973 game with Franklin College. ICC had one of its finest starts, beating its first three opponents Evansville (10-2), Alma (23-20), and Wabash (57-0). It was then time to travel to meet the Franklin College Grizzlies at what is now Faught Field.

Always a nemesis for opponents with his "run 'n' shoot" passing attack, Franklin Coach "Red" Faught seemed perpetually to have the Greyhounds' number. Indiana Central teams couldn't seem to slow down the Franklin aerial game and rarely summoned the offensive power to outscore them. At game time it seemed a typical afternoon at the Franklin College field: a large Homecoming crowd was in attendance to watch Red's boys feast on the Greyhound defense once again. In a tight struggle, ICC was surprisingly clinging to a 28-25 lead late in the fourth quarter. Then, as if scripted, Franklin connected on a long bomb to take what seemed an insurmountable lead, 32-28, with under a minute to play.

Receiving the kick-off, the Greyhounds failed to move the ball, giving it back to Franklin at mid-field. After two cautious rushes into the line by the Grizzlies, Indiana Central had spent its final timeout. With only 17 seconds left to play, all Franklin had to do to seal their win was simply run out the clock with one more innocuous play.

But for an unknown reason that Coach Faught is probably still trying to understand in the Hereafter, his quarterback decided to run a pitch-out rather than "taking a knee" to put the game safely away. The toss from the quarterback to the Grizzly running back is a basic and simple maneuver, something the duo had repeated hundreds, perhaps thousands of times. But on this occasion, the flip was a mite high and the ball slipped through the runner's fingers.

Distinction Without Pretension

For 22 seasons a coach of integrity and quiet competence, Bill Bless compiled more victories than any football coach before or since.

    Incredibly, the ball rested just an instant on the Franklin player's shoulder pad. In the Grizzly press box, the Franklin stat team, radio broadcasters, scorekeepers, and all other personnel were already celebrating the Franklin triumph. Through disbelieving eyes, I was astonished to see lead-footed defensive tackle Randy Gunyon '74 *with the ball* tucked under his arm, clomping toward the end zone! The horrified Grizzly players, realizing that a Greyhound had cleanly swiped the ball off their teammate's shoulder, desperately gave chase. But even the slow-footed Gunyon could not be caught with the head start his surprising good fortune and quick thinking had given him. The gun ending the game had already fired before Randy strode triumphantly over the goal line, giving the Greyhounds a miracle 34-32 win!
    A superb collection of skilled and tough-minded athletes came together in 1975 under head coach Bill Bless. The squad won eight games and lost three, with two of the losses by a total of four points. As yet the only Greyhound team to make the NCAA Division

James L. Brunnemer

II play-offs, this squad finished eighth in the final poll that year, the highest ranking ever for the University's footballers.

Quarterback Rod Pawlik '76, who tossed fourteen TD passes and set a season record for completion percentage (.581), led a powerful offensive attack. Hard-running Dick Nalley '77 and Steve Montgomery '76 rushed for 1,002 and 978 yards, respectively, behind one of the finest offensive lines ever to wear the Crimson and Grey. Across the line of scrimmage for the Hounds were center Rick Gardner '76 (250 pounds); guards Dave Winings '76 (220) and Tom Geffert '78 (240); and tackles Vance Stratton '76 (255) and Jett Kirkman '78 (230), brutish blockers all.

Defensively, lightweight but super-quick defensive ends Bill Willan '77 (twelve QB sacks that season) and Mike Mills '77 reaped havoc in opponents' backfields, while Don Pitman '82, Tom Zupancic '78, and Tim Lanie '78 clogged the middle. Ken Brooks '76, who ended his career as the all-time leading tackler, and burly John Peters '78 were staunch linebackers, while versatile Dave Wood '76 patrolled the Greyhound secondary.

Indiana Central received a bid for one of the eight spots in the NCAA Division II post-season play-off, lined up to play Ohio small-college powerhouse Wittenberg at the foe's home field in Springfield, Ohio. In that contest the Hounds led 13-3, smothering the Tigers' high-powered offense, until two fourth-quarter scores pushed WU into a 17-13 lead. The Greyhounds began a relentless drive in the final minutes of the contest, only to see their last chance snuffed out when Nalley's option pass was intercepted in the end zone. Two weekends later Wittenberg won the national championship.

The 1975 squad and its coaches were inducted into the U of I Athletics Hall of Fame in 2003.

Of the eleven best football seasons recorded by Greyhound teams, Bless coached six of them, including the finest three-consecutive winning years ever—1984 (8-2), 1985 (7-1-2), and 1986 (7-2)—a 22-5-2 winning run of .796.

TOP 11 FOOTBALL SEASONS

	Year	Record	Pct.	Coach
1.	1953	8-0	1.000	Dave Shaw
2.	1947	7-1	.875	Angus Nicoson
3.	1984	8-2	.800	**Bill Bless**
	1998	8-2	.800	Joe Polizzi
	1985	7-1-2	.800	**Bill Bless**
6.	1986	7-2	.778	**Bill Bless**
7.	1928	5-1-2	.750	Harry Good
8.	1975	8-3	.727	**Bill Bless**
	1997	8-3	.727	Joe Polizzi
10.	1973	7-3	.700	**Bill Bless**
	1978	7-3	.700	**Bill Bless**

The administration of 1993 and Coach Bless disagree as to whether he resigned or was fired following a 2-9 season that capped five successive years of losing teams. Bitter, but man enough to depart with his dignity intact, Bless remains atop the list of all football coaches at the university with a career mark of 114 wins, ninety-nine losses, and nine ties in his twenty-two seasons at the helm. Coach of Heartland Conference titles in 1978 and '81, and the only appearance by a Greyhound team in the NCAA playoffs (1975), Bless produced six football All-Americans, including his son Mark Bless (1983).

Distinction Without Pretension

It was a joy to witness Bill Bless's induction into the University of Indianapolis Hall of Fame in February 2003.

After a switch to the Great Lakes Intercollegiate Athletic Conference (GLIAC), a former player and Hillsdale College assistant, Joe Polizzi, took the reins of the University of Indianapolis football program. After a rough initial start, Polizzi recruited highly touted quarterback Kevin Kreinhagen and, surrounding him with a cast of small but speedy receivers, Polizzi turned the Greyhounds into an aerial circus. Winning twenty-three of thirty-two games from 1997-99, Polizzi had the third-best three-year stint in Greyhound history (8-3, 8-2, 7-4, .719). Greyhound fans were privileged to watch one of the finest passing-receiving combinations in NCAA Division II history during the 2003 season. Junior Matt Kohn, who was named GLIAC back of the Year, finished second in Division II in total offense (338 yards per game); set single-season school records in completions and attempts (239-390); and touchdown passes (21). On the receiving end, senior Cesare Manning earned first team All-GLIAC honors, while setting U of I standards for catches and receiving yards in a game, season, and career.

Baseball was the first sport in which Indiana Central played another school and the first in which the Greyhounds would complete a season without a blemish in the loss column. Led by pitchers Arville Swan '33 and Lester McCuen '33, Lowell Barnett '33 at shortstop, and captain Gordon "Frenchy" France '33 at second base, the Hounds of 1933 defeated all thirteen of their opponents.

Perhaps no team sport in ICC's history has seen one player so overpowering as was Bill Bright '54 during his three-year career. While most coaches will contend that there is no such thing as a one-man team, Bill came close to dispelling that dictum during the Hounds' 13-0 season in 1952. And no one knew how to guide a thoroughbred to the winner's circle like Angus Nicoson, the only man in school history to both play on (basketball, 1941-42, 16-0) and coach (baseball, 1952, 13-0) an undefeated Greyhound squad.

A fireballing, if somewhat wild, left-handed pitcher, Bright won ten of his squad's thirteen victories. The team earned-run average of 1.06 is a record that still stands, and Bright gave up less than one earned run per game on his way to a 10-0 individual record. Bright struck out 148 batters in ninety-two and two-thirds innings for the year, an average of 14.4 strikeouts per nine innings. Among the ten wins for the overpowering lefthander that season were complete game wins over Manchester (2-1), Earlham (4-0), Rose Poly (11-2), Taylor (2-1), Anderson (3-0), Franklin (16-2), and Hanover (2-0) for the Hoosier College Conference championship.

Backing Bill in the field and at bat were teammates like Jack Colescott '52 (a member of both the Indiana High School and University of Indianapolis halls of fame), Kenny Eiler '57, Lowell Merryman '54, Tom Potts '55, and Dick Theil '53.

Bright returned to his alma mater after a brief professional career and for twenty seasons as baseball coach would amass a record of 307 wins, 270 losses and three ties. Bill's teams won five Hoosier College Conference championships as well. His success at Indiana Central plus his overall contributions to the game earned Bill induction in 2000 to the Indiana Baseball Hall of Fame as well as into the U of I Hall of Fame (1986).

The first appearance for a Greyhound baseball team in the NCAA play-offs came in 1971, under Coach Bob Tremain '73, as the team set a season record for most wins up

James L. Brunnemer

to that time with thirty-one.

Baseball would undergo a resurgence beginning in 1994 when veteran coach Gary Vaught accepted the challenge at the U of I. With previous intercollegiate head coaching experience at Connors State (Oklahoma) Junior College (305-57), Kansas State University (61-48), and Oral Roberts University (127-47), Vaught was a proven winner. From 1998 through the 2001 seasons the Greyhounds earned a berth in the NCAA Division II National Tournament.

In 1998 the Greyhounds were ranked as high as fourth in the nation, with Marco Civelli '99 batting .466, Jason Cleary '99 belting twenty home runs and knocking in sixty-two runs, and Chad Wolff '98 breaking Bright's season pitching record with a perfect 13-0 slate.

However, the closest any Greyhound baseball team has come to a national championship came in the 2000 baseball season. After a slow start, the Greyhounds hit their stride at play-off time, sweeping the Great Lakes Valley Conference tournament to earn a spot at the NCAA Division II College World Series in Montgomery, Alabama. With its own version of the Yankees' "Murderer's Row," U of I's line-up was an opposing pitcher's nightmare. Outfielder Ryan Sorrels '01 led the Hounds with a .390 batting average and in stolen bases with twenty-nine. Fellow outfielder Champ Champanois '01 batted .351 and scored a team-high sixty-four runs. Infielders Tommy Daeger '00 (.343) and Peter Babcock '01 (.321) added punch, but the big stick was All-American catcher Al Ready '01, who batted .356 with team bests in home runs (eighteen, a school record) and RBI's with seventy-four in sixty-four games.

Top hurlers for the U of I were Scott Abercrombie '00 (eleven wins, four losses) and Chad Snyder '00 (10-2). The 42-23 Hounds finished third in the NCAA tournament after losing to champion Northeastern Oklahoma, going further in a national championship event than any team in any Greyhound sport ever had.

Expectations were high in 2001, with a veteran team returning. The Greyhound machine rolled over fifty-one opponents, more than any team in all four levels of NCAA competition. Only one other school, Tulane University (50-10), won as many as fifty games in 2001. Led by first baseman and best hitter, Peter Babcock (.437), the Greyhounds won their first conference title since 1984. Their 24-3 conference mark was among the finest single seasons of any GLVC team in history.

Senior switch-hitter Al Ready had another outstanding season at the plate, batting .330, while veterans Sorrels (.394) and Champanois (.381) again paced a high-scoring U of I line-up. Premier pitchers Rick Hummel '02 (12-1), Blake Wyatt '03 (10-3), and Brian Bigam '02 (8-1) combined for thirty wins in thirty-five decisions. So it was deeply disappointing when Southern Illinois-Edwardsville upset the Hounds in the NCAA North Regional, ending the dream of returning to Montgomery. There was some consolation for Vaught and his team when Babcock, Bigam, Ready, and Sorrels each made the Division II Academic All-American team.

To choose between Gary Vaught's baseball teams of 2000 and 2001 would be unfair to both. One appeared to overachieve its potential, while the other might have fallen short of its promise. But both teams were the equal of or better than any other Greyhounds past.

In both 2002 and 2003, Coach Vaught's teams ranked in the top twenty in the

Distinction Without Pretension

Division II poll, and exceeded thirty wins in a season for a record seven consecutive years. Eight times the Greyhounds qualified for a berth in the NCAA national baseball tournament, and seven of those were Vaught-led teams. Having won 363 games against 204 losses, Vaught has surpassed all other U of I baseball coaches in games won.

Track and field came into its own with the hiring of Jerry England '61 as coach in 1972. In twenty-seven seasons, England coached eight NCAA individual champions and twenty tracksters who earned an aggregate of forty-one All-American honors amongst them. Individual NCAA II champs were Dave Wollman '79 (shot put, 1977), who is currently head track coach at NCAA Division I-A national power Southern Methodist University; Dennis Young '81, champion in the discus (1981); Randy Heisler '86, three-time champion in the discus (1982-83-84); sprinter Chris Green '87 in the 400 meters (1986); Brian Burkhart '92 in the hammer throw (1992); Brian Evans '93, discus (1993, one-hundred ninety-nine feet, five inches); and Andy Richardson '99, the 1998 indoor champion in the shot put.

England's greatest performer in track and field, and arguably the finest athlete in the history of Greyhound lore, was Randy Heisler. Setting an NCAA record with a toss of 196' 9" in 1983 (that record is still a Greyhound standard, the oldest record on the books through 2003), Heisler won the discus event at the national finals for NCAA Division II in 1982, '83, and '84. Because of the distance of his discus throws, Randy qualified for *NCAA Division I-A* events in both '83 and '84, finishing sixth both years. He earned a spot on the United States Olympic team in 1988.

In the tradition of great "weight men" in the England program, Andy Richardson set an NCAA Division II record for indoor shot put with a toss of sixty-three feet, six and three-quarter inches in 1998, one of two years he would be named an All-American.

England's teams won one Heartland College Conference title (1973) and two Indiana Collegiate Conference championships (1980 and '81) prior to becoming the dominant team in the Great Lakes Valley league. For an incredible three-year run of domination, it would be hard to best England's U of I track teams of 1990 (31-1), '91 (34-0) and '92 (42-7) for a combined record of one-hundred-seven wins in 115 attempts.

After compiling a season record of thirty-three wins and four losses, Coach Jerry England took nine athletes to the 1992 NCAA Division II national track meet. Six Greyhounds earned All-American honors at that event and England's diminutive squad placed seventh nationally, the highest finish ever for a U of I track team. Brian Burkhardt won the national individual championship in the hammer throw, while qualifying as All-Americans were teammate (and brother) Brett Burkhardt '92 (discus); Matt Gaston '93 (hammer throw); Tom Noe '92, whose seven feet, three and one-quarter inches leap would place him fourth nationally in the high jump; Jon Uecker '96 (400-meter run); and Jim Compton '93 (110-meter high hurdles). By a margin of .01 of a second, Sam Kozyra's '92 time of 21.2 in the 200 meters fell short of becoming the seventh All-American among the nine-member squad. Chris Johnson's '93 ninth-place finish in the steeplechase, likewise, was one place out of qualifying for All-American. This surely was one of the finest collections of track and field competitors in U of I sports history.

Scott Fangman had the unenviable task of filling England's considerable shoes when he became coach in 1996. Coach Fangman has done just fine, thank you very much. Winning forty-two times against a single loss in 2002, the Greyhound men boasted NCAA

James L. Brunnemer

All-Americans Dameion Smith '04 (hammer throw), Reggie Cross '04 (400 meters three times), and GLVC Athlete of the Year Todd Mann '02 (hurdles). The 2002 squad was the first to win a GLVC track and field championship.

His team came back in 2003 even stronger. Veteran All-American sprinter Cross and two-time All-American hammer and discus thrower Smith helped the Greyhound tracksters to victory over thirty-nine of their forty foes. Senior Verizon Academic All-American Tim Mason '03, who won both the 100- and 200-meter sprints in addition to anchoring the U of I 4 X 100 relay team, was named Athlete of the Meet as the Greyhounds repeated as GLVC conference champions.

Golf, John Cunningham observed, is "a game in which a ball one-and-one-half inches in diameter is placed on a ball 27,000 miles in circumference. The object is to hit the smaller ball but not the larger." New athletics director and head basketball, football, baseball, and track coach Angus Nicoson introduced men's golf as an official sport at Indiana Central in 1948.

The men's golf team of 1961 had three dominant players: Mickey Powell '61, Don Bisesi '61, and Bob Otolski '60, each of whom became members of the U of I Hall of Fame, in 1992, 1999, and 2001, respectively. No team beat the Greyhounds linksmen that fall. As a measure of the strength of the team, Mickey Powell, its most consistent player, was an All-Hoosier College Conference selection all four years and went on to become one of Indiana's top professional golfers. Twice Mickey served as president of the Professional Golfers Association (1985 and 1986) and was inducted into the Indiana Golf Hall of Fame in 1986.

Don Bisesi was also a four-year all-conference choice, and the HCC's Player of the Year twice. Considered one of Indiana's finest teaching pros, Bisesi was for years one of the top two playing professionals in Indiana, along with Powell. The former teammates traded the state PGA championship trophy several years in a row. The personal duel for supremacy in Indiana PGA tournaments by these two, the best of friends, continued into seniors play. Powell won the individual title in 1989 and 1992, with Bisesi taking the crown in 1990.

While Otolski chose a football coaching profession, reigning as one of Indiana's premier high school coaches before going on to positions as assistant coach at Indiana University and head football coach at Illinois State University, he maintained his game on the golf course. Otolski made the All-HCC golf squad three times.

If a "dynasty" in sport refers to a school's team or teams dominating its opponents over an extended period of time, the U of I golf program under Coach Ken Partridge '58 might be considered just that. Partridge became head coach in 1967. Still the head man in 2003, his thirty-sixth year at the helm, the accomplishments of his teams have been steady and superlative.

He is the only coach in any sport at the college to win championships in four different conferences! Ken's team won its first league title—the Hoosier College Conference—in 1969. Moving to the Indiana Collegiate Conference, Partridge's linksmen were champions in 1974. With dual membership in both the Heartland College Conference and the GLVC, Ken's boys would win the championship of *both* those alliances in 1978. He grabbed a second Heartland title in 1979, and then led his golfers to an unprecedented

Distinction Without Pretension

record in the Great Lakes Valley league. From 1978 through 2001, Coach Partridge's teams claimed an even dozen titles: 1978, '82, '87, '88, '89, '90, '91, '92, '96, '97, '98, and '01. His squads have qualified for the NCAA national tournament more than any other Division II team in the Midwest, and he has produced numerous All-Americans. More than forty of his former players are now or have been PGA golf professionals.

His five greatest seasons were:

1992-93	90-7	.928
1988-89	136-11	.925
1991-92	87-9	.906
1995-96	159-19-2	.889
1987-88	79-11	.878

Scholar-athletes to be sure: Coach Ken Partridge is pictured with his 1993 golf team displaying its GLVC championship trophy. Typical of the players recruited by the coach, the members of this team excelled in the classroom, as well on the golf course. From the left, with GPA in parentheses, are Mike Mozingo (3.54), Jerry Williams (3.43), Kyle Brunnemer (3.49), Todd Clark (3.20), and Scott Richardson (3.54). That's a team average of 3.44 on the four-point grade scale.

Among golfers who played for Coach Partridge was a young man who later became a national figure in auto racing. Brian Barnhart '83 of Speedway, Indiana, is currently the director of the Indianapolis Racing League and chief steward of the Indianapolis Motor Speedway.

Coach Partridge credits one crucial recruit for lifting his program to another level.

James L. Brunnemer

"Steve Kreiger turned our program around," reminisced Partridge. "Recruiting Steve gave our program credibility it hadn't had prior to his coming. He had great heart and will to win. A bad shot or bad hole never adversely affected his next shot or hole. He remains the single finest ball-striker that I've coached in over thirty years."

Other outstanding golfers followed Krieger '91, including Kyle Brunnemer '92, who twice earned NCAA Division II All-American honors and qualified each of his four years for the NCAA Division II National Tournament.

Among Partridge's finest squads was the 1988-89 Greyhound golf team, which boasted three All-Americans in Kreiger, Brunnemer, and Todd Clark '91, plus Mike Mozingo '92, and Jerry Williams '92. They finished 136-11, with wins over numerous NCAA Division I schools. (In a shameless show at the 2003 Angus Nicoson Memorial Golf Tournament, held annually for alumni athletes and friends of the university, Partridge pulled PGA pros Kreiger and Brunnemer out of mothballs to play in his foursome. With nephew Dave Vleck '78 as his fourth member, Partridge's stacked team claimed the title in the annual scramble with an 18-under-par 54. It was the first time Kreiger and Brunnemer had teamed up in an outing since their college days. Partridge was all grins afterward.)

Led by one of Coach Partridge's finest individual players ever, Bobby Delagrange '97, the team of 1994-95 won conference and regional titles on the way to the most victories ever for Greyhound linksters, defeating 188 opponents, losing forty-one matches, with one tie.

Cross-country is a sport where student-athletes are asked to run to the point of exhaustion, and then pick up the pace. Indiana Central has produced several notable teams. Among the athletes who have run cross-country for the Hounds is Gary Romesser '73, who continued to excel into his forties and fifties as a runner of marathons and road races. Romesser led his mates to one of the nine HCC cross-country titles Bill Bright coached from 1958-76. Hoosier College Conference championship years were 1958, '59, '61, '63, and '65, while Bright-coached teams won Indiana Collegiate Conference titles in '72, '74, '75, and '76. Fritz Hohlt '72, Herman Bueno '80, and Erhard Bell '80 carried forth the legacy of such earlier stars as Marshall Goss, who retired in 2003 as head track coach at Indiana University, and John Jaroszinski '65 (U of I Hall of Fame, 1991), who became an outstanding teacher and coach in his own right.

Swimming and diving at the U of I had its most successful stretch of winning individuals and teams under Seeman Baugh. From 1984 through '94, Baugh's poolmen defeated 271 opponents, losing to only sixty-four, an .809 mark. Former University of Michigan swimmer Gary Kinkead took over the reins from Baugh in 1995 and has likewise produced outstanding teams.

Like U of I coaches in other sports, Kinkead has benefited from the emergence of international students attending the University. Setting swimming marks that may take a while to break is four-time NCAA II All-American Orel Oral '03, from Istanbul, Turkey. In 2001, Oral took two national individual titles in two days, conquering the field in the breaststroke event and winning the 200-meter individual medley with a record time of 3:57:50. The Greyhounds finished fifteenth among the twenty-six teams represented at the nationals. Oral swam for his native country in the 2000 Olympiad.

Distinction Without Pretension

In the 2003 season, the Hounds' swimmers were again led by the record-shattering performances of All-American Oral. Nationally ranked in an astounding thirteen separate events, including nine individual ones, Oral earned a number one listing in both the 200 individual medley and the 400 intermediate races. Bruno Fonseca '05 of Rio de Janeiro, Brazil, ranked first in the country in the fifty-meter free-style. The men's team competed well in the Division II national meet, finishing eighth.

Coach Kinkead's swimmers have achieved envious performances in the classroom as well. In the 2002 edition of *Swimming World Magazine*, both Greyhound *men's and women's* swimming teams tied UC-San Diego as the NCAA Division II top teams according to swimming performance in the NCAA championships combined with team grade point average.

Tennis squads at Indiana Central competed well on the courts against Hoosier College Conference foes, beginning with a 7-1 record in its first official season in 1949. When the University of Indianapolis joined the Great Lakes Valley Conference in 1978, it would take a while before the Greyhounds would compete for conference titles. Joe Gentry was an assistant when the U of I won its first conference championship in 1989. After finishing second in 1990, Gentry became head coach and his teams dominated the GLVC, winning every championship from the 1991 season through 1995. Among his finest players was Paul Buck '90, the GLVC Player of the Year in 1990. Succeeding Gentry as coach in 1996 was his number one player, Scott Riggle '00, a three-time Verizon Academic All-American.

Wrestling teams at the university have been fortunate to have two extraordinary coaches in Paul Velez (1962-69) and Terry Wetherald (1970-99 and 2000-02). Two Greyhound wrestlers achieved the remarkable feat of winning Little State individual championships four consecutive years. First, Willie Martin '61 accomplished the perfect mark at 147 pounds from 1958-61. Dave Marshall '88 equaled Martin's record, winning Little State titles each year from 1985-88. Other wrestlers who struck fear in the hearts of Greyhound opponents during the Velez reign were Cleo Moore '64, at 137 pounds; Dave Paino '67 (123); Mike Watkins '68, a two-time HCC champ in 1964 and 1965 at 115; and 145-pounder Tim Giles '66, also in '64 and '65.

Among Coach Wetherald's most outstanding wrestlers were three-time Hoosier College Conference heavyweight champion Tom Zupancic '78 (1982-83-84); career pins leader Wade Hall '83, with fifty-five from 1979-83; and heavyweight Greg Matheis '92, who won 133 times in 158 matches from 1988-92.

You might be interested to know that Mark Mastison '86, whose opponent was counted out after eight seconds in a match in the 1983 season, achieved the fastest pin ever recorded by a Greyhound wrestler.

Wetherald coached sixteen Division II All-Americans in his storied U of I coaching career.

Since my earliest association with ICC, I've been privileged to enjoy and marvel at the athletic exploits of literally thousands of those wearing the uniform of the Greyhound. Memories cascade like water over limestone in the creeks near my home in Brown County.

James L. Brunnemer

Allow me to share but a handful of those who flow out of my consciousness.

I saw Ken Brooks '75 intercept four passes against Earlham in a 1973 game, returning two for touchdowns. A 6'2" 225-pound linebacker, Brooks remains second on the all-time list for tackles thirty years after his final game. An extraordinary two-sport athlete, Ken was the first player I witnessed who regularly smashed home runs of 400-plus feet for the Greyhound baseball team.

Clark Crafton '65 amazed me with his remarkable feats on the basketball court. No less an observer than Bill Bright called Crafton "the most naturally gifted athlete we ever had here."

Dave Wollman '78, from Wawasee High School and currently head track coach at Southern Methodist University, enrolled at Indiana Central with a chip on his shoulder. As a senior in high school he thought he should have been all-state in football (he wasn't) and believed he was a better discus thrower than a rival, Mark Reiff '76. So he followed Mark to ICC to compete head-on with him. Reiff, later the head women's track coach at Stanford University, set the pace for Wollman, who won a national championship in the discus for Coach Jerry England in 1977. Dave was inducted into the U of I Athletic Hall of Fame in 1994.

Mark "Scary" Schirra '75 was a demonic defensive back for the Greyhounds, with total disregard for his own body as well as his opponents, when he initiated collisions on the gridiron. As professional wrestler "Rip Rogers," Schirra's natural madness has passed for normality in the ring.

There were moments of disbelief in Nicoson Hall when Greyhound cagers walked on air. Those present for the 1996 showdown between U of I and #1-ranked University of Southern Indiana in Nicoson Hall will recall 6'1" Jim Lindsey's '98 sky-walking slam of an "alley-oop" assist from guard Ty Barksdale '97. Defying gravity, Lindsey's forceful dunk turned the momentum of that game, leading U of I to victory and the Greyhounds to their only #1 ranking in the NCAA Division II poll.

Chris Martin '00 flew through the air in Nicoson Hall for dozens of the most amazing slam-dunks ever witnessed there. Once, as Martin soared to throw down a tomahawk dunk, Ken Partridge turned to me and said, "The last time I saw someone jump that high was when Dr. Sease asked Lynn Youngblood to fetch him a cup of coffee."

For sheer courage it was hard to surpass Randy Robertson '74 and Paul Glaspie '72. Robertson, who was an all-state football star under ICC alum Bob Otolski at Mishawaka, transferred to ICC from Western Michigan University, where he had suffered his first serious knee injury. For three years, Randy captained and played middle guard for the Hounds in excruciating pain on knees that were bereft of cartilage. Teammate Oscar Gardner '73, himself a tough hombre, confessed to tearing up at the sight of Randy hobbling in agony to the shower after a game.

Of all the dedicated and tough athletes I observed, none blended humble grace with grit like Paul Glaspie. An African-American, Paul was a goodwill ambassador with an invincible spirit. Legally blind, he astonished schoolmates with his ability to play Ping-Pong, despite the fact his vision was so impaired that he often wore his shirt inside-out. Glaspie ran cross-country and track. Coach Bright explained Paul's running strategy: "Because he could become lost on a cross country route, Paul usually let other runners lead throughout the race."

Distinction Without Pretension

Staying on the shoulder of the frontrunner, Paul would get a signal from Bright or a teammate toward the end and would kick at the finish to win.

"I once saw Paul run into a wire-mesh cable, resulting in a severe gash. But Glaspie refused to stop, finishing the race with blood pouring down his leg," reported an admiring Bright.

On another occasion, at an indoor meet, Glaspie followed the straight chalk line instead of the curve, at the end of a sixty-yard dash, running at full speed into a wall. He arose without complaint to continue the meet. Assistant coach Bill Bless recalled Paul once coming to his office to complain mildly that his new track shoes were causing him pain when he ran. Bless looked down to note that Paul had put his shoes on the wrong feet.

Among the great defenders on the football field were three Greyhound linebackers whom I watched Saturday after Saturday dismay opponents' coaches: Josh Gentry '99, Ted Liette '98, and Oscar Gardner. Of these, the greatest was Oscar. He knew the difference between "fetch" and "sic 'em!" Liette always seemed to find the man with the ball and when he arrived, he was inevitably in a bad mood. And the most likely of these to revel in separating an opposing runner's head from his shoulders? That would be Josh.

At 5'10" and 165 pounds, Chris Volz '01 was not physically impressive. He combined an exceptional understanding of the game of football with savage hitting to become one of the finest defensive backs in Greyhound lore. From Tri-West High School, Volz was a four-year starter at U of I, finishing third in pass interceptions all-time, including tying Dick Nyers' record with a 100-yard return against Mercyhurst. A two-time Verizon Academic All-District selection, Chris was chosen the GLIAC Defensive Back of the Year in 2001. A nursing major with a 3.53 GPA, Volz became the first player from a school outside of Michigan to win the Jack H. McAvoy Award. The McAvoy honor is presented to the conference player who best combines "outstanding character and leadership on the field, in the classroom and in the community."

Tyrone Barksdale, who could outrun his shadow; Tim Giles, a 145-pound wrestler called the "black panther," and Ron Rutland '91, a star in international basketball competition, were the quickest athletes I ever saw perform in the uniform of the Greyhound.

Barksdale made one of the most implausible plays I ever witnessed in Greyhound sports. In 1997, against archrival and then nationally #3-ranked Southern Indiana, Barksdale made a poor pass that was intercepted by a Screaming Eagle player. Spotting a teammate alone and heading full-steam toward the opposite end, the USI player tossed a three-quarter-court-length pass, which should have resulted in an easy, uncontested lay-up. Having made the errant pass, Ty had turned to race down court. Making a play you had to see to appreciate, he caught up with his opponent, tipped the ball just as his foe reached for it, and, continuing at blur-speed, leaped and saved the ball from going out of bounds to a teammate at half court. World-class sprinters cover one hundred yards in less than ten seconds, or ten yards per elapsed second. Barksdale, the 1997 GLVC Player of the Year, covered approximately seventy feet of basketball court in about two ticks of the clock. You do the math.

In case you're wondering about the other play: In a 1966 contest against Indiana Central, 6' 6" Dick Harris of Manchester missed a shot beneath his own basket. Surrounded by teammates and Greyhounds each fighting to get the rebound, Harris tipped that missed shot, not once, not twice, but *eight more times,* getting two points on his tenth shot attempt

James L. Brunnemer

on his *ninth consecutive offensive rebound* of the sequence.

Tim Giles, with a body fat percentage somewhere under three percent, could get at an opposing wrestler's legs and have him on his back before the poor fellow could say "Daaaaa-yam!" As a baseball teammate, I watched Tim bat .320 one season and I swear he didn't hit half a dozen balls out of the infield. A two-hop groundball to the opposing shortstop was an automatic single for Tim.

Rutland was simply, as my dad used to put it, faster than "shit through a goose."

For models of toughness, durability and supreme doggedness, my list would include at the top Herb Lepper '65 and Cleo Moore. One of my favorite ICC guys of all time, Lepper would not accept, nor give, any quarter in competition. I'll bear witness that Cleo was the most relentless competitor on a wrestling mat, ever, at Indiana Central.

If an "Adonis" award were given for the perfectly sculpted body of an athlete, my vote would go to Doug Semenick '72. Among the most superbly conditioned athletes while at Indiana Central, Doug turned his dedication in the weight room into a career. As strength and conditioning coach for the University of Louisville, he would win an NCAA Strength and Conditioning Coach of the Year honor. Later, Doug established his own private strength and conditioning consulting business.

Among the most graceful athletes was Dave Wood '76. Earning letters all four years that he played in football, basketball, and baseball, Wood did nothing spectacularly, but everything ably on all fields and was among the smartest athletes ever to play for the Greyhounds.

For the "Golden Glove" award I'd choose my former teammate Phil Paswater '66. Getting a ground ball by this slick-fielding shortstop was like sneaking a head of lettuce by a rabbit. Phil was a vacuum cleaner on the baseball field.

How about an acknowledgment for the athlete with the best voice? Yes, the finest singing athlete I ever heard in the locker room showers was ICC wrestler Larry McCloud '65. An outstanding scholar who is nearing the completion of nearly forty years of success as a high school administrator in 2003, Larry had the silky-smooth pipes of a young Nat King Cole. He brought the student convocation crowd to its feet in a 1965 talent show with his rendition of "King of the Road." If Larry had not been so committed to education, he might have accepted my not-so-tongue-in-cheek offer to be his agent and made us both rich.

My selection as the Scholar-Athlete: Bill Willan '76. A veteran of the armed forces when he chose to come to ICC, Willan was a cerebral, relentless, and brutish quarterback assassin for Bill Bless' Greyhound gridders. Still the all-time leader in quarterback sacks (thirty-five, set from 1974-76), Bill formerly served as chairman of the English Department at the University of Maine-Orono and currently is a senior executive with an educational consortium for the state of Ohio.

For passing combinations, it's hard to know whether it was the remarkable arm of quarterback Kevin Kreinhagen '98 or the amazing receiving skills of classmates Gary Isza and Craig Cothren who was responsible for the record-setting passing attack of the Greyhounds in the mid-nineties. Kreinhagen threw for 6,880 yards from (1995-98), and between them, Isza (2,489) and Cothren (2,451) were on the receiving end of nearly three-fourths of that total. Gary Izsa was a gritty little guy, who, though beaten up by bigger defenders, would get up, limp back to the huddle, and put a stake in opponents' hearts with

Distinction Without Pretension

a big reception on the next play. Lithe and almost frail-looking, Cothren seemed to glide unnoticed though opponents' secondaries, only to be found by Kreinhagen for a long gainer or a touchdown.

I can't picture ICC pass receivers, however, without mentioning the supple mitts of Jim Slavens '78. He made catches on the gridiron that defied belief.

John Peters, who at 6'1" and 240 pounds created havoc and mayhem as a linebacker for Bless, is today a skillful spine surgeon. This is a puzzlement to me, for you ought to take a look sometime at John's massive fingers and hands that used to manhandle ball carriers but are now so soft and supple.

This handful of athletes will have to serve as examples of all those I have admired, played beside, and cheered for as a student, administrator, parent, and alumnus of the college. Memories of these, and all those others unmentioned, are, as Pope intoned:

Lull'd in the countless chambers of the brain,
Our thoughts are link'd by many a hidden chain;
Awake but one, and lo, what myriads rise!
Each stamps its image as the other flies.

CHAPTER XXII

NICK

"He knew what made the mule plow."
A Hoosier maxim

"Hello, Mr. Brunnemer. My name is Mary Ann Davis, Coach Knight's secretary. Would you hold for Coach Knight?"

After a short pause, the familiar voice of then-Indiana University basketball coach Robert Knight came on the line:

"Hi, Jim. This is Coach Knight. I've been out of town for a time, and when I opened my mail I found your letter about your study of coaches. I'd like to give you an opinion."

A bit nonplussed at receiving a personal call from the coaching icon at Indiana, I stammered, "Coach, I'm really grateful that you'd take the time to call. You don't know me from Adam. I really appreciate it. What do you think of my study?"

"I think it's a bunch of bullshit."

Thus began a brief interchange between the controversial and legendary basketball coach and a nondescript IU graduate student.

It was spring of 1979. I was nearing the end of a paid sabbatical to complete my doctoral studies at Indiana University.

Because of the powerful influence of athletics coaches on my life, I had become a curious observer of those who were consistently successful. Observing certain commonalities that they seemed to share with high achievers from other walks of life especially intrigued me. So I determined to study intercollegiate coaches to determine what, if anything, set them apart from less successful, and unsuccessful, coaches. While attempting to discern a unique pattern of traits common to transcendent coaches, I was led to examine a deeper dimension of the characteristics of leadership. Intuitively, I sensed that great educators, politicians, corporate heads, religious figures, and military giants possess an almost mystical predisposition to succeed. The former longtime football coach at Florida A & M, Jake Gaither, once said of Paul "Bear" Bryant of Alabama: "He can take his'n, and beat your'n, or he can take your'n, and beat his'n."

I wanted to know *why?*

Originally, it was my intention to invite a small group of intercollegiate basketball and football coaches in America who were recognized as representative of the best in their profession to submit to a Cattell 16-Personality Factor Inventory. R. B. Cattell had developed an instrument that purportedly provided reliable data on sixteen separate personality traits, such as "a high capacity for emotional control," "general abstract ability," "ruthlessness," and "free-thinking, experimental outlook," for example.

I asked, along with Coach Knight, Indiana University coaches Doc Counsilman (swimming), Lee Corso (football), Jerry Yeagley (soccer club team, at the time), Jim

Brown (gymnastics), and Sam Bell (track), among others, to participate in a pilot study based on Cattell's theories. I requested their input prior to my soliciting coaches outside the University to gather information for my formal thesis. Within a few weeks I had received replies and helpful comments from each one of those asked, except for Coach Knight. Assuming he didn't have time to help an unknown student on this project, and only days away from approval from my doctoral committee to proceed with the Cattell study, I completed my preliminary work. It was then I received *his* telephone call.

Recovering my composure after his terse précis of my work, I asked, "Would you care to expand on your comment, Coach?"

What followed was a typical example of Coach Bob Knight's willingness to assist a graduate student at Indiana University to whom he had neither obligation nor any previous acquaintance. The subject was one about which the Coach felt informed and very passionate. It began with an invitation to visit with him at his office to fully discuss my topic.

A week later I found myself in the coaches' office complex at Indiana University's Assembly Hall. Ms. Davis escorted me into Coach Knight's quarters.

After a cordial greeting, Coach Knight told me of his high regard and affection for Jack Daugherty, my doctoral chairman whose name was on the cover letter requesting assistance from the coaches to whom I had written. Coach Knight was interested in my thesis, that of exploring personality characteristics of coaches to ascertain if one might predict coaching success by testing for such traits. What ensued was a fascinating hour-and-a-half session with Mr. Knight.

I was struck by how focused Coach Knight was on our conversation. He had made the assumption that I was sincere about learning and that I'd prepared for our discussion. He was correct on both counts. I was privileged to gain a glimpse, if only that, of his keen intelligence and his supple mind. Coach Knight dismissed the obvious to probe into areas of thought in more than a cursory fashion. The only time he let his concentration on our discussion lapse was when a knock on his office door was followed by the onrush of a round-faced, smiling child (I think it was Tim Knight) who dove into a waiting hug from his father. They exchanged a few pleasantries, the boy left, and Coach Knight got right back to task.

Essentially, I left his office with this advice: "Sport psychologists, sociologists, and sportswriters [whose work I was using for the basis of my study] don't know what makes coaches 'tick.' If I were you, spending the time, money, and effort that you are, I'd go to the great coaches themselves. Ask *them*. Get the opinions of Bo Schembechler, Woody Hayes, Clair Bee, Fred Taylor, Pete Newell, and others like them. They can tell you a helluva lot more about what it takes to be a successful coach than the writers you're reading."

So that is what I did. I went back to Professor Daugherty, shared the conversation I'd had with the Coach, and then designed an entirely different approach to the problem. The "Delphi Technique" is a research approach that is similar to having a panel of experts around a table discussing issues, except that the deliberation is handled via a series of written surveys. My study was delimited to male coaches of intercollegiate football and basketball at the NCAA Division I-A level who had won at least three-fourths of their games coached or had won a national championship. After identifying and defining twenty-

Distinction Without Pretension

three personality characteristics from the literature that related to success in coaching, I invited a list of sixty-seven of those top coaches to participate in a three-round survey. My objective was to determine a hierarchy of those characteristics for coaching success. Ultimately, forty-three of those coaches, a list that read like an NCAA Hall of Fame roster, cooperated in the study. Among those who provided thoughtful opinion on what makes highly successful coaches (and the university with which they are most closely recognized) were Frank Broyles (Arkansas); Paul "Bear" Bryant (Alabama); Denny Crum (Louisville); Duffy Daugherty (Michigan State); Dr. Tom Davis (Iowa); Bob Devaney and Dr. Tom Osborne, both of Nebraska; Notre Dame's Dan Devine and Ara Parseghian; John McKay (USC); Pete Newell (California); Barry Switzer and Bud Wilkinson of Oklahoma; and John Wooden (UCLA).

Through the pages of my doctoral dissertation, entitled *Characteristics and Attributes of Highly Successful Intercollegiate Basketball and Football Coaches**, I was privileged to record and report on the personal observations and opinions of this contingent of America's top male intercollegiate coaches.

Within each of us there seems to exist a need, emanating from whatever combination of circumstances we've experienced, to be approved by our fellow man. Overwhelmingly, the coaches collectively concluded that the most critical single key to success is an unspectacular, but insatiable, "drive to succeed." How hard are you willing to work to achieve what you want? Do you have the mental and physical capacity for work to overcome all obstacles? In any competitive endeavor, given certain innate talents and a requisite level of knowledge and understanding of the field, the level of inner drive ultimately separates winners and losers.

I couldn't help but relate the drive described by the coaches to an observation I had read by one of the founders of our country. In 1804, John Adams spoke of "man's natural 'passion for distinction,' whether they be young or old, rich or poor, high or low, wise or foolish, ignorant or learned. Every individual is seen to be strongly actuated by a desire to be seen, heard, talked of, approved and respected."

One individual whom I had been privileged to observe closely epitomized, in my view, the traits of highly successful leaders defined by my research. A playmaking guard for Coach Harry Good's undefeated Indiana Central squad of 1941-42, Angus Nicoson possessed an uncommon internal fire. After World War II and the reinstitution of athletics at ICC in 1947, Nick returned to his alma mater.

Like John George and Harry Good before him, Nick coached almost all sports at Indiana Central in addition to his duties as athletic director and instructor of physical education. While Tony Hinkle would invariably receive greater media attention, Nick's coaching accomplishments were considered by knowledgeable sports followers to be on par with the great Butler coach.

At the end of his thirty years of basketball coaching (1947-77) Nick had compiled 483 wins against 279 losses (.634). Nick's teams would win twenty or more games a record five times—1948-49 (20-9); '51-'52 (20-10); '55-'56 (23-6); '63-'64 (26-3); and '68-'69

---

* *The full study is available at the Indiana University library.*

James L. Brunnemer

(20-10)—and eight Hoosier College Conference titles. His would be the second sparkling era in Greyhound basketball, and the most enduring.

Selected to the Helms Foundation and Indiana Basketball halls of fame, Nicoson was a member of several United States Olympic basketball committees and served a term as president of the National Association of Intercollegiate Athletics as well. Nick exhibited his coaching versatility by guiding the 1947 football team to the best season in ICC history up to that time (7-1) and its first Hoosier College Conference championship. His twelve seasons of coaching baseball resulted in a record of 128-67-2 (.656) and six HCC titles.

His teams in track, cross-country, and golf were competitive, although a member of that first golf squad in 1948 still chuckles at the memory of "golf sponsor" Nicoson. As might be expected of a man coaching four sports and directing the athletics program, Nick was not always available to every team, especially when games or meets were scheduled simultaneously. Dave Stumpf '50 tells of the routine for that first golf contingent: "Nick would gather my brother, Paul '49, Lloyd Coverstone '50, Lou Sommers '49, and me—we were the entire squad—to set up the trip. He'd give us a little meal money; directions to get where we were playing (we had to arrange our own transportation); gave us each three Wilson K-28 golf balls; and bid us 'good luck.' We lost all four of our matches that year. But we were part of history!"

As is true of others who possess that elusive gift for success, whatever sports Nick coached, his teams won. Earl "Red" Blaik, legendary coach at West Point, described a winning team, and by association, its coach:

Unfortunately, too much experience in losing (gracefully) ... lowers resistance to defeat ... I have found that between equal teams the winning formula is a thin margin above which to remain requires fidelity to fundamental principles and a team faith that abhors mediocrity and moral victories.

Anyone who ever competed in any contest for or against Angus Nicoson understood he was never enamored of "moral victories."

Nick learned the game of basketball shooting at an old rim hung on the barn outside his hometown of Coal City, Indiana. A man of great personal charm with a relaxed southern Indiana exterior, Nick could, when the situation demanded, verbally peel the paint from a locker room wall. His intense competitive nature was most evident on the basketball court.

Although coaches become legitimately agitated in extracting from their players the best performance possible, all coaches, at times, are thespians. They will portray emotions of defiance, disbelief, and outrage, depending on the circumstance, to motivate their players. But there was something deeper, more threatening, in Nick's fury. His expressions and body language conjured up a foreboding of unbridled action, a frightening aura. No player branded by the heat of Coach Nicoson's blistering tongue will ever forget why. One wasted no time trying to correct whatever flaw Nick had exposed.

As with many successful coaches, Nick's actions were unpredictable. He was always cognizant of his team's confidence or lack of such. Losing was not pleasant under Nicoson; but often, when a team expected the worst after a defeat, he'd find a way to

Distinction Without Pretension

praise them. If he suspected a team of his of becoming self-satisfied, even one on a lengthy winning streak, Nick might yell and punish them with "tours" of the Greyhound basketball arena until team members would wonder if they really had been winning.

According to former player Jack Noone '67, "Even when Nick was wrong, he was right." Recalling a 1964 game in which Nick felt the Hounds were being outhustled, Noone reports that, "As only Nick could," the irate coach ranted for most of the fifteen-minute halftime intermission at Clark Crafton, Phil Honnold, and anyone else who had the courage to look into his eyes, for their lack of effort on the boards. Nick screamed that the opponents had twice as many rebounds as the Greyhounds and it was just "laziness, pure laziness!" that had placed the outcome of this game in jeopardy.

"When he'd reached the height of his indignation about our being out-rebounded," said Noone, "the student statistician quietly slipped into the steamy locker room and handed the first half statistics sheet to assistant coach Bill Bright."

A brief glance at the numbers, however, alerted Bill that something was amiss.

Glimpsing out of the corner of his eye his assistant perusing the freshly delivered information, Nick wheeled and fairly yelped at Coach Bright to give him the evidence so he could confirm before his team the truth of the first half letdown. Bill tried to discourage Nick from relying on the statistical data in his grasp, but the now livid coach was determined. He grabbed the stat sheets just as Bill tried to whisper, "Nick, we actually got thirty-two rebounds to their fourteen in the first half."

With a murderous look on his face, Nick quickly scanned the statistics. Quickly reversing his field, Nick crumpled the offending papers and, as if the numbers themselves had conspired against him, dashed them to the concrete floor and snorted, "Damned stat sheets never mean anything anyway." Though it took a Herculean effort to maintain a straight face, Noone knew he dared not laugh.

Although Nicoson's competitive verve was never, ever completely extinguished, there were times when he allowed himself not to lock in quite so tightly when coaching. As mentioned in a prior chapter, Nick coached the core of our college baseball team in the summers of 1964 and '65, with regular coach Bill Bright playing on the team. Nick was truly fun to be around.

Even then, though, Nick did have moments when his ultracompetitive nature got the best of him. This would occur if he felt we weren't respecting the game. Once, when our team was taking pre-game batting practice, Nick noticed us players standing in small groups in the outfield, engaged in idle chatter. Nick was pitching batting practice, as he occasionally did, and became angered that we weren't getting the baseballs back to him quickly enough. In fact, some of the balls out of our reach we let pass by to rest against the outfield fence. Finally, Nick barked at us, then called for every baseball to be thrown in to him. That done, he proceeded to pitch batting practice with *one ball*, making it necessary for us to retrieve the batted ball quickly, toss it back to Nick, and wait for the next.

Against the Atterbury Job Corps team, the worst players in the league, we didn't always come to the game with the best attitude. One Sunday, only eight of us showed up to play them, a few of our regulars choosing instead to go swimming or something. Nick fussed at those of us who *did* show, then announced, fearing a forfeiture of the game because we didn't have the full complement of players, that *he* would play. Once he'd been

James L. Brunnemer

*"He knew what made the mule plow"--Angus Nicoson,
Hall of Fame coach, mentor to thousands.*

a very good athlete. But as Nick was forty-five and not in top-flight condition, it seemed inevitable that no good would come from this. It didn't take long.

Nick started in right field, but on the very first ball hit to him, in an extreme effort to field it, he pulled a hamstring. Though he tried his best not to let it show, you could see Nick was really hurting. Bill Tutterow, playing second base, traded positions with Nick so the coach wouldn't have to cover so much ground. Several of us tried to get the coach to give it up, because in this league a team could legally play with only eight players. Besides, who the hell cared if we lost this forgettable game?

Nick did, that's who.

So, of course, we batted through the lineup and it became Nick's turn at the plate. Not him to flail casually at three pitches and sit down. No, he had to try to hit it and get on. So Nick gets wood on the ball from the very inept Job Corps pitcher (we would ultimately score twenty-four runs in this game), dribbling a little hopper back to the mound. In a painful, limping gait, Nick started slowly toward first base.

Wouldn't you know it? The ball skidded *under* the pitcher's glove and between his legs. The Job Corps second baseman charged in, and, with Nick chugging excruciatingly toward first, picked the ball up and fired it *wildly* toward first, out of the reach of the fielder there!

As Nick continued to plod along at the speed of molasses, the first baseman retrieved the errant throw near the first base dugout. He picked up the ball and aimed it toward the pitcher, who had come over to cover the bag. His hasty toss bounced twice, caroming off the pitcher's knee.

All the while, in such pain it was awful to watch, Nick kept lurching—*duddle-up, duddle-up, duddle-up*—toward that bag. Finally, the shortstop, who had gotten his hands on the ball, softly tossed it to the first baseman who'd come back from purgatory to cover first, and the Job Corps nipped Nick by a step, 4-to-3-to-6-to-3, if you're scoring it.

When Nick hobbled back to the dugout, he yielded at last to Bill's passionate pleas and pulled himself out of the game.

Another time when Schuster Block was playing at White River Park, Nick was upset because we were losing to a team he felt was inferior. We could see the explosion coming. With men on first and second bases, the opponent's batter bunted the ball perfectly toward first base beyond the reach of pitcher Jerry Mullinix. Holding the base runner on, I had gotten a late start on the ball. Fielding it and following the vocal orders from a teammate ("Third!") I side-armed the ball to Jack Leonard at that base. Trouble was, the runner, who had broken from second base on the pitch, was already standing on third base when my throw arrived.

Nick leaped off the bench and called the entire infield to the mound for a "conference."

"That's it! You guys aren't even *in* this game. You aren't concentrating and we're gonna get beat if you don't get your heads out of your butts! Brunnemer! Why did you throw the ball to *third*? Didn't you see that you had no play there?"

"I heard someone yell 'third,' Nick," I answered in my defense.

"Now who the *hell* would be so *dumb* as to tell you to throw it to third on *that* play?" Nick snarled indignantly.

Now the honesty bred in the genes of the Nicoson family emerged.

"*I* did, Dad," Danny Nicoson, our catcher, meekly confessed. "I yelled for Brum to throw it to third!"

Without another word, Nick stalked off.

Never saw Nick at a loss for words before that. Never after, either.

It was part of Nick's basketball coaching philosophy to prepare his Indiana Central teams with a tough pre-conference schedule. You might be surprised to learn that during Nick's tenure the Greyhounds played Kentucky (during the Adoph Rupp era, going 0-4 against the Wildcats); Harvard (0-1); Cincinnati (1-1); Louisville (0-1); St. Louis (0-1); Austin Peay (0-1); Xavier (0-1); and, of course, Butler (12-29), Ball State (20-30) and Indiana State (13-21). That strategy probably had something to do with our all-time records against Hoosier College Conference rivals Franklin (69-44), Hanover (68-18), Manchester (65-34), and Anderson (61-18).

Nicoson's first outstanding team was the 1948-49 squad that won twenty of twenty-nine games. The Greyhounds were led by Elwood "Woody" McBride '52 (still ICC's fourth all-time point maker with 1,826 points and a 1992 inductee into the U of I Hall of Fame) and Dwight Swails '51 (third all-time in points at 1,913, Greyhound Hall of Fame, 2001). Nick's teams became noted for a fast-breaking offensive attack and tenacious defensive play.

Like his mentor, Good, Coach Nicoson was an astute recruiter. In the early fifties, watching games at the fabled "Dust Bowl" in the predominantly black neighborhood on the near-northwest side of Indianapolis, Nick got his first look at a young man who would become the greatest scorer in Hounds history. Bailey "Flap" Robertson, older brother of the celebrated Oscar Robertson, entered Indiana Central in the fall of 1953. Four years later Bailey had set scoring records that endure to this day.

Nick was sly when it came to helping his players maintain their eligibility. Over the Christmas holiday, his basketball players stayed in the dormitory for practice and games that were scheduled during the break. Knowing that many faculty and staff burned wood in their stoves and fireplaces in the forties and fifties, he made a deal with Birtle Allen, head of buildings and grounds. Mr. Allen employed the team members to gather fallen limbs on the campus grounds and to fell the trees marked for destruction. The boys would then assemble loads of firewood, and, in what would appear to be an effort at team camaraderie, and a generous outreach, would then deliver wood, unannounced, to members of the ICC community.

The fact that the best lots of the wood were deposited in the homes of some of the faculty who were especially rigid in grading Nick's athletes—profs like Kenny St. Clair, Dr. Morgan, Roland Nelson and others—was surely coincidental.

Prompted by his good friend, *Indianapolis Star* sportswriter and editor Bob Collins, Angus Nicoson accepted an invitation to coach in the annual Indiana-Kentucky All-Star game, pitting the finest high school players from those states against one another. For seventeen years, Nick coached the likes of Oscar Robertson, the VanArsdale twins, George McGinnis, and other Hoosier legends in the *Star*-sponsored summer charity game against similarly touted cagers from the Blue Grass State. He won more games than any other All-Star coach in the history of the series.

Among Nick's finest teams at Indiana Central was the 1955-56 squad, which finished 23-6 and was the first Greyhound team to qualify for the National Association of Intercollegiate Athletics (NAIA) national tournament. Bailey Robertson '57 averaged 27.5 points per game to lead the squad. Other stalwarts were the great Bob Jewell '56, a 6'6" center, Indiana High School Trester Award winner in 1952 and a transfer from Michigan; Bobby Theil '57, who was named Marion County Athlete of the Year in 1953, played one season at Purdue and then returned to the Southside; and one of Indiana Central's brilliant

Distinction Without Pretension

all-around athletes, Dick Nyers.

Central fans of the mid-fifties will remember one of the most thrilling games in Greyhound lore when ICC played the mighty Purple Aces of Evansville, who would win five national small-college titles under hall of fame Coach Arad McCutchan. ICC had earned the right to host the game because of its won-lost record. Tournament officials, however, decreed that Central's ancient gym would not hold enough fans, so the game was moved to Manual High School. On March 6, 1956, McCutchan, wearing his customary florid red socks, led his team onto the floor.

Rich Reasoner '57, a reserve center on that squad, recalled Evansville's disdain for having to play the game in a high school gym.

"From the time they arrived," observed Reasoner, "their players showed a lot of attitude."

It was a fiercely contested battle. In an era when shooting forty percent from the field would be considered an unusually high percentage, Evansville hit forty-three of eighty-one field goal attempts (.531). Central showed its marksmanship from the free throw line, scorching the nets on thirty-five of forty-three free tosses. After missing his first attempt, Dick Nyers nailed seventeen consecutive free throws for what was then a state intercollegiate record. Nyers scored twenty-three points on the night and fellow guard Bill Hampton '56 added twenty-one. Jewell scored thirteen and gathered twelve rebounds; Bob Theil had double figures in both points and rebounds. The Purple Aces were led by center Clyde Cox with twenty-six points and Jim Smallins scored twenty. But it would be the matchless Bailey Robertson, launching jump shots from all over the court, who would be the difference in the game. "Flap" nailed twelve of thirty shots from the field and hit all twelve free throws for a game-high thirty-six points.

Evansville jumped out to a big lead early in the contest, but the Greyhounds rallied. Going into the dressing room at halftime Evansville was ahead 55-51. But with 11:49 remaining in the game, ICC pulled even at 73-73. Nyers' two free throws gave ICC a lead the team would never lose. The Hounds withstood a relentless rally by the Aces before coming out on top, 105-102. Local sportswriters called it one of the most exciting games they had ever seen.

Two nights later, with Robertson scoring forty-two, the Hounds earned Indiana Central's first trip to the NAIA National Tournament, at Kansas City, by beating Manchester, 96-83.

Tennesse A. & I, led by former Gary Roosevelt High School and later New York Knick Dick Barnett (22 ppg), was ICC's opponent in the first round of the single-elimination tourney. Central started Theil and Robertson, both an even 6'0", Jewell (6'6"), and Nyers and Hampton, each standing 5'10". Barnett (6'5") and Ben Jackson (6'7") were too tall and talented, scoring twenty and twelve, respectively, and wily guard Ron Hamilton had twenty-one to lead the Tigers to an 86-63 win over the Hounds. The twenty-three victories that season stood as the school record for eight years.

The 1963-64 team, brilliantly coached by Angus Nicoson, rolled to a 26-3 mark. Of all the sports teams that I have seen in more than forty years of following Greyhound athletics, no bunch had the variety of weapons, a more indomitable will, or the air of confidence than the Angus Nicoson-coached basketball team representing ICC that season. It was the finest Greyhound team I ever saw play, in any sport.

James L. Brunnemer

If you liked fast-moving, high-scoring basketball, with blitzkrieg-like defense on the hardwood, you'd love this team. In the seventy-nine seasons of Greyhound basketball through 2003, no other squad has scored more points in a season, an average of 94.3 per game. Rated all season long in the top ten of the NAIA in 1963-64, Nick's squad topped 100 points in a game nine times and scored at least ninety or more in *twenty of its twenty-nine games!*

With three members of its starting five under six feet tall (forward Tom Moran '64 at 5'11" and 5'10" guards Hank Voss '67 and Vasco Walton '66) and the other two standing a relatively slight 6'2" (Clark Crafton '65) and 6'4" (Jack Johnson '64), this team could virtually fly down the court. Usually it was ball-handling magician Hank Voss or equally sleight-of-hand Vasco Walton leading the three-lane fast break attack.

In one memorable evening in the "cracker box" gymnasium at Taylor University, each starter had at least twenty points. Led by Moran with thirty-two, Crafton twenty-eight, and Walton, Voss, and Johnson twenty each, the Hounds won a scintillating 125-101 victory over Don Odle's Trojans. A few years later at an athletic dinner, the principal speaker, Odle, recognized former Greyhounds Dave Huffman '64 and Jerry Lewis '62 in the audience. Talking of the friendly rivalry between ICC and Taylor, Coach Odle congratulated them on being fine athletes and representatives at ICC, then reminded them that Taylor had scored 101 points against them in 1964. The audience laughed at the barb at the Greyhounds. Then Odle added, "Of course, we got beat by twenty-four. My boys scored fifty-five points in the first half, which I thought was pretty good. We went to the locker room trailing by fifteen!"

The Hounds won fifteen straight games from January to mid-March, averaging ninety-seven to their opponent's seventy-eight points. Tom Moran, who is still eighth in career scoring after nearly forty seasons have passed, with 1,744 points, was perhaps the finest jump shooter Nick ever coached. A frustrated rival coach, speaking of Moran, said, "Play man-to-man and Moran will get eighteen, and the rest of the team will beat you. Play zone, and Moran will get thirty and beat you by himself!"

Crafton ended his career fourteenth in scoring (1,409) and at only 6'2" was an amazing rebounder. He remains second all-time in career rebounds (978). Vasco Walton set the standard as ICC's career assist leader with 200, including a record seventeen in one game. Walton was also the point man on the Hounds' stifling, pressing defense. Although steals were not an official statistic kept until about 1970, Walton once made ten steals in a game against St. Procopius (1963), which would surely be a school record.

That game with St. Procopius epitomized the Nicoson gift for lighting a fire under an underachieving team. The Hounds were 6-0 and the players' opinion of themselves seemed a bit elevated when St. Pro came to the Greyhound gym. At halftime, the SPC Saints led, 36-35. During the ten-minute intermission, Nick "discussed" with his players what he concluded was his team's listless play. St. Procopius matched its first half total of thirty-six points in the second stanza. With Nick's admonitions still ringing in their ears, his lads piled up sixty-four in the final twenty minutes, winning going away, 99-72.

With no disrespect intended for Johnson, who, at 6'4", was a steady performer at center and one of the most intelligent players on the squad, it was fascinating to watch how cannily Nick alternated Johnson and his talented 6'6" sophomore, Phil Honnold '67. A gifted athlete, Honnold would ultimately break all existing track and field records set a

Distinction Without Pretension

few years earlier by his outstanding older brother, Fred '64.

Phil consistently earned Nick's displeasure, however, because of his often-lackluster efforts in practice. Nick refused to put Honnold in the starting line-up, using Johnson instead. For the first five or perhaps eight minutes of the first half of a game, the lanky sophomore would sit on the bench, becoming increasingly, overtly energized. Nick would sit calmly, regardless of whether the Hounds were winning or losing, as Honnold worked himself into a lather. Finally, out would come Johnson and in his place would appear a dervish in the frame of Honnold. It wasn't uncommon for Phil to score ten points and grab an equal number of rebounds in the early minutes of his appearance in the game. With 1,366 points, Phil Honnold remains fifteenth among individual scorers for his career and picked off 862 rebounds, now fourth all-time.

Earning a berth in the thirty-two-team NAIA championship tourney at Kansas City, the 1963-64 Hounds were a high seed and the choice by many to emerge as the national champion. After dispatching Morris Harvey College 92-81 in the opening round, ICC faced powerful Rockhurst (Missouri) College. A thirty-five-foot desperation heave as time expired was the dagger that slew the Hounds in their quest for a title. With Walton, Voss, and Crafton surrounding him near the mid-court line, a Rockhurst guard threw a prayer toward the hoop that split the cords with the clock showing 00:00 remaining. Rockhurst 76, Hounds 74. Rockhurst went on to defeat handily its final two opponents to win the crown.

Once, I tried to get Nick to concede that the team of his senior year of 1941-42 (16-0) could not have beaten the 1963-64 Greyhound squad (26-3), which he coached. He replied, slyly, "Well, in 1941-42 we beat everybody that showed up." That was a claim which the 1963-64 team could not make.

In the spring of 1976 Nick invited me to accompany him on a recruiting trip to "da Region." A big, rawboned boy named Tim Bajusz was a highly sought-after prospect at Hammond High School. At 6'5" and 220 pounds, we thought Tim was a load ... until we met his father. *Mr*. Bajusz was a stunning example of Hungarian manhood. When Pater Bajusz answered our knock, I swear his body covered the entire square footage of the screened storm door. A Chicago cop, he stood about 6'4" and was at least 260 pounds of solid muscle. His raspy speaking voice growled thickly with an east-Chicago accentuation.

I learned that afternoon how nimble was Nick's response to moral challenges, when Mr. Bajusz asked what kind of beer we'd like to have before we sat down to discuss his son enrolling at Indiana Central. Ordinarily, Nick would have passed on such a beverage in the presence of a recruit. But the manner in which Mr. Bajusz phrased his question, and the knowledge that it might be seen as disrespectful if we refused, both Nick and I popped at least a couple, and maybe three cold ones. After all, "when in Rome ..." Nick was successful in recruiting Tim *and* his Dad to Indiana Central!

Nick was the central character in the saddest series of events I ever witnessed at the university. Sometime in the early seventies, Nick's behaviors were becoming unmistakably odd. His wife, Bea, fiercely loyal to Nick, told me privately one day of her worry about him. He had recently wandered for the greater part of an hour in a parking lot. He'd forgotten where the car was, she said. Bea's grace and dignity would be inspiring throughout the long

James L. Brunnemer

nightmare that was to come.

Nick's grasp on even the most ordinary mental processes increasingly diminished. Until it was named for the Dr. Alzheimer who had studied its effects, the insidious disease was generally categorized as "early senility." Most of us were not aware of the condition that was even then stealing Nick's inner light. His thinking was confused. Replies to statements that in the past would have evoked a razor-sharp observation, a clever quip, or a firm retort, passed by either to be met with Nick's addled silence and a quizzical look, or, at worst, a disjointed, nonsensical comment that bore no relevance to the original remark. The characteristic twinkle in Nick's eye was now only a hollow gaze.

During this agonizing period of time in which Angus Nicoson was sinking irreversibly into the throes of Alzheimer's disease, John Swank became a personal hero for me. As Nick increasingly fell victim to the awful effects of the insidious mind-stealer, and in what I now look back on as personal cowardice, I began avoiding Nick. I just could not accept the relentless eradication of that great mind. I curse this despicable affliction and grieve for anyone and every family who must deal with it.

As Nick's problems escalated Professor Swank became a constant companion of the coach. He patiently played golf, accompanied Nick to sports events, and made conversation with the increasingly muddled man. John nobly expended great personal sacrifice to minister to this great man. I will always be grateful for the courage and humanity of John Swank as he cared for Nick during those dark days.

Anyway, we all knew things weren't right with the coach. Nobody, however, seemed to know exactly *what* was wrong.

For the 1975-76 season, Nick had recruited an exceptionally talented freshman class, perhaps one of his best ever. Kevin Pearson '79, who was to finish tenth in scoring and first in career rebounding with 1,702 and 1,045, respectively, in his four-year career, and Rob Acord '79 were both standouts on Marion High School's 1975 Indiana State championship team. The coach of the Giants was Indiana Basketball Hall of Famer Bill Green, who played for Nick in 1953-54. Burly Tim Bajusz '79 of Hammond; sharpshooter Jeff Hanni '79, son of former player Larry Hanni; and clever playmaker Dave Ancelet '79 from Cathedral were an outstanding collection of players. Over time they became thoroughly bewildered as Nick's peculiar behaviors intensified.

David Wood '76, a three-sport standout who was a senior that year, describes one example of how pathetic practice routines became. The team would be running five-man offensive sets, against no defense, when Nick would yell, "Sag back, cut off the passing lanes!" As the coach became increasingly agitated at his team not carrying out his orders, Woody or another of the five *offensive* players would steal the ball *from his own team!* Nick would just nod in approval.

A very disheartened Steve Kahl '78 nearly quit the team. I took Steve to lunch to encourage him just to hang tough, that none of us really knew what the problem was.

In February of 1976, the Greyhound basketball team hosted the five-time small college national champion Evansville Purple Aces. Coach Arad McCutchan's lads gave the impression that playing Indiana Central was beneath them even though the Greyhounds had joined the Indiana Collegiate Conference three years before.

Characteristically, from the outset of the game the Aces played rough, suffocating defense, but the Hounds were hanging tough. Trailing by eight to ten points throughout

Distinction Without Pretension

most of the game, ICU was led by Jim Farmer '77, Wood, and Clarence Swain '77, plus Steve Kahl and Bill Rogers '78. Aided by those extraordinary freshmen, the Greyhounds rallied to take a one-point lead on a Farmer jumper with under a minute to go.

The Aces worked patiently for a shot, missed, and Kahl rebounded with less than a half minute to play. Dave Ancelet rushed up the floor, and, driving for the hoop, was fouled before the shot. He would receive one free throw and a bonus shot if he made the first. Eleven seconds remained. Plenty of time for E'ville to retrieve a missed shot and scurry to the other end to hit a game winner. It had happened to us many times before.

Ancelet hit the first of the pair. But before the referee could hand the ball to the brassy young freshman for his second try, out of the corner of my eye I caught a frantic movement near the Greyhound bench. Senior Bob Wingerter '76, all 6 feet 9 inches of him, bolted out of his seat and ran to the scorer's bench. Wingerter, who later became managing partner of the Ernst and Young accounting firm in Indianapolis and a member of the U of I Board of Trustees, was very bright and very tall, but he wasn't an especially skillful player.

But picture this: Wingerter, at 6'9", joined 6'8" regular center Steve Kahl on opposite sides of the free throw lane. This timely, tactical substitution increased ICC's chances of retrieving the rebound. Ancelet took the ball from the official, bounced it twice and let fly with a smooth stroke that was to become so familiar over the next four years. The shot was a shade long, striking the back of the rim. It caromed back toward the shooter. A large, looming figure in a white uniform intercepted the ball in its flight: WINGERTER!

His long arms outreached the more athletic, but shorter, Evansville players. Once he secured the ball, Bob tossed it quickly to Swain in backcourt. An Aces player lunged toward Clarence. Too late! He'd whipped the ball to Farmer on the side. In a millisecond Farmer rifled it to Kahl on the opposite perimeter of the court, with the Evansville players desperately, but futilely, chasing the ball. The clock moved downward. Three seconds ... two ... one ... finally, *the horn blared!*

Hounds 91, Purple Aces 89!

It was a huge win, the first over Evansville in ICC play.

But, for me, what was truly exciting—I had chills, honest to God—was the incredible coaching move by Nick. Who else but Nick would insert a player who rarely left the bench, but was perfect in that particular situation? We needed a rebound if Ancelet missed the shot. He did, and eighty-one-inches-tall Wingerter got it for us.

After the game, milling around the sidelines, I was caught up in the euphoria of the victory. Along with several other Greyhound backers I was recounting the events of those last few seconds. I was so happy for Nick. And for me. Because despite whatever wasn't right with him, he demonstrated with the Wingerter substitution that still, reflexively, intuitively, he could coach the game. That gave me comfort, somehow.

Out of the tunnel from the locker room walked #33, Dave Wood, still in his sweat-soaked uniform. Woody had come to me earlier in the year to express his frustration over Nick's behaviors. I had sympathized with him, but assured him Nick would be all right.

Congratulating the bright and thoughtful senior, I said, "Man, Woody, what a great move by Nick! He sends Wingerter in for one possible outcome and Bob gets the rebound. Incredible!"

Dave hesitated, sighed, and said quietly those words that still make me sad today

James L. Brunnemer

when I think of it: "Jim, Nick didn't put Wingerter in. I did. Farmer and me have been coaching the team for most of the year."

Nick was going through the motions, probably by instinct. But he had little idea where he was or what was happening on the court.

This was to continue for the balance of the season and on into the next before Gene Sease finally coaxed Nick into going to Florida for a vacation—in December, mid-season—thus ending the career of a man revered by those who came to know him as I did.

Recollecting that excruciating epoch, Dave Wood surmised, "Somewhere inside, Nick knew. He knew something was wrong."

"Before every game Nick called Farmer and me into his office, so we could discuss the opponent, our game plan, who would start."

Occasionally, Nick would have written in the names of Vasco Walton and Henry Voss as starting guards, both of whom had played for Nick more than ten years before.

During games, if Woody wasn't on the floor, he sat next to Nick. Everybody knew it and no one questioned it. It just "was." From there, Woody would make suggestions—whom to substitute, changes in defense. Bill Bright, Nick's loyal assistant, was reluctant to interfere. Bill coached the jayvees and Nick didn't solicit his advice.

Bill did, however, introduce an offense for the team that year. It was a crucial part of their being able to compete. Nick had little idea what was going on.

Woody learned how delicate a tightrope he had to walk with Nick. "About twice during my junior and senior years, when I crossed the line, Nick would ream me, a thorough butt-chewing as only Nick could do it." After establishing who was in charge, however, the almost surreal circumstance of Woody and Farmer leading the team continued as before. Dave also made suggestions in the huddle, but again, he had to be subtle. If he appeared to usurp Nick's authority too blatantly, Nick would lash out at him. Then, maybe a half-minute later, Nick would make whatever tactical move Woody had advocated.

Only a very close-knit aggregate of players could have continued in that quaint atmosphere. Exceptionally mature leadership by Wood, Farmer, Rex Sager '74, and other upperclassmen kept the ship going with the pilot unable to steer the course.

The long, cruel season finally ended. Emotions ran the gamut. Woody's career was over.

The following December, Dave Wood was in his first year of coaching at Pike High School and following the Greyhounds with a sense of disbelief and sorrow. He knew Nick was not in control. The team was 1-5, dispirited, and on the verge of a player rebellion.

Woody's parents, Clarence and Doris Wood, had invited a number of Dave's friends and former teammates to a Christmas party at their house in Pike Township. That evening the Greyhounds were playing Capital University of Columbus, Ohio, a perennially gritty foe known for their tenacious defensive teams under Coach Vince Chicarelli.

The party was being delayed for the arrival of Dave's close friend, Jim Farmer, now playing his final year. Knowing Farmer would be along soon, Wood and his guests tuned into Channel 6-TV to learn that the Greyhounds had upset Capital 74-73. The win would enhance the celebratory mood of the revelers.

Distinction Without Pretension

When Farmer arrived, Dave greeted him at the door. One look at Jim's somber expression told Woody something was amiss.

"Nick's done," was all a choked-up Farmer could say. President Sease had made the excruciating decision to remove Nick as coach.

It was then that Nick's former players who had assembled at the party felt crushed. Despite the dreadful scenario of deceptions and the anger and resentment, his players comprehended that the once-proud, combative, indefatigable Nick had been relieved of the one thing he lived for. Even knowing Nick *had* to be discharged from his coaching position, each one realized how very much they respected him as a man.

Nick had battled to the end. Even as the silent, treacherous disease eroded his mental faculties, Nick had remained the consummate noble warrior. And those young men knew it.

That night, in the privacy of his bedroom after everyone had gone, Woody sobbed quietly into the night.

It remained for Bob Collins, the great Indianapolis sportswriter and one of Nick's true friends and admirers, to put the exclamation point on the great Greyhound coach's career. In his daily "Sports Over Lightly" column in February 1977, under a banner proclaiming "The Last of an Excellent Breed," Collins wrote of Nick:

> [H]e came out of a town so small he got lost a couple of times himself trying to find it. And he talks with a Hoosier twang so thick his sinuses scream in pain at the end of every sentence.
>
> On the floor he was tough as steel. He fought you for every point. But, as the saying goes, he left it all in the dressing room. No man ever had a finer or more loyal friend than Angus Nicoson.
>
> Nick has enjoyed considerable public acclaim. And he has suffered much adversity. But he has taken it all—the good and the bad—with a smile. He's a guy who thinks today is great and can hardly wait to see tomorrow. He is in against a tough opponent now and has been forced to give up a big part of his life—his basketball coaching career at Indiana Central. But the other guy is up against a scrapper, too. Nick never met a guy he didn't think he could whip.
>
> He never has been anything but a winner—through his 483 victories at Indiana Central and his many years with the Indiana High School All-Stars. Some years ago the All-Star coaching job—as it is now—was passed around from year to year. Then we at The Star made a decision. Nick was the kind of person we wanted to coach our team, every year. He was an excellent teacher of the game, had a high sense of responsibility and was very much aware of the public relations aspect of the annual Indiana-Kentucky series. He coached our team from 1952 through 1965 and returned for a short tour, 1969-71. And in his tenure he straightened out more than a few young men. Let me tell you he did.
>
> Nick is one of the few men I know who is completely without

prejudice—against ill-tempered, Irish sportswriters who throw golf clubs. He accepts people for what they are. And he can spot a phony three blocks away.

Nick, like his old competitor up the street, Tony Hinkle, is the last of a breed: a man who can coach and win in any sport. He was an outstanding basketball and baseball player. When Indiana Central took up football, the job landed in his lap. It was a game he never had played and rarely watched. But he turned out winners.

He is taking on an illness with a long name. But right now he probably is studying the opponent closely—trying to figure a way to defense him. It has been written that Nick is Indiana Central to the public. He is a man without pretense, and that would embarrass him. He has never wanted to be anything more than "Angus Nicoson, basketball coach at Indiana Central."

He was. A damned good one. You don't replace an Angus Nicoson. You just go out and hire another coach.

Now, get well and get back up here, you malingerer. Soon the grass will be green and the putts will be lipping the cup. I'm not through getting into your pocket.

Nick's life ended, mercifully, on March 21 of 1982. He was sixty-two years old.

CHAPTER XXIII
THE ATHLETICISTS

Sire to sire, it's born in the blood,
the fire of the mare and the strength of the stud,
It's breeding and it's training and it's something
unknown, that drives him to carry it home.
   from "Run for the Roses"
   by Dan Fogelberg

Just over a half-century ago, February 28, 1953, two young scientists at the University of Cambridge, England, James Watson, 25, and Francis Crick, 36, unraveled the structure of DNA, "the secret of life."

Describing the double helix, Watson and Crick were the first to successfully probe into the genetic basis of inheritance and, indeed, evolution: the understanding for "how humans work."

Today, building upon the pioneering work of their predecessors' stupendous discoveries with the advantage of the most sophisticated technology, modern scientists are decoding the human genome, or the genetic blueprint "that distinguishes a man from a mouse."

What, one might ask, has the study of the most basic elements of life have to do with an observer's interest in athletics? It's a fair question.

Although millions of men and women aspire to earn a livelihood as a professional athlete, a scant percentage of the American population—less than one-tenth of one percent—reach that level of athletic performance. Two measurements of the general public's interest in those who ascend to the highest rung of the ladder are attendance figures at sports contests and the sale of products endorsed by professional athletes.

What intrigues followers of sport are those precious few athletes with similar physical stature and measurably similar strength, speed, and general athleticism who separate themselves as superior to their counterparts. "Swifter, higher, stronger" is the Olympian's quest. But many are the swift, those who leap high, and the strong. Whence comes that mysterious internal drive that sets apart transcendent athletes, that divides the great from the almost great?

As one example, millions of words have been spoken and written by sportswriters, telecasters, team owners, opponents, teammates, and fans—anyone with an opinion—in the attempt to describe the greatness of Michael Jordan, the recently retired icon of professional basketball.

Coach Bob Knight made a profound observation of and enormous compliment to Jordan, when he noted: "Michael Jordan may be the best at his sport than anyone has ever been at any other sport."

Of Jordan, performing at forty years of age in a game where a man in his early thirties is generally near the end of his career, Washington Wizards coach Doug Collins rhapsodized: "I don't know how he does it. I don't know where the will and the spirit and the energy all comes from. But he's the most resilient, proudest man I've ever been around. He's amazing."

Before Jordan, there were similar attempts to define the mystique of the superiority of Babe Ruth, Muhammad Ali, Wilt Chamberlain, and other dominant sports heroes of the twentieth century but they have always left us wanting. In describing the great Houston Oilers running back, Earl Campbell, his former coach, Bum Phillips, remarked, "Earl plays in a higher league [than most NFL players]. I'm not sure who's in that league, but I do know it doesn't take long to call the roll."

Some have coined facile clichés to describe the "something extra" that separates winners from losers. In an attempt to describe the special traits found in the peerless athlete, one coach admitted, "I can't hear it, smell it, taste it, touch or see it, but when it's inside a player in front of me, I can recognize it."

Science has advanced to frontiers inconceivable since I first began to observe sports heroes back in the 1950s. Certainly native intelligence has been researched and measured in ways that enable experts to categorize human beings by cognitive skills. Sophisticated telemetry, designed and developed by physiologists, enables them to delve into neuro-muscular systems to measure the facility and economy of effort expended by the athlete in running and jumping, and in executing the aptitude specialized to various sports or games.

But despite more than two centuries of examination of characteristics of the transcendent athlete, the complexities of the unique human experience and emotional make-up and its influence upon competitive drive is still mere speculation. Physiognomy, or attempting to discover temperament and character traits from outward appearances, remains more art than science.

The best efforts of the finest minds have still not unraveled the secret of the drive—the "something unknown" in the verse of songwriter Dan Fogelberg—of the surpassing competitor.

Webster's definition of the "athlete"—"one who is trained or skilled in exercises, sports or games requiring physical strength, agility, speed or stamina"—falls short, in my view, of describing those special few who consistently outperform other game players in a chosen athletic endeavor.

Predominant athletic skills, mental and physical toughness, and an indefinable well of competitiveness, these three define what I term the **athleticist**. To be an above-normal sportsman requires at least one of these traits. Having two of them results in a superior athlete. The truly great ones, those remembered long after they have stopped playing the games, exhibit all three.

Natural athleticism is manifested through innate physical gifts that predispose an individual to success in game playing. A stopwatch, a measuring stick or tape can measure athleticism. One's natural talent for running fast or long distances, for leaping high or far, or for lifting or thrusting great weights all are measurable against standards. Hand-eye coordination, quickness of hands and feet, flexibility of body—these, too, may be compared with other human beings'. However, one may be gifted athletically but not qualify as an *athleticist*.

Toughness is an intrinsic characteristic by which athletes are measured. Taking the easy way, pampered by doting parents, didn't harden most of the tough guys I've seen.

Distinction Without Pretension

Their physical and psychological being was tested by fire. Tough-minded young people often suffered trauma early in life, forcing them to "grow up" in advance of their chronological age. Athletes often were victims of deprivation, snubs, setbacks, or humiliating events of their past that motivate them. A physical deformity or other overt shortcoming, which the individual perceives as making him unattractive, unaccepted, or unapproved, contributes to a kind of obduracy.

Men and women of privilege, who have not grown up in desperate circumstances, are found in the sports world. But I would argue that among the world's most hardened, durable competitors, those who have had the advantages of wealth and social position are the exception to the rule.

Characteristic of the tenacious and irrepressible athlete is a high level of psychological endurance, doggedness in the face of adversity, the classic defiant response to what might seem impossible odds. The true tough guys are those who can tolerate not just physical pain (although one demonstrates one's grit by handling injuries better than most "normal" human beings) but psychological trauma as well. The stoic, expressionless response to adversity, even horror that would unravel most of us is characteristic of the truly resolute competitor.

In my view, the most intriguing trait of the athleticist is also the most complex. An extraordinary **competitiveness** refers to that inherent, inexplicable *inner drive* that separates two competitors with relatively equal athleticism according to measurable physical attributes. The supreme competitors exhibit a burning will to win that simply defies our ability to measure it.

I believe the athleticist is, to a higher degree than others, willful, uncompromising, stubborn, and intractable in his pursuit of victory. It is not enough for the superior competitor to play a game well. He must *win*. He must dominate. The athleticist may even practice a form of "denial" of his own limitations in competition. Believing he can win, or perhaps frightened beyond realistic assessment of failure, the transcendent competitor never accepts losing. His mind tells him, and he believes, that "the referees screwed us," "the ball bounced wrong," or a teammate failed in his responsibilities. "Given a little more time we would have won." That is why the superlative competitor, after losing, always wants to play again, immediately. A classic competitor will never admit defeat. Never.

Again, I would contend the mainspring of the unquenchable drive to win often comes from some dark place within the competitor. Abuse as a child, fear, deprivation, a physical limitation, or something ugly that is more fearsome for the competitor than is the challenge he finds in the competition may fuel his irrepressible drive. Often a competitor's searing fear of failure runs side-by-side an undaunting belief and confidence. I am not aware of any empirical study undertaken that identifies the top athletes in professional sports and attempts to correlate athletic success with their early life experiences. But I would contend that some interesting data might be found aligning success in athletics with troubled or difficult experiences economically, socially, and/or psychologically in childhood.

Threatened with defeat, true competitors are not nice on the field of combat. They can be acceptable socially, highly intelligent, and appreciate the arts as well as the more delicate and gentle sides of life. But in competition, challenged, they are indefatigable, often breaking down a lesser opponent with cruel efficiency. Describing his experience on the court against a Boston Celtic Hall of Famer, one NBA player commented: "When you look into Larry Bird's eyes, you see the eyes of an assassin."

Because different generations like to compare their sports heroes with those of other eras, the merits of teams and athletes from separate generations invariably ignite controversy. Attempting to compare 1930s-era Harry Good-coached basketball teams, for example, with a twenty-first century Greyhound squad of Coach Todd Sturgeon, is near folly. At 6'3" and 190 pounds, Dave DeJernett '35 was a behemoth among players in the third decade of the twentieth century. Consider that, with two players standing 6'8" and two at 6'6" with muscular frames of 230 to 265 pounds, Sturgeon's 2003 team was merely *average* in size in relation to their competition in the GLVAC. One must admit that, at least physically, DeJernett would be at a distinct disadvantage in today's game.

In 1953, Greyhound football center and linebacker John Hurrle was bigger than most of the opponents he lined up against. Hurrle was 6'3" and 215 pounds. Coach Joe Polizzi's starting offensive line for the 2002 season, tackle-to-tackle, *averaged* 6'4" and 285 pounds per man!

Anyone who believes athletes of past decades were physically equal to today's players hasn't been paying attention. Today's performers are generally bigger, stronger, and faster than players of earlier eras; collisions are far more violent in contact sports; athletes jump higher and run faster, and hand-eye coordination is more precise. Better nutrition, intense weight training and more-scientific conditioning, better and more technologically driven coaching techniques, and superior genetics through succeeding generations are among reasons that today's athletes hold physical superiority over their counterparts of earlier years.

But the inscrutable drive to win of the ascendant athlete, that combination of competitive will and toughness of the athleticist, is the equalizer of athletes of different generations. A never-changing factor that has always separated the greater performer from his less-successful counterpart, in any era, is the immeasurable inner resolve to succeed. That pertinacity always skews the issue when teams and athletes of different eras are compared. Are today's athletes, possessing preeminent physical attributes, any more driven to excel, any more tough-minded, or singular in their drive to win than athletes of the past? I doubt it. The special people of every generation seem to share an intangible hunger for victory that separates champions from the also-rans.

In all my years following Greyhound sports, I saw many, and played on teams with a few of those unique performers who are celebrated in ICC sports tradition. However, there were a number of legendary Greyhound athletes whom I know only through news accounts, school records, or stories from those who saw them play.

Among those whom I would have paid to see in their prime was the first fabled black athlete who wore the Cardinal and Grey, Dave DeJernett. Inducted posthumously into both the U of I (1993) and the Indiana Basketball halls of fame (1976), DeJernett, at 6'3" a giant of a man in the second decade of the twentieth century, led his Washington, Indiana, High School teammates to the 1930 state basketball championship.

Today, an accomplished athlete such as Dave would have had his pick of major collegiate programs. However, because of the social mores of the times, Harry Good of Indiana Central was one of the few college coaches who recruited the big center. The doors of Indiana Central were open to individuals of all races and creeds in those Jim Crow days. In addition to running dashes and throwing the shot in track, DeJernett was starting center for Good's cagers, leading his team in scoring and rebounding. According to one who played in the backcourt on the DeJernett-led squads, Bill Schaefer '35, "Big Dave was a dominant player, nearly unstoppable."

Known by later generations of ICC students more for his intellectual attributes than for his athletic prowess, Bob McBride '48 was one of the finest all-around athletes in Indiana colleges from 1945-47. After serving in the 17th and 82nd Airborne divisions in World War II, McBride returned to Indiana Central, becoming a star in four sports: football (earning Little All-American honors in 1947), basketball, track, and baseball. His 1947 season batting average of .452 was the standard for Greyhound batsmen until Mike Wishnevski hit .487 thirty-four years later. McBride's average still stands third-best on the all-time list. Following his senior year, McBride was invited to tryouts for teams from both professional football (the Browns) and baseball (New York Giants). McBride, who could have signed a pro contract, chose instead to go onto graduate work at the University of Chicago, later becoming a distinguished academician at his alma mater. From 1978-87, McBride served as president of Simpson (Iowa) College, where the baseball complex is named Robert E. McBride Stadium. He became a member of the U of I Hall of Fame in 1991.

From 1951 through 1953, Bill Bright set pitching records that stand yet today, a half-century later. The lefthander led the 1953 team to a 13-0 record, one of only two undefeated diamond squads in ICC history. Just three Greyhound hurlers have won at least ten games with no losses in a season. After completing a 10-0 slate in '53, Bright signed a professional contract with the Philadelphia Phillies following his junior season. I was privileged to play behind Bill as a first baseman during summers at Indiana Central from 1963-66. Then in his mid-thirties and obviously not as skilled as he would have been in his twenties, Bill was still the best pitcher on any team on which I played. He was elected to the Indiana Central Athletics Hall of Fame in 1988 and the Indiana Baseball Hall of Fame in 2000.

Another Indiana Basketball Hall of Famer from Indiana Central whom I would have loved to see perform was Bailey "Flap" Robertson. Graduating from Crispus Attucks High School in 1953, Bailey was much less heralded than his younger brother Oscar would be three years later. Many watchers of Indiana basketball proclaimed that "Flap" was a purer shooter than Oscar, who was selected as one of the fifty best NBA players in history in 2001. Few who watched Bailey during his four years at Indiana Central would dispute that claim.

Bailey set basketball scoring records from 1954-57 that are still on the U of I books after nearly a half-century. Robertson holds U of I records for points scored in a career (2,280) and season (754 in 1955-56); most field goals in a career (925) and season (310); and scoring average per game for career (23.3) and season (28.7 in 1956-57). In the 1,865 basketball games played in Greyhound history, only thirteen basketball players have scored as many as forty or more points in a game. Five times Flap Robertson poured in forty or more, versus Hanover (43) and Manchester (42) in 1956, and in 1957 against Hanover (40), and Manchester twice (41 and 47).

Bailey played prior to the three-point basket rule. Asked once how many points he might have scored if he had the three-pointer when he played, "Flap" quipped, "'Bout 3,000!" Those who saw or played on teams with Bailey wouldn't have found that remark

James L. Brunnemer

preposterous.

In his heyday, Bailey was a thoroughbred, but "hard to bridle," according to former teammate and 2003 Hall of Fame selection Larry Hanni. Coach Nicoson and his star player had a sometimes-contentious relationship. But Nick was able to rein "Flap" in without suffocating his greatness, a testament to Nick's genius as a coach. And Bailey's respect for his mentor was profound. Bailey left school, without his bachelor's degree, to join the professional Harlem Globetrotters in 1957. He had short stints in the National Basketball Association with the Syracuse Nationals and the Cincinnati Royals. Robertson was a Helms Foundation Little All-American in both the 1956 and 1957 seasons and was selected to the Indiana Basketball and University of Indianapolis halls of fame, both in 1990. Bailey is also a member of the National Basketball Association Hall of Fame as a former player with the Globetrotters, which was inducted as a team in a special commemoration in 2002.

Twenty-five years after leaving ICC, motivated by a promise he made to his coach before Nick died, Bailey crossed the Commencement stage at U of I to receive his diploma after completing his coursework requirements.

In 1958, Mickey Powell came to Indiana Central from Ben Davis High School to compete in golf for the Greyhounds. While serving as a caddy at the Country Club of Indianapolis, he was encouraged in his game by noted golf course architect Pete Dye. A Hoosier College Conference first team selection all four of his years at ICC, Mickey teamed with close friends Don Bisesi and Bob Otolski (each of whom later were inducted into the U of I Athletics Hall of Fame) to form the nucleus of what is arguably the finest golf team in the university's history.

Named Indiana's PGA Professional of the Year in 1972, Powell won numerous tournaments during his career. Besides winning the Indiana Senior Open (1990) and Indiana Senior PGA tournaments (1989 and '92), Powell twice qualified for the United States Senior Open. He was named Senior Player of the Year in both 1990 and 1991.

Head golf professional at Otter Creek Golf Club from 1964-74, Mickey later built the Golf Club of Indiana in Boone County in 1973, owning the facility until its sale in 1996. Inducted into the Indiana Golf Hall of Fame in 1986, Mickey twice served as president of the Indiana Section of the PGA, and was the PGA of America's twenty-fourth president in 1985 and 1986. Powell has been honored by his alma mater as a Distinguished Alumnus, elected to the athletics Hall of Fame, and currently serves as a member of the Board of Trustees. In 2003, he was honored as a "Legend of the PGA" by that international body.

In the spring of 1984, as director of development for Eastern Michigan University, I was at Lakeland, Florida, to visit alumni and friends of that institution who wintered there. Many EMU graduates gathered annually at Lakeland to watch the Detroit Tigers in spring training. Each spring, Coach Ron Oestrike's Eastern Michigan baseball squad were guests of the Tigers at the Lakeland complex. On a day when I was watching the big league club in an exhibition game, a steady rain began to fall. Seeking shelter in a storage shed along with several other fans, I overheard a couple of baseball scouts marveling about a "young kid from Indiana Central ripping the cover off of baseballs" over at the Seattle Mariners' diamond. They said the kid, "Wishnevski," was regularly bashing 500-foot rainbows and was a "can't miss prospect." Of course, my ears perked up, because even though I had not seen Mike Wishnevski '90 play, I learned he had signed with the Mariners after his junior year at ICC.

Distinction Without Pretension

A high school All-American as a fullback for Mishawaka High School, which he led to the 1978 state championship, Mike Wishnevski came to Indiana Central for the opportunity to play both football and his real love, baseball. A record-setting running back for Bill Bless's gridders, Wishnevski led Greyhound gridders to the 1981 Heartland Conference championship and was chosen as his team's Most Valuable Player for both the 1980 and 1981 seasons. Mike was even more impressive on the diamond. His .487 batting average and sixteen home runs during the 1981 season set new standards at the university. Following his junior season, after which he was named an NCAA Division II All-American, Mike signed a professional contract with Seattle, which had made him its number two pick in the baseball draft. Despite an impressive career with the Mariners' minor league affiliates and two brief trips to the big league club, Mike never got the opportunity to bat in the major leagues.

After nine years of professional baseball, Wishnevski returned to the U of I to complete his degree. While ineligible to play baseball, NCAA rules allowed the now-thirty-year old Wishnevski to compete in football. Despite diminished skills as a gridder, the "old man," as his teammates called him, still competed with the heart of a thoroughbred. He led the football team in scoring and rushing in that one final season in 1990 and was named Most Valuable back eight years after earning similar recognition in 1980 and 1981! Mike was inducted into the U of I Hall of Fame in 2000.

Another Greyhound I missed having the benefit of watching was a member of the Greyhounds' defensive secondary from 1982-85. A 1985 Kodak All-American, Tom Collins '85 set a record in his four years at ICC that remains unsurpassed by any football player in *all* NCAA divisions—I-A, I-AA, II, or III. Averaging nearly an interception *per game*, Collins set the all-time mark for picks with thirty-seven. Collins was recognized as a member of the All-time NCAA Division II "Team of the Quarter-Century" in 1997.

But when Greyhound alumni of the 1940s and 1950s talk of the paramount ICC athletes of all time, two names consistently rise to the top. Let me first tell you about Dick Nyers.

It was September 1956. The play was called "Ride 16 Power Pass." The rookie quarterback, #19, who was to cut a swath through the National Football League record book for passing over the next two decades, brought his Baltimore Colts team to the line of scrimmage. It was Johnny Unitas's first NFL action, an exhibition game against the Philadelphia Eagles.

At one halfback, wearing #21, was another rookie who was rooming with legendary Colts receiver Raymond Berry. Richard Nyers, a long way from his roots at Manual High School and Indiana Central College, nervously took his three-point stance next to Hall of Famer-to-be Alan Ameche, the fullback. At the snap of the ball, Unitas carried out a convincing fake to Ameche. Nyers swung outside as the Eagle linebacker bit on the play-action of Unitas. Sprinting now, Nyers looked over his shoulder at the perfect spiral arcing its way from Unitas's hand to his. Catching the ball in stride, Nyers outraced the Eagle defensive back to the end zone. Rookie to rookie, Unitas's first touchdown pass in NFL competition was to Indiana Central's Dick Nyers, at 160 pounds the lightest player in the league.

Later that season, defensive back Don Shula broke his ankle while tackling a Colts opponent. Nyers was switched to defensive back to replace Shula and started at that position the rest of the season. This unfortunate event for Nyers's teammate would ultimately prove a blessing, as Shula retired from playing to begin a coaching career. After thirty-three years in the NFL, Shula would retire in 1995 with more wins than any other coach in the history of the National Football League (347). His 1972 Miami Dolphins are, to date, the only undefeated team in history as they capped off a 17-0 season with a win over the Washington Redskins in Super Bowl VII. Nyers and Shula remained good friends through the years.

How did the Greyhound lightweight get from the gridiron at Indiana Central to the NFL? Following an injury-marred senior football season, Dick had an outstanding year of basketball for Coach Angus Nicoson. In the spring Nyers was preparing to start his final baseball season and found himself at Emroe Sporting Goods in Indianapolis to purchase a new mitt. He had no inkling that he might get an opportunity to play professional football. But a salesman at Emroe, Joe Kelly, asked Nyers what his plans were. Dick wasn't really sure, so Kelly asked if he might call a guy he knew with the Colts and give him Dick's name. Nyers laughed, but agreed, thinking it would never happen. That very night Weeb Eubank, who would coach both the Colts and the New York Jets to Super Bowl championships, called and made arrangements for Nyers to fly to Baltimore to try out for the team.

Injuries limited Nyers career to two-and-one-half seasons. But he had proved he could play with the best in the world despite his diminutive size.

Earning his monograms in football, basketball and baseball each of his four years, plus two more letters in track, Nyers's total of fourteen Cs have not been equaled in male sports in the forty-seven subsequent years of athletics at ICC.

He was a sprinter and pole vaulted in track. He patrolled the outfield and was a consistent hitter in baseball. And Nyers still ranks sixth on the all-time scoring list in basketball with 1,754 points. His 180 free throws in the 1955-56 season remains a record to this day. As a senior, Nyers teamed with Bailey Robertson to lead the Hounds to a 23-6 record, one of the finest teams in Greyhound basketball lore.

However, it was in football that Nyers's pronounced competitive thirst reached its zenith. In his four seasons as a varsity player ICC complied a 24-9-1 record and three Hoosier College Conference championships, one of the greatest eras of Greyhound gridiron play. The record would no doubt have been even better if Nyers had not been hampered by a hip injury the final five games of his senior season, two of which the Hounds lost by upset.

Forty-seven years after he played his last game as a Greyhound, Dick Nyers still holds these football records:

- Most points scored in a season (109, which in 1954 tied All-American Jim Swink of Texas Christian University for best in America) and career (272).
- Most touchdowns scored in a season (16) and career (43).
- Highest rushing average per carry in a game (14.2 yards versus Hanover in 1954), in a season (7.1 per carry in 1954), and career (6.3).

- Touchdown passes received in a game (four versus Centre College in 1952), in a season (10 in 1954), and career (26)
- Punt return average in a season (19.8 in 1954) and career (18.7).

Distinction Without Pretension

Additionally, Dick ranks third in total receiving yards in a career (1,937), seventh in career rushing yards (2,214), ninth in pass receptions for a career (91), and tenth in receiving yards in a season (718 in 1954). His ninety-yard run from scrimmage against Hanover in 1954 and 100-yard interception return for a touchdown versus Ferris State in 1953 were the longest in Greyhound football play. Chris Volz tied one Nyers's record when he returned an interception 100 yards against Mercyhurst in the 2000 season.

All this is simply to affirm that Nyers was setting standards four decades ago that were so far above his peers that they have lasted until today.

Dick Nyers was a gifted athlete with extraordinary speed and elusiveness. He was a tough and unbending competitor by any standard. It was that indefinable competitive verve that set him apart from other bigger and stronger athletes of his day.

"In everything I've ever done, I've been a fierce competitor," Dick mused over lunch one day. "There was a standard of performance that had to be reached, every time, and if I fell short of that level I burned inside until I could get back out on the field again. There was a fear, a fear of not meeting that self-imposed standard, that drove me."

That same tenacity propelled Dick to an outstanding coaching career at Carmel High School, and he later turned around a football program that had experienced a decade of futility when he became the Indiana Central coach in 1970.

Many would argue that Dick Nyers was the greatest athlete ever to play at ICC. Others would suggest that one other athlete at Indiana Central excelled even Nyers.

George Crowe should never have played for the Greyhounds. His fate was to be born in an era when black athletes were not welcome in many of the major universities in the north and in absolutely none in the South.

After the final game of the Indiana High School State Basketball Tournament in 1939, George had an interested visitor in the locker room. George had just played his heart out in a losing cause for the Franklin Grizzlies, which lost in the tournament finale to Frankfort, 36-22. Branch McCracken, esteemed coach of the Indiana "Hurryin' Hoosiers," had witnessed that final game.

In a 1996 conversation, George was to relate this locker room incident: Coach McCracken approached the exhausted Franklin star and said, "You played a great game, Crowe. And I'd love to have you at IU."

After a pause, McCracken sighed and added, "But I just can't do it." It would be eight more years before the first black basketball player would suit up in the Big Ten Conference, a recruit of Branch McCracken's. Bill Garrett of Shelbyville joined the Indiana University squad in 1947, opening the door for black athletes to compete at IU and other Big Ten schools.

Only weeks later, Crowe was named the *first* "Mr. Basketball" in Indiana, an honor every hoop-shooting Hoosier schoolboy would dream of becoming in succeeding years.

Harry Good, who had recruited black players to Indiana Central from the first day he returned to his alma mater, asked Ray Crowe, George's older brother, who played for Coach Good from 1935-39, to talk with George about coming to Indiana Central. George followed in Ray's footsteps to become one of Central's greatest performers.

In a discussion about race relations at Indiana Central once, I related to George

James L. Brunnemer

that my high school coach, Hank Potter, and Crowe's brother, Ray, had been roommates at Indiana Central in the 1930s, not a common occurrence in that day. I asked him how he had been treated as one of only a handful of blacks on campus in those days. He commented that he had been treated fine, that the professors were cordial and treated him just like other students. He didn't feel like that much of a novelty, but then he said, surprisingly, "I had a white roommate, too."

He went on to say that there was only one time he had heard the term "nigger" used, and it was by that roommate. The late Bill Howe, a tremendous athlete in his own right and a basketball teammate of Crowe, had told friends the Greyhounds were going to have a good team because "we have a big nigger from Franklin this year." George confronted him, and told Howe "If you use that word again I'm going to kick your ass."

Howe tried to explain that he meant it as a compliment, but George set him straight and no one used that term again in George's presence.

Stalwart center of the 1941-42 undefeated Greyhound basketball team, George Crowe would play eight seasons in the Major Leagues with the Boston/Milwaukee Braves, St. Louis Cardinals and Cincinnati Reds.

Distinction Without Pretension

George was outstanding in basketball, baseball, and track and field. ICC's version of Jesse Owens, at one meet Crowe won the shot put, high hurdles, 220-yard dash and the discus, and finished a close second in the 100-yard dash event.

He was the mainstay for Harry Good's basketball teams, which compiled a record of fifty-seven wins and six defeats during Crowe's four years, including the 16-0 team of 1941-42.

Following graduation and a two-year hitch in the army, George played professional basketball with the New York Rens, the eminent black team in the nation at that time. While in New York, George took an opportunity to try out for the all-black Yankees in the Negro League and played professional baseball the next two seasons. Finally, in 1952 at the age of twenty-nine, George had the opportunity to move up to the major league Boston Braves. Subsequently he played for the Cincinnati Reds, where he had his best season in 1958, batting .271 with thirty-one homers and ninety-six runs batted in.

In his best-selling book, *October, 1964*, about the World Series champion St. Louis Cardinals of that year, award-winning author David Halberstam described an aging but influential member of the Cardinal team:

> [O]ne of the key players in helping to create the culture of the new Cardinal clubhouse was a man few people knew. George (Big Daddy) Crowe ... played a vital role in bridging the gap from one era to another. Crowe was physically imposing, six feet two inches and about 210 pounds, and a man of immense pride and strength who was, without ever trying to be, a powerful presence in the clubhouse. If you were casting him in a movie, the writer Robert Boyle once said, you would want the young James Earl Jones. His influence on the team was vastly disproportionate to his actual contributions on the playing field. He had arrived with the Cardinals in 1959, an aging player, his skills on the decline, his legs and his feet causing him constant problems. He had played for a number of years in the Negro leagues, and the integration of major-league baseball had come more than a little late for him. What Crowe had learned in so unusual a life, filled as it was with so much success gained at so high a price, commanded the respect of his team-mates—white and black. He was someone who had a history, and that invested him with authority. He seemed to imply in what he said, and in what he did not say, and even in his body language that whatever was happening, he had seen it all before. He was certainly not going to be undone by anything he encountered. He was, thought Bob Boyle, very calm, very quiet, but his silences had as much meaning as his words.
>
> He was a man to be listened to, and, most assuredly, not to be crossed. During spring training in 1960 Big Daddy was not pleased with the calls of Ed Hurley, the home-plate umpire, who came from the American League. Crowe started getting on Hurley

early in the game, his voice strong, penetrating, and distinctive. There was no doubt when he yelled out his dissent that Hurley heard every word. Finally Hurley had enough, pointed at Big Daddy, and said, "Crowe, that's enough—you're gone! Now get the hell out of here!" That enraged Big Daddy, who started to walk the length of the dugout as if stalking Hurley. Finally, he pointed at Hurley, his words coming out now in real anger. "Ain't no meat too tough for me, Hurley." It was not a routine confrontation in baseball, where quick flashes of temper are the norm. Rather, it was something more threatening that seemed to suggest that if things went any further, if Hurley transgressed any further, his authority as an umpire might come to an end as Crowe's authority as a human being superseded it. The scene was more than a little frightening to some of the younger Cardinal players, and frightening, they suspected, to Hurley as well, who looked shaken.

In another era Crowe might well have been a manager, or even a general manager, and one of his protégés, Bill White, went on to become president of the National League. No one was going to abuse anyone or bully anyone on a team as long as George Crowe was there ... he was a black man who had lived a long time in a black man's world, and when he came to the white man's world he brought with him a distinctly black sense of dignity and pride.

Any questions about how tough George Crowe was? Big George was named a member of the Indiana Central Hall of Fame in its inaugural class of 1986.

So many great players, so little time and space. To exalt one *athleticist* above a galaxy of illustrious Greyhound athletes is folly. There seems to be no objective way to select a single athlete who stands above all the rest; so I will offer my choices regarding the best of those *whom I actually saw perform.* These are my personal favorites; and since I'm writing the book, you get to read about them. Feel free to disagree.

For pure *athleticism*, combining grace, strength, and speed, no Greyhound athlete eclipsed **Kevin Pearson** (1976-79), in my view. I first saw Kevin as a member of the 1976 Marion High School state champion basketball team, coached by Indiana Central alumnus Bill Green. In four years as a Greyhound, he averaged seventeen points per game, finishing tenth all-time in points scored in a career (1,702). His uncanny leaping ability—he would high-jump an eyelash under seven feet for Coach Jerry England in track—enabled Kevin to claim first place all-time in career rebounds (1,045), a record that stands to this day. His single-game high of forty points came against DePauw University in November 1978. He earned All-American honors in the decathlon at the 1979 NCAA Division II national track and field meet. In 1996 his alma mater honored him as a member of its athletics Hall of Fame.

For sheer *toughness*, both mentally and physically, my choice is easy. There have been hundreds of Greyhound athletes who have demonstrated steely disregard for pain and an indomitable will under arduous circumstances in competition. But in my estimation, no

Distinction Without Pretension

A superb athlete, Kevin Pearson is shown defending against Butler's Barry Collier. Pearson was elected to the U of I Athletics Hall of Fame in 1996.

one played with the reckless disregard for his own body and endured the consequences of that abandon with the stoicism of the late **Dick Nalley** '77 (1973-76).

Statistics only hint at the toughness of the Roncalli High School product. Twice he surpassed a thousand yards rushing in a season with 1,018 and 1,002 in 1974 and '75, respectively. His career total of 3,559 yards is a U of I record that still stands. He holds career standards for all-purpose yardage for both a season (1,571 in 1975) and career

James L. Brunnemer

(5,301), and set a U of I record average for returning kick-offs with 28.8 yards in 1975.

But it was his speed and punishing style that those who saw Nalley in action will forever recall. So often Dick would grasp the jersey of the blockers in front of him, usually Vance Stratton, Tom Geffert, and Dave Winings, as he sailed around the opposition end. After defensive ends and linebackers were swept away by Dick's vanguard, there remained the defensive backs closing on him. With the speed that made him Heartland Conference sprint champion three consecutive years in both the 100- and 200-yard dashes, Dick's momentum reached maximum thrust as he approached the defenders who were there to crush him to the ground. With the commitment of a kamikaze, Nalley would lower his helmet at the last instant and propel himself into the chest of his adversary. More often than not, Dick arose to find beneath him a gasping, afflicted opponent who would not be so rash next time as to take a direct hit from #24.

As mentally tough as any athlete I watched play at the U of I, it was an incident at the 1975 football game against St. Joseph's College at Renssalaer that provided insight into Nalley's genetic makeup.

Alumni Stadium at St. Joe was a hostile place, always, for opponents to play football. The field, the locker room, even the bleachers lacked the amenities of most high school facilities. Perhaps these primitive surroundings were what attracted George Halas when he started bringing his Chicago Bears teams there for pre-season training camp back in the 1960s. Players would not be motivated to slip out of the dreary dorm rooms because there was no place better to escape to. The bright lights of Chicago were a couple of hours away. Renssalaer would as well have been Nepal.

Anyway, the conditions at St. Joe were certainly below par, the student body unfriendly, and the game officials usually partisan (especially the keeper of the game clock). Puma football teams played with unusual ferocity in front of their home crowd. It was there that Dick Nalley was the unfortunate recipient of one of the most savage collisions I was to witness in all my years of watching Greyhound football.

Uncharacteristically walking the sidelines that day, I was fretting alongside Doc Dill as St. Joe was delivering its usual punishment on the field and beating us on the scoreboard as well.

On one play, quarterback Rod Pawlik sent Nalley on a screen pass out in the flat. Under intense pressure from onrushing Puma linemen, Pawlik was forced to float a lazy, arching pass to Nalley, whose back was exposed to the defense. From our position on the sideline, the play unfolded directly in front of Doc and me, Nalley not fifteen feet from us.

As Nalley awaited the pass, a 6'2", 210-pound St. Joe defensive back and their best tackler, read the play clearly. Trained to recognize opportunities such as this one, his eyes first widened, then squeezed into narrow slits as his brain processed what lay in front of him: the opportunity to legally annihilate an opponent. Rare was the chance to have an unimpeded, measured shot like this one, especially at the best player on the enemy side. Coiling like a snake ready to strike, the Puma back swiftly gathered his momentum, calculating instinctively the point at which the ball, Nalley, and he would intersect. He had committed completely to the receiver's destruction.

Well, those three did meet, simultaneously, with a frightful result.

Just as Nalley reached up for the ball, exposing his ribcage, the St. Joe player's helmet, then shoulder pads impacted, with the sound of a muffled gunshot, the Greyhound star's flanks.

"THWAAAAACK" was the first sound heard as the purple uniform of the Pumas and the Greyhounds' white and grey colors merged into one. The collision tossed Nalley backward a full five yards from where he had been the instant before.

The second sound I heard was a sickening, guttural moaning, as if from a wounded animal: "AARRRRRRRRGGGGHHHHHHH."

If he were conscious, I'm sure Dick felt he would never breathe again. His respiratory apparatus was undergoing severe stress. The concussion of that collision wasn't lost on the St. Joseph's player, either. Though he would eventually rise and walk shakily to his own sideline, the Puma back had completely sold the farm on that hit. In delivering the maximum blow, his head was scrambled a bit, as well.

Doc and I instinctually rushed forward toward the stricken heap that was Nalley, lying on the thirty-five-yard line. Coaches Bless and England quickly joined us in stooping over the prone teenager who lay retching at our feet. Gasping for air, Nalley again groaned audibly: "AARRRRRGGGHHHHHHHH!"

At just that moment, from the corner of my eye, I caught a swift movement from the nearby grandstand area. At St. Joe the visiting fans' bleachers were very close to its team's bench. All that separated onlookers from the field was a chicken-wire mesh fence, supported by a few metal posts. Now scaling that fence was a wisp of a man, not much more than five feet tall and weighing about 120 pounds. His dexterity in clearing the obstacle was impressive. He vaulted the final six feet and covered the short distance between the fence and the fallen player with amazing dispatch.

Forming a semi-circle around Nalley, we waited as the injured player agonizingly but inexorably regained his ability to draw breath. Now I was of average size, but Doc Dill and coaches Bless and England were all large men. As the diminutive, wiry stranger approached our position, he thrust himself between Doc Dill and Coach England, bouncing each aside like a couple of swinging doors in a frontier saloon. Bending slightly at the waist and looking down at #24, who was still struggling to breathe, the stolid stranger (to me) inquired, to no one in particular, "They didn't kill the little sonuvabitch, did they?"

Exploding in laughter as he recognized the intruder, Doc Dill managed to say: "No, Mr. Nalley, he'll live."

With that brief exchange, Dick's father evacuated the area, sprinting back whence he came, scaled the fence once again, and scurried into the bleachers. Dick's was a loving, but inured, paterfamilias.

I saw every yard the compact 5'10," 195-pound back gained in four years with the Hounds, but perhaps the greatest play among so many he made involved none of his record of 5,301 all-purpose yards gained on offense during his career.

James L. Brunnemer

Dick Nalley (24), carrying the football, gets my vote as the toughest hombre I ever saw in a Greyhound jersey. Nalley would die of cancer at age forty-seven.

The scene was Key Stadium and a 1974 Indiana Collegiate Conference game against St. Joe's Pumas. The Hounds were clinging precariously to a 14-12 lead late in the fourth quarter as their place-kicker, Tim Rickerd, squared up for a field goal attempt from St. Joseph's fourteen yard line. With his dependable hands, Nalley served as holder for field goals and points-after-touchdown kicks. On the signal, the ball spiraled back, Nalley placed the pigskin on the tee and Tim swung his leg forward. Reaching upward, a Puma lineman managed to deflect the kick. The football changed direction but not speed, and in a flash a startled St. Joe defensive back found the ball in his mid-section near his own goal line. Nothing but 100 yards of grass separated him and the go-ahead touchdown. He was fleet, that back, and already in full stride while Nalley was still kneeling, hands frozen in a kick-holder's position.

From the panoramic view of the press box it appeared as if the St. Joe player was in a one-man game with twenty-one uniformed spectators watching him sprint toward the distant end zone. So quickly had he bounded away, his teammates were not in position to aid him and the Greyhounds were helpless to impede his progress. It seemed a shotgun was the only thing that would bring him down.

As I watched forlornly, the one-man race to the end zone was playing itself out to its inevitable conclusion. Number 24 had left his kneeling position to take after the disappearing St. Joe runner. Football players are supposed to do that, you know. Give it the "old college try," though the effort be futile. Nalley had an obligation to give chase, even if there was no way he could catch a very fast man who had a running fifteen-yard head start to the goal line.

But as he sprang to his feet, something in Dick's manner, in his body language, communicated that he actually thought he could catch the fleet man now racing along the sideline. Legs pumping furiously now, Nalley was focused on a straight path that would carry him on the shortest route to intersect with the ball carrier at a point inside the ICC five yard line.

Distinction Without Pretension

Approaching mid-field, heading dead south toward Hanna Avenue, the St. Joe runner was still comfortably ahead of his pursuer. Moving across the Greyhound forty, he made a quick glance over his shoulder to see Nalley closing the distance between them. At the 30, less than ten yards separated the two foes.

By the time the ball carrier reached the ICC fifteen yard line, Nalley was within five yards, and still closing. Laboring now, the St. Joe runner tried desperately to outrun the willful Greyhound nearing his haunches. It would be close. At the ten, Nalley was only a stride behind. Now at the five he committed to a desperation dive. The crimson and grey #24 jersey covered the white-with-purple-trim Puma as the collision occurred. The concussion of the two speeding bodies collapsing to the ground was bestial. Entwined, the pair of competitors' momentum carried them skidding together across the grass into the end zone. The trailing official arrived on the scene and placed his foot at the spot he judged the St. Joe player to be down. Puma ball, first down, five feet from the ICC goal line. *But no TD.*

No doubt inspired by Nalley's heroic effort, the Hounds defense stiffened and over the next four downs allowed the Pumas naught. ICC regained possession on its twelve yard line. The Greyhounds scored twice in the final five minutes, one on a Nalley run, to win 28-12.

One never really got used to that kind of play, even though Dick performed the impossible over and again. Watching him perform the extraordinary, routinely, was a thrill every time.

Dick endured agonizing pain during much of his senior season, the result of a serious knee injury suffered early in the year. Corrective surgery would have ended his career prematurely, so Nalley determined to have the inevitable repairs after the season was over.

Following his final game, Dick's knee was surgically rebuilt. During rehabilitation, he was paired with a physical therapist who happened to be a manager for the United States Olympic bobsled team. Noting the extraordinary combination of speed and strength of his patient, the young therapist asked Dick if he had ever considered competing in bobsled. Dick knew next to nothing of that sport. But a few months later he found himself riding on the first bobsled he'd ever seen, in the Olympic trials at Lake Placid, New York. Dick earned a position on both the four-man and two-man teams as a "fireman." The fireman is typically the strongest and fastest of the crew who pushes the sled the longest and is last to jump aboard. In 1980, Dick Nalley represented the U.S. in the Winter Olympics, and his sled's fifth-place finish was the highest in American history to that date. Budweiser named him "Bobsledder of the Year" and Dick went on to compete for the United States World team from 1981-84.

Richard F. Nalley succumbed to cancer in 2002 at age forty-seven. To him my thoughts turn in rereading *To an Athlete Dying Young* and the melancholy verses penned by A. E. Housman (1859-1936):

> *The time you won your team the race*
> *We chaired you through the marketplace;*
> *Man and boy stood cheering by,*
> *And home we brought you shoulder-high.*

James L. Brunnemer

> *Today, the road all runners come,*
> *Shoulder-high we bring you home,*
> *And set you at your threshold down,*
> *Townsman of a stiller town.*
>
> *Smart lad to slip betimes away*
> *From fields where glory does not stay,*
> *And early though the laurel grows,*
> *It withers quicker than the rose.*

Though your trophies may now be tarnished with age and your athletic feats consigned to a few lines in an unread media guide, I won't forget you, Dick Nalley. You personified all that was noble and good and significant "between the lines," on the field of play. No, Dick, I won't forget.

It was with amazement that I watched the telecast of the 2002 Indiana State Class-AAA high school football championship. There on the screen was a muscular young man named Marcus Nalley of Roncalli High School, wearing #24 in honor of his father, whose death had come only weeks earlier. Possessing that familiar choppy-step running style of his dad, Marcus was toting the football and hunting for defensive backs.

I must admit that my eyes misted over when I read in February 2003 that Dick's youngest son had signed a national letter of intent to attend the University of Indianapolis to play football. I can't wait to see Marcus in a Greyhound uniform. According to Coach Joe Polizzi, covering Nalley's stout shoulders will be jersey number "24."

A pair of men, one of whom has been a lifelong friend and sometime teammate, the other whom I came to know intimately through athletics at Indiana Central, stand above all other Greyhounds in my mind as the personification of *competitiveness*. Both were very good, but not great, athletes. But for extraordinary competitive instincts and drive, two guys I would want on my side in any contest, including war, would unquestionably be **Vasco Walton** '66 and **Bill Tutterow** '69.

Earlier I submitted that most superior competitors I've known were driven by some earlier deprivation, childhood abuse, or a physical handicap. There are men I've known who have been called fearless. I would suggest that anyone who appears fearless is either bluffing or he isn't. One who is truly without disquietude finds few things in his external environment more frightening than that which has caused the scars within. From those unseen wounds comes the unquenchable need of the uncompromising competitor to win. I believe Vasco and "Tut" both fit this description.

Two more different individuals, externally, could hardly be found. Vasco Walton, with the sleek body of a cheetah, expressive ebony eyes, and a swarthy, Antonio Banderas-handsomeness, was a very sociable, personable man in college—except in competition. When Vasco entered a room, you knew it. He dressed fashionably for the day, knew all the cool tunes and dances of the rock 'n' roll scene, and was hip to all the fads of the popular culture.

Bill Tutterow was quiet, almost shy in social situations. Standing barely 5' 8" tall and 165 pounds in his finest athletic shape, he had little definition to his musculature. What few clothes he had were bought off the rack at Penney's or were garage sale purchases by his mother. He had a more noble than handsome face and cared little for what would be labeled "hip" in his age group.

In an arena of competition, however, the fires that drove their respective internal engines were fueled by similar stuff, and whatever drove them, it became white-hot in intensity in pursuit of victory.

Consistent with my theory that most surpassing competitors are driven by some earlier deprivation or trauma, both Walton and Tutterow had their self-concept shaped by early want and found their self-esteem through competition.

I know little about Vasco's early life. He never talked much about it, except that he had an absent father. Through adolescence and the teen-age years, he was slight of stature, below average in height and weight. As a high schooler, an extraordinary vertical jump fit well the role of a cheerleader, which he became at Manual High School after he was cut in basketball tryouts.

By his senior year he had matured to a sturdy 5'10" and 165 pounds. Suddenly his role changed in pick-up basketball games on the outdoor courts at Garfield Park on Indy's Southside. His physicality caught up with his internal drive, so he went off to Newberry College with another former Manual basketball star and hardnosed adversary, Carl Short.

After a year of seasoning at Newberry, Vasco transferred back to Indianapolis. At Indiana Central the lithe warrior would make an immediate impression on both the gridiron and the hardwood.

Labeled the "quiet assassin" by Coach Bill Bright, Bill Tutterow was the seventh of nine children reared by James and Idell Tutterow. The Tutterows were all too familiar with privation. Bill grew up in a four-room cement-block house with eight siblings. Hunger was a constant. What food found its way into the Tutterow home, Dellie cooked on a wood-burning range. A pot-bellied stove in the living room heated the house, sort of. Clothes were either hand-me-downs from relatives or made from scratch by Dellie.

But the Tutterows refused to let poverty be a humiliation, maintaining a collective dignity despite their circumstances of want. In second grade, Bill quietly went without the milk and Graham crackers that all the other kids received for their twelve cents, which was collected at the beginning of each week. Several weeks into the school term, his insensitive teacher, noting that Bill was sitting quietly as his classmates ate their snacks and drank their milk, looked at her list, then exclaimed aloud, "Oh, Billy, I'm sorry. Mr. Hussey pays for your milk and crackers." Tom Hussey owned the local Davis Cooperage, in the shadow of which was Bill's humble home. His father worked for Mr. Hussey, who would send the milk money privately to Bill's teacher, knowing the parents of the family of ten didn't have an extra twelve pennies weekly for school snacks. Bill's embarrassment was heightened as the well-meaning but misguided teacher launched into a five-minute oration about the poor and how others needed to help them.

Bill's defense manifested itself in a competitive nature that enabled him always to be a formidable opponent in any activity. A great storyteller with a robust laugh, Bill's demeanor changed utterly on the athletic field. His eyes were cold in competition, revealing nothing and missing nothing. Challenged, he intuitively sought his opponent's weakness

James L. Brunnemer

and exploited it.

Almost always at a disadvantage physically in the three sports he concentrated on—football, basketball, and baseball—Bill found ways to win that didn't require physical superiority. Bright noted, "Bill was a guy whose mind was always in and focused on the game and the moment at hand. He went quietly about his task, seldom said much, was highly respected by his teammates and opponents alike, was of extremely honorable character, but was burning inside at the opportunity and desire to cross the white line into the field of play and compete at the highest level."

I was privileged to be a teammate for two seasons of varsity baseball with Bill, despite the fact that we'd competed with and against each other since we were boys. Both times I was a senior at first base and Tut a freshman second baseman, first at Martinsville High School (1962) and then at Indiana Central College in 1966. Each time Bill would lead our team in hitting (over .400 in high school and .396 at ICC). The ball seemed to explode off Tut's bat, as his powerful forearms and wrists brought the wood through the strike zone.

Because of the success Tutterow had against his pitchers, Purdue coach Joe Sexson showed his ultimate respect for Bill's batting prowess during a game in Tut's senior season. With the score tied and Greyhound runners on second and third bases, the Purdue coach ordered his pitcher to walk the dangerous Tutterow intentionally. Always watchful "between the white lines," Bill was the cleverest of competitors, a student of the rules, continually looking at commonplace situations in creative ways. Instead of routinely standing in the batter's box, accepting a base on balls, Tut noticed the Boilermaker hurler had thrown the first pitch only slightly outside the strike zone, rather than comfortably wide of the plate, as is the normal procedure on such a play. Without tipping off the opposing pitcher or catcher, Bill coiled to swing if the next offering could be reached. Sure enough, the subsequent toss fluttered toward home plate, a full foot outside, but close enough for Tut to reach out and punch the ball into right-center field. The two startled base runners belatedly broke for home. Both scored, giving the Hounds yet another Tutterow-led victory over Purdue University.

When he became head baseball coach at Martinsville High School, Bill Tutterow turned his program into one of the most highly respected and competitive in Indiana. In 2002, Tut was honored by his fellow coaches in the Indiana High School Coaches' Association, who acknowledged his 538 wins in thirty-one seasons. Bill has won numerous sectional and regional championships and several of his players have signed professional contracts. One of those, Jason Wright, pitched four years in the Atlanta Braves farm system before enrolling at the U of I, where, as a member of Todd Sturgeon's Greyhound basketball squad, he finished second in the NCAA Division II in field goal percentage (.675) in 2002-03.

Vasco Walton was a catalyst at guard for the 1963-64 Greyhound basketball team that won twenty-six of twenty-nine games.

Vasco's mood climate could shift from a soft, gentle, and warm spring day to a vicious, dangerous thunderstorm. In a whit, his face transfigured from a relaxed, jovial, and friendly softness, to slit eyes, taut jaw, and malevolent stare. The very air around him became intense with anticipation that something uncontrollable and unpredictable had been loosed in his cauldron of emotions.

Walton played with a fury that skirted the rules of basketball. An opponent not familiar with Vasco might be unaware that #25 wasn't playing just a game, trying to help his team get more points than yours. Vasco's very life, his self-esteem, was on the line in competition, and whatever abuse he suffered at some point early in his life surfaced in the face of a challenge. Something sinister was caged inside Vasco, and that monster emerged when V perceived a threat.

I've never seen anyone compete for his life quite like Vasco did on the athletic field. He was skilled, but he was less skilled than he was competitive. Yet "competitive" is not quite a satisfactory word for what Vasco personified. No, Vasco didn't merely compete. Like a shark, he became a predator. Observing Vasco encountering a challenge, you felt as if you were watching a lion stalk his prey. It was something awful, but fascinating.

I saw Vasco back down to only one other man. ICC was playing Anderson College, an archrival in those glorious days in the mid-sixties, in a basketball game. The Ravens had a tough-acting guard named Terry Morgan. I say "tough-acting" because Morgan affected toughness but wasn't. Herb Lepper was tough. Dave Scheib was tough. Vasco was tough. Terry was a pretender.

But he was an annoyance, only an average player, and a real cheap shot artist. On this night he had gotten the better of Vasco throughout much of the first half. As the first twenty minutes expired, Morgan clearly smashed his elbow to the back of Vasco's head on a rebound. The ref missed it. As they left the floor Vasco tracked Morgan like a smart bomb. Nearing the tunnel to the dressing room, Vasco drew even with Morgan and prepared to deliver a message, which had knuckles attached to it.

Suddenly, Walton had his right arm violently ripped up behind his back in a maneuver that would have made a New York cop proud. Instantly Vasco's head jerked to see his assailant as his left arm reflexively cocked to do what came naturally to him. But when his eyes met the perpetrator, he was staring into a pair of stony eyes that were even more menacing than his own. Vasco blinked. He looked down meekly. His muscles relaxed. With his face two inches from Vasco's, Nick hissed out words that convinced Walton to proceed to the locker room forthwith.

Nick had dealt with Vasco's temperament before—used it to his advantage, actually—and he wasn't going to lose one of his most valuable assets because of that player's own irresponsibility. Nick was too much into winning to let Vasco jeopardize the outcome of this game by not finishing it.

No, Vasco didn't buck Nick. No one else did, either.

On the court, Vasco disrupted opposing offenses with his quickness and leaping ability. With his understanding of sport and his competitive drive, he became one of Indiana Central's all-time great athletes. He set records for assists and probably would still hold a standard for steals, except that steals weren't tracked statistically when he played. After graduation, Vasco twice won Most Valuable Player honors for the Indianapolis Capitals pro football team. A devout Christian whose spiritual conversion occurred during his maturation at Indiana Central, Vasco took his competitive proclivity to the business world, forming his own successful company in Indianapolis.

But there was one who donned the uniform of the Greyhound who combined, at the highest level, the mandatory athleticism *and* competitiveness *and* toughness to become a world-class performer in track and field.

My selection of the **greatest athleticist** in the history of sport at the university is **Randy Heisler '86**. I never saw Randy put the shot when he was enrolled at the University of Indianapolis. Later, when he was a member of the United States Olympic squad in 1988, I watched him on television.

Jerry England recalls scouting Heisler at a high school track meet the spring before Randy enrolled at the U of I. The veteran coach had high expectations of this athlete the day he attended the meet, and Randy's father was there eager to see his son perform in hopes that he'd earn a scholarship from Coach England. But, perhaps under the pressure of performing before the college recruiter, Randy had his most miserable event of the year. While Heisler's dad and Coach England talked quietly after the teenager fouled on his final attempt in the shot put, Randy stalked away in anger at himself. While listening to the father's effort to apologize that Randy hadn't performed up to standard, England's eyes followed the obviously distraught athlete, who approached the fence surrounding the track. The mesh-wire fence was about seven feet high. As Heisler neared the barrier, he grasped the top of the wire and, with a bound like Superman, vaulted completely over the fence whilst the astounded England blurted out, "Did you see that! Did you see what he *did?*"

Marveling at the athleticism of this young man who had the strength and vertical jump to clear what to most humans would be an impossible barrier, England couldn't get Randy's signature on a grant-in-aid fast enough!

Heisler played basketball at the U of I, but it was in track that he distinguished himself throughout his college career by establishing records for the shot put and discus. England relates another incident when Randy demonstrated his superior athleticism, one that both of them are glad athletics director Bill Bright did not witness. The Greyhound basketball team had just left the Nicoson Hall court after a practice in January 1984. Randy and his track and field teammates were completing their own practice at the top of the arena. Watching a couple of Greyhound cagers "styling" as they dunked the basketball after practice, Heisler drifted toward the basket where they were slamming the ball through the hoop. Without a word, Heisler, whose forty-inch vertical jump was extraordinary for a 250-pound athlete, leaped up from a standing start, lifting the sixteen-pound iron shot above his head with his right hand. As the basketball players watched in awe, Randy slammed the shot through the net. Of course, the heavy metal ball crashed to the floor with an explosive sound. Fortunately for England and Heisler, the shot did not break the wooden slats on the court. You might still find a dent there, though.

Heisler won the NCAA Division II national championship three consecutive years (1982, '83, and '84), earning All-American honors each time while setting a discus record that still stands twenty years later. During his junior and senior seasons, Randy also qualified for the NCAA *Division I* nationals, where he finished sixth both years. In his final season of competition, 1984, his toss of 204'1" didn't win the meet but is still the best sixth-place throw ever.

Following graduation, with England continuing as his personal coach, Heisler was a Pan American Games bronze medallist (1987) and won the gold medal in the discus at the Olympic Festival the same year.

The following summer, as a member of the United States World Championship team, Heisler defeated the best the world had to offer, winning a World University Games gold medal. At the United States National Championships, he earned the silver medal.

In 1988, Randy made the Olympic team and finished fourteenth in the world for the United States in the discus event. Named to the U of I Hall of Fame in 1999, Heisler became head coach for the Indiana University women's track team. In 2000, Randy's squad, ably assisted by England as a volunteer coach, won the Big Ten championship, and Randy was named Big Ten Women's Track Coach of the Year. Upon the retirement in 2003 of Indiana men's track coach and fellow U of I alumnus Marshall Goss, Heisler was named Director of Track and Field at IU, placing him in charge of both the men's *and* women's programs at the state's largest university.

Randy Heisler embodied the preeminently gifted athlete, who possessed the mental and physical toughness and competitive drive demanded of the winner. In my view, he was the greatest Greyhound of them all.

There is one other athlete that stands alone on my shelf of memories. He was a champion at the University of Indianapolis. But it's not for his athletic achievements that I adore him. Let me tell you about a man they call "Zup."

CHAPTER XXIV

ZUP

*You don't tug on Superman's cape,
You don't spit into the wind,
You don't pull the mask off the ole Lone Ranger,
And you don't mess around with Slim.*
                      Jim Croce
                      from "Slim"

He's part Barnum and Bailey, part Mother Teresa. A respected executive of a National Football League franchise, he is comfortable and articulate among a group of Indianapolis business leaders at the Skyline Club. But if need be, he can parry with professional athletes in the coarse language common to them in the weight room at the Colts complex. Bunyanesque in size, he can cause a grown man to lose his lunch with a menacing stare, yet any homeless, needy, or ailing child can control him. His disdain for and tolerance of physical pain is supereminent, yet he suffers wholly in his being as he weeps with the parents at the bedside of a dying child at Riley Children's Hospital. He blends an altar boy's innocence with the cunning of a safecracker.

He's among a handful of my living heroes.

The first time I encountered Thomas John Zupancic it was his mammoth physical size—at least twenty-two British stones—that made the initial awesome impression. In the three decades that have elapsed since that time, I've learned it is the *character* of the man called "Zup" (pronounced "Zoop") that sets him apart.

In 1991, H. Jackson Brown, Jr. sat down to write a few thoughts for Adam, his first-born son, as he watched him pack to leave home for a distant college. Those lines scribbled onto several pages of lined notebook paper became *Life's Little Instruction Book*, one father's values expressed to his son through 511 succinct passages of poignant, humorous, and practical wisdom.

About that same time my relationship with Tom Zupancic was being renewed after a hiatus of more than a decade. Recently, rereading Mr. Brown's aphorisms about life and love, I was struck by how often a concise analogy put me in mind of Zup and his remarkable family.

Accept pain and disappointment as part of life. (#296)

To appreciate the son, one must first become familiar with the parents. Children of immigrants, Augustus (Gus) Zupancic and Mary Debelak were wed during the Second World War, setting up housekeeping near their parents' homes in "Haughville."

A neighborhood on the near-Westside of Indianapolis bordered, roughly, by

James L. Brunnemer

Belmont Avenue on the east, Concord Street on the west, with northern and southern boundaries within Tenth and Michigan streets, respectively, Haughville has always been rife with PHDs—the Poor, the Hungry, and the Driven. Today, about ninety percent of its residents are African-American or Hispanic. Through the 1940s Haughville residents were predominantly uneducated, working class ethnic immigrants: Poles, Russians, Yugoslavians, Hungarians, Latvians, Lithuanians, and, like Tom's ancestors, Slovenians. Tough people lived in Haughville.

Coincidentally, Tom and I share Haughville as our birthplace, although early on I was adopted out of there. When my biological parents left my eight older siblings and me with a cousin, I was twenty-two months old. Ernie and Gladys Brunnemer entered my life then, along with their two daughters. That's another story for another time.

Tom, on the other hand, would spend the first eighteen years of his life in what was, and is, one of the most severe environments extant in the Hoosier capital.

Gus and Mary reared Tom and his three sisters, Mary Annette, Cindy, and Marty, in the Catholic faith. From the parents, these four would learn the value of hard work, generosity, and service to others, a creative instinct for survival, toughness, a realistic view of life, the importance of a sense of humor, and a love of music and parties that would be so evident in each of them as adults.

Gus worked long hours on the railroad, supplementing meager wages with a second and sometimes a third job. Roofing on weekends was one way to keep food on the table. Gus taught himself welding, doing small tasks for friends and neighbors, and then later taught that skill to high school students at Arsenal Technical High School at nights. The Gus Zupancic Polka Band entertained anywhere a good time was to be had, like neighborhood weddings, anniversaries, and other special gatherings.

When he eventually wound up with full-time work at Naval Avionics, Gus noticed his fellow employees constantly carped about the rancid coffee they were forced to purchase from the coin-operated dispenser there. So Gus brought an urn to work, selling his savory coffee for a tidy profit. With all this, the elder Zup still found time to volunteer as secretary for the Slovenian National Home.

Mary kept the household, providing strudel for the neighborhood widow ladies, and always prepared baskets of food and goodies for "needier" families during Christmastime. And, of course, she provided guidance for the girls and her only son. Tom was a handful as a child. Having him around, as Mary once described it, was "like having a bowling alley installed in your head." At least a measure of his over-abundance of energy was siphoned off through participation in the CYO football leagues. His size and tenacity drew attention from coaches around the city when he was but a youngster.

Remember that winners do what losers don't want to do. (#326)

It was at Cathedral High School, while wrestling and playing football, that Tom procured his ticket to higher education and, later, his professional career. Prior to the 1970s, weight training was viewed as a supplement to sport, not a necessity, as in today's sports culture. Some coaches of basketball, swimming, and golf actually discouraged athletes from lifting weights. They feared that their protégés would become "muscle-bound," detracting from the agility required to be successful. Tom and a few other Cathedral athletes were

Distinction Without Pretension

among the few high schoolers who learned earlier than most that extra strength gained through weight-lifting would give them an edge over opponents who did not increase their natural strength. And Tom always looked for an edge.

Be brave. And even if you're not, pretend to be.
No one can tell the difference. (#68)

After graduating from Cathedral, Tom talked his way into a grant-in-aid to Indiana Central while supposedly on his way for a visit with the football coach at St. Joseph's College in Rensselaer, Indiana. Stopping by the Greyhound athletic complex, he entered, without an appointment, the office of head football coach Bill Bless. He convinced Bless that he planned to attend the small Catholic college in the northwest part of Indiana on a full football scholarship, but really wanted to come to ICC.

"I won't make the trip to Rensselaer, Coach, if I can count on a scholarship here."

In 1974, a defensive lineman in the Indiana Collegiate Conference weighing 250 pounds who possessed any athletic talent was a rarity. As he inspected the young Sampson who carried more than *300 pounds* on a 6'2" frame, Bless could visualize this behemoth at middle guard on defense, suffocating the opponent's running game. So eschewing his usual practice of viewing game films of prospects, Bless offered Zup a football scholarship on the spot.

Of course, St. Joe's coaches had never heard of Tom, and he had no intention of driving to Rensselaer.

Coaches crave linemen who are "*mo*-bile, *a*-gile, and *hos*-tile." Time would prove Zup to be only the last of that trio of traits on the football field. Rare would be the time when Tom made a tackle beyond the width of his outspread arms. But woe be to the man who played across from Zup, for he would beat the crap out of the poor guy. Zupancic lettered all four of his seasons in a Greyhound football uniform.

On the wrestling mat, however, Zup dominated the heavyweight division for the Greyhound matmen his freshman, sophomore, and junior seasons. He won Little State and Hoosier College Conference championships from 1975-77 and still ranks second in number of pins in one season. He put thirteen opponents on their backs for the three-second count in 1974-75. After over a quarter of a century he also remains in third place among Greyhound wrestlers in career pins with thirty-five.

His records would be even more impressive if not for his coach ... sort of. We'll get back to that story.

If in a fight, hit first and hit hard. (#26)

Separating fact from fiction when considering the immensity of the stature and moxie of Tom Zupancic takes some doing. Bigger than life in many ways, Zup would be remembered by his former college professors and fellow students as a man-child, on the edge, if not out of, control while pursuing his education at Indiana Central. Everyone who has encountered this fun-loving (and intimidating) giant has his own favorite Zup story.

James L. Brunnemer

A respected National Football League general manager once said that "a majority of professional athletes are 'bad guys' trying to act good. They learned survival skills early on the streets and playgrounds of poor neighborhoods. Dodging the junkies, surviving the challenges and the fights, they emerged, through superior athletic ability and toughness, into the 'respectable' milieu of professional sports and its huge contracts.

However, there are many are really good guys trying to act 'bad.'" That describes Zup. He has always been a good guy. But to prove himself in the rough and callous world of athletic competition, he had to learn to be intimidating, tough, and hard-nosed. Part of conquering others in athletics, ugly as it may be, lies in putting doubt in the other fellow's mind. Particularly in the man-to-man nature of wrestling, the winner is more often determined by who is most willful, who has the greatest psychological endurance, who will not fold under pressure, than by superior athletic skill. His success in athletics enabled Zup to get where his natural instincts for service to and approbation of people has fared well in the world of business suits.

College football teammates have spoken of a routine Zup used to psych himself up for games. He would first stare off into space for a period of time. Suddenly, without warning, he emitted a barbaric roar, and then would begin to beat his head against a metal locker, over and over, until blood was pouring from his forehead. It was then he would pop on his helmet and charge out of the locker room and onto the field, presenting a gruesome spectacle to the opponent across the line of scrimmage.

I recall the 1976 football clash at Valparaiso. Tom Zupancic was probably in the best shape of his life up to that time, and he was proud of it. The first time the Greyhound defense came onto the field the Crusader lineman across from Zup looked at him and sneered, "You're in for a long day, Fat-ass!"

Zup, always subtle as a train wreck, waited only one play to retaliate with an intentional forearm to the name-caller's throat. An alert official who saw the whole thing disqualified Zupancic for the remainder of the contest.

That incident led to others, and during the entire first half both teams trashed one another with cheap shots, late hits, scuffles, elbows, and cursing, lots of cursing. Just before the half ended, a squabble between a Crusader player and a Greyhound linebacker turned into a full-scale brawl with the entire complement of both squads leaving their benches to meet in the middle of the field for a free-for-all.

Zup, who had never gone to the locker room, as the rules required of a disqualified player, gleefully joined the fray. Fighting suited him better than playing, anyway. Zup searched out and found his earlier antagonist and it was here he reverted to his Haughville-honed survival instincts. Instead of the expected confrontation, the Crusader lineman found Zup offering a right handshake of sportsmanship. Caught off guard by the show of gentlemanly behavior, the Crusader lineman relaxed, offering his hand in return.

WHOP!

Zup "sucker-punched" the naïve Valpo gridder, catching him flush in the mouth with an accurate right cross. As Zup jumped atop his nemesis to finish the job, the same official who had separated the combatants earlier in the game got between them and ordered them both off the field.

"You're gone, both of ya'," the ref yelled authoritatively. Then peering beyond the facemask of ICC's #78, said with surprise, "Hey! Didn't I kick you out once already?"

Distinction Without Pretension

Zup just smiled, spun away, and lumbered back to the sidelines. The other guy struggled to his feet. He'd been mauled—twice—by the "fat-ass."

When facing a difficult task, act as though it is impossible to fail. If you're going after Moby Dick, take along the tartar sauce. (#271)

Dave Wollman, a 6'6," 240-pound mass of muscle as a collegian, earned All-American status and a Division II national individual championship in the shot put for Coach Jerry England. Later he became head track coach at Southern Methodist University, where he has developed several NCAA Division I All-Americans.

Wollman confirms an incident that occurred his freshman year with a very terrifying Zupancic. Because Wollman also played middle guard, and, in the coaches' opinions, better than the veteran Zup, Dave was responsible for Zupancic being switched from his favored position to the offensive line. That move didn't sit well with Zup. Tom had to find some satisfaction, so he showed up late one night at Dave's dormitory door with two pairs of boxing gloves.

"Git yer ass out here, Wollman," Zup shouted through the paper-thin dormitory-room door, behind which Wollman stood assessing the perilous scenario. "We're gonna find out who the better man is!"

Knowing that Zup could splinter the plywood door with one blow from his massive forearm, Wollman nonetheless refused to give entrance to the mad bull standing only inches away on the other side. Finally Wollman answered: "If I open this door, Zup, something awful is going to happen. And I'm guessing it will happen to me."

The mad bull snorted off, realizing he would have to exact his vengeance in pads on the football field.

*Don't waste time grieving over past mistakes.
Learn from them and move on. (#213)*

Ted Polk, dining hall manager and one of the most congenial, kind men ever to grace the University of Indianapolis campus, remembers Zup, probably every time Tom shows up on campus today. Ted has received accolades from the university community for his service through the years in providing not only the daily fare for thousands of students, but for his gracious and warm hospitality to alumni and friends of the university who attend all manner of events.

Seems Zupancic, as a freshman, being approximately half again larger than the average student at Indiana Central, felt that it was not a crime to snatch an extra piece of beef during a mealtime. Recognizing that this was not a good precedent, a student server, Gary Robinson, confronted the super-sized Zup, in his usual polite manner (Robinson, Class of '74, retired as a principal of a Marion County elementary school in 2003 following three decades as an educator, beloved and esteemed by colleagues, students, and parents alike). Affronted at the challenge by this "student hash-slinger" over a measly morsel of meat, Zup reached over the counter and grabbed Gary by his collar. To emphasize his displeasure, Zup lifted the startled Robinson off the ground by his neck and onto the tray conveyor. Ted Polk arrived, just as Gary was turning blue, insisting that Zup release him. The big fella heard from Dean Watkins on that one, of course.

Years later, Tom and his family were invited to the annual Alumni Weekend festivities at which he would receive the highest honor that the University of Indianapolis Alumni Association bestows, the Distinguished Alumnus Award. The event was held in that same dining hall in Schwitzer Center where Tom had so ignominiously introduced himself to Mr. Polk. Ted was still providing food management in what was now the beautifully renovated Cyril and Mary Ober Dining Hall. Putting behind them any rancor of the past, Zup and Ted greeted one another cordially.

As he and wife, Carrie, sat with President and Mrs. Israel, Tom noticed the standard-issue and very plain dinnerware at each place setting.

"You know," he began innocently, but with that sly sparkle in his eye, "when Carrie and I were living in the married student apartments here, we had a six-piece setting of china, glass- and silverware just like these. Anytime we broke a glass or a plate I knew just where I could get a replacement. For free, too!"

I think Dr. Israel ignored this quasi-confession by Zup that he had swiped eating utensils from the college. Good presidents know when not to listen.

Zup's capacity for food and drink was legendary. This I will swear by, because I was there. I'd gone to the McDonald's on Shelby Street and ran into Zup at the counter. He was waiting for the clerk to fill his order consisting of two Big Macs, two Quarter-Pounders with cheese, two large orders of French fries, two pastries, a large Coke, and a large vanilla shake. As I prepared to order a cup of coffee, it dawned on me that Zup was eating alone!

Know how to change a tire. (#124)

The story of Zup holding up the rear end of an automobile on the berm of I-465 so a friend could change a flat tire is fiction. But Tom regularly lifts not just the back end of one, but of *two* cars during power lifting exhibitions for charity.

During their college years and afterward, Tom and his teammate, Dick Nalley, regularly traveled the circuit of power lifting competitions throughout the Midwest. Unknown in the beginning, both would gain notice with their imposing strengths. Nalley, for example, often competed in leg press, bench press, squat lifts, and other phases of weight lifting against Archie Griffin. Dick gained the respect of the Ohio State running back, who would become the only two-time winner of college football's Heisman trophy, by regularly hoisting greater amounts of weight in these exhibitions. Tom also found, through dedication and belief in his abilities, that he could compete with world-class lifters. Those long drives through the Midwest, with little to eat and barely enough money to meet the registration fees, provided a measuring stick for Zup that encouraged him to rise above what he thought he could be.

Promise big. Deliver big. (#287)

It was the accumulation of misadventures that cost Tom and his team his senior season in wrestling. Coach Terry Wetherald finally bid adieu to his champion heavyweight

Distinction Without Pretension

after a particularly egregious transgression.

In truth, Terry adored Zup. As an ex-Marine, lover of fun and the frothy ale, Terry could relate to this giant juvenile. But the final straw occurred on a road trip following a match in which Zup, as usual, had pinned his man shortly after his match had started, and the team had won a key tournament victory. The squad stayed in a motel that night before heading back to campus the next day.

A natural leader, Zup announced to his teammates, out of the hearing of Coach Wetherald, that having won the tournament they would depart for a local pizza parlor to celebrate. In addition, he'd spring for pizzas for all, to bring back to their rooms. These would be washed down with the several six-packs of Budweiser he had magically secured. Not one for details, Zup overlooked the fact that he had not a red cent to his name. Arriving at the restaurant, he refused offers by his teammates to help him carry the pizzas out. Zup went in alone. They should have known something was up when Zupancic, balancing a stack of eight boxed pizzas as he raced for the car, crawled in while urging the student behind the wheel to "get the hell outta here!"

At about midnight, Wetherald's sleep was interrupted by a knock on his door. Wondering who this visitor would be, Wetherald opened the door. An enormous human being, eyes red, smelling as if he'd practiced half-gainers in a beer vat, filled the doorframe. Zup was there to contritely confess to the coach that he'd made the acquaintance of some of the local gendarmes, and that they may appear soon to get to know Coach Wetherald as well.

Instantly surmising that something was amiss and before the man he considered one of his sons could utter a word, Wetherald spun around, presenting his back to the confused Zup.

"I didn't see you, whoever you are. And I don't want to see you. So when I turn around, *do not be there*."

The disconsolate figure shuffled off.

The friendly men in blue showed up five minutes later, allowing Coach Wetherald to pay for the shop owner's damages without arresting the miscreants.

It was ultimately to be Zup's challenging of authority and predisposition to mischief that pushed Coach Wetherald to remove Zup from the wrestling team prior to his final season.

Improve your performance by improving your attitude. (#432)

Zup completed his college work at IUPUI. But he professed later that Coach Wetherald made an important contribution to his well being by finally calling a halt to his undisciplined approach to life. Tom ultimately quelled his excesses and used that energy for other, more acceptable pursuits. He has repeatedly cited the diminutive 5'5" Coach Wetherald for much of the success he has since enjoyed.

Tom epitomizes what ICC embodies: education for service. When he arrived on campus it was an even bet he'd never graduate from college. As a wild child from a poor environment making good, his case is not exceptional at the university. He might even serve as the prototype of many Indiana Central/University of Indianapolis kids from poor circumstances who were influenced by the college and went on to improved lives.

James L. Brunnemer

Zup became the only University of Indianapolis alumnus to be booted from the wrestling squad to alight, years afterward, in a seat in the boardroom as a member of the U of I Board of Trustees.

Choose your life's mate carefully.
From this one decision will come ninety percent
of all your happiness or misery. (#93)

Of all the correct decisions Zup has made, none surpasses that which brought Carrie Oldham into his life. While at Indiana Central, Zup was recovering from knee surgery at St. Francis Hospital when he met Carrie, a sprinter from Shelbyville, who'd undergone a similar operation. I don't know if it was love at first sight, but Zup knew a good thing when he saw it. He first gained her attention by pushing Carrie in her wheelchair at precarious speeds through the halls of the hospital. She liked him, too, but would insist on his demonstrating his affection in more conventional ways in future days.

Following Zup's sophomore year, they married, and together began a journey that has led to the establishment of an admirable family, appreciated by all those who come into their midst. Petite (Tom outweighs his wife somewhere over three times), vivacious, a great sport, and an involved and admirable mother, Carrie takes absolutely no crap from the big guy. They adore one another and live their lives to the fullest.

When starting out, don't worry about not having
enough money. Limited funds are a blessing, not a curse.
Nothing encourages creative thinking in quite the same way. (#140)

Residing in the Mathews Avenue apartments while Tom was at ICC, Carrie and Tom lived hand-to-mouth as he pursued his dream of making the United States Olympic Greco-Roman Wrestling Team.

It is true that to earn money during training for the Olympic trials, Tom accepted a challenge to wrestle a circus bear. The promoters assured Tom that the smelly, frothing-at-the-mouth beast, with a coat of fur matted with unmentionable body excretions, wasn't dangerous. Even when the harness was removed from the mammoth animal's snout and mouth just before he and the bear entered the ring, Zup was comforted by the promises of the handlers that he (Zup) was safe. Nonetheless, Zupancic nearly ended up competing for a *woman's* Olympic event when the ursine animal chomped down on, and then released—after an agonizing interval—a specific part of Tom's anatomy.

Understand that happiness is not based
on possessions, power, or prestige, but on relationships
with people you love and respect. (#383)

Once, when the kids, Katie (14), Jake (11), and John (9), were complaining about something or another, as children are wont to do, Tom invited them into the car for a ride. He drove them through Haughville to show them where he grew up. He felt they needed to know that the surroundings they lived in were not divine rights but the product of hard

Distinction Without Pretension

work and sacrifice. In observing the Zupancic children, my admiration for Tom and Carrie only heightens. Both parents have been intimately involved in the nurturance of their brood, and one need be in the presence of Katie, Jake and John for only a short time to appreciate how very well bred they are. All three are polite, mature young people who are respectful of adults and are bright achievers.

*Tell your kids often how terrific they are
and that you trust them.(#102)*

While Tom and Carrie are rearing their children with care and trust, I'd pay admission to be there when Katie's first boyfriend comes a-callin' to escort her on her first date. Beware, son, beware. Oh, no, I'm not thinking of Tom, the 300-hundred pound sentinel of his daughter's virtue. It's the *she-wolf* you had better watch out for!

Call your mother. (#511)

Tom hovers protectively over his mother, Mary, and Carrie's mom, Darlene, like a personal valet. Each winter, he and Carrie pack up the kids, Mrs. Oldham, and Mom Zupancic and head south for Florida or points beyond at Tom and Carrie's expense. Zup's conscientious effort to ensure the comfort of his "two" moms is touching. Ask Mrs. Oldham if she'd trade Tom for another son-in-law.

*Remember no one makes it alone.
Have a grateful heart and be quick to
acknowledge those who help you.(#368)*

It was following his graduation from college that Zup became, for perhaps the first time, wholly committed to a goal of making the Olympic team. It was at this time, also, that Tom encountered a man who would inspire him and have a great influence on his career. Dean Rockwell lived in Ypsilanti, Michigan. Tom Zupancic was one of the young Olympic hopefuls Dean coached in Greco-Roman wrestling.

In a twist of fate, I met and became closely acquainted with Mr. Rockwell years later, while remaining totally unaware of his relationship with Zup.

In 1983, I was a member of the administrative staff at Eastern Michigan University in Ypsilanti. On perhaps my second day on the job, a raspy-voiced caller contacted me to ask for an appointment. At the scheduled time a huge block of a man, at sixty-seven years of age still in imposing physical condition, filled the door of my office. He sat down and in a bit over an hour gave me a thorough history of the University and its alumni body and advised me how to be successful in my job. Over the next three years during my stay at EMU, I spent many hours with the man many considered "Mr. Eastern Michigan."

Subsequently, I learned that others who knew Dean Rockwell held him in awe. Vague references were made to his heroism during World War II, but I never suspected that he'd played a key role in "Operation Overlord," the invasion of Normandy in 1944. Despite having become well acquainted with Mr. Rockwell, not once did he refer to any experiences he had in that cataclysmic event.

James L. Brunnemer

But when I happened across the passages below while reading *D-Day, June 6, 1944: Climactic Battle of World War II* by noted author Stephen Ambrose, I learned a lot about the young Dean Rockwell:

> [T]hirty-two-year-old Lt. Dean Rockwell was in charge of training for the LCT crews. He had been a professional wrestler and high school coach in Detroit before the war. Although he had never been on salt water, he joined the Navy after hearing a recruiting pitch from former heavyweight champion Gene Tunney.
>
> Lt. Rockwell commanded a flotilla of sixteen LCTs. Each LCT was carrying four DD tanks, scheduled to hit the beach in front of the first wave of infantry, so he was one of the first to move out of the Channel. The Germans defending the beaches from their fortifications in and atop the cliffs at Normandy were raking the beachfront with little resistance because the massive preemptive shelling from the great ships had ceased, to allow the beach to be assaulted by troops. The only firing at the Germans during this time came from the Sherman tanks on the LCTs.
>
> That those Shermans were close enough to the (Omaha) beach to fire in itself was a near miracle made possible by the courage of one man, Lieutenant Rockwell, who ... made what was perhaps the single most important command decision of any junior officer on D-Day.
>
> Eight LCTs to the left of Rockwell's flotilla launched (the tanks) as planned, but because the swells were too high, the tanks too low, the (flotable) skirts insufficient, all but three of the thirty-two tanks sank into the sea. Despite orders to launch the tanks short of the beach, Rockwell, seeing the helpless tank commanders driving, one by one, off the ramps into the sea, and sinking, signaled his flotilla to follow him, straight to the shoreline, which was laced with landmines and under withering German crossfire. Delivering his tanks directly onto the shore—imperiling his own life in the process—saved untold lives of infantryman who followed, for the tanks blasted away with 75 mm cannon and .50 caliber machine guns, silencing many of the German batteries.
>
> And then, said Rockwell, "We pulled that famous naval maneuver, known throughout history as 'getting the hell out of there.'"

That was at 0630, H-Hour, Omaha Beach, June 6, 1944.

It was Dean Rockwell who coached Tom in his quest for the Olympics, teaching Zup about the sacrifice demanded to be one of the world's best. The effect on Zup and his understanding of the demands to compete at the international level was lasting. Rockwell is another to whom Zup is indebted for his achievements in athletics.

Never give up on what you really want to do.
The person with big dreams is more powerful
than one with all the facts. (#171)

As an undergraduate, Zup had already had notable success, winning the AAU Junior Olympic heavyweight title in 1976. Under the severe tutoring of Rockwell, Tom earned a place as an alternate on the ill-fated 1980 U.S. Olympic team that President Carter prohibited from going to Russia for the Olympic games.

He would later win the Amateur Athletic Union, U.S. Wrestling Federation, and Canadian National wrestling championships. Following those triumphs, he was a finalist in the USA Greco-Roman Olympic Wrestling trials and was again selected as an alternate for the 1984 Olympic Greco-Roman Wrestling squad.

Swing for the fence. (#207)

Following his 1980 Olympic disappointment, Zup converted his years of strength training into a business. Along with former teammate Nalley, Zup opened a weight lifting and conditioning gym on the south side of Indianapolis. He continued to work at greater goals in power lifting. In 1988, Zup became one of few men in the world to bench press 600 pounds, an astonishing feat. His lift is still ranked fourteenth among all-time super-heavyweights. To this he added the 1990 WPF World Bench Press Championship and in 1993 finished second in the "world strongman" contest. I don't know this for sure, but I would wager that Tom, at age 48, still ranks among the world's one-hundred strongest men.

When you find a job that's ideal, take it
regardless of the pay. If you've got what it takes,
your salary will soon reflect your value to the company. (#458)

In 1983, the Indianapolis Colts professional football team moved to Indianapolis. That first season, Bob Irsay hired Zup as the team's strength and conditioning coach. For the next sixteen years, Tom worked with these behemoths year-round in the process of enhancing their strength and performance on the gridiron.

He authored *Strength Conditioning for Football and Then Some,* a handbook for coaches and athletes, and also consulted on a video on the subject of strength, conditioning, and motivational techniques, entitled "Building Inner Strength" (1996).

Many of the Colts' players will attest to the good work of Zup not only in the weight room but also in motivating them in rehabilitation from injury. Wil Wolford, an All-Pro offensive lineman who incurred a career-threatening shoulder injury, blesses (and curses) Zup for pushing him relentlessly during the long and lonely journey back to playing condition. The Colts' front office, coaches, and medical staff observed the offensive guard in his rehab and the day came when they announced they wished to view Wil to determine if he could continue playing for the Colts. If not, the alternative was the loss of a key player to the team, and, for Wolford, a lucrative occupation.

But before the "suits" could watch him, Wil wanted to test the shoulder in private,

James L. Brunnemer

in pads and live action. To help his buddy and rehab project, Zup donned, for the first time since college days, a helmet and pads. In the privacy of an empty Colts practice facility, Zup and Wil lined up across from one another. Chuckling as he relates the incident, Wil revealed that at first he took it easy. Still motivating his recovering Colt and by-now close friend, Zup began to "talk trash." He insulted Wolford with choice words and challenged him to give it everything he had. After a couple of soft hits, Wil burst upward on the snap count and without warning, thrust an NFL-style block on the unsuspecting giant across from him. With a violent forearm shiver under Zup's facemask, Wil ripped the helmet from Zup's massive head, clearly breaking his nose in the process.

Adhering to yet another of H. Jackson Brown's proverbs for living (#269, "Don't whine"), Zup said nothing as he picked up the helmet and placed it back on his head. Looking across to see Zup's nose lying across his left cheek and blood gushing liberally from his nostrils, Wil said, "Zup, I think your nose is broke."

"Stance!" Zup roared.

They went at it for the better part of another half an hour, with Zup's blood staining Wil's jersey. Wolford finally declared his satisfaction with the shoulder.

Both Wil Wolford and former Colt linebacker Barry Krause, who suffered a torn ACL in his knee, credit Zup with saving their careers by conveying his unconquerable spirit into them as they worked to come back from major injuries.

His career as a coach for the Colts from 1983 through 1999 reached its pinnacle when he was named by his peers as the National Football League Strength and Conditioning Coach of the Year in 1996.

Be a leader: remember the lead sled dog
is the only one with a decent view. (#505)

Recognizing Tom's potential as a representative and promoter for the Colts, Jim Irsay brought Zup out of the weight room and into the front office in 2000 as vice president for business development. Tom and the man he works for and admires, Ray Compton, have become known for their enthusiasm and creativity in promoting the Colts franchise to the public, becoming popular and beloved faces for the Indianapolis team.

Tom continues his regular engagements as a motivational speaker, and each Sunday prior to Colts games, he and his buddy Jimmy "Mad Dog" Matis can be heard on the Colts' radio network Q95 with their show, "Dog and Zup With the Pre-game Scoop."

Zup also has a regular weekly spot on a local radio station, where he trades barbs and dishes out hilarity with local deejays.

Zupancic is part owner of the Indianapolis Ice professional hockey team. He will admit that it was his brainstorm to sign former NBA center Manute Bol to a one-game contract with the Ice. At 7'7", Bol certainly will hold the record as hockey's tallest goalie. The promotional stunt ought to rank up there with that of Bill Veeck, the legendary general manager of the St. Louis Browns, who in 1951 put 3'7" and eighty-five-pound Eddie Gaedel up to bat in a major league game (the wee Gaedel received a base on balls in his only appearance in the big leagues).

Choose a charity in your community and support it
generously with your time and money. (#76)

Zup has difficulty following the charge found in Brown's #76. Choosing from among all the charities he wants to help has proved an impossible task, so he tends to say "yes" to every cause, particularly if it involves kids.

With a heart as soft as a baby's bottom, Tom has been involved in innumerable campaigns and has served scores of organizations on behalf of children. He has raised millions in charity to put hope and joy in the lives of kids—weak kids, poor kids, hungry kids, and hurting and dying kids. He serves on multiple boards for child advocacy groups such as Special Olympics; P.A.L. clubs; Broken Wagon Ranch for the handicapped; D.A.R.E. of Indiana; the Speedway Exchange Club for the prevention of child abuse; the Family Support Center of the Indianapolis Children's Bureau; the Southwest Multiservice Center; Wheeler Missions; the American Cancer Society; the Heart Association; the Julian-Springer Scholarship Fund; the Leukemia Society; and his church parish, St. Malachy.

Tom regularly makes arrangements for Riley Hospital kids and their families to attend Colts games, bringing them right down to the field in a limousine. You'll find him on Christmas Eve, not at home, but with Carrie and the kids along, dressed as Santa Claus and singing "Jingle Bells" at Riley.

On behalf of the Children's Bureau, Tom annually persuades a half dozen of his fellow former pro players and other weight-lifting enthusiasts in a "Lift for Kids" fundraiser. By the fall of 2002, Zup and his fellow strongmen lifted a total of more than 100 million pounds in four hours, raising thousands of dollars for abused kids.

As his close friend, former Colt Jim Harbaugh, has noted, "Zup could be a wealthy man if he didn't give away so much of his own earnings. Besides all the volunteer time he spends on causes for kids, his checks for radio appearances end up in the coffers of child advocacy organizations. Frequently he donates his speaking fee back to an organization if it benefits children."

Perhaps recalling his own childhood, Zup often travels into poor neighborhoods in Indianapolis, seeks out kids playing, then drives up, rolls down his window, tosses a half dozen footballs out, and drives away. He has parlayed his position with the Colts franchise into fulfilling dreams of children who suffer from poor health and economic conditions.

Be someone's hero. (#508)

The honors he has received are hard to keep track of. Governor Bayh honored him as a Sagamore of the Wabash; Mayor Stephen Goldsmith proclaimed March 26, 1996, as "Tom Zupancic Day" in Indianapolis; he has been named "Man of the Year" by numerous organizations, including the Leukemia Society, the Indiana Exchange Club, the Indianapolis Sertoma Club, and he has received the Community Heroes "Davy" Award. Each year the *Indianapolis Star* newspaper organization names ten citizens of the state of Indiana who have selflessly devoted themselves to the well being of others. With Katie, Jake, and John accompanying their father to the podium, Zup was so honored as a Jefferson Award recipient in 2001.He is both a Distinguished Alumnus honoree and a member of the

James L. Brunnemer

Athletics Hall of Fame at his alma mater, the University of Indianapolis, and a member of the university's Board of Trustees.

There is nowhere Zup won't go or anything he won't do to make little kids' eyes shine a little brighter.

Just for fun, attend a small town Fourth of July celebration. (#352)

Not Zup to *attend* an Independence Day celebration—he's got to be *in it*. Each July Fourth, Zup, Carrie, and their kids join with fellow members of the Speedway Exchange Club and hand out more than 7,000 miniature American flags to parade watchers in Brownsburg, Indiana.

Don't be deceived by first impressions. (#236)

Tom has a line of blarney from here to there. He can appear naïve as a child but sizes people up immediately. With an intuitive B.S. detector, he can smell a phony like enologists can a fine bottle of port. The size of your bankbook won't impress him, but the substance in your heart will.

Be there when people need you. (#356)

More people than he can possibly remember have been lifted by Zup showing up, when needed. Close friend and fellow U of I trustee Gary Edwards will attest from personal experience that you can count on Zup.

Be bold and courageous.
When you look back on your life, you'll regret
the things you didn't do more than the ones you did. (#346)

No one will ever accuse Zup of not having lived his life to the fullest. No one whose path I have crossed in nearly six decades comes close to Zup in terms of his zest for life. Every challenge is an opportunity for this man-child. All that has come before this combines to make for one amazing and admirable human being. My personal list of heroes is a short one. This junkyard dog from Haughville is one of them.

Never eat the last cookie. (#361)

This is one of life's little instructions Zup never has learned to abide.

CHAPTER XXV
ALL THE PRESIDENTS' (CAUCASIAN, PROTESTANT, ALUMNI) MEN

> Higher education has a role in enabling students to deal with the different ways those of different cultural, ethnic and racial backgrounds may approach the same set of circumstances. Schools that consider race and ethnicity among the many factors for admission aim to put students into an academic 'rock tumbler' that knocks the edges off their assumptions about each other's experience.
> Bobby Fong, president
> Butler University

It didn't take long after I returned as dean for Institutional Advancement to hear the whispers: "Ye, gods! Another white, Protestant, male, Indiana Central College graduate on the president's administrative council."

For those who posed as the "diversity police" among the faculty and staff of the college, it was a valid point. When I took my seat at the table of President Ben Lantz's administrative team in April 1989, the faces around me were very familiar. Save for the president and academic dean Carl Stockton, those sitting at the top of the chain of administrative leadership were (1 male; (2 Caucasian; (3 Protestant; and (4 alumni of Indiana Central. (Because neither was a graduate of the institution, Lantz and Stockton met only *three* of the categories, of course.)

Little wonder that when I arrived to head the U of I advancement office, with responsibilities for carrying out university promotions and fund raising, a small but aggrieved cluster of folks indicated a measure of concern and dismay. It seemed less an indictment of me and my qualifications for the position than a registering of chagrin that yet another opportunity had been missed to place a qualified candidate at the top of the management division with someone *other than* a white male Protestant graduate of Indiana Central.

For years, beneath a placid surface, there existed a steady current of criticism from ICC faculty and staff (and at least one team of North Central Association evaluators expressed concern) about the homogeneity of the university's leadership. An historical lack of diversity among members of the Board of Trustees and the university's presidency, plus the perceived white male hegemony within its management, made justifiable that apprehension. And there was unease, too, about the dominance of graduates of the university within the administration. Dr. Stockton, not an alumnus of Indiana Central, once commented to me: "I wonder if there were some jealousy amongst faculty who were not part of this 'in' brotherhood? I remember some murmuring ... about the Good Old Boys, meaning the alumni administrators."

Let's talk about that.

James L. Brunnemer

At the time it was established and especially in its early years, Indiana Central College was shaped by the tenets and traditions of the United Brethren Church. The values of that religious body cast its shadow over any idea considered to be outside the mainstream.

Since its founding in 1902, Indiana Central has differed little from most independent American colleges and universities in the diversity of its leadership. Like many of its counterparts across the nation,
a specific religious denomination established ICC, with at least part of the college's function intended for propagating the doctrine and values of its brand of the Christian religion. Women were esteemed as partners, but it appears they accepted their role on a lower tier in the leadership hierarchy of the Church of the United Brethren in Christ. Remember, at the time Indiana Central was established, it would be eighteen more years before the Nineteenth Amendment of the United States Constitution gave all women the right to vote. When Indiana Central was born, women in higher education were swimming upstream.

Few, if any, African-Americans were members of the UB church in Indiana, and while respect for all human beings was an expressed value of the church, I can't help but wonder how early black students at Indiana Central felt about leaders of the church and the school. Clearly a case can be made that Indiana Central was part and parcel of a racist society, but as we'll see, blacks were accepted into the fabric of the college at an earlier time than at many schools in America, including most public institutions of higher learning. On that basis, I suppose it doesn't matter now that, depending upon one's perspective, the early United Brethren influence might be seen either as promoting and defending the rights of black students by inviting them into the college, or as lords of patronage doing kindnesses with a proprietary bearing. It is, perhaps, at least a signal of the progress made within the university's church affiliation that the bishop of the United Methodist Church in Indiana is the Reverend Woodie White, an African-American.

While not specifically excluded from the college, it is unlikely that Roman Catholics and Jews would have felt comfortable in a school dominated by the Protestant overtones of Indiana Central. I clearly recall my surprise, even in 1971, learning that Roman Catholicism (twenty-seven percent) was the second most prominent denomination of the student body after the Evangelical United Brethren (forty-one percent).

Gays and lesbians? In 1902, church doctrine would, fairly I think, be described as intolerant of sexual practices other than between adult men and women. Leaders of the Church of the United Brethren in Christ and then the Evangelical United Brethren Church (1946 merger) focused on the fidelity of marriage between one man and one woman and the deleterious effect of divorce upon traditional families. The United Methodist Church (1968 merger) has struggled with the question of homosexuality within its ranks, especially in the past two decades.

In order to promote the values of the body of believers who instituted Indiana Central, the leaders, or board of trustees of the church college, would necessarily reflect that of the church. One would be hard-pressed to refute the allegation that for the greater part of its history, leadership of the institution has been predominantly in the hands of white males, mirroring the composition of almost all governing bodies of all types of American institutions. White males have dominated the U of I trustee boardroom, the presidency and the president's cabinet, and to a lesser extent, the faculty, throughout its existence. Additionally, most of those men were steadfastly Protestant and many were graduates of the institution.

With a few exceptions, such as Harriet Capehart, it has been only since the 1990s that women began to participate in policy making at the trustee level. Ann Cory Bretz '48 has been among the few alumnae who have served as trustees. In recent years, Patty Winningham Poehler '77 and Pat Polis McCrory '76 were invited to join the board. Women not having earned degrees from the U of I have been more numerous on the board of trustees than alumnae. Prominent women trustees such as Christel DeHaan, Yvonne Shaheen, Lorene Burkhart Steinmetz, Esperanza Zendejas, Carolyn Coleman, and Sue Anne Gilroy, none of whom earned a degree from the U of I, have represented the Indianapolis community on the school's trustee board. The inescapable conclusion is that for most of its history, the only unit within the university where women have been preponderant has been among the students and the clerical staff.

Few African-Americans have served as trustees and most who did were male, and U of I alumni: men like Ray Crowe '39, Emmanuel Harris '82, Murvin Enders '81 and William Raspberry '58. Ms. Coleman is the first African-American woman to serve on the board of trustees.

Trustees who are Catholic and those of Protestant denominations other than United Methodist were sparse. Rarely were Jews—Michael Maurer and Earl Harris being notable exceptions—included on the University of Indianapolis trustee board.

In 1998, Ms. DeHaan became the first female chair of the Board of Trustees, as well as the first non-EUB or United Methodist. No African-American has served that post to date.

As noted, all seven presidents of Indiana Central/University of Indianapolis have been white males. Dr. Israel is the first chief executive not to be an ordained minister.

The first black member of the president's cabinet, Dr. Everette Freeman, became vice president for academic affairs in 2001, replacing the retiring Lynn Youngblood. Note that the first African-American dean of a traditionally white college was the Reverend Dr. Howard Thurman, Dean of Chapel at Boston University in 1953. If I remember accurately, Sue Anne Gilroy, Mary Busch '62, and Karen Nirschl were each, at different times, assistants to President Gene Sease in the early seventies; but women at the cabinet level of the university have been scarce, and until Dr. Freeman, African-Americans non-existent.

An argument could be made that, like most private institutions, Indiana Central had difficulty successfully recruiting talented African-Americans who were available from the small pool of qualified candidates. (I'm not certain of the number of blacks holding the Ph.D. degree in any given year, but the number has been decidedly small in comparison to whites.) Stanford, Berkeley, Ivy League institutions, or a Big Ten school invariably recruited qualified African-American scholars who possessed competitive academic credentials, with commensurate salaries.

A conclusion that the predominance of white male trustees, chief executives, and top-line management had a way of perpetuating the status quo would appear to be well-founded.

Less overt, but certainly present, has been criticism that there were too many male *alumni* (a number of whom were clergy) among the faculty and staff. Some believed that a faculty and staff, peppered noticeably by graduates of the college, would necessarily embody a narrow set of views. That the values and experience of graduates of other institutions would provide a broader vista of exchange for student learning was seen as a way to strengthen the faculty.

In considering this criticism, it should be noted that graduates of Indiana Central have been among the school's finest instructors. Some might have taught at other, more prestigious institutions but chose to return to the college to teach or step into administrative posts. Among those who shared their scholarship and concern for and with students are W. P. Morgan '16, Donald Carmony '29, Robert McBride '48, Marvin Henricks '42, Kenneth Sidebottom '42, Marshall Gregory '62, Don Fleener '49, Dean Ransburg '54, Nathan Wooden '47, Nuel Wooden '48, Wilmer Lawrence '53, Lynn Youngblood '63, Dave Huffman '64, and Ken Hottell '62, and Steve Maple '66.

Head coaches Angus Nicoson '42, Bill Bright '54, Bill Bless '63, Terry Wetherald '63, Ken Partridge '58, Jerry England '61, and Tom Hathaway '54 were other alumni faculty whose praises are sung yet today by the literally thousands of athletes who came under their charge. This is not an exhaustive list but does demonstrate that alumni have been teaching at the university from its earliest days to the present.

In the past, the allegation that, on the average, male faculty and staff were paid more than women of relatively the same status had some basis in fact. Another injustice was that married men were paid more than single men. Husbands and fathers had to raise a family, you know. I think the record would support this. But such practices were not only acceptable in days past but were even considered mainstream management decisions. To my knowledge, those indulgences no longer exist at the university.

Nonetheless, before the 1990s and the widening presence and influence of females on the faculty and staff, there were stalwart women like Mary Huey, Virginia Sims, Sybil Weaver '19, Martha Waller, Doreen St. Clair '61, Linda Fowler '61, and Michelle Stoneburner '66, among many. In 2003, Suzanne Willey '75 became the first female athletic director at the U of I. Florabelle Wilson '49, an assistant librarian to Miss Edna Miller and later the chief librarian, was a prominent and proud African-American woman. Mary Busch '62, another African-American alumna, has served various administrative positions. As far as many students were concerned, the most influential person on campus during the 1950s through the seventies was a humble and loving African-American woman, the unforgettable Mary Streets. Daily, she oversaw the campus cupboard and dispensed common wisdom in her loving way to students who came into contact with her.

A miniscule number of Jewish women—professors Flora Valentine, Victoria Bedford, Helen Anderson, and award-winning poet and honorary degree recipient Alice Friman come to mind—found their way to the college.

In commenting on the opportunity for women to participate in U of I leadership, former university president G. Benjamin Lantz pointed with great pride in the 1990s to the gender of the deans of the five colleges within the university, not to mention a number of departments. A woman headed each college. Those included Dr. Lynne Weisenbach (School of Education); Dr. Robin Livesay (School of Business); Dr. Beth Domholdt (Krannert School of Physical Therapy); Dr. Mary Moore (School of Arts and Sciences);

Distinction Without Pretension

and Dr. Sharon Isaacs (School of Nursing). Some grumbled that this circumstance was a planned stratagem by Dr. Lantz for reasons of publicity and to shift the spotlight from his all-white-male management team. But having known each of these scholars, teachers, and administrators personally, it is my opinion that they received their positions on merit.

It might be interesting to note that it took Harvard Law School 186 years to determine that a woman was the best candidate for its top position. In April 2003 Elena Kagan was named the first female dean of that prestigious institution.

Openly gay faculty members prior to the 1990s? "Fuhgeddaboudit!" While there were gay and lesbian faculty and administrators at the college prior to the last decade of the twentieth century, public declaration of their sexual preference would have been problematic for the church. President Sease, especially, adeptly handled those situations with great sensitivity and most confidentially on behalf of his gay colleagues. Today, progress has been made toward securing the rights of gay and lesbian faculty and staff, but for those of a sexual orientation other than exclusively male-female the atmosphere remains somewhat discomfiting.

It is evident that Indiana Central was not on the cusp of promoting real diversity for the first five decades of its history. With few exceptions, the student body up until the 1960s came mostly from small towns and were white (although one may trace a thin line of black enrollees from 1916 onward), Protestant (although a surprising number of Catholics studied at ICC), somewhat evenly balanced between male and female, and heterosexual.

Economic realities, with a boost from a world war, brought to the campus the man who would initiate the first substantial movement toward cracking the academic and cultural parochialism of the institution. A visionary decision by President Esch to create the evening division following World War II had a great influence upon broadening the profile of the student body. This was partially in response to returning veterans who were armed with the GI Bill. Most had families and jobs but could attend school in the evening to advance their education and prospects for better positions. Many of the GIs helped to diminish ethnic and cultural hang-ups of the more conservative members of the church, faculty, administration, and student body.

Through the evening division, the university reached out, as well, to other sectors of Indianapolis. Many adults seeking to improve their lives and economic circumstances found opportunities to advance their education through a full schedule of courses offered after regular work hours. Indiana Central was no longer primarily a school for "preachers and teachers." Today, the University of Indianapolis offers a comprehensive array of degrees at the bachelor's, master's and doctoral levels, with students from more than sixty different countries joining their American counterparts. It has been most satisfying for those of us associated with the college to see real growth and progress on all fronts.

Another relationship that contributed to bringing students of different cultural backgrounds to Indiana Central was that of the college with the McCurdy Mission School in Espanola, New Mexico. Orphaned and underprivileged Native Americans and Hispanics were ministered to and educated there. Many of the faculty and administration were graduates of Indiana Central, including longtime principal Dale Robinson '48. Through the years, numbers of these students traveled to Indianapolis to seek higher education.

James L. Brunnemer

Later, during Gene Sease's term as president, a relationship was established between the University of Indianapolis and Intercollege at Cyprus that would bring considerable international diversity to the campus. After establishing a similar arrangement in Athens, these affiliates of the University of Indianapolis were accredited and students from countries worldwide came to Indianapolis to complete studies and degrees initiated at those international centers of education. Coinciding with the influx of international students was a steadily increasing number of African-Americans seeking enrollment. The result is that annually the U of I is near the top of the list of all Indiana colleges and universities in the percentage, per capita, of minority students.

Additionally, the university forged an association with historically black Martin Center (later University) in urban Indianapolis. At the outset, the focus was on faculty and student exchange. Later a bilateral agreement in education and nursing programs brought the U of I and Martin University into a close and collegial partnership.

As to the comfort level of students of different religious faiths, the early years of the college held to its Christian traditions. Before the traditional chapel requirement at the college was altered, then eliminated, Catholic students were kept out of the auditorium, locked in the library (as Protestant students were locked in the auditorium) during the Monday, Wednesday, and Friday sessions of chapel. The college administration probably felt, on the one hand, it should not require Catholics to attend Protestant services, but, on the other hand, could not expect its Protestant students to attend forced religious observances while letting the Catholics enjoy a free period. Nevertheless, an impression was made on students that Catholics were somehow "different" from the rest of us.

It's enough to say that the percentage of those declaring Judaism as their religion of choice barely registers among the more than 20,000 graduates of the school.

Furthermore, I'll leave it to your own determination whether the church's heritage promoted tolerance of homosexuality among its students. The few gay students attending Indiana Central tended to stay in the closet, basically until the new millennium. By the time Benjamin Lantz became president, pressure to grant official approval to PRIDE, a gay organization on campus, was intense. A vote by the Board of Trustees in 1999 (not unanimous) gave sanction to PRIDE, equal to other student confederations. Attitudes are changing, but I'm not certain it is as yet comfortable to be openly gay at U of I.

In 2003, university officials cannot, nor would they wish to, deny the lingering influence of the religious heritage upon the University of Indianapolis. Indeed, President Jerry Israel celebrates the "shared mission" and "collective history" of the school and the early United Brethren ideal. In his address to faculty and students at the President's Convocation on September 5, 2002, Israel noted the historic association of the school and the church when he proclaimed, "the church exists to serve the world. The college exists to serve the world ... it is our unequivocal collective identity."

He added:

> *[I]t seems to me that our church-connectedness begins with a parent/adult-child metaphor. The church (specifically, in our case the United Brethren) gave us life in 1902. We have doubtless grown, 100 years later, into an institution very different from the one that denomination hoped to*

> *create. And, like parents who no longer control nor make decisions for adult children, the United Methodist Church today must learn—and in many significant ways has learned—to accept, tolerate, and understand what we have become.*

The most difficult challenge, however, has been for minority students. It seems that two truths might be considered characteristic of the university relative to tolerance for black students, and perhaps to other minority groups as well. First, there has been a dominant university value that blacks should be treated with *respect*. (That value was later modified to require *equal treatment* for African-Americans with whites.) Second, most whites at the University, including those sympathetic to the cause of racial justice, did not begin to understand the difficulty and pain associated with being black and living in a white culture that thought of black persons as being inferior.

Real discrimination, prejudice, and unfairness exist in the world. No one should take lightly that there remain in our society today persons who, for reasons related only to group identification, are prohibited from enjoying the full freedoms and opportunities of the American system. It's appropriate to ask how the University of Indianapolis has handled issues of prejudice, diversity, and tolerance, especially in relation to black and minority students.

The culture of the state of Indiana has historically proven unfriendly to blacks. David Frum, author of *The Right Man*, offers convincing evidence that Indiana, most notably during the era of D. C. Stephenson and the Ku Klux Klan, "was one of the most racist states in the nation." Preparing for a trip to speak in the Hoosier state in the 1960s, Martin Luther King was alleged to have referred to traveling to Indiana as going "up South."

While population, economic, and social data would suggest that African-Americans have done reasonably well in Indianapolis, the U of I has had a veiled challenge in attracting African-American students and faculty, simply by being located in *southern* Marion County. The perception of public antipathy to blacks in certain areas of the Greater Indianapolis community has had a noticeable effect on settlement patterns in Marion County. Southside Indianapolis has been viewed, historically, as hostile to blacks. Racist actions on the part of realtors, bankers, and other organizations supposedly serving the public were perceived to be the norm well into the late twentieth century.

An *Indianapolis Star* survey appearing under the headline "Black Homes Scarce On South Side" (February 16, 2003) noted that of nine townships into which Marion County is subdivided, 34.7% of black families live in Center Township, or downtown Indianapolis. Census data shows that since the 1960s, blacks have followed whites to suburbs in the north, east, and west townships of Marion County, but not the south. Marion County townships with the lowest percentage of African-American families are Franklin (0.6%), Decatur (0.5%) and Perry (0.3%), the three southern-most townships.

Southern Marion County blends with Johnson County, which was allegedly once a haven for Klan activity. That, at least in part, seems to shed light on why blacks in Indianapolis historically have chosen to reside basically north of U.S. 40 (once Washington Street).

As noted earlier, blacks were a decided minority in the United Brethren in

James L. Brunnemer

Christ and Evangelical United Brethren churches, with which Indiana Central College was affiliated and depended upon for financial support and student recruitment. (Current Bishop Woodie White is the first African-American to have been named to that position in Indiana.) In his book, *Downright Devotion to the Cause*, University of Indianapolis historian Dr. Fred Hill alleges that some members of the United Brethren Church were members of the Klan and implies that President I. J. Good was at least tolerant of racist attitudes of the day. Hill noted that in the 1930s, white classmates delighted in a singing group of fellow students who called themselves the "Jubilee Quartet." These four African-Americans performed "songs of the Southland." Unlike white student deputation teams, which served as ICC ambassadors by singing at churches and other university-related events, Good refused to allow the "Jubilee" singers to represent the college off campus. In fairness, given the racial trends of the day, Dr. Good may have been chiefly concerned with the black students' safety, but it is difficult not to conclude that his reasons were more related to the image of the college.

Although the first black enrollee at Indiana Central, according to Dr. Hill, was Mr. F. Jones in the academy during the fall of 1916, most of the early black students were first-generation Africans. United Brethren missionaries, such as Earnest and Lota Emery, occasionally encouraged and recommended to university officials bright and promising young people from tribes to whom they had ministered. It required a brave soul to actually cross an ocean to attend our school in the early decades of the twentieth century. Read below a fascinating story of one of the first of these students, David Manley, who earned his passage to America, and Indianapolis, on an ocean steamer, as revealed in his own words in the 1920 *Oracle*:

> [I]t was five o'clock. The scorching African sun was just shedding its parting rays on the Sierra Leone mountains, and casting a deep and gloomy shadow on the peaceful waters of the bay, when I handed a check of twenty-five dollars to a half-drunken, staggering seaman who took us on board a ship that was to bring me to the land of my dreams. Very few men have had the rare privilege of paying in order to work; especially the work of a stoker in the hot and blazing furnace of a steamship. As I stood on board the vessel that evening, I noticed for the first time the beauty of my native country. To the stranger who is not accustomed to the luxuriant growth of a tropical forest, there is something in the scenery that is infinitely intoxicating. The mountains seem to grow from the very bosom of the ocean, and in their numerous valleys are small bays and inlets. The hillsides are dotted with bungalows half hidden among coconut trees and bananas; while the oil palm—the king of the country—towers above every other kind of vegetation.
>
> No one can enter that harbor, especially at this time, when all the trees and shrubs are in their utmost brilliancy, without having a profound admiration for the natural beauties of old Africa. No human language can adequately express my feelings that evening as I saw fleeting before me a panorama of my whole life, from a

few clustered mud huts to a rather large steamship ready to brave the dangers of an unknown sea. At last the anchor was weighed and we steamed for the great ocean.

What a degree of sameness and vastness the ocean presents! It was the same old ocean with the same old rolling in infinite monotony.

After a few days' steaming, the noise of the city of Freetown, and the caw of the sea-birds were left behind. Only the clatter of the engines, the shrill sound of the captain's whistle, and the commanding voice of his mate, showering oaths and curse on some delinquent member of the crew, were to be heard.

The days grew into weeks and no land could be seen; one morning the wind blew loud and strong, so that the waves rose mountain-high and came nearly tearing the ship to pieces. It swept two lifeboats away and put the wireless apparatus out of action. After two days of storm and stress the sea became calm again. You cannot imagine the happy smiles on the faces of everybody when we beheld God's blue skies again. Even the rats were glad, for that night they had a regular picnic in our cabin, perhaps to share with us some of its luxuries, which were an ample supply of old rags on which we rested our tired bodies, and a few empty cracker-barrels upon which we ate the meager food.

A few days after we left Sierra Leone the men noticed that I was a peculiar kind of a sea-boy, for I took no part in their rude talks and always said my prayers. So they excused me from further work. This is the first instance when prayer alone saved a man, at least from real hard work.

To make a long story short, we were met at the entrance to New York harbor one beautiful morning by the pilot, having been on the ocean for twenty-one days. The pealing of the bells and the bellowing of the buoys... seemed to me then as voices welcoming me to this strange and wonderful country. How I wished the ship would hurry so that I might have a peep at civilization.

As soon as we landed, the immigration officers came on board, and fearing that they might refuse my coming on shore, I hid myself in an empty cracker-barrel, making myself as comfortable as possible. Finally they left and I started on the streets of New York City. To one who has spent his little life partly in a mud-hut, what a medley of thoughts New York, where everything and everybody seem to be in a hurry, awakens. The tall mansions of Wall Street and the grim palaces of Broadway seem to be almost incredible.

David Manley '23 would return to his African land following graduation as a minister to his people.

Among the most prominent of African students who made the journey to Hanna Avenue was the late Moses Mahoi '50. He earned his bachelor's degree at ICC, attended

James L. Brunnemer

Columbia University Medical School, and received his medical degree in London, England. Dr. Mahoi then returned to his native Sierra Leone, where he practiced medicine for the benefit of his countrymen until his death in 1998.

In February of 1929, at a time when the infamous Grand Dragon D. C. Stephenson was at the height of his bigoted influence, Dean William Pickens spoke to Indiana Central students and faculty during chapel services in Kephart Memorial Auditorium. Described as "a prominent colored orator and social worker," Mr. Pickens impressed the assembly with his penetrating address on interracial good will.

Yet another singing group of black Indiana Central students composed of graduates of Crispus Attucks High School became popular during World War II at the college. But the condescending racial tone of that era is implied by a well-meaning student expressing genuine affection for his fellow black classmates in this report from the 1942 *Oracle*: " ... those little fellows from Crispus Attucks sure could sing ... the Negro race certainly is earning a place in our country."

Athletics at Indiana Central opened opportunities for minorities not available at other institutions through the mid-1940s. It has been noted that Bill Garrett of Shelbyville was the first African-American to play basketball at a school (Indiana University, 1947) in the Big Ten Conference. Over ten years previous to that Dave DeJernett, Bud Smith, and other black athletes were performing in all sports available at Indiana Central. President Good cautioned them to "avoid adverse public opinion" and insisted they not participate in student social activities. Black students' conduct was monitored and supervised in ways that would be considered outrageous and illegal today.

Among the most visible of alumni of Indiana Central, particularly in the decades of the 1950s and 1960s, was Ray Crowe. A 1939 graduate of Indiana Central, Crowe distinguished himself, first, as coach of the powerful Indianapolis Crispus Attucks High School basketball teams. Coach Crowe's Attucks Tigers was the first high school squad from Indianapolis to win an Indiana state championship (1955), repeating that feat in 1956. He has been credited with unlocking doors for blacks in a state long known for its racism.

The second oldest of the ten children of Morton and Tommi Ann Crowe of Franklin, Indiana, Ray Crowe was recruited to Indiana Central by Harry Good. I once asked Coach Crowe what life was like for him at Indiana Central in the late thirties: "I couldn't have been treated better by Coach Good and the college community," he told me in my office at Esch Hall. "Many of my closest friends today, like Hank Potter, Elmer "Bus" Linville, and Hugh Bastin, are men from my college days"—all of them white.

Any trouble? Coach Crowe told me of a Hanover player who "roughed me up in a game, and called me a name." His ICC teammates immediately came to his aid. The Hanover president called I. J. Good the next morning to apologize for the player's conduct. Also, Coach Good was always cognizant of Ray's feelings.

"Once we were refused service in a southern Indiana restaurant, because of me. Coach Good put the team back in our cars and we drove on to Columbus, where the entire team was served."

Coach Crowe, 81 at the time of our conversation, went on to reminisce about people and events of that era and closed by saying the "best days of my life were college days at ICC."

Distinction Without Pretension

That is a considerable statement considering his success and accolades in a long and successful career in education and politics.

A number of African-Americans took circuitous routes to reach Hanna Avenue and an education at Indiana Central College. Jim "Buck" Adams graduated in 1952 and later became a head coach at Talladega (Alabama) College, where he was a colleague for a time of former U of I dean Dr. Carl Stockton. From Mississippi came William Raspberry '58 to live with relatives in Indianapolis in order to seek an education better than that which he was destined to receive in the 1950s Jim Crow South. The syndicated columnist of the *Washington Post*, winner of the Pulitzer Prize, is perhaps the most prominently known and celebrated of all Indiana Central graduates.

During the 1950s, Crispus Attucks and its coach, Ray Crowe, became prominent for its extraordinary basketball success. Many African-American graduates of that high school, and other Indianapolis public high schools, began to enroll at Indiana Central. Among these were Stanley Warren '59, James Cummings '62, Bailey Robertson '57, Robert Jewell '56, William Hampton '59, Henry Taylor '59, Jon Eckels '61, and Gilbert Taylor '58.

Warren, Jewell, Raspberry, and Eckels each would receive the highest honor bestowed by the university's alumni association, the Distinguished Alumnus Award, for service and success in their respective careers.

Dr. Warren recalls the racial atmosphere on campus in the 1950s to be less congenial than he would have hoped. Following his graduation from Crispus Attucks, Stanley Warren had no notion of attending college. After a hitch in the army, he landed a job at RCA in Indianapolis, a less-than-challenging position that he loathed. Having no automobile, Warren rode the bus each day to work. One day he found himself on the same carrier as a high school friend, Henry Taylor, who was attending Indiana Central. When Stan shared his unhappiness with his former schoolmate, Taylor encouraged him to join him at the college. Eligible for the GI Bill, Warren entered Indiana Central the following semester where he encountered another close friend and former CAHS basketball teammate, Bob Jewell, who "showed me the ropes and got me involved at ICC."

A commuter, Stanley Warren encountered what he termed veiled racism among some of the faculty and students. He characterized the general demeanor of most of the white students on campus to be politely chilly: "If you leave us alone, we won't bother you, and you won't bother us."

While he felt that some faculty members were barely tolerant of blacks, many professors, recalled Dr. Warren, "openly encouraged inclusiveness of all races," using professors Marvin Henricks and Robert McBride as primary examples.

Among the white students who embraced relationships with black classmates, according to Warren, were Leo Moye '59 and Allen Morgan '59, both athletes with whom Stan became good friends.

And the student body elected Stan's high school classmate, Henry Taylor, as president of Student Council in 1958, which was the most prestigious position available to an ICC student at that time.

In observing the University of Indianapolis in the twenty-first century, Dr. Stanley Warren admires "what they've done [trustees and administrators] to make students of all races and creeds more comfortable on the campus. Seeds have been planted and strides have been made, particularly through the athletic programs, to provide equitable opportunities and a higher comfort level for students of different colors and cultures."

The issue of diversity continues to be at the forefront of challenges in America and evokes the most extreme and passionate emotions of its people. As is often the case with major social controversies, the battleground for the confrontation is the college campus. The federal government supported a lawsuit to stop admissions practices (and, generally, *all* forms of perceived affirmative action) at institutions like the University of Michigan. Factoring race into decisions to admit students to colleges, according to the complaint, violates the equal protection clause of the Fourteenth Amendment to the Constitution. In the main, affirmative action has been intended to make up for the unequal treatment of African-Americans and other minorities throughout U.S. history.

The United States Supreme Court responded on June 23, 2003, with a landmark decision. By the narrowest 5-4 majority, America's highest court of justice upheld race as a factor in admissions policies in higher education, and, in effect, hiring practices in all entities in the country.

In September 2000, at the beginning of his third year as president, Dr. Jerry Israel outlined clearly his objectives, his plan, and his commitment to aggressively promote inclusiveness at the University of Indianapolis.

Referencing the work of sixty years earlier by Swedish sociologist Gunnar Mydal and his American student and colleague Arnold Rose, President Israel described what they termed "the American dilemma." In essence, a country that "proudly proclaimed equality" of opportunity frankly was mired in a "virulent and deeply rooted racism focused primarily on the descendants of former slaves."

Dr. Israel took the opportunity at the reestablished President's Convocation to announce a bold initiative he chartered as the "Campus Diversity Team." Composed of representation of a cross-section of people and groups on the campus, reporting directly to the president, Israel challenged the new team to "be our guide, our conscience, our facilitator, and our constant reminder that the climate of race relations on this campus can, must, and will improve."

We cannot know what the university would look like if it had been a leader, at the forefront of the movement for diversity within its ranks, top to bottom. We can only know what it has been and what it is now. Despite what some might disparage as a history of provincialism in its adherence to the dictates of the church, it appears that the affiliation with the church has "cut both ways." The United Brethren, Evangelical United Brethren, and the United Methodist values system made the college more progressive in how blacks and minorities were to be regarded and treated than many other colleges. ICC seems to have managed to "do good" in spite its early lack of diversity.

In contemplating the greater question of the American racial conundrum, I find myself in sympathy with a view expressed by David A. Lips, a research fellow at Hudson Institute in Indianapolis, who wrote:

> [A]s we enter the 21st century, we should abandon
> our sad history of racial classification and differential
> treatment. Only then will the beautiful vision
> captured in the "dream" of Dr. Martin Luther King
> have the chance it deserves.

That dream of Dr. King, of course, was "that one day people would be judged, not by the color of their skin, but by the content of their character." Oh, that it might be so, one day.

CHAPTER XXVI
PRINCES I HAVE KNOWN

> All states, all powers, that have
> held and hold rule over men
> have been and are either republics
> or principalities.
>   Nicolo Machiavelli (1469-1527)
>   "The Prince"

In May of 2003 a commotion involving a young *New York Times* reporter erupted, sending shock waves outward that jolted the nation's "newspaper of record." Jayson Blair, 27, an African-American reporter, admitted that he plagiarized and fabricated scores of interviews and stories. Senior management had allegedly ignored veteran *Times* news editors' warnings of his conduct. The fallout did not end with the eventual sacking of Blair.

Only weeks later, Howell Raines, executive editor, and managing editor Gerald Boyd were caught in the maelstrom that followed. According to some experts, Raines, especially, might have survived the tempest had his autocratic "my way or the highway" management style not alienated many staffers who might have come to his defense.

"Reporters and editors probably would have rallied around a more collegial leader facing the same situation," offered Jeff Rich, ECO of Affiliated Computer Services, "but they showed no mercy for Raines."

Hinting that the moral of this story is that "autocratic leadership works, until it fails," Del Jones, *USA Today* writer, said, "autocratic leaders do not die of their own weight. They get results, often great results. Things work—until something goes wrong."

Over a period of thirty years, I worked directly for or closely with six presidents at one public and three private American colleges and universities. In my view, the characteristics of the presidents of the independent colleges with which I have been affiliated approximate, to a remarkable degree, the prince of whom Machiavelli wrote in his insightful book about governance five centuries ago. Furthermore, I would argue that while not precisely "principalities," most independent universities such as the University of Indianapolis have historically vested its primary authority in one key luminary.

While each of the more than 5,000 public and private institutions of higher learning in the United States has its own unique culture and traditions, nearly all seem to possess similarities in governance models in order to deliver education to the client. One very important companion trait is the investment of far-reaching, almost unilateral power in a sovereign leader, the college president.

By and large, successful American colleges and universities, like successful businesses, are not democratic institutions. While by repute and by charter a university is an institution of learning, it is also a business, though it might be considered an anomaly in the for-profit world.

James L. Brunnemer

The university as a corporate entity is a relatively recent and distinctly American phenomenon. "Ancient" European institutions were not meant to be business models. Oxford and Cambridge, for example, were monastic foundations that extended to education of the clergy and the sons of aristocrats and the gentry of Britain. Higher education was not, originally, intended for the masses. Even Harvard College, like most early American institutions of higher learning, was born as an outgrowth of a church movement to produce informed and literate clergy, who would then inculcate the laity with the tenets of that particular religious sect.

Governance structures of modern American colleges and universities evolved out of the rather revolutionary idea that education should be made available to every citizen. That the business of education could occur on the scale desired only if a whole spectrum of administrative duties was successfully accomplished resulted, on the whole, in the most convenient, economic, and efficient form of governance—the "benevolent autocrat."

The view of college presidents as Machiavellian is not a condemnation, because they must and do operate in the real world. Leaders, in general, would be well advised to understand and use those age-old principles to reach desirable ends. While checks and balances of presidential power exist, those are often skewed toward the chief executive, enabling an artful college head to exercise enormous influence over his environment. In fairness, university "benevolent dictators" are, for the most part, just that. The eternal struggle of this simplest form of governance—the integration of power and goodness—often found its leader blending those elements dexterously. In the case of private colleges, this may be an outgrowth of the religious temper of the institutions' origins. While I've seen presidents enrich their personal portfolios and fortunes through their positions, all with whom I have worked affected their schools for the better. I rely primarily upon personal observation, but it does seem that among major institutions in America where we find notable leaders—in business and commerce, law enforcement, military, even the clergy—the office of the university president has been the least tainted by scandal. With some exceptions—the messy situation in the late 1990s at that bastion of independent and conservative ethos, Hillsdale College, notwithstanding—college presidents appear to be among the most committed of leaders to selfless service and as models of high moral, ethical, and social standards in their daily lives.

An autarch's tolerance for advice or disagreement from others varies. Leaders are such because they stand above the common man in certain critical characteristics. Being generally smarter, more willful, or having any combination of traits that researchers have identified and defined in those whom others choose to follow, it seems natural that leaders might be insistent on having their way, or even be affronted by those "lesser" folks (including ... no, *especially* media types) who would scrutinize and criticize decisions they make. Of advice, Machiavelli wrote:

> *A prince ... ought always to take counsel, but only when he wishes and not when others wish; he ought rather to discourage everyone from offering advice unless he asks for it.*

In contrast to publicly held American corporations where CEOs must answer to shareholders, private schools generally have a voluntary board of control. Rather than a financial self-interest, the members of a university trustee board are bound primarily to due diligence in carrying out their duties by only a *moral* obligation (one would hope that is the *highest* interest of human action). Usually called "trustees," the board is composed of alumni, corporate leaders, local politicians, and perhaps representatives of the church with which the college is affiliated.

Those at the next level, the president's administrative council, oversee specific branches of the university: e.g., academic affairs, institutional advancement, and business management. These bureaucrats are paid far less than the head man and access the board only to the degree that the chief executive allows. The president can exercise control over the entire university through these lieutenants by severely limiting their association with trustees.

Often it is the president and his representatives who recommend, to a subcommittee of trustees, candidates to serve or replace other board members. In other words, the president assists in selecting his own bosses. In a large measure, this cozy arrangement between the supportive and friendly board of governance and the chief executive they have selected to run the institution is a mutually cooperative one.

The board usually gathers three or four times annually for committee meetings to hear progress reports pertaining to the school from the president and his cabinet, providing the president allows his subordinates reporting privileges at trustee meetings.

While most trustees who accept a position on the board really are concerned with and become engaged in attending to the welfare of the university, all usually have important positions elsewhere. Each allots to the internal affairs of the college some proportion of time, money, and involvement based on the priority of university activities relative to the trustee's other personal interests. For the most part, as long as the institution appears to be functioning according to its mission, trustees nod approval to the chief executive and stay out of his way.

Although the modern college administrative model, including that of the present-day University of Indianapolis, is evolving toward increased participation of the chair and the board of trustees in college affairs, the president of the past had considerable control over his own destiny. In rare instances the president might have to contend with a "rogue" or maverick trustee with an issue driven by his own personal agenda, or an occasional challenge from a concerned or naïve trustee who hasn't yet learned that the president wants his money and support but not really his advice on how to administer the university. Indiana Central/University of Indianapolis has had a few pesky, gadfly trustees, like Indiana Central alumnus and eminent Indiana University historian Don Carmony '29, who stubbornly demanded accountability from the five persons who served as president in his four decades as a member of the board.

In the final analysis, university trustees are not financial shareholders. Commitments to remain successful in their own endeavors limits the time they have to be absorbed enough to really know the essence of the issues and challenges germane to the success of the institution. Finally, trustees purposefully hire talented chief executives in order to carry forth the business of the school as expressed in the mission and trustee policymaking. Thus, by choice, trustees' real control over the administration of the college is titular.

James L. Brunnemer

But what of the faculty? At the core and within the soul of any educational institution with claims to legitimacy are those learned scholars who deliver directly to the clients (students) practical and theoretical education for which the students pay a fee (tuition).

What role *does* the faculty play in administrative decision-making—outside the classroom or faculty senate—regarding the well-being of the university?

Fortunately, not much.

(Stay with me for a few more paragraphs as the U of I faculty drags my burning effigy over Smith Mall.)

Members of a college faculty are, at the least, better educated than the average citizen. Most have impeccable academic credentials in their chosen field of endeavor, and many have mastered the art of instructing well. Although there are the occasional faculty members who have the full range of academic skills *and* administrative acuity—many become deans or even college presidents—faculty members are generally ill suited for the special challenges found in governing the institution. As members of the campus community, faculty are charged to impart knowledge within the narrow limits of their discipline to the students, while remaining current, through research and study, with trends and thought in their particular area of acumen.

The beloved former president at Indiana University, the late Herman B Wells, sagely observed that "the house of intellect is by nature averse to orders."

Dr. Wells went on:

> One of the great joys of life in a university community is the presence of many strong personalities, and these can be extraordinarily varied and can exhibit many eccentricities ... There are likely to be many people with unusual behavior in any large faculty—eccentric by ordinary standards—simply because the man who prepares for the life of scholarship and teaching is by the very nature of his vocation a person who likes independence of thought and action. He is the very antithesis of the organization man, the conventional man ... and he exhibits this difference frequently by his informal style of dress, his individuality, his behavior in many respects. I believe that an administrator should not only tolerate this idiosyncrasy but accept it and rejoice in it. He must never let a man's personal quirks obscure his true worth, scholarly distinction, or the contribution he may make to the collegial life of the academic community.

In an enterprise such as a college, tough, pragmatic, and politically charged decisions must be made, often in a very fleeting window of time. Being ordained by trustees with singular power insulates the president from too much faculty influence. Public positions taken by faculty sometimes place them in opposition to the political and financial interests that a president must account for in keeping open the doors of a university. In a

USA Today article entitled "Explosive CEOs *Passé*, But Are Nice Ones Here To Stay?" a former CEO of a major American corporation alleged, "Tough management styles are 'abhorred by the academic, nicey feelies.'" While a president cannot—and probably does not wish to—control the faculty, he *can* keep them out of the business of the institution.

In his provocative book *Put the Moose on the Table*, former Lilly Corporation chairman and CEO Randall Tobias argues that,

> [o]rganizational acceptance of a vision and a strategy in the corporate world depends on the leader's ability to build a consensus, to gain buy-in, to articulate the vision with a passion that translates to credibility and believability.

This is the fundamental difference between a corporation and a university, in my humble view. If faculty were to be included in university administration in any direct way, the tendency of the intellectual corner of the campus to subject decisions to lengthy debate and tiresome rhetoric, over minutiae that hold little bearing on the subject, except in the minds of "thinkers," would be the norm. As Jacques Barzun noted wryly, "At some point, every faculty would certainly lynch its dean—if it could agree on a date."

While it is a good thing for a university president to have the general support of that part of his workforce called "faculty," to expect to build consensus for his vision and to gain buy-in from those in the teaching profession at the college level is simply impractical.

"Spuddle" is one of my favorite words. I discovered it while scanning Charles Mackey's *Lost Beauties of the English Language,"* published in 1874. To "spuddle" is to "go about a trifling business as if it were a matter of grave importance." If you've ever observed a college faculty meeting, with a heated, heavy-browed debate about whether a comma or a semi-colon should follow a phrase describing a course in the college catalog, you know what a "spuddle" is.

Inertia in faculty discussions is a fact of life.

Additionally, faculty members are characterized by an "ivory tower" view of the world. College instructors are, indeed, a most unusual workforce over which the college president has ultimate power, but with whom he must coexist, lest there be an uprising of significant import to alarm trustees, alumni, and other key constituencies of the college.

Almost without fail, a natural tension exists between faculty and administration in higher education. Most faculty members consider themselves to be the most important entity on the campus, for without their skills and knowledge, why would the college exist? As longtime university administrator Lynn Youngblood sagely points out, "What happens in the classroom is the central issue."

Certainly the average faculty member, posed the question of who is of greater import—a teaching faculty or a member of the development team?—would likely deliver an honest, obvious, and self-serving answer: Are you kidding?

While faculties provide classroom instruction, other members of the university body undertake important tasks unrelated to instruction. But without those administrative activities taking place, instruction could not, either. In an astonishing example of verbal brevity from a president not known for such, former president Ben Lantz succinctly characterized one aspect outside the strictly educational realm—fund raising—thusly: "There is nothing more academic than the dollar."

Without private support from donors to supplement the shortfall of about forty percent that student tuition does not cover in the average college budget, the faculty member would not have a job. That really makes it no easier to convince faculty of that necessity, however, when they observe well-dressed and generally higher-paid development professionals wining and dining wealthy prospects on the college's nickel (okay, much more than that!) while the instructor scrambles to gather enough microscopes for a biology class.

This example is repeated over and again in departments called admissions, housing and food services, buildings and grounds, public relations and marketing, student services, athletics, and so on. While the college is distinctly an environment for learning, other necessities (or popular luxuries) demand attention for the institution to thrive.

So it was that early on, those responsible for the survival of American educational institutions placed presidential power and preference above even that of the faculty. Creating such a governance structure left faculty unencumbered with financial and promotional responsibilities to do what they do best: instruct and advise students. Parenthetically, it kept them out of the *business* of the college. While a president generally has considerable academic credentials plus a number of "awarded" honorary degrees, he is first a businessman whose chief responsibility is fiduciary. No less a chief executive than Gene Sease once declared his primary daily job to be the financial viability of the institution.

Examining leadership styles of American political presidents in his book, The Presidential Difference: Leadership Styles from FDR to Clinton, Princeton University professor of political science Fred I. Greenstein suggests six characteristics stand out in governmental presidential performance: "public communication, organizational capacity, political skill, vision, cognitive style, and emotional intelligence." Less flattering in his examination of corporate leaders and media rivals Ted Turner and Rupert Murdoch (Clash of the Titans), Richard Hack describes each man as "brilliant, bold, fearless, self-confident, arrogant, ruthless, grasping, and insatiable." Any of these traits may be desirable in the university chief executive, as well.

Presidents with whom I have worked closely outside of my alma mater were Neil Webb (Saint Norbert College); John Porter (Eastern Michigan University); and Melvin Vulgamore (Albion College). Each distinguished himself during his term of office at his respective institution. At Indiana Central/University of Indianapolis, I served under Gene E. Sease, G. Benjamin Lantz, and Jerry Israel. Having observed these leaders "up close," certain traits seem to be common among all university presidents.

Personal observations of those six presidents over three decades lead me to this conclusion: university presidents are a singular breed. I'm certain of it. The man really doesn't pick the job; because of the individual's very nature, the job picks the man. By this I mean the presidency does not lend itself to widely different types of personality traits that might bring different strengths to the job and perhaps re-shape it or reform it. No, our staid university leadership structure reinvents itself in its succeeding chief executives. The presidency requires someone with characteristics that are basically the same as they have been since the late nineteenth century.

To Mr. Greenstein's generalizations about attributes of leaders, I would expand on the core traits expected of the university president:

- **Superior communication skills.** An effective president is equipped to articulate concepts and visions so persuasively that an audience can be moved to tears—and to reach for their checkbooks—by an artful address. Beautiful and moving word pictures uttered through the mouths of college presidents can turn a concept diagram of cold steel, bricks, and mortar into a living, breathing entity with personality and a soul. Masterful presidential orators will convince alumni and wealthy friends that an adequate infusion of life-giving cash will provide generations of future students a facility that will maximize their potential exponentially, and, thus, the donors' influence in the world. In the October 1, 2000, edition of the *Chicago Tribune* ("Lessons in Leadership"), David McCullough surmised that, "Maybe if we could put presidential power in a pot and boil it all down, a big part of what we would find at the bottom would be language, the use of language, the potency of words. Power to persuade is power indeed."

- **A native political gyroscope.** Wading through differing political blocs in order to say the right thing to the right person or group is a monumental challenge. As Edmund Burke noted, "politics has no permanent enemies, nor permanent friends ... only permanent interests." The "art" of being a successful college president includes an ability to parry and dodge confrontation with his varied constituencies (sometimes even appearing to advocate a position in which he is in direct opposition) while doing what he needs to do in the best interests of the institution. Above all other requirements the university president must be politically astute. He cannot survive otherwise.

- **Vision.** History has shown that a small core of leaders have propelled great social movements, won wars, and changed the landscapes of societies. To me it seems that visionaries suffer from (or are *gifted with*) a form of denial. How else could one conceive and achieve dreams of projects that, on the merits, would seem to be, to a reasonable and sensible (and *ordinary*) person, impossible? That extraordinary vision common to such leaders is a special gift of discernment or foresight, enabling them to see beyond obstacles to make the impractical practical.

- **A consuming ego** (sometimes juxtaposed with tremendous insecurity). The president must have a tremendous drive and energy to keep abreast of all the demands of the job and the belief in himself to overcome the distractions, obstacles, and daily political battles one must face. The job of a college president is an exhausting commitment. Following a normal day fully scheduled with meetings and routine presidential duties, the president (often accompanied by the spouse) must choose every evening from among dozens of student, faculty, community, political, and corporate events that he should or could attend to the benefit of the university. In the presidents I have observed, that deep well of energy and drive is sustained by a robust ego.

- **General knowledge.** The philosopher opined, "He who sips of many arts, drinks of none." Mastery in varying degrees of a wide number of subjects is a requirement of the chief executive. Presidents are generalists, knowing enough about, for example, the appropriate relationship of construction managers and general contractors in building campus facilities; understanding the political content of William Hogarth etchings; fathoming the bewildering television-watching patterns of college freshmen; and knowing the record price paid for an American bottle of wine (a 1951 Penfold's Grange for $23,088, if you're wondering); all the while having the confidence to second-guess the football coach for opting to punt on fourth and inches instead of running a double reverse.

- **Vulnerability to grandiosity.** After a given period of time, many college presidents have a tendency to succumb to the allure of believing all the great things said about them by the same constituents who, if their particular interests are not served, call presidents fools behind their backs. Presidents attain their positions of leadership because they are atypically gifted. However, superior intellect and insight is a double-edged sword in that one is encouraged to trust most his own judgment, or worse, it invites the tendency for him to listen only to those who agree with his decisions. As President Wells wisely counseled presidential hopefuls, one should "strive to avoid the deadly occupational disease of omniscience and omnipotence. Only the physician, surrounded by nurses and frightened families of ill patients, is as tempted as is a president to be omniscient and omnipotent."

There is one additional, compelling trait that continually amazed me in observing presidents. These men and women of supreme intelligence, communication skills, political savvy, and *chutzpah* each possess an undisguised brass, manufacturing their own truth, regardless of what the facts are. I swear a president can point to a cow pile and not just pronounce it to be a stepping-stone, but convince you to tread upon it! And he can persuade you to that end because he *believes* it!

I have observed more than one president embrace preposterous positions on any number of issues of substance. The natural tendency to laugh was suffocated after realizing he was serious. And next thing you know the second-line management find themselves falling in rank to carry the president's position outward, like waves in a pond disturbed by a stone thrown into it. I've had more experiences with "the Emperor has no clothes" than I can report here.

And if it weren't enough that a chief executive will embrace a position that seems patently untenable, if it serves his purposes he can, without conscience or a faltering step, embrace the totally *opposite side* of the argument and seem just as convincing from that viewpoint.

> *Everyone admits how praiseworthy it is in a prince to keep faith, and to live with integrity and not with craft. Nevertheless ... those princes who have done great things have held good faith of little account, and have known how to circumvent the intellect of men by craft, and in the end have overcome those who have relied on their word. If men were entirely good this precept would not hold, but because they are bad, and will not keep faith with you, you too are not bound to observe it with them. But it is necessary to know well how to disguise this characteristic, and to be a great pretender and dissembler; and men are so simple, and so subject to present necessities, that he who seeks to deceive will always find someone who will allow himself to be deceived.*
>
> Machiavelli

This certainly sounds like cynicism at its rankest. But as a wise historian once stated " ... politics, by definition, requires blatant hypocrisy."

There is irony in how emotional equilibrium affects presidential leadership. Sentimentality is often a prime motivator in the generosity of a donor. Nostalgia touches a graduate's memories of halcyon days on campus, a misty, dreamy time, the repository of good feelings. An artful president can arouse one's need to sustain those memories, and turn that sentiment into action through contributions. However, to accomplish this, the president must be a chameleon.

> *It is not essential that a Prince should be ... merciful, faithful, humane, religious and upright ... but it is most essential that he should seem to be ... but the mind should remain so balanced that were it needful not to be so, he should be able and know how to change to the contrary.*
>
> Machiavelli

University presidents, like all leaders, may be compassionate, sympathetic, or even empathetic, but *never* sentimental. An inborn, or perhaps studied and conditioned, pragmatism always prevails in this breed.

As defined, compassion is "a sympathetic consciousness of others' distress combined with a desire to alleviate that distress." But sentimentality—"action growing out of feeling rather than reason or thought"—is taboo in the sphere of a president. Of this the university president must never be vulnerable to. As with successful leaders in any endeavor, it simply isn't a president's prerogative to allow his emotions to affect his judgment.

Now occasionally, when necessary, a president may feign a softhearted bent. If an audience of one or more donors might be persuaded by tenderness, the president can, like the chameleon, alter his color to blend into that special environment. You see, leaders have the ability to suspend pragmatism for a pseudo-sentimental response, but practicality *always* surfaces, even when disguised as compassion.

If a touching word portrait of a beloved professor needs to be painted, perhaps to fund a department chair, the president can elucidate an eloquent portrayal of that former instructor that could wrench tears from a lava rock. If a landmark facility on the campus must be replaced, a victim of age, by a modern, architectural superstructure, the university president can make that old decrepit structure of rusting iron and aged wood and bricks take on a personality, breathing its last, facing the wrecker's ball bravely and honorably. Invariably, he closes with a plea for resources to replace that perishing, but heroic landmark with a new structure to carry on its noble legacy. Even though we know exactly what he is doing, we still find ourselves reaching for our checkbook.

> *Nothing makes a Prince so well thought of as to undertake great enterprises and give striking proofs of his capacity.*
>
> Machiavelli

The most discernible means for a president to secure considerable and lasting repute lies in bricks and mortar: erecting buildings. At the opposite end of the scale, the toughest but often most important legacy a president can leave is through increasing endowment, the bedrock of a university's financial strength. Increased enrollment, favorable publicity and a heightened visibility of the school, upgraded technology, increased student services, nicely manicured campus landscaping, and congenial relations with alumni and other constituents are all important to the successful president. But nothing makes a statement like a brand-new, state-of-the-art library, fine arts center, dormitory, or athletic facility. Traditionally, constituents are most amenable to donating dollars for new construction on campus.

Fulfilling the myriad duties of a university president borders on the impossible. It seems absurd to think that one woman or man can possibly fulfill the expectations of the multitude of diverse constituencies that he or she must please. Name another job, besides the chief executive of the United States of America, that has more varied political blocs, each with its own interests and agendas, clamoring for the attention of the sovereign leader. A college president must tiptoe adroitly through a landscape filled with political land mines; by name, the board of trustees, faculty, administration, nonprofessional staff, students, parents, alumni, the church, corporations, charitable foundations, legislatures, city councils, mayors, governors, and neighborhood associations.

One or more of these interest groups is usually perturbed with the university president for his stance or policy on whatever issues it is in its interest to protest or promote. At any given time, at best, an uneasy truce exists between the president and any one or all of these groups. Invariably, animosity is publicly shielded with courtly manners. It's difficult to fathom how one individual can dance to the contrasting tunes of the varied music makers, often performing multiple dances simultaneously to please whatever constituencies need to be attended to. Ultimately, a president must abide Kipling, who said, "Let all men count with you, but none too much."

There are, of course, rewards for giving up one's life 24/7/365, not the least of which is compensation. In 2003, public college and university presidents' average pay was $356,092, with varying additional perquisites such as health care, vehicles, homes, retirement and deferred compensation. The average salary for presidents of private institutions was somewhat less, at $267,148. President Israel's base pay was $211,775.

Is the Machiavellian president a bad thing, then? Of course not. Great universities are advanced, in great measure, by adept chief executives with highly attuned communicative skills and political instincts. They are able to challenge faculty, coax and wheedle the trustee board, spur alumni to action, pacify parents, mollify students, and inspire donors.

According to Coles, "To be a moral leader is to see and to provoke, to stir others, teach them, persuade them, move them to reflection, inspire and inform them, dramatize for them the particular issues, in a given struggle, lecture, hector" all those who can make an institution reach higher and achieve more.

I salute all of those chief executives of our nation's colleges and universities, including those of my *alma mater*, who have had the vision, passion, energy, versatility, persistence, toughness, and mental acuity that has resulted in American higher education setting the standard for the world.

CHAPTER XXVII
GENIUS FUELED BY EGO

*By working faithfully eight hours a day
you may eventually get to be boss, and
work twelve hours a day.*
                                    Robert Frost

The University of Indianapolis has been blessed with extraordinary executive leadership. The institution first survived, and later thrived, in no small measure because its presidents were equal to the enormous challenge of the office each served.

Presidents J. T. Roberts, L. D. Bonebrake, I. J. Good, and, during the early years of his administration, I. Lynd Esch accomplished near-miracles against daunting odds to keep the incessantly financially strapped college alive. The modern University of Indianapolis is a tribute, especially, to President Esch, who stepped into the breech during one of the most critical periods of the school's struggle to survive and turned it around. After twenty-five years he handed to his successor a college on the cusp of genuine financial solidity and holding the promise that it could blossom into a university of distinction.

Under Gene Sease, Ben Lantz, and Jerry Israel, the challenge has not been survival of the institution, but planning expertly its proper growth and development as one of Indiana's fine independent universities. Through the astute leadership of these chief executives the profile of Indiana Central/University of Indianapolis has steadily risen.

The accomplishments of these three presidents over the last thirty-three years are impressive. Enrollment has multiplied many times since 1970. Curricula have expanded to include an array of studies far beyond the dreams of the founders, including the introduction of master's degrees and of doctoral programs in physical therapy, occupational therapy, and clinical psychology. Centers of Excellence (including Leadership of Learning, headed by executive director Dr. Lynn Weisenbach) and Aging of Community (under director Dr. Ben Dickerson) in addition to others on the horizon have been established. Sound fiscal policy has been followed consistently, while notable sums of philanthropic dollars have been raised. The annual budget, once the single most troubling challenge for the chief executive and trustees, was balanced for the fifty-sixth consecutive year in 2003. Quality of the faculty in terms of degrees and experience has never been better. Campus facilities, once embodied in a single building, now rank with the best private colleges in Indiana. Growth has been multidimensional because the flexibility of governance has enabled the university to anticipate and respond to needs within the greater Indianapolis area.

And, in part, through an accredited alliance with Intercollege (a private Cypriot organization) in Nicosia, Cyprus, and an international program in Athens, Greece, students from more than sixty countries make up one of the most diverse student bodies among all Indiana colleges and universities. Now the University of Indianapolis exists as an affiliate in those two countries, not to mention the prospect of a pending branch in the country of Israel. In August, 2003, the Committee for Higher Education in Israel approved initial accreditation for a cooperative endeavor between the University of Indianapolis and Mar

James L. Brunnemer

Elias University in Ibillin, Galilee, which will lead to Israeli students completing degrees at the Indianapolis campus of the U of I.

A skillfully conceived relationship engineered during the term of president Gene Sease between Indiana Central University and Intercollege in Greece and Cyprus brought to the Indianapolis campus students like Militsa Papadopoulou '90, (right) shown presenting an award at the 1989 Alumni Golf Outing. Ms. Papadopoulou represented her native country, Cyprus, and the University of Indianapolis at the 1989 Miss World pageant.

    In point of fact, the University of Indianapolis has taken its place among private institutions in Indiana and the Midwest as an educational enterprise worthy of high praise. For the first time, in 2000, the University of Indianapolis was included in the top echelon of similar schools in the Midwest, according to *U.S. News and World Report*, and in 2002 was recognized as an outstanding "master's college" in that same publication.
    It hasn't been easy. And no other single component has been more crucial to the school's current standing than its succession of effective leaders in the position of president.

Distinction Without Pretension

While presidential leadership at the U of I, under the men I've observed directly, has been consistent with the nondemocratic model of Machiavelli, that leadership seemed more patriarchal than Machiavellian. One might characterize the administrations of presidents Esch, Sease, and Lantz as having a "Father Knows Best" dimension, as opposed to an oppressive dictatorship, although some faculty and staff would certainly debate that in all three instances.

For example, in contrast to Dr. Esch, who was celebrated for his "patriarchal aura," the autocratic style of Gene Sease would prove to run counter to a growing independence and outspokenness of the faculty. While he was certainly no more monocratic than Esch, Dr. Sease was not viewed as the benevolent and necessarily stern father figure as was his predecessor. By the time of his departure, Sease was vilified by some members of the faculty as one whose style had become *passé*. Faculty saw in the early days of Ben Lantz's presidency a refreshing change of inclusiveness in decision-making at the college, only to discover as time went on that Ben was even more insular in his control than Dr. Sease.

Esch, Sease, and Lantz accepted the grave responsibility of being sovereign leaders with broad powers and genuinely believed they were doing their jobs in the best interests of the university and its personnel. However, as our culture has evolved from more to less acceptance of authority through the years, so, too, has the ability of a university president to rule from atop an unquestioned perch of power.

In Jerry Israel, the university community seems to have its most "consensus-friendly" president, who seeks to build coalitions or at least appears to involve those around him, more so than his predecessors, in the process of running the college. Even a casual observer would acknowledge the increased engagement in university affairs of the board chair, Christel DeHaan, and her colleagues on the board of trustees. Time will tell how this dilution of presidential prerogative will affect the chief executive's ability to lead.

Among the most fascinating personalities of my world has been Gene Sease. Bill Lyon, a scribe for Knight-Ridder newspapers, once noted, "True genius is fueled by ego." One could not be long in the company of Gene Sease without understanding that his enormous achievements were in direct proportion to his need for ego fulfillment. Gene's service ethic and commitment to excellence were genuine, but his ravenous appetite for recognition and approval impelled him to greatness.

In what could serve as a textbook model for presidential succession, Gene Sease supplanted Dr. Esch as president of Indiana Central College in 1970. Replacing himself was merely one more testimony to the greatness and remarkable selflessness of I. Lynd Esch. According to Randall Tobias, former Lilly chief who was appointed in 2003 by President Bush to head the international effort to eradicate AIDS,

> ... [I]t's *my view that when it comes to succession planning, all too often leadership transitions are handled with the principal objective of determining the best way to address ego-related concerns of the person who is leaving. Too often, the timing and the manner of a leadership change have more to do with the personal objectives of the leader who is stepping down than with a combination of other*

James L. Brunnemer

> *factors that center around what is best for the future of the enterprise. The more appropriate questions which should be asked include 'How can positive momentum best be sustained in the company?' and 'What approach will contribute most to helping the new CEO be successful?'*

Unbeknownst to most persons affiliated with the college, Dr. Esch made it his priority to prepare his successor to lead the college before he stepped down. The larger picture was, of course, his concern for the college more than for his own legacy. For approximately two years, Dr. Sease had served the college in a variety of functions, each a rehearsal for his ultimate step upward to the presidency, culminating with his serving as president-elect during President Esch's final year. This unusual arrangement was conceived and orchestrated by Dr. Esch himself, with Gene as an amenable and quite brilliant partner. When he became the fifth president of the university, Gene was as ready, willing, and able as one could possibly be.

Demonstrating both wisdom and prescience, new President Sease, in one of his first moves, recruited the then-Mayor of Indianapolis, Richard Lugar, to the Indiana Central College Board of Trustees. Today serving as a senior United States senator, Lugar's commitment to the university and contributions of wisdom, stature, and personal financial support were invaluable in the more than three decades he was a member of the ICC/U of I board. James Freeman Clarke said, "Politicans think of the next election, statesmen of the next generation." Dick Lugar is a statesman. Providing mutual guidance and support for one another, Sease and Lugar became devoted and loyal friends.

Indefatigable, willful, persuasive, and a man of enormous energy (at one time he served on more than thirty Indianapolis civic and corporate boards of directors simultaneously), Dr. Sease had presidential *éclat* unparalleled in the fraternity of Indiana Central presidents. Genius is not too strong a word to describe his brilliance.

Once, not long after I became director of alumni relations at Dr. Sease's invitation, I gained an insight into his bold political pragmatism. Aware of the delicate balancing act of presidents of church-related colleges interacting with those immersed in the popular culture, I posed the same hypothetical question to President Sease as I had to Dr. Esch when the president emeritus and I traveled together visiting alumni following his retirement. Their answers, I think, are revealing in regard to their respective stations in life at that time. One was the recently retired, the other freshly inaugurated, chief executive.

The reader should bear in mind the context of the time: the early 1970s. The question was this: "Would you accept a $2 million gift for Indiana Central from August Busch, the St. Louis beer baron (or any purveyor of alcohol)?" The appearance of accepting tainted money created the conundrum.

Those who knew Dr. Esch would not be surprised by his answer. The retiring president replied, without hesitation, "Absolutely not!"

He expanded his answer to explain that he would never accept money from anyone representing an industry "that promoted human misery," as Dr. Esch believed alcohol did. He was as unequivocal as he was terse in his response to my query.

Dr. Sease did not blink, either, in his response: "Absolutely!"

Distinction Without Pretension

He, like Dr. Esch, qualified his answer: "I wouldn't name a building for Mr. Busch," he said. Then, with the usual Gene Sease flair, added, "You see, I have a unique 'washing machine' in the basement of Esch Hall with which I will take that dirty money and clean it up to be used for a good purpose!"

I always wondered if the ethical positions expressed by these two giants of Indiana Central history would have interchanged if their time frames as president had as well.

Dr. Sease was fearless in making decisions, and he stood strong in his beliefs. When convinced he was right, nothing could turn him from his path. Once, a federal bureaucrat on a mission to chart attendance of students at schools receiving federal aid demanded to know the college's "cut policy." (Though maintaining its independent status, like most private institutions, ICC students did receive financial aid in the form of federal grants.) President Sease informed the officious government investigator that Indiana Central had no such policy.

"What do you mean? I must know how many class 'cuts' students are allowed here," replied the agent, becoming more belligerent in his self-appointed authority.

"None," answered Sease. "Our students are expected to attend *every* class meeting. If an instructor suspects a student of cutting class, he may order the student to provide written explanation or proof of his whereabouts at that time."

President Sease has plenty of assistance at the groundbreaking of Krannert Memorial Library in 1976, all kids of faculty and staff. Sitting (front row, from left) Jason Riggs, Amy Youngblood, Larissa Youngblood, Dena Riggs, Lora Hottell, Jennifer Huffman, Brian Huffman, and Dr. Sease. Second row, Brent Nicoson, Matthew Borden, Scott Nicoson, and Kyle Brunnemer. At top, Beau Brunnemer, Todd Hottell and Scott Hottell.

Try as he might, the unfriendly government agent could not induce President Sease to invent a policy in order to coincide with bureaucratic federal guidelines. Finally, the G-man vacated in frustration. To my knowledge, our federal financial aid was never affected by Gene's intransigent attitude on "class cuts."

Under Dr. Sease, what some might consider minor tremors could register as major earthquakes on his seismograph. As an example, it was better to have died a small child than to have lost your master key. Essentially, those privileged to possess the key had entree to every locked door on campus. Dave Huffman remembered Dr. Sease's forewarning whilst receiving his passage to the catacombs of Indiana Central: "If you somehow lose this key, simply report it and keep on moving, because if you can't protect this key, you no longer work here." These kinds of admonitions had a way of sticking in one's consciousness.

Lou Gerig and I once had an instructive experience with Dr. Sease that we both shudder to recall. The public relations director and I had dual supervisory duties over the editor of the alumni magazine, who doubled as a writer of news releases and other university publications. Dr. Sease had cautioned us on more than one occasion that he felt we were not getting adequate performance from this employee. He hinted that it was the responsibility of the managers to maximize that performance or get rid of the problem. Being self-assured in our ability to coax that effort out of our man, Gerig and I continued to work with him, advising and cajoling, but basically accepting inferior results.

A publication of particular importance to the president was the college catalog. After many weeks of frustration that the publication was neither done on schedule, nor done well, Dr. Sease summoned all three of us to his office. He called first for Lou and me to meet with him, as our colleague sat in the area outside the sealed inner sanctum of the president.

"In all my years with universities, I've never had a sleepless night," Dr. Sease began ominously. "Gentlemen," he continued, "last evening I almost had my first sleepless night."

With that unsettling introduction, he arose, called our employee into his office, and, explaining patiently, but firmly, "You aren't equal to the task," fired him right before our frightened and awestruck eyes. From that moment forward I never had qualms about demanding performance from one over whom I had supervisory responsibility.

Another incident demonstrating Dr. Sease's hands-on approach in dealing with special circumstances involved a brutal reprimanding of a travel agent. During my term as alumni director, a man named Karl from a local travel agency had convinced me to consider a trip to Hawaii for graduates of our school. He extolled the virtues of alumni travel, implying that such excursions were ideal means of cultivating wealthy grads who might, in appreciation, donate cash to the institution. To add a carrot to the proposal for this young and inexperienced alumni director, Karl proposed to send President and Mrs. Sease, Lu and me, all expenses paid, on the trip. When I took the proposal to Dr. Sease, he indicated that he and Joanne would be glad to accompany the group on the tour.

Over subsequent weeks I spent many hours of work promoting the travel package. Ultimately, only thirteen people, of which but four were alumni, signed up for the voyage.

There was little, if any, actual return on the investment for both the agency and the college. Just days before the trip Karl reneged on his earlier generous offer, saying, with heartfelt regret, that there was "only room for two" on the tour for university representatives, and he would naturally prefer his guests to be the Seases.

That was okay with me. I was embarrassed to have wasted so much time and effort on this fallacious venture. But when I reported the new development to President Sease so he and Joanne could prepare for the expedition without us, he got the poor agent on the telephone. What followed, as I sat wide-eyed in his office, was a scathing phone call during which Dr. Sease verbally fricasseed the poor guy. After describing in detail what he thought of an outfit that would be so crass and insensitive, he concluded, before hanging up, with this rejoinder: "I intend to tell all my friends how your company does business!"

I never promoted another alumni tour.

President Sease and his able administrative council handled routine decisions at the college, with Gene's dominance and veto power over the vice presidents assuring his own brand of quality control. It was the inevitable removal of Angus Nicoson as athletic director and basketball coach in December of 1977, necessitated by Nick's increasingly debilitating battle with Alzheimer's disease, that revealed to me President Sease's high order of political skill as well as his sensitivity. This was an especially difficult, and in some ways momentous, decision. I know of no more courageous action taken by any president on watch during my twenty-one years with the university.

Following Nick's "retirement," a groundswell of feeling arose from many of his supporters among the alumni to name the ICU gymnasium after the coach. The spokesman for the group was my predecessor as director of alumni relations, Dean Ransburg. Dean conveyed the concept to me, articulating passionately the rationale for doing so.

Being young and naïve, I thought this idea of naming the basketball venue in Nick's honor would be unchallenged, a "no-brainer." So I felt confident in asking President Sease for a meeting at which I would present the recommendation on behalf of ICU alumni.

Dr. Sease listened carefully to my brief presentation, and then replied, shockingly, "I'm adamantly opposed to the proposal."

My initial thought was that the suspected jealousy of Gene for Nick had surfaced in a most unattractive way. Nick was an institution, not just at Indiana Central, but also beyond the narrow reaches of our campus. He was the most "bulletproof" of any member of the campus community, and Sease knew it.

But the president went on: "There are only two buildings on campus that have been named without contributed capital funds attached to them. Those are Good Hall and Esch Hall. I intend that there will be no others."

"However," he continued, "in this case I will go to my key advisors on the board of trustees and tell them why I oppose naming the gymnasium for Coach Nicoson. If they advise me that it should be done, then I'll lead the parade in celebrating it."

With that satisfied, sometimes smug, expression Dr. Sease would display when he knew he had taught a subordinate a lesson in life, Gene dismissed me.

Wow. To a thirty-two-year-old neophyte in institutional politics this was a revelation. The chief executive is opposed to what unquestionably seemed to be popular sentiment among the largest group of constituents of the university community, its alumni.

James L. Brunnemer

He will seek advice from a few key board members. After testing the water, he'll dive in first. Hmmm.

I didn't say anything further about our meeting to anyone. When alumni would call about the issue I would simply murmur something about it "being under advisement of the Board," and change the subject.

Fast forward to the annual Alumni Awards banquet that May. My office planned every detail of this event, with the exception of the easel that the president's office requested to be placed near the head table that evening.

When I came in for a final check just prior to opening the doors for the 400 alumni attending, I noted a white cloth covering a rectangular item, presumably a picture frame or some such, on the easel. When the crowd began to filter in, there was Angus and Bea Nicoson, returned from their Gene Sease-imposed and university-subsidized Florida vacation.

At the conclusion of his usual "state of the college" remarks to the alumni body that evening, which always enthralled his listeners, he asked Nick and Bea to join him at the easel. As Gene unveiled a portrait of the gymnasium with **ANGUS NICOSON HALL** printed on the brickwork, I'll never forget part of one sentence of his beautifully crafted presentation: "It is only fitting that the scene of so many of Nick's triumphs should be named in his honor," Gene praised. "So *I* have proposed to the Board of Trustees—and *they* agreed—that the gymnasium be named Nicoson Hall!"

The masterful handling of this most delicate situation demonstrated Gene's insight into the desire of his constituents, his flexibility in applying principle (and where to make an exception), and the ability to secure credit for an action deemed desirable. While he initially appeared to oppose the action in order to establish and emphasize the principle of capital funding, and to control the decision-making process, Dr. Sease ultimately positioned himself to accomplish his agenda as a leader, while taking full credit for the decision.

President Sease always guarded faithfully the integrity of the university. At the time he became president, the Hoosier College Conference of Indiana Central, Franklin, Earlham, Hanover, Anderson, Taylor, and Manchester was considered to be inferior to that of the Indiana Collegiate Conference, which included Butler, DePauw, Wabash, Valparaiso, St. Joseph's, and Evansville. The image of the general public was that not only were athletics of lesser quality in the HCC as compared to the ICC, but academics were inferior, as well. When Dr. Sease and then- director of athletics Angus Nicoson explored the possibility of membership in the Indiana Collegiate Conference in the early 1970s, Gene was not about to accept entrance into that association as anything but a full and respected partner with the other institutions. The implications of aligning with the "more elite" independent schools in the ICC went far beyond the athletic field.

As with all skillful politicians, Dr. Sease tried to anticipate every eventuality to guard against any uncomfortable development. Gene always did his lobbying in advance of key political questions regarding the university. Of Lyndon Johnson, in Robert Caro's *Master of the Senate*, Hubert Humphrey, then a freshman senator from Minnesota, observed: "Some of the lessons that Johnson taught about politics were pragmatic, basic. 'Johnson said the first lesson of politics is to be able to count,' Humphrey would recall. 'I have never forgotten that.'"

Distinction Without Pretension

Gene Sease knew how to count.

Prior to the vote of the college presidents of each of the Indiana Collegiate Conference schools to consider Indiana Central for admission, President Sease did the unprecedented by meeting with each one of those chief executives about the issue. Unanimity among the other presidents in accepting Indiana Central as one of their conference brethren was important to the university. Anything less than one hundred percent concurrence among his college presidential peers and Dr. Sease would have withdrawn our petition. In what would typify his approach to practical politics, Gene knew at the time the vote was taken what it would be.

The vote was 6-0, in favor.

He wouldn't have allowed us to accept entry into the conference any other way.

Campus Queen Jena (Jones) Adrianson '74 adorns President Sease's borrowed toy, a model of the 1973 Indy 500 Pace Car. A.J. Foyt, later perched where Queen Jones sits, was not as pleasant a companion for his chauffeur, Dr. Sease.

Occasionally, his self-confidence would cross the line into hubris. Examples of that exaggerated pride and self-confidence more often than not was more humorous than harmful.

Once, around race time in May, a colleague mentioned in Gene's presence the name of A. J. Foyt, the legendary Indy 500 driver. It was apparent by his reaction that President Sease was not, like legions of others, a fan of the popular but volatile Indy racer.

Here's the reason why.

They had met once. Up close and personal.

Each was a creative genius in his respective field. One difference, however, was the size of the stage upon which each acted. Gene's domain as president of a fine private university, as a nationally recognized United Methodist educator, and member of more than thirty boards of directors of Indianapolis businesses and civic organizations, including the chairmanship of the Indianapolis Progress Committee, was not an insignificant milieu.

James L. Brunnemer

The university's fifth president commanded much respect and had a great deal of influence in the city of Indianapolis and nationally in higher education.

A. J.'s playground, and source of great fame and accolades, was international in scope. A four-time winner of the Indy 500, he was acknowledged worldwide as one of auto racing's greatest figures.

As one of the committee that planned and orchestrated the 500 Festival, Gene was entitled to use one of the official pace cars for that year's race, a brand-new convertible. Tooling around in this rather expensive loaned toy, Gene was as giddy as a teenager sixteen years and one day old. One would see him chauffeuring various members of the university community in the luxury of his car, impressing secretaries, students, faculty, and donors. Gene loved special treatment, and he was one of only thirty-three Indianapolis denizens to be so privileged.

Symbolic of Foyt's and Sease's relative positions in the world of celebrity was their respective roles in the Indianapolis 500 Festival Parade, which was the culmination of pre-race festivities in Indianapolis during Memorial Day weekend. A prerogative, or duty, depending upon how one viewed it, for entitlement to the car was serving as a chauffeur during the parade for one of the thirty-three drivers who qualified for the race. In a random distribution, President Sease would share his vehicle with the often surly, mercurial, and always firm commander of those in his presence, Anthony Joseph Foyt.

Talk about two monumental egos assembled in a small space!

Prior to the parade, the racer and the president arrived to join the entourage. A. J. greeted Dr. Sease with little more than detached disdain. Anthony Joseph Foyt wasn't then, and never became afterward, enamored of formalities, political correctness, or even civility during race week. Certainly wasting a couple of hours riding in a car for an asinine parade with someone he didn't know and cared less about did not hold promise of improving Foyt's mood.

Gene endured the initial slight and the two joined the parade in the order of the driver's qualification. Things went on without incident throughout the event with A. J. accepting cordially the adulation of his thousands of race fans and admirers in the parade crowd of some 250,000. Millions on television watched this event as well. Gene performed his less-than-glamorous duty, steering the vehicle ably, not hitting any of the other cars, parade floats, or the Shriners' mini-motorcycles swirling around him. Gene had undoubtedly never played such an invisible role before such an enormous audience.

One can understand that Dr. Sease might have been entitled to feel a bit of resentment. After all, early on in his life he committed to service to church and community, rose from a modest background to earn his Ph.D., was presented several honorary degrees from colleges and universities, and was a successful university president and model citizen. To have to defer to a high school dropout whose boorish behavior included occasionally venting his anger over a lost race by destroying groves of trees with a bulldozer on his Texas ranch would seem, to my mind, a bit of a challenge for President Sease.

One can only speculate as to his comfort level. Foyt had to have made the duty more unpalatable with his abrasive personality and lack of acknowledgment of the importance of the city mover-and-shaker behind the wheel.

It wasn't until the parade ended at the historic "brickyard" that Gene came to conclude he really didn't like Mr. Foyt.

Distinction Without Pretension

As each of the other thirty-two chauffeurs, celebrities, and lions of the Indianapolis community approached the pits, they stopped their automobiles at the entrance to fabled Gasoline Alley. From there the race car drivers would hop off their perch at the back of the convertible, thank their host chauffeur graciously, and then walk the hundred yards or so back to their assigned garage.

When Gene dutifully stopped at the appointed spot, A. J. indicated *he* would be conveyed back to his garage. When Gene diplomatically suggested to Mr. Foyt that he was to depart the car at this locality, A.J. replied, gruffly, "Back to my garage, *driver!*"

Dr. Sease? *Driver?*

That is why one doesn't speak fondly of A. J. Foyt, racer *par excellence*, in the presence of Gene Sease.

Humor, at the expense of the president, was not common. We underlings rarely made sport of Dr. Sease (in his presence, anyway). So it was especially delicious once during Homecoming festivities that his eldest son, David, portrayed his father in a comedy skit. Dave brought the house down and swept the prize for his class with a caricature of the president. The Sease mannerisms were unmistakable. It was a hoot. And Dave is still in the will, as far as I know.

During his term at the university Gene's predilection for ice cream at any hour of the day or night added to his stocky physique. Like the president, I was conscious of my weight, so we once compared our strategies for maintaining at least a manageable hold on the waistline.

I bemoaned the constant challenge of finding time for exercise and the difficulty in resisting all the calorie-laden temptations at mealtime.

Surprisingly, Dr. Sease seemed at peace with his mild rotundity. He told of a series of doctors who, when he weighed in during his annual physical exam, carped at him to lose ten, twenty, even thirty pounds.

"After about the eighth different physician scolded me about my weight, I began to consider each one and realized they had a single common denominator: All were slight of build, jogger types, weighing 150 to 160 pounds.

"So next time I went to get a physical I chose a fat doctor, a huge man, at least fifty pounds over his recommended weight. In all the times I visited him, he never once mentioned my need for a diet!"

Of course, Gene could be victimized by those innocents who didn't or couldn't fathom his commanding stature. Early in my career as alumni director, Gene and Joanne had joined my wife, Luella, and our sons, Beau and Kyle, for a gathering of alumni at the church parish home of Herman and Mary Emmert in Columbus, Ohio. The Seases flew from Indianapolis to attend the event and then planned to ride back with the Brunnemers to the university.

All went well until we prepared to leave. Kyle, who was two at the time, and Beau, 4, were playing in the den while the adults were listening to President Sease expound on the virtues of their alma mater in the living room. After all the guests had departed, we were making our expressions of gratitude to the Emmerts and preparing for our exit when Kyle refused to give up a toy he had latched onto. All usual forms of persuasion made no difference. The lad was determined to take this plaything home with him. Then, as I directed the boy to give up the prize, the parents' worst nightmare occurred: a kicking, screaming, rolling-on-the-hosts'-floor fit of temper. Lu and I were mortified, the Emmerts sympathetic, the Seases bemused and compassionate.

I finally wrested the gewgaw from the two-year-old's uncommonly strong grip, then it was in the car and onto Interstate 70 for the three-hour trip back to Indy. Gene sat in front on the passenger side, Lu and Joanne in the back seat with Kyle nestled into his mother's arms. Beau found a place to lie down on the floor of the university station wagon.

As I drove along, Gene, as was his wont, filled the silent night with stories of all kinds. He was chattering pretty much non-stop until, about Richmond, Indiana, I noted in the rear view mirror a small head pop up. It was Beau. He unceremoniously interrupted whatever comment Gene was in the middle of with "Dr. Sease, would you *be quiet!* I'm tryin' to get some shut-eye!"

Lu gasped.

Gene gaped.

Joanne giggled.

"Oh, God!" (me, to myself).

It's all hazy now, but I think I swerved off the interstate and plowed through a cornfield before I regained control of the vehicle and my emotional equilibrium. Unabashed, Beau slipped back onto the floor to renew his "shut-eye." I began to consider where I would be working next week.

That incident has been the source of much laughter through the years, but at 11 p.m. on that dark night it wasn't all that funny to me.

Dr. Sease had a bent for the flamboyant. He lit up any space with his presence. He thrived in social situations, blessed with an incredible recall of folks' names, their relatives down to the third cousins, the names of their pets, as well, and what their favorite color was. Gene was always the center of attention. That's the way he wanted it. During my corresponding years of employment at Indiana Central with those of Gene, the only time I ever saw him cede a room was to Senator Lugar.

Asked about the university budget, Gene didn't respond with boring figures. He would be apt to reply, "When I get out of bed each morning and my feet hit the floor, I know I must raise $5,000 before the day ends."

Alumni actually looked forward to normally routine speeches by Dr. Sease. His seamless "state of the college" addresses inevitably were delivered with enthusiasm and drama. There was an electrically charged aura emanating from somewhere within his core.

Having studied carefully the history of Indiana Central, Gene knew that the school's chartered name had never been legally changed. In 1921, because Indiana Central *University* had no separate "schools," only "departments," the Indiana State Board of Education reclassified it as a college rather than a university. In 1975, with the introduction of five "schools" within the college, Dr. Sease realized that the institution could now be categorized as a university. He wasted no time in recommending to the trustees that the

Distinction Without Pretension

institution's original name be restored. Thus, Indiana Central College became Indiana Central University.

However, no announcement Dr. Sease was to make in his nineteen years as president held more drama than the *second time* he changed the name of the university. Always seeking novel ways of promoting the institution, Dr. Sease coveted the idea of the school sharing the name of its home city. It rankled that many people would call the switchboard asking for Central Business College, an unaccredited school for clerical training, or would confuse our private liberal arts college with IUPUI, the mega-university in downtown Indy.

It was believed that "University of Indianapolis" was to be held for the day when Indiana University/Purdue University at Indianapolis would be subsumed under that signature. Legislators, such as State Senator Larry Borst, held tightly to that dream for the city, one that has not been fulfilled. Only Dr. Sease, his administrative council, and a handful of trustees know the intimate details, but the wily president seized an opportunity to get the name for our college. Holding it secretly for nearly an entire year, Dr. Sease announced at the 1986 commencement exercises that the students were graduating from the *University of Indianapolis*. Each was presented with his U of I diploma, signed by President Sease and the chairman of the board of trustees.

However, it would be in relation to the name change that Gene's enthusiasm for public relations gimmickry came back to haunt him. When Krannert Memorial Library was built in 1977, the initials of Indiana Central University were embedded into the brickwork of the new structure at the direction of the president. While you need to look closely to see them today, the letters "ICU" are visible on the north side of the east wall of the library, which is, of course, on the campus of the University of Indianapolis.

I once suggested to Dr. Sease that his greatest legacy would be the coup of renaming the university for the vibrant city in which it resided. He disagreed, saying his most significant contribution to the school was establishing the relationship in Cyprus and Greece that ultimately found its apex in the accreditation of the University of Indianapolis in Nicosia and Athens, respectively. The diversity of the students that this alliance brought to the campus community, the additional financial strength, and the stature of the international connection have, in his view, given the University of Indianapolis a niche unique among Indiana colleges and universities.

In the mid-eighties, Gene Sease chose to end his term as president after almost two decades of consummate and productive leadership. Ultimately, it would be an unfavorable North Central Association report that led members of the board of trustees to question Gene on some of the issues the visitation team raised. Fed in part by a few disgruntled faculty who resented President Sease's autocratic style, trustees were hearing increasingly unfavorable accounts of Gene's management. Another major point brought out in the visitation team's deliberations was the lack of diversity of the administrative team. Also there was concern that the $25-million capital fundraising campaign was stalled, at just over four million dollars committed. For the first time in his presidency, his authority to lead was challenged, and Dr. Sease was no longer invincible.

Only Dr. Sease knows why he chose to retire. But his decision to do so came to the trustees with short notice. He subsequently took his brilliance to the world of commerce,

James L. Brunnemer

having already purchased the public relations firm formerly owned by Howdy Wilcox, where he had installed son David and Lou Gerig to run the business. He would become chairman of the firm following his departure from the U of I.

The initial setback in what was to become a shared enmity with his successor, Ben Lantz, was the rejection of Gene's favored candidate to succeed him. Perhaps sensing faculty displeasure that Gene was picking his own successor, the trustees were not impressed with Dr. Sease's choice. The job was offered, instead, to Dr. Lantz. This final slight of Gene's influence alienated him. For some time afterward Dr. Sease found excuses not to attend functions at the University, despite the fact that the trustees bestowed the title of chancellor upon him.

Neither Sease nor Lantz was comfortable with the relationship. Ordinarily, a retiring president steps out of the limelight or moves to another area. Gene not only stayed in Indianapolis, but his profile remained high as he established his firm as one of the leading public relations organizations in Indiana. On those occasions when Gene and Ben did appear at a common event, the coolness in their respective demeanors was palpable. A Ben Lantz peace offering—to name one of two undesignated dormitories in his honor—was rebuffed by Dr. Sease. It took a masterstroke by Jerry Israel ten years later to promote the legacy of each in ways both Lantz and Sease found satisfying, while at the same time resolving Gene's need for closure at the university.

For nineteen years, the only man to serve as president of Indiana Central College, then Indiana Central University, and finally the University of Indianapolis, guided the institution indefatigably and with singular skill. Under his salient leadership, ICC/ICU/U of I became a legitimate partner with the city of Indianapolis.

His indelible mark will forever be upon the university.

CHAPTER XXVIII

BEN 'N JERRY

Ain't no bronc never been rode.
Ain't no cowboy never been throwed.
Anonymous

In August 1988, G. Benjamin Lantz, Jr., was inaugurated as the sixth president of the University of Indianapolis.

Ben was an able chief executive but a man of many contradictions. For those affiliated with the University of Indianapolis who initially concluded that Dr. Lantz would have a less authoritarian style than Dr. Sease, a surprise was in store. Born and reared in the mountains of West Virginia, Ben had a folksy veneer that masked an instinct for control equal to or even surpassing that of Dr. Sease.

Ben had a gift for identifying and focusing upon those areas within the institution that were crucial for success at the university. To his credit, and to the institution's everlasting benefit, Ben had an innate entrepreneurial flair and used the available assets of the university deftly.

For example, because U of I's endowment was deficient, annual operating expenses were more dependent upon student tuition than were most of our peer institutions. Wisely, Ben poured money into the admissions and financial aid operations. First Dave Huffman and later Mark Weigand orchestrated the process through which students were recruited and enrolled at the university. Both men were provided with the resources needed to get the job done. Ben was attentive to results, making almost daily phone calls seeking current admissions data. As long as classrooms continued to be full, Ben knew the bills could be paid, and more.

And this approach paid off. The record will show that startling increases in student enrollment occurred during the years of Ben's reign. By forecasting modest gains or even decreases in enrollment to the trustees when establishing annual budgets, surpluses in tuition would result when significant numbers of students beyond those predicted showed up in the fall. When Dr. Lantz proposed a budget that almost assuredly would have a healthy balance at year's end, trustee Jim Magee '74, now deceased, jovially referred to Ben, in the presence of the chief executive, as the "Great Sandbagger."

In contrast to the archconservative fiscal policies of the past (Leo Miller's "pay as you go" management of the school's resources) Ben introduced an "invest to grow" approach, adroitly using excess tuition to improve the physical aspects of the campus. He added debt, anathema to previous administrations, by refinancing current mortgages, then borrowed more millions at very favorable interest rates.

It had been the traditional financial practice to move fund balances at the close of the fiscal year to the plant fund. Repairs and replacements of roofs and parking lots and minor improvements to the grounds would be accomplished with those funds. Ben was able to finance spectacular physical changes to the campus by using balances created by "surprising" increases in student enrollment. Excitement would build among faculty, staff, students, and alumni as major renovations of existing buildings occurred or construction of impressive new structures rose on the campus landscape.

It didn't matter that they were not funded through traditional capital fund raising campaigns. And unlike Gene Sease, who insisted on including endowments for ongoing maintenance of new buildings as part of his fund drives, Ben just wanted to see the finished project and worry about how the added operational costs would affect the annual budget later. This drove financial chief Ken Hottell to distraction, of course.

President Lantz controlled the agenda of the university. When an issue arose that was deemed of critical interest to the president, all other items on deck were swept aside. Whatever the business was at that time, Ben "needed it yesterday." This caused subordinates to respond frantically to that quandary while turning away from their own programs. Ben's "crisis management" style wore people out. Privately, he once instructed me "if you demand one-hundred percent out of your people, you'll get eighty percent production. Ask for one-hundred-twenty percent and you'll get ninety. It's human nature." His insensitive approach overlooked the wake of resentment and the emotional toll taken on his employees.

While he could be boldly resolute, President Lantz was frequently slow to arrive at decisions on issues not crucial to him. Action items deemed significant to administrative staff* often would lie on his desk for days, weeks, or months, tying the hands of each of us. Ben revealed to me once that if a leader has the patience to "just wait problems out, most will prove to be far less important than others think, and will go quietly away." That isn't a fatuous notion, but it was certainly inconvenient for those of us charged with succeeding in our various responsibilities within the university. As Affiliated Computer Services CEO Jeff Rich suggests, "Purely autocratic leaders ultimately become bottlenecks because people learn that the best survival skill is to ask the boss first before making a decision. People learn to wait for directives from the boss, or worse, they become terrified about making the wrong decision. In any case, creativity is discouraged, and the most talented people eventually leave."

The first administrative council retreat that I attended as vice president was held in Louisville, Kentucky, in 1989. We frustrated aides raised the subject of Ben's tendency to delay decisions affecting our various areas. At that session, Dr. Lantz left no doubt as to who would adapt to whom: "Gentlemen," he stated forthrightly, "I will determine how and when decisions will be made here. I won't change my style, so you'd best get used to it."

That closed any and all debate about how consultative the relationship between the president and his chief lieutenants would be and was in stark contrast to an observation made about leadership by James T. Morris, onetime president of Lilly and now executive director of the United Nation's World Food Program:

> *The term "director," "dean," and "vice president" are used interchangeably to designate those who were members of the president's management team. Likewise, "cabinet" and "administrative council" connote that group of individuals who reported directly to the president.*

> *[T]he most important thing I learned in college at Indiana University is how important it is for a leader to create a consensus for a decision, so that ultimately the team can feel like they decided the issue instead of its being dictated by one person.*

Since open discussion of issues involving the school often found his vice presidents on the opposite side of the president, Ben chose to eliminate monthly administrative council meetings altogether. He monitored the effect of our advice by meeting with us, separately, when a situation demanded it, ensuring his will would always prevail.

Ben's actions in delicate matters, such as dealing with protected minorities, could be wise and judicious. When a group of African-American students approached him requesting they be allowed to establish a Black Student Association, Ben handled what could have been an explosive issue with aplomb. He agreed forthrightly to the formation of such an organization on campus, with the condition that any student—of any race or nationality—would be welcomed into membership. Likewise, when PRIDE (an organization founded by gay students on campus) was established, Ben included the same caveat: that all students, regardless of sexual orientation, be allowed to join.

While clearly understanding the need to prepare, Ben nonetheless resisted planning and mistrusted organization. Perhaps he felt constrained by a structured process where facts would be gathered and staff views would be solicited. Certainly it was my impression that Dr. Lantz believed over-analysis and too much reliance upon forethought might interfere with the ingenuity of creative thought, not to mention his ability to govern the affairs of his organization.

His tendency to exclude advice from his administrative staff was exposed, and his political acumen was tested and found wanting, during a most public event some of us later referred to as the "Great Hanna Avenue Debacle."

When ICC was founded in 1902, Hanna Avenue was a mere dirt road at the end of the interurban line. Barely wide enough for two lanes originally, the crude roadway later graduated to gravel, then to pavement. In its early years, miles of farmland separated the staid ICC campus and the "den of iniquity," the city of Indianapolis. This suited President Good and the faculty just fine.

In 1945, new president Esch foresaw prospects to increase the visibility and accessibility of the college, if only the road could be widened. If the number of cars passing by proliferated, carrying potential students, it could create a boon for the college. For more than twenty years he lobbied vainly for a four-lane throughway.

Finally, in 1968, against the wishes of the neighborhood, Dr. Esch succeeded in convincing the city government to widen the street. As a result, Hanna Avenue became a major artery for vehicular traffic passing east and west between US 31 and Keystone Avenue.

But an upgraded Hanna proved to be a double-edged sword. While greater visibility for the college was certainly a bonus as traffic grew exponentially over the years, the risk to students traversing four lanes on foot became a constant concern. As of this writing there have been no recorded pedestrian deaths at the University of Indianapolis, but frequently, students and faculty have been struck and cars have collided to avoid persons crossing Hanna Avenue.

Over the years all types of solutions were studied to resolve the problem of having a major thoroughfare through the heart of campus. No recommendation had satisfied all those who would be affected. But in 1996, under Dr. Lantz, the university was to attempt its most aggressive move to forever change Hanna and, thus, its south side neighborhood. Lantz was determined to be the president who would achieve this coup. Ben would have the satisfaction that *he,* only, of all the presidents before him, would resolve this perennial problem.

The public posture articulated by President Lantz was the noble cause of protecting the university's young people ("It's just a matter of time until a student is killed," warned Lantz). But equal to concern for student safety was Ben Lantz's desire to improve the appearance of the university and to eliminate the bifurcated campus. If the stretch of road could be made more attractive and the two parts of the school grounds were unified, it would be a most impressive accomplishment.

Combining efforts, the U of I and the city of Indianapolis commissioned studies to see what might be done. City engineers and the Odle, McGuire and Shook architectural firm explored various options, presenting their studies to the university board of trustees and administration. The neighborhood association was alerted, but not consulted, about the possibility of closing or rerouting Hanna Avenue.

One alternative that the neighborhood would seem to tolerate was a pedestrian structure over the street, the so-called "gerbil tube." Anyone who knew students, though, understood young adults wouldn't use such an inconvenient passageway. Students would simply cross the street as they always had, unless, of course, a Berlin-like wall to impede them was built along the entire length of Hanna between Shelby and State streets. Not likely.

A pedestrian tunnel *under* the street was briefly considered. The water table and exorbitant cost made this solution impracticable.

A strategy was adopted to first float a trial balloon to *completely close* Hanna. The thought was that after placing this idea on the table, if the neighborhood objected, the city and the university could compromise and achieve a more realistic goal of either rerouting Hanna or narrowing the street to one lane each way, with a turning lane in the middle. Student safety would be enhanced, not to mention a much more attractive access to and passage through the campus would be accomplished.

The proposal entailed rerouting Hanna through neighborhoods to the north (via National Avenue) or south by way of Windermire Street. The condemnation and purchase of a great deal of real estate adjacent to the street would be required because of turning ratios necessitated by law. This solution would evoke the most intense fury from the neighbors.

On the night that the required public hearing on the status of Hanna Avenue was held in the Ruth Lilly Performance Hall of the Christel DeHaan Fine Arts Center, it appeared as if every household member in the neighborhood surrounding the university was represented in the crowd that attended. There was not a seat without a butt in it and

Distinction Without Pretension

the walls were lined two deep with standing neighbors. And they were not in a joyous mood. The hostility of the locals was conspicuous in the expressions on their faces. Scowls abounded.

In contrast, we buttoned-up university administrators sat dispersed along the sides with serious but thoughtful expressions. A number of U of I students sat throughout the audience, contrasting noticeably with the blue-collar element of the crowd.

President Lantz sat on stage with the engineers and transportation experts, prepared to respond to questions. He would never have guessed how warm that seat would get before the night was over.

City representatives read a document recommending closure of Hanna, rerouting it north of the campus along National Avenue. A chorus of boos impeded the reading of the proclamation. From that high note the meeting went downhill.

Dr. Lantz began by reciting data about the thousands of vehicles traveling through the campus and the frequency of vehicle-to-vehicle and vehicle-to-people accidents. He delivered a solemn, heart-tugging discourse about the peril young university students constantly faced in crossing through the hordes of speeding vehicles on Hanna. This provoked an interruption from an incredulous young mother in the audience who shouted sarcastically, "So, instead of twenty-year old college students who ought to be able to cross a street of traffic, you'd endanger instead my five-year old?"

As Ben sputtered in an attempt to respond to that rejoinder, people began to line up at the two standing microphones that had been placed in the aisles of the Ruth Lilly Performance Hall. Each person was limited to five minutes of comments in order to accommodate all those present who desired to speak.

The city bureaucrats and Lantz became the targets of the most hostile personal invective. One by one, bellicose citizens paraded to microphones to castigate the university and the city.

Lantz hardly disguised his rage. He could control everything inside the college but found he was helpless against people who, though less formally educated, were determined not to be hoodwinked. They saw through the snobbery and elitist attitude they perceived in the president and the rest of us.

Some relief from the tension in the house came from periodic diversions provided by speechifying brethren. Those of us affiliated with the college savored one particular three hundred seconds of pomposity by a young man who presumed he was articulate, but wasn't; thought he had wisdom, but didn't; and, looking down his nose at the university, pronounced himself to be, essentially, wiser than any other individual in the hall. We couldn't believe our good fortune when the obnoxious lout announced loudly and proudly that he was a Butler grad.

But the most ludicrous scene of the evening, and perhaps *ever* in the hallowed hall, came when the temperature of the debate had reached white-hot magnitude. Someone had just called Lantz an unflattering name. Ben was obviously vexed, at times allowing his temper to overcome his political sense, as he responded to audience comments pettily and impetuously. It was at this moment that my eyes fell upon an intriguing local waiting in line to speak. He had the blissful look of one who is clueless. His demeanor was almost friendly, in contrast to the snarling neighbors ahead of and behind him in the queue leading to the mike.

James L. Brunnemer

Rosy-cheeked with a bulbous red nose, he wore a soiled, tattered windbreaker opened to reveal a tee shirt that lacked the fabric to cover his beer keg paunch. Stretched to its limit, the shirt couldn't hide the flesh leaking out over his belt. His pants were about four inches above the style of the day, which meant that the tops of his unpolished loafers and the white socks inside those shoes were on display.

When his turn came, he began to speak, at first a bit sheepishly, then boldly as the crowd reacted favorably to his concern. I don't have the transcript, but his remarks went something like this:

"Prez'dent Lands, ah'll tell ya' whut ah doan lak. 't's awl them homeruin bawls landon in mah yard."

Members of the assembly, who had been coiled like so many angry cobras ready to strike at any misstep by representatives of the university or the city, visibly relaxed. This was going to be *good*, and they didn't want to miss a word. They were pissed, but not so much that they couldn't enjoy this diversion from reality. The baggy pantsed orator continued:

"Ever tam yer skool haz a bazebawl game, they hit them bawls over the fince scarin' mah six kids, un havin' ar cats almoz plunked, let alone hittin' mah truck, which ain't runnin' but I don't need no more dents in it neither. An wun lak to kilt mah dog Bruno thuther day an mebbee you doan no ut but sum uv us is tard uv dodgin' them miss-eye'lls."

Suspecting, I believe, that he was perhaps being a bit too harsh in his assessment of a situation that wasn't entirely the president's fault, Beer Belly threw Ben a bone:

"Now Docker Lands, doan git me wrong, it ain't yer boys thass doin' it. Ther gud boys, yer team. It's them apponits that's hittin' 'em all in mah yard. (That had to make Ben feel better.) 'An sumthin' otta be dun 'bout it."

With a courteous nod to Docker Lands, and a satisfied smile across his plump face, Beer Belly turned, and with an over-the-shoulder, "An that's whut ah doan lak," retired to his seat.

He was one of their own, so the crowd politely applauded the effort.

Have you ever noticed how painful it is to stifle a full-out body-shaking laugh when you are in a place where you are supposed to adhere to appropriate decorum? I wasn't successful this time. I admit I was one who came unglued at the oratory of the innocent nincompoop.

The evening had to be a nightmare for the president of the University of Indianapolis. Ben was skewered because he stubbornly ignored the importance of applying the political finesse necessary to achieve his goal. Instead, he subjected himself to incredible personal abuse and hostility, and the school to the sneering enmity of a neighborhood of mostly working-class, uneducated, but determined and organized resistance. A deft political touch and a dash of private lobbying of the appropriate groups affected might possibly have resulted in a change in Hanna to the university's benefit.

Ben was not naïve about political machinations, but as a U of I alumnus prominent in Indianapolis government noted about such hearings: "If you wait until the meeting before completing your political groundwork, you're way too late."

To cap it off, the meeting was attended by City Council member Phil Borst and his father, State Senator Larry Borst, a couple of unctuous but powerful politicians. At one point in the evening the elder Borst infuriated Ben, tapping his pointed index finger into Ben's tie, lecturing him with a patronizing, "I'm trying to be nice to you here, *president*." As with all effective provincial politicians, the Borsts gauged the crowd, remaining mum until they saw where the people stood. Then Phil made a smarmy, opportunistic, pseudo-passionate statement against the action, as if he favored that course all along.

My personal view is that Ben's characteristic disdain for detail and planning "done him in." Also, the thinly disguised rationale for the change—that it was for student safety rather than aesthetic improvement of the campus—didn't fool the neighborhood. They saw it for what it was: a cosmetic improvement that would not help the residents of surrounding environs appreciably but would enhance Ben Lantz's personal standing as a man who got things done.

The "little people" won that fight.

Given to lengthy episodes of philosophizing, Ben was mentally supple, adroit at defending any side of a debatable question. Often, to the chagrin of Dr. Youngblood, whose office was adjacent to the president's, Ben would drift in unannounced to spend literally hours exploring ideas, leaving Lynn's work forestalled until later.

Lantz was notorious for the length and tiresomeness of his speeches and reports. He was aware of his reputation, too. He seemed to revel in his renown for protracted oratory. Dr. Brooker once said of Lantz's tedious speech-making: "Ben can give a one-minute speech in three minutes, a three-minute speech in ten, and a ten-minute speech in half an hour. It's really quite remarkable."

As chairman of the board of trustees, the very business-like and time-economy-minded David Frick finally ordered Ben to write out his reports to the trustees, I suspect because of the rambling nature of Dr. Lantz's delivery.

President Lantz recognized the necessity of building a fund raising strategy and structure, where previously Dr. Sease *was* the fund raising program at Indiana Central. During his nineteen years as president, Sease had directors of development in, first, Lynn Youngblood, and later, Dan Nicoson, to conduct the annual fund, the giving societies, and an occasional deferred gift. But Gene personally handled any significant gifts being considered by donors to the university.

When Dr. Lantz invited me back to the university as dean for institutional advancement, I was keenly aware of what my top priority would be. The lethargic "Focus on the Future" campaign, initiated by former President Sease, would have to be ended, then restarted from scratch.

I recalled the day in 1986 when my good friend Lynn Youngblood phoned me at my office at Albion College. He told me about the university's gala announcement of "Focus" at the Indianapolis Convention Center that week and of the $25 million goal.

Having kicked off our own campaign just months before, I was elated for my alma mater.

"Great, Lynn!" I responded to his announcement, "It's time our college undertook a fund raising effort of that size and ambition."

Previously, the largest campaign goal that Indiana Central had successfully achieved was approximately seven million dollars. "Focus on the Future" was a significant step upward for the trustees, President Sease, and the university community.

The most crucial step of any campaign is the "quiet phase," or that period of time when lead and major gifts, usually totaling at least half of the ultimate goal, are secured. Announcing the campaign with much of the final goal already achieved gives the positive impetus needed for success.

Fully expecting that Dr. Sease and the campaign committee had their $12 to $15 million raised, I asked, "So, Lynn, how much do you have in the bag?"

"One million dollars," he replied.

Uh-oh. At Albion, we began our thirty-five-million-dollar campaign's public phase with an announcement that more than nineteen million had been committed in advance. When we left the party two hours later we had accepted checks and commitments from, among others, Stanley Kresge and the chairman of Tecumseh Engines, adding another three million dollars. I chuckled, thinking Lynn would regale me with a stunning gift they had received.

"No, you don't, you sly dog," I teased. "Dr. Sease has to have another ten million in his hip pocket."

"If he does, I'm not aware of it," Lynn replied. It was then I knew he was serious and that "Focus on the Future" had problems.

When I arrived on campus to assume my duties in April 1989, the $25-million campaign totaled $4.6 million in cash and pledges and was headed toward the morgue. We spent several months in study, with assistance from trustees and outside counsel, to determine what we already knew instinctively: We would end "Focus" and begin the requisite planning and preparation for a new major campaign.

In order to build a professional fundraising arm of the institution, Dr. Lantz was exceptionally cooperative in providing for the plan I had presented to him for bringing our organization up to standard. The first order of business was to put into place the personnel, resources, and technology that would be needed in the advancement office to sustain a robust campaign. We purchased demographic information and identified and began cultivating the prospects we would need to be successful. Basically we set out to reload before launching another drive.

However, when it came time for Ben to become fully invested in the process of fund raising, at least the traditional method that I had learned, our relationship frayed.

Ben and I had fundamental differences in our fund raising philosophies. This would become crystal clear during a serendipitous episode that took place in Ben's office one Saturday in 1992. I had come to my office that day to complete some work. Having done so, I called Ben about a small matter. He asked that I come over to his office for a chat. When I arrived it was apparent that Ben was in a philosophizing mood, so I knew my timeframe to return home would be altered.

He began to discuss fund raising in general and capital campaigns specifically. At that time we had identified more than thirty-five million dollars in projects on the university "wish list." It was his contention that what we needed to do was embark on a series of "mini-campaigns" to raise the money for the multitude of needs specified.

Having been involved intimately in two separate and successful major fund raising campaigns of more than $50 million at other universities similar to ours, I favored the traditional comprehensive campaign approach. Such an operation addresses not just capital (bricks and mortar) projects, but annual operating needs, endowment funds, and other special objectives, as well. Because University of Indianapolis alumni and friends had never been successfully challenged to meet a goal of such magnitude, I argued that an all-encompassing crusade, led by trustees, was what our institution needed to meet its ambitious goals. Data, which we had gathered both empirically and through professional consultants, indicated that a significant number of our alumni had matured financially. Additional purposes of any major capital campaign besides surpassing the goal—refining the case for support, raising the visibility of the institution, and widening the donor base for the future—were all important in establishing our advancement program. It seemed the major campaign would best fit our challenge.

But Ben strongly believed that we couldn't be successful in a traditional campaign. It was my feeling then, as now, that Ben didn't want to put himself into a situation where a favorable outcome could not be guaranteed. All too fresh was the residual fallout of the abandoned $25-million campaign launched by President Sease. Further, it is my view that Ben didn't want to commit to the personal energy, intensity, and effort that a major campaign demands of the chief executive.

For nearly three hours we debated this issue. Finally, I unilaterally declared that I would do whatever Ben suggested and assured him I would give my best effort to the mini-campaign strategy. While I couldn't abandon my fundamental belief that the traditional campaign was the superior approach, I pledged to carry forth his plan. However, it became apparent then that he was not seeking a declaration of obedience. He needed to hear me say *I agreed with his notion.* And I just refused to do that.

Now, one can die for a principle, and in a polemic with Ben Lantz, who as president *would* prevail, starvation could become a concern. Finally, I pleaded with Ben to let me go, whimpering, practically, that I had promised Luella I would do the laundry that day. Reluctantly, and with a few parting verbal jabs intended to get me to say he was right, he allowed me to slink out of his office. I didn't concede to his mini-campaign theory, however.

Dr. Lantz simply didn't relish the drudgery of the fund raising process. His distaste for what is a university president's chief responsibility—financial viability of the school, of which private fund raising was a crucial element—surprised me. He was as persuasive one-on-one with a donor as any individual I had observed in my thirty years in the profession. Ben could become misty-eyed and his voice would falter as he described a need for the university. He could articulate a case with passion, he could paint pictures with words so inspiring as to be almost irresistible to potential donors. He just wouldn't do it often enough.

After colliding with Ben's reluctance to become more involved in donor prospect visits and solicitations, and engaging with potential donors that I had spent much time and effort cultivating for his benefit, I decided to call my counterpart at his former institution. My respected colleague Ernie Sheetz had been Lantz's vice president for advancement at Mount Union College. As I attempted diplomatically to describe my difficulty with Dr. Lantz, Ernie interrupted by asking, "Is Ben traveling a lot?"

As a matter of fact, part of Ben's legacy as president at the U of I is the extensive travel he and Mary Sue undertook. Always, he would pronounce that he was "looking for opportunities for new educational alliances" to explain his many and often prolonged absences from campus.

Certainly, legitimate trips to our programs in Cyprus and Greece were in order. And Ben was proud of the relationship established, with the assistance of Professor Phyllis Lan Lin, with Tunghai University in Taiwan, which he visited on more than one occasion. But it seemed a stretch when he returned from six weeks away on a university-financed tour of Africa and India extolling the vast, untapped potential of those countries for educational alliances with the U of I. Ditto for the potential major in oceanography he suggested after a scuba-diving excursion with a trustee in the Caribbean.

There were lesser travels to all points of the compass in the United States, often in his capacity as an evaluator of other institutions for the North Central accreditation association.

"Yes, Ernie," I answered honestly, "Ben is gone quite a bit. But that's his business. How do I get him to make calls on donors?"

Sheetz, who seemed genuinely fond of Ben, confided in me his strategy of "tricking" Ben into prospect visits, creating various ruses to get his president in the presence of prospective donors. I never proved to be as artful as Ernie apparently was in getting Dr. Lantz more involved in fund raising.

Those of us who love the university owe Ben Lantz a great debt for his insistence on a world-class performance hall within what would become the Christel DeHaan Fine Arts Center. Ms. DeHaan had given the naming gift for what was originally planned to be a center costing about seven million. To add a performance hall within the center of the quality Ben envisioned would require an additional three million dollars. Because of Ben's stubborn determination, the DeHaan Center has one of the state's aesthetically and acoustically superior and intimate venues for concert music.

We secured an appointment to discuss our need for funding a performance hall with John Kitchen, at that time philanthropist Ruth Lilly's personal counsel for her business affairs. Mr. Kitchen indicated Mrs. Lilly would provide a gift of one and one-half million dollars toward our building project, or about half of what we needed. Ben pleaded with Mr. Kitchen to double the gift, but the wily attorney was resolute in his refusal.

It was at this point that Ben and I made a wager that he would later take great glee in recalling. I bet Ben that a million and a half was all we would get from Ruth Lilly and that we should move on to other prospects. He insisted that we wait Kitchen out. For twenty-two months, as we cooled our heels in hopes of receiving a second one and a half million, Ben did virtually nothing in terms of cultivation and solicitation of major prospects. Further, he would not allow me to undertake any serious solicitation, either. He did not want to begin another major project (of which there were several on the horizon) until we had the DeHaan Center, with the performance hall, completed. Sure enough, after nearly two giving cycles by the Ruth Lilly Foundation had passed, Ben was notified that we would receive a second gift of $1.5 million to name the Ruth Lilly Performance Hall within the DeHaan Center. He framed a dollar bill I paid him regarding our wager on the $3-million gift and placed it on his credenza. How much we might have raised during that lost two-year interim will never be known.

Ben was the beneficiary of several serendipitous events (some might even say "providential") that were part of his success. With the passing of Pearl Smith in 1995, we were notified of and subsequently received the largest bequest, at four million, in the

Distinction Without Pretension

school's history. Dr. Esch had solicited that estate gift of Pat and Pearl Smith. President Sease maintained contact with Mrs. Smith up to the time of her death, officiating, I believe, at her funeral. On my occasional visits with Pearl in the retirement community at which she lived, she was always gracious and implied in our conversations that she and her late husband had "taken care of the university." I'm quite certain Ben never met her, but the officer on watch gets the credit. Thus, the parking lot that covered most of the six acres in the middle of the U of I campus was turned into a magnificent "water garden" and green space. Smith Mall was just one of many campus changes that would mark a truly astounding decade of progress at the University of Indianapolis under President G. Benjamin Lantz. In retrospect, it perhaps matters less *how* than *that* Ben Lantz achieved what he did. Always, there is more than one means to an end.

When Jerry Israel instituted planning for a major capital campaign within a year of his becoming president of the university, I confess to feeling a sense of vindication. In October of 2002, U of I announced a $50-million comprehensive campaign—*"Scholars. Partners. Friends.* The Campaign for UINDY." When President Israel and campaign chairman Norm Terry announced to the trustees in April 2003 that the goal had been met and extended to $65 million, I was personally gratified and very proud of the constituents who made it successful. My dream for the university had come true a decade later—except I wasn't in it.

It was with a mixture of elation and dread that Ben learned that business tycoon and philanthropist Christel DeHaan had accepted his invitation to chair the University of Indianapolis board of trustees. He was familiar with Christel's very personal management style and her utter belief in the principles of management by objective. After Ms. DeHaan had been elected chair of the board in 1997, a frustrated Ben revealed to me that Christel had directed him to provide her with a written set of his goals and objectives for the coming year. At first he had thought that she was simply sending a message that she intended to be involved as the chair. Later, when she gave him a deadline to have those objectives fleshed out, he realized she was serious. He never did complete the task. He retired first, surprising most of the trustees with his announcement at the spring meeting of the board in April 1998.

It is now that I need to explain a remark that has been attributed to me and that has become a mini-legend in many conversations among school personnel since Ms. DeHaan joined the board of trustees.

As we worked feverishly behind the scenes to prepare the institution and its constituents for a major fund raising venture in the early nineties, we had remarkable success in attracting noted leaders from Indianapolis businesses and corporations and from alumni of the university who were now making their own marks in high finance. We identified, recommended, and persuaded to join our effort a number of the trustees who have since played significant roles in the progress of the University of Indianapolis over the past decade and a half.

In the fall of 1992, there were several individuals we had especially coveted for our board who accepted invitations to serve. Among these were David Frick, Michael Maurer, Jim Cornelius, and Ms. DeHaan. These were the kind of folks with money and influence

James L. Brunnemer

we would need to lead the university to greater heights. One afternoon at about 5:30 p.m., Dr. Lantz, Don Tanselle, Lynn Youngblood, and I were in the president's office. Maurer had just accepted, by telephone, Ben's invitation to serve on the board, and we were all elated at the extraordinary success we had enjoyed in attracting some of Indianapolis's finest to our board. It was at that time I turned to the president and said: "Now that you've saddled this horse, I can't wait to see you ride it."

The tongue-in-cheek observation was in regard to the collection of trustees, not just Ms. DeHaan. But I understand it *has* been a source of some mirth from time to time, as the board chair occasionally asserts herself in university affairs.

One could argue that more progress, certainly to the physical campus, if not in all areas combined, occurred at the University of Indianapolis under Ben Lantz than had during the terms of his five predecessors. I'll leave it to posterity, and to others wiser than me, to assess how successful Ben truly was during his ten-year administration.

Jerry Israel had more than a passing familiarity with the U of I when he applied to succeed Ben Lantz as president. He and Ben had become acquainted as members of the United Methodist Colleges presidents association. Aware that Dr. Israel was seeking another presidential post, Ben arranged for Jerry to be a member of the North Central Association assessment team a year before Ben's retirement announcement. During his visit Dr. Israel had a most favorable impression of the institution. Additionally, as president of Morningside College in Cedar Rapids, Iowa, Dr. Israel had met and become friends with revered Indiana Central graduate and former dean Dr. Robert McBride, who only recently had retired as the president of Simpson College in Indianola, Iowa. Dr. McBride gave a strong recommendation on behalf of Dr. Israel when asked.

Surviving a rigorous selection process, Dr. Israel emerged as the favored candidate to succeed Ben. After accepting the offer from the Board, Jerry brought his wife, Carol (a Dr. Israel herself), to the U of I campus to begin his tenure as the seventh president of the university.

At a 55th birthday party for the author, The Drs. Israel--Carol (left) and President Jerry--hanging out with a member of a local motorcycle gang.

Distinction Without Pretension

My first impression of Jerry Israel was stamped as we rode together in a golf cart for an entire day at the annual Angus Nicoson Memorial Golf Outing in the summer of 1997. Although very affable and engaging, life as a Midwesterner had not completely expunged the inbred sardonic quips characteristic of his Bronx nativity. He could be enormously funny describing a catastrophic train wreck. It was also obvious he was a man of passion and terribly bright.

Aware of my disenchantment with his predecessor, Dr. Israel commented, sincerely, I believe, "I intend to be the best president you've ever worked for." As we traveled from tee to green, dispensing refreshments to the alumni golfers, I silently regretted that it was not Jerry to whom I reported when I returned to the university in 1989.

I was surprised at his casual use of profanity. Even though he employed the blue language only in private, it seemed rather unpresidential to me. Perhaps I was just jealous, because I thought part of what separated our presidents and me was that I could cuss, and they couldn't.

As I became more familiar with Jerry, I concluded that his occasional use of profanity was an intentional tactic, a means of breaking down barriers between him and those males over whom he had supervision, sort of an "I'm-really-one-of-the-guys" message. Almost purposefully, he seemed not too concerned with cultivating the presidential image; it seemed more important that he engage others on his team to a greater extent than previous presidents had. He insisted on being called "Jerry," rather than a more formal address.

Dr. Israel appears to be the most collegial of the leaders I have known. Management guru Peter Drucker insists that workers and subordinates are "not to be bossed, but conducted like an orchestra." Encouraging shared responsibility, Jerry seems to have the knack for persuading others to understand and adopt his positions on most matters. However, in his desire to be agreeable and accommodating, he sometimes wants everyone to win, which proves troublesome when two subordinates have widely divergent views on a given issue. Jerry might try to give them both blue ribbons, when there is room for only one first place.

I believe Jerry to be a very able communicator, but he has a short attention span for trivial issues. He is patient, but could and would become riled to the point of anger if he felt that was appropriate for the circumstance.

President Israel's deft handling of the sensitive issue of diversity has been especially impressive. At all levels of the university, from the trustees down, Jerry has embraced diversity and encouraged opportunity for all without scuttling the Judeo-Christian legacy of the institution.

His initial management of the delicate Sease-Lantz relationship was masterful. Bringing his two feuding predecessors together at his inaugural rite, Israel sealed his place with both through two genuine and most appropriate gestures. With stirring and heartfelt felicitations to each, President Israel concluded his inaugural address by announcing the renaming of the executive offices of Krannert Memorial Library as the Gene E. Sease Executive Wing, and the new initiative in Christian vocations as the G. Benjamin Lantz Center for Christian Vocations. With those magnanimous gestures to each of his predecessors, Jerry signaled that he desired to work with each of them, separately if not together.

Jerry is capable of great sensitivity, which he demonstrated with a kindness to me

James L. Brunnemer

at the time I decided to leave the college. With acute insight, he recognized I wasn't happy at the college after my skirmishes with Dr. Lantz. He offered to me an opportunity to serve as a special assistant to him. But, alas, Jerry had come too late for me. My decision to leave the college was firm.

Though I had spent more than twenty-one years in two separate terms at the university, I did not qualify under the rules for the school's "Bridge to Retirement" program. That required an employee to have been in the school's employ for at least fifteen consecutive years, which I had not been. Jerry was noble and most generous in acknowledging my service to the university by providing a modified version of the three-year bridge when I left at the end of September 2000. I will always be grateful to him for that kind gesture.

Dr. Israel has faced a challenge in defining the relationship between him and board chair Christel DeHaan. By the time Jerry came to his office, Ms. DeHaan had had time to learn more about the school and had begun to exercise her enormous passion on behalf of the university. Jerry walks a delicate line in administering the institution while risking alienating her. Ms. DeHaan, meanwhile, is—in her most astute way—learning that an institution of higher learning does not precisely fit the model with which she has been so successful in the corporate world. Christel DeHaan is the one person in the history of the Indiana Central/Uof I family with the philanthropic potency to position the university distinctly. Her intentions are both noble and genuine.

However, Dr. Israel's most severe challenge, and one that he seems to have handled deftly, is the unenviable task of replacing the men I call "the Big Four."

For nearly forty years, one or all of an extraordinarily loyal group of individuals, each of whom embodied the founders' mission and values, had been inordinately influential in the amazing success of Indiana Central/University of Indianapolis. It was Kenneth Partridge '58, Kendall Hottell '62, Lynn Youngblood '63, and David Huffman '64 who had a combined total of a hundred and forty-six years of service at the University of Indianapolis. Each was a walking receptacle of the institution's historical memory.

> *A university president never has all the talents required*
> *to deal with his many and varied duties ... Therefore, he*
> *must seek to have around him administrative aides of*
> *the highest competence, all of whom, if possible,*
> *complement his qualities.*
>
> Herman B Wells

Presidents Esch, Sease, Lantz, and Israel have justly received accolades for U of I's success over the years of their successive terms as president. But interestingly, each has had basically the same corps of associates at the vice president and senior-level administrative positions. Certainly rare, if not unprecedented in higher education, would be a core of top administrators serving throughout the greater part of the terms of four different presidents covering forty years. The Big Four adapted smoothly—for the most part—to the differing styles of the chief executives they served. Unwavering loyalty, dedication, and ability characterized these men, each a graduate of Indiana Central College.

Following his graduation, Ken Hottell accepted a position as a curriculum counselor at the only corporation at which he would ever be employed: Indiana Central.

Distinction Without Pretension

From the summer of 1962 through June of 2002, Ken would serve four different presidents as a curriculum counselor, instructor of business, assistant to the business manager, business manager, and vice president for business.

"ICC was the only place I ever worked," Hottell would say at his retirement dinner. Highly moral, and a true disciple of Leo Miller, Ken was driven by duty, treating his responsibilities at the university with a degree of seriousness most simply could not attain. As one in charge of the university purse strings, Ken often had to play the heavy, which was opposite of his truly kind and gentle nature. His dedication and great self-discipline led him to stick doggedly by what he thought to be right, but his inner doubts often made him feel guilty about his role. During those forty years, first through the efforts of Ken's boss, Leo Miller, and then in Leo's footsteps, Hottell compiled a remarkable fiscal record: From his first year at ICC through his retirement in 2002, the University of Indianapolis compiled forty consecutive balanced budgets. I would bet but a handful of institutions of higher learning could make the same claim.

Ken Partridge joined the faculty of Indiana Central in 1964 as associate director of industrial relations. He built the university's management program from the ground up over his thirty-six years with the school. Additionally, Partridge compiled a superb record as men's golf coach. Even after he retired from active faculty/staff status in 2000, he continued to recruit for and coach men's golf. Ken was a dependable anchor in all weathers for the university over his three score and six years as an instructor and senior administrator.

Lynn Youngblood would return to ICC in 1966 after a brief but successful high school mathematics teaching career, first as director of admissions. Subsequently, Lynn held positions as director of development, assistant to the president, and then vice president for academics and provost. A trusted advisor to four presidents, Lynn embodied the spirit of the college through his fidelity to its ideals. Following thirty-five years on the faculty and administration, Lynn retired in 2001.

Dave Huffman also taught and coached at the high school level before rejoining the university as assistant director of admissions in 1966. After he became director of admissions, then vice president for admissions, Dave was the chief architect of an enrollment program that was the envy of independent colleges in Indiana.

In 1997, President Ben Lantz, following Bill Bright's retirement as athletics director, selected Dr. Huffman to succeed Bright in that position. Recognizing that Huffman had mentored and shaped his successor in the admissions office, Mark Weigand, Dr. Lantz made the move that would benefit both athletics and admissions. He promoted Weigand to head the admissions operation and Huffman to director of athletics. As the chief administrator of athletics at the university, Dave orchestrated the extraordinary success of sports programs at the U of I for nine years from 1994-95 through 2002-03. Said President Jerry Israel of Huffman, whom he knew only as the director of athletics: "Dave is as good an administrator as I've worked with in any aspect of education. The stability and confidence he brings has created a great fountain of success for all coaches and student-athletes." Huffman retired in spring 2003 after thirty-seven years of successful administration for the university.

Such rare, extraordinary devotion and fealty from these men promoted the "family" atmosphere on the campus. These four provided uncommon stability over an

James L. Brunnemer

unusually lengthy period of time at the upper-level management of the university. Each of the presidents of that time—Esch, Sease, Lantz, and Israel—retained those men in their appropriate administrative slot.

Hottell, Partridge, Youngblood, and Huffman provided models of leadership for the presidents they served and for those employees each supervised. They have accumulated an unparalleled institutional history over the decades. To many alumni, those individuals *are* the college.

Time will tell, but there is reason to believe that those replacing the "Big Four" will accomplish great things for the university. However, it is inconceivable that anyone will surpass the performance of these men at the college. By any measurement, theirs was an era of the greatest growth, prosperity, and achievement in the school's history.

CHAPTER XXIX
GRAY HAIR AND HEMORRHOIDS

*A conclusion is the place where you
got tired thinking.*
                         Martin A. Fischer

By the time I returned to the University of Indianapolis in April 1989 as dean for institutional advancement, I had developed the requisite qualities of all fundraisers: gray hair (for the look of distinction) and hemorrhoids (for the look of concern).

Many folks look askance at those of us who work in the profession of university development, or institutional advancement (two concocted terms intended to make "fund raising" sound respectable.) Very few people I have met, even among my professional colleagues, wish to be known bluntly as solicitors of others' money. That does not include me. I'm gratified to have had a career in which I've served as a conduit between those who have the discretionary financial means to make a positive difference in the world and the noble causes that they choose to support.

Institutional advancement is essentially the sales division of a college or university. Advancement, or development, is the supporting framework for the chief sales executive of the institution, its president. Within the purview of advancement, generally, are those units that promote the university to its various publics and encourage lifetime attachments to the institution. Under the aegis of advancement are departments for marketing and public relations; publications, all periodicals and news pieces that support those efforts; and individuals assigned to the personal cultivation of prospects for charitable support, the solicitation of those prospects, and stewardship of the support received.

In 2002 more than $240 billion was contributed to not-for-profit organizations in the United States. Charitable organizations, including religious and educational institutions, health and human services, the arts, the environment, and other private entities, employ hundreds of thousands of us in fostering the welfare of our particular cause.

Most colleges and universities in America are members of the Council for the Advancement and Support of Education (CASE), a professional association for encouraging and implementing standards for advancement activities. The Code of Ethics of CASE states that no fund raiser will receive compensation through commissions, for obvious reasons. One could presume that those who engage in raising money for worthy causes have at least a modicum of interest in, if not an outright passion for, the specific service that they represent when soliciting support for it.

Most of my thirty-seven years of professional life have involved advocating the virtues of education. I firmly believe that within the educated person lies the promise for fulfillment of mankind's highest aspirations. Education—the "great equalizer" in my view—presumes to refine one's reasoning skills, promotes respect for others' views, imbues in one an appreciation of personal responsibility, and inspires a commitment to service.

I've heard it said that the only thing more costly than a college degree is not

James L. Brunnemer

having one. It is no secret that steady increases in college tuition have, for many years, outraced annual cost-of-living averages, many fold.

However, despite the concern that more and more young people are being priced out of higher education, it is a fact that tuition, fees, room, and board paid by students and their parents (and lending institutions) come nowhere near paying for a college's total costs. From half to three-quarters of an average college's operating expenses are covered by the full cost of the student's payments. The balance of operating overhead, the greatest part of which is salaries and wages for administration, faculty, and support staff, must be secured from other sources.

In the case of public colleges and universities, parts of those charges are covered by government subsidies toward which almost all of us pay taxes. Most independent or private institutions accept some direct federal subvention for student financial aid, but the greatest source of support comes from tax-deductible contributions of alumni and friends of the institution. Capital projects, equipment, and an ever-increasing reliance on technology cost a great deal of money.

At St. Norbert College, Eastern Michigan University, and Albion College, each of which I served in university advancement, I was fervent in my labors on behalf of those schools and convinced of the worthiness of each. However, at Indiana Central/University of Indianapolis, my commitment was personal. Every school acclaims its virtues, but I think an education at the University of Indianapolis encompasses a very special experience with its emphasis on both formal learning and service to others.

I first met U of I President Ben Lantz as a delegate of Albion College at his inauguration. At the time I was associate vice president for that fine liberal arts school whose president, Mel Vulgamore, had been a faculty colleague with Dr. Lantz at Ohio Wesleyan University.

Not long after that meeting, I received a call from Lynn Youngblood on President Lantz's behalf, which ultimately resulted in my return to the university as dean for institutional advancement. The challenge we faced was a daunting one. The $25-million "Focus on the Future" campaign was dead in the water with only four million raised. Professional campaign consultants hired to assess the entire advancement program concluded that the saturnine fund drive was "not well-planned or implemented." Nevertheless, I wouldn't have bet against Gene Sease successfully completing it had he remained as president.

Regardless, we had inherited an imposing test. It was necessary first to complete a comprehensive audit of the state of the advancement program and then muster the resources and the personnel to undertake the unfinished task. We set about writing a new "case for support," a document that basically expresses the purpose and objectives of a campaign. The second crucial aspect, identification of prospects with the capability to make the campaign successful, and the cultivation of those potential donors, would take time. We determined to prepare ourselves with the intention of announcing a new campaign to fulfill the goals of "Focus on the Future," plus funding additional needs Dr. Lantz and the trustees had enumerated.

During the time of my service as vice president for institutional advancement at the University of Indianapolis, new construction on campus included the Christel DeHaan

Fine Arts Center, which cost roughly $10.4 million; the Patrick and Pearl Smith Mall ($5.5 million); the Jerry and Elsie Martin Science Hall ($6.5 million); and a modern new maintenance facility ($750,000). Additionally, major refurbishments to Good Hall and Schwitzer Center (prior to the more recent and magnificent addition completed in 2002) cost approximately $2.5 million. The dining hall underwent a striking transformation thanks to a gift of $500,000 from the late Cyril and Mary Ober.

Also, the interior of Krannert Memorial Library was renovated for the insertion of the Communications Department (which moved into its shining new quarters, some would seriously contend, just before the antiquated Buxton Hall would have fallen on their heads!).

The new DeHaan facility was especially breathtaking in its architectural handsomeness, winning a trade award for the firm that designed it, Ratio Architects, Incorporated. For alumni who had not visited the campus for some time before its construction, the building surpassed in quality and attractiveness any other on the campus.

One autumn evening when I was working late, two young alumni appeared at my office to ask if I might show them around a campus that had changed significantly since their graduation.

As we set about on a walking tour, both Brian '86 and Kim '87 Fogg were especially wide-eyed in appreciation as we ambled through the elegant DeHaan Center. Observing spacious classrooms on the first floor, including special facilities for both orchestra and choir rehearsals, and abundant individual soundproof practice rooms for student musicians, Kim remarked, with a touch of awe, "Indiana Central was never like *this!*"

The couple would repeat that phrase, several times, as we proceeded through the lovely art gallery and stunning lobby and lounge area. We then entered the Ruth Lilly Performance Hall, the gem within the DeHaan Center. The Foggs were captivated by the acoustically and aesthetically superb music hall with its resemblance to classic balconied European opera houses.

"Wow!" beamed Brian as he surveyed the Lilly Auditorium, with acoustics custom-designed by internationally recognized acoustician Christopher Joffe, "Indiana Central *was* never like this!"

It was with great pride that I led the Foggs upward to the second floor where art studios and other features of the building were located. Approaching the darkened main art studio/classroom, I started to put my master key into the lock when I noticed small specks of light, like dozens of lightening bugs, inside. Pressing our faces against the glass of the double doors, Brian and I discovered that within the locked room, small individual lamps were clamped atop easels, before which art students were sketching on their respective canvases. Curiosity aroused, Brian and I simultaneously glanced to the left where sat the subject of the artists' attention.

There, posed upon a stool, sat a woman with long tresses, modeling completely in the buff, displaying ample breasts and all the rest.

Products of earlier and rather more conservative eras at the college, Brian and I blurted out, as one, "Indiana Central was *never* like this!"

In my capacity as a chief fund raiser for the university I had the privilege of

James L. Brunnemer

meeting and developing cherished relationships with generous donors and supporters. Hundreds, preferring anonymity, made contributions to the university that will remain publicly uncelebrated. For many years to come, these gracious gifts will continue to affect the lives of students, faculty, and staff. But those of us who delighted in knowing them will not forget them. Because of donors at all levels, CASE recognized the university in 1998 with its annual award for most improvement in total giving in our school classification.

Some of the gifts we received were solicited in unorthodox ways. As an example, a couple of times a year, each member school in the Associated Colleges of Indiana (forerunner of today's Indiana Grantmakers Alliance) would make available its president or chief development officer for solicitation calls on corporate executives. Early in the 1990s I found myself teamed with Father Charles Banet, the gregarious and much-respected president of St. Joseph's College, for visits to companies in Indianapolis.

Only a few weeks earlier I had been surprised to read in the sports section of the *Indianapolis Star* that the St. Joseph's basketball squad had traveled to Norman, Oklahoma, to play the NCAA powerhouse Oklahoma Sooners. It was unusual for a Division II school such as the Pumas to travel halfway across the country to take on a major Division I-A university.

After completing our final call at Indianapolis Power and Light, I commented to Fr. Banet about his school playing the University of Oklahoma a few weeks back (I didn't mention that I also noted the Pumas had been beaten rather handily).

"We've never played Oklahoma," President Banet replied, authoritatively.

"Hmmm, Father," I replied, puzzled. "I may be mistaken, but I'm sure I saw a game account and box score of a game between St. Joe and OU, just last month."

"No," replied the self-assured priest. "We've played Notre Dame before and we played Marquette once. But never Oklahoma. You must be thinking of St. Joseph of Philadelphia."

"No, Father Banet, I'm pretty certain it was your Pumas." (My wife doesn't call me "pighead" for nothing.)

A bit exasperated now at my insistence that his school had played a game of which he wasn't aware, Fr. Banet stated, with finality, "If we had played Oklahoma, I'd know it. I *am* the president, after all."

His somewhat smug retort tripped my competitive circuit breaker. Considering my options quickly, I smiled and offered this:

"Father Banet, at the University of Indianapolis an unrestricted contribution of $100 makes one a member of a giving society called the Fellows. If your basketball team has not, indeed, played the University of Oklahoma this season, I'll send a $100 check to the corresponding donors' club at SJC.

"However, if I am right, then you become a Fellow at the U of I this year. How 'bout it?"

Sensing, I think, an easy mark in his impudent fund raising partner from U of I, President Banet accepted the challenge immediately.

"You're on. And I'll know as soon as I get back to campus today." (This was before cell phones and the speedy answer to our difference that technology could have provided us.)

After we parted I drove straight back to the university and dialed my counterpart at St. Joe, vice president for development Jim Valentine. After the usual verbal amenities I inquired, "Jim, didn't your basketball team play the Oklahoma Sooners at Norman earlier this season?"

"Oh!" he chuckled, "You mean the night we had the drug problem?"

"*What?*"

"Yeah, we played the Sooners. And they drug our sorry butts up one end of the court and down the other! Beat us by forty points."

Before President Banet had arrived back at Rensselaer I knew I'd won the wager.

Two days later a letter arrived on my desk with a return address marked "Office of the President, St. Joseph's College, Rensselaer, Indiana."

A brief note accompanied a check in the amount of $100, consigned to the University of Indianapolis Fellows:

> *I'm going to find out how my damned athletic director slipped a flight to Oklahoma for the basketball team into the athletic budget without my knowledge!"*
>
> *Cordially,*
> *Fr. Charles Banet, president*

Typically presidential. Trapped, but unyielding.

So many warm memories of people, events, and achievements during my years with the college from 1989-2000 bubble up from within. The institutional advancement staff was extraordinary. So many selfless and dedicated folks in that division served the university ably. Among them was Clyde Fields '63, who established the first planned giving function and won the hearts of many of our elder alumni with his very caring and efficient counsel.

Under the creative talents of Peter Noot (hiring this incredibly able and bright young man to his first job might have been my single finest contribution as an administrator at the university), the periodical previously known as the *Alumni News* was reborn as *Portico*. Informative and aesthetically rich, *Portico* would win awards from CASE for its quality.

In a challenge to alumni graphic artists, marketing director Margaret Garrison and publications director Peter Noot received dozens of designs for a new athletic logo in 1990. Michael Schwab '84 created the contest-winning design—which became affectionately known by students as "the dog with no butt"—a version of which adorns the special U of I license plates on thousands of alumni vehicles in Indiana, as well as all athletic apparel.

Marlene Harris, once secretary to Dr. Esch, organized our office with quiet efficiency as my administrative assistant. Marlene was consistently professional, handling with grace and aplomb any situation, be it a call from an alumnus whose death we had— quite the opposite of the case of Mark Twain—greatly *underestimated* ("Why are we still getting mail from you people? My husband has been dead for seven years!"), to quietly editing my correspondence to weed out offending misspellings and incorrect grammatical usage.

James L. Brunnemer

I do recall one pair of telephone calls that challenged Marlene's ordinarily impenetrably serene demeanor. As chairman of a committee for the Council for Advancement and Support of Education (CASE) Region Five conference held annually in Chicago, it was my responsibility to recruit volunteer speakers for various and sundry sessions in our field. It was a Wednesday, I believe, and I was on the phone in conversation with Kris Kindelsperger, who was at that time vice president for development at Hanover College. As Kris and I discussed his topic for the conference, Marlene appeared at my office doorway with a bemused look on her face.

As I cupped the phone speaker with my hand to receive Marlene's message, she broke up as she requested, "When you're finished speaking with Mr. Kris Kindelsperger, Mr. Kit Klingelhoffer from I.U. is holding on the other line."

Try saying that sentence real fast.

I must admit that my two favorite alumni of Indiana Central/University of Indianapolis are Luella (Sauer) Brunnemer '69 and our second son, Kyle '93.

Kyle—whose name, by the way, is a two-syllable one in Hoosier patois ("Ky-ull")—chose to come to the U of I independent of us. He suspected we were delighted, but he enrolled here despite that because he loved Ken Partridge. He was a member of teams that recorded one of the finest four-year won-lost ledgers in U of I golf history (1988-89, 136-11; 1989-90, 140-26-2; 1990-91, 135-35, and 1991-92, 87-9), a four-year aggregate of 498 wins, 81 losses, and two ties, an .860 winning percentage. Kyle twice earned NCAA Division II All-American honors in golf and participated in the National D-II tournament all four of his years as a Greyhound.

During the first semester of his freshman year he found himself in a class of the jocular Bill Gommel, who always greeted others with a winning smile and had an unvarying cheerful disposition. Dr. Gommel became a sort of "in-house" weather forecaster who was consulted, in mock seriousness, about climatic conditions for upcoming events at the university. To my knowledge he never predicted anything but fair weather for Commencement, Homecoming, and Alumni Day events, and darned if most of the time he wasn't right.

Dr. Gommel had been an instructor more than twenty years earlier in the same course for Kyle's mother, Luella Sauer.

On the first day of class, Kyle watched as the animated professor opened his attaché case and withdrew a sheaf of yellowed, dog-eared papers that resembled the Dead Sea Scrolls. These were his lecture notes. Kyle waggishly suggested that these were likely the very same notes Bill had used to instruct this class when his mother was Kyle's age in 1966.

When I first discussed with our son the possibility that I might accept Dr. Lantz's invitation to join the administrative team at U of I, Kyle was in the second semester of his freshman year. He quelled any concerns I might have had in regard to his comfort level with the prospect of my "invading his space" at the college: "That's okay, Dad. I'll just ignore you for the next three years."

I was doubly relieved at his proposal, replying, "That's a deal, son. I've seen your grades."

Distinction Without Pretension

Prior to our moving back to Indianapolis and my taking up residency in an office in Esch Hall, our elder son, Beau, had already made his own impression at his younger brother's school.

Our boys were normal, mostly. Born innocent, they devolved into spirited little colts prior to puberty. As young adults, any semblance of our control over their behaviors was a very iffy, sometime thing. Kyle was slightly less of a behavioral embarrassment as a teenager than the more devilishly creative Beau. Some adults at the university actually considered Kyle well-mannered. Beau was considered to be, well, Beau.

Beau entered a whole new universe of freedom upon enrolling at Eastern Michigan University. Frat life suited him like a tailored suit. As with most parents in the late eighties with kids in college we wrote the checks and turned our heads, hoping our boys would come out the other end reasonably intact and ready to rejoin civilization. You can imagine our joy when Beau called us his second week at college to tell us he had been selected as the frat "social chairman." He pronounced the first fraternity bash he had orchestrated a success: "The whole *world* was there, Dad!" I was so proud.

Not long afterward, Beau, who possessed a pleasing tenor voice, called again to share with his tuition-paying parents that he had won a campus-wide talent show during "Greek Week." He couldn't understand why we were the least bit concerned when we learned that during the entire seven-day period he had not attended even one of his classes. When it came to finding fun, Beau maxed out. He is a full-bore good time guy. And I love him for it.

One Monday morning I was on the phone with Lynn Youngblood. At the time I was still at Albion College, and U of I's vice president and I frequently traded news. Lynn mentioned he'd seen Beau at the Hounds' basketball game the previous Saturday night. What he didn't tell me was what he saw Beau doing.

First, though, let me pause here to tell you a little more about our eldest son. At any contest, no matter whether the stakes be great or small, the team Beau roots for has him as its greatest fan. He will be the most vocal, the most ardent, the most unforgiving devotee, the nastiest referee baiter, and the most obnoxious winner or most embittered loser of any of the longest-standing, most loyal fans of that team. It's just in his nature to go all out in everything he does. And he does "sports fan" better than anyone I know. Whether rooting for his beloved Cubs at Wrigley Field, the Bears in Soldier Field, or the Kane County (Illinois) Cougars minor league baseball team, he becomes what I can only describe as a "fan-iac."

Allow me to emphasize my point by sharing what Beau describes as the "third greatest day" of his life. Beau has worked for the TTI Corporation in Chicago since his graduation from Eastern Michigan University. As soon as he crossed the Indiana state line and sniffed the sulfur-clogged air of the Second City, Beau became a Cubs fan. He is one of those pathetic, die-hard, long-suffering followers who consider Harry Caray one of God's saints.

Beau was sitting among the quarry of other Cubs reprobates in the left field bleachers of Wrigley one summer as Chicago played the San Francisco Giants. In the Giants line-up that day in 1992 was Barry Bonds, a reputed malcontent, not nearly as idolized as he would become ten years later when he set the major league record with seventy-three home runs.

James L. Brunnemer

In the fifth inning, Bonds clubbed a shot to the opposite field where the fly ball descended on a Budweiser-besodden cluster of young males, including one Beau Brunnemer. With a barehanded snag of the baseball, Beau's dream had come true. He caught a home run ball, and it was off the bat of Barry Bonds!

For a delirious instant, Beau was the King of Wrigley Field. His mind drifted to ESPN's SportsCenter and his chances of being seen snaring that ball on national TV. (Actually, Beau would be seen on ESPN a couple of years later, when he and his fellow left-field loonies built a pyramid eight feet high with empty beer cans. But that's another story.)

Then it started, like a distant thunderstorm, with a low rumble.

At first barely noticeable, but building louder and louder, came the monotonously rhythmical refrain: "THROW ... IT ... BACK! THROW ... IT ... BACK! **THROW ... IT ... BACK!**"

It was the famous Cubs fans' chant reserved for anyone snaring an *opponent's* home run. Tossing the ball back onto the field demonstrated disdain for the common foe and rancor for the damage he had done to the hometown Cubbies.

This was a supreme moment in my elder son's young life. How could he return this amazing memento of his trip to fantasyland? But the unrelenting chant of the crowd intensified to a deafening degree. Finally, yielding to the multitude, Beau reared back and fired the ball toward second base, nearly beaning an unsuspecting Bonds, who was in the midst of his slow home run trot around the bases.

Bedlam followed! The tumultuous cheers of the crowd washed over Beau's being, salving the invisible wound he felt in ceding the prized ball.

Why would this be his greatest day, except for the birth of my grandchildren, Noah and Nate?

At the end of the inning, as Beau mused painfully that he missed an opportunity to keep the only ball he had ever caught at a big league game, he felt a tap on his shoulder. An elderly man had awaited such a moment for more than ten years. Judd, a man Beau had never seen before, leaned over and handed him an official major league baseball, whispering in Beau's ear, "True Cubs fans *always* throw it back."

The ball, autographed by that kind and devoted Cubs follower, is displayed proudly on Beau's basement bar.

So it was only fitting that on a visit to see his kid brother at U of I, Beau became the Greyhounds' number one booster and the visiting Southern Indiana University basketball team's top nemesis in Nicoson Hall. He joined the rabid Greyhound backers of assorted football and baseball players, wrestlers, and other Cro-Magnon types in the section beneath the basket at the west end of the arena. The really insane rooters claimed seats on the first row. Of course, they never sat in the seats even once during the game, carrying on rather a standing riot.

The game proved to be a rough-and-tumble affair from the outset, with lots of contact among the players. The hotly contested game had only minutes remaining when one of the SIU star players was fouled hard on a drive to the basket. His momentum carried him into the crazies. As he tried to extricate himself from the multitude, he pushed one of the students defiantly and elbowed another, all the while sneering at these "homies" with the greatest of contempt.

This was Brer Rabbit punching forty tar babies. Surrounded by the grasping, howling horde, the SIU guy stuck to the crowd.

The other players on the floor and the officials were engaged in a heated disagreement over the foul. The Greyhounds argued it was a clean block. SIU players got into the faces of the defenders and the referees moved in to try to prevent a full-scale melee from breaking out.

Meanwhile, the distracted referees failed to notice what was happening to the poor guy engulfed by the throng in the bleachers. He was by now "wearing" the crowd of students like one of those human beehives you see on "Ripley's Believe It Or Not," only this was not a voluntary act. The U of I rabble were all over him, pinning him down.

At this point, I'll turn the story over to Dr. Youngblood: "Two of our students stood out from the rest, because one had the SIU player in a headlock while the other was pummeling him with his fists in the kidney area. I immediately recognized Todd Hottell, Ken and Georgia's son." (Todd, of course, was a Division II All-American football player who possessed Ken's athletic grace and Georgia's fiery temperament.)

"I started to lower my head in sympathy to Ken, the consummate gentleman who was always embarrassed when Todd's competitive nature spilled over. Of course, Georgia was reveling in the whole scene, calling for more violence like a lion's fan in the Roman Coliseum.

"The second student, by now aiming well-placed blows to the rib cage of the unfortunate prisoner, looked somewhat familiar to me, but I couldn't place who it was. I turned to Janis and, as a dim light bulb of recognition flashed on, said, 'That looks like Beau Brunnemer,' knowing that it couldn't be."

It not only could be, it was.

Finally, one SIU player saw his *frater* being abused. Afraid for his own welfare, he didn't wade into the frenzied mob, but he frantically called the attention of the referee to the affair. The frazzled ref, trying his best to allay the skirmish among the opposing players, now turned his attention to the scene in rows one through three in the grandstands. He rushed to the player's aid and the crowd, their bloodlust satisfied, gave up their prize with no further resistance. The lithe six-and-a-half-foot-tall cager now poured like an oil spill out of the stands and onto his back on the hardwood. After a few minutes he regained his feet, a bit sorer than when he entered the bleachers but much more wise in the ways of how not to arouse an unfriendly Greyhound crowd.

Beau and Todd melted into the seething multitude, thinking themselves invisible, and fully justified in the name of the home team, its players, fans, the university, and its alumni, living and dead, that they had done the righteous thing. What had befallen that lad in the hands of the zealous Greyhound students would have been labeled assault outside the confines of the arena. Inside, it was just jubilant college kids having fun.

And where was Kyle? Up in the sixth row, he would tell me later, "where people sit who care about their reputations."

About the Hottell lad, indulge me for another divergence, if you don't mind. Those who know her well will speak of the quiet, sweet, and gentle nature of Georgia Hottell, molder of young third grade minds during a long and efficacious teaching career. The mother of Scott, Todd, and Lora Hottell, and grandmother of their collective children,

James L. Brunnemer

is all of that—*except* at a ballgame, and most *especially* if one of her brood is involved.

At Southport High School athletic contests involving their children, Ken would often sit apart from Georgia. She could pierce the armor of the most hardened official with acid comments delivered at a couple of octaves above the noise of the "campaign of shock and awe." During one of Lora's high school games, to a basketball official who had made a series of calls that did not endear him to her, Georgia intoned, above the roar of the assembly in the stands: "Are you *blind? Where* are your eyes? In the seat of your *pants?*"

Only minutes later, on a play in which Lora appeared to have stripped the ball cleanly as her opponent attempted a shot at the basket, a whistle blew shrilly. As that same official raised his right hand to assess a foul on Georgia's favorite daughter, the ball was accidentally slapped directly at him, striking him, hard, in the groin. The poor guy toppled to the floor in agony. The crowd quieted now as a team physician attended to the fallen official. As a mortified Ken hid his face, the penetrating voice of an unforgiving Georgia sliced through the silence: "What's the problem? You don't have any of *those* either!"

For a visual of what I'm trying to convey here, check out the ICC cheerleader on page nineteen of the 1963 Indiana Central *Oracle*. Yep, that snarling young Georgia Hieb is now sweet grandmother Georgia Hottell.

Fall Saturdays often found Lu and me with President and Mrs. Lantz in the president's guest box atop Key Stadium, playing host to trustees, friends, and prospective donors of the university. Multitalented and as bright as she is, my *cum laude* graduate wife doesn't pay a lot of attention to athletics. So it didn't take long for her to develop a reputation among the regulars in the box for her incongruous observations of the action on the green field of combat spread out below us.

We had lived three years in Green Bay, Wisconsin, so perhaps, as our Greyhounds prepared to engage the football team from Ferris State University, it wasn't too audacious of Lu to inquire, of no one in particular, "Do we play the Packers this season?"

Lu never seemed to understand a coach's tactics for running the football.

"Why do they always run into the big pile in the middle?" she asked, incredulously.

It didn't occur to her straightaway that the "big pile" consistently appeared because eager tacklers from the opposing team gravitated toward and converged upon the carrier of the ball like iron filings to a magnet, rather than the reverse.

Actually, one observation made by my lovely mate, after watching a Greyhound ball carrier race seventy yards for a touchdown, might be considered astute: "Do we get more points for a longer run?"

No, Honey, there is no equivalent in football to basketball's three-point shot.

But a day came when Lu would gain the respect of all who delighted in the unintended humor she brought to her football observations. A U of I pass receiver near the home sideline went to his knees in the attempt to snare a forward pass. The ill-thrown ball, however, clearly bounced on the turf a full five yards before skipping into the receiver's waiting hands. The closest official, rushing up from behind, ruled the play a catch. First down, Greyhounds! The opposing coaches, players, and fans howled in indignation at such an obvious indiscretion by the referee.

Silent, smirking satisfaction at the obvious miscall pervaded most of us in our

Distinction Without Pretension

private box, until Lu posed this:

"Are we allowed to catch it on one bounce now?"

Peals of laughter arose from those of us gathered there, startling some fans sitting in the bleachers outside our window. Lu was vindicated. Even *she* noticed that something not quite according to Hoyle had happened down there.

On the eve of the Homecoming game against Butler in 1992, Margaret Garrison, our very able director of marketing and public relations, approached me late Friday afternoon. She was convinced she had a marketing masterstroke to embellish festivities on what was always a red-letter day. She had been in contact with a member of an association that advocated the adoption of retired racing greyhounds. Only that afternoon, she had engaged a man to bring four of the sleek canines to perform a race during halftime of the game.

With expansive enthusiasm my colleague described how appreciative the home crowd would be, especially when the brand-new athletic mascot would be introduced as—here's the punch line—"Big Ben!"

Get it? *"Big Ben!"*

If Margaret had an X-ray contraption capable of projecting the images passing through my mind at that moment she would have known her truly creative marketing idea was not going to happen.

There were a number of practical reasons I could cite for nixing this brainstorm, beginning with "Have you checked this out with the athletic director?" ("No, but ... ")

Bless her heart, Margaret wasn't aware that I had experienced a greyhound mascot before.

Yep. Dixie, the three-legged brown-hound.

As a young alumni director in the seventies, I was approached by a gaggle of cheerleaders who had found a greyhound mascot for our teams. The girls had gone through all the appropriate administrative hoops for approval, even finding a home for Dixie with congenial faculty member Ken Borden and his wife, Jane. The girls were looking to me to promote the mascot to our alumni. Seemed like a sound idea to me, then.

What I didn't anticipate prior to our mascot's debut before a home basketball crowd still gives me heartburn. Dixie wasn't the dashing symbol of speed, strength, and grace that Lynn Turner and his fellow ICC classmates had in mind in 1926 when they adopted the Greyhound as the athletic archetype.

As the cheerleaders proudly led Dixie, tethered by a lengthy leash, onto the basketball court, one couldn't fail to notice she was missing a hind leg. Trembling in terror before the assembly of fans, the poor creature, with her pronounced limp, skulked reluctantly behind the peppy pompon team, her fear-filled eyes scanning the arena for somewhere to hide.

At first a few students rose to applaud, grateful that Indiana Central had a real live Greyhound mascot. Dulling their initial ardor was the frightened demeanor of the animal and the realization that she couldn't have beaten a healthy gerbil in a 100-yard sprint.

The final indignity? Dixie wasn't grey. She was an ugly, mottled brown! While most of the students chose to politely ignore the miscast canine, a few derisive whistles and hoots spoke volumes about the choice of Dixie as the living logo of Greyhound honor

James L. Brunnemer

in the athletic arena.

But this was only part of the equation that was forming in my mind as I considered Margaret's request.

The Homecoming crowd was traditionally the largest of the year in Key Stadium. The fact that the hated Butler Bulldogs were the opponent assured us of an even larger and more raucous assembly than usual, and it would be almost evenly divided between Greyhound and Bulldog rooters. I was aware, as well, that Butler's president, Geoffrey Bannister, and his wife, Margaret, had accepted the Lantzs' invitation to join them in the president's guest box for the game.

My mind drifted back to the time only a few years earlier when I was a member of the administrative staff at Eastern Michigan University. A few friends and I were in attendance at a football game between EMU and the Western Michigan Broncos at Kalamazoo. WMU had acquired a full-grown stallion, which would race from end zone to end zone whenever the Broncos scored a touchdown, a cowboy-clad student rider waving his Stetson wildly from atop the horse.

On this particular evening WMU celebrated many scores, as the Hurons of Eastern had a hapless team. It was, I believe, following the fourth Western touchdown that "Bronc," no doubt well kept and well fed, left a trail of road-apples on the Astroturf of the stadium as he galloped the length of the field. The horse dung was strewn rather evenly between the ten and forty-five-yard lines, to the absolute delight of students of both schools. The administration, however, wasn't amused.

As these two dreaded visions morphed into one in my head, I could see a scrawny and scared brown greyhound with an amputated limb, named "Big Ben" after the university president, squat to take a huge dump at the fifty yard line. The thought of that occurring, in front of an overflow football crowd made up of not only U of I alumni and students but followers of our despised rivals and a contingent of Indianapolis sportswriters, was enough to make me muzzy.

"No, Margaret," I said decisively, "We'll not introduce 'Big Ben' tomorrow. Or any day that I'm still vice president for the institution."

As I consider my combined twenty-one years at Indiana Central College/Indiana Central University/University of Indianapolis, if there is one area of my modest accomplishments that I am duly proud, it is this: the role I was privileged to play in identifying and recommending some of the outstanding members of the board of trustees serving the institution so ably today.

A strong university board of regents or trustees is one with great diversity, wisdom, commitment, and wealth. Further, I would argue that, especially crucial in a university setting, a good balance between alumni and non-alumni is necessary. While each group brings multiple perspectives to the work of the board, alumni possess the added ingredients of historical insight and a personal commitment to preserve the unique experience they encountered there.

As I follow with great interest the affairs of the University of Indianapolis in 2003, I am comforted that its primary caretakers, beyond the administration and staff—its board of trustees—sets an enormously high standard for quality and commitment. Of those who serve today, I played a role, to a greater or lesser degree, in an invitation to the board, these: Gary Edwards, a graduate of Ball State University, David Frick (Indiana University), Sue Anne Gilroy (DePauw University); and U of I alumni Steve Carson '68, Ann Cory Bretz '48 (after whom Cory Bretz Hall is named), Murvin Enders '81, Cary Hanni '69, Emmanuel Harris '82, D. J. Hines '73, Tom Martin '72, Pat Polis McCrory '76, Gene Perkins '59, Patty Poehler '77, Mickey Powell '61, William Raspberry '58 (for whom Lynn Youngblood and I lobbied over Dr. Lantz's objections), Rick Stierwalt '78, Norm Terry '64, Larry Thompson '63, Jerry Throgmartin '78, Mike Watkins '68, Bob Wingerter '76, and Tom Zupancic '78.

These people and their fellow trustees James Bear, Lorene Burkhart Steinmetz, Carolyn Coleman, Christel DeHaan, Oscar Gardner '74, James Jones, Bill Kiesel '63, Jerry Martin, Carolene Mays, Kent Millard, David Roberts, Yvonne Shaheen, Gordon St. Angelo, Lorenzo Tallarigo, Don Tanselle, Bishop Woodie White, Gordon Wishard, and Esperanza Zendejas are as formidable a collection of leaders as will be found on any college board in Indiana. The University of Indianapolis is truly favored to have each one of those listed above considering its present and future welfare. As an alumnus, I am so very gratified by the work they are doing to make our alma mater the best that it can be.

Let me conclude this chapter by sharing with you Saturday, September 30, 1999. Having served twenty-one years in two terms at the university, and a most generous President Israel providing a modified version of the university's "bridge to retirement" benefit, I determined to retire from the University that fall. So, I set about requesting my own retirement gift. What I wanted more than anything on the eve of my departing the University of Indianapolis after a nearly forty-year association was the Faculty Flops to meet again on the Nicoson Hall basketball court.

In August, I wrote to the core members of the Flops with an offer I knew would be irresistible: basketball and pizza. Returning, mostly fat and grossly out-of-condition, were Huffman, Youngblood, Collins, Hottell, England, Wetherald, Hanni, Watkins, Partridge, Borden, Kistler, and honorary Flop Bill Coffee. Possessing graying temples and balding pates, these now middle-aged to elderly gentlemen had seemingly matured with the years, until the scrimmage started.

Actually, the expected began even before the games. Cary Hanni sneaked up behind Larry Collins as Larry was launching a practice shot from forty feet away, trying to playfully block his shot. Unfortunately, Dr. Hanni, the surgeon, broke the fourth finger on his right hand, which I would assume, that being his dominant hand, was of significance when he practiced surgery on someone. Predictably, Cary sucked it up and played the entire afternoon.

The intent was to play *one game*, to ten hoops, with baskets scored from behind the three-point line counting as two. After that exhausting spectacle, we'd move into the showers and on to the Pizza Hut, where all of us now excelled.

First, however, we argued over who would be shirts versus skins. Of course, not one of us wanted to be seen in public (there was actually a bit of an audience who gathered for this momentous occasion), or in one another's presence, for that matter, without a shirt on. Our pale obesity was truly an ugly sight. So a "shoot-off" was held to decide this important detail. I missed the shot for my team, so was instantly excoriated by my teammates for forcing them to display their horrendous bellies and abundant cellulite to the multitude.

Now we began the contest. It was light-hearted at the outset. We joshed one another, feigned coronaries, and muttered in amazement at how much of our former athleticism (at least as we perceived it) had eroded with age. My "skins" team won, 10-8. That was supposed to be the end of it.

But given that no one seemed to be on the verge of collapse, and there were no serious injuries (we wouldn't learn until later that Hanni had broken his finger), we decided to play another game.

The shirts won this time, 10-9.

Now, tongues *are* hanging out. Flops are leaning over, gasping for air, sweat flowing out of every pore; but no one is laughing. We have returned to 1973. We *must* play the "rubber match," to fifteen hoops this time.

All hell breaks loose in this, the third game.

Pride surfaces. Faces are taut in exertion. The pace of the game quickens. Defense is actually attempted. Watkins goes for a rebound and is whacked, severely, in the eye. Time-out. Bruised and bloody is Watkins, but no stitches. Hell, he's okay. Let's go.

Huffman breaks the unspoken code of the competition by sneaking in to steal the ball and makes the winning basket for the "shirts" team. Youngblood emerges as the Star of Stars, hitting five three-pointers at distances from which he had never shot before.

No tempers flared, but play was serious. The only Flop throughout the event who maintained his joyful countenance, who was not drawn into the competitive maelstrom in the press for victory? Yours truly!

I went 0-for-the-day—didn't make even *one* basket—in many, many tries. And *loved* it! I got to watch the other guys slip into a contentious mode without going there myself. I didn't defend hard when the game got close, nor did I try to wrestle for rebound position. No attempts to steal the ball by me. Against all odds, I generally maintained a mature outlook. *Me!* I had my own private victory.

So, at the end, physically wrecked, we proceeded to the Pizza Hut, where we spun tales of glories past, and Larry Collins showed he hadn't lost his touch in the three decades since we had last gathered for basketball and pizza.

No one ever had a more enjoyable retirement party than I did that day.

CHAPTER XXX
ARE THERE NO MORE HEROES?

> [W]hat the people need and demand is that
> their children shall have a chance—as good
> a chance as any other children in the world—to
> make the most of themselves, to rise in any and
> every occupation, including those occupations
> which require the most thorough training. What
> the people want is open paths from every corner
> of the state, and the best things which men can
> achieve. To make such paths, to make them
> open to the poorest and lead to the highest, is
> the mission of democracy.
> William Lowe Bryan, president
> Indiana University (1903-38)

Those who would embrace the mission of democracy as articulated so eloquently by Dr. Bryan so many years ago accept a high and serious calling, indeed. The ideal described above becomes a *noblesse oblige* that presumes that each generation, having received opportunities for a better life from its antecessors will, in turn, provide pathways to opportunities for those who come after them.

Individuals who have influenced other people and events to an uncommon degree invigorate, and, often, advance history. The general populace has typically admired persons who demonstrate courage, commitment, persistence and self-sacrifice in fulfilling a high purpose or attaining a noble end. Some of us would call them heroes.

One concept of the hero is a romantic, idealized one. The family of Man recognizes—or creates—heroes and heroines, real or imagined, in all areas of our society. Typically, we tend to think of heroic behavior in terms of isolated, dramatic acts that alter the course or outcome of an event. Those who die in an act of heroism may be eulogized and lionized for all time. Living heroes face a more formidable transformation, for each is a human being vulnerable to behaviors not consistent with whatever actions resulted in their being embraced as living legends. Human beings may act heroically, but they are not necessarily saints.

Popular culture in America tends to appoint celebrities as icons. Athletes and entertainers have been admired out of all proportion to their importance in the larger picture of life. As the late author Erma Bombeck cautioned a graduating class in an address at Wellesley, "Don't confuse fame with success. Madonna is one, Mother Teresa, the other."

The idols of the boys of my adolescence were born of the relative frivolity of sports and movies. In our innocence, we idolized Gene Autrey, "the Singing Cowboy," who always got the bad guy without a trace of bloodshed. We revered Stan "the Man"

James L. Brunnemer

Musial of the Cardinals, whose grand feats on the baseball field were portrayed by a thirty-something Harry Caray, brought to central Indiana via KMOX radio in St. Louis. In March of 1954, I saw history and an Indiana high school basketball hero born on our grainy, black-and-white television screen. Bobby Plump of tiny Milan, Indiana, held the ball for more than three minutes as the Butler Fieldhouse crowd of 15,000 screamed continuously, then arced a jump shot at the last second over Muncie Central's Jimmy Barnes that they speak of with awe fifty years later.

Our school texts taught us of heroic presidents like Washington, Jefferson, and Lincoln. We learned of military heroes, significant artists and authors, and of others whose boldness and moral courage propelled historic social movements.

The portraiture of the hero underwent a seismic alteration in the 1960s, an American era of great social turmoil. The birth of the antihero, mostly young firebrands who rebelled against the "establishment" and upset the traditional social order, was chronicled with devastating effects. In the modern age of pitiless and uncompromising scrutiny by print and electronic media, the standard image of the hero faced off with a skeptical public. Under the harsh scrutiny of gigantic, and manic, media conglomerates, conventional heroes were revealed to be all too human.

As antiwar activists and proponents of racial, gender, and gay rights took to the streets, prevailing heroes were likely to be publicly castigated in a frenzy to unmask their darker natures in contrast to heretofore-admired characteristics and accomplishments. For example, veterans returning from Vietnam, unlike those who served in wars past, were sometimes spat upon and derided as "baby killers" by many in the American civilian population.

There seemed to be no boundaries in the examination of doyens of American socio-political figures. President Nixon became the exemplar for those who would stress the moral bankruptcy of America's political leaders. As the trend to accentuate the perceived failures of public persons accelerated, information about extramarital affairs tarnished such icons as John F. Kennedy and Martin Luther King, Jr. Reports on the lives of athletes and entertainers more often were about drug use, sexual improprieties, and criminal behavior rather than their artistry or talent. Religious figures, always held to a higher standard and looked upon by many as unassailable, suddenly plunged in the public eye as sordid scandals—quietly shielded by church leaders for decades—were exposed.

On and after September 11, 2001, heroic acts and selfless conduct by men and women of the New York and Washington, D.C. fire and police departments, of government officials such as Mayor Rudy Guiliani, and thousands of faceless men and women gripped the nation. Overnight, heroism was in vogue again.

I have always believed in heroes. As American author Bernard Malamud (1914-1986) sagely advised: "Without heroes, we are all plain people and don't know how far we can go."

However, the delineation of my idols has undergone a drastic overhaul as I've grown to adulthood. To me, the exhaustive test of heroic behavior is found in a lifetime of lesser acts toward a high ideal, performed consistently, day in and day out. While pop artist Andy Warhol spoke of everyone having "his fifteen minutes of fame," Mother Teresa commended those humble folk who would never receive public acclaim: "We realize that what we are accomplishing is a drop in the ocean. But if this drop were not in the ocean, it would be missed."

In retrospect, the *real* heroes of my youth were of a common sort, masked in the unimposing cloth of familiar people, rather than the pinstripes of athletic darlings. My parents, and the wider circle of family and friends, modeled behaviors in countless imperceptible ways, providing for me opportunities to grow and mature in an acceptable fashion. Patient and caring teachers and coaches contributed, beyond my ability to fully appreciate it, to a debt of gratitude I can never repay. My heroes shaped opportunities for me to advance to a place I might not have achieved otherwise, and thus, to an obligation to help those who follow me.

In ways uncountable, the little educational institution on Hanna Avenue has been blessed with an uncommon abundance of quiet sacrifice from a host of common folk. Hundreds of individuals, many of whom have already been referenced in preceding pages, acted in ways that may be described as *heroic*.

The current and temporary caretakers of the University of Indianapolis—President Jerry Israel, the board of trustees, faculty, administrators, and staff—are each making their own contributions to the legacy of an institution that has a part of each of us graduates woven into its fabric. President Israel, especially, has demonstrated an unwavering resolve to diversity, providing opportunity and fairness to all who pass beneath the portals of Good Hall. The university is the sum of all the dreams of those whose passion, devotion, and sacrifice in the past has contributed to its present growth and vitality.

The school continues to spread a special brand of education to its students, imbuing them with the service-centered component one can scarcely escape while walking its halls alongside the shadows of students who came before.

On October 6, 2002, the university celebrated the one-hundredth anniversary of the signing of the charter that brought Indiana Central University into being. Thousands of congratulatory notes and comments, written by alumni, current students, parents and friends, were received extolling the school during the yearlong commemoration. These few, gleaned from the pages of *Portico*, serve as expressions of personal gratitude to those who helped to make their education fulfilling:

> *It's hard to recognize that this is the same campus I attended; but it's wonderful to see the growth. I received a great education.*
> Deanna Foster Baumer '64

> *In our next century, may U of I leave an even greater mark on society than it has in its first 100 years. We have much to be proud of in our first century of serving.*
> Richard E. Stierwalt '80

> *As an international student, I saw the beginnings and growth of the International Division, and many people and countries gained*

James L. Brunnemer

> *from this. I also thank Mimi Chase so much for supporting me and being a great friend which made my life at U of I a great one!*
> Ricardo Bombonatti Bonganhi '96

> *This is such a wonderful school. It has blessed the community for 100 years and I pray it will bless for 100+ more! God bless all of the people who have been involved in keeping the dream alive!*
> Michelle Armstrong (current student)

High praise for an educational enterprise now incorporated as the University of Indianapolis was received from all over the world during the celebration of its centennial anniversary. The nation's president, congressional leaders, Indiana's government and legislature, and educators, as well as graduates, current students, and parents have all hailed the centennial milestone attained by the little university that not only could, but did.

Were it not for those that I dare to call heroes, Indiana Central University might not have survived the lean early years to become Indiana Central College in 1921. Without the courage and conviction of resolute leaders during the Great Depression, through the second worldwide war of the twentieth century, and into the years of constant challenge for financial viability, Gene Sease and his board of trustees would not have had an institution to restore to its original name of Indiana Central University in 1977. And nine years later, when that same President Sease ventured to incorporate the namesake city of the school, he was standing on the shoulders of the thousands of servants like him whose talents and devotion were embodied in the University of Indianapolis.

Heroic leaders seem to have a quality to lift those around them, to inspire others to be better than they think they might be. Who, at the U of I, has contributed most to the ideal expounded by President Bryan at the head of this chapter? Which persons should be saluted?

It's an impossible task. Without question the *ad hoc* committee composed of leaders of the United Church of the Brethren in Christ from the St. Joseph, White River, and Indiana conferences, who entered into the original contract with Indianapolis realtor and land developer William L. Elder, deserve the first salute.

The original trustees, who had the foresight and dedication to their vision in establishing the school, shall forever occupy a venerated place in the hierarchy of heroes at Indiana Central. The names of J. T. Roberts (who accepted the position as first president of ICU), W. M. Karstedt, M. F. Dawson, Charles J. Wheeler, A. R. Nicholas, Jacob J. Butcher, J. Simons, O. F. Landis, J. W. Hindbaugh, J. E. Newell, Ephraim Wells, J. N. Schnell, J. T. Hobson, A. W. Arford, J. H. Walls, C. C. Dawson, George A. Hottell, and H. E. Ward are scrolled in indelible ink upon the soul of Indiana Central.

Others who have followed in their footsteps, such as Gordon France, Don Carmony, Don Earnhart, Ray Crowe, Bill Kiesel, Ottis Fitzwater, Zane Todd, and Christel DeHaan, to name but a handful, have emulated the example of those early trustees, whom they never met, in the high calling of service to the U of I.

Each chief executive, in his turn, contributed to the growth and progress of the university, some more dramatically than others. The seven—John T. Roberts (1905-07);

Distinction Without Pretension

Lewis D. Bonebrake (1909-15); Irby J. Good (1915-44); Isaiah Lynd Esch (1945-70); Gene E. Sease (1970-88); G. Benjamin Lantz, Jr. (1988-98); and Jerry Israel (1998-) —all affected the evolution of Indiana Central University (1902) into Indiana Central College (1921), to Indiana Central University again (1977), and then to the University of Indianapolis (1986). The college seems to have had the right president in charge at the right time to provide the leadership qualities necessary to meet the challenges of their respective administrations.

The more than twenty thousand alumni of the institution could each sing praises of favorite faculty and staff. But it was early faculty members whom we should recognize for planting the seeds of trees under which they would never sit to enjoy the shade.

Not long ago I turned the pages of a borrowed copy of the first University of Indianapolis yearbook, the 1909 *Oracle*. On pages eight through twelve were individual pictures of the entire faculty of nine (forty-four percent of whom were women, a significant statement given the limitations placed upon women in that day), with accompanying information about their educational credentials.

Pictured with flecks of gray at his temples and an abundant moustache was the senior member of that faculty, John Abijah Cummins, instructor of science and philosophy and graduate of Otterbein University (1887) in Westerville, Ohio.

Studious and serious-looking was the principal of the Teacher's Training Department, William Carter Brandenburg. A teaching certificate earned at Indiana State Normal School (1894) accompanied his bachelor of arts degree from Westfield College (1896).

Wearing the high collar in the style of that day, a dapper young Irby J. Good was the lone graduate of Indiana Central University on the 1909 faculty. He taught German and mathematics.

From the 1904 class at Indiana University, Gertrude Colescott taught in the Department of History and Economics. Her grandson, Jack Colescott, would star on the athletic field at Indiana Central College from 1950-52, earning induction into both the Indiana Basketball (1997) and University of Indianapolis (2001) halls of fame.

Demure-looking Ora Fay Shatto, Ph.D. from Otterbein (1899) was an instructor in both Latin and French.

The college pastor and teacher of English, Bible, and Greek, J. Ernest Paddock earned degrees at Iowa Christian College (1905), Westfield College (1906) and Union Biblical Seminary (1907).

Instructing her students in Piano, Harmony, Musical History, Musical Form and Analysis, General Theory, and Ensemble Playing must have kept Ivy May Smith out of mischief. She was a graduate of both the Academy of Music and the Metropolitan School of Music in Indianapolis.

Youthful Guston P. Roberts came to Indiana Central from Ohio Normal University (1898) and Oberlin Business College (1900) as instructor in the Commercial Department. Because he had taught in the Shorthand Department of the Modern School of Business Training in Cleveland, Ohio, and the Business Department of Central College in Huntington, Indiana, it is fair to assume he taught business to ICU students.

The final member of the faculty was a very beautiful Martha Feller King, instructor in Drawing. Her credentials were degrees from Shortridge High School (1902) and the Indianapolis Normal School (1904), with a state license as a supervisor in drawing.

James L. Brunnemer

We of a later age fondly remember instructors like Dr. McBride, Prof Henricks, coaches Nicoson and Bright, Miss Huey, Dr. Warden, Miss Weaver, Dr. Morgan, Mrs. Martha Waller, Dr. Brooker—you construct your own list. These teachers were the Cummins and Brandenburgs, the Kings and the Smiths of a later era.

Without able administrators and loyal support staff, the work of the faculty could not have taken place. Of particular note was an unbroken string of dedicated business managers, from Good through Kek to Miller and Hottell, men of high character and uncommon dedication. Serving four presidents (Esch, Sease, Lantz, and Israel) through the better part of forty years were the men I term the "Big Four": Hottell, Youngblood, Huffman, and Partridge, whose stamp upon the institution is profound.

When I think of colleagues who, through devotion to duty, unfailing competence, and their agreeable presence went quietly about making a difference in their respective positions with the university during my twenty-one years as an administrator there, the names of Peter Noot, Linda Handy (to whom literally thousands of students owe a debt of gratitude for her untiring efforts in securing financial aid for those deserving and in need), Paul Washington-Lacey (a champion of and for minority students), Jim Ream (whose exemplary work in theatre at the university was only surpassed by his devotion to his students), and Marlene Harris come immediately to the forefront. In all probability, the noble behavior of Pete, Linda, Paul, Jim, and Marlene will not be immortalized in the legacy of U of I heroes, but without their humble but effective service, the institution would be less than it is today. And there were many more unsung servants like them.

I recall beloved friends like Doc Dill, Mary Streets, Bill Bless, Lynne Weisenbach, LeAlice Briggs, and Beth Domholdt, each of whom affected lives in ways and numbers they will never know.

Philanthropists and friends too numerous to recall have blessed the University of Indianapolis with their talents and treasures. The university should never forget Ted Plum, perhaps President Esch's closest associate over the quarter-century he served the college. Not a graduate himself, Mr. Plum came to ICC as a "loaned executive" from an Indianapolis business, and through his admiration for Dr. Esch and his love of the ICC ideal, stayed on to seek private financial support that is numbered in the millions of dollars.

Among the most gentle and caring souls I had the joy of knowing, and loving, was Mary Elizabeth Ober, widow of Cy. A servant of God and man, Mary spent her entire life as an exemplification of common sense, service to others, and devotion to family.

There have been alumni families like the Hiatts, the Hannis, the Peters, the Milhouses, and the Thompsons, to name a handful, featuring patriarchs and matriarchs who believed that Indiana Central was the only college for their family members to attend.

Distinguished alumni who have brought honor and prestige to their alma mater include Bill Breneman '30, considered one of Indiana University's finest faculty members in the history of that institution; Dr. Raymond Lee '54, world-renowned physician on the staff of the Mayo clinic; and noted journalist and Pulitzer Prize-winner William Raspberry '58, who was selected in 2003 as one of Indiana's "Living Legends" by the Indiana Historical Society.

Where does one leave off? It pains me to know weakened memory and lack of space will not permit what should be a personal tribute to all of the ICC/ICU/U of I heroes.

Distinction Without Pretension

Let me try to resolve my dilemma by sharing briefly about four who studied, and then passed beneath the portals of Good Hall with diploma in hand, who might best convey the effect on many graduates of the educational experience at Indiana Central. These alumni may serve as representatives of the hundreds of dedicated servants from Indiana Central who have contributed toward making life on this earth better for those around them. Their names are Dr. Moses Mahoi '50, Master Sergeant Polly Horton Hix '72, Dr. Henry Martinez '51, and the Reverend George Jacobs '42.

Children of the Depression, Indiana Central graduate Charles Leader '35 and his wife located in Sierra Leone, Africa, to serve as missionaries for the United Brethren Church. During their term of service there, they met a bright teenager whose desire was to become a healer for his people. The Reverend Mr. Leader made the appropriate contacts and encouraged Moses Musa Mahoi to attend Indiana Central College. The young African arrived at his new home in Indianapolis in late summer of 1946. An outstanding student, Moses' enchanting smile, sense of humor, and kind presence captivated his classmates, among whom was Louise Dragoo (Barnett).

"Moses was so bright and funny," Mrs. Barnett recalled recently. "I recall the first time he saw snow, and how he went outside to roll around in this new phenomenon."

He was extolled by the late Dr. Robert Brooker as "the best lab assistant I ever had."

After graduation, Mahoi studied medicine at Columbia University and at the Cleveland Medical School, later earning his degree in London, England. He eventually returned to his native land in Freetown, Sierra Leone, to practice medicine.

Named a Distinguished Alumnus of Indiana Central in 1971, Moses occasionally visited his alma mater. Following one such visit in 1995, Dr. Mahoi wrote to friends Don and Esther Fleener. One can almost hear Moses chuckling as he reminisced about the very different university he returned to:

> [I] recall my short visits in your home and was really amazed at the changes at ICC. Co-educational dormitories? I am sure that Miss Cravens will flip in her grave. What will Miss Huey do? And "Andy," our mascot, will bark at anyone holding hands ... And for that matter, using words—dance, drinks, rather than folk game and Cokes ... time and tide waits for no man, ICC keeps marching on!

In the 1990s, Dr. Mahoi was the chief physician at a mining company when a deadly civil war broke out in Sierra Leone. His friends in Indiana were concerned for his safety at the hands of the rebels. Despite the fact that danger lurked within the civil distress in his country, Dr. Mahoi left the mining company to establish a family clinic treating the poor and needy.

With buildings burning and explosions rocking Freetown, Moses and his family lived above his clinic, where indigent tribe members would come for medical attention. As the number of patients with war injuries increased dramatically, Dr. Mahoi worked from sunrise to well after sunset for years. It was during that time that he suffered great fatigue

James L. Brunnemer

and finally diagnosed himself as having prostate cancer. He returned to the U.S. for a brief time for surgery but hurried quickly back to Sierra Leone and his patients.

From that same letter to the Fleeners, Dr. Mahoi described his family clinic:

> [I] have a group of patients who cannot afford the necessary medical care ... I class[ify] them as D.F.G. (Do for God), the Creole expression which means do it in the name of God. And I still recall in our Chapel devotion [at Indiana Central] and doing my year of seminary before I went to medical school 'that which you have done for the least of these, you have done it for me.'
>
> All of this confirms the basis of my highest convictions: medicine is an art and not necessarily a science as much as I had the Western-type of medical education. I continue to respect the traditional healer and through the years I have had the satisfaction of the Golden Rule, a satisfaction of helping others to help themselves. <u>This is a great hobby!</u>

As the bloody civil war surged around and through the capital city, Moses ignored his deteriorating condition (there were no other qualified physicians in the area), choosing not to return to the U.S. for checkups. He ignored his own malignancy because he was too busy with his patients. Moses Mahoi continued to work at an unbending pace until he was no longer mobile. Toward the end of his life, family and friends would carry Dr. Mahoi on a pallet every day from his second-floor bedroom down the stairs to his clinic, where he continued to administer to the suffering. Angela Allie, sister of Moses' wife, Elizabeth, noted that Dr. Mahoi literally "worked himself to death."

After her husband died in 1998, Elizabeth Mahoi continued the clinic in Moses' name, catering to the grass roots community unable to afford medical care elsewhere.

Polly Horton Hix '72 is not widely known and she would certainly be reluctant to accept a hero's laurels. An adoptee, Polly was reared in Porter County by a loving couple that encouraged her to make college a priority. She came to Indiana Central in 1968 with the intent of studying German. While she fondly recalls Marga Meier, chair of the languages department, by her senior year Polly had changed her major to education. Following graduation, however, no teaching positions were available for her. After a series of jobs, she settled on law enforcement as a career.

For the past twenty-five years, she has served the Marion County Sheriff's Department, becoming the first woman Zone Commander in 1989. Master Sergeant Hix has had an extraordinary career in a profession she loves, entering her squad car at nine p.m. five nights a week. From evening until five a.m. the next day, she helps to keep Indianapolis safe, on the shift that she prefers.

Polly was a principal figure in a controversial incident about five years ago that resulted in publicity she would just as soon not have had. Members of the Sheriff's

Department were engaged in a high-speed chase of a bank robber during a time of heavy traffic on I-465 around Indianapolis. Officer Hix was cruising ahead of the chase, preparing to move in to assist her fellow deputies. She received an order from her superior officer to use the "stop stick," an instrument with sharp spikes, which is placed across a road to blow out a fleeing perpetrator's tires.

Noting the danger to innocent and unaware travelers, Ms. Hix recommended that tactic not be used. Her supervisor repeated the order to employ the equipment. Again, she advised against it. Another officer beyond her location was then commanded to use the instrument, and did so. When the speeding offender's vehicle crossed the stick, his tires blew, and he careened at high speed into a van, instantly killing a mother and her young daughter. While Polly was disciplined for failing to obey a direct order, the *Indianapolis Star* editorial page was filled for some time afterward with letters of support for her judgment in the incident.

Polly Horton Hix's contributions to the city of Indianapolis would be sterling if one considered only her dedication as a police officer. But to reflect on Polly's distinguished police work would be to tell only part of her story. The intriguing aspect of her life that is least apparent to the public, yet which most defines her character, is her charitable giving.

Crediting her father, Arthur Horton, with "teaching me at an early age to have a giving attitude," Polly inherited a substantial amount of money at her father's passing. She placed the greatest portion of his fortune into a charitable trust, "because it was the right thing to do," she said. From that trust, Polly annually makes gifts to the Indianapolis Children's Museum, the Human Society, the University of Indianapolis, the African Fund for Endangered Wildlife, and her favorite charity, the Indianapolis Zoo.

This woman, who has "seen it all" on the mean streets of Indianapolis, was honored in 1993 by the Indiana Chapter of the National Society of Fund Raising Executives as "Philanthropist of the Year."

Anyone riding the miniature train that traverses the grounds of the Zoo will pass by the Polly Horton Hix Animal Hospital, made possible in 1992 through a substantial gift by Ms. Hix.

In March 2003 Master Sergeant Polly Horton Hix finished her nine-p.m.-to-five-a.m. shift for the Sheriff's Department, arrived at a scheduled appointment with officials of the Zoo, and completed arrangements for an *$8 million gift* from her trust for improvements to the Indianapolis Zoo.

Later that evening, she was back in her patrol car, cruising the byways of Indianapolis to make them safer for you and me.

A child of Hispanic parents, Henry Martinez was born in the small village of Vallecitos in the arid and hardscrabble land of north-central New Mexico. Martinez attended the McCurdy School, a boarding institution in Espanola, New Mexico, that was founded and supported, in part, by Evangelical United Brethren Church missions. McCurdy was established to provide opportunity in education for Native Americans and Hispanics.

After high school, Martinez traveled to Indianapolis to accept an academic scholarship at Indiana Central College. Later he was followed to ICC by brother John Martinez '54 and sister Carlotta Martinez Thompson '56. While at ICC Henry studied under Dr. William P. Morgan, who found him to be a bright and eager learner. After he

James L. Brunnemer

graduated *cum laude* in 1951, Henry received Dr. Morgan's recommendation to the Indiana University Medical School. Martinez earned his M.D. degree there in 1956.

After an internship and residency in general surgery at the University of Texas Medical Branch in Galveston, Dr. Martinez studied in the relatively new field of thoracic and cardiovascular surgery at the U of T Southwestern Medical School in Dallas.

Once serving on a surgical team led by the eminent Dr. Michael DeBakke in Houston, Dr. Martinez later developed revolutionary new techniques to improve open-heart surgery. His interest in thoracic surgery, which at the time was both risky and not fully explored, led him ultimately to the Medical Center in Amarillo, Texas, not far from his boyhood home.

It was at Amarillo that Dr. Martinez applied for one of the limited number of heart-lung machines available at that time. The heart-lung contraption did the work of the patient's organs during open-heart surgery. After a series of frustrating failures in securing one of the very few machines available, Dr. Martinez and fellow surgeon Dr. W. R. Klingensmith purchased the apparatus themselves, setting it up in Dr. Martinez's garage. With Dr. Martinez's wife Ann, an RN, operating the mechanism, Henry and Dr. Klingensmith practiced on dogs and other small animals in the makeshift O.R. at home to perfect their skills, prior to putting the technology to use on humans.

On October 14, 1964, Dr. Martinez performed the first successful operation, using the heart-lung machine in Amarillo on twenty-one-year-old Richard Bills. From that initial surgical procedure, Henry Martinez introduced the first thoracic surgery program in the Southwest. Thousands of lives were saved and prolonged through the tireless work of this graduate of ICC.

Dr. Henry Martinez, honored as a Distinguished Alumnus of Indiana Central in 1976, was forced to stop practicing in 1992 after being struck by amyotrophic lateral sclerosis, more commonly known as Lou Gehrig's disease. He would die seven years later.

Four of Dr. Martinez's five daughters became physicians, emulating their beloved father in his dedication to serving others.

I first met George '42 and Dorothy Milhouse Jacobs '39 in 1971, during my first year as alumni director at Indiana Central. It was apparent from that first encounter that the Jacobses were a team in the business of making others' lives better. It seemed that simply by breathing, George became intoxicated with positive enthusiasm. And Dorothy supported him in all his endeavors.

In 1943, following George's graduation, he and Dorothy were married. They will celebrate their sixtieth wedding anniversary in 2003. The couple moved to Dayton, Ohio, where George completed his work at Bonebrake (later, United Theological) Seminary.

A series of pastorates in small churches, including United Brethren denominations in Elliott, Peoria, Casey, and Aurora, Illinois, preceded his becoming minister at Freeport, Illinois. This was his first charge as an Evangelical United Brethren pastor, resulting from the merger. George spent the rest of his career prior to retirement as the beloved pastor of this lovely church body.

Thousands of ministers, serving all over the United States and in many foreign lands, are alumni of Indiana Central/University of Indianapolis. George exemplifies the

Distinction Without Pretension

quiet, humble, unspectacular service to mankind that has been the lot of so many of those servants. And while guiding his congregations, George has been among the most enthusiastic and faithful recruiters of students for his alma mater. The number of young people he has personally encouraged to consider and accompanied on visits to Indiana Central is unknown, but it has to be in the many hundreds. Scores of ICC alumni owe their first exposure to the school to George Jacobs.

And what was good for the youth of Pastor Jacobs's churches was good for his own children, as well. Daughter Carolyn '67 wed Reverend Jack Hartman '67, and younger sister Joyce '68 is now Mrs. Richard Erfert. Son Mark '76 is a pastor in Oregon, Illinois, with his wife, Janet French Jacobs '76, assisting him in his ministry.

In recognition of his life of service to his alma mater, George was the recipient of an honorary degree from the University of Indianapolis in 1977.

Retired and living at the United Methodist Community in Franklin, Indiana, George and Dorothy have been exemplary models of all those who have served God after leaving the halls of Indiana Central. Celebrity and fortune were not in the plans for George Jacobs. He toiled in relative anonymity throughout his life. But for anyone who has ever had George Jacobs pass into or through their lives, you are better for it. He is a true hero of Indiana Central.

As with so many of their fellow alumni heroes, Dr. Moses Mahoi, Sgt. Polly Hix, Dr. Martinez, and the Rev. George Jacobs possessed noble qualities before ever entering Indiana Central. When they left the confines of the college each was just over twenty years of age. None of them had an inkling, then, that one day they would be revered alumni of ICC and of the greater community of mankind. Only now, after a lifetime of service, do we recognize their gallantry.

But during their lives, each would remember the people and the lessons that they received during four years at Indiana Central, and recall those who reminded them of the motto of ICC/ICU/U of I that embodies the selflessness of the giver: "Education for Service."

Martinez, Mahoi, Horton Hix, and Jacobs became heroes after lifetimes of service. So who among the senior class of 2003 might be the Mahois, the Martinezes, the Horton Hixes, and the Jacobses of the coming century? Who, now viewing the world behind the eyes of a twenty-something graduate of the University of Indianapolis, will we one day salute as a special achiever in the vein of those celebrated above?

Let me suggest one who, during her four years at the U of I, has demonstrated the innate characteristics of those who achieve greatness.

A 1999 graduate of Ft. Wayne Dwenger High School, Kim Moore was recruited by then-coach of the U of I women's golf team, Larry Bledsoe. Kim's golf scores were impressive, so she had been invited to campus, sight unseen, to discuss the possibility of earning an education while performing for the Lady Greyhound golf squad.

Four years later, Kim has graduated with her degree in pre-medicine. The fact that she became the greatest female golfer in U of I history, however, is not the rationale for suggesting she has heroic tendencies. It is true that Kim recorded the lowest stroke average in the history of the school (79.3, ranking seventeenth among all women golfers in NCAA Division II in 2003); shot the lowest single round (70) ever by a Lady Greyhound;

finished second (by one stroke) in the GLVC conference meet; and performed well in the NCAA regional post-season tournament. That she averaged 250 yards on her drives as a senior (the LPGA's finest player in 2003, Annika Storenstam, averaged 275 off the tee) was impressive. But all of this is not why we think she may one day walk in the steps of Martinez, Mahoi, Horton Hix, and Jacobs.

You see, Kim Moore was born with a clubfoot at the end of her left leg, and her right leg ended just below her knee. She had corrective surgery at least once in each of her first sixteen years of life and has worn a prosthesis to replace the missing portion of her right leg since she was a toddler. But as Coach Bledsoe noted, Kim "overcame a handicap and never complained. Contrary to a lot of people who let little injuries get the best of them, she had a lifelong situation she had to adjust to and she's done it quite remarkably."

Born into an athletic family, Kim naturally gravitated to sports, despite her disadvantage, playing soccer, volleyball, basketball, and softball as a youth. In high school, she settled on golf, applying all her energies and competitive instincts to the game.

The culmination of her hard work came in the spring of 2003 when she earned a slot in the NCAA women's golf tourney. The event was set up with the women golfers playing seventy-two holes on consecutive days, *sans* caddies, of course. Several players, citing back problems from toting their heavy golf bags, asked for exemptions in order to use a pull cart. Moore carried her own bag more than eight hours each day, without complaint. NCAA East Region officials were so inspired by Moore's achievements and attitude that they instituted the Kim Moore Award to be presented annually to "a student-athlete who has demonstrated a positive attitude, determination and perseverance to overcome personal challenges."

And Moore's assessment of the attention she has received?

"I don't even consider my leg in the equation. I'm so used to it. Other people think it's really remarkable, but it's something I've had all my life, so it's normal for me. I'm just out there playing golf."

Steve Rushin, veteran sportswriter for *Sports Illustrated* magazine, is one who has taken note of Ms. Moore. Kim was cited in the September 22, 2003, edition of the national weekly in Rushin's column after she won the women's National Amputee Golf Championship that month.

Yes, there are heroes in our midst today at the University of Indianapolis. In the coming century, more names will be added to the hallowed list like those above. What will the U of I look like in 2102? We have no more notion of that than those bold founders of 100 years ago had of what today sits on 67 acres on the south side of Indianapolis.

But I am confident, knowing that people with the character of Kim Moore grace the campus, that whatever is there on Hanna Avenue will be an institution of which all of us, living and dead, may be proud. Heroes still walk among us, on the grounds of the University of Indianapolis.

ACKNOWLEDGMENTS

At our home at Sweetwater Lake near Nineveh, Indiana, Luella and I are blessed to live on an acre containing nearly one hundred trees, mostly of the mature pin oak variety. Through our living and dining room windows we may look out through the trees at a lovely one-hundred-eighty feet of shoreline on the 450-acre lake.

Very little of what you have read was created in that comfortable, serene setting. No, my preferred environments for musing about and writing of the past are the usually-crowded and often raucous inner sanctums of truck stops, bars, coffee shops, and small family-owned eating establishments. I can drift off into other worlds amidst the clamor of these gathering places.

So, I'd like to acknowledge those tables and booths and barstools where the greater number of the thoughts and memories in this book seeped out of my mind and onto paper.

A corner booth at Hal and Karis Johnson's coffee shop in Nashville, Indiana—The Daily Grind—was a favored haunt. Over glasses of merlot, I viewed the tree-smothered Cloudcrest Ridge south of Nashville while writing from a booth in the Overlook Bar in Season's Lodge. I holed up in the Corncrib saloon at Nashville's Brown County Inn many Sunday afternoons to pen thoughts. Many Saturday mornings found me at Rob Wilson's Collector's Corner General Store in Nineveh, the only spot in a thirty-mile radius of my home that opened by five a.m., when I routinely arise to begin the day.

To all the other coffee houses, barrooms, truck stops, fast-food emporiums, shopping mall food courts, and small family restaurants along the roadways of the Midwest, where me and my Goldwing rested, I salute and thank you. Expressions of gratitude are due, as well, to the barkeeps, waitresses, and proprietors (who didn't require of me a cover charge for the use of their space) for tolerating a stranger with a note pad and thesaurus on their tables.

Special thanks go out to a host of others, including:

- Professor Ray Warden, who was the first to convince me that having something to tell and telling it well was worthy in itself.
- Gene Lausch and Carl Stockton, two sturdy ships, between which this pugnacious PT-109 hovered alee. When my rebellious and adventuresome spirit threatened to sail into dangerous waters, these two coaxed me back into safe harbor.
- Peter Noot, the sweetest-natured Hun of an editor one could ever encounter. Brutal and uncompromising when it comes to a dangling participle, Peter's sharp eye is reflected in what you'll find to be a rather consistent style in the book.
- Former classmates, teachers and coaches, colleagues, and friends I met through my association with the university, from whom I learned so much.
- Dr. Patrick Loehrer, loyal friend whose life defines the essence of service.
- And Zup, Mike Watkins, and Steve Baber, three confidants who have believed in me.

James L. Brunnemer

    To those most beloved by Lu and me: Beau and Vera, Noah and Nathan, and Kyle and Susan, Julia, Sam, and Kaitlyn, you are my inspiration every day.

    And to my late Mom, Gladys, and my sisters, Lois and Joyce, and their families, words aren't enough.

    But most of all, this book belongs to my greatest hero, Dad.

    As I wrote this book, I was reminded of an incident that occurred on a raw November day in 1958. Dad and I were slogging through brambles and briars and the muck of the sloughs of a farmer's woods in Shelby County, Indiana, our shotguns in hand. It was the first time that I accompanied my father, Ernie, on a rabbit-hunting venture. Dad was a marksman with his Browning automatic, having been a hunter since his youth in the 1920s.

    Above us, strolling comfortably along a well-worn path atop a knoll, was a friend of Dad's, Harlan Hicks. Unlike me, Harlan had hunted rabbits before. But not with Dad. Up to that time on this day, Dad had bagged three rabbits on three shots. I had gotten shots at two of the scurrying animals, hitting one, while Harlan hadn't even seen a cottontail.

    Finally, Dad signaled Harlan, who was obviously not a descendant of Dan'l Boone, hollering, "Them rabbits don't follow the path, Harlan."

    Dad showed me, in ways other than hunting, that life is richer away from the well-trodden lanes and that to find life's rewards, one must be bold and brave enough to go where others are uncomfortable, to be unafraid to risk. He taught me that life isn't about money and acquiring things, but about being happy with where and who you are.

    This book is dedicated to my wife, Luella. It *happened* because of Ernie.